Standard	Key Elements of the Standard	Chapter and Topic	MyEducationLab Topic
3. Observing, Documenting, and Assessing to Support Young Children and Families	3a. Understanding the goals, benefits, and uses of assessment 3b. Knowing about and using observation, documentation, and other appropriate assessment tools and approaches 3c. Understanding and practicing responsible assessment to promote positive outcomes for each child 3d. Knowing about assessment partnerships with families and with professional colleagues	2: Voice from the Field: How to Help Eng[...] Learners Succeed: Competency Build[...] 3: What Is Assessment? 3: Classroom Assessment 3: The Power of Observation 3: Assessment for School Readiness 3: What Are Critical Assessment Issues? 6: The Teacher's Role 6: Curriculum and Practices 6: Active Learning 7: Program Accreditation 9: Accommodating Diverse Learners 10: School Readiness and Young Children 10: Early Intervention 11: The Changing Kindergarten 11: Retention 11: The Kindergarten Curriculum 12: State Standards 12: Teaching Practices 12: Figure 12.2: The Three Tiers of Continuous Intervention/ Instruction 15: Assess Your Attitudes Toward Children 15: Select Appropriate Instructional Materials 15: Teaching English Language Learners 15: Accommodating Diverse Learners 16: Individuals with Disabilities Education Act (IDEA) 16: Instructional Strategies for Teaching Children with Disabilities 16: Voice from the Field: How to Teach in an Inclusive Classroom: Competency Builder	[...]nity [...]ntent
4. Using Developmentally Effective Approaches to Connect with Children and Families	4a. Understanding positive relationships and supportive interactions as the foundation of their work with children 4b. Knowing and understanding effective strategies and tools for early education 4c. Using a broad repertoire of developmentally appropriate teaching/learning approaches 4d. Reflecting on their own practice to promote positive outcomes for each child	2: Voice from the Field: How to Help English Language Learners Succeed: Competency Builder 4: Theories of Learning and Development 5: Piaget and Constructivist Learning Theory 5: Vygotsky and Sociocultural Theory 5: Maslow and Self-Actualization Theory 5: Erikson and Psychosocial Development 5: Gardner and Multiple Intelligences Theory 5: Bronfenbrenner and Ecological Theory 6: The Montessori Method 6: HighScope: A Constructivist Model 6: Reggio Emilia 6: The Project Approach 11: Alternative Kindergarten Programs 11: Developmentally Appropriate Practice 13: Technology and Special Childhood Populations 13: Implementing Technology in Early Childhood Education Programs 13: Voice from the Field: How to Use Technology as a Scaffolding Tool in the Preschool Classroom: Competency Builder 14: A Social Constructivist Approach to Guiding Children 14: Ten Steps to Guiding Behavior 14: Figure 14.1: The Zone of Proximal Development Applied to Guiding Behavior 15: Teaching English Language Learners 15: Selecting Appropriate Instructional Materials 17: Entire Chapter 17	5: Program Models 6: Curriculum Planning 8: DAP/Teaching Strategies 9: Guiding Children 10: Cultural & Linguistic Diversity 11: Special Needs/Inclusion

continued

Standard	Key Elements of the Standard	Chapter and Topic	MyEducationLab Topic
5. Using Content Knowledge to Build Meaningful Curriculum	5a. Understanding content knowledge and resources in academic disciplines 5b. Knowing and using the central concepts, inquiry tools, and structures of content areas or academic disciplines 5c. Using their own knowledge, appropriate early learning standards, and other resources to design, implement, and evaluate meaningful, challenging curricula for each child	7: What Constitutes Quality Care and Education? 8: Head Start Programs 8: Federal Legislation and Early Childhood 8: Federal Involvement in Literacy Education 9: Research and Infant/Toddler Education 10. What Are Preschoolers Like? 10: The Future of Preschool 11: The Kindergarten Curriculum 11: Lesson Plan: A Literacy 5E Lesson 11: Voice from the Field: How to Integrate Science and Literacy In Kindergarten: Competency Builder 11: Figure 11.1 Reading/Literacy Instructional Terminology 11: Figure 11.2 NCTM's Curriculum Focal Points of Kindergarten 12: Curriculum Content Areas 12: Voice from the Field: How to Use Literature Circles in the Elementary Grades 12: Lesson Plan: 5E Model Lesson in Math 13: Voice from the Field: Carolina Beach Elementary: Technology Across the Curriculum: Competency Builder 15: Teaching and Multicultural Infusion 15: Implement an Antibias Curriculum and Activities All Chapters: Accommodating Diverse Learners	1: History 6: Curriculum Planning 7: Curriculum/Content Areas
6. Becoming a Professional	6a. Identifying and involving oneself with the early childhood field 6b. Knowing about and upholding ethical standards and other professional guidelines 6c. Engaging in continuous, collaborative learning to inform practice 6d. Integrating knowledgeable, reflective, and critical perspectives on early education 6e. Engaging in informed advocacy for children and the profession	1: The CDA Program 1: The Future: You and the Early Childhood Profession 2: Professional Staff Development 4: Why Is the Past Important? 4: History and Historical Figures 4: Views of Children Through the Ages 5: Theories of Learning and Development 5: Applying Theory to Practice 6: The Teacher's Role 7: Professional Staff Development 7: Program Accreditation 9: Research and Infant/Toddler Education 9: Implications for Professionals 12: State Standards 12: Teaching Practices 15: America the Multicultural All Chapters: Activities for Professional Development	4: Observation/Assessment 12: Professionalism/Ethics

twelfth edition

Early Childhood Education Today

GEORGE S. MORRISON
University of North Texas

Boston   Columbus   Indianapolis   New York   San Francisco   Upper Saddle River
Amsterdam   Cape Town   Dubai   London   Madrid   Milan   Munich   Paris   Montreal   Toronto
Delhi   Mexico City   São Paulo   Sydney   Hong Kong   Seoul   Singapore   Taipei   Tokyo

Vice President and Editor in Chief:
Jeffery W. Johnston
Senior Acquisitions Editor: Julie Peters
Development Editor: Bryce Bell
Editorial Assistant: Nancy Holstein
Senior Marketing Manager:
Christopher D. Barry
Senior Managing Editor: Pamela D. Bennett
Senior Project Manager: Linda Hillis Bayma
Senior Operations Supervisor:
Matthew Ottenweller
Senior Art Director: Diane C. Lorenzo
Cover and Text Designer: Candace Rowley

Photo Researcher: Lori Whitley
Permissions Administrator:
Rebecca Savage
Cover Image: Shutterstock
Media Producer: Autumn Benson
Media Project Manager: Rebecca Norsic
Full-Service Project Management: Thistle Hill
Publishing Services, LLC
Composition: Integra Software Services, Inc.
Printer/Binder: Courier/Kendallville
Cover Printer: Lehigh-Phoenix
Color/Hagerstown
Text Font: Garamond

Credits and acknowledgments borrowed from other sources and reproduced, with permission, in this textbook appear on appropriate page within text.

Every effort has been made to provide accurate and current Internet information in this book. However, the Internet and information posted on it are constantly changing, so it is inevitable that some of the Internet addresses listed in this textbook will change.

Photo Credits: Photo credits appear on page 573, which constitutes a continuation of this copyright page.

Library of Congress Cataloging-in-Publication Data
Morrison, George S.
    Early childhood education today / George S. Morrison.—Twelfth ed.
        p. cm.
    Includes bibliographical references and index.
    ISBN-13: 978-0-13-703458-1 (casebound)
    ISBN-10: 0-13-703458-X (casebound)
    1. Early childhood education—United States.   I. Title.
LB1139.25.M66 2012
372.21—dc22

                                                    2010047287

www.pearsonhighered.com

10 9 8 7 6 5 4 3 2 1
ISBN-13: 978-0-13-703458-1
ISBN-10:   0-13-703458-X

To **BETTY JANE**—whose life is full of grace and who lives the true meaning of love every day.

About the Author

George S. Morrison is professor of early childhood education at the University of North Texas where he teaches child development and early childhood classes to undergraduate and graduate students. He is an experienced teacher and was a principal in the public schools.

Professor Morrison's accomplishments include both a Distinguished Academic Service Award from the Pennsylvania Department of Education and Outstanding Service and Teaching Awards from Florida International University. His books include *Early Childhood Education Today,* Eleventh Edition; *Fundamentals of Early Childhood Education,* Sixth Edition; and *Teaching in America,* Fifth Edition. Professor Morrison has also written books about the education and development of infants, toddlers, and preschoolers; child development; the contemporary curriculum; and parent/family/community involvement.

Dr. Morrison is a popular author, speaker, and presenter. He is senior contributing editor for the *Public School Montessorian.* His research and presentations focus on the globalization of early childhood education, the influence of contemporary educational reforms on education, and the application of best practices to early childhood education. Professor Morrison also lectures and gives keynote addresses on topics of early childhood education in Thailand, Taiwan, China, South Korea, and the Philippines.

Professor Morrison having fun reading with children at the Child Development Laboratory on the campus of the University of North Texas.

Preface

Changes are sweeping across the early childhood landscape, transforming our profession literally before our eyes! These changes create exciting possibilities for you and all early childhood professionals. We discuss these changes in every chapter of *Early Childhood Education Today*, Twelfth Edition, which is designed to keep you current and on the cutting edge of early childhood teaching practice.

Changes in early childhood education bring both opportunities and challenges. Opportunities are endless for you to participate in the ongoing re-creation of the early childhood profession. In fact, creating and re-creating the early childhood profession is one of your constant professional roles. This also means you have to create and constantly re-create *yourself* as an early childhood professional. *Early Childhood Education Today*, Twelfth Edition, helps you achieve this professional goal. The challenges involved in reforming the profession include collaboration, hard work, and constant dedication to achieving high-quality education for *all* children. I hope you will take full advantage of these opportunities to help all children learn the knowledge and skills they need to succeed in school and life. I believe how you and I respond to the opportunities we have in front of us today will determine the future of early childhood education. This text will help you learn what it takes to understand and teach young children and how to provide them the support they and their families need and deserve.

New to This Edition

- More student-friendly, **streamlined chapter content and design** provide for smoother and more accessible reading. The author engages readers with information and practices they can apply to their teaching.

- Revised and new **Accommodating Diverse Learners** sections in every chapter provide specific and explicit examples for accommodating children with diverse and special needs, including English language learners. Coverage of inclusion practices is enhanced and expanded in areas such as Response to Intervention (RTI), embedded instruction, differentiated instruction, and universal design (UD). An overall increased emphasis on diversity includes autism spectrum disorders, ADHD, and ranges of family compositions headed by or including individuals who are lesbian, gay, bisexual, or transgender.

- The discussion of assessment practices (Chapter 3) is expanded with authentic **examples of assessment tools** used by teachers in classrooms today. Teaching is a constant practice of assessing what children know and have learned in order to inform practice, adhere to standards and accountability, and ensure that all children learn at high levels.

- Stronger emphasis is given to **lesson planning** (Chapters 10–12) using the highly adaptable 5E Model in grades K–3, as well as preschool lesson planning based on current preschool practices.

- Newly revised **NAEYC** *Standards for Early Childhood Professional Preparation Programs* begin each chapter.

- A **redesigned approach to the history** of early childhood education provides a clear distinction between history (Chapter 4) and theory (Chapter 5) while emphasizing the importance of historical figures and their influence on current educational theory.

This provides for a more comprehensive understanding of the history of early childhood education and how it impacts the field today.

- An emphasis on **green curriculum, green schools, and ecological topics** in contemporary society and classrooms helps students become aware of and involved in the latest educational trends and practices that emphasize environmental thinking and eco-friendly lifestyles and practices.

- An enhanced and expanded discussion of how to **integrate technology** in the classroom prepares students for teaching in an increasingly high-tech world.

- Seven new *Voice from the Field* features continue the text's practice of providing **authentic teacher voices** in every chapter, allowing students to gain insight into classroom and program practices.

Students and early childhood instructors who use *Early Childhood Education Today* are enthusiastic about it for many reasons, including the following:

- **Comprehensive coverage.** This text offers comprehensive coverage of the field of early childhood education. From inclusive classrooms, to teaching ELLs, to the latest instructional strategies, to how to apply the latest technologies to your classroom, *Early Childhood Education Today*, Twelfth Edition, leads the way! It provides you with the knowledge, skills, and tools you need to be a consummate professional and leader.

- **Timeliness.** This text provides you up-to-the-minute coverage of the latest changes in the field, from how to accommodate diverse learners to how to collaborate with the many different kinds of families rearing children in America today.

- **Professional practice.** This text is known for its coverage of professionalism and equips you to take your place as a practicing, confident professional equipped to make a difference in the classrooms of today as you teach children and collaborate with parents and families. It acts as your professional guide as you grow and develop as an early childhood professional.

- **Insightful coverage of the latest issues and trends.** As society changes, so do early childhood practices and programs. *Early Childhood Education Today,* Twelfth Edition, keeps you on the cutting edge of these changes, informing you on political and social issues that influence how and what you teach.

Early Childhood Education Today, Twelfth Edition, integrates ten critical themes that are foundational to the field today. These themes are:

1. The growing number of **diverse children** in America's classrooms today and implications of this demographic shift for your teaching and learning.

2. The importance of **Developmentally Appropriate Practices (DAP)** and the application of these practices to all aspects of early childhood programs and classroom activities. With today's emphasis on academic achievement, *Early Childhood Education Today*, Twelfth Edition, anchors your professional practice in DAP, beginning in Chapter 1.

3. The effects of the economic recession on children and their families. More children and families have slipped below the **poverty** line. Many of your children will come to school unprepared to meet the challenges of preschool or kindergarten. This text helps you educate these children and close the achievement gaps that exist between children in poverty and their more advantaged peers.

4. The integration of the fields of **special education** and early childhood education. Increasingly, special education practices are influencing early childhood practices. This text helps you understand the integration of the two fields and how this integration provides enhanced opportunities for you and the children you teach.

5. The **inclusive classroom** movement. You will teach in an inclusive classroom. This text prepares you to be an inclusive teacher of all young children regardless of disability, in the least restrictive environment possible.

6. **School readiness**. How to help families get their children ready for school and how to promote children's school readiness is at the forefront of issues facing society today. This text provides you with helpful information, ideas, and strategies that enable you to close the readiness gaps that exist across racial, gender, linguistic, and socioeconomic backgrounds.

7. The emphasis on **teacher accountability for student achievement**. Today early childhood teachers—indeed, all teachers—are accountable for how, what, and to what extent children learn. This text helps you meet this challenge confidently and boldly; it provides you with step-by-step strategies for helping all children learn.

8. The use of **technology** to support children's learning. Contemporary teachers are savvy users of technology to promote children's learning and their own professional development. This text helps you gain the technological skills you need to teach in today's classroom. Practicing teachers provide you practical technological examples for how to use technology to support teaching and learning.

9. **Ongoing professional development**. As an early childhood professional you will be constantly challenged to create and re-create yourself as society and professional practices change. *Early Childhood Education Today* helps you be the professional you need to be in the classroom today.

10. Eco-friendly/environmental curriculum and practices. More schools, classrooms, and teachers are embracing **eco-friendly practices**. The eco-friendly movement is a big part of the contemporary curriculum and of social consciousness today. This text provides you with knowledge, information, and classroom strategies you can use to make your classroom and school ecologically and environmentally friendly.

- **Coverage of Professionalism.** What does it mean to be a practicing early childhood professional today? This text answers this question and helps you become a high-quality professional. Chapter 1, "You and Early Childhood Education: What Does It Mean to Be a Professional?" discusses in detail the many dimensions of professionalism. In addition, three core attributes of professional practice—collaboration, ethics, and advocacy—are highlighted throughout the text.

Voice from the Field
Reggio Emilia

Boulder Journey School, a private school for young children in Boulder, Colorado, welcomes 250 children, six weeks to six years of age, and their families.

The philosophy of education and pedagogy of Boulder Journey School stems from the constructivist, social-constructivist, and systems thinking theories of John Dewey, Jean Piaget, Lev Vygotsky, Jerome Bruner, David Hawkins, Howard Gardner, Loris Malaguzzi, Carlina Rinaldi, and Boulder Journey School's Theory of Supportive Social Learning.

The work of the school community has evolved through our dialogue with the educators in Reggio Emilia, Italy and educators throughout the world who are inspired by the world-renowned Reggio Emilia approach to early childhood education.

Our values are based on a strong image of children as curious, competent, and capable of co-constructing knowledge with other children and adults. From the moment of birth, children are engaged in a search for the meaning of life, seeking to understand the world that surrounds them and the relationships that they form and develop with others in their world. Educators and families, as partners in the research of the children, seek to encourage, enhance, and extend children's thinking and learning, thereby creating a relational community.

We value our school as a community of learners who think reflectively and who collaborate in dialogue with one another as they

in order to . . .

- solve problems
- define meanings based on values
- build new understandings
- experience life
- generate hypotheses, test theories and ask more questions
- project further investigations

ultimately co-constructing a knowledge base that continues to evolve and grow.

The co-construction of knowledge is afforded by an environment that is filled with myriad resources and supported by time. Provocations designed to enhance experiences offer endless possibilities for creativity, imagination, symbolization, and representation in the classrooms, studios, theater, and outdoors.

Children and adults interact in relationships formed and maintained within the school. We think that this system of relationships is critical because it provides a basis for the development of a culture in the school that reflects the unique cultures of the individuals within the school.

During meetings together we revisit, interpret, and make predictions about our learning, weaving daily moments into long-term investigations. Children, families, and educators dialogue in small and large groups, leading to the development of a rich, diversified and contextual curriculum. We give visibility to our work and our relationships through the use of technology, leaving traces of our daily experiences in photographs, slides, videos, commentaries, and examples of children's representations. We

---

- **Voice from the Field.** Teachers' authentic voices play a major role in illustrating authentic practices. Voice from the Field features enable practicing teachers to explain to you their philosophies, beliefs, and program practices. These teachers mentor you as they relate how they practice early childhood education. Among the contributors are professionals who are Teachers of the Year, have received prestigious awards, and have National Board Certification.

Voice from the Field
COMPETENCY BUILDER
How to Guide Children to Help Ensure Their Success

Kenneth entered the kindergarten classroom on the first day of the school year, trailing several feet behind his mom, who appeared to be unaware of his presence. She called out a greeting to another mom, and the two of them had an extended discussion about events in the neighborhood. Kenneth glanced around the room and headed purposefully toward the housekeeping center, where he grabbed a baby doll, threw it out of the doll bed, and then ran to the block box and grabbed a large block in each hand. At this point I deflected his trail of destruction and redirected his progress. "Good morning, welcome to my class. My name is Ms. Cheryl. What's your name?" The whirlwind stopped briefly to mumble a response that I could not understand and glared at me in open hostility. "Let's go talk to Mom," I suggested, touching his shoulder and directing him toward his mom.

Understanding Behavior

In our opening scenario, what important facts should we as educators recognize as signals that Kenneth has some behaviors that require adjustment to ensure his success in school?

- He seems unaware of the expected protocol for entering a classroom.
- His mother's apparent lack of interest in her child's behavior could be an indicator that Kenneth does not expect the adults around him to be involved with his activities.
- He may have been in an atmosphere that requires very little from him when it comes to following rules and, as

STEP 1 Plan
Plan what activities you will offer your children. What part of the day will I use for centers? How can I show my students the best ways to use materials? Where will your children keep their belongings?

STEP 2 Be explicit
Be sure that all of your children fully understand the classroom expectations. For example, I give my children opportunities to practice how we are to walk in the hallways, play on the playground, eat in the cafeteria, and move about the classroom. Many behaviors that inhibit success in school occur because students are not made aware of appropriate and inappropriate school procedures.

STEP 3 Model behavior
Model appropriate behaviors and use sociodramatic play to give children an opportunity to "act out" inappropriate behaviors. Lead a class discussion on appropriate versus inappropriate behaviors and allow children to discuss how they feel. Teach children how to handle these issues through conflict resolution methods. Remember, it takes numerous rounds of modeling and role playing to make an impact on behavior that has been ingrained for five years at home and is still the norm when students return home.

- **Competency Builder.** The Voice from the Field features that are labeled as Competency Builders are just what their name implies; they are designed to *build your competence* and confidence in performing essential teaching tasks, step by step. In college coursework, students are increasingly required to demonstrate strategies and provide explicit details that enable them to do the key professional tasks expected of early childhood teachers. These features are user friendly and can be immediately applied to your professional practice.

- **Portraits of Children.**   In a text about children, it is sometimes easy to think about them in the abstract. The Portraits of Children found in Chapters 9 through 12 are designed to ensure that you consider children as individuals as we discuss how to teach them. The features present authentic portraits of real children from all cultures and backgrounds, enrolled in real child care, preschool, and primary-grade programs across the United States. Each portrait includes developmental information across four domains: social-emotional, cognitive, motor, and adaptive (daily living). Accompanying questions challenge you to think and reflect about how you would provide for these children's educational and social needs if they were in your classroom.

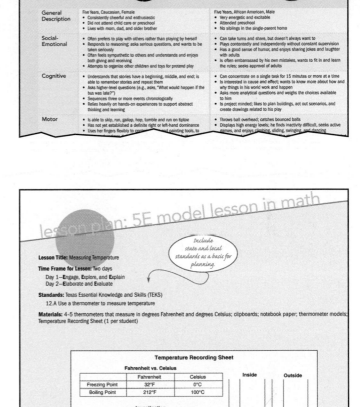

- **Lesson Plans.**   Planning for teaching and learning constitutes an important dimension of your role as a professional. This is especially true today, with the emphasis on ensuring that children learn what is mandated by state standards. The lesson plans in this text follow the 5E Model (Engage, Explore, Explain, Extend, and Evaluate). They enable you to look over the shoulder of experienced teachers and observe how they plan for instruction. These award-winning teachers share with you how they plan to ensure that their children will learn important knowledge and skills. In addition, Voice from the Field Competency Builders in Chapters 9, 11, and 12 discuss the specific competencies necessary to effectively plan learning activities and lessons for infants and toddlers, kindergartners, and primary-grade students.

- **Ethical Dilemmas.**   As an early childhood professional you will inevitably face difficult choices in your career that require you to have a solid understanding of ethical responsibility and best practices. To that end, each chapter includes an ethical dilemma based on facts, current issues, and real-life situations faced by early childhood professionals today. They present difficult decisions early childhood professionals have to make. These ethical dilemmas help build a better understanding of what it means to think like a professional and to respond appropriately in complicated and potentially compromising situations.

skill deficit When a child has not learned how to perform a particular skill or behavior.

inclusive classroom, you can achieve this goal by creating a positive management plan that addresses skill deficits. A skill deficit is the inability to perform a skill because the child does not possess the skill. For example, a child with a disability may have a social skill deficit associated with making friends and gaining popularity. Motivational deficits involve the unwillingness or lack of cooperation of children to perform a skill they possess, either entirely or at an appropriate level. For example, some children may be reluctant or hesitant to engage in an activity because of their disability. In contrast, some children may lack motivational self-control and be aggressive and intrusive in their behavior.

- *Rules:* State rules positively; limit their number; and make sure they are observable and measurable. Ensure that children's rules don't involve academic or homework issues that can unfairly impact students with disabilities or who are linguistically diverse.
- *Physical arrangement:* The four-desk cluster provides the most opportunities for students with disabilities to be included in the classroom. You can efficiently move from child to child, and at the same time the children support socialization, cooperation, and group work.
- *Grouping:* Grouping in the inclusive classroom is an excellent way to differentiate instruction in order to meet each child's needs. Appropriate assessment enables you to form appropriate groups.

Activities for Professional Development

Ethical Dilemma

"Caught in the middle."

Julia Le is a second grade teacher. One day, she, her colleagues, and her students are stunned to learn that, Greg, a nine-year-old third grader, just committed suicide at school. The whole school community is shocked and grieving. Julia's students pepper her with tearful questions. "Why did he do it? How did he do it? Where will he go? But why?" Julia struggles to answer their questions. When Julia goes to her teaching mentor for advice on how best to help her students through this terrible time, her mentor empathizes but says, "It's not really your job to answer questions like that. That's what school counselors are for. If they keep asking you questions, just send them to the counselor." In addition, the principal tells Julia, "It's inappropriate for eight-year-olds to be talking about suicide." Julia just doesn't feel right about it. She did some research and found that the

- **Margin Glossary Terms and Definitions.** Keeping track of important key terms is a problem often associated with reading and studying. Key terms and concepts are defined in the text as they are presented and are also placed in page margins. In this way, you have immediate access to them for reflection and review, and they maximize your study time by helping you retain essential knowledge.

- **Glossary.** A glossary of terms at the end of the book incorporates all of the definitions and terms found in the margin notes. The glossary provides a quick and useful reference for study and reflection.

Supplements to the Text

The supplements package for the twelfth edition is revised and upgraded. All online ancillaries are available for download by adopting professors via www.pearsonhighered.com from the Educator screen. Contact your Pearson sales representative for additional information.

Online Instructor's Manual   This manual contains chapter overviews and activity ideas to enhance chapter concepts, as well as instructions for assignable MyEducationLab material.

Online Test Bank   The Test Bank includes a variety of test items, including multiple choice, true/false, and short answer items.

Pearson MyTest   This powerful assessment generation program helps instructors easily create and print quizzes and exams. Questions and tests are authored online, allowing ultimate flexibility and the ability to efficiently create and print assessments anytime, anywhere. Instructors can access Pearson MyTest and their test bank files by going to www.pearsonmytest.com to log in, register, or request access. Features of Pearson MyTest include:

Premium assessment content
- Draw from a rich library of assessments that complement your Pearson textbook and your course's learning objectives.
- Edit questions or tests to fit your specific teaching needs.

Instructor-friendly resources
- Easily create and store your own questions, including images, diagrams, and charts, using simple drag-and-drop and Word-like controls.
- Use additional information provided by Pearson, such as the question's difficulty level or learning objective, to help you quickly build your test.

Time-saving enhancements
- Add headers or footers and easily scramble questions and answer choices—all from one simple toolbar.
- Quickly create multiple versions of your test or answer key, and when ready, simply save to MS-Word or PDF format and print.
- Export your exams for import to Blackboard 6.0, CE (WebCT), or Vista (WebCT).

Online PowerPoint Slides   PowerPoint slides highlight key concepts and strategies in each chapter and enhance lectures and discussions.

PEARSON
myeducationlab

The Power of Classroom Practice

In *Preparing Teachers for a Changing World*, Linda Darling-Hammond and her colleagues point out that grounding teacher education in real classrooms—among real teachers and students and among actual examples of students' and teachers' work—is an important, and perhaps even an essential, part of training teachers for the complexities of teaching in today's classrooms. MyEducationLab is an online learning solution that provides contextualized interactive exercises, simulations, and other resources designed to help develop the knowledge and skills teachers need. All of the activities and exercises in MyEducationLab are built around essential learning outcomes for teachers and are mapped to professional teaching standards. Utilizing classroom video, authentic student and teacher artifacts, case studies, and other resources and assessments, the scaffolded learning experiences in MyEducationLab offer pre-service teachers and those who teach them a unique and valuable education tool.

For each topic covered in the course you will find most or all of the following features and resources:

Connection to National Standards

Now it is easier than ever to see how coursework is connected to national standards. Each topic on MyEducationLab lists intended learning outcomes connected to the appropriate national standards. And all of the activities and exercises in MyEducationLab are mapped to the appropriate national standards and learning outcomes as well.

Assignments and Activities

Designed to enhance student understanding of concepts covered in class and save instructors preparation and grading time, these assignable exercises show concepts in action (through video, cases, and/or student and teacher artifacts). They help students deepen content knowledge and synthesize and apply concepts and strategies they read about in the book. (Correct answers for these assignments are available to the instructor only under the Instructor Resource tab.)

Building Teaching Skills and Dispositions

These learning units help students practice and strengthen skills that are essential to quality teaching. After presenting the steps involved in a core teaching process, students are given an opportunity to practice applying this skill via videos, student and teacher artifacts, and/or case studies of authentic classrooms. Providing multiple opportunities to practice a single teaching concept, each activity encourages a deeper understanding and application of concepts, as well as the use of critical thinking skills.

IRIS Center Resources

The IRIS Center at Vanderbilt University (http://iris.peabody.vanderbilt.edu), funded by the U.S. Department of Education's Office of Special Education Programs (OSEP), develops training enhancement materials for pre-service and in-service teachers. The Center works with experts from across the country to create challenge-based interactive modules, case study units, and podcasts that provide research-validated information about working with students in inclusive settings. In your MyEducationLab course we have integrated this content where appropriate.

Teacher Talk

This feature emphasizes the power of teaching through videos of master teachers, all telling their own compelling stories of why they teach. These videos help teacher candidates see the bigger picture and consider why what they are learning is important to their career as a teacher. Each of these featured teachers has been awarded the Council of Chief State School Officers Teachers of the Year award, the oldest and most prestigious award for teachers.

Study Plan Specific to Your Text

A MyEducationLab Study Plan is a multiple-choice assessment tied to chapter objectives, supported by study material. A well-designed Study Plan offers multiple opportunities to fully master required course content as identified by the objectives in each chapter.

- **Chapter Objectives** identify the learning outcomes for the chapter and give students targets to shoot for as they read and study.
- **Multiple Choice Assessments** assess mastery of the content. These assessments are mapped to chapter objectives, and students can take the multiple choice quiz as many times as they want. Not only do these quizzes provide overall scores for each objective, but they also explain why responses to particular items are correct or incorrect.
- **Study Material: Review, Practice, and Enrichment** gives students a deeper understanding of what they do and do not know related to chapter content. This material includes text excerpts, activities that include hints and feedback, and interactive multimedia exercises built around videos, simulations, cases, or classroom artifacts.

Course Resources

The Course Resources section on MyEducationLab is designed to help students put together an effective lesson plan, prepare for and begin their career, navigate their first year of teaching, and understand key educational standards, policies, and laws.

The Course Resources tab includes the following:

- The **Lesson Plan Builder** is an effective and easy-to-use tool that students can use to create, update, and share quality lesson plans. The software also makes it easy to integrate state content standards into any lesson plan.
- The **Preparing a Portfolio** module provides guidelines for creating a high-quality teaching portfolio.
- **Beginning Your Career** offers tips, advice, and other valuable information.

- *Resume Writing and Interviewing*: Includes expert advice on how to write impressive resumes and prepare for job interviews.
- *Your First Year of Teaching*: Provides practical tips to set up a first classroom, manage student behavior, and more easily organize for instruction and assessment.
- *Law and Public Policies*: Details specific directives and requirements teachers need to understand under the No Child Left Behind Act and the Individuals with Disabilities Education Improvement Act of 2004.

Certification and Licensure

The Certification and Licensure section is designed to help students pass their licensure exam by giving them access to state test requirements, overviews of what tests cover, and sample test items.

The Certification and Licensure tab includes the following:

- **State Certification Test Requirements:** Here students can click on a state and will then be taken to a list of state certification tests.
- Students can click on the **Licensure Exams** they need to take to find:
  - Basic information about each test
  - Descriptions of what is covered on each test
  - Sample test questions with explanations of correct answers
- **National Evaluation Series™** by Pearson: Here students can see the tests in the NES, learn what is covered on each exam, and access sample test items with descriptions and rationales of correct answers. They can also purchase interactive online tutorials developed by Pearson Evaluation Systems and the Pearson Teacher Education and Development group.
- **ETS Online Praxis Tutorials:** Here students can purchase interactive online tutorials developed by ETS and by the Pearson Teacher Education and Development group. Tutorials are available for the Praxis I exams and for select Praxis II exams.

Visit www.myeducationlab.com for a demonstration of this exciting new online teaching resource.

Acknowledgments

In the course of my teaching, service, consulting and writing, I meet and talk with many early childhood professionals who are deeply dedicated to doing their best for young children and their families. I am always touched, heartened, and encouraged by the openness, honesty, and unselfish sharing of ideas that characterize my professional colleagues. I thank all the individuals who contributed to the Voice from the Field features and other program descriptions. They are all credited for sharing their personal accounts of their lives, their children's lives, and their programs.

I am blessed to work with my colleagues at Pearson. My editor, Julie Peters, is bright, savvy, and always relentless in her efforts to make *Early Childhood Education Today* the best. Julie continues to be a constant source of creative and exciting ideas. Development Editor Bryce Bell is a pleasure to work with. He is attentive to details, conscientious, and provides many insightful suggestions for making this text better. Project Managers Linda Bayma and Angela Williams Urquhart (Thistle Hill Publishing Services) are very attentive to detail and make sure every part of the production process is done right and that we meet all production deadlines. Lori Whitley helps me select the best possible photos. She is always patient and accommodating with my requests for more photos to pick from. Becky Savage is informative and works collaboratively to make sure permissions are done right.

I want to thank the "A-Team," Brittany Flournoy, Haley Garth, Destine'e Davis, and Jasmine Montgomery. Brittany's positive energy keeps us all laughing and the pages turning. Haley is the spine of the book. Thanks Haley for staying late many days to make sure all details were taken care of. Thank you Destine'e for being the glue that holds the book and team together. Jasmine is hardworking, intelligent, and our problem solver.

Finally, I want to thank the reviewers: Michelle Amodei, Grove City College; Nurun N. Begum, East Stroudsburg University; Szu Yin Chu, University of Texas, Austin; Mary Cordell, Navarro College; Benita Flores, Del Mar College; Shernaz B. Garcia, University of Texas, Austin; Rhonda D. Richardson, Sam Houston State University; and Anne M. Slanina, Slippery Rock University. Many of the changes in this twelfth edition are the result of their suggestions.

Brief Contents

Contents

Special Features

*Voice from the Field: *Competency Builders* outline specific steps, strategies, or guidelines to guide early childhood professionals as they develop competencies or skills in these areas.

PART
I

EARLY CHILDHOOD EDUCATION AND PROFESSIONAL DEVELOPMENT

1

YOU AND EARLY CHILDHOOD EDUCATION

What Does It Mean to Be a Professional?

focus questions

1. How is the early childhood profession changing?
2. Who is an early childhood professional?
3. What are the six standards for being an early childhood education (ECE) professional?
4. What is developmentally appropriate practice (DAP) and how do you apply it to your professional practice?
5. How can you prepare for a career in early childhood education?
6. What is a philosophy of education and how can you use it in your professional practice?
7. What new roles are expected of you as an early childhood professional today?

naeyc standards

Standard 1. Promoting Child Development and Learning

I use my understanding of young children's characteristics and needs, and of multiple interacting influences on children's development and learning, to create environments that are healthy, respectful, supportive, and challenging for each child.[1]

Standard 2. Building Family and Community Relationships

I know about, understand, and value the importance and complex characteristics of children's families and communities. I use this understanding to create respectful, reciprocal relationships that support and empower families, and to involve all families in their children's development and learning.[2]

Standard 3. Observing, Documenting, and Assessing to Support Young Children and Families

I know about and understand the goals, benefits, and uses of assessment. I know about and use systematic observations, documentation, and other effective assessment strategies in a responsible way, in partnership with families and other professionals, to positively influence the development of every child.[3]

Standard 4. Using Developmentally Effective Approaches to Connect with Children and Families

I understand and use positive relationships and supportive interactions as the foundation for my work with young children and families. I know, understand, and use a wide array of developmentally appropriate approaches, instructional strategies, and tools to connect with children and families and positively influence each child's development and learning.[4]

Standard 5. Using Content Knowledge to Build Meaningful Curriculum

I understand the importance of developmental domains and academic (or content) disciplines in early childhood curriculum. I use my knowledge and other resources to design, implement, and evaluate meaningful, challenging curricula that promote comprehensive developmental and learning outcomes for every young child.[5]

Standard 6. Becoming a Professional

I identify and conduct myself as a member of the early childhood profession. I know and use ethical guidelines and other professional standards related to early childhood practice. I am an informed advocate for sound educational practices and policies.[6]

Ever since she was in high school, Renee Comacho wanted to teach young children. Not just any children, but children with disabilities. "During my junior year, I joined a summer volunteer intern program at my local child care center that had five children with disabilities. I really enjoyed working with them! That experience got me hooked on early childhood special education!" Today, Renee teaches K–3 in a public early childhood center of two hundred children that includes children with many kinds of disabilities. Renee is working on her master's degree and wants to earn National Board Certification as an exceptional needs specialist. "I work with teams of teachers and we are always learning how to accommodate lessons and activities to assure that we are meeting the needs of all children—especially those with disabilities. At the beginning of this school year, we all received training in how to accommodate the curriculum and classroom environments to support learning and how to involve families of children with disabilities. My colleagues and I have high expectations for all the children, so we want to make sure we do the best we can for them."

"Contributing to the teaching profession has been my **personal goal** since entering the doors of my first classroom. My classroom is **academically rigorous**, and regardless of circumstances and challenges, **I have hope for my students**, their potential, and their abilities to become change agents."

ROBERT KELTY
2008 Arizona Teacher of the Year, second and third grade teacher at Puente de Hozho Elementary School, Flagstaff, Arizona

Changes in the Early Childhood Profession

This is an exciting time to be a member of the early childhood education profession. Early childhood education, which includes children from birth to age eight, has changed more in the last ten years than in the previous fifty years, and more changes are in store. Why is early childhood education undergoing dramatic transformation and reform?

First, there is a tremendous increase in scientific knowledge about young children and the ways they grow, develop, and learn. This new knowledge enables professionals to view young children as extremely capable and naturally eager to learn at very young ages. Second, educators have developed research-based programs and curricula that enable children to learn literally from the beginning of life. Third, influential research, such as the HighScope Perry Preschool Project, validates the theory that high-quality education in the early years has positive and lasting benefits for children throughout their lives.[7] The way children are reared and educated in the early formative years makes a significant difference in the way they develop and learn. When families, teachers, and other caring adults get it right from the start of children's lives, all of society reaps big dividends. Fourth, more than 80 percent of all four-year-olds attend some kind of preschool program.[8] Fifth, nearly 54 percent of white children, 14 percent of African American children, 25 percent of Hispanic children, 3 percent of Asian children, 1 percent of American Indian children, and 4 percent of other races born in 2001 entered kindergarten for the first time in 2006 and 2007.[9] More than 1.1 million children attended state-funded preschool education, 973,178 at age four alone.[10] The demand for teachers and the ongoing public and professional attention will continue to focus attention on the early years and the importance they play in lifelong education.

A New Era of Early Childhood Education

Combined, these changes are dramatically altering our understanding of how young children learn; how teachers teach; and professional roles and responsibilities. As a result, the field of early childhood education is entering a new era, which requires professionals who are up-to-date and willing to adapt so that all children will learn and succeed in school and life. You and other early childhood professionals have a wonderful opportunity to develop new and improved programs and to advocate for best practices for all young children. Change and how you can respond to it is one of the themes of this book.

Who Is an Early Childhood Professional?

Like Renee, you are preparing to be a highly qualified and effective early childhood professional, who teaches children from birth to age eight. You are going to work with families and the community to bring high-quality education and services to all children. How would you explain the term **early childhood professional** to others? What does *professional* mean?

early childhood professional An educator who successfully teaches all children, promotes high personal standards, and continually expands his or her skills and knowledge.

A high-quality early childhood professional has the professional characteristics, knowledge, and skills necessary to teach and conduct programs so that all children learn and the ability to inform the public about children's and families' issues. Early childhood professionals are those who promote high standards for themselves, their colleagues, and their students—they are continually improving and expanding their skills and knowledge. Professionals also think about and reflect on their teaching and collaborations with colleagues and families. Being a reflective practitioner is an important part of being a professional. Later in this chapter, we will discuss more in depth your role as a reflective professional.

You will discover in your work as an early childhood professional that as a result of the changing field of early childhood education there are many new job opportunities. Your role as teacher, aide, or administrator will constantly change in response to new jobs created by the expanding field of early childhood education. You can expect that you will participate in many professional development activities and that you will be constantly involved in new programs and practices; and you will have opportunities to engage in new and different roles as a professional. As Renee in our chapter opener illustrates, the fields of early childhood and early childhood special education are merging, creating jobs and opportunities not available five years ago.

The Six Standards of Professional Development

Being a professional goes beyond any academic degrees and experiences you may earn. High-quality professionalism in early childhood education has six integrated standards, all of which are important and necessary dimensions of your professional experience. These are located at the beginning of each chapter. Figure 1.1, "The Six Standards of Professional Practice," shows how each of these standards plays a powerful role in determining who and what a professional is and how professionals implement practice in early childhood classrooms. Let's review each of these standards and see how you can apply them to your professional practice.

Standard 1: Promoting Child Development and Learning

As an early childhood professional you will need to know how to promote child development and learning. Learning how to do this includes knowledge and understanding of young children's characteristics and needs and the multiple influences on children's development and learning.

Child Development.   Knowledge of child development is fundamental for all early childhood educators regardless of their roles or the ages of the children they teach. It allows you to confidently implement developmentally appropriate practices with all children. All early

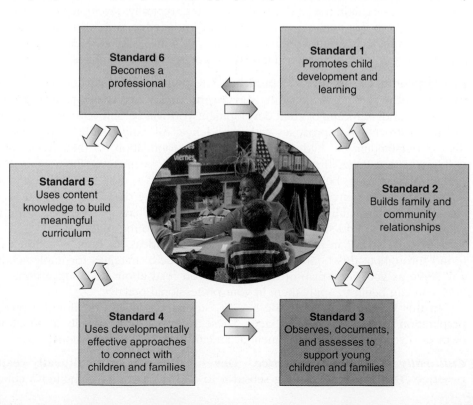

FIGURE 1.1 The Six Standards of Professional Practice

These standards of professional preparation provide guidelines for what you should know and be able to do in your lifelong career as an early childhood professional.

Source: National Association for the Education of Young Children, NAEYC Standards for Early Childhood Professional Preparation Programs, July 2009. Photo by Ariel Skelley/Getty Images, Inc. – Blend Images.

childhood professionals "use their understanding of young children's characteristics and needs, and of multiple interacting influences on children's development and learning, to create environments that are healthy, respectful, supportive, and challenging."[11] Child development knowledge enables you to understand how children grow and develop across all developmental domains—cognitive, linguistic, social, emotional, physical, language, and aesthetic domains and also to understand children's play, activity, learning processes, and motivation to learn.[12]

Knowledge of individual children, combined with knowledge of child growth and development, enables you to provide care and education that is developmentally appropriate for each child. DAP means basing your teaching on how children grow and develop, and DAP is the recommended teaching practice of the early childhood profession. Appendix A contains the new, revised, NAEYC Position Statement on Developmentally Appropriate Practice in Early Childhood Programs. Now would be a good time for you to read it and reflect on how DAP applies to your professional practice.

Tania Harman, 2009 Indiana Teacher of the Year, a first and second grade English as New Language (ENL) teacher, believes "Every student does not learn the same way, at the same pace, nor do they have the same schema to build on for meaningful lessons. My lessons reflect that knowledge. I present information to my students based on the effort I make to get to know them, and I differentiate instruction in order to teach to their differing strengths. Knowing my students is a powerful way to get to the heart of a lesson for each individual."[13]

Early childhood special education is becoming part of the field of early childhood education as more children with disabilities are included in the regular classroom. The blending, or integration of these two fields has been going on for the last decade and we will continue to see this trend. For example, kindergarten teacher Julie Sanders has in her classroom a child with autism and a child with attention deficit hyperactivity disorder (ADHD). As a result, she has to apply knowledge of typical and atypical child development. As a teacher of young children, you will more than likely have at least one child with a disability in your classroom. Consequently, it is important that you, like Julie, know the developmental characteristics of children with disabilities as well as typically developing children.

Throughout this text, I provide you with knowledge and information necessary to also meet standards when working with children with disabilities. Each chapter also has specific ideas and skills for accommodating children with disabilities.

Developmentally Appropriate Approaches.   Knowledge of child development provides the foundation for you to conduct **developmentally appropriate practices (DAP)**. With your understanding of child development you will be able to select essential curricula and instructional approaches with confidence. All early childhood professionals use their understanding of child development as the foundation for their work with young children. Carol Foltz, first grade teacher at Neil A. Armstrong Elementary School in Mooresville, Indiana, believes "Each and every child is special and deserves a safe and respectful learning environment. Students learn in many different ways and in teaching we need to address all of the learning styles that they have. In the classroom, children should be able to find success no matter what their learning style may be."[14]

We discuss DAP in more detail in this chapter. Ideas for how to conduct DAP are found throughout this book. These ideas and specific strategies for implementing DAP will serve as your road map of teaching. As you read about DAP suggestions, consider how you can begin to apply them in your professional practice.

In this book you will see the NAEYC standards for early childhood professional preparation on chapter-opening pages. These are provided to identify information of relevance to you and your development as an early childhood professional.

Culturally Appropriate Practice.   **Developmentally and culturally responsive practice (DCRP)** includes being sensitive to and responding to children's cultural and

developmentally appropriate practice (DAP) Practice based on how children grow and develop and on individual and cultural differences.

developmentally and culturally responsive practice (DCRP) Teaching based on the ability to respond appropriately to children's and families' developmental, cultural, and ethnic backgrounds and needs.

ethnic backgrounds and needs. The United States is a nation of diverse people, and this diversity will increase. Children in every early childhood program represent this diversity. When children enter schools and programs, they do not leave their uniqueness, gender, culture, socioeconomic status, and race at the classroom door. Children bring themselves and their backgrounds to early childhood programs. As part of your professional practice you will embrace, value, and incorporate **culturally appropriate practice** into your teaching. Learning how to teach children of all cultures is an important part of your professional role.

Antibias Education.   Conducting a developmentally and culturally appropriate program also means you will include in your curriculum activities and materials that help challenge and change all biases of any kind that seek to diminish and portray as inferior any children based on their gender, race, culture, disability, language, or socioeconomic status. You can accomplish this goal by implementing an **antibias education (ABE)**. The book *Anti-Bias Curriculum: Tools for Empowering Young Children*, by Louise Derman-Sparks, provides the profession's foundation for understanding antibias curriculum and how to implement it in your classroom.[15]

Anti-Bias Education for Young Children and Ourselves, by Louise Derman-Sparks and Julie Olsen Edwards, extends the research and practices featured in the first edition and provides a set of strategies for teachers who want to see themselves as champions for all children.[16] Antibias education has four goals that can be applied to children of diverse backgrounds and influences to provide a safe, supportive community for all children.

Goal 1   Each child demonstrates self-awareness, confidence, family pride, and positive social identities.

Goal 2   Each child expresses comfort and joy with human diversity; accurate language for human differences; and deep, caring human connections.

Goal 3   Each child increasingly recognizes unfairness, has language to describe unfairness, and understands that unfairness hurts.

Goal 4   Each child demonstrates empowerment and the skills to act, with others or alone, against prejudice and/or discriminatory actions.[17]

If you have not read these books, put them at the top of your list of professional books to read.

Critical tasks of developmental identity include developing an *individual identity* and a *cultural identity*. Individual identity involves learning about the self—"Who am I?" Cultural identity involves learning about the culture of which the child is a part and how she or he relates to and functions in that culture. This is why you have to provide activities and an environmental context in which children can learn about their cultures, identify with them, and feel comfortable about being a part of their culture.

Here are a few antibias strategies to follow in your classroom:

- *Evaluate your classroom environment and instructional materials to determine if they are appropriate for an antibias curriculum.*   Get rid of materials that are obstacles to your antibias goals, such as books that include children of only one race. In my visits to early childhood classrooms, I observe many that are "cluttered," meaning they contain too many materials that do not contribute much to a multicultural learning environment. Include photos and representations from all cultures in your classroom and community.

- *Redesign your classroom.*   For example, you may decide to add a literacy center that encourages children to read and write about multicultural themes. Remember that children need the time, opportunity, and materials required to read and write about a wide range of antibias topics. Make sure you provide children with books relating to gender, culture, and ethnic themes.

culturally appropriate practice An approach to education based on the premise that all peoples in the United States should receive proportional attention in the curriculum.

antibias education (ABE) An approach that seeks to provide children with an understanding of social and behavioral problems related to prejudice and seeks to provide them with the knowledge, attitude, and skills needed to combat prejudice.

The United States is a pluralistic society and will continue to be a nation of diverse cultures and ethnic backgrounds. It is important for you to promote racial and cultural awareness and to help children live in harmony with others.

• *Evaluate your current curriculum and approaches to diversity.* Review your curriculum to see how it is or is not supporting antibias approaches. Learning experiences should be relevant to your students, their community, and their families' cultures. When you are diversifying your curriculum, consider two categories: how you teach and what you teach.

• *Make sure all children are accepted and valued.* For example, some children of different cultural backgrounds may not be included in particular play groups. Anti-bias information enables you to develop plans for ensuring that children of all cultures and genders are included in play groups and activities. For example, Anne Borys, a physical therapist from Drexel University, suggests that teachers can promote disability awareness and acceptance in childhood by having a "disability for a day" in your classroom. Have children wear mittens and attempt to button their shirt, play with play dough with rubber bands on fingers, and put Vaseline on plastic glasses to help your inclusive classroom gain awareness and understanding of children who have disabilities.[18]

• *Reflect on your interaction with all children.* You may unknowingly give more attention to boys than to girls. Also, you may be overlooking some important environmental accommodations that can support the learning of children with disabilities. How do you interact with children of different cultures? Children with disabilities?

• *Include antibias activities in your lesson plans.* Intentional planning helps ensure that you are including a full range of antibias activities in your program. Intentional antibias planning also helps you integrate antibias activities into your curriculum for meeting national, state, and local learning standards.

• *Work with families to incorporate your antibias curriculum.* Remember, families are valuable resources in helping you achieve your goals.[19] For example, Figure 1.2 shows a parent survey used by teacher Renee Comacho to learn more about her student's ethnic and cultural backgrounds so she can incorporate them into her classroom.

Implementing an antibias education will not be easy and will require a lot of hard work and effort on your part. However, this is what teaching and being a professional is all about. You owe it to yourself, your children, and the profession to conduct programs that enable all children to live and learn in **bias-free** programs.

bias-free An environment, classroom setting, or program that is free of prejudicial behaviors.

Knowledge and understanding of young children's characteristics and needs enable you to develop and implement meaningful learning experiences that promote learning for all children. Say, for example, you were a beginning teacher with a group of English language learners (ELLs) in your class. You would want to know how ELLs learn best and how to teach them so they learn at high levels. Effective pedagogical approaches include using developmentally appropriate practices; selecting and using bias-free and culturally appropriate learning materials; promoting children's oral language and communication; supporting child-initiated learning; guiding children's learning and behavior, promoting responsive relationships; establishing and using learning centers; using play as a foundation for children's learning; and using technology as a teaching and learning tool.

The featured Voice from the Field "Multiculturalism and Professionalism: You Can't Have One Without the Other" on page 10 shares some important suggestions to guide you in making sure your professional practice is multicultural. This Voice from the Field is also a Competency Builder. Competency Builders are features of this text designed to help you increase your teaching competence and performance in specific professional areas. By

FIGURE 1.2

Parent Survey

Dear Parents,

   In our classroom, I want the children to learn about and appreciate different cultures and family traditions. Please join me in teaching your children to view cultural similarities and differences in positive ways and to experience a community of diverse learners collaborating and working together. Please complete the survey and return it to me as soon as possible.

Your Name _____   Child's Name _____

Countries of your family's heritage:

1. _____   2. _____

3. _____   4. _____

Describe any traditions that may be important to your family (i.e., holiday events, foods, clothing, languages, etc.):

_____

_____

_____

_____

What suggestions do you have for me for how to include your culture in my classroom?

Thank you for helping me,

Renee Comacho

completing the Competency Builder activities, you will enhance your professional development and contribute to your qualifications as a high-quality and highly effective teacher.

Creating Healthy, Respectful, Supportive, and Challenging Learning Environments. Research consistently shows that children cared for and taught in enriched environments are healthier, happier, and more achievement oriented.[20] To attain this goal for all children, you must provide them with environments that are healthy, respectful, supportive, and challenging.

- **Healthy Environment:** *Provide for children's physical and psychological health, safety, and sense of security.* For example, the Austin Eco School in Austin, Texas, creates an environment for its students where they can learn and play in an environment that is free from chemical toxins typically found in cleansers, paint, and flooring.

healthy environments
Environments that provide for children's physical and psychological health, safety, and sense of security.

Voice from the Field

Multiculturalism and Professionalism: You Can't Have One Without the Other

Think for a moment about all of the classrooms of children across the United States. Consider these data about America's children:

- In 2009, 56 percent of U.S. children were white, non-Hispanic; 22 percent were Hispanic; 15 percent were African American; 4 percent were Asian; and 5 percent were all other races.
- The percentage of children who are Hispanic has increased faster than that of any other racial or ethnic group.*

This increase in racial, ethnic, and cultural diversity in America is reflected in early childhood classrooms, which are also receiving increased numbers of children with disabilities and developmental delays. Consider the current student population at Susan B. Anthony Elementary School in Sacramento, California: 19 percent are Hispanic, 63 percent are Asian, 12 percent are African American, and 3 percent are white. Moreover, 98 percent of the children receive free lunches, and 41 percent are English-language learners.[†]

Meeting the Challenge

This diverse composition of early childhood classrooms challenges you to make your classroom responsive to the various needs of all your children, which is part of your professional responsibility. Let's look at some of the things you can do to be a responsible professional who is multiculturally aware and who teaches with respect and equity:

STRATEGY 1 Be Concerned About Your Own Multicultural Development

- Honestly confront your attitudes and views as they relate to people of other cultures. You may be carrying baggage that you have to get rid of to authentically and honestly educate all of your children to their fullest capacity.
- Read widely about your multicultural role as a professional.
- Learn about the habits, customs, beliefs, and religious practices of the cultures represented by your children.
- Ask some of your parents to tutor you in their language so you can learn basic phrases for greeting and questioning, the meaning of nonverbal gestures, and the way to address parents and children appropriately and respectfully.

STRATEGY 2 Make Every Child Welcome

- Make your classroom a place where diversity is encouraged and everyone is treated fairly. Create a classroom environment that is vibrant and alive with the cultures of your children. You can do this with pictures, artifacts, and objects loaned by parents.
- Support and use children's home language and culture. Create a safe environment in which children feel free to talk about and share their culture and language. Encourage children to discuss, draw, paint, and write about what their culture means to them.

STRATEGY 3 Make Every Parent Welcome

- Invite parents and families to share their languages and cultures in your classroom. Music, stories, and customs provide a rich background for learning about and respecting other cultures.
- Communicate with parents in their home languages.
- Work with parents to help them (and you) bridge the differences between the way schools operate and the norms of their homes and cultures.

STRATEGY 4 Collaborate with Colleagues

- Ask colleagues to share with you ideas about how to respond to questions, requests, and concerns of children and parents.
- Volunteer to form a faculty study group to read, discuss, and learn how to meet the cultural and linguistic needs of all children.

STRATEGY 5 Become Active in Your Community

- Learn as much as you can about your community and the cultural resources it can provide. Communities are very multicultural places!
- Collaborate with community and state organizations that work with culturally and linguistically diverse families and populations. Ask them for volunteers who can help you meet the diverse needs of your children. Children need to interact with and value role models from all cultures.
- Volunteer to act as a community outreach coordinator to provide families with services, such as family literacy and school readiness information.

You can't be a complete early childhood professional without a multicultural dimension. As you become more culturally aware, you will increase your capacity for caring and understanding—and you and your students will learn and grow together.

*ChildStats.gov, "America's Children: Key National Indicators of Well-Being 2009," www.childstats.gov/americaschildren/tables/pop3.asp?popup=true
[†]http://www.greatschools.net/cgi-bin/ca/other/4675#students.

Increasingly, child care programs are using eco-friendly diapers, non-toxic methods to control pests, and organic baby foods.

- **Respectful Environment:** *Show respect for each individual child, and for their culture, home language, individual abilities or disabilities, family context, and community.* Marcy Henniger, author of *Setting the Stage for Learning*, encourages parents and teachers to promote learning through cooking. Teachers can have an "exploration center" filled with learning activities and materials from different cultures such as foods and recipe books, where children can experiment and interact with cooking.[21]

  Santos Ramirez is a first grader at Jay Shideler Elementary School in Topeka, KS and a child with ataxic cerebral palsy. He uses a DynaVox Vmax, an augmentative and alternative communication device that helps individuals with speech and learning challenges communicate. Santos is in a regular, inclusive classroom with other first graders and enjoys physical education and recess along with his friends. Santos's teacher, Lisa Hamilton, was initially nervous about having Santos in her class; however, "He won everyone over. He's a regular kid trapped in a body that won't work the way he wants it to. He is capable of the first grade curriculum. He is very intelligent."[22]

- **Supportive Environment:** *Believe each child can learn and help children understand and make meaning of their experiences.* Discovery Elementary School in Meridian, Idaho, encourages and supports its students by offering a program which pairs students who have autism with typically-developing children. The goal of the program is to "ease autistic students into the traditional classroom and bring the regular school experience to students who spend most of their day in the autistic classroom," says Discovery Principal Ken Marlowe.[23]

- **Challenging Environment:** *Provide achievable and "stretching" experiences for all children.* Sherry Grimes, a third grade mathematics teacher at Medina Elementary in Medina, Tennessee, uses praise statements for her students such as "clap one time" and "pop like popcorn" to encourage them in their understanding of math skills. Sherry says, "Our teachers and support staff are committed to students; we look at the whole child, work in small groups, and relate the subject matter to real life for students."[24]

respectful environments Environments that show respect for each individual child and for their culture, home language, individual abilities or disabilities, family context, and community.

supportive environments Environments in which professionals believe each child can learn, and that help children understand and make meaning of their experiences.

challenging environments Environments that provide achievable and "stretching" experiences for all children.

Standard 2: Building Family and Community Relationships

Families are an important part of children's lives. Creating a collaborative relationship with your students' families and the community makes sense to give your students the best opportunity to succeed. To do this, you need to know and understand the characteristics of children's families and the communities in which they live and become an advocate for parents and families. Your collaboration with families will also involve supporting and empowering them. In addition, you will need to know how to involve families and communities in all aspects of children's development and learning.[25] It is very important to be respectful of children and their families in order to build strong relationships.

Saying that you are respectful of children and families is one thing; putting respect into practice means you will use your knowledge and skills of child development and family involvement to make respectfulness a reality. Here are some things you can do to demonstrate your respectfulness for children and families:

- When you plan cooking activities, talk with parents who have children with restricted diets to determine acceptable foods and recipes so all children can participate.
- Validate children's home languages by learning words and teaching them to the other children. For example, when counting the days on the calendar, you can count in English, Spanish, Vietnamese, and so on.[26]
- Keep expectations clear between your students and their families. For example, at the beginning of the school year, kindergarten teachers Gretchen Rohrer and Jessie McPeck at Demmitt Elementary School in Vandalia, Ohio, send out a newsletter titled the "ABC's of

Early childhood educators are professionals who collaborate and work with families and communities to help children of all backgrounds and abilities to learn.

Kindergarten" for parents which includes information such as attendance, behavior, classroom expectations as well as content areas taught, and roles of the parent in the classroom.[27]

- Gina Pace, second grade teacher of Estes Hills Elementary, Chapel Hill, North Carolina, says, "What I think makes me an outstanding teacher is the sincere and loving relationships I form with the children I have the honor to teach. When children know you love them, they feel like they can do anything. When parents know you love their children, there is trust. This is a recipe for success on all levels."[28]

- ELL Teacher Janet Davis-Castro, also from Chapel Hill, says she earns the respect of students because she gives it: "I earn their trust because I keep my word; I earn their affection because they know my commitment to them and their family. My favorite compliment by a former student was, 'Mrs. Castro, we love you because you don't give up on us. You don't let us get away with not doing stuff. You talk to our moms all the time.' "[29]

Learn and find out about families' child-rearing practices and how they handle routines relating to toileting, behavioral problems, and so on. Learning how to build family relationships is an important part of your professional development. Respectful and reciprocal relationships with parents and families empower them to be involved in their children's educations.

Standard 3: Observing, Documenting, and Assessing to Support Children and Families

assessment The process of collecting information about children's development, learning, behavior, academic progress, need for special services, and achievement in order to make decisions.

One of your most important responsibilities as an early childhood professional will be to observe, document, and assess children's learning. The outcomes of your **assessment** will help guide you in making decisions about what and how to teach young children, and they will also provide you abundant information with which to share with parents and families. You can consider assessment as the three-way process that you will use as a professional shown in Figure 1.3.

FIGURE 1.3 Three-Way Process of Assessment

As more research emerges about the importance of early childhood education, observing and assessing in your own classroom will also become more important. In Chapter 3, you will learn how observing and assessing will guide you in making decisions in your classroom.

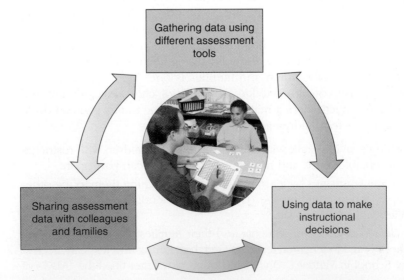

Gathering data using different assessment tools

Using data to make instructional decisions

Sharing assessment data with colleagues and families

In your professional development, you can integrate methods for achieving your professional goals. You can sharpen your observation skills to help you also learn about child development. Observation and documentation are just two forms of assessment that you will use in ongoing systematic ways. In fact, observation is one of your main means for gathering information about young children.

Through your assessment, observation, and documentation practices, you can provide accommodations for children with disabilities and also involve parents in the process. For example, first grade teacher Addie Hare asks parents to fill out a short survey about their child's interests and learning needs. Parents know their children best and you can learn a lot when you listen to what they have to say. Ask parents what their children like to do outside of school, any special accommodations the child may need, and how the parents would like to be involved. Finish your survey with an open-ended question such as, "Is there anything else you would like me to know?" This often yields helpful information that might not emerge from previous questions.[30]

One of the most important professional classroom skills is the ability to observe and assess children's learning.

Standard 4: Using Developmentally Effective Approaches to Connect with Children and Families

As an early childhood professional, you will want to integrate your understanding of and relationships with children and families; your understanding of developmentally effective approaches to teaching and learning; and your knowledge of academic disciplines to design, implement, and evaluate experiences that promote positive, developmentally appropriate learning for all children.[31] To be a professional in this area, you will want to demonstrate positive relationships with children and families. In the final analysis, all of education is about relationships: how you relate to your colleagues, how you relate to parents and other family members, and how you relate to children. In **responsive relationships**, you are responsive to the needs and interests of children and their families. Throughout the book, I provide you examples of suggestions for creating responsive relationships.

responsive relationships The relationship that exists between yourself, children, and their families where you are responsive to their needs and interests.

Standard 5: Using Content Knowledge to Build Meaning Curriculum

Research shows that students benefit when teachers develop a more in-depth understanding of content areas, of effective means of gathering and using formative assessment data, and of how to differentiate instruction to address needs.[32]

Content Areas.   Content areas are important to children's learning. Content areas form the basis for children's learning to read, write, do mathematics and science, and be creative. Consequently, early childhood professionals understand the importance of each content area in children's development and learning, demonstrate the essential knowledge and skills needed to provide appropriate environments that support learning in each content area, and demonstrate basic knowledge of the research base underlying each content area.[33] The content areas in early childhood are:

- Language, Literacy, and Reading
- Music and the Arts

- Mathematics
- Science
- Health and Physical Education
- Social Studies

Types of Knowledge.   To effectively teach your students, you must gain a better understanding of how your students will learn and how you will teach them. To teach all students according to today's standards, teachers need to deeply understand content and be able to conform to each child so they can help students create useful, meaningful experiences and connect across subject matter and to everyday life. The four types of knowledge are described below.

content knowledge The content and subjects teachers plan to teach.

Content Knowledge.   The knowledge that comes from content areas is known as **content knowledge**. Teachers must understand the content they teach (e.g., math, science, social studies) and what constitutes the essential knowledge and skills of each content area. This is where state standards are important and helpful; you will want to be familiar with your state standards.

Pedagogical Content Knowledge.   In addition to knowing content, teachers also must know *how* to teach students so they learn content knowledge. This is called **pedagogical content knowledge**, knowing how to teach children so the content knowledge is accessible to them. For example, Sarah Becker, first grade teacher at Evergreen Elementary School in Carol Stream, Illinois, created a Blooming Earth Garden, an outdoor classroom that provides an exciting hands-on learning experience across all grade levels and covers several school curriculum areas such as science, writing, math, and art. Students study the importance of Illinois prairies, documenting, and photographing, and by the end of the year students are able to identify the differences between living and nonliving things and have an increased understanding of plant and animal growth.[34]

pedagogical content knowledge The teaching skills teachers need to help all children learn.

Second grade students at Robert E. Clow Elementary School in Naperville, Illinois, learn social studies by building a model community resembling their city out of cardboard and shoe boxes. The students learn about how to use map grids and keys, and use the telephone book to look up addresses and descriptions of actual landmarks in Naperville, such as the town hall, stores, and roads.[35]

pedagogical knowledge The ability to apply pedagogical and content knowledge to develop meaningful learning experiences for children.

Pedagogical Knowledge.   A third type of knowledge, general **pedagogical knowledge**, has to do with how to effectively teach and to facilitate learning regardless of the content area. This knowledge involves considering school, family, and community contexts, and children's prior experiences, to develop meaningful learning experiences. It also involves reflecting on teaching practice, and includes the variety of ideas, methods, and technologies teachers use to help each child learn.

knowledge of learners and learning Understanding students and how they learn (DAP); managing classroom environments and guiding children.

Knowledge of Learners and Learning.   Finally, high-quality teachers must know about and understand the students they teach. This is called **knowledge of learners and learning**.[36]

Third grade teacher at Warrenwood Elementary School Sarah Hennessey, 2009–2010 North Carolina Teacher of the Year, is constantly aware that words, deeds, and actions are creating memories in her students' minds. She knows firsthand how powerful an educator's influence and example can be. Caring teachers and a valued sense of education led her out of the inner city to one of the most rewarding life experiences that she has had, becoming an educator.[37]

Robert Stephenson, 2009–2010 Michigan Teacher of the Year and third grade teacher at Wardcliff Elementary School in East Lansing, Michigan, knows it is important to treat each child with respect and dignity; to accept each child with understanding; and to have faith in his or her abilities. He also wants to help students learn to value themselves, value others, and develop a love and enthusiasm for learning. He believes in connecting with individuals and challenging them to reach their highest potential.[38]

Collaborative Planning.   You will engage in **collaborative planning**, meeting collaboratively in grade level teams or across grade level teams in order to examine student data together and to plan and develop instructional strategies. In your planning, you will incorporate and align your curriculum with local and state standards.

Reflective Practice.   Building meaningful curriculum for young children also involves reflective practice. **Reflective practice** helps you think about how children learn and enables you to make decisions about how best to support their development and learning. Thinking about learning and understanding how children learn makes it easier for you to improve your teaching effectiveness, student learning, and professional satisfaction. In addition, thinking about learning and thinking about teaching are part of your reflective practice. Reflective practice involves deliberate and careful consideration about the children you teach, the theories on which you base your teaching, how you teach, what children learn, and how you will teach in the future. Although solitary reflection is useful, the power of reflective practice is more fully realized when you engage in such practice with your mentor teacher and your professional learning community. The reflective teacher is a thoughtful teacher. Reflective practice involves the three steps shown in Figure 1.4.

Standard 6: Becoming a Professional

Early childhood professionals conduct themselves as professionals and identify with their profession.[39] Your identification with and involvement in your profession enables you to

collaborative planning Planning used by groups of teachers at the grade levels or across grade levels to plan curriculum daily, weekly, and monthly. Also called *team planning*.

reflective practice The active process of thinking before teaching, during teaching, and after teaching in order to make decisions about how to plan, assess, and teach.

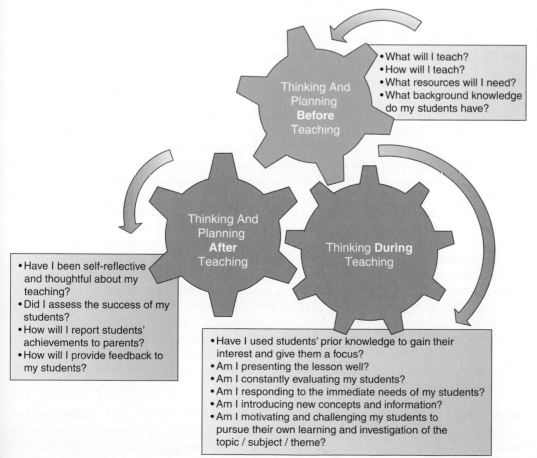

FIGURE 1.4 The Cycle of Reflective Practice: Thinking, Planning, and Deciding

Thinking And Planning **Before** Teaching
• What will I teach?
• How will I teach?
• What resources will I need?
• What background knowledge do my students have?

Thinking And Planning **After** Teaching
• Have I been self-reflective and thoughtful about my teaching?
• Did I assess the success of my students?
• How will I report students' achievements to parents?
• How will I provide feedback to my students?

Thinking **During** Teaching
• Have I used students' prior knowledge to gain their interest and give them a focus?
• Am I presenting the lesson well?
• Am I constantly evaluating my students?
• Am I responding to the immediate needs of my students?
• Am I introducing new concepts and information?
• Am I motivating and challenging my students to pursue their own learning and investigation of the topic / subject / theme?

say proudly that you are a teacher of young children. Being a professional means that you (1) know about and engage in ethical practice; (2) engage in continuous lifelong learning and professional development; (3) collaborate with colleagues, parents, families, and community partners; (4) engage in reflective practice; and (5) advocate on behalf of children, families, and the profession.[40] These competencies represent the heart and soul of professional practice. You should be committed to increasing your knowledge in these areas throughout your career. Carole D. Moyer, a National Board Certified teacher, provides these ten powerful tips for molding yourself into a high-quality professional:

1. *I am honest and trustworthy.*
2. *I am fair and strive diligently not to discriminate.*
3. *I respect the privacy of others.*
4. *I honor confidentiality.*
5. *I acquire and maintain professional competence.*
6. *I know and respect existing laws pertaining to my profession.*
7. *I honor contracts, agreements, and assigned responsibilities.*
8. *I improve public understanding of teaching and the profession.*
9. *I communicate effectively.*
10. *I am cognizant of my appearance.*[41]

Continuous and Lifelong Professional Development Opportunities.   A professional is never a "finished" product; you will always be involved in **professional development**, a process of studying, learning, changing, and becoming more professional. Early childhood educators are always in the process of becoming more professional. Professional development involves participation in training and education beyond the minimum needed for your current position. You will also want to consider your career objectives and the qualifications you might need for positions of increasing responsibility.

professional development A process of studying, learning, changing, and becoming more professional.

Professional Learning Communities.   As we previously discussed, you and your colleagues and administrators will engage in collaborative planning in which you develop curricula and instructional processes. This process is often accomplished through a **professional learning community (PLC)**, a team of early childhood professionals working collaboratively to improve teaching and learning. Professional learning communities support a school culture that recognizes and capitalizes on the collective strengths and talents of the staff. They are designed to increase student achievement by creating a collaborative school culture focused on learning. Many schools benefit from the use of professional learning communities. The promise of PLCs to improve practice and contribute an ongoing emergence of knowledge supports their growing use and acceptance at the early childhood level.

professional learning community (PLC) A team of early childhood professionals working collaboratively to improve teaching and learning.

Peer Coaching.   I'll bet all of you had experience with coaches—little league, soccer, softball, or whatever other sport you participated in. Coaches provide invaluable assistance and support. They help guide, direct, model, and encourage others to use their talents and abilities. Just as coaches play an invaluable role in the field of sports, coaches also play an important role in teaching and learning. Peer coaching is a process whereby teachers agree to learn from each other through observation, interaction, and discussions. In peer coaching, teachers work in pairs with each other to observe and identify areas in which they would like to improve. Peer coaching is powerful and enables you to grow and develop as you collaborate with your colleagues.

Mentoring.   Mentoring is the process in which an experienced and highly qualified teacher works with a novice or beginning teacher in order to help the new teacher be successful. More than likely, as a new beginning teacher, you will be assigned to a mentor teacher who will act as a leader, guide, sponsor, and role model for you. Generally, the mentor teacher works with the new early childhood professional during his or her first year of teaching.

Just in Time Professional Development. We have talked about how professional development is increasingly playing a more powerful role in helping teachers gain the knowledge and skills they need in order to help each student be successful. While some professional development occurs grade wide and school-wide, oftentimes, teachers need help and assistance in their classroom implementing instructional strategies. Increasing numbers of school districts provide "just in time" staff development, in which instructional leaders work with teachers in the classroom to help them implement effective teaching methods. For example, first-year teacher Ashley Higgins is having difficultly implementing guided reading in her first grade classroom. Instructional specialist Amanda Murphy works with Ashley in her classroom to develop the skills she needs to effectively implement guided reading.

Engaging in Ethical Practice. **Ethical conduct**—the exercise of responsible behavior with children, families, colleagues, and community and society—enables you to engage confidently in exemplary professional practice. The profession of early childhood education has a set of ethical standards to guide your thinking and behavior. NAEYC has developed a Code of Ethical Conduct (see Appendix A) and a Statement of Commitment, which follows:

> As an individual who works with young children, I commit myself to furthering the values of early childhood education as they are reflected in the NAEYC Code of Ethical Conduct. To the best of my ability I will:

- Never harm children
- Ensure that programs for young children are based on current knowledge and research of child development and early childhood education
- Respect and support families in their task of nurturing children
- Respect colleagues in early childhood care and education and support them in maintaining the NAEYC Code of Ethical Conduct
- Serve as an advocate for children, their families, and their teachers in community and society
- Stay informed of and maintain high standards of professional conduct
- Engage in an ongoing process of self-reflection, realizing that personal characteristics, biases, and beliefs have an impact on children and families
- Be open to new ideas and be willing to learn from the suggestions of others
- Continue to learn, grow, and contribute as a professional
- Honor the ideals and principles of the NAEYC Code of Ethical Conduct[42]

You can begin now to incorporate professional ethical practices into your interactions with children and colleagues. To stimulate your thinking, the Activities for Professional Development at the end of each chapter include an ethical dilemma.

> An ethical dilemma is a situation an individual encounters in the workplace for which there is more than one possible solution, each carrying a strong moral justification. A dilemma requires a person to choose between two alternatives; each has some benefits but also some costs. Typically, one stakeholder's legitimate needs and interests will give way to those of another.[43]

As you reflect on and respond to each dilemma, use the NAEYC Code of Ethical Conduct as a valuable guide and resource.

> The goal of the NAEYC Code of Ethical Conduct is to inform, not prescribe, answers in tough decisions that teachers and other early childhood professionals must make as they work with children and families. The strategy inherent in the Code is to promote the application of core values, ideals, and principles to guide decision making.[44]

Collaborating with Parents, Families, and Community Partners. As a part of becoming a professional, you will encounter many experiences with parents, families, and the community. These experiences will allow you to gain a better understanding of the

ethical conduct
Responsible behavior toward students and parents that allows you to be considered a professional.

complex characteristics of families and communities as well as begin to create respectful, reciprocal relationships that support and empower families. Parents, families, and the community are essential partners in the process of schooling and a relationship that should be allowed to be nurtured. Knowing how to collaborate effectively with these key partners will serve you well throughout your career.

advocacy The act of engaging in strategies designed to improve the circumstances of children and families. Advocates move beyond their day-to-day professional responsibilities and work collaboratively to help others.

Advocacy.   **Advocacy** is the act of pleading the cases of children and families to the profession and the public and engaging in strategies designed to improve the circumstances of those children and families. Advocates move beyond their day-to-day professional responsibilities and work collaboratively to help others. Children and families today need adults who understand their needs and who will work to improve the health, education, and well-being of all young children. You and other early childhood professionals are in a unique position to know and understand children and their needs and to make a difference in their lives.

Kristi Luetjen, kindergarten teacher at Whiting Lane Elementary in West Hartford, Connecticut, and 2010 Teacher of the Year, has moved fluidly in and out of special education and is praised for integrating students with special needs into her classroom. She dedicated herself to improving the services for kindergartners with special needs. She blended the lines of regular and special education and created a new co-teaching model with incorporated yoga practice with the West Hartford curriculum to create a yoga program for kindergartners. Luetjen adds "I am grateful for the opportunity to continue to advocate for our youngest students, our students with disabilities, and the general importance of a kindergarten education."[45]

There is no shortage of issues to advocate for in the lives of children and families. Some of the issues in need of strong advocates involve providing high-quality programs for all children; reducing and preventing child abuse and neglect; closing the achievement gap between socioeconomic and racial groups; and providing good health and nutrition for each child. You must become actively engaged to change policies and procedures that negatively impact children. The following are some of the ways in which you can advocate for children and families:

- *Join an early childhood professional organization that advocates for children and families.*   Organizations such as NAEYC, the Association for Childhood Education International (ACEI), Children's Defense Fund (CDF) and the Council for Exceptional Children (CEC) have local affiliates at colleges and universities and in many cities and towns and are very active in advocating for young children. You can serve on a committee or be involved in some other way.

- *Volunteer in community activities that support children and families.*   Donate to an organization that helps children and families and volunteer your time at a local event that helps children get ready for school. For example, the Georgia Justice Project hosts its annual "Back-2-School" event in order to help their clients be prepared for their first day of school. The community of Atlanta, Georgia, supplies families with backpacks, school supplies, and health and dental screenings.[46]

   Early childhood major Chris Sayen, through his college, volunteers in a program called Success for Life through Reading. Chris reads books to children in child care programs serving children from low-income families. Chris also helps raise funds to purchase new books for the children.

- *Investigate the issues that face children and families today.*   Read the news and become informed about relevant issues. For example, subscribe to Early Childhood News and receive a bi-weekly electronic newsletter from a group that informs you of news affecting children ages birth through eight and their families; news updates are automatically sent on current issues. Then share the news with colleagues, family, and friends.

- *Seek opportunities to share your knowledge of young children and the issues that face children and families.* Inform others about the needs of young children by speaking with groups. For example, volunteer to meet with a group of parents at a local child care program to help them learn how to share storybooks with their young children, or meet with a local civic group that maintains the community park to discuss appropriate equipment for younger children. Identify a specific concern you have for children and families, and talk to others about that issue. For example, if you are concerned about the number of children who do not have adequate health care, learn the facts about the issue in your community, and then talk to people you know about ways to solve that problem in your community. Begin with your own circle of influence: your colleagues, friends, family members, and other social groups in which you are a member.
- *Enlist the support of others.* Contact others to help you disseminate information about an issue. For example, enlist the help of your local PTA in a letter-writing effort to inform town leaders about the need for safety improvements at the local playground.
- *Be persistent.* Identify an issue you are passionate about, and find a way to make a difference. There are many ways to advocate for children and families. Change takes time![47]

Within your own program or classroom, you will face many issues that should inspire you to advocate for your children and their families.

Professional Dispositions

In addition to the six professional standards previously discussed in this chapter, professional dispositions play an important role in assuring that you will be a well-rounded and highly qualified professional. **Professional dispositions** are the values, commitments, attitudes, and professional ethics that influence behaviors toward students, families, colleagues, and communities and affect student learning, motivation, and development as well your own professional growth. Dispositions are guided by beliefs and attitudes related to values such as caring, fairness, honesty, and responsibility. For example, they might include a belief that all students can learn; a vision of high and challenging standards for all children; or a commitment to a safe and supportive learning environment. We have already discussed other dispositions such as ethical practice, collaborating with colleagues and families, and reflective practice. All programs that prepare professionals for the early childhood profession have a set of dispositions that are important for professional practice.[48]

professional dispositions The values, commitments, and professional ethics that influence behaviors toward students, families, colleagues, and communities and affect student learning, motivation, and development as well as the educator's own professional growth.

Caring: The Most Important Disposition

For every early childhood professional, *caring* is the most important of any professional dispositions. Professionals care about children; they accept and respect all children and their cultural and socioeconomic backgrounds. As a professional, you will work in classrooms, programs, and other settings where things do not always go smoothly—for example, children will not always learn ably and well and they will not always be clean and free from illness and hunger. Children's and their parents' backgrounds and ways of life will not always be the same as yours. Caring means you will lose sleep trying to find a way to help a child learn to read and you will spend long hours planning and gathering materials. Caring also means you will not leave your intelligence, enthusiasm, and other talents at home but will bring them into the center, the classroom, administration offices, boards of directors' meetings, and wherever else you can make a difference in the lives of children and their families. The theme of caring should run deep in your professional preparation and in your teaching.

The Voice from the Field feature "Caring and Kindness Are Keys to the Profession" illustrates the importance of caring and kindness with many examples that you can use in your classroom.

Caring and Kindness Are Keys to the Profession

Kindness is a simple eight-letter word that has the extraordinary power to make the world a better place. We practice what we teach by inspiring our students to share kindness with one another and to spread kindness wherever they go. To achieve that goal, we model kindness in these ways:

- Show enthusiasm for the subject matter and the children.
- Take time to know each child, both personally and academically (e.g., likes, dislikes, strengths, weaknesses, home environment).
- Be friendly and courteous, knowing that our attitudes can change children's attitudes.
- Be supportive and encouraging (e.g., saying "I am very proud of you," "Keep trying," "You're a great example for others").
- Avoid the use of criticism and ridicule.
- Don't choose favorites.
- Be sensitive to children's responses.
- Encourage mutual respect and trust.
- Create nurturing interactions with the children. (Our classroom motto, "Effort Creates Ability," makes students feel secure in trying new things.)

Classroom Pledges

Each morning we begin the day by reciting three pledges. The first pledge is our Kindness Promise:

Every day, in every way,
I will show kindness to others.

When an unkind act occurs in our classroom, we ask the students involved to repeat the Kindness Promise and to make an apology to the parties involved.

Our second pledge is our Helping Hands pledge. It is a quote from Helen Keller:

I am only one, but still I am one.
I cannot do everything, but still I can do something.
And because I cannot do everything, I will not refuse to do the something that I can do.

This is our motto for community service projects in our classroom.

Our third pledge is our Learning Cheer.

L—Listen to others.
E—Expect to learn each day.
A—Act kindly toward others.
R—Remember the class rules.
N—Never give up on yourself.
1, 2, 3—First grade's cool!

All three pledges remind us that there is more to our classroom than the three Rs.

We show acts of kindness in our classroom through these special activities. We:

- Pause each morning for a moment of silence. We think kind and happy thoughts for our students who are absent, as well as for friends, family, pets, and situations that could benefit from our actions.
- Make a kindness critter, which is like a caterpillar. Each day our class thinks of one new way to show kindness. We write the idea on a new segment of the caterpillar. By the end of the school year, we have a very long critter with almost two hundred ways of showing kindness to others.
- Have regular class meetings to discuss situations in the classroom that relate to kindness (or its absence) and brainstorm solutions for those situations.
- Insist that each student say please and thank you. We also remind our students to say, "I'm sorry."

DAP and the Early Childhood Education Professional

The NAEYC's Position Statement on Developmentally Appropriate Practice (see Appendix B) represents a commitment to promote excellence in the constantly evolving field of early childhood education and early childhood special education. The Position Statement provides a framework for best practices rooted in numerous research studies on child development and learning—which promotes each child's optimal learning and development.

- Encourage students to compliment each other (e.g., "I like your picture," or "Congratulations, your team won the game.").
- Display a rainbow fish in the classroom. Each time the teacher catches a child showing kindness, she can add a shiny scale to the rainbow fish.
- Form partnerships with organizations in the community. Our local chapter of Parent-Wise has developed a Bee Kind program, which comes to our school, sharing stories and creating hands-on activities that remind the students about the importance of kind acts, no matter how big or small.
- Host our "Have Lunch with Someone You Love" day! Each Friday in February, families are invited into our classroom to have lunch with their children. When parents cannot attend, grandparents, babysitters, or other family members fill in. Our intention is to provide kind and caring comments about their children. It is not a time for an academic or behavioral conference. It is just a time to let the parents know just how special their children are to us.
- Take pictures of our students, as they are involved in the classroom, and especially with our community service projects. At the end of the year, we give each student a "First Grade Memory Book."
- Make our own "smiley face" classroom t-shirts. We wear them to special events in our school, and when we participate in community service projects outside of our school.

Kindness Outside the Classroom

There is no better way to promote and foster kindness and compassion in our world than by participating in community service projects. Here are ways we have taken caring and kindness outside our classroom:

- We made a lemonade stand and sold lemonade after each physical education class. We sent the proceeds of the sale to former President George W. Bush to be given to the children of Afghanistan.
- We traced the handprint of each of the students in our school onto red, white, or blue pieces of felt. We formed a six-by-eight-foot American flag from those hands and gave it to our state representative. It is now proudly displayed in our state capitol building.
- We raked leaves of veterans who live near our school on Veterans Day. We made patriotic wreaths for their doors and made no-bake cookies as a way of saying "thank you" to our veterans.
- We visited the pediatric floor of our local hospital. We used the bonus points from our book club to acquire age-appropriate books and prepared gift bags of hot chocolate, cups, and student-made bookmarks. Our theme was "Warm up with a good book; you'll feel so much better!" The books were given to each sick child as he or she was admitted to the hospital.
- We collected chewing and bubble gum and sent care packages to soldiers stationed in Iraq. Our theme "We Stick with Our Soldiers" was an inexpensive yet effective project that promoted kindness and caring attributes.
- We decorated lunch bags for our local Meals on Wheels program during our inside recess times. We were able to make 180 lunch bags per month for the elderly residents that live near our school and depend on Meals on Wheels for a nutritious meal. Meals on Wheels provided the bags and it cost us nothing but our recess time to make many elderly and, often, lonely people happy!
- We collected cans of soup and donated them to our local food bank for our own "Souper Bowl." As a culminating activity, we had a "tailgate party," complete with hot dogs, popcorn, and root beer!

Let your light shine! "All the darkness in the world cannot extinguish the light of a single candle."

Source: Contributed by Christa Pehrson and Vicki Sheffler, 2002 USA Today *First-Team Teachers, Amos K. Hutchinson Elementary School, Greensburg, Pennsylvania.*

The NAEYC Position Statement on Developmentally Appropriate Practice (DAP) is clear about what constitutes DAP:

- Developmentally appropriate practice requires both meeting children where they are—which means that teachers must get to know them well—and enabling them to reach goals that are both challenging and achievable.
- All teaching practices should be: (a) appropriate to children's age and developmental status, (b) attuned to children as unique individuals, and (c) responsive to the social and cultural contexts in which children live.
- Developmentally appropriate practice does not mean making things easier for children. Rather, it means ensuring that goals and experiences are suited to children's learning and development *and* challenging enough to promote their progress and interest.[49]

Knowledge of Social and Cultural Contexts in Which Children Live

The values, expectations, and behavioral and linguistic conventions that shape children's lives at home and in their communities that practitioners must strive to understand in order to ensure that learning experiences in the program or school are meaningful, relevant, and respectful for each child and family.

Knowledge of Child Development

Knowledge of age-related characteristics that permit general predictions about what experiences are likely to best promote children's learning and development.

Knowledge of the Child as an Individual

What practitioners learn about each child that has implications for how best to adapt and be responsive to that individual variation.

FIGURE 1.5 Core Considerations in Developmentally Appropriate Practice

Source: Adapted and reprinted with permission from the National Association for the Education of Young Children (NAEYC). Full-text versions of all NAEYC position statements are available at www.naeyc.org/positionstatements. Photo by Dreamstime LLC – Royalty Free.

Figure 1.5 further clarifies these dimensions and illustrates how they are related.

Pathways to Professional Development

The educational dimension of professionalism involves knowing about and demonstrating essential knowledge of the profession and professional practice. This knowledge includes the history and ethics of the profession, understanding how children develop and learn, and keeping up to date on public issues that influence early childhood and the profession.

Training and certification is a major challenge facing all areas of the early childhood profession and those who care for and teach young children. Training and certification requirements vary from state to state, and more states are tightening personnel standards for child care, preschool, kindergarten, and primary-grade professionals.

Many states have career ladders that specify the requirements for progressing from one level of professionalism to the next. For example, Figure 1.6 outlines a career pyramid of professional development. What two things do you find most informative about this career pyramid? How can you use pyramid to enhance your professional development?

Advanced Degrees—M.S., M.A., Ph.D., Ed.D., J.D., M.D., R.N.

Traditional:
- Early care and education Instructor at technology centers
- Teacher educator at a two year college or four year university
- Instructor/curriculum specialist
- Child development specialist
- Child guidance specialist
- Research/writer
- Early intervention
- Director/specialist in a child care resource and referral
- Family support and education

Related: with further education/training/certifications
- Social worker
- Teacher/administrator/special educator in a public or private elementary school—certification required
- Child advocate/lobbyist
- Librarian
- Pediatric therapist—occupational and physical
- Human resources personnel in industry
- Child life specialist in a hospital

- Speech and hearing pathologist—health department, public/private school, private practice, university teaching
- Early childhood consultant
- Entertainer/musician/song writer for children
- Career coach
- Agency administrator/director
- Author and illustrator of children's books
- Physician/Pediatrician
- Pedodontist (works only with children)
- Dietitian for children

- Counselor
- Child psychologist
- Psychiatrist
- Dietetic assistant
- Recreation supervisor
- Children's policy specialist
- Dental hygienist
- Scouting director
- Hospice care
- Domestic violence counselor
- Positions in elder care
- Child care center or playground/recreation center designer

- Probation officer
- County extension educator with 4-H
- Adoption specialist
- "Friend of the Court" counselor
- Psychometrist
- Attorney with primary focus on children/elderly
- Faith-based community coordinator and educator
- Family mediator
- Marriage and family therapy
- Infant/Child mental health specialist

Baccalaureate Level (4 yr)—Bachelors of Science, Bachelors of Arts, Bachelors of Education

Traditional:
- Early childhood teacher in public school, Head Start or child care settings—certification required
- Special education teacher
- Family child care home provider
- Nanny
- Administrator in a Head Start program
- Child care center director/owner/coordinator
- Child care center director in the armed services

Related: Some positions will require additional coursework at the baccalaureate level which will be in a field other than early childhood:
- Parent/family educator
- Family advocate
- Case manager in a state agency/recourse coordinator
- Parents as teachers coordinator
- Director of school-age (out of school time) program
- Mentor/coach
- Child advocate/lobbyist
- Recreation director/worker/leader
- Web master
- Adult educator
- Journalist/author/publisher/illustrator of children's books
- Children's librarian
- Retail manager of children's toy or book stores
- Licensing worker

- Human resource personnel in industry
- Music teacher, musician/entertainer for children
- Recreation camp director
- Camp counselor/scouts camp ranger
- Domestic violence prevention and education
- Sex education and prevention
- Resource and referral trainer/data analyst
- Referral specialist/child care food program consultant

- Childbirth educator
- Gymnastic or dance teacher
- Pediatric nurse aide
- Child and parenting practitioner certification
- Producer of children's television shows and commercials
- Faith community coordinator and educator
- Substance abuse educator
- Foster care services

Associate Level (2 yr)—Associate of Arts, Associate of Science and Associate of Applied Science

Traditional:
- Child care center director
- School-age provider
- Early intervention/special needs program
- Para-professional assistant

- Parent educator

Related: in addition to those listed at the core level:
- Family and human services worker
- LPN–specialized nurse training

- Entertainer for children at theme restaurants, parks or parties
- Social service aide
- Youth services
- Playground monitor

- Physical therapy assistant
- Nursing home aide/worker/technician
- Faith community coordinators for families and children

National Credential Level and Certificate of Mastery

Traditional:
- Family childhood care home provider
- Nanny

- Family childhood care home provider
- Nanny

- Child care center director
- Home visitor

- Nursing home aide/worker
- Teacher assistant in public school classroom

Core Level—These positions require minimim education and training depending on the position.

Traditional:
- Head Start teacher (CDA required)
- Child care teacher—master teacher

Traditional:
- Child care teaching assistant
- Family child care home provider
- Head Start teacher assistant
- Nanny
- Foster parent
- Church nursery attendant

Related positions which involve working with children in settings other than a child care center, family child care home, Head Start or public school program
Related positions may require specialized pre-service training:
- Children's storyteller, art instructor or puppeteer
- Recreation center assistant
- Salesperson in children's toys, clothing or bookstore
- School crossing guard

- Children's party caterer
- Restaurant helper for birthday parties
- Van or transportation driver
- Children's art museum guide
- Receptionist in pediatrician's office

- Camp counselor
- Special needs child care assistant
- Live-in caregiver
- Respite caregiver
- Cook's aide, camp cook, Head Start or child care center cook

FIGURE 1.6 Career Pyramid

Source: Reprinted with permission of the Center for Early Childhood Professional Development, College of Continuing Education, University of Oklahoma. Funded by the Oklahoma Department of Human Services.

Associate Degree Programs

Many community colleges provide training in early childhood education to qualify recipients to be **child care** aides, primary child care providers, and assistant teachers. Associate degree programs provide a foundation for knowledge in child development and working with children and families. These programs usually last two years and could provide the following early childhood education career opportunities: child care instructor, director, owner, director of a family day home, or manager of a corporate child care facility.[50]

Baccalaureate Degree Programs

These programs provide more extensive knowledge on early childhood education and work to ensure their students or "candidates" have mastered the six professional preparation competencies, with differences expected in depth and breadth of competencies for the bachelor's level. The ages and grades to which the certification applies vary from state to state. Four-year colleges provide programs that may result in early childhood teacher certification. Some states have separate teacher certification for **pre-kindergarten** and grades K–3 and grades 4–6. In other states, early childhood and elementary teacher certification are combined in a K–6 program. This is the way it is at my university, the University of North Texas. However, some other early childhood career opportunities for this level include teacher educator/researcher, administrator, and public policy and advocacy specialist.

Master's Degree Programs

Depending on the state, individuals may gain initial early childhood certification at the master's level. Many colleges and universities offer master's programs for people who want to qualify as program directors or assistant directors or may want to pursue a career in teaching. Linda Smerge graduated with a bachelor's and master's degree in elementary education from Northern Illinois University, as well as a juris doctorate. She taught second grade and kindergarten before practicing transactional law for thirteen years in Chicago. Smerge felt the calling to return to the classroom and satisfy her desire to work with young children. Now Smerge is the 2009 Illinois Teacher of the Year from Wilson School in Cicero, Illinois, and is on a year-long journey around Illinois and the United States as an educational ambassador.[51]

The CDA Program

The **Child Development Associate (CDA)** National Credentialing Program is a competency-based assessment system that offers early childhood professionals the opportunity to develop and demonstrate competence in their work with children ages five and younger. Since its inception in 1975, the CDA program has provided a nationally recognized system that has stimulated early childhood training and education opportunities for teachers of young children in every state in the country and on military bases worldwide. The credential is recognized nationwide in state regulations for licensed child care and preschool programs as a qualification for teachers, directors, and/or family child care providers. The standards for performance this program has established are used as a basis for professional development in the field.

The CDA program offers credentials to caregivers in four types of settings: (1) center-based programs for preschoolers, (2) center-based programs for infants/toddlers, (3) family child care homes, and (4) home visitor programs.

Evidence of ability is collected from a variety of sources including firsthand observational evidence of the CDA candidate's performance with children and families. This evidence is weighed against national standards. The CDA national office sets the standards for competent performance and monitors this assessment process so it is uniform throughout the country.

Developing a Philosophy of Education

Professional practice entails teaching with and from a philosophy of education, which acts as a guidepost to help you support your teaching on what you believe about children.

A **philosophy of education** is a set of beliefs about how children develop and learn; what children should know, learn, and do; and how to best teach young children. Your philosophy of education is based in part on your philosophy of life. What you believe about yourself, about others, and about life determines your philosophy of education. For example, we previously talked about caring. If you care about others, chances are you will be a caring person for your children. We know that when teachers care about and have high expectations for their children, then children achieve at higher levels. Core beliefs and values about education and teaching include what you believe about children, what you think are the purposes of education, how you view the teacher's role, and what you think you should know and be able to do.

In summary, your philosophy of education guides and directs your daily teaching. As you reflect on your philosophy of education, think about what makes it special. What are some critical elements that you can incorporate into yours? The following guidelines will help you develop your philosophy of education.

philosophy of education A set of beliefs about how children develop and learn and what and how they should be taught.

Read

Read widely in textbooks, journals, and other professional literature to get ideas and points of view. A word of caution: when people refer to philosophies of education, they often think of historical influences. This is only part of the information available for writing a philosophy. Make sure you explore contemporary ideas as well, for these will also have a strong influence on you as a professional. The Activities for Professional Development section at the end of the chapter will help you get started. Below are a few books that will assist you in developing your philosophy of education.

- Copple, C., & Bredekamp, S. (2009). *Developmentally Appropriate Practice in Early Childhood Programs,* 3e. Washington, DC: National Association for the Education of Young Children.
- Noddings, N. (2006). *Philosophy of Education,* 2e. Boulder, CO: Westview Press.
- Sennett, F. (2003). *Teacher of the Year: 400 Quotes of Insight, Inspiration, and Motivation from America's Greatest Teachers.* Chicago: McGraw-Hill Companies.
- Canfield, J. & Hansen, M.V. (2002). *Chicken Soup for the Teacher's Soul: Stories to Open the Hearts and Rekindle the Spirit of Educators.* Deerfield Beach, FL: Health Communications.

Reflect

As you read through and study this book, make notes and reflect about your philosophy of education. The following prompts will help you get started:

- I believe the purposes of education are . . .
- I believe that children learn best when they are taught under certain conditions and in certain ways. Some of these are . . .
- The curriculum—all of the activities and experiences—of my classroom should include certain "basics" that contribute to children's social, emotional, intellectual, and physical development. These basics include . . .
- Children learn best in an environment that promotes learning. Features of a good learning environment are . . .

- All children have certain needs that must be met if they are to grow and learn at their best. Some of these basic needs are . . .
- I would meet these needs by . . .
- A teacher should have certain qualities and behave in certain ways. Qualities I think important for teaching are . . .

In addition, reflect on these philosophy statements of teachers of the year as a context for expanding and enriching your philosophy.

- The philosophy of teaching of Michelle Lacombe, 2009–2010 Teacher of the Year at Carrie Downie Elementary School in New Castle, Delaware, includes these key points:
  - Providing consistency and stability for students in a safe learning environment
  - Establishing clear expectations and consequences
  - Motivating all students to be the best they can be
  - Promoting a "Yes I Can!" attitude
  - Maintaining good communication with parents and students
  - Differentiating instruction so all students can learn
  - Helping students to realize the importance of education[52]
- Blythe Turner, 2008–2009 New Mexico Teacher of the Year and second grade teacher at Rio Rancho Elementary School in Santa Fe, New Mexico, prides herself on her efforts to increase her knowledge and, in turn, increase her power as an educator. "I aspire to bestow upon my students a drive to become a lifelong learner and to share their knowledge with others. All students should be proud of who they are and where they come from, and have the opportunity to share their heritage and individuality with others."[53]

Discuss

Discuss with successful teachers and other educators their philosophies and practices. The personal accounts in the Voice from the Field boxes in each chapter of this text are evidence that a philosophy can help you be a successful, effective teacher. They also serve as an opportunity to "talk" with successful professionals and understand how they translate theory into practice. Join or create an on-line discussion group to share your thoughts and ideas about teaching. For example, Second Grade Teachers (http://second-grade-teachers.ning.com) is an interactive website for second grade teachers and support staff which enables you to blog, chat, post photos, and collaborate with other teachers across the world to exchange ideas, activities, and resources.[54]

Write and Share

Once you have thought about your philosophy of education, write a draft and have others read it. Writing and sharing helps you clarify your ideas and redefine your thoughts because your philosophy should be understandable to others (although they do not necessarily have to agree with you).

Evaluate

Finally, evaluate your philosophy using this checklist:

- Does my philosophy accurately relate my beliefs about teaching? Have I been honest with myself?
- Is it understandable to me and others?
- Do I clearly state what I believe are the key essentials of teaching?

- Do I clearly state what the essentials children should learn are? For example, in this book, I stress that literacy—learning to read, write, and communicate—is fundamental to all early childhood programs.
- Does it provide practical guidance for my teaching?
- Are my ideas consistent with one another?
- Does what I believe make good sense to me and others?

Now finalize your draft into a polished copy. A well-thought-out philosophy will be like a compass throughout your career. You will modify your philosophy throughout your career, but it will be your GPS system and point you in the right direction and keep you focused on doing your best for children.

What Are New Roles for Early Childhood Professionals Today?

The role of the early childhood professional today is radically different from what it was even two or three years ago. Although the goals of professionalism and the characteristics of the high-quality professional remain the same, responsibilities, expectations, and roles have changed and will continue to change. Here are some of these new roles of the contemporary early childhood professional:

- *Teacher as an instructional leader.* Teachers have always been responsible for classroom and program instruction, but this role is now reemphasized and given a much more prominent place in what early childhood teachers do, such as planning for what children will learn, guiding and teaching so that children learn, assessing what children learn, and arranging the classroom environment so that children learn. The professional learning community we previously discussed will play a more prominent role throughout your teaching career.
- *Teacher of federal, state, district, and program goals and standards.* Federal and state standards provide a framework for what teachers should be teaching and students should be learning. Intentional teaching occurs when teachers teach for a purpose, are clear about what they teach, and teach so that children learn specific knowledge and skills. In this context, teachers spend more time during the day planning activities that involve the children in active learning while making a conscious effort to be more involved in each child's learning process. Intentional teaching to standards can and should occur in a child-centered approach for specified times and purposes throughout the school day.
- *Teacher that maximizes full-instructional time.* Teachers are expected to maximize the full length of instructional time with activities and content that will provide students with a valuable learning experience every day. Teachers emphasize engaging children in learning activities, spend more time on instruction, actively involve themselves in children's learning, and increase the amount of time spent on learning.
- *Teacher of performance-based accountability for learning.* Teachers today are far more accountable for children's learning. Previously, the emphasis was on the process of schooling; teachers were able to explain their role as "I taught Mario how to. . . ." Today the emphasis is on "What did Mario learn?" and "Did Mario learn what he needs to know and do to perform at or above grade level?"
- *Teacher of literacy and reading.* Although the teaching of reading has always been a responsibility of early childhood professionals, this role has greatly expanded. Today, every early childhood teacher is now a teacher of literacy and reading, skills necessary in all content areas, including math and science.

- *Teacher of STEM—Science, Technology, Engineering, and Math.*   National leaders want schools to teach STEM subjects beginning in preschool. As a result, more early childhood programs are devoting more time to STEM activities.

- *Teacher of twenty-first century skills.*   The role of the contemporary teacher to be able to improve and advance students' knowledge of twenty-first century skills is becoming more and more important in early childhood education. Teachers are expected to be advocates of these special skills and to be able to reform their teaching to incorporate these skills. The Partnership for 21st Century Skills believes "To build a strong economy, we must ensure young people are prepared to succeed both in the jobs of today and those that haven't been created yet. We can do this by fusing the three Rs and the four Cs, which represent the skills (such as critical thinking and problem solving, collaboration, communication, and creativity and innovation) required for success in today's and tomorrow's world."[55]

- *Teacher in inclusive classrooms.*   Teaching in an inclusive classroom offers many new opportunities for you and your students. With the fields of early childhood and early childhood special education merging together, there is a greater demand for all teachers to have knowledge and skills for how to teach in inclusive classrooms. This may at first seem challenging for some teachers. However, with collaborative teamwork, this experience can be very successful for all involved. School district Teacher of the Year Laura Ditman teaches second grade at Jefferson Elementary School. When Laura began her teaching career three years ago, she did not expect she would have three children in her classroom with disabilities. Laura is fortunate to have the help and support of her principal and special education personnel as she meets the demands of teaching two children with learning disabilities and a third with attention deficit hyperactivity disorder (ADHD). Laura believes all children can be successful and welcomes diversity in her classroom. "I adapt the curriculum and design instructional strategies to meet each student's needs. I think the inclusive classroom is the best way to teach all children."

- *Teacher as a continuous learner.*   As we have discussed in this chapter, you will participate in ongoing professional staff development. Secretary of Education Arne Duncan wants to transform the teaching profession, and continuous learning is a way to achieve this goal in an effort to increase children's achievement.

- *Teacher as a reflective professional.*   As we have discussed previously in this chapter, a reflective professional possesses the ability to think before, during, and after teaching in order to make decisions about how to plan, assess, and teach children. As a teacher of young children, you will rely heavily on reflective practice as a valuable tool that will assist you in the way you teach your children.

As the field of early childhood education continues to change, the details of your role as an early childhood professional will continue to be refined. You will want to devote the time and energy necessary to keep yourself in the forefront of your field. Figure 1.7 contains a development checklist for becoming a professional. Complete this checklist now, and review it throughout your teaching career to further refine your professional teaching role.

The Future: You and the Early Childhood Profession

It is always risky to predict what the future holds for you and me as early childhood professionals. However, if the past is any indication of the future, I expect that we will practice our profession under the following conditions:

- *Rapid change.*   The field of early childhood education will continue to undergo rapid and dramatic change. New ideas and methods will challenge old ways of doing things. This means that you will have to adapt to embrace change as the field changes. And, you will have to transform your thinking continually as new ways make old habits obsolete.

- *Increased use of technology.*   Technology will play an increasingly important and prominent role in how you teach, what you teach, and how children learn. Growing numbers of teachers across the country are embracing technology as a powerful means of helping them teach so that each student learns.

- *Politicization of early childhood education.*   Politics have always influenced education in one way or another. However, in the years to come, politics and politicians will play an even greater role in determining what to teach and how to teach it. This means that advocacy will be a major dimension of your professional practice, allowing you to influence decisions on public policy at all levels regarding what is taught in early childhood classrooms.

- *Increased emphasis on young children.*   The public and politicians are recognizing the critical importance that the early years play in children's school and life success. As a result, preschool programs are expanding and will continue to do so. These programs help children gain the knowledge and skills they need for school and learning readiness. Early childhood will continue to be a time of interest, attention, and action.

- *Acceleration of early childhood teacher education and training.*   As the field of early childhood changes, so do the knowledge and skills associated with it. This means that constant and continuous education will play a central role in your professional development. Many teachers will spend as much time educating themselves and being educated as they spend on teaching their children. One way you can continue to educate yourself is by exploring the Linking to Learning section at the end of each chapter in this book. Each Linking to Learning section offers a list of professional organizations and information sites, many of which have been mentioned in the chapter. Each entry includes a website where you can access additional information and helpful ideas that will enhance your teaching abilities.

The future of early childhood education holds many opportunities and exciting changes for you. It is important for you to keep up with the changing times and to align your teaching with current practices and new ideas.

Changes that the future holds for the field of early childhood education and for you as a professional are not to be feared but are to be welcomed and embraced. This is a wonderful and exciting time to be in the field of early childhood education. A bright future awaits you and your children.

Accommodating Diverse Learners

When you consider the makeup of pre-K–3 classrooms today, every classroom is an inclusion classroom. Teachers have always taught to all kinds of children with diverse needs. For example, in most classrooms you will find children of different developmental levels and capacities; different races and ethnicities; diverse religions and cultural beliefs and backgrounds; with different fears, hopes, and dreams; with diverse strengths and differences; different health levels and health-specific needs; with different family configurations; with different income levels; and with different learning styles and needs. In addition, all children, by the time they come to you, have a history of experiences, of feelings, pains and triumphs, all of which you have to consider as you plan and teach. As an early childhood professional you will be responsible for accommodating the naturally occurring diversity of your classroom.

The Division for Early Childhood (DEC) and the National Association for the Education of Young Children (NAEYC) have issued a joint statement of inclusion and inclusionary practices. They define inclusion as education that:

embodies the values, policies, and practices that support the right of every infant and young child and his or her family, regardless of ability, to participate in a broad range of

FIGURE 1.7

Seventeen Competencies for Becoming a Professional: A Professional Development Checklist

NAEYC Standard	Desired Professional Goals
Standard 1	**Promoting Child Development and Learning** I use my understanding of young children's characteristics and needs, and of multiple interacting influences on children's development and learning, to create environments that are healthy, respectful, supportive, and challenging for each child.
Standard 1	**Delivering Education and Child Care** I am familiar with a variety of models and approaches for delivering education and child care, and I use this knowledge to deliver education and child care in a safe, healthy learning environment.
Standard 1	**Guiding Behavior** I understand the principles and importance of behavior guidance. I guide children to be peaceful, cooperative, and in control of their behavior.
Standard 1	**Theories of Early Childhood Education** I understand the principles of each major theory of educating young children. The approach I use is consistent with my beliefs about how children learn.
Standard 2	**Building Family and Community Relationships** I know about, understand, and value the importance and complex characteristics of children's families and communities. I use this understanding to create respectful, reciprocal relationships that support and empower families, and to involve all families in their children's development and learning.
Standard 3	**Observing, Documenting, and Assessing to Support Young Children and Families** I know about and understand the goals, benefits, and uses of assessment. I know about and use systematic observations, documentation, and other effective assessment strategies in a responsible way, in partnership with families and other professionals, to positively influence the development of every child.
Standard 4	**Using Developmentally Effective Approaches to Connect with Children and Families** I understand and use positive relationships and supportive interactions as the foundation for my work with young children and families. I know, understand, and use a wide array of developmentally appropriate approaches, instructional strategies, and tools to connect with children and families and positively influence each child's development and learning.
Standard 4	**Educating Diverse Students** I understand that all children are individuals with unique strengths and challenges. I embrace these differences, work to fulfill special needs, and promote tolerance and inclusion in my classroom. I value and respect the dignity of all children.
Standard 4	**Developmentally Appropriate Practice** I understand children's developmental stages and growth from birth through age eight, and use this knowledge to implement developmentally appropriate practice. I do all I can to advance the physical, intellectual, social, and emotional development of the children in my care to their full potential.
Standard 4	**Technology** I am technologically literate and integrate technology into my classroom to help all children learn.
Standard 5	**Using Content Knowledge to Build Meaningful Curriculum** I understand the importance of developmental domains and academic (or content) disciplines in early childhood curriculum. I know the essential concepts, inquiry tools, and structure of content areas, including academic subjects, and can identify resources to deepen my understanding. I use my own knowledge and other resources to design, implement, and evaluate meaningful, challenging curricula that promote comprehensive developmental and learning outcomes for every young child.
Standard 6	**Becoming a Professional** I identify and conduct myself as a member of the early childhood profession. I know and use ethical guidelines and other professional standards related to early childhood practice. I am a continuous, collaborative learner who demonstrates knowledgeable, reflective, and critical perspectives on my work, making informed decisions that integrate knowledge from a variety of sources. I am an informed advocate for sound educational practices and policies.
Standard 6	**Ongoing Professional Development** I have a professional career plan for the next year. I engage in study and training programs to improve my knowledge and competence, belong to a professional organization, and have earned or am working on a degree or credential (CDA, AA, BS, or BA). I strive for positive, collaborative relationships with my colleagues and employer.
Standard 6	**Philosophy of Teaching** I have thought about and written my philosophy of teaching and caring for young children. My actions are consistent with this philosophy.
Standard 6	**Keeping Current in an Age of Change** I am familiar with the profession's contemporary development, and I understand current issues in society and trends in the field. I am willing to change my ideas, thinking, and practices based on study, new information, and the advice of colleagues and professionals.
Standard 6	**Professional Dispositions** I work with students, families, and communities in ways that reflect the dispositions expected of professional educators as delineated in professional, state, and institutional standards. I recognize when my own dispositions may need to be adjusted and am able to develop plans to do so.
Standard 6	**Historical Knowledge** I am familiar with my profession's history, and I use my knowledge of the past to inform my practice.

Note: These professional development outcomes are consistent with the core values of the NAEYC and the competencies of the CDA.

Level of Accomplishment? (Circle One)	If High, Provide Evidence of Accomplishment	If Needs Improvement, Specify Action Plan for Accomplishment	Target Date of Completion of Accomplishment	See the following for more information on how to meet the desired professional outcomes
High Needs Improvement				Chapters 1, 4, 5, 6, 7, 8, 9, 10, 11, 12, and 13
High Needs Improvement				Chapters 3, 4, 7, 8, 9, 10, 11, and 12
High Needs Improvement				Chapter 12
High Needs Improvement				Chapters 3 and 4
High Needs Improvement				Chapter 2, 11, and 13
High Needs Improvement				Chapter 16
High Needs Improvement				Chapters 1, 2, 3, 4, 5, 6, 7, 8, 9, 10, 11, 12, and 13
High Needs Improvement				Chapters 1, 2, 4, 6, 7, 8, 9, 10, 11, 12, and 13
High Needs Improvement				Chapters 1, 2, 3, 4, 5, 6, 7, 8, 9, 10, 11, 12, and 13
High Needs Improvement				Chapters 7 and 9
High Needs Improvement				Chapters 1, 2, 3, 4, 6, 7, 8, 9, 10, and 11
High Needs Improvement				Chapters 1, 5, 6, and 13 and all Ethical Dilemma features
High Needs Improvement				Chapter 1 and 7 and all Ethical Dilemma features
High Needs Improvement				All Activities for Professional Development and Ethical Dilemma features
High Needs Improvement				Chapters 1, 2, 3, 4, 5, 6, 7, 8, 9, 10, 11, 12, and 13
High Needs Improvement				Chapters 1, 2, 5, 11, and 12 and all Ethical Dilemma features
High Needs Improvement				Chapters 3 and 6

activities and contexts as full members of families, communities, and society. The desired results of inclusive experiences for children with and without disabilities and their families include a sense of belonging and membership, positive social relationships and friendships, and development and learning to reach their full potential. The defining features of inclusion that can be used to identify high quality early childhood programs and services are access, participation, and supports. [56]

True inclusion, as the NAEYC and the DEC defines it, involves providing for the needs of all children of different abilities ranging from the developmental to the social, from the academic to emotional and behavioral. To do so, the NAEYC and DEC recommend that you and your early childhood programs

1. *Create high expectations for every child to reach his or her full potential.*   A definition of early childhood inclusion creates high expectations for each child, regardless of ability.

2. *Develop a program philosophy on inclusion.*   Programs need a philosophy on inclusion as a part of their broader program mission statement to ensure that teachers and staff operate under a similar set of assumptions, values, and beliefs about the most effective ways to support infants and young children with disabilities and their families.

3. *Establish a system of services and supports.*   A system of services and supports for children with disabilities and their families should respond to the needs and characteristics of children with varying types of disabilities and levels of severity, including children who are at risk for disabilities.[57]

As an early childhood professional, you have a unique role in making antibias education a reality, promoting diversity in all aspects of children's lives, giving each child a chance to thrive and succeed in school and in life.

Activities for Professional Development

Ethical Dilemma

"My principal rewards her favorite teachers . . ."

First year kindergarten teacher Emily Wittmer is happy in her classroom teaching. She loves her children and enjoys helping them learn and grow. However, she is having second thoughts about whether or not she wants to continue teaching at her school next year. The problem is that Emily's principal, Sunny Mariglow, has her favorite teachers and involves them, and only them, in school-based decisions. For example, last week Sunny and five of her favorite teachers went off campus for a day-long retreat to develop plans for new school programs. Several days later at a faculty meeting, Sunny announced that "she and her faculty representatives set goals for the rest of the school year." Emily thinks that this process is unfair and she is upset that only the principal's favorites get to make any decisions.

What should Emily do? Should Emily schedule a meeting with her principal and tell her that she does not approve of how decisions are made—possibly risking her career as a kindergarten teacher? Or, should Emily keep quiet and do nothing? Or, should Emily inquire about procedures for making a transfer to another school? What do you recommend that Emily do?

Activities to Apply What You Learned

1. Throughout this chapter, we have discussed changes in the early childhood profession. Create an account on Blogger to voice your opinions on the changes in the field. Which policies have your support and which do not? Share this information with friends and classmates and ask for their opinion as well.

2. Develop a professional resource notebook, portfolio, or a professional resource folder on your computer. A professional resource notebook contains your philosophy of education, lesson plan ideas, reflections, book lists, DVDs, and other classroom experiences and resources that will help you as a beginning teacher and demonstrates your abilities and knowledge. Using the six NAEYC Standards for Professional

Preparation Programs, organize your professional resource notebook to show how you have met the six standards. Create a resource log to record websites that have information useful for early childhood education professionals. You may wish to include websites such as www.naeyc.org; www.earlychildhoodnews.com and the others listed at the end of each chapter.

3. Developmentally appropriate practice is a skill that you will constantly use throughout your early childhood education career. Log on to YouTube and search videos of teachers using developmentally appropriate practice in their classrooms. Create a video to share with your colleagues on the importance of DAP and how you will use it to help children and families.

4. Recall a teacher who had a great influence on you. Make a PowerPoint presentation or write a one-page statement describing the characteristics of this teacher and some examples that you plan to imitate. Share your product with your classmates in small-group sessions.

5. Review your teaching philosophy draft. Evaluate your strengths and areas in which you hope to improve. As you review your professional teaching philosophy statement, reflect on Renee Comacho, at the beginning of the chapter. What were some of the qualities you admire about Renee? What are the qualities that make her a professional? What dimensions of Renee's background can you apply to your professional development?

Linking to Learning

Children's Defense Fund
www.childrensdefense.org/

Provides research and persistent advocacy for children's rights on issues including poverty, discrimination, and gun violence to ensure every child a healthy, fair, and safe start in life and successful passage to adulthood with the help of caring families and communities.

Council for Early Childhood Professional Recognition
www.cdacouncil.org

Offers a nationally recognized, competency-based child development associate credential that provides training, assessment, and certification of child care professionals; also offers bilingual specialization.

Council for Exceptional Children (CEC)
www.cec.sped.org

Offers a variety of information regarding children with disabilities and serves as an advocate for these exceptional children. Also acts as the largest international professional organization dedicated to improving the educational success of individuals with disabilities and/or gifts and talents.

National Association for the Education of Young Children
www.naeyc.org

Publishes brochures, posters, videotapes, books, and journals discussing teaching and program ideas, ways to improve parent–teacher relations, and resources for students about safety, language arts, and learning. Offers training opportunities through national, state, and local affiliate groups.

Promising Practices Network
www.promisingpractices.net/

Provides unique resources that offer credible, research-based information on programs that work to improve the lives of children and families. Offers additional research information in all areas related to child well-being, including their physical and mental health, academic success, and economic security. The Institute offers independent research-based advice and technical assistance to policy makers, journalists, researchers, and educators.

myeducationlab

Go to Topic 12 (Professionalism/Ethics) in the MyEducationLab (www.myeducationlab.com) for your course, where you can:

- Find learning outcomes for Professionalism/Ethics along with the national standards that connect to these outcomes.
- Complete Assignments and Activities that can help you more deeply understand the chapter content.
- Apply and practice your understanding of the core teaching skills identified in the chapter with the Building Teaching Skills and Dispositions learning units.
- Access video clips of CCSSO National Teachers of the Year award winners responding to the question, "Why Do I Teach?" in the Teacher Talk section.
- Hear viewpoints of experts in the field in Professional Perspectives.
- Check your comprehension on the content covered in the chapter by going to the Study Plan in the Book Resources for your text. Here you will be able to take a chapter quiz, receive feedback on your answers, and then access Review, Practice, and Enrichment activities to enhance your understanding of chapter content.

2

CURRENT ISSUES AND PUBLIC POLICY
Contemporary Influences on Children and Families

focus questions

1. What are public policy and current issues?
2. How can you provide for cultural diversity?
3. How have policy and programming trends impacted early childhood?
4. How can you accommodate diverse learners in your classroom?
5. What are some of the hot topics in early childhood education?

naeyc standards

Standard 1. Promoting Child Development and Learning

I use my understanding of young children's characteristics and needs, and of multiple interacting influences on children's development and learning, to create environments that are healthy, respectful, supportive, and challenging for each child.[1]

Standard 6. Becoming a Professional

I identify and conduct myself as a member of the early childhood profession. I know and use ethical guidelines and other professional standards related to early childhood practice. I am a continuous, collaborative learner who demonstrates a knowledgeable, reflective, and critical perspective on my work, making informed decisions that integrate knowledge from a variety of sources. I am an informed advocate for sound educational practices and policies.[2]

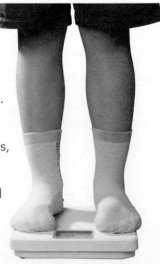

In this chapter we discuss public policy and current issues as they influence early childhood education. At no time in U.S. history has there been so much interest and involvement by early childhood professionals in the development and implementation of public policy. *Public policy* refers to the proposed or actual actions of government and nongovernmental organizations (NGOs) to address and solve social issues. It includes such things as laws; federal, state, and local government guidelines; position statements of professional organizations (e.g., NAEYC's position statement on ethical conduct in Appendix A); and court decisions.

President Obama is advocating reform in America's public schools to deliver a twenty-first century education that will prepare children for success in the workplace.[3] The Children's Defense Fund (CDF) is an example of a national NGO that develops and implements public policy on behalf of children and families. CDF provides a strong, effective voice for all the children of America who cannot vote, lobby, or speak for themselves, and endeavors to educate the nation about the needs of children.[4]

Some states have policies designed to ensure that all children's progress is tracked and they meet achievement goals.[5] These policies give rise to programs to improve children's health and education while also enhancing their abilities to achieve at high levels. For instance, the federal government through the Child Nutrition Act is starting to crack down on school programs that do not have their cafeterias inspected at least two times a year.[6] In addition, the public is asking for better quality and safety of the food their children consume at school.

School readiness for all children is becoming a high priority for the federal government. Secretary of Education Arne Duncan cites these exemplary school readiness programs that states and school districts can emulate: the Chicago Parent Centers; Oklahoma's universal pre-kindergarten program, and the Pennsylvania Pre-K Counts program.[7] You very well may be involved in some of these school readiness programs. At the local level, public schools have developed policies regarding the admittance and education of three- and four-year-old children. According to the National Institute for Early Education Research more than one million three- and four-year-old children attend state-funded preschool education programs.[8] More school districts are hiring preschool teachers, and you might be one of them. Public policy drives public and private education from pre-kindergarten through grade twelve.

public policy All the plans that local, state, and national governmental and nongovernmental organizations have for implementing their goals.

Contemporary Family and Social Issues

Agencies develop **public policy** in response to critical societal issues; public policy, in turn, frequently creates public issues. For example, the federal government through the No Child Left Behind Act changed the way states and local school districts teach children to achieve high standards. The federal government's policy on standards and testing created issues about developmentally appropriate testing and teaching of young children. Teachers and parents expressed concern about how schools and teachers teach and test children. On the other hand, all children and families, especially children and families from diverse backgrounds and with disabilities, face many issues that dramatically place at risk their education and life outcomes. As a result, governmental agencies and NGOs develop and seek to implement appropriate programs to service the

> At the desk where I sit in Washington, I have learned one great truth: The answer for all our national problems, the answer for all the problems of the world, comes down, when you really analyze it, to one single word—education.
>
> **LYNDON B. JOHNSON**

educational, health, and social needs of children and families. For example, the NAEYC promotes national, state, and local public policies that support a system of well-financed, high-quality early childhood education programs in a range of settings, including child care centers, family child care homes, and schools. In addition, the federal government is very much involved in aligning federal and other early childhood programs with the public schools in order to assure quality programming and seamless K–3 programs.

Current issues affect how you, as a professional, provide for children's development, education, and care. They influence every dimension of practice from how we teach children to read, to the health care we provide, to special education services, to the quality of our teaching. We cannot ignore these issues or pretend they do not exist. We must be part of the solution to make it possible for all children to achieve their full potential. Education today is very political, and politicians look to early childhood professionals to help develop educational solutions to social problems.

Family Issues

A primary goal of early childhood education is to meet children's needs in culturally and developmentally appropriate ways. Early childhood professionals agree that a good way to meet the needs of children is through their families, whatever their family unit may be. Family-centered practice is one of the cornerstone features of early childhood education and early childhood special education. This follows the fundamental notion that children's development is influenced by their environment: their family, teachers, school, town, media, governmental systems, and so on.[9] Review Figure 2.1, which shows the potential benefits of working with children and their families.

Benefits of Family-Centered Programs.   Providing for children's needs through and within the family system makes sense for a number of reasons. First, helping families function better means that everyone stands to benefit. When the other people in the family unit—mother, father, grandparents, and relatives—function better, children in the family function better, too.

Second, professionals frequently need to address family problems and issues to help children effectively. For example, helping parents gain access to adequate, affordable health care means that the whole family, including the children, will be healthier. And when children are healthy, they achieve more.[10]

Third, early childhood professionals can do many things concurrently with children and their families that benefit both. Literacy is a good example. Early childhood professionals take a family approach to helping children, their parents, and other family members learn to read, write, speak, and listen. Teaching parents to read helps them understand the importance of supporting their children in the learning process. For example, Pinewood Elementary in Stuart, Florida, has a Family Literacy Night to help enhance students' reading skills while also instilling in families a love of reading and lifelong learning.[11]

Fourth, addressing the needs of children and their families as a whole (i.e., the holistic approach to education and the delivery of services) enables early childhood professionals and others to address a range of social concerns simultaneously. Programs that provide education and support for literacy, health care, nutrition, obesity prevention, healthy living, abuse prevention, and parenting are examples of this family-centered approach. A major trend in early childhood education is that professionals are expanding the family-centered approach to meeting the needs of children and families.

Thus, keeping children healthy becomes an important aspect of early childhood programs. In addition to nutrition and health information children can use at home, early childhood professionals can include daily activities in the classroom to support healthy lifestyles.

FIGURE 2.1 A Model for Meeting the Needs of Children and Families

Early childhood professionals provide:

- Parent education to help parents learn basic child-rearing knowledge and skills
- Literacy programs to help children and families learn literacy skills
- Readiness activities and programs designed to get children ready for school
- Family referrals to community agencies that can provide help (e.g., the Special Supplement Nutrition Program for Women, Infants, and Children (WIC), a health and nutrition program that provides services
- Assistance with problems of daily living such as food, clothing, and shelter

Family and child outcomes as a result of professionals' efforts:

- Less family and child stress
- Healthier families and children
- More involvement of families in their children's education
- Increased school achievement and success
- Reduced child abuse and neglect
- A better quality of life for children and families

Changing Family Units.   Families are in a continual state of change as a result of social issues and changing times. Even the definition of what a family is varies as society changes. Consider the following ways families are changing:

1. *Structure.*   Families now include arrangements other than that of the traditional nuclear family:
   - Single-parent families, headed by mothers or fathers
   - Stepfamilies, including individuals related by either marriage or adoption
   - Heterosexual, gay, or lesbian partners living together with children
   - Extended families, which may include grandparents, uncles, aunts, other relatives, and individuals not related by kinship

2. *Roles.*   As families change, so do the roles of parents, family members, and others:
   - More parents work and have less time for their children and family affairs.
   - Working parents combine the roles of parents and employees. The number of hats that parents wear will increase as families change.
   - Grandparents and non–family members must learn new parenting roles.

As families continue to change, you and other early childhood professionals must develop creative ways to provide services to children and families of all kinds.

FIGURE 2.2 Mothers in the Workforce with Children of Varying Ages

Unlike previous generations, today the majority of mothers with young children are employed.

Source: United States Department of Labor, "Employment Characteristics of Families in 2008" (2008) Available at http://www.bls.gov/news.release/famee.nr0.htm. Photo by Prentice Hall School Division.

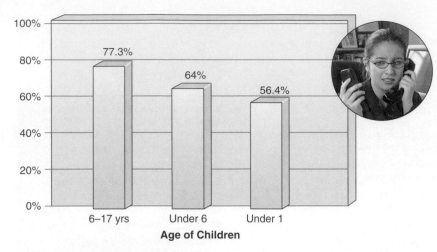

Age of Children
- 6–17 yrs: 77.3%
- Under 6: 64%
- Under 1: 56.4%

When families are involved in their children's education, everyone benefits. What are some culturally appropriate ways you can reach out to the families of the children in your care?

Working Parents. More and more families find that both parents must work to make ends meet. An increasing percentage of mothers with children under six are currently employed (nearly 64 percent in 2008; see Figure 2.2), thereby creating a greater need for early childhood programs.[12] This demand focuses increased attention on early childhood programs and encourages early childhood professionals to meet working parents' needs. You can help working parents by effectively communicating with them and providing ways for them to be connected to their children's learning.

Collaborating with Families. Early childhood professionals agree that a good way to meet the needs of children is through their families, whatever the family units may be. As families change, early childhood professionals have to develop new and different ways of meeting parents' and children's needs. Providing for children's needs through and within the family system makes sense for a number of reasons:

- The family system has the primary responsibility for meeting children's many needs. Parents are children's first teachers, and the experiences and guidance they do or do not provide shapes their children for life. It is in the family that basic values, literacy skills, and approaches to learning are set and reinforced. This is why it is important to work with families and help them get a good start on parenting. For example, teachers can encourage parent phone calls or plan regular conferences to promote family collaboration.[13]

- Teachers frequently need to address family problems and issues simultaneously as they help children. For example, working with family services agencies to help parents access adequate, affordable health care means that the whole family, including children, will be healthier. Alma Family Service Preschool in Los Angeles, California, has an onsite family service center which refers families to community service agencies for help and assistance.[14]

- Early childhood professionals can work with children and their families and benefit both. Family literacy is a good example. Helping children, their parents, and other family members learn to read and write helps the whole family. Many early childhood

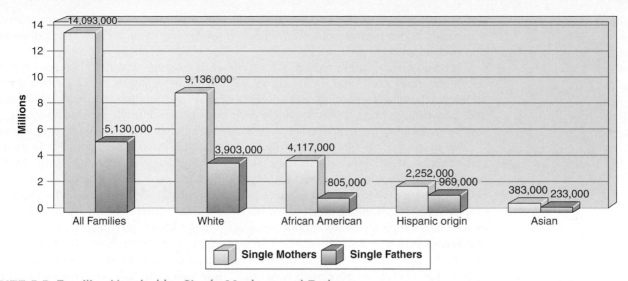

FIGURE 2.3 Families Headed by Single Mothers and Fathers

Families headed by single mothers and fathers are now a way of life for parents and children across the United States.

Source: Data from U.S. Census Bureau, Current Population Survey (2007) and Monthly Labor Review, *Labor Force Status of Families: A Visual Essay*, Stella Potter Cromartie, (July/August 2007).

programs have literacy programs for parents and children. For example, the Toyota Family Literacy Program (TFLP) partners with the National Center for Family Literacy and addresses the growing needs of Hispanic and other immigrant families by increasing English language and literacy skills for adults while also supporting parents' involvement in their children's education.[15] Families matter in the education and development of children. Working with parents becomes a win–win proposition for everyone. You are the key to making family-centered education work.

Fathers and Early Childhood.   Fathers are rediscovering the joys of parenting and working with young children, and early childhood education is discovering fathers! Men are now playing a more active role in providing basic care, love, and nurturance to their children. Fathers are more concerned about their role and their participation in family events before, during, and after the birth of their children. Fathers want to be involved in the whole process of child rearing. For example, kindergarten teacher Lauren Gonzales's husband is a full-time stay-at-home dad. He bathes, feeds, diapers, and cares for their five-month-old child. He also helps their nine-year-old child with homework and takes her to extracurricular activities.

Figure 2.3 shows the number of single-parent families headed by mothers and fathers of certain races. Also increasing in number are the full-time stay-at-home dads; estimates are as high as 159,000.[16] And fathers are receiving some of the employment benefits that have traditionally gone only to women, such as paternity leaves, flexible work schedules, and sick leave for family illness.

Because so many men feel unprepared for fatherhood, early childhood programs and agencies such as hospitals and community colleges are providing courses and seminars to introduce fathers to the joys, rewards, and responsibilities of fathering. In addition, more agencies are promoting the roles of fathers.

Single Parents.   An important part of your professional preparation is to develop the knowledge and skills necessary for collaborating with single-parent families. The number of one-parent families continues to increase, and certain ethnic groups are disproportionately represented, as suggested by Figure 2.3. These increases are attributable to several factors. First, pregnancy rates are higher among lower socioeconomic groups. Second, teenage pregnancy rates in poor white, Hispanic, and African American populations are sometimes higher because of lower education levels, economic constraints, and fewer life opportunities.[17]

People become single parents for a number of reasons: About 35 percent of all marriages end in divorce;[18] and some parents, such as many teenagers, are single by default. In addition, liberalized adoption procedures, artificial insemination, surrogate childbearing, and increasing public support for single parents make this lifestyle an attractive option for some individuals. The reality is that more women are having children without marrying.

No matter how people become single parents, they have tremendous implications for early childhood professionals. In response to growing single parenthood, early childhood programs are developing curricula to help children and their single parents. In addition to needing assistance with child care, single parents frequently seek help in child rearing, especially in regard to parenting practices. At Maplebrook Elementary School in Naperville, Illinois, early childhood professionals conduct seminars to help parents gain skills that will maximize children's learning and social growth.[19] In seminars parents learn things like how to praise, how to disapprove, time-out procedures for misbehavior, and how to set up special incentive systems for motivating cooperative behavior.[20] How well early childhood professionals meet the needs of single parents can make a difference in how successful single parents are in providing for the needs of their children and other family members. Thus your support of single parents can impact how well their children progress in your programs and classroom.

Teenage Parents.   Teenage pregnancies continue to be a societal problem. Although over the past decade, the teen birthrate has declined, in the past few years it has risen. This upswing in teen pregnancies raises concerns among policy makers and early childhood professionals.[21] The following facts about teenage pregnancy dramatically demonstrate its continuing extent and effects:

- In 2009, for women ages fifteen through nineteen, there were 40.5 births per 1,000.[22]
- The only states with a decrease in teenage birth rates were North Dakota, Rhode Island, and New York.[23]
- Teenage birthrates are highest in the South and Southwest. They are highest in Mississippi, New Mexico, and Texas. The states with the lowest teenage birthrates are in the Northeast. They are New Hampshire, Vermont, and Massachusetts.[24]

Concerned legislators, public policy developers, and national leaders view teenage pregnancy as a loss of human potential. They worry about the demand for public health and welfare services and about an increased number of school dropouts. From an early childhood education point of view, teenage pregnancies create greater demand for infant and toddler child care and programs to help teenagers learn how to be good parents. The staff of an early childhood program must often provide nurturance for both children and parents because the parents themselves may lack the emotional maturity necessary to engage in a giving relationship with children. Early childhood professionals must help teenage parents develop parenting skills.

Social Issues

It is almost a given in early childhood education that substandard, unhealthy living conditions are major contributors to poor school achievement and life outcomes.[25] A number of social issues facing children today put their chances for learning and success at risk.

poverty The condition of having insufficient income to support a minimum standard of living.

Poverty.   Living in **poverty** means that individuals don't have the income to purchase adequate health care, housing, food, clothing, and educational services. In 2009 poverty for a nonfarm family of four meant an income of less than $20,050.[26] The federal government annually revises its poverty guidelines, which are the basis for distribution of federal aid to schools and student eligibility for academic services, such as

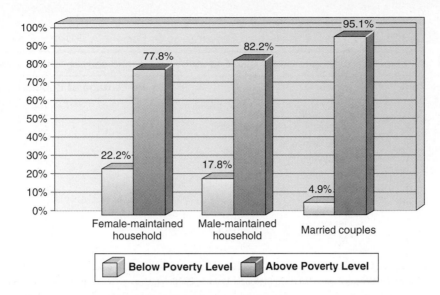

FIGURE 2.4 Families with Children Living in Poverty

Female-headed families are linked to poverty, which is also linked to poor school achievement.

Source: Adapted from U.S. Census Bureau, "Table 3. People and Families in Poverty by Selected Characteristics: 2006 and 2007" (2007).

Head Start, **Title I** (a program that provides additional help in math and reading), and free and reduced-price school breakfasts and lunches. Over 75 percent of children enrolled in Medicaid/CHIP coverage are in families with income less than double the federal poverty level ($40,100). Over 48 percent are in poor families and 29.3 percent are nearly poor.[27] School districts are struggling to cover their share of school lunches' rising cost. Currently, nearly 20 million children receive free or reduced-price lunches in the nation's schools.[28]

Children comprise approximately 39 percent of the 28 million individuals living in poverty. Of those, 5.6 million are under the age of six. Poverty is a greater risk for children living in single-parent homes with female heads of household (see Figure 2.4). Approximately 29 percent of African American children under the age of five live in poverty. Poverty rates for Hispanic American children under the age of six are 32 percent overall.[29] Poverty's children face many risks in school and life. Research shows that low-income children achieve poorly in school; are less healthy; and are more prone to school dropout and delinquency.[30] You and your early childhood colleagues are on the front lines in helping children and their families.

Poverty's Effect.   Living in rural communities and in rural southern states also increases the likelihood that families will live in poverty. As Table 2.1 illustrates, the majority of the ten states with the highest poverty rates are in the South. In Mississippi 29 percent of all children are poor.[31] In addition, living in the inner city increases the chances of being poor. And both rural and urban poverty lead to decreased support for education, meaning that children living in poverty will likely attend schools that have fewer resources and poorer facilities.

The effects of poverty are detrimental to students' achievement and life prospects. For example, children and youth from low-income families are often older than others in their grade level, move more slowly through the educational system, are more likely to drop out, and are less likely to find work. Children in poverty are also more likely to have emotional and behavioral problems and are less likely than others to be "highly engaged" in school.[32] These detrimental effects of living in poverty are further compounded for families raising children with disabilities. Furthermore, parents in low-income families are less likely to help their children complete homework assignments.[33]

Low-income families may also have trouble providing food for their children. A nationwide hunger report estimates that nearly seventeen million children in the United States are living in homes where food sometimes runs short. That is one in four kids facing hunger today! This is an increase of more than four million children in one year. Sixty-two percent

Title I A program that provides additional help in math and reading, and free and reduced-price school breakfasts and lunches

TABLE 2.1 States with Highest Percentage of People in Poverty, 2008

What implications do these data have for public policy and early childhood education?

Rank	State	Percentage of Population in Poverty
1	Mississippi	21.2
2	Arkansas, Kentucky, Louisiana	17.3
3	New Mexico	17.1
4	West Virginia	17.0
5	Oklahoma	15.9
6	Texas	15.8
7	Alaska, South Carolina	15.7
8	Tennessee	15.5
9	Montana	14.8
10	Arizona	14.7

Source: U.S. Census Bureau, *The 2008 Statistical Abstract*, 2008; http://www.census.gov/compendia/statab/ranks/rank34.htm.

of teachers say that they see children who regularly come to school hungry each week because they are not getting fed at home. More than three-quarters of teachers say they respond to hunger in the classroom by helping families sign up for free or reduced-price lunches. Furthermore, 63 percent report that they spend money from their own pocket to buy food for children in their classrooms.[34] Living in poverty means children and their families don't have the income that allows them to purchase adequate health care, housing, food, clothing, and educational services. Cities with the highest school-age poverty rate are in the South and East.[35] Poor children are more likely to be retained in school, and students who have repeated one or more grades are more likely to become school dropouts. Poverty affects students' health prospects as well. For example, in 2008 the number of children under age eighteen without health insurance was 11 percent, or 8.1 million.[36] Also, children living in poverty have poorer health and shorter life spans. The longer children live in poverty, the less efficient their bodies become in handling environmental demands.[37]

If all of these risk factors associated with childhood poverty were not enough, poverty and childhood obesity are also linked. Part of this link can be explained by the fact that people living in poverty tend to have less healthy diets because food is more expensive. Also, maternal obesity and child obesity are linked, and we know that maternal obesity rates are higher in low-income families. Part of your role as an early childhood professional will be to help families develop and practice good nutrition habits.[38]

Socioeconomic Status and Children's Development.   Throughout the course of their in-school and out-of-school lives, children's successes and achievements are greatly influenced by their family's socioeconomic status (SES).[39] SES consists of three broad but interrelated measures: parents' education levels, parents' employment status, and family income. These three measures, acting individually and as an integrated whole, influence (1) how children are reared; (2) family–child interactions; (3) home environments and the extent to which they do or do not support language development and learning; (4) the kind and amount of discipline used; and (5) the kind and extent of future plans involving children's education and employment.[40]

Housing.   Children's homes and the environments of their homes can have a tremendous impact on their growth, development, and educational achievement. Let's look at some of the ways homes affect young children.

Almost 60 percent of U.S. children ages three to eleven are exposed to secondhand smoke. About 25 percent of children at this age live with at least one smoker, with estimates ranging from 9.8 percent in Utah to 28.6 percent in Kentucky.[41] Secondhand smoke, also known as environmental tobacco smoke (ETS), is a mixture of the smoke given off by the burning end of tobacco products and the smoke exhaled by smokers. Children exposed to secondhand smoke have an increased risk of serious respiratory problems such as a greater number and severity of asthma attacks and lower respiratory tract infections, and an increased risk for middle ear infections. For children with certain physical disabilities, exposure to secondhand smoke can further complicate the manifestations of their disability. Here are some things you can do to help children in the battle with secondhand smoke:

- *Quit.* If you are a smoker, become a nonsmoker.
- *Advocate.* You can be in the forefront of efforts to make sure schools and child care centers are smoke free.
- *Protect.* Ask people not to smoke around children.
- *Educate.* Use newsletters and other forms of family communication to inform parents of the dangers of secondhand smoke to themselves and their children.

Beyond the dangers of secondhand smoke, 2.32 million families with children in the United States live in substandard housing.[42] Lead poisoning and asthma, discussed in the next section, are chronic children's health conditions that are related to the quality and condition of children's homes.[43]

In addition, 5 percent of poor households with children live in crowded housing. Crowded households will have 1.01–1.50 people in each room.[44] In certain geographic areas, crowding can be much worse; 2.7 percent of households are classified as crowded in the Midwest while 8.4 percent of households are classified as crowded in the West.[45] Inadequate, crowded, or costly housing can pose serious problems to children's physical, psychological, and material well-being.[46] Furthermore, crowding puts higher levels of stress on parent–child relationships and parents in crowed homes are less responsive to children.[47]

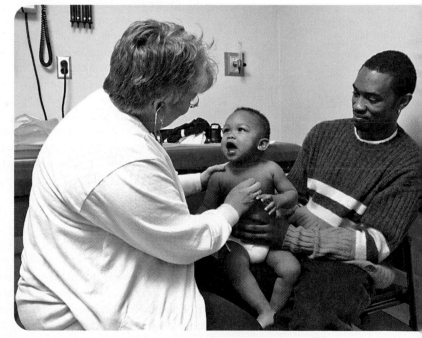

Knowing how housing affects children and families will help you be alert to ways that you can work with families and community agencies to improve the quality of housing wherever it is inferior. For example, I worked with a group of urban teachers who undertook a letter-writing campaign about a slum landlord who ignored the pleas of residents to repair roof leaks and broken plumbing. The campaign attracted public attention and eventually resulted in some relief for the families.

Wellness and Healthy Living. As you know, when you feel good, life goes much better. The same is true for children and their families. Poor health and unhealthy living conditions are major contributors to poor school achievement and life outcomes. A number of health issues facing children today put their chances for learning and success at risk.

Illnesses. When you think of children's illnesses, you probably think of measles, chicken pox, and strep throat. Actually, asthma, lead poisoning, and obesity are the three leading childhood diseases.

Readiness includes physical growth and general health, such as being well rested and fed and properly immunized. How does children's health status affect their readiness for learning?

Asthma.   Asthma is a chronic inflammatory disorder of the airways, characterized by breathlessness, wheezing, coughing, and chest tightness. It is the most common chronic childhood illness in the United States; according to the Centers for Disease Control and Prevention (CDC), an estimated 6.9 million children suffered from asthma in 2007. These soaring rates of asthma have many ill effects, including children missing school days and loss of learning, physical exercise, and healthy development for the affected children.[48]

Asthma is caused in part by poor air quality, dust, mold, animal fur and dander, allergens from cockroaches and rodent feces, and strong fumes. Many of these causes are found in poor and low-quality housing. In your role as advocate you can work with the American Lung Association, which has two initiatives designed to help children with asthma. One program is the Asthma Friendly School Initiative (AFSI). The other is the Kids with Asthma Bill of Rights, designed to help children with asthma talk to their parents and teachers about asthma management.

You will want to reduce asthma-causing conditions in your early childhood program and work with parents to reduce the causes of asthma in their homes. In your school environment, you can prohibit smoking around children, keep the space clean and free of mold, reduce or eliminate carpeting, and have children sleep on mats or cots. You can also work with parents to ensure that their children are getting appropriate asthma medication.

Lead Poisoning.   The CDC estimates that approximately 250,000 children ages one to five years have elevated blood lead levels.[49] These children are at risk for lower IQs, short attention spans, reading and learning disabilities, hyperactivity, and other behavioral problems.

The major source of lead poisoning is lead-based paint that still exists in many homes and apartments. Lead based paints were banned in 1978. Since then, lead has not been used in paint. Approximately 24 million housing units have deteriorated leaded paint and accumulated levels of lead-contaminated dust, and children live in at least 4 million of those homes belong to children.[50] Other sources of lead are car batteries, cheap children's jewelry, and dust and dirt from lead-polluted soil. Lead enters the body through inhalation and ingestion. Young children are especially vulnerable because they put many things in their mouths, chew on windowsills, and crawl on floors.

The threat of lead poisoning in the lives of children continuously lurks. In 2009 Mattel was fined for importing and distributing tainted toys. These toxic toys included the "Sarge" car, GeoTrax toys, Go Diego Go Boat, Sesame Street toys, Dora the Explorer, Batman, Polly Pocket and many Barbie toys and accessories.[51] The U.S. Consumer Product Safety Commission has outlawed paint containing lead for use on U.S. toys since 1978.[52]

Cadmium in children's jewelry is another toxic threat. Cadmium is a known carcinogen. Like lead, it can hinder brain development in the very young. Swallowing an item is not the only way children can expose themselves to cadmium. If they get persistent low-level doses of cadmium by regularly sucking or biting jewelry, this can expose them as well.[53]

The seriousness with which the United States considers lead poisoning is reflected in federal legislation to prevent it. In 2007, then-U.S. Senator Barack Obama and Representative Louise M. Slaughter introduced legislation in the Senate and House, respectively, to protect children from lead poisoning. The Lead Poisoning Reduction Act of 2007 requires that all non-home-based child care facilities, including Head Start program locations and kindergarten classrooms, be lead safe within five years. The bill establishes a five-year, $42.6 million grant program to help local communities pay to make these facilities safe, and sets up "best practices" standards for communities to test for and reduce lead hazards.[54]

Obesity.   Over the past five years, researchers, nutritionists, and politicians have been calling attention to the growing national crisis of childhood obesity. This generation of children is frequently referred to as the Supersize Generation. Indeed, during the past three decades, the childhood obesity rate has more than doubled for children ages two to five and twelve to nineteen, and it has more than tripled for children ages six to eleven. At present, approximately 12.4 percent of children ages two to five are considered obese.[55]

Obesity refers to excess fatty tissue in relation to lean body mass.[56] Children are deemed obese if their weight is more than 20 percent greater than the ideal weight for a boy or girl of their age and height.[57] Even though the terms *obesity* and *overweight* are frequently used interchangeably, there are actually three ways of accurately determining obesity:

- Height and weight plotted on a growth chart
- Skin-fold thickness measured on the back of the upper arm with special calipers
- Body Mass Index (BMI) determined by a mathematical calculation involving height and weight[58]

To counteract the national epidemic of childhood obesity in the United States, early childhood professionals are increasingly turning to physical exercise and activities to help children lead healthy lives, now and in the future.

Obesity is prevalent in both developed and developing countries, reflecting changes in behavioral patterns such as decreased physical activity and overconsumption of high-fat, energy-dense foods. Many other individuals become obese because of a biological predisposition to readily gain weight. Genetic predispositions toward obesity are typically triggered by poor eating habits.[59] Current research into childhood obesity reveals numerous causes:

- Limited amount of physical activity
- Obesity in one or both parents
- Changes in schools' food offerings
- Not eating at the dinner table with family increases risk of children being overweight
- Eating high-calorie snacks
- Drinking high-calorie soft drinks
- Eating too much fast food
- Inability to determine proper portion sizes[60]

What can you, as an early childhood professional, do to help children and parents win the obesity war? You can start by following these ten suggestions and commit to supporting them in your early childhood program:

1. *Encourage breakfast.* If your school or program does not provide breakfast for children, be an advocate for starting to do that. Providing school breakfasts can be both a nutritional and an educational program.
2. *Provide healthy snacks instead of junk food.* Also, advocate for healthy foods in school and program vending machines.
3. *When cooking with children, talk about foods and their nutritional value.* Cooking activities are also a good way to eat new foods and talk about them.
4. *Integrate literacy and nutritional activities.* For example, reading and discussing labels is a good way to encourage children to be aware of and think about nutritional information.
5. *Make meals and snack times pleasant and sociable experiences.*[61] Provide opportunities to help children develop positive attitudes about healthy foods and learn

appropriate eating patterns, mealtime behavior, and communication skills. Encourage children to eat slowly. Do not use food as punishment or reward.

6. *Provide parents with information about nutrition.*   For example, you can make parents aware of the U.S. Department of Agriculture's individualized food pyramid (Figure 2.5). You might access the pyramid online, have children enter their own data, and then have them share their individualized pyramids with their parents.

7. *Help families understand and practice healthy eating habits.*   Encourage parents to set a healthy example for their families so that they can help their young children develop healthy eating habits.[62]

8. *Encourage exercise.*   You can provide daily opportunities for physical exercise and physical activities in your program, maximizing large-motor muscle activity, such as jumping, dancing, marching, kicking, running, riding a tricycle, or throwing a ball.[63] National Association for Sport and Physical Education experts now recommend that toddlers engage in at least 60 minutes of physical activity a day.[64]

9. *Be a role model.*   You can set a good example for children to follow by modeling appropriate behaviors, such as promoting healthy eating patterns, routinely promoting physical activity, and putting limitations of television and video time to a maximum of 2 hours per day.[65]

10. *Use classroom examples and movement.*   For example, Christine Williams developed Animal Trackers to build children's motor skills as a way to present obesity.

Animal Trackers.   Animal Trackers (AT) was designed as a developmentally appropriate, fun, and skill-building physical activity, movement, and play program for two- to five-year-old children, building on and enhancing the natural acquisition of gross-motor skills during the preschool years.

The AT curriculum accomplishes the following:

- Increases the frequency and duration of preschool physical activity targeted toward learning and practicing gross-motor skills in a fun and active play format
- Increases the performance of age-appropriate gross-motor skills for preschoolers who participate
- Educates preschool teachers to teach the AT motor-skills activities in an effective and enjoyable way
- Involves parents in the AT program through AT-at-Home child and parent activities

AT activities can easily be integrated into traditional preschool content areas, through innovative cross-curricular content and objectives in math, language, and social skills, designed to build a variety of educational skills through structured active play. Examples include counting, sorting, alphabet recognition and other language skills, following directions, taking turns, and partnering with others. The following Creepy-Crawly Things activity enhances both locomotor and literacy skills.

> Have children alternate crawling and creeping by asking them to move like the following animal and repeat the sound of the letter that begins the name. For example, "Can you creep like a sssss . . . snake? Snake starts with the letter S. Can you crawl like a bbbbbbb . . . baby? Baby starts with the letter B." Can you creep like a . . . CATERPILLAR?; Can you crawl like a . . . SPIDER?; Can you creep like a . . . WORM?; Can you crawl like a . . . DOG?; Can you creep like a . . . SNAIL?; Can you crawl like a . . . CRAB (or lobster)?
>   An alternative is to set up an obstacle course that requires crawling in some places and creeping in others, depending on the obstacle under which the children must move.[66]

There are a lot of things you can do to promote children's health. Review Figure 2.5, "Mypyramid.gov," and think of ways you can use this as a guide in your classroom and with parents.

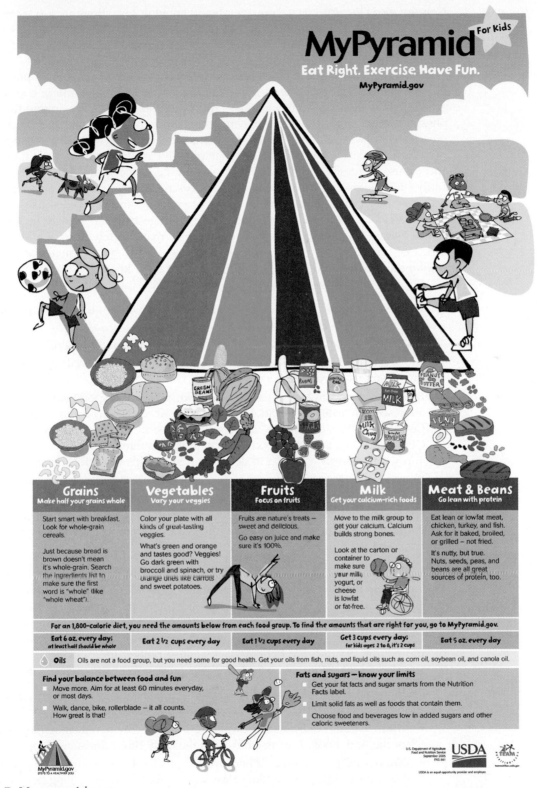

FIGURE 2.5 Mypyramid.gov

Go to www.mypyramid. gov to individualize the pyramid according to each child's age, gender, and physical activity level.

Source: U.S. Department of Agriculture, Food and Nutrition Service, "MyPyramid for Kids" (August 2007), http://www.mypyramid.gov.

Gender and Obesity.   Have you ever heard an adult say, "Boys are just more active than girls; they need more time to run and play outdoors" or "The girls are content to play inside; it's the boys who have to get out on the playground"? Knowledgeable preschool and primary teachers know that vigorous physical activity is very important for girls as well as for boys. Both girls and boys need and deserve plenty of time to be physically active indoors and out. Improved aerobic endurance, muscular strength, motor coordination, and growth stimulation of the heart, lungs, and other vital organs are among the benefits of physical activity for all children. Giving equal opportunity to girls and boys—starting in preschool—is what Title IX of the Educational Amendments of 1972 is all about.

Physical activity, for both genders, helps build and maintain healthy muscles, bones, and joints; increases the body's infection-fighting white blood cells and germ-fighting antibodies; helps control weight; and reduces the risk of developing such illnesses as diabetes, heart disease, and many types of cancer. Sandy Hopkins uses an electronic game called Dance Dance Revolution to encourage physical activity in her classroom. Dance Dance Revolution operates using a dance mat and television. Children dance to a series of dance steps that the screen displays until they complete the song. One of Hopkins's children said, "It was so fun, I did not even know I was even working out."[67]

Physical activity has additional benefits for girls:

- Because osteoporosis is more prevalent among women, it's especially important for girls to build strong bones when they're young.
- Exercise has been shown to significantly increase strength in girls.
- Estrogen-dependent cancers (breast, ovarian, and endometrial) may occur less often in women who exercise.
- Exercise can positively impact depression, which is experienced twice as often by adolescent females as by adolescent males. According to a report of the President's Council on Physical Fitness and Sports ("Physical Activity and Sport in the Lives of Girls"), participation in physical activity helps counteract the feelings of hopelessness and worthlessness common to depression and helps instill feelings of success.
- Physical activity and exercise also positively affect self-esteem, self-concept, and body image.
- Studies show that many high school female athletes receive higher grades and standardized test scores than their nonathletic counterparts. They also drop out at lower rates and are more likely to go on to college.[68]

Bullying.   Programs to prevent and curb bullying are another example of how educators are combating the effects of violence on children. Although in the past bullying has been dismissed as normal or kids' play, bullying is now related to school and other violence. Bullying includes teasing, slapping, hitting, pushing, unwanted touching, taking personal belongings, name calling, and making sexual comments and insults about looks, behavior, and culture. Schools are fighting back against bullies and bullying.

Here are some things you can do to help prevent bullying in your classroom:

- Read books about bullying during story time and group reading lessons, guided reading, and shared reading. Here are some books you might want to read:
  - *Arthur's April Fool* by Marc Brown. Arthur worries about remembering his magic tricks for the April Fool's Day assembly, and the bully Binky threatens to pulverize him.
  - *Blubber* by Judy Blume. When overweight Linda gives an oral report on whales, the cruel and power-wielding class leader, Wendy, starts calling her "Blubber," and the name-calling escalates into more intense bullying and humiliation.
  - *Dealing with Bullying* by Marianne Johnston. This book describes what is meant by bullying, and explains why bullies act as they do, how to deal with them, and how to stop being one.

- *Nobody Knew What to Do* by Becky R. McCain. When bullies pick on Ray, a boy at school, a classmate is afraid but decides he must do something.
- *Stop Picking on Me* by Pat Thomas. This picture book helps kids accept the normal fears and worries that accompany bullying, and it suggests ways to resolve this upsetting experience.
- *The Berenstain Bears and the Bully* by Stan Berenstain. When she takes a beating from the class bully, Sister Bear learns a valuable lesson in self-defense—and forgiveness.

- Talk to children individually and in groups when you see them engage in hurtful behavior. For instance, "Chad, how do you think Brad felt when you pushed him out of the way?"
- Intervene immediately when you see children starting to, or attempting to, bully others. Do not ignore it.
- Be constantly alert to any signs of bullying behavior in your classroom.
- Teach cooperative and helpful behavior, courtesy, and respect. Much of what children do, they model from others' behaviors. When you provide examples of courteous and respectful behavior in your classroom it sets a good example for children.
- Have children work together on a project. Then, have them talk about how they got along with each other and worked together.
- Make children and others in your classroom feel welcome and important.
- Talk to parents and help them understand your desire to have a bully-free classroom. Conduct a workshop for parents on anti-bullying behavior.
- Send books home on anti-bullying themes that parents can read with their children.

A good book for you to read to help you learn more about how to deal with bullying is *The Anti-Bullying and Teasing Book* by Barbara Sprung, Merle Froschl, and Blythe Hinitz. This text uses activities, the classroom environment, and family involvement to develop empathy in children and create a climate of mutual respect in the classroom.

Cyber Bullying.   With the widespread use of the Internet, iPhones, texting devices, and social networking sites used by young children, cyber bullying is becoming more of a problem. Cyber bullying is the threat, stalking, harassment, torment, and humiliation of one child by another through electronic means. Cyber bullying is often anonymous, and sometimes occurs between cliques and a single victim. Girls are the victims of cyber bullying more often than boys.[69] For example, Sydney received an anonymous e-mail that said, "You are fat, stupid and ugly."

How to Prevent Cyber Bullying.   Some ways you can prevent cyber bullying in your classroom:

- Educate your staff, students, and families about cyber bullying during open house and parent meetings.
- Update and post anti-bullying policies.
- Use filtering and tracking software on computers.
- Closely monitor students' use of computers.
- Investigate and report any and all signs of cyber bullying.[70]

In addition, because most cyber bullying takes place outside the classroom, you can work with parents to help them educate their children about cyber bullying. Here are some ways that parents can prevent cyber bullying at home:

- Learn what cyber bullying is and how technology is used to bully others.
- Contact their Internet service provider to see what parental controls are provided.

- Monitor what their children are doing online.
- Immediately notify school officials when they suspect any form of cyber bullying.[71]

When you are alert for signs of cyber bullying, then you can lessen the likelihood that children will be the victims of the electronic age version of the playground bully.

Providing for Cultural Diversity

As a result of changing demographics, more students will require special education, bilingual education, and other special services. Issues of culture and diversity shape instruction and curriculum. These demographics also have tremendous implications for how you teach and how your children learn.

Diversity

The population of the United States is changing and will continue to change. For example, projections are that by 2050, minorities will constitute more than 47 percent of the American population.[72] The population of young children in the United States reflects the population at large and represents a number of different cultures and ethnicities. Thus, many cities and school districts have populations that express great ethnic diversity, including Asian Americans, Native Americans, African Americans, and Hispanic Americans. For example, the Charlotte-Mecklenburg school district in North Carolina has children from 141 countries, each with their own culture.[73] Across the United States, seismic demographic changes herald how diverse populations are transforming regional geographic areas, states, school districts, and schools. For example, the South has become the first region in the country where more than half of public school students are poor. Additionally, more than half of students in the South are members of minorities (Arizona, 56%; California, 71%; Florida, 54%; Georgia, 54%; Louisiana, 51%; Mississippi, 54%; Nevada, 57%; New Mexico, 70%; and Texas, 65%). This shift is fueled by an influx of Latinos and other ethnic groups; the return of African Americans to the South; and higher birth rates among African American and Latino families. The numbers also herald the future of the United States as a whole, as minority students are expected to exceed 50 percent of public school enrollment by 2020 and the numbers of students poor enough to qualify for free or reduced-price lunches continues to rise.[74] The constantly changing population demographics mean you have to understand diversity and embrace it in your classroom. You can design your classroom and teaching to address issues relating to the needs of diverse populations in the accompanying Voice from The Field, "The Kindergarten Achievement Gap Begins Before Kindergarten."

Thinking and Acting Multiculturally

cultural competency The process of developing proficiency in effectively responding in a crosscultural text. It is the process by which individuals respond respectfully and effectively to diverse cultures.

As an early childhood professional, keep in mind that you are the key to the classroom environment that promotes **cultural competency** for all children. The following guidelines will help you foster cultural understanding and acceptance in young classrooms:

- *Recognize that all children are unique.*   Children have special talents, abilities, and styles of learning and relating to others. Make your classroom a place in which children are comfortable being who they are. Always value uniqueness and diversity.
- *Get to know, appreciate, and respect the cultural backgrounds of your children.*   Visit families and community neighborhoods to learn more about cultures and religion and the ways of life they engender.
- *Use authentic situations to provide for cultural learning and understanding.*   For example, a field trip to a culturally diverse neighborhood of your city or town provides children an opportunity for understanding firsthand many of the details about how

people live. Such an experience provides wonderful opportunities for involving children in writing, cooking, reading, and dramatic play activities. What about setting up a market in the classroom?

- *Use authentic assessment activities to assess fully children's learning and growth.* Portfolios are ideal for assessing children's learning in nonbiased and culturally sensitive ways.
- *Infuse culture into your lesson planning, teaching, and caregiving and make it a foundation for learning.* Use all subject areas—math, science, language arts, literacy, music, art, and social studies—to relate culture to children's lives and cultural backgrounds. This approach makes students feel good about their backgrounds, cultures, families, and experiences.
- *Be a role model by accepting, appreciating, and respecting other languages and cultures.* In other words, infuse multiculturalism into your personal and professional lives.
- *Be knowledgeable about, proud of, and secure in your own culture.* Children will ask about you, and you should be prepared to share your cultural background with them.

It is up to you to help your children to accept and respect all people and their cultures.

Cultural Infusion

Cultural infusion means that culturally aware and culturally sensitive education permeates the curriculum to alter or affect the way young children and teachers think about diversity issues. In a larger perspective, infusion strategies are used to ensure that culture becomes a part of the entire center, school, and home. Infusion processes foster cultural awareness; use appropriate instructional materials, themes, and activities; teach to children's learning styles; and promote family and community involvement.

cultural infusion Culturally aware and culturally sensitive education permeates the curriculum to alter or affect the way young children and teachers think about diversity issues.

Cultural Awareness. **Cultural awareness** is the appreciation for and understanding of people's cultures, socioeconomic status, and gender. It includes understanding one's own culture. Cultural awareness programs and activities focus on other cultures while making children aware of the content, nature, and richness of their own. Learning about other cultures concurrently with their own culture enables children to integrate commonalities and appreciate differences without inferring inferiority or superiority of one or the other. Promoting cultural awareness in an early childhood program has implications far beyond your school, classroom, and program. Culture influences and affects work habits, interpersonal relations, and a child's general outlook on life. Being a culturally aware teacher means that you are sensitive to the socioeconomic backgrounds of children and families. For example, we know that low family socioeconomic status tends to dampen children's school achievement. The same is true with children's school achievement and level of maternal education. Research shows that children that have educated parents enter school with a higher level of academic skills and continue to perform better than other children.[75] By learning about family background you can provide children from diverse backgrounds the extra help they may need to be successful in school.

cultural awareness The appreciation for and understanding of people's cultures, socioeconomic status, and gender.

Early childhood professionals must take these influences into consideration when designing curriculum and instructional processes for the impressionable children they teach. One way to accomplish the primary goal of cultural infusion and awareness—to positively change the lives of children and their families—is to infuse acceptance of diversity in early childhood activities and practices. Children must be culturally competent. They need to develop proficiency to respond respectfully and effectively to diverse cultures.[76]

Using Appropriate Instructional Materials. You need to carefully consider and select appropriate instructional materials to support the infusion of cultural education. The following are some suggestions for achieving this goal.

Voice from the Field

The Kindergarten Achievement Gap Begins Before Kindergarten

In the opening pages of the new third edition of NAEYC's *Developmentally Appropriate Practice: Serving Children from Age Birth–8*, the authors discuss the early childhood achievement gap as one of the critical issues faced by children and early childhood professionals. Here is what they say:

> All families, educators, and the larger society hope that all children will achieve in school and go on to lead satisfying and productive lives, but that optimistic future is not equally likely for all of the nation's school children. Most disturbing, low income and African American and Hispanic students lag significantly behind their peers on standardized comparisons of academic achievement throughout the school years, and they experience more difficulties while in the school setting.[1]

The achievement gap between students of various races, cultures, and socioeconomic backgrounds is a serious issue that all of us as early childhood educators must address. Many children come to school already behind their more advantaged counterparts because they are not prepared to meet the demands of contemporary schooling. For example, as the following chart shows, children from low-income families are already well behind children in the highest socioeconomic groups.

The extent and seriousness of the achievement gap is further illustrated in the results of a survey of Michigan kindergarten teachers.

- Thirty-two percent of kindergarten teachers were not satisfied with the abilities of their kindergarten students when they started school, with an additional 50 percent being only somewhat satisfied.

- According to the teachers, only 65 percent of children entered kindergarten classrooms ready to learn the curriculum.
- Eighty-six percent of teachers report that students who are behind academically at kindergarten entrance have an impact on their teacher's ability to effectively provide instruction to the rest of the class.[2]

Awareness of the extent of the problem is only one part of our efforts to reduce and eliminate achievement gaps. Taking effective action is the other part of the solution. Here are some things for you to advocate for:

- The opportunity for all children, but particularly children from low-income backgrounds and English language learners, to participate in preschool programs. There is a growing consensus that providing universal preschool will help all children socially and academically as they continue through the elementary grades.
- High-quality preschool and other early education programs for all children. Unfortunately, not all children have high-quality programs available to them; this is particularly true for students from low-income families.
- "Ready schools and ready communities" means that the schools children attend and the communities they live in are united in their efforts to provide the health, nutrition, and educational experiences all children need in order to be successful in school and life. Ready schools are those that have strong leadership, have continuity between early child care and education, promote smooth transitions between home and school, and are committed to the success of every child as well as every teacher and adult who interacts with children at school. Ready communities

- *Multicultural Literature*. Choose literature that embraces similarities and welcomes differences regarding how children and families live their *whole lives*.
- *Themes*. Early childhood professionals may select and teach thematic units that help strengthen children's understanding of themselves, their culture, and the cultures of others. Here are some appropriate theme topics, all of which are appropriate for meeting various state standards and the standards of the National Council for the Social Studies (NCSS):
  - Getting to Know Myself, Getting to Know Others
  - What Is Special About You and Me?
  - Growing Up in the City
  - Tell Me About Africa (or South America, China, etc.)
- *Personal Accomplishments*. Add to classroom activities, as appropriate, the accomplishments of people from different cultural groups, women of all cultures, and individuals with disabilities.

Children's Achievement by Socioeconomic Status

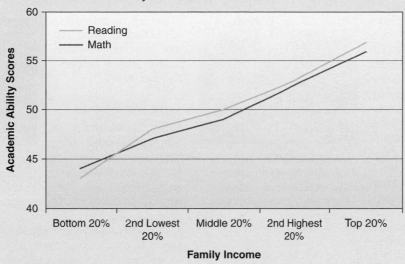

Source: U.S. Department of Education, National Center for Education Statistics, *Early Childhood Longitudinal Study, Kindergarten Class of 1998–99,* September 2009; http://nces.ed.gov/pubs2009/2009003.pdf.

provide neighborhoods that are safe; have high-quality schools; have safe homes free of lead paint; and have amenities such as parks, playgrounds, and libraries.[3]

In addition, there are many specific things that preschool and kindergarten teachers can do to help children catch up with their more advantaged peers. Children need specific language and literacy skills such as oral language, vocabulary, listening comprehension, and print awareness skills to be successful. Intentional teaching of these skills will go a long way to help eliminate the achievement gap.

[1]*Carol Copple and Sue Bredekamp, Developmentally Appropriate Practice in Early Childhood Programs: Serving Children from Birth Through Age 8, 3rd edition (Washington, DC: National Association for the Education of Young Children, 2009), 8.*

[2]*Lansing, MI: Early Childhood Investment Corporation. A Summary of Michigan kindergarten teachers' beliefs about the school readiness of kindergarten children and other issues related to school readiness. August 2009.*

[3]*Wisconsin Council on Children and Families, "Ready Kids, Ready Schools and Ready Communities," Spring 2004; accessed February 22, 2010 at www.wccf.org/pdf/schoolreadiness.pdf.*

When you select materials for use in a cultural curriculum for early childhood programs, make sure of the following:

- Represent people of all cultures fairly and accurately.
- Include people of color, many cultural groups, and people with exceptionalities.
- Verify that historical information is accurate and nondiscriminatory.
- Do not use materials that include stereotypical roles and languages.
- Ensure gender equity—that is, boys and girls are represented equally and in non-stereotypic roles.

Promoting Family and Community Involvement.   In your work with children and families of diverse cultural backgrounds, you should not assume values and beliefs just because a family speaks a particular language and is from a different country of origin. Take time to discover the particular values, beliefs, and practices of the families in the community.

You will teach children from different cultures whose first language is not English. Educating students with diverse backgrounds and individual needs makes for a challenging

Voice from the Field

How to Help English Language Learners Succeed

My attempts to learn Spanish have given me a lot of empathy for English language learners. Perhaps you have had the same experience of frustration with comprehension, pronunciation, and understandable communication. English language learners face these same problems and others. Many come from low socioeconomic backgrounds. Others come to this country lacking many of the early literacy and learning opportunities we take for granted.

Picture yourself in this classroom. Which of the activities suggested here would you select to help your student learn English?

a number of approaches you can use to ensure that your children will learn English and be academically successful.

Tips for Success

Judith Lessow-Hurley, a bilingual expert, says, "It's important to create contexts in which kids exchange meaningful messages. Kids like to talk to other kids, and that's use-

Classroom activities such as those suggested here can help English language learners gain important skills.

ful."[2] Lessow-Hurley also supports sheltered immersion. She says, "A lot of what we call 'sheltering' is simply good instruction—all kids benefit from experiential learning, demonstrations, visuals, and routines. A lot of sheltering is also common sense—stay away from idioms, speak slowly and clearly, [and] find ways to repeat yourself."[3]

Here are some other general tips Lessow-Hurley offers for assisting English language learners, along with some explicit classroom strategies:

Increasing Numbers

Many school districts across the country have seen their numbers of English language learners skyrocket. For example, in the Winston-Salem/Forsyth County School District in North Carolina, more than 9 percent of the 51,325 student population are English language learners, representing seventy-seven different native languages. In the Springdale School District in Northwest Arkansas, 40 percent of the 17,400 student population are English language learners.[1]

The chances are great that you will have English language learners in your classroom wherever you choose to teach. There are

STRATEGY 1

Develop Content Around a Theme

The repetition of vocabulary and concepts reinforces language and ideas and gives English language learners better access to content.

and rewarding career. Learning how to constantly improve your responses to children's needs and improve learning environments and curricula will be one of your ongoing professional responsibilities. Given the high number of students from diverse backgrounds, today it is more important than ever before that educators be aware of cultural differences. Lack of knowledge of these differences can lead to the overrepresentation of students from diverse backgrounds in special education programs.[77]

The accompanying Voice from the Field, "How to Help English Language Learners Succeed" will provide you with six strategies for becoming a successful teacher of linguistically and culturally diverse children.

Policy and Programming Trends

As you might suspect, all of the issues confronting the field of early childhood education today result in increased public attention. Federal and state policy makers are constantly considering reforms and programs that will improve teaching and learning.

STRATEGY 2 — Use Visual Aids and Hands-On Activities to Deliver Content

Information is better retained when a variety of senses are used.

- Rely on visual cues as frequently as possible.
- Have students create flash cards for key vocabulary words. Be sure to build in time for students to use them.
- Encourage students to use computer programs, books with accompanying DVDs, and electronic books (e-books).

STRATEGY 3 — Use Routines to Reinforce Language

This practice increases the comfort level of second-language learners; they then know what to expect and associate the routine with the language. Daily reading is one such helpful routine. Pictures, gestures, and a dramatic voice will help convey meaning.

STRATEGY 4 — Engage English Language Learners with English Speakers

Cooperative learning groups of mixed language abilities give students a meaningful context for using English.

- Pair English language learners with native speakers to explain and illustrate a specific word or phrase frequently heard in the classroom.

- Ask the students to make a picture dictionary of the words and phrases they are learning, using pictures they have cut out of magazines.
- Have small groups make vocabulary posters of categories of common words, again using pictures cut from magazines.

STRATEGY 5 — Allow Students to Use Nonverbal Responses

Permit students to demonstrate their knowledge and comprehension in alternative ways. For example, one teacher has early primary students hold up cardboard "lollipops" (green or red side forward) to indicate a yes or no answer to a question.

STRATEGY 6 — Don't Correct All Nonstandard Responses

It's better to get students talking; they acquire accepted forms through regular use and practice. A teacher can always paraphrase a student's answer to model Standard English.[4]

Photos by Hope Madden/Merrill.

[1] Lesli Maxwell, "Immigration Transforms Communities," Education Week (January 8, 2009.)

[2] "Acquiring English Schools Seek Ways to Strengthen Language Learning," Curriculum Update, Association for Supervision and Curriculum Development (Fall 2002), 6.

[3] Ibid.

[4] Ibid., 7.

Educational Reform

At the same time that states are exerting control over education, so is the federal government. One of the dramatic changes occurring in society is the expanded role of the federal government in the reform of public education. We are currently witnessing more federal dollars allocated for specific early education initiatives than ever before. For example, the federal government is providing increased funding to reform Head Start by making it more academic and emphasizing the development of early literacy skills. The critics of federal support for such programs argue that the federal government should not allocate dollars for specific, targeted programs. However, the number and size of federal allocations for reform initiatives will likely continue for the following reasons:

- Politicians and the public recognize that the early years are the foundation for future learning.
- Spending money on children in the early years is more cost effective than trying to solve problems in the teenage years, because there is more support for funding research that

Accommodating Diverse Learners

Now that you have read about public policy and current issues affecting children who are typically developing in early childhood today, let's look at one issue that has many policy implications as well as an issue about which many early childhood teachers have questions: *inclusion,* typically defined as educating children with and without disabilities in the same classroom. While the Division for Early Childhood (DEC) of the Council for Exceptional Children (CEC) and the National Association for the Education of Young Children (NAEYC) have identified inclusion as the preferred service delivery option for young children with special needs, there is no agreed-on model for developing and delivering these services. A classroom template for inclusion is not available, but it is essential that teachers believe that preparing all children to function in society is best achieved by creating environments that include children whose diversity includes varying abilities and disabilities and backgrounds.

Once teachers support the philosophy of inclusion, they must be able to plan for and provide for the needs of the diverse children in their classroom. Creating a successful inclusive environment requires a well-planned and well-organized classroom. Teachers who plan and evaluate the different aspects of the classroom setting can construct classrooms that meet the needs of all students. You will gradually gain the skills, awareness, and dispositions to do this. The following list provides some examples of ways to create, implement, evaluate, and modify classrooms so optimal learning conditions are created for all students:

- *Classroom schedule:* A consistent schedule helps students feel secure and adds to the predictability of the environment. A visual schedule that is reviewed orally every day benefits all children. In addition, some students will need their own individual schedules, particularly if their day includes therapists who provide services for them.
- *Routines:* Routines for different times of the day and scheduling a particular activity at the same time every day or on the same day every week is beneficial for students who need the stability of knowing what their day will entail.
- *Classroom curriculum:* Classroom curriculum that is appropriate for all children does not mean each child will do the same things every day. The curriculum must include activities that can be modified and adapted to meet the needs of each child.
- *Classroom management:* Teachers must support and encourage appropriate behavior, prevent inappropriate behavior, and guide or redirect misbehavior when it does occur. In the inclusive classroom, you can achieve this goal by creating a positive management plan that addresses skill deficits. A **skill deficit** is the inability to perform a skill because the child does not possess the skill. For example, a child with a disability may have a social skill deficit associated with making friends and gaining popularity. Motivational deficits involve the unwillingness or lack of cooperation of children to perform a skill they possess, either entirely or at an appropriate level. For example, some children may be reluctant or hesitant to engage in an activity because of their disability. In contrast, some children may lack motivational self-control and be aggressive and intrusive to others.
- *Grouping:* The inclusive classroom can include heterogeneous and homogeneous grouping, depending on the activity. Teachers must have explicit individual behavioral and academic expectations for each child depending on his or her needs.
- *Physical arrangement:* In the early childhood classroom, the four-desk cluster provides the most opportunities for students with disabilities to be included in the classroom. Teachers can move efficiently from child to child, and socialization, cooperation, and group work are optimized.
- *Rules:* Rules should be stated positively, limited in number, observable, measurable, and applied to behavior only. Rules should not address academic or homework issues that could unfairly impact students with disabilities or who are linguistically diverse.

skill deficit When a child has not learned how to perform a particular skill or behavior.

- *Transitions:* Strategies that support smooth transitions between activities include verbal cues (e.g., "Five minutes before clean-up"), visual cues (e.g., picture schedules), auditory cues (e.g., timers), and praise after successful transitions.

Teachers who actively prepare for all students are better able to provide accommodations, supports, and instruction where needed. Organizations such as DEC (www.dec-sped.org), CEC (www.cec.sped.org), and NAEYC (www.naeyc.org) are excellent sources for position papers, instructional resources, and other documents that will assist you with this endeavor.

Hot Topics in Early Childhood Education

The issues facing early childhood education today are many and varied and have considerable consequences, both positive and negative, for young children. The following hot topics are discussed throughout this book to help you be on the cutting edge of your professional practice.

- *Globalization of early childhood education.* Countries around the world are using education and language to muscle their way into the top tier of world economic influence. Nowhere is this more evident than in Asia. Early childhood education has emerged as a tool of economic competitiveness.[86]
- *Early literacy and reading.* Early childhood professionals regard providing children with the foundation for literacy as one of the key factors necessary for their school success.
- *Emphasis on science, technology, engineering, and math (STEM).* Children need an education with a foundation in STEM areas so that they are prepared to both work and live in the twenty-first century. For example, Scales Technology Academy, located in Tempe, Arizona, provides a laptop for each student from kindergarten through fifth grade and focuses on a high technology curriculum.[87]
- *The politicization of early childhood education.* There has been a dramatic increase in state and federal involvement in the education of young children, as discussed earlier. President Obama and his administration have initiated various programs and are providing funding to improve early education learning.
- *Use of early childhood programs to promote and support children's readiness for school and learning.* Increasingly, there is a recognition that if children are ready to learn when they enter school, they are more likely to succeed. The Even Start program provides funding to support school readiness for children from birth through age seven. This opens the educational opportunities for students in low-income areas by integrating early childhood education, adult education, parenting education and interactive literacy activities between parents and their children.[88]
- *Public schools and early childhood programs.* The alignment of public schools with early childhood programs is becoming increasingly popular. Some think it makes sense to put the responsibility for educating and caring for the nation's children under the sponsorship of one agency—the public schools. For their part, public school teachers and the unions that represent them are anxious to bring early childhood programs within the structure of the public school system. However, a growing vocal minority views federal funding of preschool programs as a movement to "standardize childhood." They argue that with federal funding comes federal control and a standardized one-size-fits-all approach to preschool education. This tension between local and federal funding and control of early childhood education will continue to give both sides opportunities to advocate for which approach they think best meets the needs of children and families.

It seems inevitable that the presence of public schools in early childhood education will continue to expand. Given that so many public schools offer programs for three- and four-year-olds, can programs for infants and toddlers be far behind?

- *The increasing use of testing to measure achievement and school performance in the early years.* At the same time, increasing numbers of parents, professionals, and early childhood critics are advocating for less emphasis on high-stakes testing in the early years.

- *The use of research results to inform and guide program and classroom practice.* Another name for this is *evidence-based practice*. Throughout this text, I discuss the importance and influence of research on teaching and learning. I also discuss how to apply research as you care for and teach young children. In addition, you can use research results as part of your advocacy agenda. For example, research that shows the benefits and lifelong value of children's participation in early childhood programs enables you to advocate for additional high-quality programs. The application of research to practice is one of the hallmarks of the "new" early childhood education.

- *The return of whole-child education.* There is definitely a trend toward rethinking what is an appropriate education for all children. There has been a tendency, in many sectors, to look at education as consisting of primarily achievement as measured by test scores. Now, more people are coming to support what early childhood educators have always known and held dear: We must educate the whole child in all developmental dimensions—physical, social, emotional, cognitive, linguistic, and spiritual!

- *Inclusive classrooms.* Teachers must be educated for and prepared to provide for the needs of the diverse children in their classroom. You can count on having children with disabilities in your classroom.

This is a great time for early childhood education and a wonderful time to be a teacher of young children. The numerous changes in the field and the compelling issues that accompany them provide many opportunities for you to become even more professional and for all children to learn the knowledge and skills necessary for success in school and life.

Activities for Professional Development

Ethical Dilemma

"My child's not dangerous!"

Zachary Christie, a six-year-old, was suspended for forty-five days after he was found with a camping utensil that was ruled a weapon. Zachary got the camping utensil after joining Boy Scouts and was excited to use it at lunch, using it as a spoon, fork, and knife.

Local school districts' zero tolerance policy restricts students from bringing weapons to school. Regardless of Zachary's intent, school officials proclaimed that they had to penalize him because bringing knives to school is against school policy. There is a growing debate over whether or not zero tolerance policies have gone too far. Although Zachary may not have intended to harm anyone, administrators argue that it is hard to decipher between pranks, innocent mistakes, and serious threats. In order to ensure the safety of all children they must adhere to strict rules. Zachary's mom started a website to gain support and persuade others that "he is not some sort of threat to his classmates."

Do you think that the zero tolerance policies are too strict? Or should administrators have the final say and make decisions on a case-by-case basis? Do you agree with the decision to suspend Zachary from school? What would you have done?

Activities to Apply What You Learned

1. Think about and list five ways you can create a healthy and safe classroom for the grade level you plan to teach. Log on to MySpace and share with other classmates by creating an online blog. To do this, go to www.myspace.com and click on create blog. Take a look at the number of people that have viewed your blog and their comments. What do their comments tell you?

2. Many young children live in diverse families. Conduct online research about the challenges of providing for different types of families. Think about diverse families, the challenges families face, and what you can do as an early childhood professional to support contemporary families. Log on to Twitter and share with a small group of classmates your findings through Twitter's online website. To do this, go to www.twitter.com and type "diverse families" in the search box.

3. Recall some of the reasons that parents support early childhood education programs. Create an online wiki that will allow you to share your thoughts and ideas on why parents want, need, and support public early childhood education programs. To do this go to www.wikidot.com and after you have typed in the name of your online wiki that you would like to create, click "get it now."

4. How can you create and modify classrooms to accommodate diverse learners? Go online and find ways teachers in inclusive classrooms accommodate their diverse learners. Next, discuss your findings with classmates in a chat room. Finally, develop a list of ways you will support students with disabilities in your classroom.

5. Think about ways to incorporate some of the hot topics we discussed in the chapter. Log on to www.facebook.com and share your ideas by posting a note. Tag your classmates to get their feedback.

Linking to Learning

Annie E. Casey Foundation
www.aecf.org
Presents the latest information on issues affecting America's disadvantaged children; a friendly, newly updated resource.

Council for Exceptional Children (CEC)
www.cec.sped.org
A national organization dedicated to improving educational outcomes for individuals with exceptionalities, students with disabilities, and/or the gifted.

The Division for Early Childhood (DEC)
http://dec-sped.org
A division of the Council for Exceptional Children that promotes policies and advances evidence-based practices that support families and enhance the optimal development of young children who have or are at risk for developmental delays and disabilities.

U.S. Department of Agriculture—Food Pyramid
www.mypyramid.gov
Provides useful information on current nutrition guidelines, including the food pyramid, which promotes a healthy diet.

Zero to Three
www.zerotothree.org
Promotes the healthy development of the nation's infants and toddlers by supporting and strengthening families, communities, and those who work on their behalf.

PEARSON myeducationlab

Go to Topic 3 (Family/Community) in the MyEducationLab (www.myeducationlab.com) for your course, where you can:

- Find learning outcomes for Family/Community along with the national standards that connect to these outcomes.
- Complete Assignments and Activities that can help you more deeply understand the chapter content.
- Apply and practice your understanding of the core teaching skills identified in the chapter with the Building Teaching Skills and Dispositions learning units.
- Check your comprehension on the content covered in the chapter by going to the Study Plan in the Book Resources for your text. Here you will be able to take a chapter quiz, receive feedback on your answers, and then access Review, Practice, and Enrichment activities to enhance your understanding of chapter content.

3

OBSERVATION AND ASSESSMENT FOR TEACHING AND LEARNING

Effective Teaching Through Appropriate Evaluation

naeyc standards

Standard 3. Observing, Documenting, and Assessing to Support Young Children and Families

I know about and understand the goals, benefits, and uses of assessment. I know about and use systematic observations, documentation, and other effective assessment strategies in a responsible way, in partnership with families and other professionals, to positively influence the development of every child.[1]

Teachers use assessments daily and each teacher uses assessments differently. First grade teacher Kylie Shipley says, "I use assessments in different ways to help improve student learning. I use performance-based assessments that are fun for the students, such as playing *Jeopardy*, *Who Wants to Be a Millionaire*, *Deal or No Deal*, and other PowerPoint games with them. The children really enjoy it and learn a lot while they 'play.' These are wonderful ways to assess especially when you have a SMART Board."[2] Veteran kindergarten teacher Michaele Sommerville says, "Some schools include preliminary formal assessments for incoming kindergarten students. . . . My own preference is to refrain from putting barely-five-year-olds through additional performance stress."[3] Instead, Michaele uses observational assessments to get to know her students in their own time. "I'm writing down thoughts and observations about each of the children as they familiarize themselves with their environment. *What is the child's size, and how does she/he use physical space? Does the child squint, or say 'huh' or ask for directions to be repeated again? Does the student only demonstrate parallel play? Does the child recognize and choose to acknowledge and cooperate with transitions? Is the student a watcher or a do-er? A little of both? How long does it take him/her to come out of a comfortable shell?*"[4]

Teachers' minutes, hours, and days are filled with such assessment questions and decisions. Assessment is continuous. Questions abound: "What is Jeremy ready for now?" "What can I tell Maria's parents about her language development?" "The activity I used in the large-group time yesterday didn't seem to work well. What can I do differently?" Appropriate assessment can help you find the answers to these and many other questions about how to teach, how to assess, and what is best for each child.

What Is Assessment?

"Teaching without assessment is like driving a car without headlights."[5] Teaching in the dark does not benefit you or your children. Assessment casts light on what children know and can do. It is an invaluable tool to guide your teaching and your students' learning.

Your children's lives, both in and out of school, are influenced by your assessment and the assessment of others. As an early childhood professional, assessment influences your professional life and is a vital part of your professional practice. Effective assessment is one of your most important responsibilities.

Assessment is the ongoing, continuous process of collecting, gathering, and documenting information about children's development, learning, health, behavior, academic progress, need for special services, and achievement in order to make decisions about how to best educate them. Teachers and early childhood programs are

> . . . informed by ongoing systematic, formal, and informal assessment approaches to provide information on children's learning and development. These assessments occur within the context of reciprocal communication with families and with sensitivity to cultural contexts in which children develop. Assessment results are used to benefit children by informing sound decisions about children, teaching, and program improvement.[6]

In addition, teachers use assessment to identify children who may need specialized services and instruction. Figure 3.1 outlines the purposes of assessment. Student assessment occurs primarily through observation, performance-based assessment with commercial and

assessment The process of collecting information about children's development, learning, behavior, academic process, need for special services and attainment of grade level goals in order to make decisions.

> We need to set high standards for students and teachers. . . . This is the time to shed the old conflicts and come together.
>
> **RANDI WEINGARTEN**

FIGURE 3.1 Purposes of Assessment

For Children, Assessment:
- Identifies what they know
- Identifies their special needs
- Determines their appropriate placement
- Refers them and their families for additional services to programs and agencies

For Families, Assessment:
- Provides information about their children's progress and learning
- Relates school activities to home activities and experiences to promote at-home learning
- Enables teachers and families to work collaboratively to benefit children and family members

For Teachers, Assessment:
- Informs lesson and activity plans and establishes goals
- Creates new classroom arrangements
- Selects materials
- Monitors and improves the teaching–learning process
- Groups for instruction

For Early Childhood Programs, Assessment:
- Informs policy decisions regarding what is and is not appropriate for children
- Determines how well and to what extent programs and services children receive are beneficial and appropriate
- Aligns curriculum and teaching with children's needs

For the Public, Assessment:
- Informs them of children's achievement
- Provides information relating to students' school-wide achievements
- Provides a basis for public policy (e.g., legislation, recommendations, and position statements)

teacher-made tests, and evaluation of students' portfolios and work samples. You will use all three of these assessment procedures to inform your teaching so you can help all children be successful.

Developmentally Appropriate Assessment

Early childhood professionals do their best to use assessment in appropriate ways to support children's learning. We apply the framework of developmentally appropriate practice to assessment. You can develop a broad background of information about developmentally appropriate assessment by reviewing now the Early Childhood Curriculum, Assessment, and Program Evaluation Position Statement of the National Association for the Education of Young Children (NAEYC) and the National Association of Early Childhood Specialists in State Departments of Education (NAECS/SDE) at www.naecs-sde.org. This important document provides you with many essential guidelines to follow as you assess young children.

Ensuring that your assessment practices are developmentally appropriate is challenging because children develop and learn in ways that are embedded within their specific cultural and linguistic contexts.[7] You need to consider such factors as children's age and development in addition to how well children can or cannot use English and their stages of linguistic development in the language they speak at home.[8] Developmentally appropriate assessment is:

- Ongoing and purposeful
- Used to inform planning and teaching
- Appropriate to the developmental status and experiences of young children
- Responsive to individual differences in learners and allows children to demonstrate their competence in different ways
- Conducted using appropriate tools and practices[9]

Selecting Developmentally Appropriate Assessment Practices

Selecting appropriate assessment methods and instruments is an important part of the assessment process. You will know that the assessment practices and tools that you're using are appropriate when they meet these criteria:

- Addresses all developmental domains
- Measures developmentally appropriate skills, learning strategies, and learning styles
- Is conducted in natural authentic situations
- Is ongoing and closely related to curriculum development and program planning
- Provides early childhood teachers with guidance for how to design child-centered curriculum
- Results in information that is useful in planning children's experiences and making decisions
- Involves the family and yields understandable information that is easily related to families and other teaching team members
- Helps teachers modify environments and practices in order to maximize child learning
- Helps program staff identify children for more focused intervention[10]

Classroom Assessment

In the classroom, you will be using formative assessments on a regular if not daily basis. **Formative assessments** are informal means of gathering data about students.[11] Formative assessments are incorporated into the classroom practice and are a part of the instructional process.[12] They provide information to inform teachers what is needed to adjust teaching and learning while they are happening. Any type of assessment that obtains information that can be used to make judgments about children's learning behavior and characteristics or programs using means other than standardized instruments is considered to be *informal* because it does not entail standard guidelines for administration and use. Formative assessments are considered to be the most *authentic,* or truest, means of evaluating children's actual learning and the instructional activities in which they are involved. The terms *informal assessments*, *formative assessments*, and *authentic assessments* are often used interchangeably.

formative assessment
The ongoing process of gathering information about students during learning and teaching. Also called informal assessment, performance assessment, and authentic assessment.

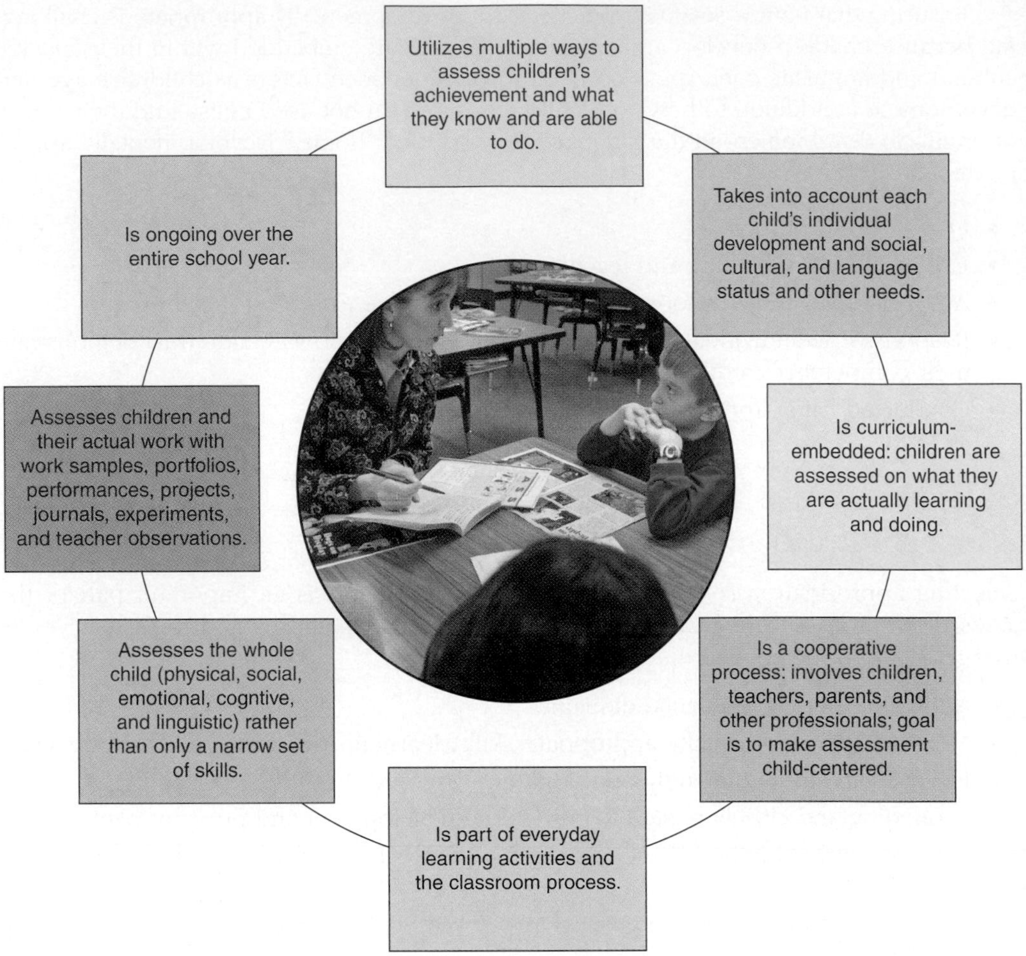

FIGURE 3.2
Characteristics of
Authentic Assessment

Utilizes multiple ways to assess children's achievement and what they know and are able to do.

Takes into account each child's individual development and social, cultural, and language status and other needs.

Is ongoing over the entire school year.

Assesses children and their actual work with work samples, portfolios, performances, projects, journals, experiments, and teacher observations.

Is curriculum-embedded: children are assessed on what they are actually learning and doing.

Assesses the whole child (physical, social, emotional, cogntive, and linguistic) rather than only a narrow set of skills.

Is a cooperative process: involves children, teachers, parents, and other professionals; goal is to make assessment child-centered.

Is part of everyday learning activities and the classroom process.

Authentic Assessment.   Figure 3.2 outlines characteristics of authentic assessment. As you examine these characteristics, think about how you will apply them to your professional practice. Following the authentic assessment strategies shown in Figure 3.2 will help ensure the information you gather will be useful and appropriate for all children. Authentic assessment relies heavily on informal procedures. Observations, checklists, and portfolios are just some of the informal methods of authentic assessment available to early childhood educators, as discussed in the following sections. *Informal screening* is what you and other professionals do when you gather information to make decisions about small-group placements, instructional levels, and so forth.

Part of authentic assessment includes *performance-based assessment*. In performance-based assessment, children *demonstrate* by doing what they know and are able to do. Authentic assessments are particularly useful when teaching children who are from diverse backgrounds as well as for children with disabilities because you can gain a good picture of what they can do. For example, second grade teacher Robert Brooks uses authentic assessment in his inclusion classroom, particularly at the beginning of the school year, to determine what each of his students is capable of doing. From there, he designs activities and sets goals for each individual student. First grade teacher Marisa Cortez uses authentic assessments to keep track of her students' progress. If her assessment shows that a student is falling behind, she individualizes the material, re-teaches, and provides more one-on-one attention.

Authentic Assessment Guidelines.   Here are some guidelines to follow as you authentically assess young children:

- *Assess children based on their actual work.*   Use work samples, exhibitions, performances, learning logs, journals, projects, presentations, experiments, and teacher observations.
- *Assess children based on what they are actually doing in and through the curriculum.*   For example, children demonstrate skills, behaviors, and concepts as evidence of their learning.
- *Assess what each individual child can do.*   Evaluate what each child is learning, rather than comparing one child with another or one group of children with another.
- *Make assessment part of the learning process.*   Encourage children to show what they know through presentations and participation.
- *Learn about the whole child.*   Make the assessment process an opportunity to learn more than just a child's acquisition of a narrow set of skills. Learn about many of the children's domains of development, such as their social development, as they work with other children to solve a math problem, or their emotional development as they analyze a story.
- *Involve children and parents in a collaborative assessment process.*   Authentic assessment is child centered.
- *Provide ongoing assessment over the entire year.*   Assess children continually throughout the year, not just at the end of a grading period or at the end of the year.
- *Use developmentally appropriate assessments and techniques.*   Assessment procedures are most authentic and results are most accurate when assessments and techniques are developmentally appropriate.

Methods of Authentic Assessment

Authentic assessment plays a major role in helping you understand what students can do and what they have learned. Table 3.1 provides a list of the different types of informal, authentic assessments that you can use in your classroom practice.

Observation.   Early childhood professionals recognize that children are more than what is measured by any particular standardized test. Observation is an authentic means of learning about children—what they know and are able to do, especially as it occurs in more naturalistic settings such as classrooms, child care centers, playgrounds, and homes, and it is the most widely used method of assessment. **Observation** is the intentional, systematic act of looking at the behavior of a child or children in a particular setting, program, or situation. As we have said, observation is sometimes referred to as "kid-watching" and is an excellent way to find out about children's behaviors and learning.

Anecdotal records, running records, event sampling, time sampling, rating scales, and checklists are all excellent authentic assessment tools used to authentically observe children and record observations for assessment purposes.

Anecdotal records.   Teachers use **anecdotal records** to write down brief reports of students' behavior and what they see and hear. Marisa Rodriguez likes to use anecdotal records in her kindergarten classroom because they provide insight into a particular behavior and give a basis for planning a specific teaching strategy. In order for an anecdotal record to be considered authentic, Marisa knows to record only observed facts, not her inferences or opinions. For example, she records where and when a behavior occurred, and who said what to whom. Figure 3.3 is an example of an anecdotal record. As you can see in Figure 3.3, Marisa does not record her opinions about Amy's behavior.

observation Observation is the intentional, systematic act of looking at the behavior of a child in a particular setting, program, or situation.

anecdotal record A brief written recording of student behavior that includes only what a teacher sees or hears, not what he or she thinks or infers.

TABLE 3.1 Informal Methods of Authentic Assessment

Method	Purpose	Guidelines
Observation Kid-watching—looking at children in a systematic way	Enables teachers to identify children's behaviors, document performance, and make decisions	Plan for observation and be clear about the purposes of the observation.
Anecdotal record Gives a brief written description of student behavior at one time	Provides insight into a particular behavior and a basis for planning a specific teaching strategy	Record only what is observed or heard; should deal with the facts and should include the setting (e.g., where the behavior occurs) and what was said and done.
Running record Focuses on a sequence of events that occur over time	Helps obtain a more detailed insight into behavior over a period of time	Maintain objectivity and try to include as much detail as possible.
Event sampling Focuses on a particular behavior during a particular event (e.g., behavior at lunchtime, behavior on the playground, behavior in a reading group)	Helps identify behaviors during a particular event over time	Identify a target behavior to be observed during particular times (e.g., fighting during transition activities).
Time sampling Record particular events or behaviors at specific time intervals (e.g., five minutes, ten minutes)	Helps identify when a particular child demonstrates a particular behavior; helps answer the question, "Does the child do something all the time or just at certain times and events?"	Observe only during the time period specified.
Rating scale Contains a list of descriptors for a set of behaviors	Enables teachers to record data when they are observed	Make sure that key descriptors and the rating scale are appropriate for what is being observed.
Checklist A list of behaviors identifying children's skills and knowledge	Enables teachers to observe and easily check off what children know and are able to do	Make sure that the checklist includes behaviors that are important for the program and for learning (e.g., counts from 1 to 10, hops on one foot).
Work sample Piece of children's work that demonstrates what they know and are able to do	Provides a concrete example of learning; can show growth and achievement over time	Make sure that the work sample demonstrates what children know and are able to do. Let children help select the items they want to use as examples of their learning.
Portfolio Collection of children's work samples and other products	Provides documentation of a child's achievement in specific areas over time; can include test scores, writing work samples, videotapes, etc.	Make sure the portfolio is not a dumpster but a thoughtful collection of materials that documents learning over time.
Interview Engaging children in discussion through questions	Allows children to explain behavior, work samples, or particular answers	Ask questions at all levels of Bloom's taxonomy in order to gain insight into children's learning.
Rubric Scoring guides that differentiate among levels of performance	Enables teachers to assess performance based on pre-established criteria, makes teachers' expectations clear, and enables children to participate in evaluation of own work	Provide children with models or examples of each level of work and encourage them to revise their work according to the rubric assessment. Give children opportunities to contribute to the rubric criteria.

FIGURE 3.3

Authentic Assessments: Excerpt of an Anecdotal Record

. . . Today we had a lesson on letter recognition. I had the children write their abc's with their fingers in shaving cream on their desks. Amy started immediately and wanted to start spelling whole words. She spelled Cat, Dog, and Cow on her own. Once she had written the abc's several times and the words she already knew, she began to ask for other words to spell. We talked about how to spell Mom, Dad, and Rob, her brother's name. She asked three or four times, "Ms. R, Ms. R, how do you spell farm?" from across the room. When I was helping another student, she fidgeted and raised her voice to get my attention. At one point she grabbed me by the hand to lead me to her table and wanted to know how to spell House . . .

You can tell she isn't recording her opinions or inferences because she does not use phrases such as "she seems to," "she liked/disliked," "she felt," "she understands," or "she can't." Instead, Marisa reports only what she sees and hears.

Marisa uses the anecdotal record to gain insight about Amy's strengths and weaknesses. Marisa infers that Amy has a strong basis for language acquisition, likes to be challenged, isn't afraid to get messy, and isn't turned off by the texture of shaving cream. Marisa also notices that Amy shows a lot of interest in farm animals and decides that using animals as a means of gaining Amy's interest and participation may be helpful in lessons that Amy finds difficult. Based on this assessment, Marisa decides to teach Amy with a lot of hands-on activities that are on or slightly above her level of knowledge so that Amy stays interested and challenged. Marisa also uses the anecdotal record to inform her opinion that Amy feels a need for a lot of individual attention. Marisa will help her learn to wait her turn and raise her hand.

Running record.   We refer to a **running record** as a detailed narrative of a child's behavior that focuses on a sequence of events that occur over a period of time. Anna Beatty uses running records frequently in her kindergarten classroom to assess her students' social skills. Running records are useful in assessing more abstract behaviors and skills because they help obtain a more detailed insight into behavior in general, rather than specific events like the anecdotal record. When using running records, Anna maintains objectivity and includes as much detail as possible. Running records should include objective observations, and unlike anecdotal records, they provide Anna an opportunity to write down her comments concerning the sequence of events. Figure 3.4 is an example of a running record Anna kept in her classroom.

As you can see in Figure 3.4, Anna objectively records what each child says while focusing on Ali's behavior. She separately records her own ideas and questions about Ali's social skills. Using both her observations and her comments, Anna can infer a lot about Ali's social skills, his problem-solving capabilities, and even his fine motor skills. For example, she can infer that Ali is flexible in his play schemes, that he knows how and when to compromise, and that he has the fine motor skills to build intricate systems with the blocks. From here, she can design instruction. She pairs Ali with a more rigid classmate to help the classmate become more flexible and to help Ali continue practicing his compromising skills.

Event sampling.   Dustin Kramer often uses event sampling as a method to informally but authentically assess his first graders. **Event sampling**—a form of assessment that systematically observes a specific behavior during a particular period of time—allows Dustin to identify students' behaviors, document their performance, and then make

running record A detailed narrative of a child's behavior that focuses on a sequence of events that occur over a period of time. Includes both factual observations and teacher's inferences.

event sampling A form of assessment that systematically observes a specific behavior during a particular period of time that is based on the ABC model.

FIGURE 3.4

Authentic Assessments: Example of a Running Record

Teacher _Anna Beatty_

Student _Ali R._

Age _5_

School _Reed Elementary_

Date _04/08/2011_

Time _10:00am – 10:20am_

Observations	Comments
Ali is playing the block center with Jake and Travis. Ali has surrounded himself with the blocks and begins stacking them. The blocks are about waist high. Jake is playing with cars with Travis.	Ali has spent a lot of time building with the blocks and is very careful about stacking them just right. But he seems to be looking at Jake and Travis a lot.
A: "I'm building a fort!"	Travis and Jake play together a lot. It doesn't look like Ali knows how to join them. Maybe that's why Ali told them it was a fort?
J: "That doesn't look like a fort."	
A: "It's a fort; I made it to be a fort."	
T: "I think it's a garage for our cars!"	Aki definitely doesn't look like he likes them putting cars on his fort. What will he do?
Travis and Jake start to push their cars along Ali's fort. Ali keeps stacking blocks.	Shows good compromising skills! The red car is a favorite of most of the boys. Good way to get what he wants and still get to play with J & T.
A: "I said it's a fort. I built it so I get to pick. It's a fort, not a garage."	
T: "Why can't it be a garage?"	
A: "I don't have a car." Ali pauses. Then says, "If you let me be the red car, the fort can be a garage. It can be a garage first, then a fort!"	Pretty flexible of Ali to let J & T change his fort. Another good play skill.
Jake gives Ali the red convertible car and they start to zoom the cars all over the "garage."	
J: "Let's add a ramp."	
A: "That's a good idea. Put it here."	

decisions about teaching methods, lesson plans, partner groupings, and such. Use event sampling clearly and purposefully. In order for event sampling to be an authentic assessment you must repeat it several times. For example, during math time, which follows physical education (P.E.), Dustin realizes that Keith has difficulty paying attention to directions and he tends to be rowdy and distracts other students. Dustin decides to use the ABC observation system during the 45-minute period to observe Keith for a week.

Figure 3.5 shows an example of an ABC observation system. The A (antecedent) column, or the precursor to a behavior, enables Dustin to watch for what happens *before* Keith's distracting behavior begins. Does Keith seem to enjoy P.E? Is he readily a part of P.E. teams or is he picked last? Does Keith get along with the coach? How does Keith look: happy, grumpy, sweaty? Dustin then documents his observations in the A column. The B (behavior) column allows Dustin to target the behavior that he

FIGURE 3.5

Authentic Assessments: Example of Event Sampling Using the ABC Method

Teacher: _D. Kramer_

Student: _Keith C._

Grade: _1st_

School: _DUPont Elementary_

Date: _10-17-09_

A	B	C
	Tuesday	
1:15 pm: Keith just finished P.E. He looks a little upset. Ask if he's ok. I ask class to get out pencils and look at the board.	1:20 pm: Keith fidgets a little but is mostly calm, says he's fine	1:22 pm: lessons continued
1:24 pm: told class we would do a group project with cubes first, then they will work individually	1:27 pm: Keith fidgets and scoots around in his chair. Some classmates giggle & turn to watch, others ignore	1:28 pm: I ignore it, hand out rubix cubes to groups
1:33 pm: Keith stopped fidgeting; I show class how to count by 5s with rubix cubes.	1:40 pm: Keith participates with group, seems to enjoy	1:42 pm: tell class only a few more minutes with the group before move on to individual work
1:43 pm: told class to clean up cubes and start own work	1:44 pm: Keith plays with blocks, tossing them in the air, throwing at friends	1:46 pm: ask Keith to clean up, classmates laugh with Keith
1:50 pm: asked Keith to clean up, he is still playing with cubes	1:55 pm: Keith making silly faces at me and classmates, playing with blocks	1:57 pm: Take the cubes away and give Keith a warning
1:59 pm: gave Keith worksheet, but realize we're out of time, class will be late for art	2:01 pm: assign Keith the worksheet for homework	2:02 pm: Keith lines up for art without a problem, walks quietly in the hallway on way to art.

wants to assess—in this case, Keith's distractibility and disruptiveness. What exactly is Keith doing? Talking, fidgeting, fighting, joking? Is he involving other students? Does the behavior occur at the beginning of the lesson when Dustin gives verbal information or at the end when Keith is expected to work independently? Was math a group effort today or an individual project? Whatever it is, Dustin writes the behavior down in the B column. The C (consequences) column, or the results of the behavior, helps Dustin to understand what Keith gets out of his behavior. Is Keith getting peer recognition, more individual attention? Is the lesson disrupted and thus less time is spent on math? What happens after math? Is the following activity difficult for Keith or does Keith settle into the activity easily? This time Dustin writes his observations in the C column.

Dustin systematically monitors Keith for a week during the 45 minutes of math. As Figure 3.5 shows, Dustin is careful to document the time and the nature of the ABCs. After a week of observations, Dustin looks for a pattern in Keith's behavior. He realizes that Keith is calmer and paying attention at the beginning of math, but when the class generally works independently, Keith becomes increasingly disruptive. Keith is often so disruptive that the class runs out of time to do the independent work and Keith has extra homework as a result. Dustin decides to talk to Coach Culp about Keith's behavior in P.E. Coach Culp reports that some of the students had teased Keith about asking for "so much" help with his math work and that Keith seemed embarrassed. Dustin uses this information to ask himself more questions. If Keith needs more help on individual work, does that mean that he doesn't understand the instructions? Is Dustin relying too much on verbal teaching instead of differentiating the information in a lot of different ways? Does Keith need more one-on-one attention in math? But, how to keep the other kids from teasing Keith? How does Keith learn best? Isn't Keith a *tactile* (hands-on or concrete) learner?

Using the results of ABC.   As a result of these explorations, Dustin uses the event sampling information to tailor his teaching methods to Keith's needs; he makes sure to encourage and praise students who ask questions, and he provides Keith individual directions on individual work to build his confidence and competency. For example, Dustin gives directions to the class as a whole first and then slowly gives them again to Keith. He stops frequently to make sure Keith follows them. Dustin makes sure to incorporate as many tactile exercises in math lessons as possible so that Keith can use his hands to better understand math concepts. Also, Dustin starts giving high-fives to students when they ask questions or for help and uses encouraging phrases such as, "Wow, what a great question," and "Asking questions means you really care about learning."

Time sampling.   Another authentic means to assess children that involves focusing on a particular behavior over a continuous period of time is called **time sampling**. For example, Charlotte Lu wants to know if her first grade student Amanda is as distractible as she thinks Amanda is. Charlotte decides to use time sampling to determine how on-task or off-task Amanda is during center time. She and Benjamin Woods, her teaching assistant, first sit down together to determine what exactly on-task behavior looks like and what off-task behavior looks like. Then they both observe Amanda during center time and specifically watch for the previously specified behavior, such as wandering around the room or staring into space. Afterwards, Charlotte and Benjamin compare their samples to determine how often they agree on Amanda's behavior. Figure 3.6 is the time sample Charlotte and Benjamin used.

From their sample, shown in Figure 3.6, Charlotte and Benjamin can see that they agreed that Amanda was off task 7 out 10 minutes of center time. Their collaboration established a mutually-agreed-upon means of observing and collecting data. It also prevented sampling bias by getting more than one opinion. For more reliable results, as with event sampling, Charlotte and Benjamin should repeat their time sampling several more times. To gain an even more accurate picture of Amanda's behavior, Charlotte and Benjamin should take time samples of Amanda in various settings. For example, they should assess Amanda not just in centers, but during reading lessons, library time, P.E., math lessons, and so on.

Charlotte and Benjamin know the more data they have about Amanda's behavior the more they can use their assessment to teach to her needs. If they find that Amanda is off task only during centers, they may decide to change the way that the centers are structured, rearrange Amanda's group, or institute a pictorial schedule to help keep her on task. However, if Charlotte and Benjamin find from their multiple samples that Amanda is in fact off task for most of the day across multiple settings and situations and that her off-task behavior is detrimental to her social and academic growth, they may decide to refer Amanda to the district Special Education services or to recommend to Amanda's parents that they seek an evaluation from her pediatrician for possible developmental, neurological, or cognitive delays or deficits.

time sampling Authentic means to assess children that involves focusing on a particular behavior over a continuous period of time.

Authentic Assessments: Example of a Time Sample

Charlotte Lu—Teacher			
Event	**time**	**On task**	**Off Task**
Center time	10:01 am	✔	
	10:02 am	✔	
	10:03 am		✔
	10:04 am		✔
	10:05 am		✔
	10:06 am	✔	
	10:07 am		✔
	10:08 am		✔
	10:09 am		✔
	10:10 am		✔
		Total: 3	Total: 7

Benjamin Woods—Tech Assistant			
Event	**time**	**On task**	**Off Task**
Center time	10:01 am	✔	
	10:02 am	✔	
	10:03 am	✔	
	10:04 am		✔
	10:05 am		✔
	10:06 am	✔	
	10:07 am		✔
	10:08 am		✔
	10:09 am		✔
	10:10 am		✔
		Total: 4	Total: 6

Rating scale. **Rating scales** are usually numeric scales that contain a list of descriptors for a set of behaviors or goals. They usually begin with the phrase, "On a scale of (a number) to (a number), you rate the (behavior) as . . ." Rating scales enable teachers to record data when they are observed. When using rating scales, make sure that the key descriptors and the rating scales are appropriate for what is being observed.

Bess Stensel uses rating scales in her preschool classroom to gain a broad picture of her students' development. Figure 3.7 is an example of a rating scale that Bess uses to gauge the degree of Rebecca's language development. As the figure shows, Bess is not only able to assess the appearance of a skill set, but also the *degree* to which it is present. From her rating scale, Bess concludes that Rebecca has gained some mastery, if not full

rating scales Usually numeric scales that contain a list of descriptors for a set of behaviors or goals.

FIGURE 3.7

Authentic Assessments: Example of a Rating Scale

Teacher: _Bess Stensel_

Student: _Rebecca M., Pre-K_

School: _Stephen F. Austin Elementary School_

Date: _11-10-11_

Skill Set	No Mastery		Developing Mastery		Full Mastery
Demonstrates knowledge that print carries a message in a book	1	2	3	4	⑤
Orally retells a story	1	2	③	4	5
Listens with interest and comprehension when a story is read aloud	1	2	3	④	5
Sequences the events of a story in proper order	1	2	3	④	5
Answers questions concerning the meaning of a story	1	2	3	4	⑤

mastery, in most areas of early literacy skills, but that she still is developing her skills in orally retelling information. Now that she has assessed Rebecca, Bess can plan for how to provide for her needs in reading and language skills.

Checklist.   An excellent and powerful tool for observing and gathering information about a wide range of student abilities in all settings are checklists. **Checklists** are lists of behaviors identifying children's skills and knowledge and can be used as a regular part of your teaching on a wide variety of topics and subjects. Some checklists, such as those in Figure 3.8 and Figure 3.9, are cognitive or social; others can help you assess behaviors, traits, skills, and abilities. In addition, using the same checklists used over a period of time enables you to evaluate progress and achievement. Figure 3.10 is a checklist for assessing children in inclusive classrooms and can be used as a template or model to make other checklists. How could you modify Figure 3.10 to assess children's technology use and skills in your classroom?

Keep in mind that many skills or behaviors assessed by checklists may have a cultural or religious connotation. You should take cultural factors into context when using any form of assessment. For example, in Figure 3.8, one item denoting proper social development is eye contact. While in the United States eye contact is considered a demonstration of respect and engagement, this is not true for all people. In some Eastern cultures such as South Korea and China, children are taught to show respect to adults by refraining from making eye contact. Here in the United States, eye contact is a sign of paying attention and respecting the listener; in addition, not making eye contact is often a cause for concern as it may indicate developmental delays. As a result, you may be tempted to considerer some children as lagging developmentally when in fact they are trying to show you respect according to their cultural norms. Therefore, you should be careful to use checklists, and indeed, all forms of assessment, within the larger context of a student's

checklists Lists of behaviors identifying children's skills and knowledge.

FIGURE 3.8

Authentic Assessments: Example of a Social-Emotional Developmental Checklist

Social-Emotional Checklist First Grade		
Social Behavioral Skills	**Yes(Y)/No(N)**	**Date**
Student is able to ask for what he/she needs and wants from caregivers.	Y	11-05-12
Student is able to follow directions and general expectations of caregivers.	Y	11-05-12
Student has good eye contact with peers.	Y	11-05-12
Student is able to express feelings appropriately to peers.	N	11-05-12
Student is able to share and interact cooperatively with peers.	N	11-05-12
Student is able to start conversations with peers.	Y	11-05-12
Student is able to ask questions of peers.	Y	11-05-12
Student is able to listen to peers.	N	11-05-12
Student is able to ignore peers when he/she should.	Y	11-05-12
Student is not passive with peers.	Y	11-05-12
Student is not aggressive with peers.		11-05-12
Social and General Problem-Solving Skills	**Yes(Y)/No(N)**	**Date**
Student thinks about what he/she is doing.	Y	11-05-12
Student understands the consequences of behavior.	Y	11-05-12
Student behavior is goal oriented.	N	11-05-12
Student is aware when he/she is having a problem.	Y	11-05-12
Student learns from past mistakes and does not repeat them.	Y	11-05-12
Student uses good strategies to solve problems.	Y	11-05-12
Student knows when he/she is having a social problem.	Y	11-05-12
Student is knowledgeable of how he/she affects others.	Y	11-05-12
Student uses appropriate strategies to solve interpersonal difficulties.	N	11-05-12
Student uses nonaggressive solutions to solve disagreements with others.	Y	11-05-12
Emotional Well-Being and Level of Self-Esteem	**Yes(Y)/No(N)**	**Date**
Student acknowledges his/her own feelings.	Y	11-05-12
Student expresses feelings in appropriate ways. Student is able to tell others about his/her concerns/troubles.	N	11-05-12
Student thinks and verbalizes positive thoughts about self and others.	Y	11-05-12
Student seems to like him/herself (can identify positive self qualities).	Y	11-05-12
Student focuses on positive things and manages negative things.	Y	11-05-12
Student is able to take responsibility for achievements and mistakes.	Y	11-05-12

Source: From Child Care Resource & Referral of Central Iowa, www.centraliowachildcare.org/healthconsulting/schoolagescreentoolkg.pdf. Used with permission.

Authentic Assessments: Example of a Cognitive Developmental Checklist, Ages 4–5

✔ Can correctly name several colors (4+)

✔ Tries to solve problems from a single point of view

✗ Follows three-part commands   *Will follow two-part commands, is working on three.*

✔ Recalls parts of a story

✔ Understands the concepts of "same" and "different"

✔ Engages in fantasy play

✔ Can count 10 or more objects *Is up to 13!*

✔ Better understands the concept of time

✔ Knows about things used every day in the home (money, food, appliances)

Sources: www.cdc.gov/ncbddd/actearly/interactive/milestones/cognitive_5years.html; www.cdc.gov/ncbddd/actearly/interactive/milestones/cognitive_4years.html

---

FIGURE 3.10

Authentic Assessments: Example of an Inclusion Classroom Checklist

Teacher: *Graciela Gomez*   **School:** *Mission Hill Elementary*

Student: *Tenisha B.*   **Class:** *First grade*

Number of children in class: *16*   **Number of children with disabilities in class:** *1*

Date: *09-08-11*   **Types of disability:** *Tenisha has moderate cerebral palsy (CB), and must use a wheelchair.*

Physical Features of the Classroom

1. Are all areas of the classroom accessible to children with disabilities?

   No, Tenisha cannot access the library/literacy center.

2. Are learning materials and equipment accessible for all children?

   There is not enough room for Tenisha to manipulate her wheelchair past the easel and the shelf with art materials.

3. Are work and play areas separated to minimize distractions?

   Yes, but pathways are too narrow for Tenisha's wheelchair.

4. Are special tables or chairs necessary to accommodate children's disabilities?

   Tenisha has a large work board/table that attaches to her wheelchair.

Academic Features of the Classroom

1. What special accommodations are necessary to help children with disabilities achieve state and local standards?

   I need to check on this.

2. Are principles of developmentally appropriate practice applied to all children, including those with disabilities?

   Yes.

3. Is there a wide range of classroom literature on all kinds of disabilities?

   I have a few books but not enough. I would like more.

Classroom Interaction

1. Are children with disabilities included in cooperative work projects?

   I will work on this next week.

2. Do children without disabilities interact positively with children with disabilities?

   Tenisha is a very sociable person. Students interact well with her. Tenisha could not reach the crayons by herself, so she asked Billy for help. She and Billy seem to get along well.

Play Routines

1. Are children with disabilities able to participate in all classroom and grade-level activities?

   I need to talk with the P.E. teacher. I also need to observe Tenisha during lunch and recess to see if she is involved in play and social activities during these times.

Conclusions

1. *I need to rearrange my classroom to make sure that Tenisha has access to all learning centers and materials.*

2. *The children are not as helpful to Tenisha as I want them to be*

3. *The classroom library/lit center needs more books relating to children with disabilities.*

4. *There are a lot of questions I don't have the answer to at this time (i.e., meeting state standards).*

5. *I need to include more group work and cooperative activities in my planning*

Recommendations

1. *I will ask a custodian to help me move a heavy bookshelf. I can move and rearrange the other things. I'll give the new arrangement a trial run and see how it works for all the children.*

2. *In our daily class meetings, I will talk about helpful behaviors and helping others.*

   a. *We can read books about helping.*

   b. *I plan to start a class buddy system; I can pair Tenisha and Billy!*

3. *In my lesson plans, I need to include activities for learning helpful behaviors.*

4. *I will search for books about children with disabilities.*

   a. *I'll consult with the school librarian.*

   b. *I'll talk to my grade-level leader and ask for money for books.*

5. *I will talk with the director of special education about meeting state standards. Tenisha is very smart so I don't anticipate any problems.*

6. *I will develop a lesson involving group work and projects. I will include Tenisha and observe the children's interactions.*

7. *I will observe Tenisha at lunch and during recess.*

religious, cultural, and ethnic background. Here are some other things for you to keep in mind when making and using checklists:

- Each checklist should contain the qualities, skills, behaviors, and other information you want to observe. In other words, "tailor" each checklist to a specific situation.
- File all checklists in students' folders to track their progress and for future reference and use.
- Use checklists as a basis for conferencing with children and parents.
- Use the information from checklists to plan for small-group and individual instruction.

work sample, or **student artifact** An example of children's work that demonstrates what they know and are able to do. Such examples are used as evidence to assess student abilities. Work samples can be physical or electronic and come in many different forms.

Work sample.   A **work sample**, or a **student artifact**, is an example of children's work that demonstrates what they know and are able to do and are used as evidence to assess students' abilities. They are often included to document a child's accomplishments and achievements. Work samples can be physical or electronic and come in many different forms. Figure 3.11 is an artifact that demonstrates kindergartener Brittney's ability to write to a prompt (tell about something you like to do and why you like to do it), and her ability to use English language conventions. Examples of artifacts like Brittney's are artwork; paper documents such as written work; electronic documents and electronic images; DVD recordings or excerpts of daily behavior; photographs of projects; voice recordings of oral skills (i.e., reading, speaking, singing); video recordings of performances (i.e., sports, musical, theatrical); scanned images of 3-D or large-scale art; and multimedia projects or web pages exploring curriculum topics, current events, or social problems.

portfolio A compilation of children's work samples, products, and teacher observations collected over time.

Portfolios.   Today many teachers use **portfolios**—a compilation of children's work samples, products, and teacher observations collected over time that attest to what children are able to do—as a basis for authentic assessment.[13] Examples of what to put in

FIGURE 3.11 Authentic Assessments: Example of a Work Sample

Voice from the Field

Creating Student Portfolios Based on Authentic Assessment

Assessment Portfolios

Assessment portfolios are more than just a scrapbook or collection of children's work. And, although they may contain photographs of the child in action, they are much more than a photo album. An assessment portfolio is a representation of what teachers are learning about each child's performance in selected domains. It includes observation notes, photographs and work samples with clear connection to learning outcomes. The portfolio items are collected at least twice across a year to show progress.

Portfolio Samples

You can't possibly collect evidence to go with every single skill or outcome in the curriculum. Therefore, you need to identify important, key outcomes that are best documented in a portfolio. Teachers of young children report that the following are informative portfolio items through which they can assess many capabilities of their students.

- Writing samples
- Responses to reading experiences
- Mathematical problem-solving activities
- Creations that require mathematical understanding (patterning, geometrical creations)
- Scientific explorations and experiments
- Self-reflections
- Art/Drawing samples

Good portfolio samples, if chosen well, represent how the child is progressing related to selected curricular goals and development expectations. Work samples and photos are always accompanied by a teacher observation note explaining the significance of the sample or photo, as well as giving contextual information about what the child was doing and saying at the time.

Good Portfolio Samples

Good portfolio items are rich in information about HOW the child applies a variety of skills. For example, a writing sample can demonstrate multiple goals such as:

- fine motor control of a writing tool
- eye hand coordination
- understanding that writing has meaning

- communicating ideas through writing
- scribbling and beginning letter formation for preschoolers and kindergartners
- writing of words, sentences and paragraphs and understanding of punctuation and capitalization as children progress into the primary grades
- recognition of conventions of print (left to right, top to bottom, etc.)
- beginning sound/letter correspondence for kindergartners and first graders
- use of spelling conventions for second and third graders

The goal in assessment portfolios is to show evidence of the child's performance. Therefore, the items in the portfolio should represent the child's TYPICAL work (not only the best). By saving children's typical work, teachers are building an authentic case about the child's on-going performance and are able to document what the child does most of the time in the classroom. Also include some "shining moments" in a portfolio. These items can show particular progress or unique ways the child is demonstrating her learning. They can be informative as well—but are not the primary focus of the portfolio collection process.

Develop a Plan

Assessment portfolios are a way to capture children's progress. To do so, set up a systematic plan to collect similar items at least twice during the year. Two to four collection periods are needed in order to compare items and assess the child's progress related to specific goals. Such periods should be several weeks in length so that children have a variety of opportunities to demonstrate their typical work. Have a clear idea of what you are looking for and pay attention across time as children demonstrate their capabilities. Items in children's assessment portfolios will not all look the same. Rather, they will reflect the uniqueness of each child as well as a variety of curricular activities.

At first, portfolio collection can feel like a daunting task. However, as you identify key items that show how each child is learning and growing, assessment portfolios become a vital component in determining each child's capabilities and a wonderful way of showing parents and family members what each child can do.

Source: Contributed by Gaye Gronlund.

portfolios vary, but examples include the several types of artifacts and work samples discussed above. Each teacher compiles a portfolio differently. Jonathon Barrio lets his third grade students put their best work in their portfolios; while Megan LeBlanc decides with her second graders what will be included. Portfolios are very useful, especially during parent–teacher conferences. The accompanying Voice from the Field above provides specific suggestions for creating student portfolios based on appropriate and authentic assessment.

Also, websites such as TeacherVision and books such as *Developing Portfolios in Education: A Guide to Reflection, Inquiry, and Assessment* by Johnson et al. (2010) and *The Portfolio Connection: Student Work Linked to Standards* by Belgrad et al. (2008) may be helpful to you in designing and implementing portfolios as a means of authentic assessment in your early childhood classrooms.

Some teachers use technology to develop digital portfolios, which can stand alone or supplement the traditional portfolio. Digital portfolios include books and journals that children keep on computers and then illustrate with digital cameras. However, it is important to remember that portfolios are only one part of children's assessment.

interview A common way that observers and researchers engage children in discussion through questions to obtain information.

Interview.   **Interviewing** is a common way that observers and teachers use to engage children in discussions through questions to obtain information. Carla Silliman likes to use interviews in her second grade classroom because it allows her students to explain their own behavior, work samples, and particular answers. Interviewing gives an eyewitness account to obtaining information and can describe more visible information otherwise not shown through written records such as portfolios or checklists. Figure 3.12 is an excerpt of Carla's interview with Jorge.

Bloom's Taxonomy Refers to a classification of different objectives that educators set for students in three domains: affective, psychomotor, and cognitive. Within the taxonomy, learning at higher levels is dependent on having mastered foundational knowledge and skills at lower levels of skills.

When Carla uses interviewing as a form of assessment, she makes sure to use the hierarchy of questions in Bloom's Taxonomy to gain further insight into children's learning. **Bloom's Taxonomy** refers to a classification of different objectives that educators set for students in three domains: affective, psychomotor, and cognitive. Within the taxonomy, learning at higher levels is dependent on having mastered foundational knowledge and skills at lower levels (i.e., you must be able to add and subtract before you can multiply or divide). For example, Carla assesed Jorge's knowledge, the first level of the cognitive domain, by using questions such as, "What happened in the story?" In her interview, Carla can see that Jorge has mastered the second level, comprehension,

FIGURE 3.12

Authentic Assessments: Excerpt of an Interview Assessment

Teacher: Carla Silliman

School: Dewberry Elementary

Student: Jorge V.

Grade: 2nd

Date: 02-26-11

CS: Jorge, do you remember the "Yellow School Bus" story we read on Wednesday?

JV : Yeah, they took the bus to Antarctica.

CS: Who all went to Antarctica in the story?

JV : Well, the Friz, and Arnold, and Ralphie . . . Dorothy Ann, Carlos, and Phoebe. And the uncle. Phoebe's uncle went on this trip too.

CS: That's right, Jorge. Can you tell me what happened in the story?

JV : Well, like, the school bus turns into a ship and they go to Antarctica. And it's really cold, right? They have to wear parkas. That's like a really big coat. And, um, the class gets off the boat to look at penguins and they all complained about how bad it smelled.

CS: Mmhmm, then what happened next?

JV: Oh! Phoebe's uncle accidentally turns some of the kids into penguins. Some of the kids thought it was cool and some of them were afraid. Ralphie was afraid. He's always the one that's afraid. That'd be so cool to turn into a penguin. I'd be one of those giant penguins. Well, then they all go swim in the ocean. Penguins fly in the ocean but not in the air.

CS: Why do you think that's important?

JV: Most birds fly in the air. But in class we talked about how penguins can't fly because their feathers are made differently. Regular birds' feathers are, like, empty, hollow. But penguins are too heavy and they have all this extra fat on them. But penguins are special. I mean, unique, because they swim like they're flying. They're special that way. And remember, you said that that made penguins unique, and I said I didn't know what unique meant so I used the dictionary to look it up. So yeah, but anyway, penguins swim so fast they can get away from sea lions and stuff.

CS: So penguins are unique. Tell me, why do you think Ralphie was afraid when they got turned into penguins?

JV: I don't know. Well, maybe because it was an accident. Or, maybe he was nervous. Um, I think maybe he was afraid he couldn't turn back into a kid again . . .

because he can summarize the main ideas of the story. She can also see that he has mastered application, the third level, because he solved his problem of not knowing what "unique" meant and synthesized it into his understanding of the content of the story. Carla moved onto the fourth level, analysis, by asking questions such as, "Why do you think . . ."

As a result of her interview with Jorge and her use of Bloom's Taxonomy, Carla sees that Jorge meets several standards set forth in the Texas English Language Arts and Reading Grade 2 Standards. For example, Carla can tell that Jorge can listen critically to interpret and evaluate language and that he can use vocabulary to clearly describe ideas and feelings. She is also pleased to see that Jorge discusses the meaning of words to develop his vocabulary, and that he successfully uses problem-solving skills and reference tools to enhance his knowledge and comprehension. From her interview, Carla is able to assess Jorge's reading comprehension, vocabulary growth, and overall literacy fluency.[14]

Rubric. **Rubrics** are performance and scoring guides that differentiate among levels of performance. Conventional rubrics use a range of three or more levels—for example, beginning, developing, and proficient. Each of the levels contains specific, measurable performance characteristics, such as "makes few/occasional/frequent spelling errors." Checklists, which provide specific steps for completing tasks to the highest level, are similar to rubrics.[15]

rubric Scoring guide that differentiates among levels of performance.

Rubrics have a number of purposes:

- To enable teachers to assess performance based on pre-established criteria
- To make teachers' expectations clear
- To enable children to participate in the evaluation of their own work
- To enable children to distinguish between levels of performance and strive to do their best

To use rubrics effectively in your classroom, provide children with models or examples of each level of work and encourage them to revise their work according to the

FIGURE 3.13

Authentic Assessments: Example of Rubric

Conventions	Punctuation	Capitalization	Word Use	Ideas
My letters are written clearly. ✔	I use a period at the end of each sentence. ✔	I use both capital and lowercase letters. ✔	I use synonyms for words I write a lot. ✔	I describe where my story takes place. ✔
I leave white spaces between my words. ✔	I use a question mark at the end of each question. ✕	I use a capital letter to start the names of people, pets, and places. ✔	I use new spelling words. ✔	I describe what characters feel. ✔
My sentences go from left to right. ✔	I use an exclamation point at the end of an exclamation. ✔	I use a capital letter to start the first word of a sentence. ✔	I use the right action word form with my nouns. ✕	My story has a beginning, middle, and end. ✔

rubric assessment. You should also give children opportunities to contribute to the rubric criteria.

First grade teacher Emily Cherry, for example, created a writing rubric for her students. She believes that her students will gain a beginning understanding of what is expected of them in a clear and concise manner. Figure 3.13 is an example of Charlie's, a student in Emily's class, writing rubric.

Note how each example can be checked against the rubric by the student. This involves the student in the informal assessment process. Rubrics allow children to know what is generally expected of them and help them complete a specific piece of work. By adapting the rubric for writing, the child's progress is acknowledged. Over several weeks, as Charlie improved in his writing, Emily created rubrics that became more specific and more challenging so that she could assess how Charlie performed as expectations rose.

The Power of Observation

As we discussed before, observation is one of the most widely used methods of assessment.[16] Table 3.1 provided information on and guidelines for observation and other informal methods of authentic assessment.

Purposes of Observation

Observation is designed to gather information on which to base decisions, make recommendations, develop curriculum, plan for teaching, select activities and learning strategies, and assess children's growth, development, and learning. When professionals and parents look at children, sometimes they do not really see or concern themselves with what the children are doing or why, as long as they are safe and orderly. Consequently, the significance and importance of critical behaviors may go undetected if observation is done casually and is limited to unsystematic looking.

Systematic observation has these specific purposes. It is used to:

- *Determine the cognitive, linguistic, social, emotional, and physical development of children.* Using a developmental checklist is one way you can systematically observe and chart the development of children.
- *Identify children's interests and learning styles.* Today, teachers are very interested in developing learning activities, materials, and classroom centers based on children's interests, preferences, and learning styles.
- *Plan.* The professional practice of teaching requires daily ongoing planning. Observation provides useful, authentic, and solid information that enables you to plan intentionally for activities rather than to make decisions with little or no information.

Observing children at play enables teachers to learn about children's developmental levels, social skills, and peer interactions. How might you use such information to plan play-based activities?

- *Meet the needs of individual children.* Meeting the needs of individual children is an important part of teaching and learning. For example, a child may be advanced cognitively but overly aggressive and lacking the social skills necessary to play cooperatively and interact with others. Through observation, you can gather information to develop a plan to help that child learn how to play with others.
- *Determine progress.* Systematic observation, over time, provides a rich and valuable source of information about how individuals and groups of children are progressing in their learning and behavior.
- *Provide information to parents.* Teachers report to and conference with parents on an ongoing basis. Observational information along with other information, such as test results and child work samples, provides a fuller and more complete picture of individual children.
- *Provide professional insight.* Observational information helps professionals learn more about themselves and what to do to help children.

Advantages of Intentional, Systematic Observation

There are a number of advantages to gathering data through observation. Observation:

- *Enables teachers to collect information that they might not otherwise gather through other sources.* Many of the causes and consequences of children's behavior can be assessed only through observation and not through formal standardized tests, questioning, or parent and child interviews.
- *Is ideally suited to learning more about children in play settings.* Observation affords the opportunity to note a child's social behavior in a play group and discern how cooperatively he or she interacts with peers. Observing a child at play gives you a wealth of information about developmental levels, social skills, and what a child is or is not learning in play settings.
- *Reveals a lot about children's prosocial behavior and peer interactions.* It helps you plan for appropriate and inclusive activities to promote the social growth of young children. Additionally, your observations can serve as the basis for developing multicultural activities to benefit all children.

- *Is a useful accompaniment to other assessments for children who may not typically respond.* For some students with certain disabilities, observation is used to support or refute the results of other assessment measures. These children may have a limited capability for the appropriate response or they may fatigue quickly. This fatigue may cause them to not complete the assessment, and their scores are affected.
- *Provides a basis for assessment of what children are developmentally able to do.* Many learning skills are developed sequentially, such as the refinement of large-motor skills before small-motor skills. Through observation, you can determine if children's abilities are within a normal range of growth and development.
- *Is useful to assess children's performance over time.* Documentation of daily, weekly, and monthly observations of children's behaviors and learning provides a database for the cumulative evaluation of each child's achievement and development.
- *Provides concrete information for use in reporting to and conferencing with parents.* Increasingly, reports to parents involve professionals' observations and children's work samples so that parents and educators can collaborate to determine how to help children develop cognitively, socially, emotionally, and physically.

Intentional observation is a useful, informative, and powerful means of guiding teaching and helping to ensure the learning of all children.

Steps for Conducting Observations

Four steps are involved in the process of systematic, purposeful observation (review and reflect on Figure 3.14).

Step 1: Plan for Observation. Planning is an important part of the observation process; everything you do should be planned in advance of the observation. A good guide to follow in planning is to ask *who, what, where, when,* and *how* you will observe.

Setting goals for observation is also an important part of the planning process. Goals allow you to reflect on why you want to observe and thus direct your efforts to what you will observe. Your goal might include observing the physical classroom environment for effectiveness, social interactions, or improvements to children's learning activities. Stating a goal focuses your attention on the purpose of your observation. For example, to focus on providing an inclusive classroom or program and fully including an exceptional child, your goals might read like this:

Goal 1: To determine what modifications are necessary in the classroom to provide Tenisha and her wheelchair access to all parts of the classroom
Goal 2: To assess the kinds of prosocial behavior other children display to Tenisha while they interact in the classroom

Planning also involves selecting the type of observational tool you will use; one that will meet your goal for observing. To assess the physical modifications necessary to accommodate Tenisha and to examine students' social interactions with her, you might select an observational tool similar to the checklist in Figure 3.10. Review that figure to see how the teacher, Graciela Gomez, used the checklist to achieve Goals 1 and 2 above.

Step 2: Conduct the Observation. While conducting your observation, it is imperative that you be objective, specific, and as thorough as possible. There are many ways to

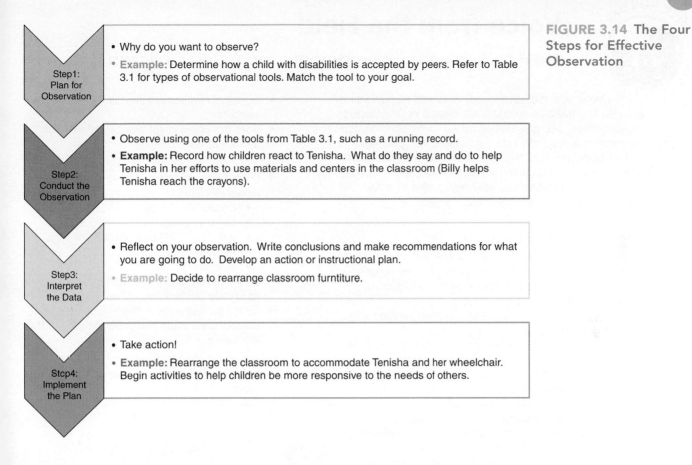

FIGURE 3.14 The Four Steps for Effective Observation

Step1: Plan for Observation
- Why do you want to observe?
- Example: Determine how a child with disabilities is accepted by peers. Refer to Table 3.1 for types of observational tools. Match the tool to your goal.

Step2: Conduct the Observation
- Observe using one of the tools from Table 3.1, such as a running record.
- **Example:** Record how children react to Tenisha. What do they say and do to help Tenisha in her efforts to use materials and centers in the classroom (Billy helps Tenisha reach the crayons).

Step3: Interpret the Data
- Reflect on your observation. Write conclusions and make recommendations for what you are going to do. Develop an action or instructional plan.
- Example: Decide to rearrange classroom furntiture.

Stcp4: Implement the Plan
- Take action!
- **Example:** Rearrange the classroom to accommodate Tenisha and her wheelchair. Begin activities to help children be more responsive to the needs of others.

record your observations, including taking notes, using a checklist or a tally sheet, making a sketch of an indoor or outdoor environment, making a video recording, or an audio recording. Here are some suggestions for collecting observation data:

- Record information on self-stick notes, which are easily transferred to student files and folders.
- Use a clipboard to hold a checklist and other forms to record data as you observe.
- Take photographs of children's accomplishments or infants' milestones. Take other photos of room arrangements (such as play areas, storage, and circle-time area), children's interactions, teacher-child interactions, and student artifacts. Digital camera images are easily manipulated and transferred to student files.
- Use technology whenever possible. For example, a laptop loaded with student files makes it easier to record, store, and manage data after an observation session. In addition, video cameras are a good way to capture certain events and activities.

Step 3: Interpret the Data. All observations should result in some kind of **interpretation**. Interpreting data includes drawing conclusions about what you have observed and making recommendations for the actions you will take based on what you have observed. This serves several important functions. First, interpretation enables you to use your professional knowledge to make sense of what you have seen. Second, interpretation can help you learn to anticipate behaviors associated with normal growth and development and to recognize what is not representative of appropriate growth, development, and learning for each child. Third, interpretation provides direction for the implementation or modification of programs and curriculum. Review again the

interpretation Forming a conclusion based on observational and assessment data with the intent of planning and improving teaching and learning.

Voice from the Field

How to Evaluate Environments for Young Children

One of your roles as an early childhood professional is to create and maintain environments that are healthy, respectful, supportive, and challenging for all young children. This Competency Builder will help you achieve this goal, which is part of Standard 1 of NAEYC's Standards for Professional Development. In addition, you will learn to assess and evaluate environmental strengths and weaknesses, and to reflect and make decisions for improvement and changes.

STEP 1 — Plan for the Observation

- Decide what you will observe, how you will observe, and where you will observe. In our case, we are observing environmental features of classrooms and child care centers.
- Write your goals for observation. Our goals for observing environments are to:
    - Assess the features of environments that contribute to their being healthy, respectful, supportive, and challenging for each child.
    - Make recommendations for what features of environments do not contribute to these criteria.
    - Make recommendations for what to include in environments so that they do meet these criteria.
- Select your observation tool. For our observation, a checklist will achieve our goals and provide the data necessary to make conclusions and recommendations. Our checklist is as follows:

    Healthy
    - Does this environment provide for children's physical and psychological health?
    - Does this environment provide for children's safety?
    - Does this environment provide children with a sense of security?

    Respectful and Supportive
    - Does this environment show respect for each individual child's:
        - culture
        - home language
        - individual abilities or disabilities
        - family context
        - community?
    - Do the professionals in this environment believe each child can learn?
    - Do the professionals in this environment help children understand and make meaning of their experiences?

    Challenging
    - Does this environment provide achievable expectations?
    - Does this environment encourage children to try to new things?

STEP 2 — Conduct the Observation

- As you conduct your observation, look for each of the items on your checklist. As you go through the checklist, take notes about what you are seeing and ask yourself specific questions so that you will be prepared to make recommendations in the steps that

---

observational checklist in Figure 3.10, and note the teacher's interpretation of data—that is, her conclusions and recommendations.

implementation
Committing to a certain action based on interpretations of observational data.

Step 4: Implement a Plan. The **implementation** phase is the time that you act on the results or the findings of your observation. For example, although Tenisha's behavior is appropriate for her, the other children can benefit from activities designed to help them recognize and respond to the needs of others. In addition, the physical environment of the classroom requires the rearrangement of furniture to make spaces more accessible for Tenisha. Implementing—doing something with the results of your observations—is the most important part of the process.

The Voice from the Field "How to Evaluate Environments for Young Children" on pages 86–87 is a Competency Builder that will help you learn how to observe in a classroom setting and use your observations as a basis for making decisions about how to structure your classroom to benefit young children.

follow. Examples of specific questions concerning healthy environments might include:

- What are three characteristics of this environment that would make it safe, healthy, and supportive for children?
- What environmental features promote children's physical and psychological security?
- What evidence is there that this is conducting healthy environment practices?

- In addition, as you observe, you should ask yourself the following about respectful and supportive environments:
  - Is the teacher using positive interactions with the children?
  - Does the teacher show interest in children's ideas and activities?
  - Is the teacher supporting children's learning?
  - What evidence is there that the teacher is supporting learning and wants children to succeed?
  - What background evidence can you identify in the classroom that would lead you to believe that this classroom environment is/is not respectful and supportive?
- Observe for the following when assessing how challenging the environment is:
  - What evidence is there that this environment contains materials that would provide challenging activities for the children?
  - What evidence do you observe that the children are being challenged to succeed in their learning?
  - What evidence do you observe that individual children are being challenged to learn?

STEP **3** **Interpret the Data**

- Review your goals for observing.
- Look at the observation data as a whole. Place your observation in the context of all that you know about young children and all that you know about healthy, respectful, supportive, and challenging environments.
- Reflect on your observation and look for patterns.
- Make decisions about what actions you want to pursue based on your conclusions from the data.
- Your decision-making process can include consulting with other colleagues and professionals. Who are some people who could coach and mentor you in observing and developing environments that are healthy, respectful, supportive, and challenging?

STEP **4** **Implement the Plan**

- Make recommendations for what needs to be included in order to make the environment more healthy, supportive, respectful, and challenging.
- Make recommendations for what needs to be removed from the environment in order for it to be more healthy, supportive, respectful, and challenging.
- Make recommendations for what needs to continue in order for the environment to meet these criteria.
- Take action based on your interpretation of the data.

Assessment for School Readiness

Because of federal mandates and state laws, many school districts formally assess children in some manner before or at the time of their entrance into school. Table 3.2 shows formal methods of assessment. Some type of screening occurs at the time of kindergarten entrance to evaluate learning readiness. Unfortunately, children are often classified on the basis of how well they perform on these early screenings. When assessment is appropriate and the results are used to design developmentally appropriate instruction, assessment is valuable and worthwhile.

Formal methods of assessment that involve the use of standardized tests with set procedures and instructions for administration and have been normed, meaning it is possible to compare a child's score with the scores of a group of children who have already taken the same exam, are called **summative assessments**. Summative

summative assessments
Assessments given periodically to determine at a particular point in time what students know and are able to do. Examples of summative assessments include: state, end of year, and end of grading period assessments.

TABLE 3.2 Examples of Formal Measures of Assessment Used in Early Childhood Education

Assessment Instrument	Age/Grade Level	Purpose
Early Childhood Environment Rating Scale Revised (ECERS-R) http://www.fpg.unc.edu/~ECERS/	Ages $2\frac{1}{2}$ to 5 years	Assesses the space and furnishings, personal care routines, language-reasoning, activities, interactions, program structure and parents and staff of group programs
Early Literacy Inventory (ELI)	Kindergarten through third grade	Assesses writing level, phonemic awareness, rhyming, syllable segmentation, concepts about print, letter/sound identification, sight word identification
Dynamic Indicators of Basic Early Literacy Skills (DIBELS) https://dibels.uoregon.edu/	Kindergarten through sixth grade	Assesses three of the five Big Ideas of early literacy: Phonological awareness, alphabetic principle, and fluency with connected text
BRIGANCE® Screens and Inventories www.curriculumassociates.com	Prekindergarten to ninth grade	Obtains a broad sampling of children's skills and behaviors to determine initial placement, plan appropriate instruction, and comply with mandated testing requirements
Developmental Indicators for the Assessment of Learning, 3rd edition (DIAL-3) www.pearsonassessments.com	Ages 3 to 6 years	Identifies children who may have special educational needs
Preschool Child Observation Record, 2nd edition www.highscope.org	Ages $2\frac{1}{2}$ to 6 years	Measures children's progress in all early childhood programs

assessments are given periodically to determine what students do and do not know at particular points in time.[17] Examples of summative assessments are state assessments such as the the TAKS (Texas), the FCAT (Florida), and the OCCT (Oklahoma); and district benchmark or interim assessments such as the Early Literacy Inventory and the DIBELS (Dynamic Indicators of Basic Early Literacy Skills).[18] Summative assessments are most often used for accountability for schools, such as making Adequate Yearly Progress (AYP), a measurement mandated by No Child Left Behind.[19] In the following pages we discuss screening procedures, which are also a type of summative assessment.

Screening

screening A type of summative assessment that gives a broad picture of what children know and are able to do, as well as their physical health and emotional status.

Screening is an investigation of a large number of children that looks for a specific problem or feature, such as vision impairments. Screening gives you and other school personnel a broad picture of what children know and are able to do, as well as their physical and emotional status. As gross indicators of children's abilities, screening procedures provide much useful information for decisions about placement for initial instruction, referral to other agencies, and additional testing that may be necessary to pinpoint a learning or health problem. In special education, screening measures are used to determine if further, more in-depth assessment measures and techniques are needed to make final determinations about student placement.

Many school districts conduct comprehensive screening programs for children entering preschool and kindergarten. For example, in Colorado, vision and hearing screenings must be provided to all children in kindergarten.[20] In addition, each school district must assess the reading readiness or literacy reading comprehension level of each pupil enrolled in kindergarten.[21] These screening programs are conducted in one day or over several days. Data for each child are usually evaluated by a team of professionals who make instructional placement recommendations and, when appropriate, suggest additional testing and make referrals to other agencies for assistance.

Screening programs can involve the following:

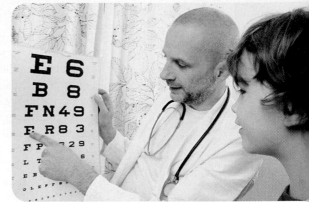

- Interviewing parents to gather information about their children's health, learning patterns, learning achievements, personal habits, and special problems
- Conducting health screenings including a physical examination, a health history, and a blood sample for analysis
- Conducting vision, hearing, and speech screenings
- Collecting and analyzing data from former programs and teachers, such as preschools, Head Start, and child care programs
- Administering a cognitive and/or behavioral screening instrument such as those shown in Table 3.2.

Many school districts conduct a comprehensive screening for children entering kindergarten, which may include assessment of readiness skills, vision, hearing, and speech.

Though the screening process itself is important, just as important is communicating the results to parents and families. Parents are more likely to accept information when they have good communication with the person doing the screening. For example, Head Start, in its ongoing partnerships with families, uses family conferences as an opportunity to communicate screening and assessment results to parents in a manner that recognizes the child's strengths while systematically responding when a concern warrants it.[22]

Screening Instruments.   Screening instruments provide information for grouping and planning instructional strategies. Most can be administered by people who do not have specialized training. However, some instruments require administration by someone who is specifically trained to administer assessment instruments, such as a psychologist. Parent volunteers often help administer screening instruments, many of which are administered in about thirty minutes. See Table 3.2 for examples of these screening instruments.

In addition to participating in the formal assessment of young children, you will have many opportunities to engage in informal assessment of children with disabilities in your classroom. For example, some children with disabilities such as dyslexia may also have ADD. Another example would be that some children with disabilities, though certainly not all, in addition to their particular disability, may exhibit behavioral problems. Learning how to assess children's behavior in order to provide appropriate intervention is one of your key roles.

What Are Critical Assessment Issues?

With almost everything we talk about in this book, essential questions surround what constitutes appropriate and inappropriate practice and what is best for children and families. Assessment is no exception.

Assessment and Accountability

There is a tremendous emphasis on assessment and the use of tests to measure achievement in order to compare children, programs, school districts, and countries. This emphasis will likely continue for a number of reasons. First, the public, including politicians and legislatures, sees assessment as a means of making schools and teachers accountable for teaching all children so they achieve at or above grade level. Second, assessment is seen as playing a critical role in improving education: assessment results are used to make decisions about how the curriculum and instructional practices can increase achievement. For example, the Good Start, Grow Smart Early Childhood Initiative in the No Child Left Behind Act calls for an accountability system to ensure that every Head Start center assesses standards of learning in early language and numeracy skills. Therefore, as long as there is a public desire to improve teaching and achievement, we will continue to see an emphasis on the use of assessment for accountability purposes.

Blurring the Line Between Assessment and Teaching.   As an early childhood professional you are constantly multitasking. You are simultaneously assessing and teaching children. But many believe that the emphasis on assessment leads to "teaching to the test." This leads to children knowing how to bubble in a scantron sheet, but not necessarily *really understanding* the material. This phrase refers to teachers spending valuable instruction time teaching how to answer certain questions children will find on an upcoming summative assessment rather than interpreting content, learning to reason and debate, or take another perspective. Many fear that the emphasis on accountability is creating an educational culture that puts test scores ahead of intellectual growth.

Performance-Based Pay.   Many school districts give their teachers extra compensation or bonuses if their schools meet certain student achievement goals. Such plans are based on measuring student achievement with standardized tests, and this means more testing for students of all ages. While performance-based pay programs are not popular with all teachers, they are a part of many districts' pay plans and are growing in popularity.[23]

President Obama and Secretary of Education Arne Duncan's education plan focuses on four points, one of which is alternative pathways for teacher certification and performance-based pay.[24] Performance-based pay is a contentious topic for some because they fear that performance-based pay encourages teaching to a standardized test. However, Randi Weingarten, president of the 1.4 million-member American Federation of Teachers, is supportive of the plan, saying, "We finally have an education president."[25] Many critics of performance-based pay are excited about Obama and Duncan's plan because, as the president of the 3.2 million-member National Education Association Dennis Van Roekel said, Obama's call for teacher performance pay does not mean that raises or bonuses would be tied only to student test scores.[26] It also means more pay for teachers who acquire extra knowledge and skills, or who take on leadership roles in their schools, attain credentials such as national board certification, or those who work in high-poverty, hard-to-staff schools.[27] Secretary Duncan says, "What you want to do is really identify the best and brightest by a range of metrics, including student achievement."[28]

Standards and Testing.   While there is no national curriculum in the United States, states are federally required to adhere to certain standards and to use these standards to guide school instruction. In addition, federal law mandates that state standards be developed and improved in order for states to receive federal assistance.

Standardized tests are the main means of determining if schools are meeting state and federal guidelines.[29]

State Standards.   Each state mandates what is taught in their public schools in order to achieve accountability in relation to the terms set forth by NCLB. For example, in the state of Texas the Texas Essential Knowledge and Skills (TEKS) is a set of skills that the state has determined are essential for each student to learn. Each grade level has a specific set of TEKS for each content area, ranging from technology and science to literature, art, and physical education. The state's standardized test, the TAKS (Texas Assessment of Knowledge and Skills) test, is based on the TEKS. The state of Texas requires that its textbooks teach the TEKS as well, which means that the major textbook publishers tailor their content for Texas, in many cases creating textbooks that are different from those purchased by the other states. As a result, the curriculum in Texas is heavily dependent upon the TEKS because the TEKS builds on skills established in the preschool and kindergarten and throughout the high school years. Now would be a good time for you to learn about procedures of standardized testing and how standardized testing affects the curriculum in your state.

High-Stakes Testing.   **High-stakes testing** occurs when standardized tests are used to make important and often life-influencing decisions about children. Standardized tests have specific and standardized content, administration and scoring procedures, and norms for interpreting scores. High-stakes outcomes include decisions about whether to admit children into programs (e.g., kindergarten), whether children will have to attend summer school, and whether children will be retained or promoted. Generally, the early childhood profession is opposed to high-stakes testing for children through grade three. Take, for example, kindergarten teacher Michael Kenney, who says, "We are testing them so much that I barely have time to teach the curriculum. These are 5- and 6-year-olds, and there is so little time for them to be kids."[30] This pretty well sums up how many early childhood teachers feel!

> **high-stakes testing** An assessment test used to either admit children into programs or promote them from one grade to the next.

Despite early childhood professionals' opposition, as part of the accountability movement, many politicians and school administrators view high-stakes testing as a means of making sure children learn and that promotions from one grade to another are based on achievement. Many school critics maintain that in the pre-K and primary grades there is too much social promotion—that is, passing children from grade to grade merely to enable students to keep pace with their age peers.

With so much emphasis on tests, it is understandable that the issue of testing and assessment raises many concerns on the part of teachers, parents, and the public. Some argue that testing reduces teaching and learning to the lowest common denominator—teaching children what they need to know to get the right answers. Many early childhood professionals believe that standardized tests do not measure children's thinking, problem-solving ability, creativity, or responsibility for their own learning. Furthermore, critics believe that group-administered, objectively scored, skills-focused tests—which dominate much of U.S. education—do not support (indeed, may undermine) many of the curricular reforms taking place today.

As an early childhood professional, part of your responsibility is to be an advocate for the appropriate use of assessment (see the Ethical Dilemma at the end of this chapter). You will make ongoing, daily decisions about how best to assess your children and how best to use assessment results.

Assessment of Children with Disabilities

As an early childhood professional, you will have many opportunities to assess or participate in the assessment of young children with disabilities. Assessment is a pivotal event for families and their children because assessment results are used to include or exclude children from specialized intervention that can change their developmental and academic destinies.[31]

Let's look at assessment considerations for students with special needs and English language learners (ELLs). The Individuals with Disabilities Education Act (IDEA) mandates that children with disabilities be included in state- and district-wide assessments unless alternate assessments are more appropriate. For many students with disabilities, participation in classroom, district, or state assessments will not necessitate any changes in the manner in how teachers administer assessments. Assessment and evaluation for children with special needs must be fair and equitable for all children, and teachers must adhere to the mandates required by IDEA. Tests must:

- Be administered in the child's native language or other mode of communication.
- Be validated for the purpose they are being used for.
- Be administered by trained personnel in conformance with instructions from the test publisher.
- Cannot be used as the only basis of special education eligibility.
- Provide information about the students' educational needs, not simply intelligence.

In addition, in this chapter you have learned about the various ways teachers assess children that go beyond state, district, or standardized tests. Children both with and without disabilities will require accommodations to those assessments and the more informal assessments given by classroom teachers. These accommodations do not change the content of the test but usually fall into one of five categories. Using these accommodations will help you and other teachers equitably assess all children:

1. *Format Accommodations:*   The assessment directions or content are altered to include visual (such as large print), tactile (such as Braille or raised print), or auditory (such as an audio recording) presentations depending on the needs of the child.
2. *Response Accommodations:*   Children can respond in different ways such as using an assistive communication device, typing, sign language, or pointing.
3. *Setting Accommodations:*   The location of an assessment is changed so it is free from distractions and other interruptions. For example, a child might be moved to a room that is quiet or has fewer children moving about.
4. *Timing Accommodations:*   These accommodations change the allowable length of the testing time and provide students with the time and breaks they need.
5. *Scheduling Accommodations:*   These accommodations may change the particular time of day, day of the week, or number of days an assessment is given.

Test Bias and Test Generalizability

Sometimes school district testing programs do not enable all children to demonstrate what they know and are able to do. There are many gender and ethnic biases in test performance. Testing programs should include assessments of multiple types of intelligence and use different ways of testing children, such as portfolios and modeling, so that all students are able to demonstrate what they know and are able to do.

Furthermore, in addition to inherent test bias, teachers and administrators can quickly forget issues of individuality and differences in culture, ethnicity, home language, age, home and community environment, maternal and paternal psychological well-being, and socioeconomic background. Children simply do not come to the assessment or testing situations with equal chances for success. For example, consider the language of the test. Was the test given to a non-English-speaking child developed for English-speaking children? Is the test linguistically appropriate for the children with whom it is used? Also, think about the developmental age of the children being assessed. For example, with the trend to test younger children, schools use tests that were developed for older children. You should ask yourself these questions: Is this test appropriate for this age group; and is this test developmentally appropriate for students who may be a certain age but are developmentally behind? Can the test be administered in sections or does it have to be administered all in one setting? If a child is developmentally four years old, even at the age of seven or eight, is it appropriate to expect that child to attend to a test that requires sitting for an hour and a half to complete? Also, consider how children's socioeconomic status influences their achievement and test performance. For example, children who live in families with high incomes tend to score better on achievement tests and have fewer behavior problems in general than do children from low-socioeconomic households.[32] Ask yourself, "Did my students who are economically disadvantaged receive high-quality preschool programs? Are they as ready to take this test as their more advantaged peers or do they need extra help?" In essence, you are not only asking if there is a bias inherent in the assessments you use, you are asking if the assessment *generalizes* to each of your students accurately and fairly.

You will want to make sure that all of your assessments of young children generalize and are as unbiased as possible. To do so, get to know each of your students. How can you expect to administer an accurate assessment if you do not know the language Daniel speaks at home; if Hailey is sleepy in class because she has been living out of the family van for the past three weeks; if Tyler's learning disability is being effectively monitored; or if Maria, an inclusion student, is developmentally and chronologically the same age? If you make a habit of asking questions such as these, you will get to know each child well.

Reporting to and Communicating with Families

Part of your responsibility as a professional is to report to families about the growth, development, and achievement of their children. Communicating with parents and families is one of the most important jobs of the early childhood professional. The following guidelines will help you meet the important responsibility of reporting assessment information to family members:

- *Be honest and realistic.*   Too often, we do not want to hurt parents' feelings, so we sugarcoat what we are reporting. However, families need our honest assessments about their children and what they know, are able to do, and will be able to do.

- *Communicate clearly.*   What we communicate to families must make sense to them; they have to understand what we are saying. Reporting to families often has to be a combination of written (in their language) and oral communication. Use a translator when necessary and be sure to have someone who is fluent in the other language to check and double check any written translations for cultural errors and grammatical mistakes.

- *Share student work samples and portfolios.*   Documentation of student progress is a concrete, tangible way to report and share information with family members.

- *Provide ideas and information to help them assist in their children's learning.* Remember that you and families are partners in helping children be successful in school and life.

Report assessment findings accurately and honestly to parents. How can such communication build trust? What are other advantages of honest, open communication?

How Young Is Too Young?

There are many issues involved in testing young children. For example, one report cautions early childhood professionals about testing young children and the misuse of test results from young children.

> All assessments, and particularly assessments for accountability, must be used carefully and appropriately if they are to resolve, and not create, educational problems. Assessment of young children poses greater challenges than people generally realize. The first five years of life are a time of incredible growth and learning, but the course of development is uneven and sporadic. The status of a child's development as of any given day can change very rapidly. Consequently, assessment results—in particular, standardized test scores that reflect a given point in time—can easily misrepresent children's learning.[33]

Accommodating Diverse Learners

Though not speaking English is not a disability, like children with disabilities, English language learners (ELLs) are often at a disadvantage when it comes to testing. It is a troubling fact that ELLs' academic performance is well below that of their peers and that ELLs have excessively high dropout rates.[34] Contributing to the difficulty many ELLs face in reaching achievement performance scores comparable to those of non-ELLs is that assessing students in English is required by law, and as a result, assessments are often not authentic.[35]

ELLs and Assessment Issues. Assessments are often inauthentic for many reasons. First, ELLs are expected to master content in English before they have reached a certain level of English proficiency. For example, Marisol is expected to read and write in English even though she only understands and speaks Spanish.[36] Second, each state, and frequently several districts, has divergent policies concerning ELLs.[37] As a result, the accommodations ELLs receive often vary from school to school, district to district, and state to state. Third, standards for what ELLs should know are not matched with a corresponding test.[38] In other words, ELLs are held accountable to one set of standards, like those specified in accommodating for level of language, but then are assessed with a test that is normed for children who are fluent speakers of English. When it comes to ELLs, the standards are not standardized! This contributes to the difficulty ELLs face when it comes to accurate and authentic assessments, equal education, and chances to succeed in an educational setting.

Cultural Issues and Accommodation. In addition to issues of alignment of standards with assessments, ELLs may also have cultural differences that make achievement difficult. For example, the activities and learning behaviors fostered in U.S. schools are often based on individual achievement and behavior while many ELLs come from schools where the desired achievement and behaviors are based on a collectivistic perspective.[39] For example, in the United States, the phrase "Pull yourself up by your own bootstraps" is indicative of American culture, emphasizing personal achievement without help from others; but in some other countries, the phrase might better be applied as "You help me, I'll help you, and we'll both benefit." In such cultures, individual accomplishment is not as important as the group equally achieving or benefiting. As a result, children from a different cultural background may not understand the importance placed on their own academic achievement because they are used to thinking about themselves as a member of the greater whole. Also, while U.S. schooling encourages creativity, problem solving, and analysis, schooling in other cultures often emphasizes recitation and rote memorization.[40] Furthermore, academic communication in speech and writing in U.S. schools is mostly linear; we tell stories in a straight line with a beginning, middle, and end; in some other cultures it is often circular or digressive.[41] For example, conversations in other cultures may not be straightforward but instead circle around a topic in order to emphasize its importance or make a point. The pattern of communicating is different, and as a result, translations from other languages into English often don't make sense or appear to be disjointed. With such barriers, it is no wonder that ELLs are struggling in areas of academic performance achievement!

Guidelines for ELL Success.   To help ELLs in your classroom, consider the following:

- Review the standards and assessments used to determine ELL achievement performance in your state. Do the standards and assessments align? If they do not, become an advocate for your students. For more information, go to the World-Class Instructional Design and Assessment Consortium (WIDA) website, as well as the Center for Research on Education, Diversity, and Excellence.

- Use a variety of assessment types and techniques. We have already discussed how standardized tests are often not accurate representations of what ELLs know and can do. Therefore, a diverse array of assessments is especially important in order for you to get an accurate picture of your students' progress, knowledge, and abilities. Portfolios are particularly helpful to achieve this goal because they include work samples collected over time. Interviews also increase language fluency and teacher-student relationships.

- Make sure your ELLs receive a high-quality education so that they can perform their best on assessments. For example:
  - In addition to the traditional American education emphasis on individual learning and achievement, include plenty of activities like group projects and group discussions to appeal to many ELLs' preference for working with others.
  - Encourage ELLs to utilize memorization and recitations, as these are the more common learning modes in many of their cultures. At the same time, also teach creative thinking, problem solving, and analysis.
  - Get to know your ELLs well. The more you know about your students and the more you are involved in their lives, the better you can teach to their needs. Conduct home visits, talk with providers, and talk with your students.

Conclusion

Today there is a great deal of emphasis on accountability. Teachers are asked to be accountable to parents, legislators, and the public. Providing for and conducting developmentally appropriate assessment of young children and their programs is one of the best ways for you to be accountable for what you do. Conducting appropriate assessment not only makes you accountable to parents and the public, but it also enables you to be accountable to young children. You have accepted a sacred trust and have dedicated your life to helping children learn and develop. Effective assessment practices will help you achieve this goal.

Activities for Professional Development

Ethical Dilemma

●●●●●●

"To test or not to test?"

Recently, a large east coast school district suspended two special education teachers without pay for refusing to give a state-mandated test to children with cognitive disabilities. Janice Morris and Sally Sutton teach at Blue Lake Elementary in a special education classroom. They were concerned about the authenticity and appropriateness of a grade-level based test that their students had already failed the previous semester. Janice and Sally agreed to parents' request that their students not be tested. They also believed the test was not in the best interests of the children. Both teachers maintain they have high expectations for their children, but when a test is inappropriate to children's needs it is wrong to administer it. Janice and Sally think the test was a one-size-fits-all assessment. The parents are very supportive of Sally and Janice's actions, saying, "They stood up for our children and what's best for them." The school district's superintendent maintains that although he understood the teachers' position, they should have administered the test because it is state mandated.[42]

What do you think? Do you agree with Janice and Sally, or do you agree with the superintendent? Should Janice and Sally have administered the test because it is the law, even though they believed that it was unethical? What would you have done?

●●●●●●

Activities to Apply What You Learned

1. Write a journal or a blog entry detailing three reasons why assessment is important. Which reason is the most important to you?
2. We have discussed the importance of choosing the most appropriate assessments possible. What questions can you ask in order to choose the most appropriate assessment? List three questions you can ask your students for each of these areas: culture, home life and discipline, social interactions with peers and adults, and handling conflict (i.e., "Juan, when Mommy reads you a story at night, does she read to you in Spanish or in English?"). E-mail these to two of your friends and ask them to comment.
3. Observation is an important professional skill. For example, you could use it to learn more about three- and four-year-old children's toy preferences. Using ideas from this chapter, develop an observation form and write guidelines for how you would collect your data. Share this information with two or three of your classmates and ask for feedback.
4. Of the summative assessments described in this chapter, which would you prefer to use in a classroom of ELLs? Gifted and talented learners? How about an inclusion classroom? For each setting, provide evidence to support your answer.
5. Pick an issue from the "What are Critical Assessment Issues?" section of the chapter. Write a pro or con position statement in a note on Facebook, then tag several of your friends in the note and engage them in a debate on the issue.
6. Go to the World-Class Instructional Design and Assessment Consortium (WIDA) website (www.wida.us/index.aspx). Is your state a member of WIDA? Why or why not? Explore the website. Then, conduct an Internet search for the ways your state is currently working to accommodate ELLs. Do you think your state's efforts are sufficient?

Linking to Learning

ARCNet
http://arc.missouri.edu/
Created for anyone interested in the world of assessment.

Assessing Young Children's Progress Appropriately
www.ncrel.org/sdrs/areas/issues/students/earlycld/ea500.htm
Another good source for looking at critical issues relating to the appropriate assessment of children's progress.

A Guide to the Developmentally Appropriate Assessment of Young Children
www.beyond-the-book.com/strategies/index.html
This guide to the developmentally appropriate assessment of young children provides useful information about the appropriate uses of assessment and assessment results.

Linking Assessment and Teaching in the Critical Early Years
www.nea.org/ and a related site:
www.keysonline.org/
Excellent sources for additional information about assessment through documentation and about linking assessment and teaching.

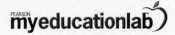

Go to Topic 4 (Observation/Assessment) in the MyEducationLab (www.myeducationlab.com) for your course, where you can:

- Find learning outcomes for Observation/Assessment along with the national standards that connect to these outcomes.
- Complete Assignments and Activities that can help you more deeply understand the chapter content.

- Apply and practice your understanding of the core teaching skills identified in the chapter with the Building Teaching Skills and Dispositions learning units.
- Hear viewpoints of experts in the field in Professional Perspectives.
- Check your comprehension on the content covered in the chapter by going to the Study Plan in the Book Resources for your text. Here you will be able to take a chapter quiz, receive feedback on your answers, and then access Review, Practice, and Enrichment activities to enhance your understanding of chapter content.

PART II

FOUNDATIONS: HISTORY AND THEORIES

4

THE PAST AND THE PRESENT
Prologue to the Future

focus questions

1. Why is the history of early childhood education important?
2. Which people have had the greatest influence on early childhood education throughout history?
3. How has society viewed children through the ages?
4. What can early childhood professionals do to encourage inclusion practices?

naeyc standards

Standard 4. Using Developmentally Effective Approaches to Connect with Children and Families

I understand and use positive relationships and supportive interactions as the foundation for my work with young children and families. I know, understand, and use a wide array of developmentally appropriate approaches, instructional strategies, and tools to connect with children and families and positively influence each child's development and learning.[1]

Standard 6. Becoming a Professional

I know and use ethical guidelines and other professional standards related to early childhood practice. I am an informed advocate for sound educational practices and policies.[2]

Why Is the Past Important?

When we read of the hopes, ideas, and accomplishments of people whom our profession judges famous, we realize that many of today's ideas are built on those of the past. There are at least five reasons to know about the ideas and theories of great educators who have influenced and continue to influence the field of early childhood education.

Rebirth of Ideas

Old ideas and theories are often reborn. Good ideas and practices persist over time and are recycled through educational thought and practices in ten- to twenty-year periods. For example, many education initiatives that started in the 1980s and the 1990s are widely implemented today. For example, the public concern over the condition and quality of education of the 80s and 90s has matured into the current full-fledged accountability movement. Also, the suggestion of the adoption of standards to improve education has transformed into the adoption of state standards and now the adoption of Common Core national standards designed to improve education in the United States.

However, old ideas and practices seldom get recycled in exactly their previous form; they are changed and modified as necessary for contemporary society and current beliefs. When you know about former ideas and practices you can more easily recognize how they are recycled. This knowledge enables you to be an active participant in the recycling process of applying good practices and ideas of previous years to contemporary practice. And, you can more fully appreciate this recycling if you understand the roots of the early education profession. Take a moment to look at the time line in Appendix C; it will help you understand how ideas about early childhood education have been reborn through the years.

Building the Dream—Again

Many of today's early childhood practices have their roots in the past. In this sense, building the dream seems like a never-ending process. For example, the idea of universal preschool in the United States has been around since 1830, when the Infant School Society of Boston submitted a petition to incorporate infant schools into the Boston Public Schools.[3]

We are *still* trying to implement universal preschool education. We have inherited the ideas and dreams of a long line of early childhood educators, which we use as a base to build meaningful teaching careers and programs for children and their families. You are both a builder of dreams and an implementer of dreams as you join the ranks of all early childhood professionals.

Implementing Current Practice

Understanding the ideas of early educators helps you know how to implement current teaching strategies, whatever they may be. For instance, Rousseau, Froebel, and Montessori all believed children should be taught with dignity and respect. This attitude toward children is essential to an understanding of good educational practice and contributes to good teaching and quality programs. You and any program you are involved in should include respect for children and families— among many other dispositions—as one of your core values.

> "Today, we begin in earnest the work of making sure that the world we leave our children is just a little bit better than the one we inhabit today."
>
> **PRESIDENT BARACK OBAMA**

Empowering Professionals

Theories about how young children grow, develop, and learn shape educational and child-rearing practices. Studying the beliefs of the great educators helps parents, you, and all early childhood educators clarify what to do and gives insight into educational practice. In this sense, knowing about theories liberates the uninformed from ignorance and empowers professionals and parents. Those who understand historical ideas and theories are able to confidently implement developmentally appropriate practices.

Inspiring Professionals

Exploring, analyzing, and discovering the roots of early childhood education help inspire professionals. Recurring rediscovery forces professionals to contrast current practices with what others have advocated. Examining sources of beliefs helps clarify modern practice, and reading about and studying others' ideas make us rethink our own beliefs and positions. Thus knowledge of the great educators and their beliefs helps keep us current. When you pause long enough to listen to what they have to say, you frequently find a new insight or idea that will motivate you to continue your quest to be the best you can be.

History and Historical Figures

The contributors to the American education system are many and distinguished. In the following, you will read about some of the most notable contributors to education as we know it today. As you read, consider how the contributions of the past play a part in the work you will do in the early childhood education field. Take a moment to refer to Figure 4.1 as you read this chapter. In Figure 4.1, you will be able to trace how historical figures and important moments in education have influenced one another and how events from the distant past influence us even today. As you read, you should be wondering, "How will I contribute to the field? How will I continue or influence and modify the ideas of the founders of the field?"

1500–1700: The Foundations

The primary impact of the Protestant Reformation in Europe was religious. However, other far-reaching effects were secular. Two of these effects involved *universal education*, or education for all, and *literacy*, both of which are very much in the forefront of educational practice today. In addition, the advent of the printing press made the written word accessible to a wide population, making literacy education more necessary on a larger scale than ever before.

Martin Luther.   The question of what to teach is an issue in any educational endeavor. Does society create schools and then decide what to teach, or do the needs of society determine what schools it will establish to meet desired goals? This is a question early childhood professionals wrestle with today. In the case of sixteenth-century European education, Martin Luther (1483–1546) emphasized the necessity of establishing schools to teach children to read. Prior to the Reformation, most of the people who could read were clergy members, but not the general populace. Luther replaced the authority of the hierarchy of the Catholic church with the authority of the Bible in his landmark *Ninety-Five Theses*. He believed that individuals were free to work out their own salvation through the scriptures. This meant that people had to learn to read so that they could access the Bible.

This concept marked the real beginning of teaching and learning in people's native languages, or vernacular, as opposed to Latin, the official language of the Catholic church. After Luther translated the Bible into German, other translations followed, finally making the Bible

Martin Luther (1483–1546)

FIGURE 4.1 Education Over Time

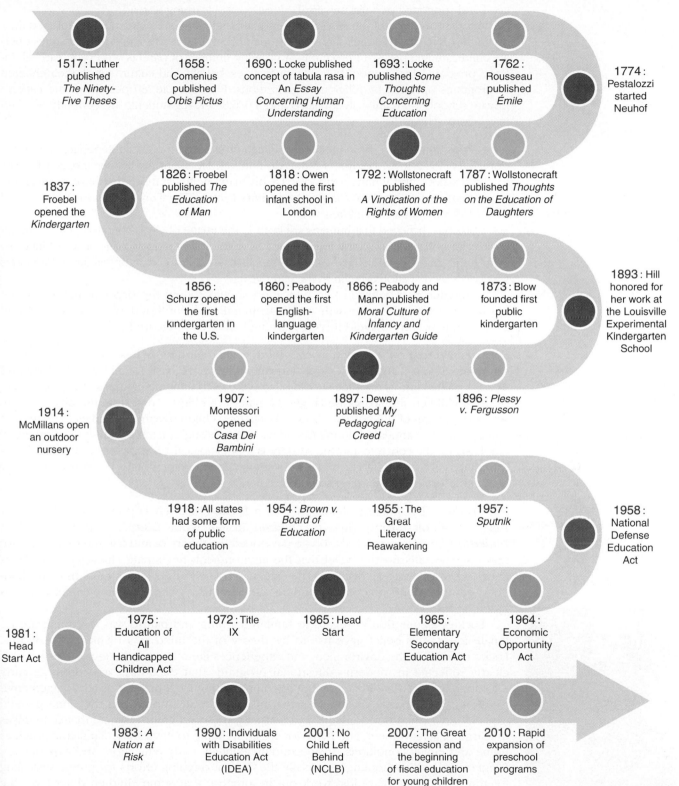

1517: Luther published *The Ninety-Five Theses*

1658: Comenius published *Orbis Pictus*

1690: Locke published concept of tabula rasa in An *Essay Concerning Human Understanding*

1693: Locke published *Some Thoughts Concerning Education*

1762: Rousseau published *Émile*

1774: Pestalozzi started Neuhof

1787: Wollstonecraft published *Thoughts on the Education of Daughters*

1792: Wollstonecraft published *A Vindication of the Rights of Women*

1818: Owen opened the first infant school in London

1826: Froebel published *The Education of Man*

1837: Froebel opened the *Kindergarten*

1856: Schurz opened the first kindergarten in the U.S.

1860: Peabody opened the first English-language kindergarten

1866: Peabody and Mann published *Moral Culture of Infancy and Kindergarten Guide*

1873: Blow founded first public kindergarten

1893: Hill honored for her work at the Louisville Experimental Kindergarten School

1896: *Plessy v. Fergusson*

1897: Dewey published *My Pedagogical Creed*

1907: Montessori opened *Casa Dei Bambini*

1914: McMillans open an outdoor nursery

1918: All states had some form of public education

1954: *Brown v. Board of Education*

1955: The Great Literacy Reawakening

1957: *Sputnik*

1958: National Defense Education Act

1964: Economic Opportunity Act

1965: Elementary Secondary Education Act

1965: Head Start

1972: Title IX

1975: Education of All Handicapped Children Act

1981: Head Start Act

1983: *A Nation at Risk*

1990: Individuals with Disabilities Education Act (IDEA)

2001: No Child Left Behind (NCLB)

2007: The Great Recession and the beginning of fiscal education for young children

2010: Rapid expansion of preschool programs

available to people in their own languages. In this way, the Protestant Reformation encouraged and supported popular universal education and learning to read.

Another outcome of the Reformation was that religious denominations developed their own schools to preserve their faith. Today, many churches, synagogues, and mosques operate child care and pre-K–12 programs. A growing number of parents who want early childhood programs that support their religious values, beliefs, and culture enroll their children in programs operated by religious organizations. For example, 80 percent of the nation's private schools are religiously affiliated and 4,086,880 K–12 students are currently enrolled in religious schools.[4]

John Amos Comenius.   Born in Moravia, then a province of the Czech Republic, John Amos Comenius (1592–1670) became a Moravian minister. He spent his life serving as a bishop, teaching school, and writing textbooks. Of his many writings, those that have received the most attention are *The Great Didactic* and **Orbis Pictus** (*The World in Pictures*), considered the first picture book for children.

Orbis Pictus (*The World in Pictures*) Considered the first picture book for children.

Comenius believed that humans are born in the image of God. Therefore, each individual has an obligation and duty to be educated to the fullest extent of his or her abilities so as to fulfill this God-like image. Since so much depends on education, as far as Comenius was concerned, it should begin in the early years.[5]

Comenius also believed that education should follow the order of nature, which implies a timetable for growth and learning. Early childhood professionals should observe this pattern to avoid forcing learning before children are ready.

sensory education
Learning experiences involving the five senses: seeing, touching, hearing, tasting, and smelling.

Sensory Education.   Comenius also thought that learning is best achieved when the senses are involved and that **sensory education** forms the basis for all learning. Comenius said the golden rule of teaching should be to place everything before the senses—for example, that children should not be taught the names of objects apart from the objects themselves or pictures of the objects. *Orbis Pictus* helped children learn the names of things and concepts as they appeared during Comenius' time, through pictures and words. Comenius' emphasis on the concrete and the sensory is a pedagogical principle early childhood professionals still try to fully grasp and implement. Many contemporary programs, especially Montessori programs, stress sensory learning.

blank tablet The belief that at birth the mind is blank and that experience creates the mind.

environmentalism The theory that the environment, rather than heredity, exerts the primary influence on intellectual growth and cultural development.

John Locke.   The English philosopher John Locke (1632–1704) popularized the *tabula rasa*, or **blank tablet**, view of children in his work *Essay Concerning Human Understanding*. More precisely, Locke developed the theory of and laid the foundation for **environmentalism**—the belief that the environment, not innate characteristics, determines what children will become. The extent of Locke's influence on modern early childhood education and practice is unappreciated by many who daily implement practices based on his theories.

Locke's assumption in regard to human learning and nature was that there are no innate ideas. This belief gave rise to his theory of the mind as a blank tablet. By this, Locke meant that the environment and experiences literally form the mind. This belief is clearly reflected in modern educational programs that encourage and promote early education as a means of overcoming or compensating for a poor or disadvantaged environment. Based partly on the idea that all children are born with the same general capacity for mental development and learning, these programs assume that differences in learning, achievement, and behavior are attributable to environmental factors, such as home and family conditions, socioeconomic context, early education, and experiences. Programs of early schooling, especially the current ongoing efforts for public schooling for three- and four-year-olds, work on the premise that some children don't have the readiness experiences necessary for kindergarten and first grade and are at risk for failure in school and life.

John Locke (1632–1704)

1700–1850: From Naturalism to Kindergarten

The foundation laid by philosophers like Luther and Locke paved the way for others to focus on education as a humanistic imperative. With this foundation, the world of education was able to evolve with the sometimes revolutionary ideas of Rousseau, Wollstonecraft, Owen, and Froebel.

Jean-Jacques Rousseau.   Best remembered by educators for his book *Émile*, Jean-Jacques Rousseau (1712–1778) raises a hypothetical child from birth to adolescence. Rousseau's theories were radical for his time. The opening lines of *Émile* set the tone not only for Rousseau's educational views but for many of his political ideas as well: "God makes all things good; man meddles with them and they become evil."[6]

Naturalism.   Rousseau advocated a return to nature and an approach to educating children called **naturalism**. To Rousseau, naturalism meant abandoning society's artificiality and pretentiousness. A naturalistic education permits growth without undue interference or restrictions. Rousseau would probably argue against such modern practices as dress codes, compulsory attendance, frequent and standardized testing, and ability grouping on the grounds that they are "unnatural." On the other hand, more early childhood programs are incorporating outdoor activities, nature education, and gardening as ways of getting children involved in more natural approaches to education. We will discuss Rousseau's influence on environmental education later in this chapter.

American education tends to emphasize ideas associated with naturalism. For example, family grouping seeks to create a more natural, family-like atmosphere in schools and classrooms; literacy programs emphasize literature from the natural environment (e.g., using menus to show children how reading is important in their everyday lives); and conflict resolution programs teach children how to get along with others.

According to Rousseau, natural education promotes and encourages qualities such as happiness, spontaneity, and the inquisitiveness associated with childhood. Rousseau felt that Émile's education occurred through three sources: nature, people, and things.

Unfolding.   Rousseau believed that although parents and others have control over education that comes from social and sensory experiences, they have no control over children's natural growth. In essence, this is the principle of **unfolding**, in which the nature of children—what they are to be—develops as a result of maturation according to their innate developmental schedules. We should observe the child's growth and provide experiences at appropriate times. Some educators interpret this as a laissez-faire, or "let alone," approach to parenting and education. On the other hand, understanding unfolding is also important to our understanding of developmentally appropriate practice.

The belief in unfolding can be seen today in high-stakes testing. With the trend toward testing children at younger and younger ages, even in kindergarten, there is a heightened concern about the developmental appropriateness of such practices. Many critics say that kindergarten is a time of developmental fluctuation, not just between children, but on a daily basis in an individual child, and that high-stakes tests are therefore inappropriate. As a result, proponents of developmental unfolding are in a deadlock with proponents of testing for accountability.

Another example of the use of unfolding in today's education scene is *redshirting*, the act of holding a "young" five-year-old back from entering kindergarten for a year so that he or she is more developmentally capable to meet the demands of the increased rigor of school. Redshirting is becoming ever more popular.[7] Parents who hold back their children hope that the extra year will give their children an opportunity to further *unfold* and perform to higher standards when they do enter school.

Rousseau maintained that a natural education encourages spontaneity and inquisitiveness. What should families and teachers do to provide experiences in which children can develop their natural abilities?

Émile Jean-Jacques Rousseau's famous book that outlines his ideas about how children should be reared.

naturalism Education that follows the natural development of children and does not force the educational process on them.

unfolding Process by which the nature of children—what they are to be—develops as a result of maturation according to their innate developmental schedules.

Rousseau established a way of thinking about young children that is reflected in the educational practice of Pestalozzi and Froebel. Rousseau's concept of natural unfolding echoes Comenius' concept of naturalness and appears in current programs that stress children's readiness as a factor in learning. Jean Piaget's cognitive developmental stages also reinforce Rousseau's thinking about the importance of natural development.

Johann Heinrich Pestalozzi.   Impressed by Rousseau's back-to-nature concepts, Johann Heinrich Pestalozzi (1746–1827) purchased a farm and started a school called Neuhof. There Pestalozzi developed his ideas about the integration of home life, vocational education, and education for reading and writing.

Rousseau's influence is most apparent in Pestalozzi's belief that education should follow children's natural development. Pestalozzi reared his only son, Jean-Jacques, using *Émile* as a guide and on harmonizing nature and educational practices.

Object Lessons.   Pestalozzi believed that all education is based on sensory impressions and that through the proper sensory experiences, children can achieve their natural potential. This belief led to his development of object lessons. As the name implies, Pestalozzi thought the best way to learn many concepts was through manipulatives—counting, measuring, feeling, touching. Pestalozzi believed the best teachers were those who teach children, not subjects. He also believed in multiage grouping.[8]

Mary Wollstonecraft.   In 1787, Mary Wollstonecraft (1759–1797), a British philosopher and early feminist, published *Thoughts On The Education Of Daughters: With Reflections On Female Conduct, In The More Important Duties Of Life*. With this work, published in the wake of the Declaration of Independence and the French Revolution, Wollstonecraft became one of the first philosophers to extend the burgeoning ideals of equality and independence to women through education. Wollstonecraft emphasized education as a means to better society. In *Thoughts on the Education of Daughters*, Wollstonecraft offered advice on female education as well as basic child-rearing instructions, such as how to care for babies. Wollstonecraft was significantly influenced by Locke's *Some Thoughts Concerning Education* and Rousseau's *Émile*. Wollstonecraft followed Locke's example in emphasizing a parent-directed domestic education and built on Rousseau's beliefs in natural abilities.

Later, Wollstonecraft published *A Vindication of the Rights of Woman: with Strictures on Political and Moral Subjects*, in which she responded to those educational and political theorists of the eighteenth century who argued against educating women. In the eighteenth century, it was argued by most European educational philosophers that women were incapable of thinking clearly because they were too susceptible to following their feelings rather than rationality. Wollstonecraft, along with other reformers, maintained that women were capable of rational thought and deserved to be educated. In the *Vindication of the Rights of Women*, she argued that women ought to have an education because they are essential to the nation as educators of its children. Wollstonecraft's work is essential because it was one of the first arguments for truly educating all people, an idea that we are still very much influenced by and are striving toward today. In addition, she paved the way for women to become educators, not only of their own children, but of other children as well.

Robert Owen.   Quite often, people who affect the course of educational thought and practice are also visionaries in political and social affairs. Robert Owen (1771–1858) was no exception. Owen's influences on education resulted from his entrepreneurial activities associated with New Lanark, Scotland, a model mill town he managed. Owen was an environmentalist; that is, he believed the environment in which children are reared is the main factor contributing to their beliefs, behavior, and achievement. Consequently, he maintained that society and persons acting in the best interests of society can shape children's individual characters.

He also was a **Utopian**, believing that by controlling the circumstances and consequent outcomes of child rearing, it was possible to build a new and perhaps more perfect society. Such a deterministic view of child rearing and education pushes free will to the background and makes environmental conditions the dominant force in directing and determining human behavior. Owen believed that good traits were instilled at an early age and children's behavior was influenced primarily by the environment.

Infant Schools.   To implement his beliefs, Owen opened an infant school in 1816 at New Lanark, designed to provide care for about a hundred children ages eighteen months to ten years while their parents worked in his cotton mills. This led to the opening of the first infant school in London in 1818. Because part of Owen's motivation for opening the infant schools was to get children away from their uneducated parents, he also opened a night school for his workers to provide them an education and transform them into "rational beings."

Although we tend to think that early education for children from low-income families began with Head Start in 1965, Owen's infant school came more than a hundred years before. Owen's legacy also lives on in the infant schools and kindergartens of England. In addition, during World War II, as an extension of Owen's ideas, the Kaiser Company built shipyard child care centers for working mothers in Richmond, California and Portland, Oregon. These were 24-hour child care centers and served nearly 4,000 children.[9]

Friedrich Wilhelm Froebel.   Friedrich Wilhelm Froebel (1782–1852) devoted his life to developing a system for educating young children. Whereas Pestalozzi, a contemporary with whom he studied and worked, advocated a system for teaching, Froebel developed a curriculum and educational methodology. In the process, Froebel earned the distinction of being called the *Father of Kindergarten.*

Froebel's primary contributions to educational thought and practice are in the areas of learning, curriculum, methodology, and teacher training. His concept of children and how they learn is based in part on the idea of unfolding. According to Froebel, the educator's role, whether parent or teacher, is to observe this natural unfolding and provide activities that will enable children to learn what they are ready to learn when they are ready to learn it. The teacher's role is to help children develop their inherent qualities for learning. In this sense, the teacher is a designer of experiences and activities.

Kindergarten.   Consistent with his idea of unfolding, Froebel compared the child to a seed that is planted, germinates, brings forth a new shoot, and grows from a young, tender plant to a mature, fruit-producing one. In so doing, he likened the role of educator to that of gardener. In his **kindergarten**, or *garden of children*, he envisioned children being educated in close harmony with their own nature and the nature of the universe. Children unfold their uniqueness in play, and it is in learning through play that Froebel makes one of his greatest contributions to the early childhood curriculum.

In 1876, a model kindergarten was on display in the first World's Fair in the United States in Fairmount Park, Pennsylvania. Ruth Burrit, a member of the Froebel Society of Boston, was the teacher and demonstrator in the Kindergarten Cottage that was a live exhibit of Froebelian kindergarten principles. Three days a week, Burrit explained and demonstrated the system to visitors to the fair as a group of orphans followed a typical kindergarten routine including games, singing, playing, and manipulating Froebel's gifts.[10]

Owen believed that infant schools were an ideal way to provide for the needs of young children while their families worked. What are some issues facing early childhood professionals today as they try to provide quality infant care for working families?

utopian The belief that by controlling circumstances and consequent outcomes of child rearing, it is possible to build a new and more perfect society.

kindergarten The name Friedrich Froebel gave to his system of education for children ages three through six; means "garden of children."

From there, parents and teachers alike took Froebel's ideas, and his gifts, back with them to their homes and schools and applied them to their lives and teaching.

Gifts and Occupations.   Froebel knew from experience that unstructured play doesn't work and that children left to their own devices may not learn much. Without guidance, direction, and a prepared environment in which to learn, there was a real possibility that little or the wrong kind of learning would occur. According to Froebel, the teacher is responsible for guidance and direction so children can become creative, contributing members of society, a value all early childhood teachers today should embrace. Today there is an emphasis on teachers having instructional leaders and intentional teachers.

As a result, Froebel developed a systematic, planned curriculum for the education of young children. Gifts, occupations, songs, and educational games were its basis. Froebel's **gifts** were objects for children to handle and explore with a teacher's supervision and guidance. Figure 4.2 identifies all ten gifts. The children formed impressions about the shapes and materials, relating them to mathematics, design (symmetry), and their own life experiences. Froebel himself named only the first six materials as gifts; his followers have since included other materials that Froebel used in his kindergarten.

Currently, there are ten sets of learning materials, or gifts, designed to help children learn through play and manipulation. The first six gifts are meant to represent solid forms, gift seven represents surfaces, gift eight represents line, gift nine represents the point, and gift ten completes the cycle with the use of point and line to represent the framework of solid forms.

Froebel's most well-known gift, the second, consists of a cube, a cylinder, and a sphere, all able to be suspended in such a way that children can examine their different properties by rotating, spinning, and touching. The sphere, because of its symmetry, has only one loop hole by which it is to be suspended. But the cube and the cylinder have multiple loop holes, so children can suspend the solids in different ways and examine the complexity of these seemingly simple shapes.

A significant idea behind the gifts is the importance for developing children's minds for examining things around them in a free but structured manner. It is not difficult to imagine three- or four-year-olds playing with the wooden solids and learning from their play.[11] Froebel's traditional gifts are still used throughout preschools and kindergartens throughout the world. In fact, can you even imagine a young child's classroom without a block center or manipulatives? Over the years, Froebel's gifts have given rise to an entire modern toy industry. Consider Lincoln Logs; oversized, large cardboard building blocks; 3-D puzzles and alphabet sets; construction sets; and Build N Roll sets.

In addition to his gifts, Froebel used **occupations**, which provide materials for craft activities, such as drawing, paper weaving, folding paper, modeling with clay, and sewing. These activities were intended to be extensions of the gifts and would enable children to create and explore different materials.

Father of the Kindergarten.   Froebel was the first educator to develop a planned, systematic program for educating young children. He envisioned the kindergarten as a place where children could and would learn through play. The idea that children could learn through play was as radical in Froebel's time as the idea that children don't need to play in order to learn is radical for today.

Froebel's supporters imported his ideas and kindergarten program, virtually intact, into the United States in the last half of the nineteenth century. Even though Froebel's ideas seem perfectly acceptable today, they were not acceptable then to those who subscribed to the notion of early education. Especially innovative and hard to accept was the idea that learning could be child centered, based on play and children's interests. Most European and American schools were subject oriented and emphasized basic skills. In addition, Froebel was the first to advocate a communal education for young children outside the home. Until Froebel, most young children were educated in the home by their

gifts Ten sets of learning materials designed to help children learn through play and manipulation.

occupations Materials designed to engage children in learning activities.

Gift 1:
Six colored balls of soft yarn or wool

Gift 2:
Wooden sphere, cylinder, and cube

Gift 3:
Eight cubes, presented together as a cube

Gift 4:
Eight rectangular pieces,
presented as a cube

Gift 5:
Twenty-one cubes, six half-cubes, and
twelve quarter-cubes

Gift 6:
Twenty-four rectangular pieces, six
columns, and twelve caps

Gift 7:
Parquetry tablets derived from the
surfaces of the gifts, including
squares, equilateral triangles, right
triangles, and obtuse triangles

Gift 8:
Straight sticks of wood, plastic, or metal
in various lengths, plus rings and half-
rings of various diameters made from
wood, plastic, or metal

Gift 9:
Small points in various colors made of
plastic, paper, or wood

Gift 10:
Materials that utilize rods and
connectors, similar to Tinker Toys

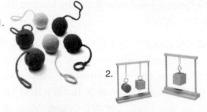

FIGURE 4.2 Froebel's Gifts

Froebel's concept of learning through play remains one of the basic principles of early childhood practice.

Source: Used by permission of Scott Bultman, Froebel Foundation USA, www.froebelfoundation.org.

mothers. The idea of educating children as a group in a special place outside the home was revolutionary.

1850–1950: From a Garden of Children to the Children's House

Contemporary early childhood programs have their roots in the past and continue to be influenced by twentieth and twenty-first century people and their ideas. For example, contrary to the popular perception that environmentalism is recent grassroots movement, "going green" has long been a part of the evolution of education. In addition, environmentalism as we know it can in part be traced back to Rousseau and his belief in going "back to nature."

Henry David Thoreau.   In 1854, Henry David Thoreau (1817–1862), an American philosopher and writer much influenced by Rousseau, published *Walden*, an exploration of people's connection to the environment, and extolled the respect and conservation of the environment. *Walden* came at a time when people were increasingly removed from the environment as the United States underwent industrialization, urbanization, and westward expansion, often to the detriment of the environment. *Walden* has been used as both an educational and environmental treatise because it establishes a connection between children and their environments. As *Walden* set the foundation for green schools, Schurz set the foundation for kindergarten in the United States.

Margarethe Schurz.   Margarethe Schurz (1833–1876) established the first kindergarten in the United States. After attending lectures in Germany on Froebelian principles, she returned to the United States and in 1856 opened her kindergarten in Watertown, Wisconsin. Schurz's program was conducted in German, as were many of the new kindergarten programs of the time. Schurz was instrumental in converting Elizabeth Peabody to the Froebelian kindergarten system.

Elizabeth Peabody.   Elizabeth Peabody (1804–1894) opened the first English-speaking kindergarten in the United States in Boston in 1860. She and her sister, Mary Mann, also published *Kindergarten Guide*. Peabody realized almost immediately that she lacked the necessary education to implement Froebel's ideas so she visited kindergartens in Germany and then returned to the United States to popularize Froebel's methods. Peabody is credited as being kindergarten's main promoter in the United States.

Susan Blow.   The first public kindergarten was founded in St. Louis, Missouri, in 1873 by Susan E. Blow (1843–1916) with the cooperation of the St. Louis superintendent of schools, William T. Harris. Endorsement of the kindergarten program by a public school system did much to increase its popularity and spread the Froebelian influence within early childhood education. Harris, who later became the U.S. Commissioner of Education, encouraged support for Froebel's ideas and methods.

progressivism Dewey's theory of education that emphasizes the importance of focusing on the needs and interests of children rather than teachers.

Patty Smith Hill.   The kindergarten movement in the United States was not without growing pains. Over a period of time, the kindergarten program, at first ahead of its time, became rigid and teacher centered rather than child centered. By the beginning of the twentieth century, many kindergarten leaders thought that programs and training should be open to experimentation and innovation rather than rigidly tied to Froebel's ideas. Susan Blow was the chief defender of the Froebelian approach. In the more moderate camp was Patty Smith Hill (1868–1946), who thought that kindergarten should remain faithful to Froebel's ideas but nevertheless be open to innovation. She believed that to survive, the kindergarten movement had to move into the twentieth century, and she was able to convince many of her colleagues of the value of kindergarten reform. More than anyone else, Hill is responsible for the kindergarten as we know it today.

John Dewey.   John Dewey (1859–1952) was very influential on education in the United States. Through his positions as professor of philosophy at the University of Chicago and Columbia University, and his extensive writing, such as *My Pedagogical Creed*, Dewey redirected the course of education in the United States.

Dewey's theory of schooling, called **progressivism**, emphasizes children and their interests rather than subject matter. From this emphasis come the terms *child-centered curriculum* and *child-centered schools*. The progressive education philosophy maintains that schools should prepare children for the realities of today rather than for some vague future time. As expressed by Dewey in *My Pedagogical Creed*, "Education, therefore, is a process of living and not a preparation for future living."[12] Thus, out of daily

John Dewey (1859–1952)

life should come the activities in which children learn about life and the skills necessary for living.

In a classroom based on Dewey's ideas, children are involved in physical activities, hands-on learning, intellectual pursuits, and social interaction. The growing child learns to use tools and materials to construct things. Dewey felt that an ideal expression for this interest was daily home and work occupations such as cooking and carpentry. Dewey also believed that social interactions with children and adults is encouraged in a democratically run classroom.

Maria Montessori.   Maria Montessori (1870–1952) devoted her life to developing an educational system that has influenced virtually all early childhood programs. She chose medicine as her career and became the first woman in Italy to earn a medical degree. She was then appointed assistant instructor in the psychiatric clinic of the University of Rome, where her work brought her into contact with children who were believed to be mentally retarded and had been committed to insane asylums.

Maria Montessori
(1870–1952)

Montessori soon became interested in educational solutions for problems such as deafness, paralysis, and "idiocy." As she said, "I differed from my colleagues in that I instinctively felt that mental deficiency was more of an educational than medical problem."[13] She wrote of her initial efforts to educate children:

> I succeeded in teaching a number of the idiots from the asylums both to read and to write so well that I was able to present them at a public school for an examination together with normal children. And they passed the examination successfully.[14]

This was a remarkable achievement, which aroused interest in both Montessori and her methods. Montessori, however, was already considering something else:

> While everyone else was admiring the progress made by my defective charges, I was trying to discover the reasons which could have reduced the healthy, happy pupils of the ordinary schools to such a low state that in the intelligence test they were on the level with my own unfortunate pupils.[15]

In 1906 Montessori was invited by the director general of the Roman Association for Good Building to organize schools for the young children of the families who occupied the tenement houses constructed by the association. In the first school, named Casa dei Bambini, or **Children's House**, she tested her ideas and gained insights into children and teaching that led to the perfection of her system.

children's house
Montessori's first school especially designed to implement her ideas.

The McMillan Sisters.   In the 1900s, President Theodore Roosevelt advanced environmentalism when he advocated for responsible use and conservation of the environment. In 1914, the McMillan sisters, Rachel and Margaret, built on Rousseau's, Thoreau's, and Roosevelt's foundation and incorporated environmentalism into their education of young children by opening an **open-air nursery school** and training centre in Peckham, England. The McMillan sisters believed in education where young children could explore their imaginations, develop their sensory and perceptual faculties, and care for gardens and pets. The first open-air nursery is recognized as a milestone in the history of the early years of education and in environmental education.

A modern and innovative equivalent to the McMillans' nursery is an educational approach to outdoor play and learning called Forest Schools. The idea, inspired by the open-air nursery, originated in Scandinavia where it is now embedded into practice, especially in the early years. British educators also became interested in the model and have for some time created similar experiences in their own education systems. The **Forest Schools** pedagogy believes that by participating in engaging, motivating, and achievable tasks and

open-air nursery school
School established by the McMillan sisters, who believed in education where young children could explore their imaginations, develop their sensory and perceptual faculties, and care for gardens and pets.

forest schools Programs with the belief that by participating in engaging, motivating, and achievable tasks and activities in a woodland environment, each child has an opportunity to develop intrinsic motivation and sound emotional and social skills.

activities in a woodland environment, each child has an opportunity to develop intrinsic motivation, and sound emotional and social skills.[16]

1950–1962: From Politics to Education

After the World Wars, education in the United States became much more influenced by political and social trends than individuals. With the advent of mass communication through radio and television, education became a movement motivated by large groups of people rather than single influential individuals. As such, it is important to understand that education always occurs within a social and political context and is often a direct outgrowth of social and political trends. The purposes of education, how we view children, and how we teach them are all influenced by what is going on in the world around us. Social and political trends of the last fifty years have created an educational culture that influenced your education and will influence you as a teacher.

Education as National Defense.   After the end of World War II in 1945 the United States and the Soviet Union became embroiled in a heated competition consisting of a nuclear arms race, a race to be first in space, and a race for world dominance. Out of this Cold War came *Sputnik.*

Sputnik The world's first satellite.

National Defense Education Act (NDEA) Provided federal funding for science, technology, engineering, math (S.T.E.M.), and foreign language education and is considered by many to be the beginning of federal standards in education.

Sputnik.   In 1957, The Soviet Union launched ***Sputnik***, the world's first satellite. *Sputnik* sparked a nationwide fear of Soviet dominion, the spread of communism, and the fall of the United States as a world power. In response to this national fear, Congress passed the **National Defense Education Act (NDEA)** of 1958. NDEA's founding idea was that the best defense is a good (educational) offense. NDEA provided federal funding for science, technology, engineering, math (S.T.E.M.), and foreign language education and is considered by many to be the beginning of federal standards in education.

The launch of *Sputnik* is important to you today because the current emphasis on science, math, and technology was born out of the race for world superiority. It resulted in amazing scientific discoveries that impact how we think about education and teaching children. Today, the worldwide race for science, technology, engineering, and mathematic superiority continues. The idea that education is a nationalistic imperative also continues. As Mark Yudof, president of the University of California, says, "The race today involves genomes and stem cells and climate models and microchips, but the goal has not changed: keep America strong in a competing world and stable and prosperous at home. And the staging ground for success also remains the same"—the education system.[17]

21st Century Skills.   The race for superiority on a global scale is also continued today by the emphasis on teaching and encouraging twenty-first century skills. Essentially, twenty-first century skills are those that are necessary for working and living in a technological environment and a rapidly changing global society. Twenty-first century skills include core subjects such as language arts, mathematics, science, global awareness, and financial literacy; but emphasize learning and invocation skills such as creativity, innovation, critical thinking, and problem solving. Other twenty-first century skills are information, media, and technology skills; and life and career skills such as taking initiative and self direction.[18]

1962–The Present: From Civil Rights to the Education of Today

In the 1960s the Civil Rights Movement permanently altered the course of education as we know it today. With the Civil Rights Movement, the federal government became ever more involved in ensuring education for all and in altering the environments of education as a whole.

Environmentalism.   Modern environmentalism is largely a product of the social movements of the 60s and 70s and the progressive politics of the federal government at the time.

In 1962, Rachel Carson published *Silent Spring*, which described and decried the environmental impacts of the spraying of DDT, a pesticide used on crops. Following the widespread popularity of *Silent Spring* between 1963 and 1968, President Johnson signed into law almost three hundred conservation and beautification measures that were supported by more than $12 billion in authorized funds. In 1969, the first Earth Day revealed the environment to be a potent political issue and one of importance to schools and children around the world.

Environmentalism is still strong in the United States today. Some might say environmentalism is stronger than ever as it is now a part of the curriculum for many schools and thus has the potential to grow and effect change on a national level from the ground up, or rather, from the child up. Based on the environmental movement, eco issues around the world, and the McMillans' pioneering efforts, schools in the United States are responding by going green! Going green in the school setting represents an attempt to save energy; conserve resources; infuse curricula with environmental education and awareness; build school gardens; and offer more healthy school lunches. Green schools are those in which the building creates a healthy environment conducive to learning while saving energy, resources, and money.

Education as Equalizer.   In the 1960s, society began to stress civil rights and the education system played a large part in assuring equality for everyone. The **Civil Rights Act of 1964** included a provision that protects the constitutional rights of individuals in public facilities, including public education. Congress amended the Civil Rights Act in 1972. The most famous of these amendments is Title IX, later discussed on page 118. The education amendments of the Civil Rights Act are now called The Equal Opportunity in Education Act.

The Economic Opportunity Act.   A part of President Lyndon B. Johnson's war on poverty was the **Economic Opportunity Act of 1964 (EOA)**. The EOA implemented several social programs to promote the health, education, and general welfare of people with low socioeconomic status and was designed to put them to work. Most of the initiatives in the act have since been modified, weakened, or altogether rolled back, but remaining programs include Head Start, Early Head Start, and the Job Corps.

The EOA provided for the beginning of Head Start in 1965. The EOA was later updated as The Head Start Act of 1981. **Head Start** is one of the longest-running programs to address systemic poverty in the United States. Its programs include Early Head Start; Head Start; Family and Community Partnerships; Migrant and Seasonal Head Start; and American Indian–Alaska Native Head Start.

Elementary Secondary Education Act.   In 1965, Congress passed the **Elementary Secondary Education Act (ESEA)** which served to more fully fund primary and secondary education. At the time, ESEA prohibited the establishment of a national curriculum. Implementing a national curriculum continues to be a hot debate topic today and is gaining full steam, as demonstrated by the Adoption of Common State Standards. As one editorial commented, the "common standards mean teaching to the best global standards of the 21st century."[19] An article in *Time* magazine agreed that, "without national standards for what our students should learn, it will be hard for the us to succeed in the 21st century economy."[20] Opponents to a national curriculum and national standards argue that the federal government is exceeding its authority and eroding state sovereignty.

Civil Rights Act of 1964
Included a provision that protects the constitutional rights of individuals in public facilities, including public education.

Economic Opportunity Act of 1964 (EOA)
Implemented several social programs to promote the health, education, and general welfare of people of low socioeconomic status, and was designed to put them to work.

Head Start One of the longest-running programs to address systemic poverty in the United States.

Elementary Secondary Education Act (ESEA)
Designed to more fully fund primary and secondary education

Head Start addresses systemic poverty in the United States. It provides comprehensive education, health, nutrition, and parent involvement services to low-income children and their families.

Title I Provided monies to help educate children from low-income families under the Elementary Secondary Education Act.

No Child Left Behind The current reauthorization of ESEA; provides federal funding for schools that accrue high test scores and meet adequate yearly progress (AYP).

Education of All Handicapped Children Act (EAHC) Mandated that in order to receive federal funds, states must develop and implement policies that assure a Free Appropriate Public Education (FAPE) for all children with disabilities.

Individuals with Disabilities Education Act The current reauthorization of the Education of All Handicapped Children Act; provides for inclusion, universal design, response to instruction and differentiated instruction.

universal design (UD) A broad-spectrum solution that produces buildings, products and environments that are usable and effective for everyone, not just people with disabilities.

response to instruction (RTI) A multi-tiered approach to the early identification and support of students with learning and behavior needs.

differentiated instruction (DI) An approach that enables teachers to plan strategically to meet the needs of every student in order teach to the needs of each child and allow for diversity in the classroom.

The ESEA of 1965 provided monies to help educate children from low-income families. This portion of the ESEA is known as **Title I**. Eligibility for Title I funds is based on children's eligibility for free or reduced-price school lunches. Funds are used to provide additional academic support and learning opportunities so that children can master challenging curricula and meet state standards in core academic subjects. For example, funds support extra instruction in reading and mathematics, as well as special preschool, after-school, and summer programs to extend and reinforce the regular school curriculum. More than 30,000 schools use Title I funds for the whole school, and at last count, Title I served more than 17 million children. Of these students, approximately 60 percent were in kindergarten through fifth grade. Therefore, it is likely that you will teach children served by Title I and teach at a Title I school.[21]

No Child Left Behind.   The current reauthorization of ESEA is the No Child Left Behind Act of 2001. The **No Child Left Behind Act (NCLB)** continues the standards movement established by the National Defense Education Act and emphasizes accountability through testing. Currently, all fifty states have standards that specify what children should know and do. NCLB provides federal funding for schools that accrue high test scores and meet adequate yearly progress (AYP), an accountability measurement. Opponents of NCLB and the accountability movement argue that it relies too heavily on standardized testing rather than authentic means of assessment. There is an ongoing discussion in the country right now concerning the reauthorization of NCLB in 2011. Bob Wise, president of the Washington-based Alliance for Excellent Education, summed up the ongoing discussion of NCLB in saying that, "in many ways, [No Child Left Behind] is a compact disc in an iPod world. It's still around, but it is in desperate need of an upgrade."[22]

The Education of All Handicapped Children Act.   In 1975, Congress passed Public Law 94-142: **The Education of All Handicapped Children Act (EAHC)**. The EAHC mandated that in order to receive federal funds, states must develop and implement policies that assure a Free Appropriate Public Education (FAPE) for all children with disabilities.

The Individuals with Disabilities Education Act.   In 1990, the Education of All Handicapped Children Act was reauthorized and renamed the **Individuals with Disabilities Education Act (IDEA)**. IDEA was reauthorized again in 1997 and 2004, and is still in effect today. IDEA provides for inclusion, **universal design (UD)** (a broad-spectrum solution that produces buildings, products, and environments that are usable and effective for everyone, not just people with disabilities); **response to instruction (RTI)** (a multi-tiered approach to the early identification and support of students with learning and behavior needs); and **differentiated instruction (DI)** (an approach that enables teachers to plan strategically to meet the needs of every student in order teach to the needs of each child and allow for diversity in the classroom). IDEA was the foundation for the integration and blending of early childhood education and early childhood special education. Today, every early childhood teacher is a special education teacher.

Providing equality education for all of the country's children continues to be one of the larger purposes of federally funded education. However, as our following discussion on the views of children shows, we are still fighting the battle of equality in the education system.

National Commission on Excellence in Education and Developmentally Appropriate Practice.   An emphasis on developmentally appropriate practice emerged in the 1980s as the nation became alarmed at the state of education. The alarm arose when the National Commission on Excellence in Education published a federal report titled *A Nation at Risk* in 1983. The report found that students in the United States were not studying the right subjects, working hard enough, or learning enough; that teachers were ill prepared; and the schools suffered from slack and uneven standards. The emphasis on developmentally appropriate practice (DAP) arose partially in response to *A Nation at Risk* in order to counterbalance the claim that "America will soon be engulfed by a rising tide of mediocrity in elementary and secondary schools" and the fear that "our social structure will crack, our culture erode, our economy totter and our national defenses weaken."[23]

Since then, education reform has become a permanaent item on the national agenda and DAP has emerged as the center of good educational practices. DAP consists of four essentials. One, DAP requires meeting children where they are so that they can reach their goals. Two, DAP is also appropriate to age and development, and is responsive to various social and cultural contexts of children's lives. Three, DAP is not only appropriate to age and development, it challenges and promotes children's growth as members of a larger society. Four, DAP is based on knowledge—research and systematic observation—not assumptions. In order for the education field to meet these four essentials of DAP, it must incorporate essentials of learning, teaching, and families.[24]

Views of Children Through the Ages

How we think about children determines how we rear them and how society responds to their needs. As you read here about how society views children, try to clarify, and change when appropriate, what you believe. Also, identify social, environmental, and political factors that tend to support each particular view. Sometimes views overlap, so it is possible to integrate ideas from several perspectives into your own particular view of children.

Miniature Adults

Childhood as we know it has not always been considered a distinct period of life. During medieval times, the notion of childhood did not exist; little distinction was made between children and adults. This concept of **children as miniature adults** was logical for the time and conditions of medieval Europe. Economic conditions did not allow for a long childhood dependency. The only characteristics that separated children from adults were size and age. Children were expected to act as adults in every way, and they did so.[25]

In many respects, twenty-first century society is no different. Children are still viewed and treated as adults. Concern is growing that childhood as we knew or remembered it is disappearing. Children are viewed as pseudo adults; they even dress like adults, in designer clothes and expensive footwear designed especially for them. Doctors are warning parents about the dangers of high heels on children's feet and minds.[26] Children as young as four years old are frequenting boutiques where they are pampered with manicures, pedicures, and the latest hair and clothing styles. Others fear that, even when allowed a childhood, children are forced to grow up too fast, too soon.[27] Lisa Spiegel, a resource center counselor, concurs, saying, "We really, really try to help families hold on to their better instincts that kids should be children and not little adults."[28]

Encouraging children to act like adults and hurrying them toward adulthood causes conflicts between capabilities and expectations, particularly when early childhood professionals demand adultlike behavior from children and set unrealistic expectations.

Sinful Children

Based primarily on the religious belief of original sin, the view of the **child as sinful** was widely accepted in the fourteenth through the eighteenth centuries, particularly in colonial North America during the Puritan era of the sixteenth and seventeenth centuries. Misbehavior was a sign of this inherent sin. Those who sought to correct misbehavior forced children to behave and used physical punishment whenever necessary. Misbehavior was taken as proof of the devil's influence, and "beating the devil out" of the child was an acceptable solution.[29]

This view of inherent sinfulness persists, manifested in the belief that children need to be controlled through strict supervision and insistence on unquestioning obedience to

children as miniature adults Belief that children are similar to adults and should be treated as such.

child as sinful View that children are basically sinful, need supervision and control, and should be taught to be obedient.

and respect for adults. Many private and parochial or religious schools emphasize respect, obedience, and correct behavior, responding to parents' hopes of rearing children who are less susceptible to the temptations of crime, drugs, and declining moral values. Many Christian religious conservatives advocate a biblical approach to child rearing, encouraging parents to raise their children to obey them. Thus, disobedience is still viewed as sinful, and obedience is promoted, in part through strict discipline, and when deemed necessary, physical punishment.

Blank Tablets

children as blank tablets View that presupposes no innate genetic code or inborn traits exist and the sum of what a child becomes depends on the nature and quality of experience.

Earlier we discussed John Locke's belief that children were born into the world as *tabulae rasae*, or blank tablets.[30] Locke believed that children's experiences determined what they learned and, consequently, what they became. The **children as blank tablets** view presupposes no innate genetic code or inborn traits; that is, children are born with no predisposition toward any behavior except what is characteristic of human beings. The sum of what a child becomes depends on the nature and quality of experience; in other words, environment is the primary determinant.

The blank tablet view has several implications for teaching and child rearing. If children are seen as empty vessels to be filled, the teacher's job is to fill them—to present knowledge without regard to needs, interests, or readiness for learning. What is important is that children learn what is taught. Children become what adults make of them.

Growing Plants

children as growing plants View of children popularized by Froebel, which equates children to plants and teachers and parents to gardeners.

A perennially popular view of children, which dates back to Rousseau and Froebel, likens them to **growing plants**, with teachers and parents performing the role of gardeners. This is why Froebel named his program kindergarten—garden of children. Classrooms and homes are gardens in which children grow and mature in harmony with their natural growth patterns. As children grow and mature, they unfold, much as a flower blooms under the proper conditions. In other words, what children become results from natural growth and a nurturing environment. Two key ingredients of this natural unfolding are play and readiness. The content and process of learning are included in play, and materials and activities are designed to promote play. Children become ready for learning through maturation and play. Lack of readiness to learn indicates that children have not sufficiently matured and the natural process of unfolding has not occurred.

Property

children as property Belief that children are literally the property of their parents.

The view of **children as property** has persisted throughout history. Its foundation is that children are the property of their parents or institutions. This view is justified in part by the idea that, as creators of children, parents have a right to them and their labors; parents have broad authority and jurisdiction over their children. Interestingly, few laws interfere with the right of parents to control their children's lives, although this situation is changing somewhat as children are given more rights as courts protect and extend children's rights.

Although difficult to enforce, laws protect children from physical and emotional abuse. In addition, where there are compulsory attendance laws, parents must send their children to school. Generally, however, parents have a free hand in dealing with their children. Legislatures and courts are reluctant to interfere in what is considered a sacrosanct parent–child relationship. A widely publicized Supreme Court decision, *Troxel v. Granville*, reaffirmed this right and declared that parents have a "fundamental right to make decisions concerning the care, custody, and control" of their children.[31] Parents are generally free to exercise full authority over their children; within certain broad limits, most parents feel their children are theirs to do with as they please.

Investments in the Future

Closely associated with the notion of children as property is the view that children represent future wealth or potential for parents and the nation. Since medieval times, people have viewed child rearing as an investment in their future. Many parents assume (not always consciously) that, when they are no longer able to work or must retire, their children will provide for them.

This view of **children as investments**, particularly in their parents' future, is being dramatically played out in contemporary society as more middle-age adults are caring for their own aging and ill parents. Also, as a result of the Great Recession of 2007–2010, many parents have found that the investment they thought they were making in their children's education is reversed with many children moving back home with their parents. About 40 percent of 2008 college graduates live with their parents and 42 percent of 2006 graduates moved back home with their parents and still live there.[32]

Over the last several decades, some U.S. social policies have been based on the view that children are future investments for society in general. Many programs are built on the underlying assumption that preventing problems in childhood leads to more productive adulthood. And many federal programs, such as Head Start, are based on the idea of conserving one of the country's greatest resources—its children.

Native American Education.   For several centuries, Native American children were not seen as part of this nation's great resource, and their appropriate education was given little attention. Today, however, attitudes are changing, and programs focus on providing high-quality education for Native American children. One such program in California, Project Nee-Sim-Pom, which is a collaborative effort that acknowledges the importance of the entire "family"—including home, school, and community—to the academic success of American Indian children.[33] There are several such projects in the United States today. Go to page 118 and read the Voice from the Field: Teaching Children Who Are Native American.

African-American Education.   As with Native Americans, African Americans have a long history of unequal early childhood education. In 1896 the case of ***Plessy v. Ferguson*** established the "separate but equal" doctrine.[34] This doctrine determined that as long as the opportunities and accommodations were equal for both races, that segregating people in public places, including schools, was lawful. This ruling legitimized a legal tradition in which the races were kept separated under the pretense of equality. However, education, as well as many other opportunities, was not equal.

The 1954 case ***Brown v. Board of Education*** overturned the *Plessy v. Ferguson* ruling and paved the way for the civil rights movement and the integration of schools and other public thoroughfares. The *Brown v. Board* ruling states,

> Segregation of children in public schools solely on the basis of race deprives children of the minority group of equal educational opportunities, even though the physical facilities and other "tangible" factors may be equal. The "separate but equal" doctrine adopted in *Plessy v. Ferguson* has no place in the field of public education.[35]

However, even since *Brown v. Board* and the Civil Rights Movement, education of African American and other minority children remains unequal. Classes of mostly minority children are "less likely than their white counterparts to be taught by teachers who know their subject matter; they are less likely to be exposed to a rich and challenging curriculum; and the schools that educate them typically receive less state and local funding than the ones serving mainly white students."[36] Many of the nation's public schools today have a minority majority and minorities are rapidly emerging as the majority of public school students.[37] Schools that are minority-heavy and of lower-income remain highly unequal in terms of funding, qualified teachers, and curriculum. As a result, Latinos and African Americans are actually more segregated today than during

children as investments
View that investing in the care and education of children reaps future benefits for parents and society.

Plessy v. Ferguson Court ruling that established the "separate but equal" doctrine, which determined that so long as the opportunities and accommodations were equal for both races, that segregating people in public places, including schools, was lawful.

Brown v. Board of Education
Court ruling that stated, "Segregation of children in public schools solely on the basis of race deprives children of the minority group of equal educational opportunities, even though the physical facilities and other 'tangible' factors may be equal. The 'separate but equal' doctrine adopted in *Plessy v. Ferguson* has no place in the field of public education."

Voice from the Field

Teaching Children Who Are Native American

As we discussed on page 117, teaching children who are Native American is very different than it used to be. Programs now focus on honoring culture and language as well as academics. For example, Irene Jones, a Native American Navajo, teaches seventeen kindergarten students who are Native American at Kenayta Primary School. Kenayta Primary serves 450 children who are Native American in kindergarten through second grade on the Navajo Nation in Kenayta, Arizona. Irene offers the following insights about what it is like to teach children who are Native American today.

My children are not as well prepared for school as I would like them to be. Half of my children come to school not knowing any alphabet or their numbers. The other half of my children know their alphabet and numbers. It is really like teaching two classes. Some of my children speak Navajo. At our school we encourage children to retain their language and culture.

I make a lot of modifications in textbooks and materials so that my children understand what they are to do. My children are very visual learners—I can't just talk—I show them everything. I show my children how to do things—I don't tell them.

Darlene Smith teaches in the Navajo Culture and Language Acquisition Program at Kenayta and has dedicated her teaching career to the preservation of Navajo culture and language.

The Navajo tribe wants to have the young children learn their language and culture. I am Navajo and I have taught bilingual now for ten years. The emphasis now is to get more Navajo people to go into teaching. This wasn't always true. This emphasis on Native Americans teaching Native Americans began in the 1980s and 1990s, and I hope it continues. We need to preserve our culture and language.

I teach students to read and write in Navajo, using a Navajo language curriculum that we developed here at Kenayta. The first thing we do is have the children learn their clans. Every child has a clan. For example, Harry Yazzie, a kindergartner, is a member of the Bitter Water Clan. By knowing his clan, he knows his heritage and where he comes from. He also learns respect for the people who he is related to.

I think it is important for Navajo children to learn their language and culture. Our language is slowly dying, and if this generation doesn't learn it, I am afraid it will be lost. This is why I am so passionate about teaching our children our culture and language.

At San Felipe Pueblo Elementary School in San Felipe Pueblo, New Mexico, all 490 children are Native American. Anna Beardsley, a native Navajo, teaches twenty-two children who are Native American.

There is a difference here at San Felipe because some of our teachers are native language speakers, so we are helping our children retain their native language. In the village and school, we encourage the students to retain the language and the culture.

We try our best to have all children achieve to their greatest potential. Our entire curriculum is aligned to the state standards, so we make sure our children are learning what the standards specify. If our children achieve at high levels, then they are more likely to be successful in the real world.

Source: Contributed by Irene Jones, Darlene Smith, and Anna Beardsley through telephone interviews with the author.

---

the Civil Rights Movement and that the most severe segregation in public schools is in the western states, including California.[38]

This inequality shows up in test scores. Review Figure 4.3 to see for yourself the correlation between school achievement and students' race/ethnicity. Minority students have lower reading and mathematics achievement scores than do Caucasian children and the nation on average. This is due in large part to the history of unequal education and opportunities, testing bias, cultural bias, and other sociocultural factors. This has a profound effect on children and our country. Research shows that the underutilization of human potential reflected in the achievement gap is very costly. In fact, the existing achievement gaps impose the economic equivalent of a permanent national recession.[39]

Gender and Education. Discrimination on the basis of gender persisted long after it was illegal on the basis of race or ethnicity. **Title IX** of the Education Amendments of 1972 stated that

> No person in the United States shall, on the basis of sex, be excluded from participation in, be denied the benefits of, or be subjected to discrimination under any program or activity receiving federal financial assistance.[40]

Title IX Amended the constitution to state, "No person in the United States shall, on the basis of sex, be excluded from participation in, be denied the benefits of, or be subjected to discrimination under any program or activity receiving federal financial assistance."

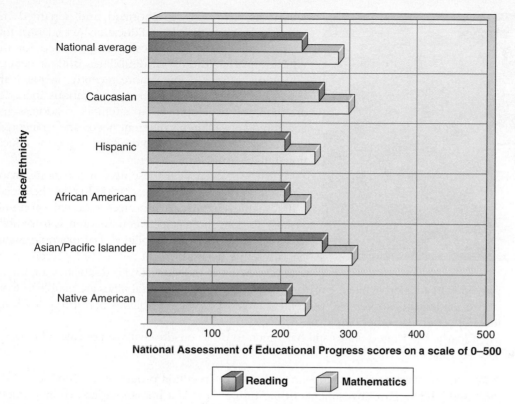

FIGURE 4.3 Reading and Mathematics Achievement Scores by Race/Ethnicity

Source: National Center for Education Statistics, National Assessment of Educational Progress (NAEP), NAEP Data Explorer, Reading Grade 4, 2007, from http://nces.ed.gov/nationsreportcard/naepdata/report.aspx.

However, even with Title IX in place, research indicates that the genders are still not equal in education. For example, there are still gaps in the test scores in areas of math and science between girls and boys[41] and there is a shortage of girls in certain science, technology, engineering, and math, or STEM-related, classes and career fields.[42] Research shows that in countries with high levels of gender equality, like Iceland, Sweden, and the UK, the math gender gap is significantly smaller, has disappeared entirely, or is even reversed.[43] Countries with low levels of gender equality have larger gender gaps in mathematics.[44] Gender inequality has a direct effect on the performance of children and gender inequality still persists in the United States with negative effects for all our children.

Children with Disabilities.   Attempting to improve the lives of those with differences is relatively new in the United States and other countries. It has not always been an American priority to accommodate differences. People with mental impairments were put in group homes, out of the public eye, and often abused. Deaf and mute children were often considered "idiots" and not worth teaching. Most communities did not have schools for children with disabilities, so if parents wanted their children with disabilities to be educated, they often had to send their children away to live in state-run (and often unregulated) group homes.[45]

The history of disabilities education has been one mostly of exclusion and separation. In attempts to address individual children's needs, separate educations were considered to be best practice. It was not until the Education for All Handicapped Children Act of 1975 that the trend slowly began to reverse.[46] This act required local education authorities to provide educational services within the community, which allowed children with disabilities to remain living with their families.[47]

Although the Education for All Handicapped Children Act might be considered the beginning of the inclusion movement and children with disabilities were finally provided access to schools within their districts, this still created two educational tracks—one for non-disabled children and a second for children with disabilities. It was not until 1990,

The Individuals with Disabilities Education Act (IDEA) supports and provides services for the education of children who have disabilities in a general education setting. What can teachers and families do to ensure children benefit from IDEA as much as possible?

when the law was reauthorized and renamed the Individuals with Disabilities Education Act (IDEA), that support and related services were provided for the education of children with disabilities in their general education settings.[48] Even more recently, inclusionary classroom practices, medication, and various therapies are the latest developments in attempts to address and accommodate children's different needs and to incorporate and accept children with disabilities into the educational mainstream.

However, even with these accommodations, many children still fall through the cracks. Just as the racial/ethnic achievement gap produces national economic results, so does the gap between children with disabilities and those without disabilities. For example, while nationally the unemployment rate is 10.1 percent, more than 62 percent of individuals with disabilities are unemployed.[49] In addition, while the myth persists that people with disabilities are unable to work or are inadequate workers, 90 percent of employees with disabilities perform at the same level or better than other employees.[50]

Clearly, the United States still has much to do to ensure that we educate all children to their fullest capacity.

A Return on Investment.   Head Start and child intervention programs are products of the view that children are investments in the future. This is a human capital, or investment, rationale for child care, preschools, and other services. Research about the HighScope Perry Preschool program is frequently cited to demonstrate how high-quality preschool programs save taxpayers money. The latest HighScope preschool research study reports that for each dollar invested, $17.07 is returned to taxpayers. This monetary return results from students who attend high-quality preschools being involved in less crime, staying in school longer, and paying higher taxes as adults.[51]

Child-Centered Education.   As the public increasingly reexamines its views of children and comes to see children as a return on investment, educators are responding by implementing more child-centered approaches. **Child-centered** is a term that means every child is a unique and special individual; all children have a right to an education that helps them grow and develop to their fullest; children are active participants in their own education and development; and teachers should consider children's ideas, preferences, learning styles, and interests in planning for and implementing instructional practices. The Whole Child Initiative, put forth by the Association for Supervision and Curriculum Development (ASCD), promotes child-centered practices because they will lead to children who are healthy, safe, engaged, supported, and challenged in their education. We redefine what a successful learner is and how we measure success by keeping in mind these guiding principles about child-centered education:[52]

child-centered Term meaning that every child is a unique and special individual; that all children have a right to an education that helps them grow and develop to their fullest; that children are active participants in their own education and development; and teachers should consider children's ideas, preferences, learning styles, and interests in planning for and implementing instructional practices.

- All children have a right to an education that helps them grow and develop to their fullest. This basic premise is at the heart of our understanding of child-centered education. Base your daily interactions with children on the fundamental question, Am I teaching and supporting each child in his/her growth and development across all domains—social, emotional, physical, linguistic, and intellectual? Such teaching is at the heart of developmentally appropriate practice.

- Every child is a unique and special individual. Consequently, teach individual children and be respectful of and account for their individual uniqueness of age, gender, culture, temperament, and learning style.

- Children are active participants in their own education and development. This means that they should be mentally involved and physically active in learning what they need to know and do.
- Consider children's ideas, preferences, learning styles, and interests in your planning for and implementation of instructional practices.

Child-centered education has been an important foundation of early childhood education since the time of Froebel. As a professional, you will want to make your teaching and practice child centered. In addition, you will want to advocate for the inherent right of every child to a child-centered education. The Voice from the Field, "How to Teach in a Child-Centered Program," on pages 122–123 is a Competency Builder that describes a real-life program and includes guidelines for involving children in active learning. After you read the feature article, look at the observation checklist. It can be a valuable tool to help you assess whether programs support child-centered learning.

All great educators have believed in the basic goodness of children; the teacher is to provide the environment for this goodness to manifest itself. A central theme of Luther, Comenius, Pestalozzi, Froebel, Montessori, and Dewey is that we must do our work as educators well, and we must really care about those whom we have been called to serve. This indeed is the essence of child-centered education.

Accommodating Diverse Learners

In this chapter, we have already discussed some of the ways in which society's views of children affect the education they receive. Throughout American history, concepts of children as a whole and of subgroups based on individual differences such as race, culture, and disability status in particular, have kept many children from receiving their rightful education. In the past, exclusionary practices were more formal. Today, exclusionary practices are not socially accepted, yet in many ways they still persist and affect children's education as revealed by the achievement and gender gaps we previously discussed.

Inclusion practices are considered by many to be in the best interest of children both with and without developmental disabilities. **Inclusion** is generally defined as educating typically developing students in the same classroom as students who have various disabilities. Although inclusion has been identified as the preferred method of delivering services to children with special needs by the Division for Early Childhood of the Council for Exceptional Children and the National Aassociation for the Education of Young Children, teachers and policy makers have yet to determine a universal model for delivering inclusive services.

Here is something you should consider: Inclusion is not just a school issue; it extends to the communities in which children and their families live. This means that you must consider not only the varying abilities and disabilities of your students, but also the context in which they occur on a larger societal level. Children's differences exist not only in the classroom, but in their homes and communities. This means that children's disabilities occur within the context of various cultures, religions, ethnicities, and socioeconomic backgrounds. As a result, like any other classroom, diversity is as much a consideration as the abilities and disabilities of your students. You should support and nourish diversity in the inclusive classroom.

You may be faced with parents and possibly other teachers who are uncomfortable with inclusion practices. "I know Ella needs to be in the classroom, too," Katherine Morris, a mother of a typically developing kindergartener in Houston, Texas, says of her daughter's classmate, Ella, who has autism. "But, sometimes I really think that she disrupts the classroom and my daughter's education gets interrupted. My daughter's education shouldn't be put in jeopardy just because Ella has autism." As a teacher, it can be difficult juggling the needs of typically developing children and children with learning differences, especially when parents are not supportive or may have concerns about

inclusion Generally defined as educating typically developing students in the same classroom as students who have various disabilities.

Voice from the Field

How to Teach in a Child-Centered Program

Observation Checklist for Child-Centered Programs

	Yes	No
Physical environment:		
Are learning centers accessible to the children?	✓	
Does the classroom arrangement support children's active learning?	✓	
Learning environment:		
Are there opportunities for cooperative learning?	✓	
Are children engaged in projects and other extended activities?	✓	
Do the learning materials . . .		
Support a wide range of children's interests?	✓	
Provide for children's different academic and social abilities?	✓	
Teaching environment: Does the teacher . . .		
Support children's efforts to explore, discover, and pursue their interests?	✓	
Make children the center of learning?	✓	
Act as a guide, facilitator, and coach?	✓	
Provide for children's individual differences based on cognitive and physical ability, culture, and gender?	✓	

The City and Country School believes an educator's greatest challenge isn't to teach children, but rather to create an environment that keeps their inherent curiosity intact. The C&C classroom serves as an ideal place for children to explore, experiment, learn, and grow, both as individuals and as a group.

In the partnership of learning among children and teachers, community is lived through purposeful experiences that foster responsibility, cooperation, active participation, care, and respect—qualities necessary to the life of a democratic society.

Lower School classrooms are equipped with ample space and an abundant supply of carefully chosen, open-ended materials, including blocks, paint, clay, paper, wood, sand, and water. These materials, along with teachers who expertly guide their use, promote children's active involvement and independence while also inspiring creativity and cooperation. Children use the materials to explore, experiment, and in the process, build a foundation in the academic disciplines of social studies, reading, writing, math, and science. As the children move through the Lower School, academic skills are taught more formally. Systematic teaching of reading begins in kindergarten.

GUIDELINE 1 Arrange the Classroom to Support Child-Centered Learning

Example: C&C teachers, rather than filling the room with teacher-driven materials, display the work and current interests of the children, such as child-created murals that may depict their social studies. Furthermore, the design of the room provides materials and space that allow children to experiment with sand and water; research their interests with books; and recreate their learning through blocks, clay, woodshop materials, artwork, writing, and dramatic play.

GUIDELINE 2 Provide Easily Accessible Materials and Supplies

Example: The classrooms at C&C are simple in design, with child-accessible shelves filled with clearly

the quality of their children's education. But inclusion teacher Meredith Brandon-Garcia maintains that the children in her classroom benefit from inclusion. "Ella has really improved. She used to have meltdowns almost every day. In the beginning, it was really difficult—it took a lot of work on my part, but I think it's paying off. Ella is learning and is a part of the group. She's getting the education and the peer interaction she deserves. But the others are doing well, too. At first, the other students weren't sure about Ella. But now Ella is a part of the group, and I've really noticed that the other kids are much more

labeled and organized open-ended materials and tools. The children keep their spaces orderly, and are responsible for classroom tasks such as distributing snacks and cleaning tables. In this and other ways, the children have ownership of their space.

3 Provide Opportunities for Children to Move Around and Engage in Active Learning

Example: Woodworking, block, and dramatic play offer children opportunities to use their bodies and minds. For example, starting in the fours, children start working with real woodworking tools in their classroom. If they want a boat or a car to use in their play, they can create one. By trusting children to achieve their visions in such a substantial way, they gain a tremendous sense of autonomy, accomplishment, and respect. Furthermore, children at C&C are not restricted to sitting at a desk or table as they find a comfortable way to work.

4 Provide Materials and Space for Focused Hands-On Activities

Example: As social studies topics are explored in-depth, children engage in active learning by first exploring their ideas through research, such as trips, and then reconstructing their knowledge in any number of ways. For example, as the sixes learn about transportation, they may visit Grand Central Station, where they use research logs to take notes of their observations (in pictures or writing). They later might create books based on their research, and then plan, build, and accessorize a large-scale Grand Central Station and railroads with blocks and art materials.

5 Arrange Furniture so That Children Can Work and Play Together

Example: Tables and workspaces are provided so children can work together, side by side and across from one another, rather than in desks and rows. C&C classrooms also provide ample open space for children to work with blocks and on large-scale group work, such as murals.

6 Support Cooperative Learning

Example: Our youngest children share materials, space, and group responsibilities. When children ages four and older recreate their research and interests in blocks or plays, they share and discuss what they've learned as a group, then plan the layout and design, or scripts and sets, together as a whole group, and work on smaller, discrete tasks in small groups. In this way, the goals of the whole group are achieved in a variety of social configurations and contexts for democratic decision making.

7 Provide for Individual Differences and Individualized Instruction

Example: After studying the operations of a restaurant, the six-year-old children plan the opening of a real restaurant in the classroom. They can work on areas of specific interest to them, such as cooking, menu creation, organizing the space, practicing communicating with their customers, and writing down orders, thus allowing each child to take ownership of his or her learning. Teachers work alongside the child and challenge each child to explore his or her strengths and take time to work on areas where he or she is less experienced.

8 Provide Ample Time for Children to Engage in Cooperative Activities

Example: As the eights learn multiplication tables, they are also working on opening the school post office. In order to quickly tally orders, they must know their multiplication tables. This real-world need for a rote skill solidifies the knowledge in a concrete activity, while group-mates are relying on them to keep the post office running smoothly. The motivation to learn the math facts is intrinsic to the group's need and to the job at hand.

City and Country School remains committed to its founding principles and continues to promote and exemplify progressive education.

....
Source: Contributed by Jennifer Moran, Director of Publications and Archives, City and Country School, New York, New York.

responsive and respectful of differences. I think this arrangement has improved education for everyone—not just Ella."

How can you make inclusion work in your classroom? Here are some pointers from Meredith:

- Inclusive classrooms don't exist in isolation; cooperation is key. Adults—teachers, parents, administrators, and other professionals—must collaborate to train one another, plan, support, and respond to challenges.

- Get the parents involved. Inclusion cannot occur just in the classroom. If a concerned parent like Katherine either explicitly or implicitly discourages the inclusion of Ella into the classroom, her attitude will likely be picked up by her daughter and may be reflected in the classroom. Inclusion, like all social movements, starts at home.

  - At the beginning of the year, invite the parents of your classroom to a meeting and encourage the parents of children with differences to discuss their story. What has it been like for Ella? What have been her struggles and triumphs? What are Ella's gifts that make her special? The more parents can identify with Ella as a child and with her parents as advocates, the more they can empathize and approach inclusion as a positive experience.
  - Assure your parents that you consider the needs of all of the children to be of equal and paramount importance. Your goal is to make the school year beneficial and positive for everyone. Encourage parents to come to you with their concerns or questions and remember to respect their roles as parents.
  - The process of building an inclusion experience may be rocky at times. Ask for patience and support, and be up-front about your needs as a teacher. Do you want volunteers or parent aides? Let the parents know. Frustration on the parents' part is likely to come from a sense of powerlessness or inactivity. If you let parents know that you not only value their concerns and time, but would value their help, input, and contributions, the road will be much smoother.
  - Tell parents that you have a zero-tolerance policy when it comes to bullying and teasing. Ask that they help to carry over this policy in their homes.

- The inclusive classroom is a starting point for children, not something they have to earn. Remember, each child has the right to an equal education. This means that if a child lacks certain skill sets, like toilet training, has a communication deficit, or has difficulty transitioning, the program needs to accommodate the child; the child does not accommodate the program. Inclusion classrooms are a place in which children are encouraged, and when necessary, helped, to participate.

- Support inclusion in your classroom in these ways:

  - Arrange the classroom in a way that is accessible to a student like Ella. Make sure that his or her schedule is individualized, visual, and easily accessible. Be sure to provide a quiet place where he or she can recuperate from meltdowns or sensory overload.
  - On the first day of class, have students sit in a circle and share about themselves. Let children tell their classmates their names, where they are from, something they are good at and something that is difficult for them. This sharing establishes from the beginning a positive sense of differences and similarities.

Activities for Professional Development

Ethical Dilemma

"More segregated than ever."

Amy Mendez is a second grade teacher at Westside Elementary School. The majority of her students are minority children from low socioeconomic families. Amy believes in the potential of her students, but she is continually frustrated by her students' educational opportunities. Her 43 students have to share texts that are outdated. Her classroom activities are limited by the fact that Amy doesn't have enough materials. As a school, the students don't perform well on achievement tests, so Amy hasn't had a raise in five years because pay is related to student achievement, and she can't make rent. Amy visited classrooms in an area of town that is more affluent and predominantly Caucasian. Amy found the classroom well supplied with SMART Boards, laptops, and books of every description. In addition, the class sizes average half of

Amy's. Amy also learns that in one of the schools, a teacher is retiring and she wonders if she should apply for the job.

Should Amy stay with her children that desperately need and deserve a high-quality education? Or, should Amy make a career move to the other side of town that will pay more and provide her with exciting teaching possibilities?

What should Amy do? Should she complain to her principal? The Board of Education? Apply for a new job or stay? What would you do?

Activities to Apply What You Learned

1. Take a closer look at Froebel and the kindergarten at www.froebelfoundation.org/index.html. Create an online discussion with your classmates and explore these topics: (a) why the history of early childhood education is important; (b) why play and learning were considered a radical idea in Froebel's time; (c) the religious basis for Froebel's gifts and occupations; and (d) how and why the kindergarten as envisioned by Frobel is so different from kindergarten in the United States today.
2. Which two historical figures do you think have had the greatest influence on early childhood education throughout history? State your opinion as your status on Facebook and ask your friends to comment. What is the general consensus?
3. Using an online image search engine such as Google or Bing, look for current photos that reflect how society has viewed children through the ages (i.e., type in the search bar, "sinful children," or "children as miniature adults," etc.). Which one is the most prevalent today? Share your findings with your classmates in a Facebook note.
4. Skype with an inclusion teacher in your local school district. Take the opportunity to ask him/her any questions or concerns you may have about inclusion practices. Then use Skype to observe the classroom. What are some ways that the environment reflects the teacher's inclusion practices? Post your findings on your blog.

Linking to Learning

John Amos Comenius
www.comeniusfoundation.org/
Biographical information with facts and quotes about Comenius.

John Dewey
www.siu.edu/~deweyctr/

The Center for Dewey Studies; offers online documents about Dewey, numerous links, and instructions for joining a mailing list.

Friedrich Wilhelm Froebel
www.infed.org/thinkers/et-froeb.htm
Biography and bibliography of the father of the kindergarten.

John Locke
www.iep.utm.edu/locke/
The Internet Encyclopedia of Philosophy's entry on John Locke, including his writings and a list of sources.

Martin Luther
www.educ.msu.edu/homepages/laurence/reformation/Luther/Luther.htm
Provides links to many of Luther's writings online.

Maria Montessori
www.webster.edu/~woolflm/montessori.html
Historical perspective of her life and teaching methods.

Robert Owen
www.infed.org/thinkers/et-owen.htm
A bibliography of writings by Robert Owen.

Jean Heinrich Pestalozzi
www.infed.org/thinkers/et-pest.htm
A page about Pestalozzi similar to that about Rousseau.

Jean-Jacques Rousseau
www.infed.org/thinkers/et-rous.htm
Contains a brief statement on education by Rousseau and links to other Rousseau sites.

Go to Topic 1 (History) in the MyEducationLab (www.myeducationlab.com) for your course, where you can:

- Find learning outcomes for History along with the national standards that connect to these outcomes.
- Complete Assignments and Activities that can help you more deeply understand the chapter content.
- Apply and practice your understanding of the core teaching skills identified in the chapter with the Building Teaching Skills and Dispositions learning units.
- Check your comprehension on the content covered in the chapter by going to the Study Plan in the Book Resources for your text. Here you will be able to take a chapter quiz, receive feedback on your answers, and then access Review, Practice, and Enrichment activities to enhance your understanding of chapter content.

5

THEORIES APPLIED TO TEACHING AND LEARNING
Foundations for Practice

naeyc standards

Standard 1. Promoting Child Development and Learning

I apply my knowledge of contemporary theory and research to construct learning environments that provide achievable and stretching experiences for all children—including children with special abilities and children with disabilities.[1]

Standard 4. Using Developmentally Effective Approaches to Connect with Children and Families

I understand the theories and research that support the importance of relationships and high quality interactions in early education. I ground my curriculum in a set core of approaches to teaching that are supported by research and are closely linked to the processes of early development and learning.[2]

This chapter discusses the pioneering work of theorists who have contributed to our knowledge and understanding of how children learn, *grow*, and develop. They have laid the foundation for the practice of *constructivism*, which is based on the theory that children literally construct their knowledge of the world and their level of cognitive functioning. Constructivist theorists include Jean Piaget, Lev Vygotsky, and Howard Gardner. In addition, this chapter discusses the psychosocial theory of Erik Erikson, the basic needs theory of Abraham Maslow, and the cultural context theory of Urie Bronfenbrenner.

Theories of Learning and Development

Teaching without an understanding of learning theories and about how children learn and develop is like driving off the highway with no idea of where you are going. Learning theories guide and direct us on the roadways of teaching. Sure, off-roading can be good weekend fun, but when you are serious about where you want to go, you can't beat an interstate highway! The same is true of using theories of learning to guide your professional practice.

Learning

How do you learn? How do children learn? We take learning for granted and frequently don't pay much attention to *how* learning occurs. But your beliefs about how children learn plays a major role in the curriculum you select for them and the way you teach them. Think for a moment about how you would define *learning* and what learning means to you. For some the ability to learn is a sign of intelligence. For others it means the grades children bring home on their report cards. For many parents, learning is the answer to the question, "What did you learn in school today?"

For our purposes, **learning** refers to the cognitive and behavioral changes that result from experiences. The experiences that make up the curriculum are at the core of the learning process. The experiences you provide for children should be based on a theory or theories of how children learn.

learning Cognitive and behavioral changes that result from experiences.

How will you know whether or not children are learning? How will you know what children are learning? You can determine whether learning occurs in a number of ways: by observing what each child is doing, by noting how a child is interacting with other children, by interpreting the results of achievement tests, and by reading stories children have written.

Theories

A **theory** is a statement of principles and ideas used to explain how things happen. In our case, theories explain how children learn and develop. For example, many professionals use Jean Piaget's theory of cognitive development as a basis for developing curriculum and guiding practice. His theory is very influential and is applied to many early childhood programs, such as HighScope. In fact, Piaget's theory is used more often than any other theory to explain children's thinking and learning and to guide program development.

theory A set of explanations of how children develop and learn.

Learning theories such as Piaget's are an important part of your professional practice for a number of reasons. Let's review them.

- *Communication:* Theories enable you to explain to others, especially families, the complex process of learning and what you and they can expect of children. Communicating with clarity and understanding to parents and others about how children learn is one of the most important jobs for all early childhood professionals. To do this, you need to know the theories that explain how children develop and learn.

> " Children's minds, if planted in fertile soil, will grow quite naturally on their own. "
>
> **JEAN PIAGET**

- *Evaluation:* Theories enable you to evaluate children's learning. Theories describe behaviors and identify what children are able to do at certain ages. You can use this information to evaluate learning and plan for teaching. Evaluation of children's learning is another important job for all teachers.

- *Guidance:* Theories help us understand how, why, where, and when learning occurs. As a result, they guide you in developing programs for children that support and enhance their learning. For example, what Piaget believed about how children learn directly influences classroom arrangements and what is taught and how it is taught. Developing programs and curriculum is an important part of your professional practice.

Children are dynamic individuals. Their learning involves the dynamic interaction of all developmental areas—physical, social/emotional, linguistic, cognitive, and spiritual. So, while we learn about children's cognitive development, we cannot forget that cognitive development is influenced by the other domains of development as well. Children are in a constant state of being influenced and changed by their environment, their experiences, their health and nutrition, and their genetic backgrounds, which influence how they think. Thinking serves an adaptive purpose: it enables children to devise plans for attaining goals. However, attaining goals also requires the ability to take action; without this ability, thinking would be pointless. What purpose would it serve for an infant to figure out that she needed to remove an obstacle to get a toy if she were incapable of moving an obstacle and reaching for and grasping a toy? As this analysis implies, any variable that influences an infant's ability to execute the plan—for example, her ability to accurately perceive the toy's position and to maintain a stable posture while reaching—would influence her likelihood of achieving the goal. This connection between thinking and acting is very important in our discussion of cognitive development and constructivism.[3]

Constructivism

constructivism Theory that emphasizes the active role of children in developing their understanding and learning.

Constructivism is the cognitive theory of development and learning based on the ideas of John Dewey, Jean Piaget, and Lev Vygotsky. The *constructivist approach* supports the belief that children actively seek knowledge; it explains children's cognitive development, provides guidance for how and what to teach, and provides direction for how to arrange learning environments.

> Constructivism is defined in terms of the individual's organizing, structuring and restructuring of experience—an ongoing lifelong process—in accordance with existing schemes of thought. In turn, these very schemes become modified and enriched in the course of interaction with the physical and social world.[4]

Basic Concepts. These are basic constructivist concepts you can use to guide your work with young children:

- Children construct their own knowledge based on what they already know (their prior knowledge).
- Children are active agents who problem-solve and think for themselves.
- Children's experiences with people, places, and things provide a framework for their construction of knowledge.
- Children learn best through experiences and activities that they initiate and find interesting.
- Teaching and learning are child centered.

The Constructivist Classroom. The constructivist classroom is child centered and learning centered. Children in a constructivist classroom:

- Are physically and mentally active.
- Are encouraged to initiate learning activities.

- Are partners with teachers in learning.
- Carry on dialogues and conversations with peers, teachers, and other adults.

Teachers in a constructivist classroom:

- Create and support children's social interactions with peers, teachers, and other adults to provide a context for cognitive development and learning.
- Provide rich social environments characterized by children's collaboration, projects, problem solving, and cooperative learning.
- Arrange classroom desks, tables, and learning centers to support student collaboration and social interaction.
- Create a classroom climate of mutual respect and cooperation.
- Are partners with children in learning.
- Provide guided assistance (see scaffolding discussion later in this chapter).
- Link children's prior knowledge and experiences with current classroom activities and experiences.

We discuss constructivism more throughout the chapter and show how to apply it to your teaching and classroom practice.

Piaget and Constructivist Learning Theory

Jean Piaget's (1896–1980) theory is about cognitive development; it explains how children think, understand, and learn. His theory is basically a logicomathematical theory; that is, cognitive development is perceived as consisting primarily of logical and mathematical abilities, such as numeration, seriation, clarification, and temporal relationships.

Generally, the term *intelligence* suggests intelligence quotient, or IQ—that which is measured on an intelligence test. But this is not what Piaget means by intelligence. Instead, intelligence is the cognitive, or mental, process by which children acquire knowledge; hence intelligence is "to know." It is synonymous with thinking in that it involves the use of mental operations developed as a result of acting mentally and physically in and on the environment.

Active involvement is basic to Piaget's cognitive theory; through direct experiences with the physical world, children develop intelligence. Other basic concepts of Piaget's theory include *active learning*, *adaptation*, *schemes*, *assimilation*, and *accommodation*.

Active Learning

Active learning is an essential part of constructivism. Active learning means that children construct knowledge through physical and mental activity and that they are actively involved in problem-setting and problem-solving activities.

Think for a minute about what would happen if you gave six-month-old Emily some blocks. What would she try to do with them? More than likely, she would put them in her mouth; she would try to eat the blocks. But if you gave blocks to Emily's three-year-old sister Madeleine, she would try to stack them. Both Emily and Madeleine want to be actively involved with things and people as active learners. Active involvement comes naturally for all children and is an essential part of how they learn.

active learning theory The view that children develop knowledge and learn by being physically and mentally engaged in learning activities.

Adaptation

The adaptive process operates at the cognitive level much as it does at the physical level. A newborn's intelligence is expressed through reflexive motor actions such as sucking,

adaptation The process of building schemes through interaction with the environment. Consists of two complementary processes—assimilation and accommodation.

schemes Organized units of knowledge.

grasping, head turning, and swallowing. Children develop their intelligence through this process of **adaptation** to the environment via reflexive actions.[5]

Through interactions with their environment, children organize sensations and experiences. The quality of the environment and the nature of children's experiences play a major role in the development of their intelligence.

Schemes.   **Schemes** refer to organized units of knowledge that children develop through the adaptation process. Infants use their reflexive actions such as sucking and grasping to build their concepts and understanding of the world.

In the process of developing new schemes, Piaget ascribed primary importance to physical activity. Physical activity leads to mental stimulus, which in turn leads to mental activity. There is not a clear line between physical and mental activity in infancy and early childhood. Consequently, early childhood teachers provide for active learning by arranging classrooms to allow children to explore and interact with people and objects.

assimilation The process of fitting new information into existing schemes.

Assimilation and Accommodation.   **Assimilation** is the taking in of sensory data through experiences and impressions and incorporating this information into existing knowledge of people and objects as a result of previous experiences.[6] Through assimilation, children use old methods or experiences to understand and make sense of new information and experiences. Emily used assimilation when she put a block in her mouth and ended up sucking on it. The block was fine for sucking but not for eating.

accommodation Changing or altering existing schemes or creating new ones in response to new information.

Accommodation is the process by which children change their way of thinking, behaving, or believing to come into accord with reality. Accommodation involves changing old methods to adjust to new situations. Whereas Emily tried to eat the blocks, Madeleine wanted to stack them. Through accommodation she had learned not to try to eat them. Bobby, who is familiar with kittens and cats because he has several cats at home, may, upon seeing a dog for the first time, call it a kitty. He has assimilated dog into his organization of kitty. However, Bobby must change (i.e., accommodate) his model of what constitutes "kittyness" to exclude dogs. He will start to construct, or build, a scheme for dog and thus what "dogness" represents.[7] The twin processes of assimilation and accommodation, viewed as an integrated and functioning whole, constitute adaptation. Figure 5.1 demonstrates the assimilation and accommodation process as Santiago learns to ride a bike.

equilibrium A balance between existing and new schemes, developed through assimilation and accommodation of new information.

Equilibrium.   **Equilibrium** is a balance between assimilation and accommodation. Children assimilate, or fit, new data into their already-existing knowledge (i.e., scheme) of reality and the world. If the new data can be immediately assimilated, then equilibrium occurs. However, if children are unable to assimilate the new data easily, they try to accommodate their way of thinking, acting, or perceiving to account for the new data and restore equilibrium to their intellectual system.

Children have difficulty with assimilation and accommodation when new experiences are radically different from their past experiences. For this reason Piaget insisted that new experiences must have a connection to previous experiences. It is imperative that you learn and understand as much as possible about the children you teach—their culture, family, and community—so that you can tap into and expand on their past experiences.

Developmentally Appropriate Practice

The National Association for the Education of Young Children believes, as Piaget believed, that children are thinking, moving, feeling and interacting human beings.[8] As such, developmentally appropriate practice involves considering and fostering children's cognitive development. Piaget believed development occurred in stages and the NAEYC supports this belief in stating that "development proceeds toward greater complexity, self-regulation, and symbolic or representational capacities."[9] Developmentally appropriate teaching involves reaching children at their developmental level, or stage, while challenging them to grow, and when ready, to proceed to their next stage of development. As you read about Piaget's

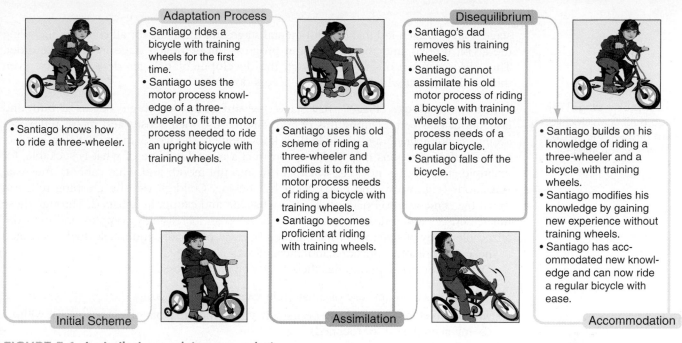

FIGURE 5.1 Assimilation and Accommodation

stages, reflect upon how Piaget's theory of progressive intellectual development influences modern concepts of what is developmentally appropriate practice.

Piaget's Stages of Intellectual Development

Figure 5.2 summarizes Piaget's first three developmental stages, provides examples of stage-related characteristics, and gives suggestions of ways that teachers can support each

I. The Sensorimotor Stage (Birth to about two years)

Characteristics:
Children use their innate sensorimotor systems of sucking, grasping, and gross-body activities to build schemes. In addition, children "solve" problems by playing with toys and using everyday "tools" such as a spoon to learn to feed themselves.

Teachers' Role:
- Provide interactive toys, such as rattles, mobiles, and pound-a-peg.
- Provide many and varied multisensory toys to promote investigation and sensory involvement; include household items such as pots, pans, and spoons.
- Provide environments in which infants and toddlers can crawl and explore, keeping infants out of their cribs as much as possible.

II. The Preoperational Stage (2–7 years)

Characteristics:
Children depend on concrete representations and "think" with concrete materials. Children in this stage enjoy accelerated language development. They are very egocentric in thought and action and therefore tend to internalize events. Children think everything has a reason or purpose. Children are perceptually bound and therefore make judgments based primarily on how things look.

Teachers' Role:
- Provide many and varied kinds of manipulative materials, such as puzzles, counters, and clay.
- Provide many concrete learning materials and activities.
- Provide many developmentally appropriate language opportunities involving speaking, listening, reading, and writing.

III. The Concrete Operations Stage (7–17 years)

Characteristics:
Children are able to reverse their thought processes and conserve and understand numbers. They begin to structure time and space and to think logically. In this stage, children can apply logic to concrete situations.

Teachers' Role:
- Give students a chance to manipulate and test objects.
- Use familiar examples to explain more complex ideas.
- Give opportunities to classify and group objects and ideas on increasingly complex levels.

FIGURE 5.2 Piaget's Stages of Cognitive Development

Source: Based on Anita Woolfolk, *Educational Psychology*, 11th ed. (Upper Saddle River, NJ: Prentice Hall, 2009). Photos by Krista Greco/Merrill (top) and courtesy of the Centenary of the Montessori Movement (center and bottom).

stage. Piaget contended that developmental stages are the same for all children, including the atypical child, and that all children progress through each stage in the same order. Thus the sequence of growth through the developmental stages does not vary, even though the ages at which progression occurs do vary.

sensorimotor stage The stage during which children learn through the senses and motor activities.

Sensorimotor Stage.   Piaget's first stage, the **sensorimotor stage**, begins at birth and lasts about two years. During this period children use their senses and motor reflexes— seeing, sucking, grasping—to build their knowledge of the world and to develop intellectually. Reflexive actions help children construct a mental scheme of what is suckable, for example, and what is not (i.e., what can fit into the mouth and what cannot) and what sensations (e.g., warm and cold) occur by sucking. Children use the grasping reflex in much the same way to build schemes of what can and cannot be grasped. Through these innate sensory and reflexive actions, they develop an increasingly complex and individualized hierarchy of schemes. What children become physically and intellectually is related to these sensorimotor functions and interactions.

The sensorimotor period has these major characteristics:

- Dependence on and use of innate reflexive actions
- Initial development of object permanency (i.e., the idea that objects can exist without being seen, heard, or touched)
- Egocentricity, whereby children see themselves as the center of the world and believe events are caused by them
- Dependence on concrete representations (i.e., things) rather than symbols (i.e., words, pictures) for information
- By the end of the second year, less reliance on sensorimotor reflexive actions, and a beginning use of symbols for things that are not present

preoperational stage The stage of cognitive development in which young children are capable of mental representations.

Preoperational Stage.   Piaget's second stage, the **preoperational stage**, begins at age two and ends at approximately seven years.

Representation.   During the preoperational stage, one of the child's major accomplishments is the ability to use symbols to represent objects and events—symbols such as language, pictures, picture books, maps, drawings, and make-believe play. At about age two, children's ability to use language rapidly accelerates, and at about age three they begin to understand that a picture of a house, for example, stands for a house in the real world. This ability to think symbolically, to visualize things mentally, opens many opportunities for children to develop cognitively and increases their knowledge of their environment.

Children in the preoperational stage make judgments based on how things look. When they look at an object that has multiple characteristics—such as a long, round, yellow pencil—they see whichever of those qualities first catches their eye. Thus their knowledge is based mainly on what they are able to see, simply because they do not yet have *operational* intelligence, or the ability to think logically.

Conservation.   The absence of operations makes it impossible for preoperational children to *conserve*, or determine that the quantity of an object does not change simply because a transformation occurs in its physical appearance. For example, if you show preoperational children two identical rows of coins (see Figure 5.3) and ask whether each row has the same number of coins, the children should answer affirmatively. If you then space out the coins in one row and ask whether the two rows still have the same number of coins, they might insist that more coins are in one row because it's longer. These children are basing their judgment on what they can see—namely, the spatial extension of one row beyond the other row. This example also illustrates that preoperational children are not able to *reverse* thought or action, which requires mentally putting the row back to its original length. Figure 5.3 shows other examples of conservation tasks.

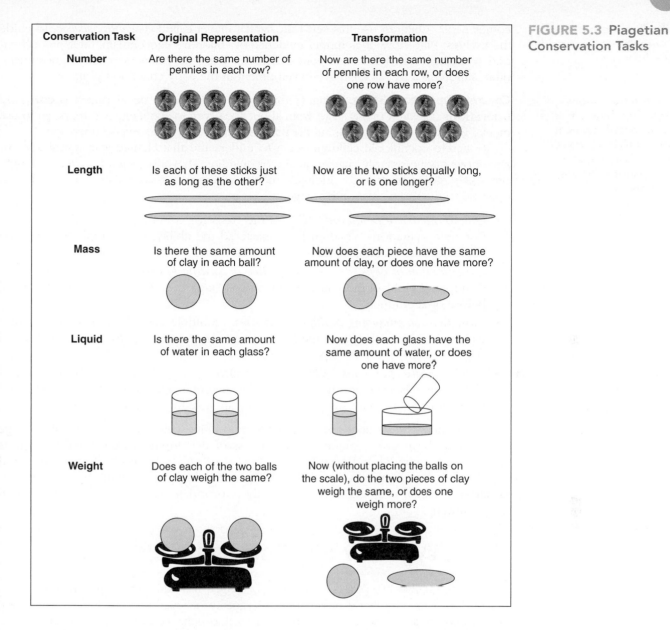

FIGURE 5.3 Piagetian Conservation Tasks

Conservation Task	Original Representation	Transformation
Number	Are there the same number of pennies in each row?	Now are there the same number of pennies in each row, or does one row have more?
Length	Is each of these sticks just as long as the other?	Now are the two sticks equally long, or is one longer?
Mass	Is there the same amount of clay in each ball?	Now does each piece have the same amount of clay, or does one have more?
Liquid	Is there the same amount of water in each glass?	Now does each glass have the same amount of water, or does one have more?
Weight	Does each of the two balls of clay weigh the same?	Now (without placing the balls on the scale), do the two pieces of clay weigh the same, or does one weigh more?

In addition, preoperational children believe and act as though everything happens for a specific reason or purpose. This explains children's constant and recurring questions about why things happen and how things work.

Egocentrism. Preoperational children believe that everyone thinks as they think and acts as they do for the same reasons. They have a hard time putting themselves in another's place, and it is difficult for them to be sympathetic and empathetic. The way preoperational children talk reflects their *egocentrism.* For example, in explaining about his dog running away, three-year-old Matt might say something like this: "And we couldn't find him . . . and my dad he looked . . . and we were glad." Matt assumes you have the same point of view he does and know the whole story. The details are missing for you, not for Matt.

Young children's egocentrism also helps explain why they tend to talk at each other rather than with each other and why they talk to themselves. Perhaps you have observed a four-year-old busily engrossed in putting a puzzle together and saying, "Which piece

self-talk Speech directed to oneself that helps guide one's behavior.

comes next?" Children use this **self-talk**, which Piaget called *egocentric speech*, to guide themselves. Piaget saw it as further evidence of children's egocentrism, their preoccupation with their own needs and concerns rather than the views of others. Egocentrism, quite simply, is a fact of cognitive development in the early childhood years.

Concrete Operations Stage.   Piaget's third stage of cognitive development is **concrete operations**. Children in this stage, from about age seven to about age twelve, begin to use mental images and symbols during the thinking process and can reverse operations.

concrete operations stage The stage of cognitive development during which children's thought is logical and can organize concrete experiences.

Concrete operational children begin to understand that change in physical appearance does not necessarily change quality or quantity. They also begin to reverse thought processes, going back and undoing a mental action just accomplished. Other mental operations are also typical of this stage:

- *One-to-one correspondence.*   This is the basis for counting and matching objects. Concrete operational children have mastered the ability, for example, to give one cookie to each classmate and a pencil to each member of their work group.
- *Classification of objects, events, and time according to certain characteristics.*   For example, a child in the concrete operations stage can classify events as occurring before or after lunch.
- *Classification involving multiple properties.*   Multiple classification occurs when a child can classify objects on the basis of more than one property, such as color and size, shape and size, or shape and color.
- *Class inclusive operations.*   Class inclusion also involves classification. For example, if children in this stage are shown five apples, five oranges, and five lemons and asked whether there are more apples or fruit, they are able to respond with "fruit."

The concrete stage does not represent a period into which children suddenly emerge after having been preoperational. The process of development from stage to stage is gradual and continual and occurs over a period of time as a result of maturation and experiences. No simple sets of exercises will cause children to move up the developmental ladder. Rather, ongoing developmentally appropriate activities lead to conceptual understanding.

Vygotsky and Sociocultural Theory

Lev Vygotsky (1896–1934), a contemporary of Piaget, has had increasing influence on the practices of early childhood professionals. Vygotsky believed that children's mental, language, and social development is supported by and enhanced through social interaction. This view is the opposite of the Piagetian perspective, which sees children as much more solitary developers of their own intelligence and language. For Vygotsky, "Learning awakens a variety of developmental processes that are able to operate only when the child is interacting with people in his environment and in collaboration with his peers. Once these processes are internalized, they become part of the child's independent developmental achievement."[10] Vygotsky further believed that beginning at birth, children seek out adults for social interaction and that development occurs through these interactions.

Zone of Proximal Development

zone of proximal development (ZPD) The range of tasks that are too difficult to master alone but that can be learned with guidance and assistance.

For early childhood professionals, one of Vygotsky's most important concepts is the **zone of proximal development (ZPD),** which he defines as follows:

> The area of development into which a child can be led in the course of interaction with a more competent partner, either adult or peer. [It] is not some clear-cut space that exists independently of joint activity itself. Rather, it is the difference between what the child can

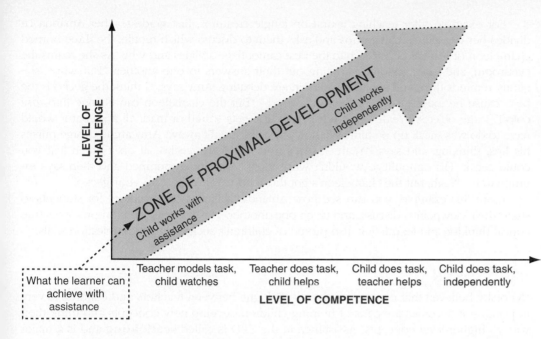

FIGURE 5.4 Teaching and Learning in the Zone of Proximal Development

Scaffolding occurs through the support of the more competent other. Think about some of the ways you and other more competent persons—such as peers, siblings, and parents—can help children master tasks within this zone.

accomplish independently and what he or she can achieve in conjunction with another, more competent person. The zone is thus created in the course of social interaction.[11]

Thus the zone of proximal development represents the range of tasks that children cannot do independently but can do when helped by a more competent person—teacher, adult, or another child. Tasks below the ZPD children can learn independently. Tasks, concepts, ideas, and information above the ZPD children are not yet able to learn, even with help. Figure 5.4 illustrates the ZPD.

In addition, Vygotsky believed that learning and development constitute a dynamic and interactive process:

> Learning is not development; however, properly organized learning results in mental development and sets in motion a variety of developmental processes that would be impossible apart from learning. Thus, learning is a necessary part and universal aspect of the process of developing culturally organized, specifically human, psychological functions.[12]

In other words, learning drives or leads development; the experiences children have influence their development. For this reason it is important for teachers and parents to provide high-quality learning experiences for all children.

In addition, teachers have to create zones of proximal development by creating environments in which children can learn new behaviors and skills in collaboration with others.

Intersubjectivity

Intersubjectivity, another Vygotskian concept, is based on the idea that

> [I]ndividuals come to a task, problem, or conversation with their own subjective ways of making sense of it. If they then discuss their differing viewpoints, shared understanding may be attained. . . . In other words, in the course of communication participants may arrive at some mutually agreed-upon, or intersubjective, understanding.[13]

The implication for early childhood education is that social interaction among students and between teachers and students in the classroom promotes learning.[14] When you provide opportunities for children to socially engage in small groups, you support intersubjectivity.

intersubjectivity A Vygotskian theory based on the idea that individuals come to a task, problem, or conversation with their own subjective experiences and ways of thinking. Through discussing their different viewpoints, children can build a shared understanding.

For example, after teaching a unit on jungle creatures, first grade teacher Amanda Le divides her class into small groups and asks them to discuss which reptile, the three-horned chameleon or leaf-tailed gecko, had the best camouflage abilities and why. As she roams the classroom, she hears children shouting out their answers to one another. "But why?" she gently reminds them and soon the children are debating. Amy says, "I think the gecko is the best 'cause he looks just like a leaf and wood." "But the chameleon can change into *any* color!" Jorge objects. "Yeah, but it turns black if it gets scared or mad; all a predator would have to do was sneak up on him and then you'd see it right away," Amy argues. Jorge purses his lips, thinking, and says, "Yeah . . . that's true. But if the gecko sat on a green leaf you could see it. His camouflage wouldn't work then!" Amy looks stumped and then says triumphantly, "Yeah, but the chameleon's got those horns! He'd beat up your gecko!"

From this example, you can see how Amanda facilitates opportunities for students to share their viewpoints, discuss, and teach one another. This social interaction promotes true critical thinking and learning; it also promotes children's social and communication skills.

Scaffolding

scaffolding The process of providing various types of support, guidance, or direction during the course of an activity.

Vygotsky believed that communication or dialogue between teachers and children is very important; it becomes a means of helping children develop new concepts and think their way to higher-level concepts. Assistance in the ZPD is called **scaffolding** and is a major component of teaching; it enables children to complete tasks they could not complete independently. When adults assist toddlers in learning to walk, they are scaffolding them from not being able to walk to walking. Teachers guide and support children's language learning by building on what they are already able to do, and moving them to a higher level of language use. For example, kindergarten teacher Candace Tegler reviews the concept of nouns with her class, something they learned last week. Then she tells them about verbs. She brings out a stack of magazines and asks them to look for action word pictures. She motivates them by using their pictures to create a collage to hang in the hallway. As the children apply what they already know about nouns, they expand their knowledge to include verbs. Next week, Candace plans to start working on sentence structure!

Scaffolding is a gradual process of providing different levels of support during the course of an activity. At the beginning of a new task, scaffolding should be concrete and visible; Vygotskian theory maintains that learning begins with the concrete and moves to the abstract. Then, as the child masters the task, the leader slowly withdraws her scaffolding support. Thus, scaffolding builds on children's strengths and enables them to grow cognitively and become independent learners. The Voice from the Field, "How to Scaffold Children's Learning," is a Competency Builder that can help you become a knowledgeable and confident participant with children in their learning. Figure 5.5 provides you with the steps of scaffolding.

Maslow and Self-Actualization Theory

Abraham Maslow (1890–1970) developed a theory of human motivation called *self-actualization*. His theory is based on the satisfaction of human needs and he identified self-actualization, or self-fulfillment, as the highest human need. However, Maslow said that children and adults cannot achieve self-fulfillment until other basic needs are satisfied. These essential human needs are:

- Life essentials, such as food and water
- Safety and security

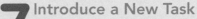

Voice from the Field

How to Scaffold Children's Learning

Vygotsky believed that cognitive development occurs through children's interactions with more competent others—teachers, peers, parents—who act as guides, facilitators, and coaches to provide the support children need to grow intellectually. Much of that support is provided through conversation, examples, and encouragement. When children learn a new skill, they need that competent other to provide a scaffold, or framework, to help them—to show them the overall task, break it into doable parts, and support and reinforce their efforts.

The Scaffolding Process

Here are the basic steps involved in effective scaffolding. Study them carefully and then look for them in the example that follows:

STEP 1 Observe and Listen

You can learn a great deal about what kind of assistance is needed.

STEP 2 Engage the Child

Ask what he or she wants to do, and ask for permission to help.

STEP 3 Talk About the Task

Describe each step in detail—what is being used, what is being done, what is seen or touched. Ask the child questions about the activity.

STEP 4 Adjust Support

Remain engaged but adjust your support. Allow the child to take over and do the talking.

STEP 5 Gradually Withdraw Support

See how the child is able to perform with less help.

STEP 6 Child Performs Independently

After you have withdrawn all support, check to be sure the child continues to perform the task successfully.

STEP 7 Introduce a New Task

Present the child with a slightly more challenging task, and repeat the entire sequence.

Example—Working a Puzzle

Celeste picks a puzzle to work and dumps the pieces out. She randomly picks up a piece and moves it around inside the frame. She tries another. Look at her face: Is she smiling or showing signs of stress? Is she talking to herself?

Perhaps Celeste needs a puzzle with fewer pieces. If so, you can offer her one. But from prior observation, you may know she just needs a little assistance. Try sitting with Celeste and suggesting that you will help. Start by turning all the pieces right side up. As you do this, talk about the pieces you see: This one is red with a little green, this one has a straight edge, this one is curved. Move your finger along the edge.

Ask Celeste whether she can find a straight edge on the side of the puzzle and then whether she can find a piece with a straight edge that matches the color. Ask what hints the pieces give her. Repeat with several other pieces. Then pause to give Celeste the opportunity to try one on her own. As she does, describe what she is doing and the position, shape, and color of the piece. Demonstrate turning a piece in different directions while saying. "I'll try turning it another way." (If you just say, "Turn the piece," she will most likely turn it upside down.) By listening to you verbalize and by repeating the verbalizing, Celeste is learning to self-talk—that is, to talk herself through a task. By practicing this private speech, children realize they can answer their own questions and regulate their own behavior. When the puzzle is complete, offer Celeste another of similar difficulty and encourage her to try it on her own while you stay nearby to offer assistance as needed, allowing her to take the lead.

Source: Contributed by Catherine M. Kearn, EdD, early childhood professional and adjunct professor, Carroll College, Waukesha, Wisconsin. Also contributing were Elena Bodrova, senior researcher at Mid-Continent Research for Education and Learning, Denver, Colorado; and Deborah Leong, professor of psychology and director of the Center for Improving Early Learning.

- Belonging and love
- Achievement and prestige
- Aesthetic needs

Maslow maintained that everyone has these basic needs, regardless of race, gender, sexual orientation, socioeconomic status, or age. The satisfaction of basic needs is essential for children to function well and to achieve all they are capable of achieving.

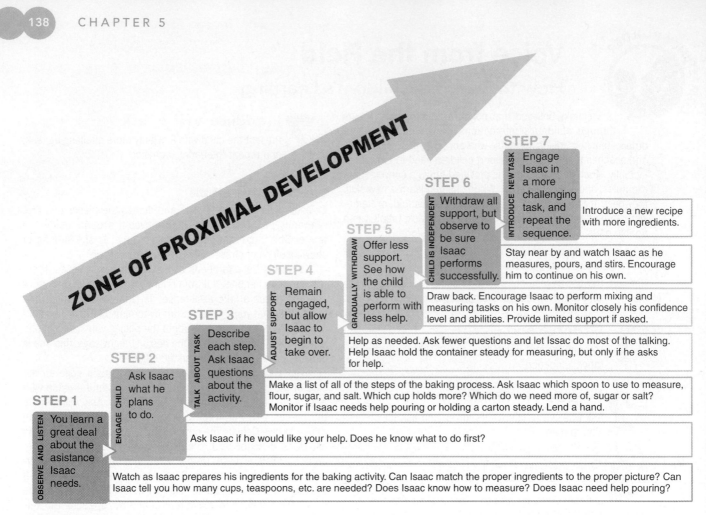

ZONE OF PROXIMAL DEVELOPMENT

STEP 1
OBSERVE AND LISTEN
You learn a great deal about the asistance Isaac needs.

Watch as Isaac prepares his ingredients for the baking activity. Can Isaac match the proper ingredients to the proper picture? Can Isaac tell you how many cups, teaspoons, etc. are needed? Does Isaac know how to measure? Does Isaac need help pouring?

STEP 2
ENGAGE CHILD
Ask Isaac what he plans to do.

Ask Isaac if he would like your help. Does he know what to do first?

STEP 3
TALK ABOUT TASK
Describe each step. Ask Isaac questions about the activity.

Make a list of all of the steps of the baking process. Ask Isaac which spoon to use to measure, flour, sugar, and salt. Which cup holds more? Which do we need more of, sugar or salt? Monitor if Isaac needs help pouring or holding a carton steady. Lend a hand.

STEP 4
ADJUST SUPPORT
Remain engaged, but allow Isaac to begin to take over.

Help as needed. Ask fewer questions and let Issac do most of the talking. Help Isaac hold the container steady for measuring, but only if he asks for help.

STEP 5
GRADUALLY WITHDRAW
Offer less support. See how the child is able to perform with less help.

Draw back. Encourage Isaac to perform mixing and measuring tasks on his own. Monitor closely his confidence level and abilities. Provide limited support if asked.

STEP 6
CHILD IS INDEPENDENT
Withdraw all support, but observe to be sure Isaac performs successfully.

Stay near by and watch Isaac as he measures, pours, and stirs. Encourage him to continue on his own.

STEP 7
INTRODUCE NEW TASK
Engage Isaac in a more challenging task, and repeat the sequence.

Introduce a new recipe with more ingredients.

FIGURE 5.5 Scaffolding a Baking Lesson

hierarchy of needs
Maslow's theory that basic needs must be satisfied before higher-level needs can be satisfied.

Figure 5.6 depicts Maslow's **hierarchy of needs**. As you review and reflect on it, identify ways you can help children meet their needs.

Life Essentials

Just as water is essential for proper brain functions,[15] the same is true of food.[16] We know that when children are hungry, they perform poorly in school. UNICEF executive director Ann M. Veneman reported, "Undernutrition diminishes the ability of children to learn and earn throughout their lives. Nutritional deprivation leaves children tired and weak, and lowers their IQs, so they perform poorly in school. As adults they are less productive and earn less than their healthy peers, and the cycle of undernutrition and poverty repeats itself, generation after generation."[17] Thus children who begin school without eating breakfast, don't have a healthy lunch, or eat improperly at home don't achieve as well as they should and experience difficulty concentrating on their school activities. They can even drop in IQ![18] Additionally, obesity, malnutrition, and diabetes also come from improper nutrition. For these reasons, many early childhood programs provide children with breakfast, lunch, and snacks throughout the day.[19] For some children with disabilities or other health impairments that affect their ability to ingest or digest food, these conditions may also impact their performance in school.

The state of children's nutrition today has caused growing concern on a national level. The statistics are shocking: More than 16 percent of children and adolescents in the United

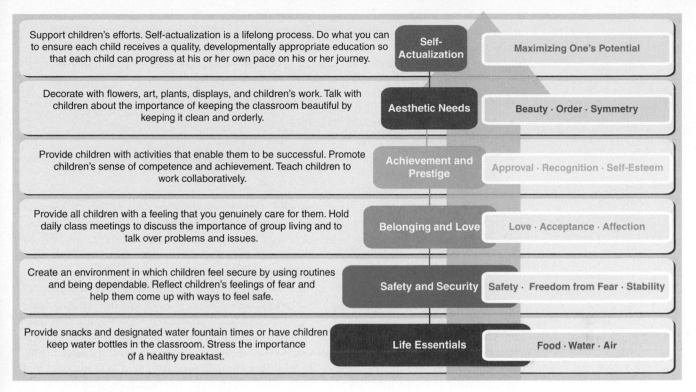

FIGURE 5.6 Maslow's Hierarchy of Needs

Source: Maslow's hierarchy of needs data reprinted by permission from Abraham H. Maslow, *Motivation and Personality*, 3rd ed., rev. Robert Frager et al. (New York: Addison Wesley, 1970).

States are overweight,[20] while nearly 16 percent of households with children are food insecure, meaning they went hungry one or more times sometime during the year.[21] For many children, both obese and food insecure, the National School Lunch Program (NSLP), a federally assisted meal program, provides some of the only nutritionally balanced meals children eat each school day.

Safety and Security

Safety and security needs also play an important role in children's lives. When children think that their teachers do not like them or children are fearful of what their teachers or others may say and how they may treat them, these children are deprived of a basic need. As a consequence, they do not do well in school, and they become fearful in their relationships with others. In addition, classrooms that have routines and predictability can provide children with a greater sense of security.[22] For some children who live in homes and environmental conditions that do not support their basic need for safety and security, such as neglectful/abusive homes and impoverished neighborhoods, their ability to learn and achieve in school may also be affected.

Belonging and Love

Children also need to be loved and feel that they belong within their home and school in order to thrive and develop. All children have a need for affection that teachers can help satisfy through smiles, hugs, eye contact, and nearness. For example, in my work with three- and four-year-old children, many want to sit close to me and want me to put my arms around them. They are seeking love and are looking to their teachers and me to satisfy this basic need.

Think for a minute about your social relations with others. How others treat you affects you emotionally, physically, and cognitively. The same is true for the children you teach. How you relate to them really matters and affects how well they achieve, as well as how well they do and will behave. What are teacher behaviors that really matter in preventing children's behavior problems? Consider these:

- Responding to children in a timely fashion
- Anticipating student needs and emotions
- Giving frequent feedback
- Providing strong supports for children's academic and social competence in the classroom setting

Teacher-Child Interaction. Researchers have found that the extent to which children can access the instructional and socialization resources of the classroom environment may be, in part, predicated on teacher–child interactions: "The association between the quality of early teacher–child relationships and later school performance can be both strong and persistent. The association is apparent in both academic and social spheres of school performance."[23]

In addition, teacher–child closeness, such as having an affectionate and warm relationship, can reduce the tendency for aggressive behavior. "Closer teacher–child relationships may provide young children with resources (e.g., emotional security, guidance, and aid) that facilitate an 'approach' orientation—as opposed to an 'avoidant' or 'resistant' stance—toward the interpersonal and scholastic demands of the classroom and school."[24] The implication for you and other early childhood professionals is that you need to really care for your children and develop strong and affectionate relationships with them.

In one study regarding teacher–child closeness, "females tended to develop higher levels of cooperative participation, school liking, and achievement than did males."[25] This might indicate gender differences in teacher–child relations and suggest that boys are at greater risk of not having a close teacher relationship. Thus, a close teacher–child relationship is particularly important for males; for low-socioeconomic children and minorities; and for all children who might not experience a close relationship with another caring adult.

These findings mean that you need to provide a classroom context that is supportive of and responsive to children's social and affectional needs. This, of course, can be a challenging task, but one that is necessary. How we teachers relate to children helps determine their behavioral outcomes now and in the future.

Achievement and Prestige

Recognition and approval are self-esteem needs that relate to success and accomplishment. Children who are independent and responsible and who achieve will have high self-esteem. Today, many educators are concerned about how to enhance children's self-esteem; a key way is through increased achievement.

It is important that teachers use encouragement to increase achievement rather than praise. Praise is evaluative and conveys that it is the product that is important, rather than the effort put into it. Praise and encouragement differ in the following ways:

- Praise stimulates rivalry and competition; encouragement stimulates cooperation and contribution for the good of all.
- Praise focuses on quality of performance; encouragement focuses on the amount of effort and joy of a performance.
- Praise is evaluative and judgmental and a child feels judged; encouragement involves little or no evaluation of a person or act, which allows the child to feel accepted.
- Praise fosters selfishness at the expense of others; encouragement fosters self-interest, which does not hurt others.

- Praise emphasizes global evaluation of the person ("You are better than/worse than others"); encouragement emphasizes specific contributions ("You helped in this way").
- Praise creates frustration and quitters; encouragement creates children that try and persist.
- Praise fosters a fear of failure or disappointment; encouragement fosters acceptance of being imperfect.
- Praise fosters dependence on others' evaluation of their self; encouragement fosters self-sufficiency and independence.[26]

First grade teacher Tatiana Herrera says, "I try hard to not use praise phrases like, 'Good job, that's awesome work,' or even, 'I really like that.' Instead I try to encourage kids by saying, 'You worked really hard on that, I bet you feel proud of yourself, you are trying so hard even though it's really difficult.' It was hard at first! After all, it's instinctual to want to make kids feel good, and we all grew up hearing praise phrases, but I can see a difference in the children's self-confidence already."

Aesthetic Needs

Children, just as all of us, like and appreciate beauty. They like to be in classrooms and homes that are physically attractive and pleasant. As an early childhood professional, you can help satisfy aesthetic needs by being well dressed and providing a classroom that is pleasant to be in, one that includes plants and flowers, art, and music.[27] For example, second grade teacher Allen Hamilton says, "I always have some flowers or potted plants around the room; it makes it feel homey and the kids like it. They get a charge out of helping to care for them and being responsible for the beauty in the classroom. I like having classical music on during the day, too. It encourages children to talk about the music they like, why they like it. By the end of the semester, I have students bringing in their favorite music. We'll play their music if they can talk with me about why they like it, and not just because it's 'cool'!"

When teachers and parents support children to meet their basic needs, they promote self-actualization. As a result, children have a sense of satisfaction, are enthusiastic, and are eager to learn. Such children want to engage in activities that will lead to higher levels of learning. The Voice from the Field on page 142 will show you how one teacher implements Maslow's hierarchy in her classroom.

Erikson and Psychosocial Development

Erik H. Erikson (1902–1994) developed his *psychosocial development* theory based on the premise that cognitive and social development occur hand in hand and cannot be separated. According to Erikson, children's personalities and social skills grow and develop within the context of society and in response to its demands, expectations, values, and social institutions, such as families, schools, and child care programs. Parents and teachers are key parts of these environments and therefore play a powerful role in helping or hindering children in their personality and cognitive development. For example, school-age children must deal with the demands of learning new skills or risk a crisis of *industry*—the ability to do, be involved, be competent, and achieve—versus *inferiority*, marked by failure and feelings of incompetence. Many of the cases of school violence in the news today are connected to children who feel inferior and unappreciated and who lack the social skills to get along with their classmates.[28] Figure 5.7 outlines Erikson's stages of psychosocial development and provides suggestions for you to follow and use in each of the four stages.

Voice from the Field

Applying Maslow's Hierarchy to a Third Grade Classroom

I stand in the classroom doorway and watch as my class of new third graders wanders wide-eyed through the hallway of their new school. Last year they were the big kids in their K–2 school. This year will be very different. I think of the changes they will go through during this year. Can they handle the changes? Will they be ready emotionally to learn what needs to be learned? When you think of these changes as a gradual continuum outlined by Abraham Maslow in his hierarchy of needs, and if you keep in mind the levels of these needs, you can apply them throughout the year and help your children become comfortable and confident learners, willing and able to take the risks necessary to stretch and grow.

Physiological Needs

I make sure my students know where to put their things in their cubby and desk. We take a tour of the school to find the closest restrooms, cafeteria, main office, and nurse's office. We go over the classroom sign-out process. I explain that I really need to know where they are at all times because I care about them. We talk about snack and lunch and what they can do if they're thirsty. It is impossible to ask a child to pay attention to a math lesson if he or she is worried about going to the restroom or when he or she will be eating lunch.

Safety

We also to talk about what students can do to help make our classroom a safe and secure place for learning. We talk about "Double D behaviors" (dangerous and destructive) as well as my only nonnegotiable rule: "Hands, feet, and objects to ourselves at all times." We practice the fire drill and lock-down drill procedures. Children's safety needs are related to their physiological needs and are just as important. I've learned students respond well to the structure and they really want to know they are safe.

Belonging

Only after we have talked about our basic needs do we talk about how we will learn together as a classroom community. We talk about classroom courtesies and what it means to be part of a group of learners. We set up our first cooperative groups of four, five, or six students. I initially allow students to sit with friends, but I tell them that these groupings change as I get to understand each of their strengths and weaknesses. Each group establishes a group name and I use this name to recognize good group behaviors or exceptional group thinking throughout the day during team-building activities and classroom lessons.

Esteem

Within each cooperative group, students are assigned specific roles they will play or jobs they will do when we engage in group activities such as math problem solving. Roles like time keeper, facilitator, materials handler, recorder, and note taker are important to ensure group success. It is essential early on to help students see the benefits of working together to achieve a common goal. After each group problem-solving activity I always include a group assessment piece in which students think and talk together about what went well and what didn't. I remind students to keep their comments positive. The goal is to help students build their individual self-esteem while learning and celebrating what they're good at as a group.

Self-Actualization

As my students learn to work together and contribute to each other's success, they begin to become aware of their own strengths and weaknesses. I change the roles and reassign group members from time to time to help bring about continuous improvement as my students work to achieve individual potential. I tell my students in the real world, we often don't have the luxury of knowing or even liking who we work with. We all need to learn strategies to help us be successful.

Maslow's hierarchy stresses the potential for each individual student to achieve self-actualization. I see their progress as my third graders learn and become comfortable in each level.

Source: Contributed by Robert Cote, third grade teacher at Jordan Jackson School, Mansfield, Massachusetts.

Children's Social Development and School Success

Children's appropriate and wholesome social development is an extremely important social issue today. Increasing numbers of children lack the social skills necessary for school readiness and success.[29] Social skills and other developmental issues play a huge part in why more preschoolers are expelled from school each year than teenagers![30] This is why early childhood programs are doubling their efforts to appropriately meet children's psychosocial needs in the first five years of life.

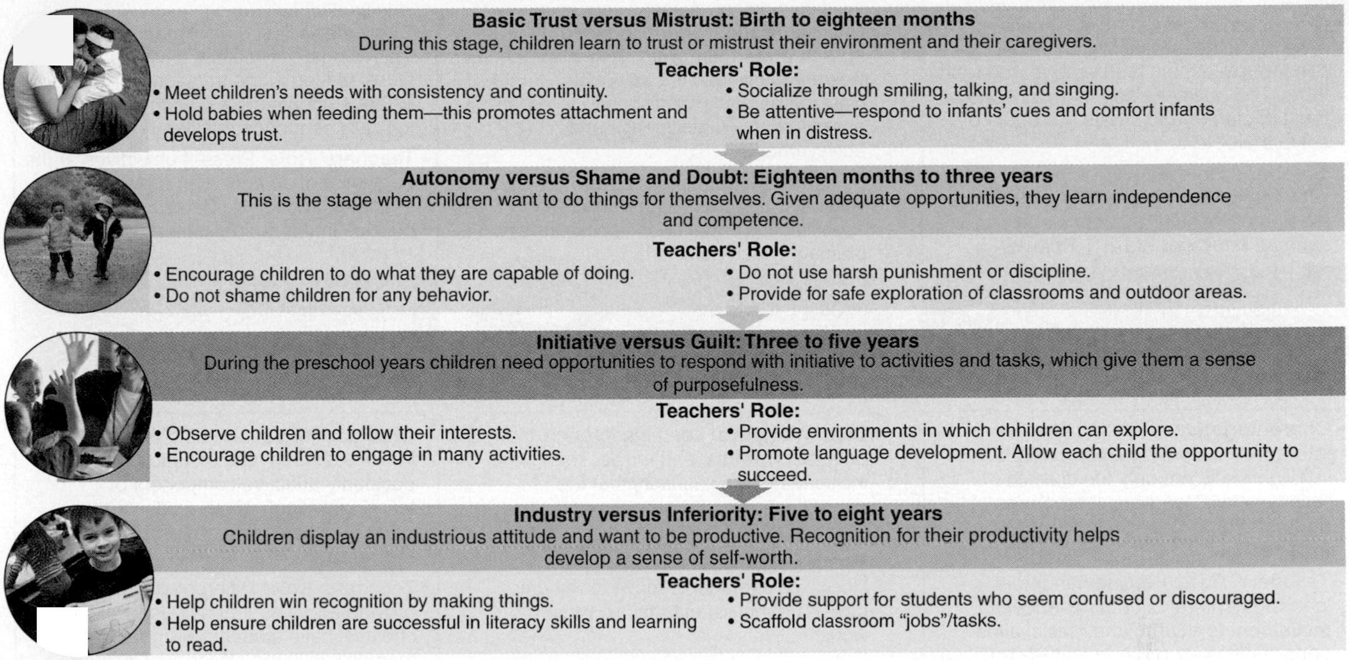

Basic Trust versus Mistrust: Birth to eighteen months
During this stage, children learn to trust or mistrust their environment and their caregivers.
Teachers' Role:
- Meet children's needs with consistency and continuity.
- Hold babies when feeding them—this promotes attachment and develops trust.
- Socialize through smiling, talking, and singing.
- Be attentive—respond to infants' cues and comfort infants when in distress.

Autonomy versus Shame and Doubt: Eighteen months to three years
This is the stage when children want to do things for themselves. Given adequate opportunities, they learn independence and competence.
Teachers' Role:
- Encourage children to do what they are capable of doing.
- Do not shame children for any behavior.
- Do not use harsh punishment or discipline.
- Provide for safe exploration of classrooms and outdoor areas.

Initiative versus Guilt: Three to five years
During the preschool years children need opportunities to respond with initiative to activities and tasks, which give them a sense of purposefulness.
Teachers' Role:
- Observe children and follow their interests.
- Encourage children to engage in many activities.
- Provide environments in which chhildren can explore.
- Promote language development. Allow each child the opportunity to succeed.

Industry versus Inferiority: Five to eight years
Children display an industrious attitude and want to be productive. Recognition for their productivity helps develop a sense of self-worth.
Teachers' Role:
- Help children win recognition by making things.
- Help ensure children are successful in literacy skills and learning to read.
- Provide support for students who seem confused or discouraged.
- Scaffold classroom "jobs"/tasks.

FIGURE 5.7 Erikson's Stages of Psychosocial Development

Gardner and Multiple Intelligences Theory

Howard Gardner (b. 1943) plays an important role in helping educators rethink what constitutes basic intelligence. Gardner's theory of *multiple intelligences* proposes that children are smart in many ways. Gardner has identified nine different intelligences: visual/spatial, verbal/linguistic, mathematical/logical, bodily/kinesthetic, musical/rhythmic, intrapersonal, interpersonal, naturalistic, and existential. His view of intelligence and its multiple components will undoubtedly continue to influence educational thought and practice. Review Figure 5.8 to learn more about these nine intelligences and their implications for teaching and learning.

Bronfenbrenner and Ecological Theory

The ecological theory of Urie Bronfenbrenner (1917–2005) looks at children's development within the context of system of relationships that form their environment. There are five interrelating environmental systems—the microsystem, the mesosystem, the exosystem, the macrosystem, and the chronosystem. Each system influences and is influenced by the others. Figure 5.9 shows a model of these environmental systems and the ways each influences development.

The **microsystem** encompasses the environments of parents, family, peers, child care, schools, neighborhood, religious groups, parks, and so forth. The child acts on and influences each of these and is influenced by them. For example, four-year-old April might have a physical disability that her child care program accommodates by making the classroom more accessible. Five-year-old Mack's aggressive behavior might prompt his teacher to initiate a program of bibliotherapy.

The **mesosystem** includes linkages or interactions between microsystems. Interactions and influences there relate to all of the environmental influences in the microsystem. For example, the family's support of or lack of attention to literacy influences a child's school

microsystem The environmental settings in which children spend a lot of their time (e.g., children in child care spend about thirty-three hours a week there).

mesosystem Links or interactions between microsystems.

- **Characteristics:** Learning visually and organizing ideas spatially. Seeing concepts in action in order to understand them. The ability to "see" things in one's mind in planning to create a product or solve a problem.
- **Teachers' Role:** Provide a visually stimulating environment; work with manipulatives; utilize technologies such as KidPix or SMART Boards.

Visual/Spatial

- **Characteristics:** Learning through the spoken and written word. This intelligence was always valued in traditional classrooms and in traditional assessments of intelligence and achievement.
- **Teachers' Role:** Introduce new vocabulary; provide opportunities for speaking in front of class; incorporate drama in classroom.

Verbal/ Linguistic

- **Characteristics:** Learning through reasoning and problem solving. Also highly valued in the traditional classroom, where students are asked to adapt to logically sequenced delivery of instruction.
- **Teachers' Role:** Present objectives at the beginning of an activity to provide structure; encourage debates; incorporate puzzles into learning centers.

Mathematical/ Logical

- **Characteristics:** Learning through interaction with one's environment. This intelligence is not only the domain of "overly active" learners. It promotes understanding through concrete experiences.
- **Teachers' Role:** Provide hands-on learning centers; offer experiences in movement to rhythm and music; allow opportunities for building and taking apart.

Bodily/ Kinesthetic

- **Characteristics:** Learning through patterns, rhythms, and music. This includes not only auditory, but the indentification of patterns through all the senses.
- **Teachers' Role:** Work with pattern blocks; have students move to rhythm; have students listen to music while working.

Musical/ Rhythmic

- **Characteristics:** Learning through feelings, values, and attitudes. This is a decidedly affective component of learning through which students place value on what they learn and take ownership for their learning.
- **Teachers' Role:** Differentiate instruction; provide activities that offer learner choices; have students set goals for themselves in the classroom; include daily journal writing.

Intrapersonal

- **Characteristics:** Learning through interaction with others. Not the domain of children who are simply "talkative" or "overly social." This intelligence promotes collaboration and working cooperatively with others.
- **Teachers' Role:** Allow interaction among students during learning tasks; include group work tasks; form cooperative groups so each member has an assigned role.

Interpersonal

- **Characteristics:** Learning through classification, categories, and hierarchies. The naturalist intelligence picks up on subtle differences in meaning. It is not simply the study of nature; it can be used in all areas of study.
- **Teachers' Role:** Use graphic organizers; provide sorting and grouping tasks; build portfolios of student work.

Naturalistic

- **Characteristics:** Children who learn in the context of where humankind stands in the "big" picture of existence. They ask, "Why are we here?" and "What is my role in my family, school, and community?" This intelligence is seen in the discipline of philosophy.
- **Teachers' Role:** Offer an overview before starting new instruction; discuss how topics are important to the classroom, school, and community; bring in resource people or offer additional perspectives on a topic.

Existential

FIGURE 5.8 Gardner's Nine Intelligences

Source: Reprinted with permission from Walter McKenzie, "Multiple Intelligences Overview," 1999; available online at http://surfaquarium.com/MI/overview.htm.

exosystem Environment or setting in which children do not play an active role but which nonetheless influences their development.

performance. Likewise, school support for family literacy will influence the extent to which families value literacy.

The **exosystem** is the environmental system that encompasses those events with which children do not have direct interaction but which nonetheless influence them. For example, when a local school board enacts a policy that ends social promotion in favor of grade failure, this action can and will influence children's future development. From

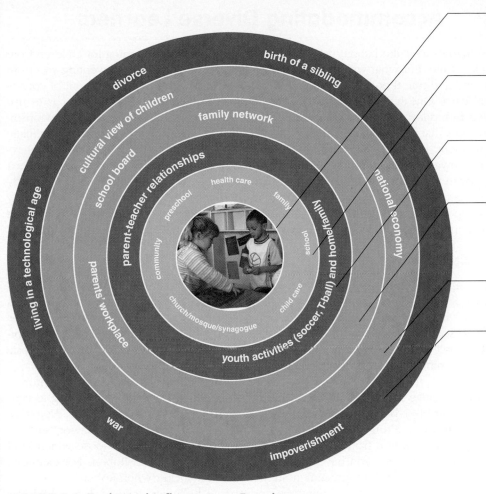

Individual children:
Includes genetic background, temperament, physical characteristics.

Microsystem:
Any setting in which children have direct experiences.

Mesosystem:
Linkages between microsystems.

Exosystem:
Social settings that do not include children but affect their microsystems and influence them indirectly.

Macrosystem:
Larger cultural influences.

Chronosystem:
Temporal changes in life events, environmental events, and life transitions.

FIGURE 5.9 Ecological Influences on Development

research, we know that children who are retained suffer academically and developmentally in the long run![31] And when a parent's workplace mandates increased work time (e.g., a ten-hour workday), this may decrease parent–child involvement, and have a negative impact on development.

The **macrosystem** includes the culture, customs, and values of society in general. How children are viewed, ideas of gender-appropriate behavior, and the emphasis on individualism over collectivism are all a part of the macrosystem. For example, contemporary societal violence and media violence influence children's development. As a result, many children are becoming more violent, and many children are fearful of and threatened by violence.

The **chronosystem** includes environmental influences over time and the ways they impact development and behavior. For example, today's children are technologically adept and are comfortable using technology for education and entertainment. In addition, we have already referred to how the large-scale entry of mothers into the workforce has changed family life and children's developmental outcomes.

Clearly, as Bronfenbrenner's theory illustrates, there are many influences on children's development. Currently there is a lot of interest in how these influences shape children's lives and what parents and educators can do to enhance positive influences and minimize or eliminate negative environmental influences as well as negative social interactions.

macrosystem The broader culture in which children live (e.g., democracy, individual freedom, and religious freedom).

chronosystem The environmental contexts and events that influence children over their lifetimes, such as living in a technological age.

Accommodating Diverse Learners

In this chapter we talked about using constructivism to structure learning for children from all walks of life. But what will you do when a student's behaviors are preventing you from using tried and true theories of learning? After all, a child whose behavior is out of control cannot learn. One way to effectively and (relatively) quickly modify behavior is to use **applied behavior analysis (ABA)**. ABA is based on the learning theory of behaviorism, which states that all behavior is motivated by a purpose and is learned through systematic reinforcement. In other words, when behavior is rewarded, it continues; but when behavior is not rewarded or is ignored, the behavior will stop. For example, a child who wants a candy bar in the grocery store has *learned* that screaming, crying, and kicking in the candy aisle will get her what she wants. Her mother *reinforces* that behavior by giving her a candy bar to stop her tantrum. If the mother had ignored the tantrum or removed the child from the store instead of reinforcing the behavior, would the behavior continue? Probably not.

Applying ABA

You can apply ABA to your classroom to accommodate a variety of behavioral disturbances. Let's consider Robert, a five-year-old who protective services removed from his home last year because his parents were physically abusive. Robert has learned from his parents to solve his problems by hitting. For example, if he is trying to get your attention and you don't provide it right away, he hits you. This pattern of behavior seriously affects Robert's learning and social development.

Using ABA, there are two ways you can modify Robert's behavior: positive reinforcement and negative reinforcement. **Positive reinforcement** is adding something to promote or diminish a behavior, such as giving a high-five for a job well done. **Negative reinforcement** is taking away something to promote or diminish a behavior, such as removing your attention from someone (ignoring them). In order to choose which kind of reinforcement to use, you have to know what is meaningful to Robert. For example, providing Robert positive reinforcement in the form of a sticker when Robert doesn't care anything about stickers will not reinforce appropriate behavior. Instead, for a child like Robert who has had nothing but negative and painful relationships, social interactions that are positive, consistent, and satisfying may be very rewarding.

You decide to use both positive and negative reinforcement. You will ignore Robert when he hits you and reward him when he uses his words. At the beginning of the day you pull Robert aside and tell him, "I know that it's hard for you to remember to use your words and wait to get my attention. But if you hit me instead of using your words, I'm not going to listen to you. If you use your words, you will earn story time with me at the end of the day."

After lunch, Robert is frustrated and he has not gotten your attention; he forgets the plan and hits you. You ignore him. You give him no other reaction and continue to focus on the other children. Remember, consistency is the only way to make ABA techniques work. With ABA, it is important to have a plan for your intervention and to *follow it every time*. It is likely that after Robert hits you and gets no response, he will hit you again, harder. His behavior will likely escalate because it is the only behavior he has learned.

If you break down, turn around, and shout, "STOP!" you have positively reinforced his behavior by giving him a reaction and your attention. It is not the kind of reaction or the attention he wants, but it is still a reaction, and a negative reaction is better than no reaction or attention at all. In this way, you are teaching him that his behavior is *working*. If you continue to ignore his behavior, and it does not work, Robert will be forced to learn a new behavior to meet his needs because the old behavior is not working.

When Robert does not hit you, immediately and consistently provide positive reinforcement. Genuine verbal encouragement, high-fives, and hugs are all positive reinforcements. At the end of the day make sure to have the special story time between the two of

applied behavior analysis (ABA) A technique based on the learning theory of Behaviorism, which states that all behavior is motivated by a purpose and is learned through systematic reinforcement.

positive reinforcement Adding something to promote or diminish a behavior, such as giving a high-five for a job well done.

negative reinforcement Taking away something to promote or diminish a behavior, such as removing your attention from someone (ignoring them).

you as you planned with him. In this way, you are teaching Robert that there are other ways of getting attention. Robert can get nurturing and meaningful attention by following the rules, waiting patiently, and using his words.

You have to develop and modify your plan to fit the child. For example, going all day without hitting you may be impossible for Robert because the behavior is so ingrained in him. Instead of rewarding him at the end of the day, break the day into smaller, more manageable segments. In other words, if Robert has not hit you in one hour, reinforce his accomplishment with five minutes of special Robert and Teacher time. You can also help Robert develop patience by reassuring him that you aware of his needs without giving him overt attention with nonverbal clues, such as a wink to communicate, "I'm thinking about you;" holding up a finger as if to say, "I hear you, but I need a minute to finish with someone else;" or even a gentle hand on the shoulder to communicate closeness and responsiveness along with his need to wait patiently. As Robert develops new skills and begins to phase out his hitting behavior because it isn't working, you can extend the time for his behavioral expectations, pushing back the reinforcement period to two hours, then three, and eventually the whole day. Changing children's behavior can be difficult, but it is worth it! And, in Robert's case, you put theory into action.

As we said at the beginning of the chapter, theories are very helpful—indeed necessary—for your professional practice. Applying theory to practice will give you a rewarding teaching experience and will help your children achieve.

Activities for Professional Development

Ethical Dilemma

"I don't buy into that stuff!"

Deborah and her teaching partner Michelle are attending a professional development session on instructional strategies. The principal has brought a Vygotskian scholar from the local university to teach the second grade teaching teams how to scaffold learning. After the meeting, Michelle storms out and tells Deborah, "I don't buy into that stuff! It just adds a whole bunch of steps to my lessons and I'm already rushed as it is! It doesn't even work. Well, they've got another think coming if they think I'm going to go through all that for each kid!" Deborah is shocked; she feels like she got a lot out of the presentation and can't wait to try it. "But it's school policy, Michelle. And I've seen it work wonders!" Deborah replies. "Well, you teach your lessons your way, and let me teach mine my way." Deborah and Michelle are both irritated with one another. Deborah can't believe how oppositional Michelle is toward scaffolding. Deborah isn't sure what to do, but she is concerned that their argument will affect their professional relationship. Just as she's about to head back to her classroom, the principal approaches her. "Everything all right, Deborah?"

What should Deborah do? Should she try to talk to Michelle to resolve their personal conflict? What if Deborah and Michelle cannot come to an agreement about how to teach in their classroom? Should she confide in her principal and ask for her help in repairing the teaching relationship? But if Deborah tells the principal that Michelle isn't scaffolding, won't she get Michelle in trouble? What would you do if you were Deborah?

Activities to Apply What You Learned

1. Think back on your own days in elementary school—would you characterize your classroom and learning experience as constructivist? Make a list of the ways in which your first grade experience was constructivist; then add a column detailing the ways it was not constructivist. Post your findings on an education blog and ask for others to contribute their own experiences.

2. Piaget believed old and new experiences needed to be linked in order to maintain equilibrium. What are some ways you can make sure children are not in a constant state of disequilibrium in your classroom? Select a subject area such as math or science and outline a few ways you can connect new subject matter to children's experiences (i.e., the idea of counting by fives to multiplication). Share your ideas online.

3. Vygotsky's theory says that social interaction is a key process for cognitive development. However, for some children with disabilities, behavioral problems, and those

whose home language is other than English, social interactions can be difficult. Conduct an Internet research and make a list of five things you could do to support children's social interactions with others. Share and compare your list with your classmates online.

4. On pages 136–141, we discussed Maslow's hierarchy of needs. At the bottom of the pyramid in Figure 5.6 are life essentials (food, water, and air), without which children cannot survive; and safety and security, without which learning and positive development is next to impossible. Read online newspapers (*New York Times*, *Boston Globe*, *Houston Chronicle*, etc.). Read articles about children who are neglected or abused. How does abuse and neglect impact children's development? How could you target the most basic needs in your classroom? Write a Facebook note and tag your friends. What do they suggest?

5. Which of Erikson's stages of social development seems most important to you? Why? What aspects of Erikson's theory would you suggest are most important for parents to understand? Considering how important it is to keep parents involved in their children's education, create a PowerPoint presentation designed to inform parents about Erikson's stages and include tips for how parents can support each stage at home. Post your presentation to the class discussion board.

6. Pick a grade level and consider the ways you teach to children's different types of intelligences. Select two of Gardner's intelligences and outline how teaching to those intelligences is impacted by each level of Bronfenbrenner's ecosystems. Share your findings with your classmates.

7. Skype with an ABA therapist and ask for tips on how to effectively incorporate ABA in your classroom. Post your findings and compare/contrast them with your classmates' findings.

Linking to Learning

Building an Understanding of Constructivism
www.sedl.org/scimath/compass/v01n03/2.html
Describes the basic tenets of constructivism and gives a list of resources.

Constructivism and the Five Es
www.miamisci.org/ph/lpintro5e.html
A description of constructivism and the five Es—engage, explore, explain, elaborate, and evaluate.

Jean Piaget and Genetic Epistemology
www.gwu.edu/~tip/piaget.html
Detailed description of Piaget's theories concerning genetic epistemology; contains a QuickTime video clip of Piaget discussing this topic.

Multidisciplinary/Cognitive Skills
www2.ed.gov/pubs/EPTW/eptw10/index.html
Contains a complete list of projects on cognitive skill development approved by the U.S. Department of Education.

Resources for the Constructivist Educator
http://sites.google.com/site/assocforconstructteaching/
Website for the Association for Constructivist Teaching; provides a rich problem-solving arena that encourages the learner's investigation, invention, and inference.

PEARSON **myeducationlab**

Go to Topic 2 (Child Development/Theories) in the MyEducationLab (www.myeducationlab.com) for your course, where you can:

- Find learning outcomes for Child Development/Theories along with the national standards that connect to these outcomes.
- Complete Assignments and Activities that can help you more deeply understand the chapter content.
- Apply and practice your understanding of the core teaching skills identified in the chapter with the Building Teaching Skills and Dispositions learning units.
- Check your comprehension on the content covered in the chapter by going to the Study Plan in the Book Resources for your text. Here you will be able to take a chapter quiz, receive feedback on your answers, and then access Review, Practice, and Enrichment activities to enhance your understanding of chapter content.

PART III

PROGRAMS AND SERVICES FOR CHILDREN AND FAMILIES

6

EARLY CHILDHOOD PROGRAMS
Applying Theories to Practice

focus questions

1. Why is there a growing demand for quality early childhood education programs?
2. How does the Montessori method provide for the needs of young children?
3. How does the HighScope program model provide for the needs of young children?
4. How does the Reggio Emilia approach provide for the needs of young children?
5. How can you use the Project Approach to create a unique learning experience for young children?
6. Why is it important for you to know and understand early childhood programs?

naeyc standards

Standard 1. Promoting Child Development and Learning

I use my understanding of young children's characteristics and needs, and of multiple interacting influences on children's development and learning, to create environments that are healthy, respectful, supportive, and challenging for each child.[1]

Standard 4. Using Developmentally Effective Approaches to Connect with Children and Families

I understand and use positive relationships and supportive interactions as the foundation for my work with young children and families. I know, understand, and use a wide array of developmentally appropriate approaches, instructional strategies, and tools to connect with children and families and positively influence each child's development and learning.[2]

Parents want their children to attend high-quality programs that will prepare them for school and provide them with a good start in life. They want to know that their children are being well educated and cared for. Parents want their children to get along with others, be happy, and learn. How best to meet these legitimate parental expectations as well as federal, state, and local expectations is one of the ongoing challenges of early childhood programs and professionals.[3]

The Growing Demand for Quality Early Childhood Programs

The National Association for the Education of Young Children (NAEYC), the nation's largest organization of early childhood educators, accredits over 7,000 early childhood programs serving approximately 623,000 children.[4] These programs are only a fraction of the total number of early childhood programs in the United States. Think for a minute about what goes on in these and other programs from day to day. For some children, teachers and staff implement well-thought-out and articulated programs that provide for children's growth and development across all the developmental domains—cognitive, linguistic, emotional, social, and physical. In other programs, children are not so fortunate. Their days are filled with aimless activities that fail to meet their academic and developmental needs.

With the national spotlight on the importance of the early years, the public is demanding more from early childhood professionals and their programs. On one hand, the public is willing to invest more heavily in early childhood programs, but on the other hand, it is demanding that the early childhood profession and individual programs respond by providing meaningful, high-quality programs.[5] The public wants high-quality early childhood programs that:

- *Help ensure children's early academic and school success.* The public believes that too many children are being left out and left behind. The achievement gap—the differences in school achievement between children or different socio-economic and social groups is a serious national problem. We will see more resources devoted to programs to close and erase achievement gaps.[6]

- *Provide the inclusion of early literacy and reading readiness activities in programs and curricula that enable children to read on grade level in grades one, two, and three.* Early literacy is the key to much of school and life success, and school success begins in preschool and before.[7] Early literacy is everything children know about reading and writing before they can actually read and write. Because children develop much of their capacity for learning in the first three years of life, when their brains grow to 90 percent of their eventual adult weight, early childhood programs are challenged with the opportunity to assist parents in laying the foundation for children's early experiences with books and language for success in learning to read.[8]

- *Learning environments that meet the needs of each child.* The public wants its early childhood programs to be inclusive and meet the learning, behavioral, cultural/ linguistic, socioeconomic, and disability differences that are reflected in children and families.

- *Promote the national good.* The nation and politicians see the early years as one way to keep America politically and economically strong. In many ways, world leadership begins in the preschool. As a result, President Obama and other national leaders want to make sure

> Education cannot be effective unless it helps a child to open up himself to life.
>
> **MARIA MONTESSORI**

our children are prepared for kindergarten by investing in early childhood education and dramatically expanding programs to ensure that each young child is ready to enter kindergarten.[9] There is a substantial amount of research that shows that a well-educated, high-performing workforce is the key to maintaining the nation's competitive advantage and leadership in the global economy of the twenty-first century.[10] Some of the benefits of investing in early childhood programs are listed below.

- *Contribute positively to today's workforce.* A public investment in early childhood programs allows parents to enter the workforce more easily; decrease their absenteeism; earn higher wages; move between jobs less frequently; and achieve higher productivity.[11]
- *Generate high payoffs for state and local governments and taxpayers.* Students who get off to a good start with high-quality early childhood care require fewer additional resources in school, and as adults, draw on fewer social services and pay more in taxes.[12]
- *Research documents high returns on public investment in early care and education.* Rigorous peer-reviewed longitudinal studies show that high-quality programs offer one of the largest returns on investment of any public spending for economic development with payoffs in education, crime, earnings, employment, tax revenue, and health and social services.[13]

Model Programs

model early childhood program An exemplary approach to early childhood education that serves as a guide to best practices.

In this chapter we examine and discuss some of the more notable programs for use in early childhood settings designed to address children and family needs. As you read about and reflect on each of these, think about their purposes and curriculum and the ways each tries to meet the needs of children and families. Pause for a minute and review Table 6.1, which outlines and compares three of the **model early childhood programs** discussed in this chapter: Montessori method, HighScope educational model, and Reggio Emilia.

Models are guides that provide us with instructions, ideas, and examples. We use models to guide a lot of what we do in life. We model our lives after others we respect and admire. We adopt the fashions of models in advertisements, and in early childhood education, we model our programs after highly respected models such as Montessori, HighScope, and Reggio Emilia. While none of these individual models are a perfect fit for all children, they nonetheless are widely used in the United States and around the world as a blueprint to better serve young children and families. In addition, other programs such as Head Start and Early Head Start and for-profit companies such as Knowledge Learning Corporation, the nation's largest provider of child care, also provide ideas for how to implement high quality early childhood programs.

The Montessori Method

The Montessori method continues to be very popular in the United States and around the world with early childhood professionals and parents. The Montessori approach is designed to support the natural development of children in a well-prepared environment. This method is attractive to parents and early childhood professionals for a number of reasons. First, Montessori education has always been identified as a quality program for young children. Second, parents who observe a good Montessori program like what they see: orderliness, independent children, self-directed learning, a calm environment, and children at the center of the learning process. Third, some public schools include Montessori as one of their program options, giving parents choices in the education of their children.

TABLE 6.1 Comparing Three Models of Early Childhood Education

Model	Main Features	Teacher's Role
Montessori	• Theoretical basis is the philosophy and beliefs of Maria Montessori. • Prepared environment supports, invites, and enables learning. • Children educate themselves—self-directed learning. • Sensory materials invite and promote learning. • Has a set curriculum regarding what children should learn. Montessorians try to stay as close to Montessori's ideas as possible. • Children are grouped in multiage environments. • Children learn by manipulating materials and working with others. • Learning takes place through the senses.	• Follows the child's interests and needs. • Prepares an environment that is educationally interesting and safe.* • Directs unobtrusively as children individually or in small groups engage in self-directed activity.* • Observes, analyzes, and provides materials and activities appropriate for the child's sensitive periods of learning.* • Maintains regular communications with the parent.
HighScope	• Theory is based on Piaget, constructivism, Dewey, and Vygotsky. • Plan-do-review is the teaching-learning cycle. • Emergent curriculum is not planned in advance. • Children help determine curriculum. • Developmental indicators guide the curriculum in promoting children's active learning.	• Plans activities based on children's interests. • Facilitates learning through encouragement.* • Engages in positive adult-child interaction strategies.*
Reggio Emilia	• Theory is based on Piaget, constructivism, Vygotsky, and Dewey. • Emergent curriculum is not planned in advance. • Curriculum is based on children's interests and experiences. • Curriculum is project oriented. • *Hundred Languages of Children* is the symbolic representation of children's work and learning. • Learning is active. • Atelierista—a special teacher is trained in the arts. • Atelier—an art/design studio is used by children and teachers.	• Works collaboratively with other teachers. • Organizes environments rich in possibilities and provocations.* • Acts as recorder for the children, helping them trace and revisit their words and actions.*

*Information from C. Edwards, "Three Approaches from Europe: Waldorf, Montessori, and Reggio Emilia," *Early Childhood Research & Practice 4*, no. 1 (2002). Available online at http://ecrp.uiuc.edu/v4n1/edwards.html

Five basic principles fairly and accurately represent how Montessori educators implement the Montessori method in many kinds of programs across the United States. Figure 6.1 illustrates the five basic principles of the **Montessori method**.

Respect for the Child

Respect for the child is the cornerstone on which all other Montessori principles rest. As Montessori said,

> As a rule, however, we do not respect children. We try to force them to follow us without regard to their special needs. We are overbearing with them, and above all, rude; and then

Montessori method
A system of early childhood education founded on the ideas and practices of Maria Montessori.

FIGURE 6.1 Basic
Montessori Principles
These basic principles are
the foundation of the
Montessori method. Taken
as a whole, they constitute
a powerful model for helping all children learn to
their fullest.

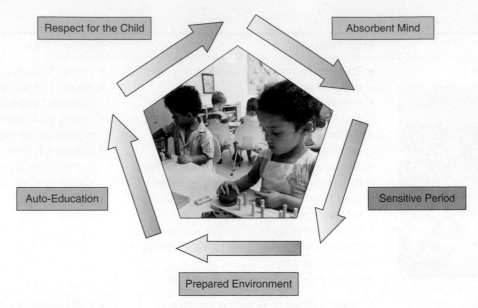

Respect for the Child

Absorbent Mind

Auto-Education

Sensitive Period

Prepared Environment

we expect them to be submissive and well-behaved, knowing all the time how strong is their instinct of imitation and how touching their faith in and admiration of us. They will imitate us in any case. Let us treat them, therefore, with all the kindness which we would wish to help to develop in them.[14]

Teachers show respect for children when they guide and scaffold their learning and enable them do things and learn for themselves. When children have choices, they are able to develop the skills and abilities necessary for effective learning, autonomy, and positive self-esteem.

The Absorbent Mind

absorbent mind The idea that the minds of young children are receptive to and capable of learning. The child learns unconsciously by taking in information from the environment.

Montessori believed that children educate themselves: "It may be said that we acquire knowledge by using our minds; but the child absorbs knowledge directly into his psychic life. Simply by continuing to live, the child learns to speak his native tongue."[15] This is the concept of the **absorbent mind**.

Montessori wanted us to understand that simply by living, children learn from their environment. Children are born to learn, and they are remarkable learning systems. Children learn because they are thinking beings. But what they learn depends greatly on their teachers, experiences, and environments.

Today, as early childhood professionals, we are reemphasizing Montessori's ideas that children are born to learn and have a constant readiness and ability to learn.

Sensitive Periods

sensitive period In the Montessori method, a relatively brief time during which learning is most likely to occur. Also called a critical period.

Montessori believed there are **sensitive periods** (or critical periods) when children are more susceptible to certain behaviors and can learn specific skills more easily:

A sensitive period refers to a special sensibility which a creature acquires in its infantile state, while it is still in a process of evolution. It is a transient disposition and limited to the acquisition of a particular trait. Once this trait or characteristic has been acquired, the special sensibility disappears. . . .[16]

Although all children experience the same sensitive periods (e.g., a sensitive period for writing), the timing varies for each child. One role of the teacher is to use observation to detect times of sensitivity and provide a prepared setting that supports optimum learning.

Prepared Environment

Montessori believed that children learn best in a **prepared environment**, a place in which children can *do things for themselves*. The prepared environment makes learning materials and experiences available to children in an orderly and organized format. Classrooms Montessori described are really what educators advocate when they talk about child-centered education and active learning. Freedom is the essential characteristic of the prepared environment. Since children within the environment are free to explore materials of their own choosing, they absorb what they find there. Maria Montessori was a master at creating environments for young children that enabled them to be independent, active, and learn on their own.

In a prepared environment, materials and activities provide for three basic areas of child involvement:

1. Practical life or motor education
2. Sensory materials for training the senses
3. Academic materials for teaching writing, reading, and mathematics

All these activities are taught according to a prescribed procedure.

Practical Life. The prepared environment supports basic, **practical life** activities, such as walking from place to place in an orderly manner, carrying objects such as trays and chairs, greeting a visitor, and learning self-care skills. For example, *dressing frames* are designed to perfect the motor skills involved in buttoning, zipping, lacing, buckling, and tying. The philosophy for activities such as these is to make children independent and develop concentration.

Practical life activities are taught through four different types of exercise:

1. *Care of the person*—activities such as using dressing frames, polishing shoes, and washing hands
2. *Care of the environment*—for example, dusting, polishing a table, and raking leaves
3. *Social relations*—lessons in grace and courtesy
4. *Analysis and control of movement*—locomotor activities such as walking and balancing

Sensory Materials. The **sensory materials** described in Figure 6.2 are among those found in a typical Montessori classroom. Materials for training and developing the senses have these characteristics:

- *Control of error.* Materials are designed so that children can see whether they make a mistake; for example, a child who does not build the blocks of the pink tower in their proper order does not achieve a tower effect.
- *Isolation of a single quality.* Materials are designed so that other variables are held constant except for the isolated quality or qualities. Therefore, all blocks of the pink tower are pink because size, not color, is the isolated quality.
- *Active involvement.* Materials encourage active involvement rather than the more passive process of looking.
- *Attractiveness.* Materials are attractive, with colors and proportions that appeal to children.

Sensory materials have several purposes:

- To help sharpen children's powers of observation and visual discrimination as readiness for learning to read.

The Montessori prepared environment makes materials and experiences available for children to explore for themselves. Why is it important to prepare such an organized environment?

prepared environment A classroom or other space that is arranged and organized to support learning in general and/or special knowledge and skills.

practical life Montessori activities that teach skills related to everyday living.

sensory materials Montessori learning materials designed to promote learning through the senses and to train the senses for learning.

Material	Illustration	Descriptions and Learning Purposes
Pink tower		Ten wooden cubes of the same shape and texture, all pink, the largest of which is ten centimeters. Each succeeding block is one centimeter smaller. Children build a tower beginning with the largest block. (Visual discrimination of dimension)
Brown stairs		Ten wooden blocks, all brown, differing in height and width. Children arrange the blocks next to each other from thickest to thinnest so the blocks resemble a staircase. (Visual discrimination of width and height)
Red rods		Ten rod-shaped pieces of wood, all red, of identical thickness but differing in length from ten centimeters to one meter. The child arranges the rods next to each other from largest to smallest. (Visual discrimination of length)
Cylinder blocks		Four individual wooden blocks that have holes of various sizes and matching cylinders; one block deals with height, one with diameter, and two with the relationship of both variables. Children remove the cylinders in random order, then match each cylinder to the correct hole. (Visual discrimination of size)
Smelling jars		Two identical sets of white opaque glass jars with removable tops through which the child cannot see but through which odors can pass. The teacher places various substances, such as herbs, in the jars, and the child matches the jars according to the smells. (Olfactory discrimination)
Baric tablets		Sets of rectangular pieces of wood that vary according to weight. There are three sets—light, medium, and heavy—which children match according to the weight of the tablets. (Discrimination of weight)
Color tablets		Two identical sets of small rectangular pieces of wood used for matching color or shading. (Discrimination of color and education of the chromatic sense)
Cloth swatches		Two identical swatches of cloth. Children identify them according to touch, first without a blindfold but later using a blindfold. (Sense of touch)
Tonal bells		Two sets of eight bells, alike in shape and size but different in color; one set is white, the other brown. The child matches the bells by tone. (Sound and pitch)
Sound boxes		Two identical sets of cylinders filled with various materials, such as salt and rice. Children match the cylinders according to the sound the fillings make. (Auditory discrimination)
Temperature jugs or thermic bottles		Small metal jugs filled with water of varying temperatures. Children match jugs of the same temperature. (Thermic sense and ability to distinguish between temperatures)

FIGURE 6.2 Montessori Sensory Materials

- To increase children's ability to think, a process that depends on the ability to distinguish, classify, and organize.
- To encourage and support children's readiness for writing and reading.

Academic Materials. The third area of Montessori materials is more academic. Exercises are presented in a sequence that encourages writing before reading. Reading is therefore an outgrowth of writing. Both processes, however, are introduced so gradually that children are never aware they are learning to write and read until one day they realize they are writing and reading. Describing this phenomenon, Montessori said that children "burst spontaneously" into writing and reading. She anticipated contemporary educational literacy practices by integrating writing and reading and maintaining that writing lays the foundation for learning to read. Children use their writing to learn to read, a practice duplicated in preschool today.

Montessori believed that many children were ready for writing at four years of age. Consequently, children who enter a Montessori system at age three have done most of the sensory exercises by the time they are four. It is not uncommon to see four- and five year olds in a Montessori classroom writing and reading.

Following are examples of Montessori materials that promote writing and reading:

- *Ten geometric forms and colored pencils.* These introduce children to the coordination necessary for writing. After selecting a geometric inset, children trace it on paper and fill in the outline with a colored pencil of their choosing.
- *Sandpaper letters.* Each letter of the alphabet is outlined in sandpaper on a card, with vowels in blue and consonants in red. Children see the shape, feel the shape, and hear the sound of the letter, which the teacher repeats when introducing it.
- *Movable alphabet with individual letters.* Consonants are blue, vowels are red. Children learn to put together familiar words, such as *pat* and *rat*.
- *Command cards.* A set of red cards with a single action word printed on each card. Children read the word on the card and do what the word tells them to do (e.g., run, jump).

Auto-Education

Montessori named the concept that children are capable of educating themselves **auto-education** (also known as self-education). Children who are actively involved in a prepared environment and who exercise freedom of choice literally educate themselves. Montessori teachers prepare classrooms in which children educate themselves.

auto-education The idea that children teach themselves through appropriate materials and activities.

The Teacher's Role

Montessori believed that "it is necessary for the teacher to guide the child without letting him feel her presence too much, so that she may be always ready to supply the desired help, but may never be the obstacle between the child and his experience."[17]

The Montessori teacher demonstrates key behaviors to implement this child-centered approach:

- *Make children the center of learning* because, as Montessori said, "The teacher's task is not to talk, but to prepare and arrange a series of motives for cultural activity in a special environment made for the child."[18]
- *Encourage children to learn* by providing freedom for them in the prepared environment.
- *Observe children* so as to prepare the best possible environment, recognizing sensitive periods and diverting inappropriate behavior to meaningful tasks.
- *Introduce learning materials,* demonstrate learning materials, and support children's learning. The teacher introduces learning materials after observing each child.
- *Prepare the learning environment* by ensuring that learning materials are provided in an orderly format and the materials provide for appropriate experiences for each child.
- *Respect each child* and model ongoing respect for all children and their work.

Montessori and Contemporary Practices

The Montessori approach supports many methods of instruction used in contemporary early childhood programs:

active learning Involvement of the child with materials, activities, and projects in order to learn concepts, knowledge, and skills.

- *Integrated curriculum.* Montessori involves children in actively manipulating concrete materials across the curriculum—writing, reading, science, math, geography, and the arts.
- *Active learning.* Montessori classrooms practice **active learning**, the involvement of children using concrete, manipulative materials in order to learn concepts, knowledge, and skills.
- *Individualized instruction.* Montessori individualizes learning through children's interactions with the materials as they proceed at their own rates of mastery. Montessori materials are age appropriate for a wide age range of children in mixed-age classrooms.
- *Independence.* The Montessori environment emphasizes respect for children and promotes success, both of which encourage children to be independent.
- *Appropriate assessment.* In a Montessori classroom, observation is the primary means of assessing children's progress, achievement, and behavior. Well-trained Montessori teachers are skilled observers of children and are adept at translating their observations into appropriate ways of guiding, directing, facilitating, and supporting children's active learning.
- *Developmentally appropriate practice.* The concepts and process of developmentally appropriate curricula and practice are foundational in the Montessori method. The Montessori method emphasizes the uniqueness of each child and the importance of independent learning.

You can gain a good understanding of the ebb and flow of life in a Montessori classroom by reading and reflecting on the Voice from the Field, which describes a day at Children's House.

Providing for Diversity and Disability

Montessori education is ideally suited to meet the needs of children from diverse backgrounds, those with disabilities, and those with other special needs such as giftedness. Montessori believed that all children are intrinsically motivated to learn and that they absorb knowledge when they are provided appropriate environments at appropriate times of development. Thus Montessorians believe in providing for individual differences in enriched environments.

This child is learning independence and active learning—two of the many methods that Montessorian programs use in contemporary early childhood programs. Montessori believed it was important for children to learn the arts as a basis for learning about their world.

Raintree Montessori in Lawrence, Kansas, provides inclusive services for its children. Several teachers have special education training as well as Montessori certification. Pam Shanks, inclusion coordinator and primary classroom teacher comments, "We believe all students have the right to high-quality educational programs designed to allow them, regardless of their abilities or disabilities, to thrive and develop."[19]

Further Thoughts

In many respects, Maria Montessori was a person for all generations who contributed greatly to early childhood programs and practices. Many of her ideas—such as preparing

Voice from the Field

Children's House Daily Schedule

This sample schedule is typical of a Montessori program. It is structured to allow for activities in all three basic areas of involvement—life, sensory materials, and academic materials—and includes a rest period for the youngest children.

	Classroom Activities	Benefits for Children
8:00–10:45 **Work Period**	Children spend this uninterrupted time working on individual or small-group activities at a table or on a rug on the floor. Many activities require a lesson from the teacher. Others, such as puzzles, can be used without a lesson. Children who choose an activity that is too difficult for them are offered something that better matches their abilities.	These activities allow children to improve their attention span and concentration skills, small-motor control, eye–hand coordination, attention to detail, perseverance, and the joy of learning. Responsibility for one's own learning is developed as the children make their own choices.
10:45–11:15 **Circle Time**	This group activity includes calling the roll, a peace ceremony, grace and courtesy lessons, stories, songs, games, or lessons on something new in the classroom. Children help set the tables for lunch, feed the animals, water the plants, and perform other chores.	Whole-group lessons are an important time for children to learn how to take turns, participate appropriately in a larger society, share feelings and ideas, enjoy each other's company in songs and games, and learn respect for others.
11:15–11:45 **Outside Play**	Climbing on the play apparatus, sand play, and gardening are a few of the activities available on the playground.	Large-motor control, participation in group games, and learning about the wonders of nature take place as the children play outside.
11:45–12:25 **Lunchtime**	The children wash their hands, wait until all are seated before beginning, concentrate on manners and pleasant conversations at the table, take a taste of everything, pack up leftovers, throw away trash, and remain seated until everyone is finished and excused. After lunch, children help clean the tables and sweep the floor.	Respectful behavior at mealtime is learned through modeling and direction from the teacher. Discussions can include manners, healthy nutrition, and family customs. Cooperation and teamwork are fostered as children help each other clean up and transition to the next activity.
12:25–12:50 **Outside Play**	Climbing on the play apparatus, sand play, and gardening are again available on the playground.	See earlier outside play.
12:50–3:00 **Age-Appropriate Activities**	Nappers—Children under the age of four and a half sleep or rest in a small-group setting.	Rest rejuvenates these young children for participation in the remainder of the day.
	Pre-kindergarten—Children between four and a half and five rest quietly for thirty minutes and then join the kindergarten group.	Working alongside kindergartners encourages pre-kindergarten children to emulate their classmates in academic as well as social skills.
	Kindergarten—Children who are five years old by September 30 and are ready for the kindergarten experience continue to work on the lessons that were begun in the morning; they also have more extensive lessons in geography, science, art appreciation, writing, and music.	Kindergarten children benefit from being part of a small group and working to their full potential in any area of their choosing. The joy of learning comes to life as they concentrate on works of intrinsic interest to them.
3:00–3:45 **Outside Play**	Climbing on the play apparatus, sand play, and gardening are again available on the playground.	See earlier outside play.
3:45–4:00 **Group Snack**	Children share a snack before starting the afternoon activities.	A snack provides another opportunity to encourage manners and healthy eating.
4:00–5:30 **After-School Fun**	Activities at this time can include games, art, drama, music, movement, cooking, an educational video, or the continuation of Montessori work begun earlier in the day.	Cooperation, teamwork, and creative expression are fostered as children build self-esteem.
5:30 **End of Day**	All children should be picked up by this time.	Pick-up time offers the children an opportunity to say good-bye to the teacher and each other. It also gives the teacher a chance to speak briefly with parents.

Source: Contributed by Keturah Collins, owner and director, Children's House Montessori School, Reston, Virginia, www.childrenshouse-montessori.com.

the environment, providing child-size furniture, promoting active learning and independence, and using multiage/mixed-age grouping—are fully incorporated into early childhood classrooms. As a result, it is easy to take her contributions for granted. We do many things in a Montessorian way without thinking too much about it!

What is important is that early childhood professionals use the best of Montessori for children of the twenty-first century. As with any practice, professionals must adopt approaches to fit the children they are teaching while remaining true to what is best in that approach. Respect for children is never out of date and should be accorded to all children regardless of culture, gender, or socioeconomic background.

HighScope: A Constructivist Model

HighScope educational model A program for young children based on Piaget's and Vygotsky's ideas.

The **HighScope educational model** gears curriculum to children's stages of development and promotes constructive processes of learning that broaden children's emerging intellectual and social skills.[20] The HighScope model is based on Piaget's cognitive development theory and fits well with Vygotsky's theory of social development.

Basic Principles and Goals of the HighScope Model

Three of the principles of the HighScope model are:

- Active participation of children in choosing, organizing, and evaluating learning activities, which are undertaken with careful teacher observation and guidance in a learning environment with a rich variety of materials located in various classroom learning centers.
- Regular daily planning by the teaching staff in accord with a developmentally based curriculum model and careful child observations.
- Developmentally sequenced goals and materials for children based on HighScope's "key developmental indicators."[21]

The HighScope program strives to develop in children a broad range of skills, including problem solving, interpersonal, and communication skills that are essential for successful living in a rapidly changing society. The curriculum encourages student initiative by providing children with materials, equipment, and time to pursue activities they design themselves. At the same time, it provides teachers with a framework for guiding children's independent activities toward sequenced learning goals. The teacher plays a key role in instructional activities by selecting appropriate, developmentally sequenced material and by encouraging children to adopt an active problem-solving approach to learning. This teacher–student interaction—teachers helping students achieve developmentally sequenced goals while also encouraging them to set many of their own goals—uniquely distinguishes the HighScope curriculum from direct instruction and teacher-centered curricula.[22]

Five Elements of the HighScope Model

Professionals who use the HighScope curriculum are fully committed to providing settings in which children actively learn and construct their own knowledge. Teachers create the context for learning by implementing and supporting five essential elements: active learning, classroom arrangement, the daily schedule, assessment, and the curriculum/content.

Active Learning.   Teachers support children's active learning by providing a variety of materials; making plans and reviewing activities with children; interacting with and carefully observing individual children; and, leading small- and large-group active learning activities.

Classroom Arrangement.   The classroom contains five or more interest centers that encourage choice. The classroom organization of materials and equipment supports the daily routine. Children know where to find materials and what materials they can use. This encourages development of self-direction and independence.

The teacher selects the centers and activities to use in the classroom based on several considerations:

- Interests of the children (e.g., preschool children are interested in blocks, housekeeping, and art)
- Opportunities for facilitating active involvement in seriation (e.g., big, bigger, biggest), numbers (e.g., counting), time relations (e.g., before–after), classification (e.g., likenesses and differences), spatial relations (e.g., over–under), and language development
- Opportunities for reinforcing needed skills and concepts and functional (real-life) use of these skills and concepts

Classroom arrangement is an essential part of professional practice in order to appropriately implement a program's philosophy. This is true for every program with which you may be involved. A well-organized classroom provides a rich context for children's learning.

Assessment.   Teachers keep notes about significant behaviors, changes, statements, and things that help them better understand a child's way of thinking and learning. Teachers use two mechanisms to help them collect data: (1) the key developmental indicators note form and (2) a portfolio. In addition, teachers use the child observation record (COR) to identify and record children's progress in key behavioral and content areas.

Curriculum/Content.   The HighScope educational method is based on **key developmental indicators (KDIs)** in five curriculum content areas. The KDIs are early childhood milestones that guide teachers as they plan and assess learning experiences and interact with children to support learning.[23] The five curriculum content areas are: (1) approaches to learning; (2) language, literacy, and communication; (3) social and emotional development; (4) physical development, health, and well-being; and (5) arts and sciences (math, science and technology, social studies, and arts). You can review all KDIs by accessing the website at the end of the chapter.

key developmental indicators (KDIs) Activities that foster developmentally important skills and abilities.

Daily Routine.   HighScope preschool programs follow a predictable sequence of events known as the daily routine. This framework provides for the day's events that support children's security and independence. The daily routine consists of these components:

- *Plan-do-review sequence (planning time, work time, recall time).* The **plan-do-review** sequence is unique to the HighScope curriculum. It includes a 10- to 15-minute period during which children plan what they want to do during work time (the area to visit, materials to use, and friends to play with); a 45- to 60-minute work time for children to carry out their plans or shift to new activities that interest them; and another 10- to 15-minute period for review and recall. This review permits children to reflect on what they did and how it was done. It brings closure to children's planning and work time activities. Putting their ideas and experiences to words also facilitates children's language development and it enables children to represent to others their mental schemes.
- *Small-group time.* During this time, a small group of children meet with an adult to experiment with materials, try out new skills, and solve problems.
- *Large-group time.* Large-group time builds a sense of community. Up to twenty children and two adults come together for movement and music activities, interactive storytelling, and other shared experiences.

plan-do-review A sequence in which children, with the help of the teacher, initiate plans for projects or activities; work in learning centers to implement their plans; and then review what they have done with the teacher and their fellow classmates.

- *Outside time.* Children and adults spend at least thirty minutes outside every day, enjoying vigorous play in the fresh air.
- *Transition times.* Transitions are the minutes between other activities of the day, as well as arrival and departure times. Teachers strive to make transitions pass smoothly, since they set the stage for the next segment in the day's schedule.
- *Eating and resting times (if applicable).* Meals and snacks allow children to enjoy eating healthy food in a supportive social setting. Rest is for quiet, solitary activities.
- *Adult team planning time.* This time occurs every day in a HighScope program. It can happen during children's nap time, before children arrive, or after they leave. The teaching team meets to discuss their observations of children's developing abilities and interests.

Notice the facial expressions of these children as they engage in active, hands-on learning with manipulative materials. Certainly this picture is worth a thousand words in conveying the power of active learning.

Further Thoughts

Implementing the HighScope approach has several advantages. First, it offers you a method for implementing a constructivist-based program that has its roots in Piagetian cognitive theory. Second, it is widely popular and has been extensively researched and tested. Third, a rather extensive network of training and support is provided by the HighScope Foundation. You can learn more about HighScope through its website located in the Linking to Learning section. Reviewing the website will help you to determine which characteristics of the HighScope program you would like to implement in your classroom.

Providing for Diversity and Disability

The HighScope curriculum is a developmentally appropriate approach that is child centered and promotes active learning. The use of learning centers, active learning, and the plan-do-review cycle, as well as allowing children to progress at their own pace, provides for children's individual and special needs. HighScope teachers emphasize the broad cognitive, social, and physical abilities that are important for each child, instead of focusing on a child's deficits. HighScope teachers identify where a child is developmentally and then provide a rich range of experiences appropriate for that level. For example, they would encourage a four-year-old who is functioning at a two-year-old level to express his or her plans by pointing, gesturing, and saying single words, and they would immerse the child in a conversational environment that provides many natural opportunities for using and hearing language.[24]

Many early childhood programs for children with special needs incorporate the HighScope approach. For example, Regional Early Childhood Center in Rockburn Elementary School in Elkridge, Maryland, operates a half-day multiple-intense-needs class for children with disabilities and typically developing peers and uses the HighScope approach. The daily routine includes greeting time, small groups (e.g., art, sensory, preacademics), planning time (i.e., picking a center), work time at centers, cleanup time, recall (i.e., discussion about where they "worked"), snacks, circle time with stories, movement and music, and outside time.[25]

Voice from the Field

Reggio Emilia

Boulder Journey School, a private school for young children in Boulder, Colorado, welcomes 250 children, six weeks to six years of age, and their families.

The philosophy of education and pedagogy of Boulder Journey School stems from the constructivist, social-constructivist, and systems thinking theories of John Dewey, Jean Piaget, Lev Vygotsky, Jerome Bruner, David Hawkins, Howard Gardner, Loris Malaguzzi, Carlina Rinaldi, and Boulder Journey School's Theory of Supportive Social Learning.

The work of the school community has evolved through our dialogue with the educators in Reggio Emilia, Italy and educators throughout the world who are inspired by the world-renowned Reggio Emilia approach to early childhood education.

Our values are based on a strong image of children as curious, competent, and capable of co-constructing knowledge with other children and adults. From the moment of birth, children are engaged in a search for the meaning of life, seeking to understand the world that surrounds them and the relationships that they form and develop with others in their world. Educators and families, as partners in the research of the children, seek to encourage, enhance, and extend children's thinking and learning, thereby creating a relational community.

We value our school as a community of learners who think reflectively and who collaborate in dialogue with one another as they . . .

- explore and discover
- organize and interpret information
- ask questions and build answers
- propose ideas and strategies
- make choices and negotiate decisions
- develop and test hypotheses

in order to . . .

- solve problems
- define meanings based on values
- build new understandings
- experience life
- generate hypotheses, test theories and ask more questions
- project further investigations

ultimately co-constructing a knowledge base that continues to evolve and grow.

The co-construction of knowledge is afforded by an environment that is filled with myriad resources and supported by time. Provocations designed to enhance experiences offer endless possibilities for creativity, imagination, symbolization, and representation in the classrooms, studios, theater, and outdoors.

Children and adults interact in relationships formed and maintained within the school. We think that this system of relationships is critical because it provides a basis for the development of a culture in the school that reflects the unique cultures of the individuals within the school.

During meetings together we revisit, interpret, and make predictions about our learning, weaving daily moments into long-term investigations. Children, families, and educators dialogue in small and large groups, leading to the development of a rich, diversified and contextual curriculum. We give visibility to our work and our relationships through the use of technology, leaving traces of our daily experiences in photographs, slides, videos, commentaries, and examples of children's representations. We view communication and participation as essential forums for the expression of our connections, the history of our work, and the story of our lives together at the school.

Source: Contributed by Dr. Ellen L. Hall, founder and executive director of Boulder Journey School, Boulder, Colorado. Photos courtesy of Boulder Journey School, Boulder, Colorado.

Reggio Emilia

Reggio Emilia, a city in northern Italy, is widely known for its approach to educating young children.[26] Founded by Loris Malaguzzi (1920–1994), **Reggio Emilia** sponsors programs for children from three months to six years of age. Certain essential beliefs and practices underlie the Reggio Emilia approach. These basic features define the Reggio approach, make it a constructivist program, and enable it to be adapted and implemented in many U.S. early childhood programs. Read the Voice from the Field "Reggio Emilia" to understand how this model is implemented at the Boulder Journey School.

Reggio Emilia An approach to education based on the philosophy and practice that children are active constructors of their own knowledge.

Beliefs About Children and How They Learn

As we have discussed, your beliefs about young children determine how you teach them, what kind of programs you provide for them, and your expectations for their learning and development. This is the case with Reggio. Their beliefs drive their program practices.

Respect for Children.   Respect for each child is a foundational theme in Reggio. Teachers do not impose adult ideas or daily schedules on children. Rather, the program places each child at the center of learning and the hundred languages are child centered and emerge from children, not adults.

Relationships.   The Reggio approach focuses on each child and is conducted in relation to the family, other children, teachers, environment of the school, community, and the wider society. Each school is viewed as a system in which all these interconnected relationships are reciprocal, activated, and supported. In other words, as Vygotsky believed, children learn through social interactions. In addition, as Montessori indicated, the environment supports and is important to learning.

When preparing space, teachers offer the possibility for children to be with the teachers and many of the other children, or with just a few of them. Also, children can be alone when they need a little niche to stay by themselves.

Teachers are always aware, however, children learn a great deal in exchanges with their peers, especially when they interact in small groups. Such small groups of two, three, four, or five children provide possibilities for paying attention, listening to each other, developing curiosity and interest, asking questions, and responding. Also, groups provide opportunities for negotiation and ongoing dynamic communication.

Hundred Languages.   Malaguzzi wrote a poem about the many languages of children. Here is the way it begins:

> *The child is made of one hundred.*
> *The child has a hundred languages, a hundred hands, a hundred thoughts.*
> *A hundred ways of thinking, of playing, of speaking.*[27]

The hundred languages Malaguzzi was referring to include drawing, building, modeling, sculpturing, discussing, inventing, discovering, and more. However, art and artistic products is the main medium for representing children's thinking. Teachers are encouraged to create environments in which children can literally use all hundred languages to learn. Access the Hundred Languages on the Reggio Emilia website at the end of the chapter and read the poem in its entirety.

Time.   Reggio Emilia teachers believe time is not set by a clock and that continuity is not interrupted by the calendar. Children's own sense of time and their personal rhythms are considered in planning and carrying out activities and projects. The full-day schedule provides sufficient time for being together among peers in an environment that is conducive to getting things done with satisfaction.

Teachers get to know the personal rhythms and learning styles of each child. This is possible in part because children stay with the same teachers and the same peer group for three-year cycles (infancy to three years and three years to six years).

Adults' Roles

In the Reggio approach, adults play a very powerful role in children's lives; children's well-being is connected to the well-being of parents and teachers. One of the essential things you notice from the three programs in this chapter is that high-quality teachers are essential for high-quality programs.

The Teacher.   Teachers observe and listen closely to children to know how to plan or proceed with their work. They ask questions and discover children's ideas, hypotheses, and theories. They collaboratively discuss what they have observed and recorded and make flexible plans and preparations. Teachers then enter into dialogues with the children and offer them occasions for discovering and also revisiting and reflecting on experiences, since they consider learning an ongoing process. Teachers are partners with children in a continual process of research and learning.

The Atelierista.   A teacher trained in the visual arts, the **atelierista**, works closely with teachers and children in every preprimary school and makes visits to the infant/toddler centers. The atelier (the studio area, see below) is the focal point for the atelierista and children.

atelierista A teacher trained in the visual arts, who works with teachers and children.

Parents.   Parents are an essential component of the program and are included in the advisory committee that runs each school. Parents' participation is expected and supported and takes many forms: day-to-day interaction, work in the schools, discussion of educational and psychological issues, special events, excursions, and celebrations.

The Environment

The infant/toddler centers and school programs are the most visible aspect of the work done by teachers and parents in Reggio Emilia. They convey many messages, of which the most immediate is that this is a place where adults have thought about the quality and the instructive power of space.

The Physical Space.   The layout of physical space, in addition to welcoming whoever enters, fosters encounters, communication, and relationships. The arrangement of structures, objects, and activities encourages choices, problem solving, and discoveries in the process of learning.

The centers and schools of Reggio Emilia are beautiful. Their beauty comes from the message the whole school conveys about children and teachers engaged together in the pleasure of learning. There is attention to detail everywhere: in the color of the walls, the shape of the furniture, the arrangement of simple objects on shelves and tables. Light from the windows and doors shines through transparent collages and weavings made by children. Healthy green plants are everywhere. Behind the shelves displaying shells or other found or made objects are mirrors that reflect the patterns that children and teachers have created.

The environment is also highly personal. For example, a series of small boxes made of white cardboard creates a grid on the wall of a school. On each box the name of a child or a teacher is printed with rubber-stamp letters. These boxes are used for leaving little surprises or messages for one another. Communication is valued and favored at all levels.

The space in the centers and schools of Reggio Emilia is personal in still another way: it is full of children's own work. Everywhere there are paintings, drawings, paper sculptures, wire constructions, transparent collages coloring the light, and mobiles moving gently overhead. Such things turn up even in unexpected spaces like stairways and bathrooms. Although the work of the children is pleasing to the eye, it is not intended as decoration, but rather to show and document the competence of children, the beauty of their ideas, and the complexity of their learning processes.

The Atelier.   A special workshop or studio, called an **atelier**, is set aside and used by all the children and teachers in the school. It contains a great variety of tools and resource materials, along with records of past projects and experiences. For example, the College School Atelier in St. Louis, Missouri, is equipped with easels, paints, drawing materials, clay, wire, collage objects, and a multitude of natural and recycled materials. Technology resources and a workshop for documentation are also present.[28]

atelier A special area or studio for creating projects.

The activities and projects, however, do not take place only in the atelier. Smaller spaces called mini-ateliers are set up in each classroom. In fact, each classroom becomes an active workshop with children involved with a variety of materials and experiences that they have discussed and chosen with teachers and peers. In the view of Reggio educators, the children's use of many media is not art or a separate part of the curriculum but an inseparable, integral part of the whole cognitive/symbolic expression involved in the process of learning.

Program Practices

Cooperation is the powerful working mode that makes the achievement of the goals Reggio educators set possible. Teachers work in pairs in each classroom. They see themselves as researchers gathering information about their work with children by means of continual documentation. The strong collegial relationships that are maintained with teachers and staff enable them to engage in collaborative discussion and interpretation of both teachers' and children's work.

Documentation.   Transcriptions of children's remarks and discussions, photographs of their activity, and representations of their thinking and learning using many media are carefully arranged by the atelierista, along with the other teachers, to document the work and the process of learning. **Documentation** has many functions:

documentation Records of children's work, including recordings, photographs, art, work samples, projects, and drawings.

- Making parents aware of children's experiences and maintaining their involvement
- Allowing teachers to understand children better and to evaluate their own work, thus promoting professional growth
- Facilitating communication and exchange of ideas among educators
- Making children aware that their effort is valued
- Creating an archive that traces the history of the school and the pleasure of learning by many children and their teachers

Curriculum and Practices.   The curriculum is not established in advance. Teachers express general goals and make hypotheses about what direction activities and projects might take. Based on these discussions, teachers make appropriate preparations for their individualized

These documentation panels include children's artifacts, photos, and descriptive captions written by teachers or children. The panels document block work, literacy development, and other activities that the children experience in a day.

curriculum. Then, after observing children in action, teachers compare, discuss, and interpret together their observations. Teachers then make choices that they share with the children about what to offer and how to sustain the children in their exploration and learning. In fact, the curriculum emerges in the process of each activity or project and is flexibly adjusted accordingly through this continuous dialogue among teachers and with children.

Further Thoughts. Keep a number of things in mind as you consider the Reggio Emilia approach and how it might relate to your work as an early childhood educator. First, its theoretical base rests within constructivism and shares ideas compatible with those of Piaget, Vygotsky, Dewey, and Gardner, and the process of learning by doing. Second, there is no set curriculum. Rather, the curriculum emerges or springs from children's interests and experiences. This approach is, for many, difficult to implement and does not ensure that children will learn basic academic skills valued by contemporary American society. Third, the Reggio Emilia approach is suited to a particular culture and society. How this approach works, flourishes, and meets the educational needs of children in an Italian village may not necessarily be appropriate for meeting the needs of contemporary American children. The Italian view of education is that it is the responsibility of the state, and the state provides high levels of financial support. While education is a state function in the United States, traditionally local community control of education is a powerful and sacred part of American education.

Providing for Diversity and Disability

The Grant Early Childhood Center in Cedar Rapids, Iowa, meets the challenge of inclusion through Prizing Our National Differences (POND), a program based on the Reggio Emilia approach. The POND program includes all children with disabilities as full participants in general education classrooms with their age-appropriate peers. Two core ingredients of the Reggio approach facilitate successful inclusion at Grant Early Childhood Center:

1. *Encouraging collaborative relationships.* For example, children older than five years of age who need special education services are included with kindergarten and first grade classes.
2. *Constructing effective environments for each child.* For example, members of Grant's support team include a counselor, speech therapist, occupational therapist, physical therapist, psychologist, resource teacher, nurse, and two Title I teachers. The support team attempts to address the individual needs of students through the PSS (POND Support Sessions) and IDM (Instructional Decision Making) processes to ensure children are getting the proper services needed to succeed.[29]

The Project Approach

The **Project Approach** is another very popular method used in early childhood education. The Reggio Emilia program is an excellent example of the project approach in action. However, the Project Approach has been an important part of early childhood and traces its modern roots back to John Dewey's use of projects in his laboratory school at the University of Chicago.

With the Project Approach, an investigation is undertaken by a small group of children within a class, sometimes by a whole class, and occasionally by an individual child. The key feature of a project is that it is a search for answers to questions about a topic worth learning more about, something the children are interested in.[30]

Projects provide the backbone of the children's and teachers' learning experiences. These projects are based on the strong conviction that learning by doing is of great importance and that to discuss in groups and to revisit ideas and experiences is the premier way of gaining better understanding and learning.

Project Approach An in-depth investigation of a topic worth learning more about.

Voice from the Field

How to Use the Project Approach

Students in the K–1 classroom at University Primary School in St. Louis, Missouri, begin their day reading a daily sign-in question that is intended to provoke a thoughtful response:

Have you ever eaten the flowers of a plant?
Do you think a van is more like a car or a bus?

Such questions are related to the topic under study and are used to engage children in discussing different views during their whole-group meeting later in the morning.

Opportunities for children to express themselves abound at University Primary School. In addition to an hour of systematic literacy instruction, authentic opportunities to read and write occur throughout the day in the course of the children's regular activities.

Integrating Language Arts with the Project Approach

The Project Approach involves students in in-depth investigation of worthy real-world topics;* learning becomes meaningful for them as they pursue answers to their own questions. Students can carry out specific literacy-related activities in each phase of project investigation:

PHASE 1

Exploring Previous Experiences

- Brainstorm what is already known about a project topic
- Write or dictate stories about memories and experiences
- Categorize and label experiences

Activities you can incorporate into Phase 1 that allow children to explore previous experiences are:

- Memory drawings or stories

- Concept webs or maps of student ideas (e.g., Venn diagrams)
- Questionnaires that children develop to ask their peers or parents

PHASE 2

Investigating the Topic

- Write questions, predictions, and hypotheses
- Write questions to ask experts
- Write questionnaires and surveys
- Write thank-you letters to experts
- Record findings
- Record data
- Make all types of lists (what materials need to be collected, what will be shared with others, who will do which tasks)
- Listen to stories and informational texts read aloud
- Read secondary sources to help answer questions
- Compare what was read with what the experts shared

For example, students at the University Primary School work in small groups on subtopics of the larger topic and share what they find with the other students in the class, giving them authentic reasons to express what they have newly learned during Phase 2. Fieldwork includes interviewing experts, visiting places

Ideas for projects originate in the experiences of children and teachers as they construct knowledge together. Projects can last from a few days to several months. They may start from a chance event, an idea, or a problem posed by one or more children or from an experience initiated directly by teachers.

The Voice from the Field "How to Use the Project Approach" is a Competency Builder that shows how you can use projects effectively to involve children in activities that interest them and teach young children traditional academic subjects, such as literacy.

Early Childhood Programs and You

As an early childhood teacher it is important for you to know about various programs for young children. Knowing about programs enables you to talk knowledgeably with colleagues and parents and to critically compare and contrast features of one program with another. As

of interest, and delving into secondary sources including Internet resources, books, or artifacts.

PHASE 3 Sharing the Project with Parents and Others

- Make charts, displays, and PowerPoint presentations
- Write reports or plays that demonstrate new understanding
- Write invitations to a culminating event
- Host a culminating event as an open house

In Phase 3, children share findings with other students and their families. See for example how students at University Primary School have explored music, construction, communication, and measurement through project investigations described fully on the website: www.ed.uiuc.edu/ups/projects/.

Throughout all phases of their project investigation, students have authentic contexts to read, spell, write words, and build their vocabulary. In addition, comparing what they knew with what they have learned from the primary and secondary sources, they develop their analytical thinking and comprehension skills. And they become more fluent readers and writers by using their skills to answer their own questions.

Providing Direct Instruction in Reading and Writing

The five reading components articulated in the No Child Left Behind Act—phonemic awareness, phonics, fluency, vocabulary, and comprehension—are taught throughout the students' day within the context of project investigation and during small-group direct literacy instruction. Direct instruction includes a whole-group meeting during which the teacher reads books aloud (i.e., shared reading) for specific purposes. The teacher may choose to highlight the project topic or specific authors or illustrators or to focus on rhyming words or specific patterns of phonemes.

Following the shared reading time, students engage in writing activities related to the books they heard read aloud. These activities may include literature extensions that encourage students to write creatively. They may write a different ending to a story or write a related story from a different point of view. Students may also write their own stories, using the principles of writer's workshop, in which students learn to edit and extend their language skills. The teacher may also introduce extended mini-lessons on tools of writing, such as alliteration, similes, metaphors, or syllabic rhythms.

After their noon recess, students choose books to read quietly while the teacher provides individual guided reading. Project-related books may be a popular choice. Students conclude their silent reading with approximately ten minutes to engage in buddy reading. During the buddy reading time, students talk about what they have just read with their buddy and read favorite excerpts of their books to their buddy. This collaboration reinforces comprehension skills and instills the love of literature that motivates all children to read. At University Primary School, students are always improving and using their literacy skills to learn.

Source: Contributed by Nancy B. Hertzog, associate professor, Department of Special Education, and director, University Primary School at the University of Illinois at Urbana-Champaign; and by Marjorie M. Klein, former head teacher in the K–1 classroom at University Primary School and now an educational consultant in St. Louis, Missouri. Photo by Patrick White/Merrill.

*L. G. Katz and S. C. Chard, Engaging Children's Minds: The Project Approach, 2nd ed. (Norwood, NJ: Ablex, 2000).

you engage in this reflection and critical analysis you will be able to identify what you think are the strengths and weaknesses of each program and what features of each program you like the best. Knowing about early childhood programs enables you to always be clear about what you believe is best for children and families and to think, talk, and act as a confident professional.

Even though all of the program models we have discussed in this chapter are unique, at the same time they all have certain similarities. All of them, regardless of their particular philosophical orientation, have as primary goals respect for each child and how to provide the best education for all children.

Here are some critical decisions to make now. First, identify which features of these program models you can and cannot support. Second, decide which of these models and/or features of them you can embrace and incorporate into your own practice. An ongoing rule of the early childhood professional is to decide what you believe is best for children and families before you make decisions about what to teach.

Accommodating Diverse Learners

Meet Esmeralda, an energetic and precocious Mexican American four-year-old. She loves to read and play outside with her older brother and with trucks and dolls. But for all of Esmeralda's intrinsic gifts, she faces a great disadvantage due to the achievement gaps that exist in American education today. Research on the achievement gaps reveals that, on average, African American and Latino students are two to three years of learning behind Caucasian students of the same age.[31] Furthermore, in math and reading scores across the fourth and eighth grades, 48 percent of African Americans and 43 percent of Latinos are "below basic," while only 17 percent of Caucasians are below basic.[32] These gaps exist in every state and in more pronounced extremes in large urban school districts.[33]

It is certain you will have children from different backgrounds in your early childhood classroom. You and other early childhood professionals must help close the achievement gap. You have the power to make a difference in children's lives.

Closing the Gaps

The most important thing you can do is be the most effective teacher you can be. You can use effective educational strategies that respond to and are sensitive to the diversity of families and children. You create effective educational strategies when you:

- *Use developmentally appropriate practice.*   DAP serves as a framework for you to plan the environment and the curriculum. This allows you to create individualized activities and instruction that builds on each child's strengths. For children with disabilities of any kind, accommodate and differentiate. For example, because Esmeralda is economically disadvantaged, she may not have had the same resources available to her as her peers to support her development. You may have to spend extra time with Esmeralda to "play catch up," or offer one-on-one time a few days a week before school starts in the morning to ensure she achieves school and state standards.

- *Create accessible physical environments.*   Environments that are healthy, safe, respectful, supportive, and challenging support children's independence and interaction and increase achievement. Be familiar with the principles and practices of **universal design (UD)**, the design of products, services, and environments so they are usable and accessible for all children. Universal design is intended to make all environments accessible for all people regardless of age, situation, or ability. For example, new paper towel dispensers and faucets that are now common in many restrooms and classrooms operate on a motion sensor. This assists young children with mobility or strength issues, and even when they have to hold something in one hand!

You can make environments physically accessible for children by following the principles of UD in these ways:

- *Equitable use:*   Make high-quality resources available to all. Ensure that all children have the opportunity and the knowledge to use classroom materials, technology, and networks.
- *Flexibility in use:*   Classrooms and materials should be movable, malleable, and manageable. You should be flexible enough to allow students to rearrange materials, chairs, and so on, if they need to.
- *Simple and intuitive:*   Classrooms should be arranged simply enough so that even young children can navigate and understand how things work and where to find and store materials, books, and so on.

universal design (UD)
A broad-spectrum solution that produces buildings, products, and environments that are usable and effective for everyone, not just people with disabilities.

- *Perceptible information:*   Children should find it easy to look around a classroom and gather the information they need. For example, objects should be clearly labled and/or color coded. Avoid clutter to prevent confusion, mobility problems, and sensory overload.
- *Tolerance for error:*   Physical environments should be forgiving. Materials should be sturdy but not dangerous. For example, do not use a toy chest in your classroom unless it has a lid support to hold the lid open in any position. Make sure the toy box or chest has ventilation holes.

- *Create accessible social environments.*   Universal design is intended to make all environments accessible for all people regardless of age, situation, or ability. This pertains to social environments as well as physical environments. You can make environments socially accessible to Esmeralda and others by following the principles of UD.
  - *Equitable use:*   Include material and subject matter that is culturally inclusive. For example, provide information that goes home in Spanish, study Spanish stories, poetry, and songs as well as other cultural contributions that typically make up the curriculum. Also, ensure that Esmeralda's family is encouraged and supported by the school community. For example, introduce families to one another, encourage parents to join activities, and help to resolve hurdles to their involvement.
  - *Flexibility in use:*   Be sure to remain flexible in your understanding and approach to children from all backgrounds, cultures, languages, and developmental level. Accept children for who they are, but also challenge them to grow. Help classmates develop flexibility through modeling and discussion.
  - *Simple and intuitive:*   Follow your gut and listen to what your intuition tells you about a child. For example, if you sense a child is falling behind, has trouble at home, or has difficulties with friends or peers, don't ignore your intuition. Listen to yourself, observe the child closely, and check with the child on a one-to-one basis. Whatever you do, don't just assume the problem will go away on its own. A child who is struggling in one area is usually struggling in another, and often the struggles are connected. Sometimes the simplest or smallest things, like an extra moment of encouragement or even asking the child directly, can brighten a day and improve chances of success.
  - *Perceptible information:*   Make social expectations and guidelines clear and accessible. Classroom rules should be posted clearly and yours should always be a model for positive social interactions and behavior.
  - *Tolerance for error:*   Accept mistakes. Children from different cultures and socioeconomic status may have different cultural and educational backgrounds. You may have to help these children play "catch up" so that they can succeed. This means that you need to be patient, encouraging, and tolerant of perspectives and experiences different from your own.
- *Collaborate with other professionals.*   Collaboration enables you to develop activities and opportunities designed to promote student success. Collaboration with local agencies and institutions facilitates interactions that benefit children, families, and schools. For example, you can work closely with food banks, local Big Brother Big Sister chapters, libraries, Salvation Army, and others; all of which can be tapped to benefit Esmeralda and other children at your school. In addition, appeal to local advocacy lawyers, pediatricians, psychiatrists, and family counselors to provide pro bono services to children, families, and schools.

Even though the program models discussed in this chapter are unique, at the same time they all have certain similarities. All of them, regardless of their particular philosophical orientation, have as a primary goal to provide the best education for all children. Universal design helps you achieve this goal.

Activities for Professional Development

Ethical Dilemma

"That money is ours!"

Students at Walker Early Childhood Center are running out of supplies for projects. You and your colleagues spent many hours writing grants to various agencies for support to purchase the much needed school supplies. Finally, you were successful! The Cy Dickerson Foundation awarded you $500. However, when your director, Tammy Earhart, heard about the grant, she said the money was needed for "more important things." She plans to write a letter to the Dickerson Foundation to ask them if she can use the grant money for a renovation of the infant classroom. You and your colleagues feel betrayed and that your efforts have gone to waste because the money will not be used the way you intended.

What should you do? Go to Tammy and demand that the grant money be used for supplies? Report Tammy to the Board of Directors for unethical conduct? Should you contact the parents' group and "blow the whistle" on Tammy? Or should you and your colleagues look for more grants for the children's supplies and let Tammy have the $500 for the infant room? What do you recommend?

Activities to Apply What You Learned

1. The push for high-quality early childhood programs is becoming more prevalent and important worldwide. Research several current newspapers and professional publications such as *USA Today* and *Education World* concerning early childhood education and the issues facing the profession today. How can you address these issues? Log on to Twitter and share with a small group of classmates your findings through Twitter's online website.
2. In this chapter, you have read about the Montessori model. Use an online search engine to look up Montessori material sites on the Internet such as *MontessoriMaterials.org* and create a list of materials you would buy for inclusion in your early childhood program. Share your ideas and activities by making a Wiki and encouraging your classmates and other experienced teachers to post different activities that incorporate various Montessori materials.
3. The HighScope program model impacts the lives of many children. What components of the model would you incorporate into your classroom? Blog with other classmates and share your ideas!
4. One of the implications the Reggio approach has for all early childhood professionals is how to make all classrooms more aesthetically pleasing. List five things that you would recommend to others. For example, you could invite an artist to your classroom and ask for ideas. Share your five suggestions with others on Facebook.
5. Preschool teacher Marilyn Griffin's children were experimenting with mixing colors. Suddenly, Kiley screamed, "Mrs. Griffin! My hands are green!" This event led to many ongoing projects about the color green. Think of two experiences you had with children that could be the catalyst for a project.
6. In the years to come, there will be an increased need for educators who are aware and knowledgeable of inclusive classrooms and how to reach children with special needs. How can you advocate for children with disabilities to get the services they will need in your classroom using the early childhood models you studied in this chapter? Show your ideas in an online discussion with your classmates.

Linking to Learning

American Montessori Society
www.amshq.org
Serves as a national center for Montessori information, both for its members and for the general public—answering inquiries and facilitating research wherever possible.

ERIC Reggio Emilia Page
http://ceep.crc.uiuc.edu/poptopics/reggio.html
Contains information and resources related to the approach to early childhood education developed in the preschools of Reggio Emilia, Italy.

HighScope Educational Research Foundation
www.highscope.org
Official site for the HighScope Educational Research Foundation. Provides information on HighScope curriculum, assessment, and research as well as e-tools, lists of trainings and conferences, and an online store for purchasing HighScope classroom materials.

International Montessori Society
http://imsmontessori.org
Founded to support the effective application of Montessori principles throughout the world; provides a range of programs and services relating to the fundamental principles of (a) observation, (b) individual liberty, and (c) preparation of the environment.

North American Montessori Teachers' Association
www.montessori-namta.org
A membership organization open to parents, teachers, and anyone else interested in Montessori education.

The Project Approach
www.projectapproach.org/

Provides information about Project Approach and how you can implement its practices in your classroom. Offers an array of project examples to use for inclusion in the classroom, according to grade level.

Reggio Emilia Approach—The Preschool Child's Languages of Learning
http://reggioemiliaapproach.net/

Contains information and resources related to the Reggio Emilia approach, history, and learning environment.

Universal Design
www.design.ncsu.edu/cud/

The Center for Universal Design (CUD) is a national information, technical assistance, and research center that evaluates, develops, and promotes accessible and universal design.

PEARSON myeducationlab

Go to Topic 5 (Program Models) in the MyEducationLab (www.myeducationlab.com) for your course, where you can:

- Find learning outcomes for Program Models along with the national standards that connect to these outcomes.
- Complete Assignments and Activities that can help you more deeply understand the chapter content.
- Apply and practice your understanding of the core teaching skills identified in the chapter with the Building Teaching Skills and Dispositions learning units.
- Check your comprehension on the content covered in the chapter by going to the Study Plan in the Book Resources for your text. Here you will be able to take a chapter quiz, receive feedback on your answers, and then access Review, Practice, and Enrichment activities to enhance your understanding of chapter content.

7

CHILD CARE
Meeting the Needs of Children and Families

naeyc standards

Standard 1. Promoting Child Development and Learning

I use my understanding of young children's characteristics and needs, and of multiple interacting influences on children's development and learning, to create environments that are healthy, respectful, supportive, and challenging for each child.[1]

Standard 4. Using Developmentally Effective Approaches to Connect with Children and Families

I understand and use positive relationships and supportive interactions as the foundation for my work with young children and families. I know, understand, and use a wide array of developmentally appropriate approaches, instructional strategies, and tools to connect with children and families and positively influence each child's development and learning.[2]

The World of Child Care

Child care is the comprehensive out-of-home care and education of children that supplements the care and education children receive from their families. Child care programs address a variety of needs. They provide

- For children's safety and health needs
- A comprehensive array of services that meet children's physical, social/emotional, and intellectual needs
- Educational and readiness programs and activities that support children's abilities to learn and that get them ready for school
- Collaboration with families to help them care for and educate their children

Child care has many faces and dimensions. Like the children they serve, child care programs have many similarities and differences; no two are the same. Each program is unique in its location, its teachers and administrators, and the children and families it serves. Parents and other primary caregivers make their decisions about using child care based on its affordability, accessibility, and quality. Consider the following real-life scenarios:

- Maria Gloria is a young single parent with two children ages two and four. Maria works for minimum wage in a local convenience store. "I really can't afford child care, but I have to work. A woman in the apartment three floors up from me keeps my kids and five others while I work. I give her twenty-five dollars a week. It's all I can afford. I'm lucky to have someone to take care of my kids."
- Charlie and Beth Cosdale have jobs that enable them to just get by on their combined incomes. Charlie drops off their children, one-year-old Amanda and three-year-old Jesse, at the Children's Barn Child Care Center on his way to work. "It's not the best, but it's about what we can afford. I have to leave twenty minutes early because the child care is out of the way. We're looking for something closer, but we haven't found it yet. With the recession, we are lucky to have work."
- Seven-year-old Chantel Harris walks home and lets herself into the family apartment after school each day. There is no one else at home. Her mother wishes she had more choices. "I know it isn't the best or safest thing for Chantel to do. I can't afford anyone to take care of her, and the school doesn't offer any kind of programs after school. What am I supposed to do? My cousin's kids have after-school care at their school. Me and my kids, we're stuck."
- Amy Charney is a stay-at-home mom. Three mornings a week she takes her four-year-old daughter, Emily, to a Mothers' Day Out (MDO) program at a local church. "It's a great arrangement and very reasonable, in terms of cost. When Emily is in MDO I volunteer in the community, and still she and I get to do a lot of things together. The staff is great and is up-to-date on the latest trends, and I feel Emily is definitely getting ready for school."
- Abby Belanger is an up-and-coming attorney in a prestigious law firm. She is a single mother by choice. Abby's four-year-old daughter, Tiffany, is enrolled in a high-quality, high-end preschool program. "I want Tiffany to have the best, and I can afford the best. I want her to have a good start in life so she can go to whatever schools she wants to attend. Education is important to me."

> "As a former teacher, I believe the best way to prepare our youth for success in their academic and professional lives is to provide every child with quality early education."
>
> **U.S. REP. DALE KILDEE**
> Chair of the Early Childhood Subcommittee

Child care arrangements such as these are duplicated countless times each day all across the United States. During the swine flu epidemic of 2009, many child care centers closed.[3] Parents scrambled to find child care to avoid taking time off from work. Think for a moment about the child care arrangements you know about or are involved with. Child care in the United States is often referred to as a patchwork of programs and arrangements of varying costs and quality, combining the good, the bad, and the unavailable. The reality is that America's families need and depend on child care.

To thrive, children need nurturing families and high-quality early care and learning experiences. Securing child care is particularly important for working parents with young children. Research shows that child care assistance is positively associated with the long-term employment and financial well-being of parents.[4] In addition, programs that target families with infants and toddlers, such as Early Head Start, improve children's social and cognitive development, and parenting skills.[5]

Part of our job as early childhood professionals is to advocate and work for high-quality, affordable and accessible child care for all children and families. We will discuss the kind and quality of care children receive outside their homes, which makes a big difference in their lives and the lives of their parents and families. As Table 7.1 illustrates, 47.3 percent of children under the age of 5 are cared for by relatives and 39.5 percent are in organized and nonrelative child care centers.

The Popularity of Child Care

Child care is popular, receives much public attention, and will continue to do so for these reasons:

Working Parents.   There are more dual-income families and working single parents today than ever before. For example, 64 percent of mothers with children under six are

TABLE 7.1 Children in Different Types of Child Care Arrangements

What implications do these data have for you as an early childhood professional?

	Number of Children (In Thousands)	Percent in Arrangement
Total children under 5	11,300	100.0
Relative care	**5345**	**47.3**
Mother	486	4.3
Father	1944	17.2
Other		
Grandparent	2192	19.4
Other	723	6.4
Organized care facility	**2701**	**23.9**
Day care center	2045	18.1
Nursery or preschool	565	5.0
Head Start/School	90	0.8
Nonrelative care	**1762**	**15.6**
In provider's home	1356	12.0
Other	**1492**	**13.2**
Other arrangement	283	2.5
No regular arrangement	1220	10.8

Source: National Child Care Information and Technical Assistance Center, Statistical Information on Child Care in the United States, March 2008, www.nccic.acf.hhs.gov/poptopics/statistics.pdf.

employed, and it is not uncommon for mothers to return to work as early as six weeks after giving birth.[6] Families are paying on average $8,150 per year for an infant, $6,423 per year for a toddler and $5,000 per year for a school-aged child in child care, which makes it hard for working parents who are trying to make ends meet in the current economy.[7]

The current unprecedented entry of large numbers of mothers into the workforce has greatly impacted the care and education of children in the early years. And, the number of working mothers will likely continue to increase and create an even bigger demand for child care for children from six weeks to their entry into public school programs.[8] More parents than ever are balancing work and raising children.

Public Policy.   Child care is an important part of this country's solution to the nation's economic and social problems. Child care is an instrument of public policy; it is used to address political and social issues and is an essential part of enabling parents to be productively employed.

Politicians also view quality child care as a way of addressing many of the country's social problems through early intervention in children's lives. The reasoning is that if we provide children with quality programs and experiences early in life, we reduce the possibility that they will need costly social services later in life.

As the demand for child care increases, the challenge to you and other early childhood professionals is clear. You must participate in advocating for and creating quality child care programs that meet the needs of children and families.

Placement in Child Care Programs

Decisions to place children in child care are personal, individual, and complex. We can say with some assurance that because parents work, they place their children in child care. But it could also be the other way around: because child care is available, some parents choose to work. Decisions relating to child care are not necessarily straightforward but depend on many factors. Consider some of these interesting facts:

- Approximately 2.3 million individuals earn a living caring for and educating children under age five in the United States, of which about 1.2 million are providing child care in formal settings, such as child care centers or family child care homes. The remaining 1.1 million caregivers are paid relatives, friends, or neighbors. [9]

- Children from lower-income families, children whose mothers have less education, and Latino children are significantly less likely than others to attend center based early care and education programs, even though they are among the groups that consistently show a lack of readiness for school.[10]

- Three- and four-year-old preschoolers in center-based settings are recieving different quality early learning experiences because of quality of caregivers and the setting where the children are enrolled.[11]

- On average, children under age five of working mothers spend 36 hours a week in child care.[12]

- Among low-income children under age five in any type of child care arrangement nationwide, three-quarters are cared for in a home setting.[13]

Types of Child Care Programs

Child care is offered in many places and by many persons and agencies that provide a variety of services (see Table 7.2). Of the 12 million children birth to age six, about one third spend 37 hours a week in multiple child care arrangements.[14] The options for child care are almost endless. However, regardless of the kind of child care provided, the issues

TABLE 7.2 Variety of Child Care Programs

Child Care Type	Description
Relatives and friends	Children are cared for by grandparents, aunts, uncles, other relatives, or friends, providing both continuity and stability.
Family	An individual caregiver provides care and education for a small group of children in his or her home.
Intergenerational	Child care programs integrate children and the elderly in an early childhood and adult care facility.
Center-based	Center-based child care is conducted in specially designed and constructed centers, churches, YMCAs and YWCAs, and other such facilities.
Employer-sponsored	To meet the needs of working parents, some employers are providing child care at the work site.
Proprietary	Some child care centers are run by corporations, businesses, or individual proprietors for the purpose of making a profit; these programs often emphasize an educational component.
Before- and after-school	Public schools, center-based programs, community and faith-based agencies, and individuals all offer programs that extend the school day with tutoring, special activities, and a safe space.

of *quality, affordability,* and *accessibility* are always part of the child care landscape. For parents of children with disabilities, *inclusivity* is an added dimension on this landscape. Table 7.2 outlines the placement of children in child care programs.

Child Care by Relatives and Friends

Child care is frequently arranged within extended families or with friends, and parents handle these arrangements in various ways. In some cases, children are cared for by grandparents, aunts, uncles, or other relatives. For example, Marie Harvey takes care of her granddaughter while her daughter works. "I'll pitch in wherever it's needed. I truly enjoy taking care of my granddaughter."[15] In addition, approximately 2.5 million—30 percent—of grandparents provide primary child care to the grandchildren who live with them.[16] In Texas 448,439 children live with grandparents (7.6% of all children in the state)[17] and in California 625,934 children live with grandparents (6.8% of the children in the state).[18] Grandparents are taking over the parenting role for their grandchildren because of divorce, child abuse, negligence/abandonment, incarceration, HIV/AIDS, substance abuse, teenage pregnancy, or parental death.[19]

Relative and friend arrangements satisfy parents' needs to have their children cared for by people with similar lifestyles and values. It also meets the needs of working parents to have child care beyond normal working hours and on weekends. Such care may also be less costly, and the caregiver-to-child ratio is low. These types of arrangements allow children to remain in familiar environments with people they know, benefiting from both continuity and stability.

Family Child Care

family child care Home-based care and education provided by a nonrelative outside the child's home; also known as *family care.*

When home-based care is provided by a nonrelative outside a child's home but in a family setting, it is known as **family child care**, or *family care.* In this arrangement an individual caregiver provides care and education for a small group of children in the caregiver's home. Nine percent of children under five in child care are in family care.[20] Family child care is the most preferred type of care for young children, especially infants and toddlers.[21] Family child care offers several benefits to parents that are not necessarily available in other early care settings:

- Smaller ratio of children to adults
- Mixed-age groups of children, allowing siblings to be together
- Consistent primary caregivers
- Flexibility to meet the family's needs
- The nurturing environment of a home[22]

Both the quantity and the quality of specific services provided in family homes vary from state to state and home to home. For example, because of the high-quality family child care she is in, four-year-old Sarah is able to recognize and identify diverse cultural worlds. She observes the differences in her culture and the cultures of the other children. Family child care providers spend a substantial amount of time in direct interaction with the children.[23] Consider the unique features of Family Child Care homes and the ways the issues of quality, accessibility, and affordability are addressed. The Family Child Care Home:

- Is convenient neighborhood care that is close to home or work
- Provides a cozy homelike environment
- Provides stability by assigning one consistent caregiver to children
- Has a low provider-to-child ratio
- Builds leadership skills, social skills and self esteem by providing mixed ages of children in small groups
- Offers flexible days and hours
- Conducts personal communication between teachers and parents and promotes caring relationships
- Provides children school readiness skills with enriched activities and educational learning experiences
- Provides an inclusive environment for children with special needs[24]

Child care providers should aspire to provide these services to all children and families. On the other hand, family child care can be detrimental for some children. Consider a recent case in which a seventy-year-old man operating a child care home was accused of sexual contact with a four-year-old child which allegedly included sexual intercourse.[25] You can probably find similar cases in your city in which children were abused.

Intergenerational Child Care

Intergenerational child care programs integrate children and the elderly in an early childhood and adult care facility. The elderly derive pleasure and feelings of competence from interacting with children, and young children receive attention and love from older adults. Intergenerational programs blend the best of two worlds: children and the elderly both receive care and attention in a nurturing environment. ONEgeneration in Van Nuys, California is an intergenerational child care that incorporates senior citizens into its child care programs, which serve children six weeks to six years old. In ONEgeneration, seniors and children work together to help one another. For example, three-year-old Joanna Ray and sixty-one-year-old Keith Mullins work together to stir muffin mix in a bowl. Joanna has not developed the strength and coordination to accomplish this task, whereas Keith's legs became paralyzed after a car accident. They work together to strengthen their skills. Research has found that contact with young children improves adult mood interaction and that children who interact with seniors are more advanced in their social development.[26]

Voice from the Field

A Spanish Immersion Program

Bright Years Child Learning Center, a child care program in League City, Texas, provides children the opportunity to learn Spanish through a Spanish immersion program. Children range from six weeks to twelve years of age, and the Spanish immersion program begins at the age of two. Most of our students speak English only. Parents enroll their children in the program because they want them to benefit from learning Spanish.

In the Spanish immersion program, children are taught in Spanish using a regular school curriculum. Spanish is the medium of instruction, and not the subject of instruction. Through daily exposure, children incorporate knowledge information and are able to process it and comprehend it. The children's ability to accept and understand Spanish comes as they progress through the program. As they become more familiar and comfortable hearing, understanding, and speaking Spanish, it becomes a natural part of their thought process and eventually, their speaking process.

Our curriculum is themed by month, and every week we incorporate a subtheme. Every day, we begin the morning with circle time. During this time, we review the calendar, numbers, colors, shapes, and the alphabet. We also sing songs and read books in English and Spanish. The incorporation of English and Spanish during this time is important so that children learn the basic skills in both languages. Spanish is spoken the rest of the day, in all learning domains. In order for children to achieve their fullest potential, it is important to remember some things.

GUIDELINE 1 Avoid English Translation

As easy as it may be, do not translate into English. If information is translated into English after it's already been given in Spanish, students will wait until they hear it in English and entirely ignore the Spanish. This will limit the acceptance of the new language tremendously, hindering any possibility of grasping it. In order to avoid translation, it is important to remember that children learn through all senses, which brings us to point number 2.

GUIDELINE 2 Incorporate All Senses

Children learn through various learning styles. Some children are auditory learners, others learn through seeing or doing, but children pick up cues through all of the senses. Because of this they learn to understand the meaning of words spoken in Spanish very quickly.

Center-Based Child Care

center-based child care
Child care and education provided in a facility other than a home.

As the name implies, **center-based child care** is provided to groups of children and families in specially constructed or renovated facilities. Out of 11.3 million children in different childcare arrangements, 15.6 percent of children are cared for in center-based child care centers.[27] For example, KIDCO Child Care Centers in Miami, Florida, operate as a nonprofit corporation out of four renovated warehouses and a former public school. The centers provide care for 450 children, from birth to age five, who are from primarily moderate and low-income families. Seventy percent of the children come from single parent families with primarily women who need to work in order to raise their children.[28] The Voice from the Field feature, "A Spanish Immersion Program," illustrates another multicultural high-quality child care program, where staff and administrators strive to provide

Include Auditory Learning

- Pronounce and articulate words clearly so that children can identify sounds, especially those that are not common to the English language, such as ll (elle), ñ (eñe) and rr (erre).
- The tone of your voice and expression when trying to convey an idea or emotion is also important. For example, if a story is being read about a sad bear, the face and tone should be gloomy and the body posture should be poor when saying *triste* or sad.
- Repetition is critical in order for children to learn new words, commands, or phrases. A good guideline is to repeat words in threes. For instance, if children are being instructed to wash their hands for snack time, say *lavar las manitas, lavar las manitas, lavar las manitas* (wash hands, wash hands, wash hands).
- Singing words and phrases daily to establish routine and familiarity with scheduling is also very important. For example, you can sing *Vamos a recoger* or "Clean Up" whenever playtime is over.
- Music, dance, and body movement are especially important to convey ideas and allow freedom of expression. Dancing to slow and fast music, for example, allows children to learn the vocabulary *despacio y rápido* and also gives them the opportunity to speak the words without stressing about the pronunciation.

Provide Visual Learning

It is important to incorporate a large variety of visual aids for a successful Spanish immersion program.

- Use prompts, books, puppets, flannel boards, and any other creative learning tools.

- Act out feelings by using body language and facial expressions.
- Use students as examples. If you have a child wearing a red t-shirt, use him or her to demonstrate the color red or *rojo*.
- Use flashcards, posters, drawings, and real pictures. If children can relate to it, they will learn it easier.
- Use drawings created by teachers and students.
- Smiling goes a long way. If students see the teacher's joyful and optimistic attitude, they will follow.

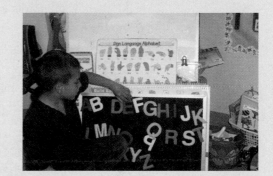

Go Outside the Classroom

Take field trips to places where Spanish is spoken, such as Mexican restaurants or Mexican grocery stores. This will help children take chances speaking the language and give them the opportunity to build confidence, not to mention learning about the culture and real-life situations.

Children will learn the second language much the same as they learned the first. Therefore, continue to expose students to as many ideas and information as possible; simply do it in Spanish, and before you know it, they will be bilingual!

Source: Photos and text contributed by Iris Ochoa, Director, Bright Years Child Learning Center.

children and families with quality, affordable, and accessible child care, while immersing them in English and Spanish.

Because each state has its own definition of a center-based program, you should research your state's definitions and regulations regarding child care, center care, and other kinds of care. In addition, learn about your state's child care licensing and child-to-staff ratio requirements.

Employer-Sponsored Child Care

As more parents enter the workforce, child care programs provide new responses. The current economic recession is pushing many highly educated women who had left work to stay at home with their children to dive back into the labor pool.[29] In a survey of

5,000 employees at five companies, 57 percent of women and 33 percent of men with children under six years old report that they spend unproductive time at work because of child care concerns. Eighty percent of employers report that child care problems force many employees to lose work time.[30] To meet the needs of working parents, employers are increasingly called on to provide affordable, accessible, quality child care. According to the U.S. Chamber of Commerce, corporate-supported child care is one of the fastest growing employee benefits. But employer-sponsored child care is not new: The Stride Rite Corporation started the first on-site corporate child care program in Boston in 1971.[31]

On-site child care provides a number of advantages for parents:

- Parents can drop in on breaks for lunch to tend to babies.
- Mothers with infants can stop in to breast-feed.
- Parents can carpool with their children, saving time in the drop-off and pick-up process.
- Parents have the peace of mind knowing their children are close, safe, and well cared for.

Many corporations have child care management programs that operate their child care programs for them. Other employers provide different types of child care assistance. Some employers offer flexible work arrangements to make it easier for parents to make child care arrangements. Some employers allow their employees to take paid time off to care for mildly ill children. They see this as a positive return on the investment.[32] Aetna Insurance Company estimated the savings realized from parental leave policies to be about $1 million per year. The company cut post-childbirth turnover by 50 percent by extending parental leave to six months, allowing a part-time return, and training supervisors to manage maternal leaves.[33]

Bristol-Myers Squibb continues to be a leader in employee work-life programs and was named one of the 2010 *Working Mother* "100 Best Companies for Working Mothers" for its dedication to family-friendly benefits. They are building their fifth child care center for employees based in New Brunswick, New Jersey because they realize the importance of having work-life programs and services in place to help employees achieve both their personal and professional goals. The company believes, "It's good business—helping us recruit and retain the top talent we need to help patients prevail against serious disease." Bristol-Myers Squibb offers a comprehensive array of work-life programs and services to meet the needs of working families over the course of their career with the company, including:

- Dependent care services—on-site child care centers, free infant formula, access to backup child care centers, and referral services.
- Time away from work policies—adoption, foster care, birth, and leaves for spouses and partners.
- Flexible work options—flex time, job sharing, telecommuting, compressed work-weeks, remote work, and part-time schedules.
- Financial support—adoption assistance, higher education scholarship programs for employees' children, and tuition reimbursement.[34]

Military Child Care

The Department of Defense (DoD) military child development system (CDS) provides daily services for the largest number of children of any employer in the United States. Military child care is provided in 742 centers in more than 300 geographic locations, both within and outside the continental United States.[35]

Military families face challenges that are not found in other work environments. Shifting work schedules that are often longer than the typical eight-hour day and the requirement to be ready to deploy anywhere in the world on a moment's notice require a child development system that is flexible in nature yet maintains high standards. Mike Mullen, chairman of the Joint Chiefs of Staff, says the Department of Defense Educational Activity (DoDEA) teachers have "been a big part of the glue that is holding us together in an enormously stressful time." Mullen feels that it is important for military parents "to know that their kids are in good schools and are being well taught."[36] Frequent family separations and the need to move, on average, every three years place military families in situations not often experienced in the civilian world. For this population, affordable, high-quality child care is paramount if they are to be ready to perform their missions and their jobs. It is also important to military personnel that child care services be consistent at installations throughout the military.

Four main components make up the DoD CDS: child development centers, family child care, school-age care, and resource and referral programs. Through these four areas, the DoD serves more than 200,000 children (ages six weeks to twelve years) daily.[37] The system offers full-day, part-day, and hourly (i.e., drop-in) child care; part-day preschool programs; before- and after-school programs for school-age children; and extended-hour care, including nights and weekends.

Before- and After-School Care

In many respects, public schools are logical places for before-school and after-school care; they have the administrative organization, facilities, and staff to provide such care. In addition, many taxpayers and professionals have always believed that schools should not sit empty in the afternoons, evenings, holidays, and summers. Using resources already in place for child care makes good sense.

The before- and after-school child care programs of Broward County, Florida, provide students with:

- An inclusive child care program that is safe and nurturing in a comfortable environment
- A culturally enriching program that promotes the physical, intellectual, emotional, and social development of each child
- A program that meets the highest quality of child care standards

Currently Broward County serves more than 23,000 children in 170 before- and after-school child care programs. Programs at elementary schools and centers are either school district operated or operated by private providers.[38]

Nadine Rudek-Kelly leads a kindergarten before- and after-school program in Raynham, Massachusetts, that offers a curriculum of a variety of activities including academics, arts, crafts, stories, and physical activities. The student-to-teacher ratio for this program is 10:1. In the before-school program children engage in quiet activities and eat a light breakfast before the start of the school day. In the after-school program the children do homework, participate in games, science projects, and outdoor play, and receive homework help.[39]

The Maricopa School District located in Maricopa, Arizona, has a before- and after-school program that offers a loving, safe, fun, and educational learning environment. Their curriculum includes science, homework help, art, music, crafts, creative dramatic play, games, and group projects. During the summer months children take field trips as well. The goal of their programs is to provide a nurturing, friendly, and safe environment that encourages children to build on their classroom experiences and expand their horizons.[40]

Before- and after-school care programs play an increasingly important role in school-based programs and in the lives of children and families. Although opportunities for play and exercise are important in these programs, more and more parents want them to provide help with homework, time to study, and enrichment activities such as music and the arts.

Proprietary Child Care

Some child care centers are run by corporations, businesses, and individual proprietors for the purpose of making a profit. Some for profit centers provide before- and after-school programs for school-age children as well. Many of these programs emphasize their educational component and appeal to middle-class families who are willing to pay for the promised services. Knowledge Learning Corporation (KLC) is the nation's leading private provider of early childhood and school-age education and care with 1,746 centers.[41] Its KinderCare Learning Centers comprise approximately 1,250 community-based centers in 38 states and the District of Columbia, serving more than 250,000 children and employing approximately 47,000.[42] About 35 percent of all child care centers in the United States are operated for profit, and the number is likely to grow. Child care is a $38 billion service industry, with more and more entrepreneurs realizing they can make money in caring for the nation's children. Some of the other largest child care management organizations in the United States are the Learning Group, Inc. with 1,105 centers, Bright Horizons Family Solutions with 675 centers, and Nobel Learning Communities with 178 centers.[43]

What Constitutes Quality Care and Education?

As child care grows and expands across the nation, it focuses our attention on a number of critical issues. One of these is how to provide and maintain high-quality care for *all* children. Although there is much debate about quality and what it involves, we can nonetheless identify the main characteristics of quality programs that provide care and education for children and families. Some critical components of high-quality care include:

- Low staff to child ratios and small groups of children (the fewer the children for each adult, the better it is for each child)
- Primary caregiver assignments for each small group of children
- Continuity of care (the same primary caregiver remains with a cohort of children for more than one year)
- Caregivers actively and regularly involve and communicate with families
- An emphasis on good nutrition and nutrition education for both children and parents
- Proper health maintenance and safety (e.g., making sure child care settings have safe and well maintained playgrounds)
- Cultural and linguistic continuity.[44] For example, a caregiver who shares a cultural background with a child is much more likely to naturally engage in practices which are in harmony with those of the home. The ability to place children directly under the care of a provider who shares their cultural heritage can help increase the capacity of a child care facility to provide appropriate care.[45]
- Teachers who are responsive to young children and interact in warm and caring ways
- Teachers who know how each child learns, grows, and develops, and engage in developmentally appropriate practices

Each of these components is a necessary part of providing for high-quality education. FIO360's child care program in Atlanta, Georgia, adds to the dimension of high quality by providing an eco-friendly building and curriculum (see the Voice from the Field feature on pages 186–187).

Healthy Child Care Environments

At all age levels, a healthy environment supports children's physical and mental health. The environment should also be attractive and pleasant. The rooms, home, or center should be clean, well lit, well ventilated, cheerful, well maintained, and with separate areas for toileting (and for changing diapers), eating, and sleeping. Caregivers teach infants and toddlers healthy habits such as hand washing after toileting, before and after meal time, and after other appropriate activities. Frequent handwashing is one of the most important factors in maintaining children's health and avoiding illness.[46]

A healthy environment also provides a relaxed and happy eating environment. Areas should be disinfected properly before eating. Substantial research clearly indicates that a healthy diet and environment contribute to children's overall health and well being.[47] Early childhood is a stage of life in which lifelong nutritional habits are developed and obesity is prevented. For infants and children, a major source of chemical pesticide exposure is through their food. Research shows that children's levels of chemical pesticide exposure drops quickly and significantly when they are switched from a normal diet to an organic one.[48] The Little Dreamers, Big Believers Daycare in Columbus, Ohio uses ingredients that are 70 percent organic. Children eat meals with foods such as rigatoni with tomato sauce, garlic bread, and broccoli, all designed to provide healthy habits in accord with the MyPyramid nutritional guide.[49]

A healthy environment also supports children's mental health. Caregivers support children's mental health when they provide responsive and loving care and create environments that have a balance of small and large open areas. Small areas provide the opportunity for infants and toddlers to be alone or in small groups. The open areas encourage active involvement with larger numbers of children. In addition, child care staff collaborate with and involve parents to help them know about and understand the importance of children's mental health and how they can help their children.

Lead-Free Environment.   In general, children less than six years old are more likely to be affected by lead than adults because of increased contact with lead sources in the environment, such as lead-contaminated house dust and soil. Children also absorb lead more easily. Children's developing nervous systems are also more susceptible to the unfavorable health effects of lead including developmental delay and behavioral problems.[50] The Centers for Disease Control and Prevention recently found lead in artificial turf in Newark, New Jersey. They recommend taking these precautions in the classroom to keep children healthy and minimize any potential risk in the future:

1. Wash children's hands frequently and always before they eat.
2. Do not let children eat food or use pacifiers that have been dropped on the floor or outside.
3. Remove all shoes when entering the center or use doormats.[51]

Cadmium is also a harmful lead product. Cadmium was recently found in bracelets and charms sold in stores across the United States.[52] Child care providers have to be ever vigilant in their role of providing lead-free environments.

Nontoxic Pesticides.   Exposure to pesticides at schools is associated with illnesses among employees and students. Rates of illness from pesticide exposure at schools are higher in school staff than in children because staff members are more likely to handle pesticides. However, children may be particularly susceptible to pesticide toxicity because their organ systems have not reached developmental maturity. Exposure to pesticides can produce coughs, shortness of breath, nausea, vomiting, headaches, and eye irritation.[53]

In child care programs, keep all surfaces free of food and water, and reduce opportunities for pests to enter the building. Sanitary food habits, properly handling garbage, and sealing food in airtight containers help prevent problems with pests. Also, periodically vacuuming furniture and draperies can reduce dust mites and other pests.[54]

Voice from the Field

The Eco-Environment in Early Childhood Settings

Philosophy

FIO360 is an eco-friendly early learning boutique located in Atlanta, Georgia. The supportive, eco-friendly environment is home to 140 children ages six weeks to five years. *Fio* is the Latin verb for "to become," 360 represents "whole." Our name means, "to become whole." The FIOlosophy is that, "Children learn when supported in a healthy, nurturing environment where caring adults intentionally encourage exploration of the environment." Our learning process encourages children to be aware of their thoughts, actions, and decisions, which is the beginning step in meta-cognitive awareness.

Environment

The inside environment is filled with natural light. Soft colors on the walls showcase children's art that is displayed at eye level for them to enjoy. Water play along with sand and dirt are available to children, incorporating the inside and outside environment. Familiar items, including manipulatives, dress-up clothing, books, and soft cozy areas for small gatherings and quiet reflection at each developmental age group, are arranged in an inviting setting. Photos of the children, their families, and pets encourage interaction while focusing on each child's attention and feelings.

At the nucleus of the FIO360 environment, supportive adults are woven into the natural course of the day to provide an unmistakable positive contribution to the development of each young child. Nurturing, experienced early childhood specialists prepare activities and lessons that enrich the daily experiences of each child.

Outside

Outside children interact with nature through planting, digging, climbing, riding, jumping and exploring on the rooftop play yard. Paint, books, music, and bubbles complete the outdoor experience.

The environment has a lasting effect on growth and development. The physical environment in an early childhood setting sends messages to children: about what's important, what they are to do, and how they might do it.[78] Children spend an average of eight to ten hours per day in a child care setting.[79] The colors, textures, smells, light, sounds, and food, along with the touch and tones of adults with whom they interact, support development and growth. "Sensory integration is a neurobiological process in which the brain analyzes, interprets, and acts on sensory stimulation taken from the environment."[80]

Safe Environment

The physical environment provides for safe exploration and individual learning. Protection from environmental toxins and healthy nutrition promotes optimal growth and brain development. Toys made of wood, play dough made from flour and salt with fresh fruit extract such as pomegranate, naturally engage the children in activities that will support development and exploration. Our eco-environment reduces overstimulation from outside sources such as very loud music and voices, overpowering smells from air fresheners and perfume, bright, glaring colors with adult-made art, and by using filtered water.

Air Quality

The healthy FIO360 eco-environment offers superior indoor air quality through a filtration system that reduces the exposure to

---

The more that you can do to promote high-quality healthy programs, the better it will be for you, children, and families.

Safe Environments

Safe and healthy environments go together. In addition to what we have discussed, healthy environments also include keeping children safe emotionally. Caregivers provide safe environments through responsive relationships and by developing close and nurturing bonds with the children they care for. Responsive and close relationships enable infants and toddlers to experience trust and feel safe with you and in your program. More and more research tells us that healthy development depends on safe experiences during the first few years of life.[55]

harmful pollutants. Poor indoor air quality can aggravate asthma and poses a threat to a child's respiratory system. Filtered pure water, free of added chemicals, fluoride and harmful bacteria is used for all cooking and drinking, significantly reducing unsafe toxins. All disinfectants and cleaning products have little or no harmful gases. No VOC (volatile organic compounds), which is found in most paint and, minimal PVC (polyvinyl chloride), that is commonly used in building construction materials, reduces the exposure to dangerous toxins.

Organic Food

Organic, unprocessed freshly prepared food significantly reduces the amount of chemicals and toxins ingested by children.

Respect for the Environment

In an eco-environment, children are taught by example to respect the earth and its resources. It is important to expose young children to the benefits of eco-friendly practices. The children participate in planting a garden full of vegetables, plants, herbs, and flowers. The herbs and vegetables are used to cook meals. Children plant seeds and care for the budding plants by watering them and ensuring that they are exposed to natural light. The harvest of vegetables and herbs are proudly delivered to the kitchen where the chef incorporates them into meals that showcase the hard work of each child. Families and teachers are invited to share a delicious meal that includes corn, green beans, parsley, and tomatoes. The plants and flowers are cared for by the children and provide a safe haven for small earthly creatures including ants and earthworms. Children begin to realize that nature's creatures have a purpose and are valued.

Recycling

Recycling plastic water and soda bottles, aluminum cans and paper support the belief that respecting the earth is a responsibility that we all must support. **Re-purposing** old and worn books into pictures, making papier-mâché objects, and using clean empty food containers and boxes for dramatic play activities is a great way to recycle. The intentional interactions and choices that are made achieve our purpose of providing interactive opportunities for the children to respect the earth and all living creatures. For example, our preschool children created "recycle-o-bots" from paper towel holders, aluminum foil, cereal boxes, CDs, and some wire. Toddlers enjoy taking worn books and placing some of the pages in a hand-made frame to view their favorite story in a place of importance in the classroom. This type of activity also promotes language development.

Children do not have a say where they spend their day. We have an obligation to provide a place where children can breathe clean air, drink safe water, and eat healthy, nutrient-rich food. All children deserve the best environment possible. Raising the bar and supporting healthy environments for young children is the responsibility of all early childhood professionals.

Source: Text contributed by Linda Owens; photos contributed by Jeff Kaminski/Linda Owens, FIO360 Director, located in Atlanta, Georgia.

Safe child care centers supervise children at all times.[56] Safe centers enforce strict security measures and install security cameras so that staff can monitor traffic. For example, Kiddie Academy buildings are equipped with secure entries and exits that require a pass or identification card for entry. Some buildings also utilize fingerprint verification and video monitoring. They also conduct background checks on all employees. [57] Keeping children safe physically contributes to their feeling safe and trusting emotionally.

re-purposing To use or convert for use in another product.

Respectful Environments

A respectful environment is one in which caregivers deeply care about children and families. Caregivers create respectful environments by listening, observing, and being aware

of children's verbal and nonverbal communications. Arranging the classroom in a way that maximizes social interaction promotes a safe, supportive, and engaging classroom climate. For example, if children are seated in a circle or horseshoe shape this maximizes the eye contact you have with them and that they have with each other.[58] Closely looking at and observing children enables you to "read" children's behavior by asking yourself: "How will I respond to what the child is saying to me?"

A respectful environment also honors and supports children's unique individualities. Each child's unique individuality is a product of the interactions of such dimensions as temperament, gender, race, language, culture, and socioeconomic status.

Child care providers need to give children opportunities to learn social and academic skills through daily activities such as mealtime. What are some ways that you could provide opportunities to ensure that children are learning important nutritional concepts and skills?

Culturally Appropriate Practice.   Respectful environments include culturally appropriate practices. Children who are Hispanic remain the largest minority group of underserved children, and the child care issues of access, affordability, and quality are of critical concern to their community. Fewer than half of Hispanic children birth to age three attend a center-based early education childhood program, compared to 66 percent of African American children and 59 percent of white children.[59] Because of limited access to high-quality programs, Hispanic children start kindergarten well behind their peers.[60]

Here are some things you can do to create a culturally respectful environment for your children.

- Greet families in a culturally sensitive manner. For example, some Hispanic families prefer the father to be greeted first, then the mother, and the children last.
- Provide inclusive artwork. For example, murals include children with different skin and hair colors.
- Use linguistically appropriate materials and provide books in English and Spanish.
- Adjust teacher-infant interaction style according to culture. Although most infants who are Hispanic are calmed with quick, repetitive, choppy phrases and back patting, infants who are Latin, for example, are calmed through soft, smooth talking, cradling, and gentle rocking.
- Apply limits to cultural accommodation when necessary. Discuss compromises with parents. For example, some cultures allow infants to eat items they could choke on such as hot dogs. In this case, explain the dangers of certain foods and ask parents to bring alternative snacks.
- Communicate with parents and other family members in your program. You must place a high priority on daily communication about children's progress. In addition, share with parents how your program and community agencies provide information in such critical areas as child development and nutrition.[61]

Supportive Environments

A supportive environment means that you will spend time with children, pleasantly interact with them, and encourage and help them. Supportive environments encourage and promote children's routine social interactions. A supportive environment accommodates children's individual differences and provides for active play. The Read, Play, and Learn program in Baltimore, Maryland, provides a supportive environment for their children. Children engage in games, songs, experiments, reading, dramatic play, and projects. In the Sensory Area, children explore and manipulate various textures and devices to support their psychological needs. Teachers use story themes to support children's needs. For example, *The Kissing Hand* storybook helps children adjust to leaving home for the first time. Family involvement components help children incorporate materials and favorite items from home into their day.[62] A supportive environment also offers a wide range of learning materials. This type of environment also promotes children's mental health and encourages child-centered activities.

Supportive programs should have written, developmentally based curricula for meeting children's needs. A program's curriculum should specify activities for children of all ages. Caregivers can use these activities to stimulate infants, provide for the growing independence of toddlers, and address the readiness and literacy skills of four- and five year-olds. All programs include curricula and activities that meet the social, emotional, and cognitive needs of all children. Supportive programs use developmentally appropriate practices to implement the curriculum and achieve their program goals.

Child care involves much more than merely providing physical care. All caregivers should provide children with love and affection and should meet each child's full range of social, emotional, and physical needs.

Challenging Environments

A challenging environment provides opportunities for infants and toddlers to be actively involved with other children, staff, and parents. These interactions are extremely important as children learn about their world and themselves. A child care program is not developmentally appropriate if it does not offer sufficient challenges to growing children. A challenging environment supports children's social interaction and lays the foundation for school readiness and other life outcomes. A challenging environment provides materials and activities that are matched to the needs, interests, and abilities of children and provide for many hands-on activities that support seeing, touching, feeling, and moving. Supportive and challenging environments complement each other.

Good care and education provides for children's needs and interests at each developmental stage. For example, infants need good physical care as well as continual love and affection and sensory stimulation. Toddlers need safe surroundings and opportunities to explore. They need caregivers who support and encourage active involvement. However, within these broad categories of development, individual children have unique styles of interacting and learning that you must also accommodate.

Caregivers and Environments.   Caregivers are the key to all environments. They are the ones who passionately care about children and create the environments that are safe, healthy, supportive, respectful, and challenging. Every child wants and needs a teacher who is inspired and willing to do what it takes to create appropriate environments for them. This means that you will engage in ongoing professional development and gain the knowledge you need to grow as a professional in order to promote the educational environment all children need.

Caregiver-to-Child Ratio

The ratio of adults to children is an important part of high-quality child care and ratios also influence the environments used for children. The ratios should be sufficient to give children the individual care and attention they need. NAEYC guidelines for the ratio of

TABLE 7.3 Child Care Ratios and Group Size

Age	Maximum Child-to-Staff Ratio	Maximum Group Size
Birth–24 Months	3:1	6
25–30 months	4:1	8
31–35 months	5:1	10
3-year-olds	7:1	14
4–5-year-olds	8:1	16
6–8-year-olds	10:1	20

Source: U.S. Department of Health and Human Services. Office of Human Services Policy. 13 Indicators of Quality Child Care: Research Update, 2002. Available at http://aspe.hhs.gov/hsp/ccquality-ind02/#Staff1.

caregivers to children are 1:4 for infants and toddlers and 1:6 to 1:10 for preschoolers, depending on group size.[63]

The American Academy of Pediatrics recommends the ratios and standards shown in Table 7.3. You should check the ratios for the state and city in which you live.

Research shows that when programs meet these recommended children-to-staff ratios and recommended levels of caregiver training and education, children have better outcomes.[64] Teachers have to provide attentive care for all children. When they have too many children either individually or in a group, they cannot do this, and this contributes to low-quality child care. Low-quality care for all children—regardless of whether they were in child care centers or homes—are associated with poorer school readiness and language performance.[65]

Professional Staff Development

Staff and professional development is another dimension of high-quality child care. All teachers should be involved in an ongoing program of training and development. The Child Development Associate (CDA) certification program is a good beginning for staff members to become competent and maintain necessary skills. Program administrators should also have a background and training in child development and early childhood education. Knowledge of child growth and development is essential for all child care professionals. They need to be developmentally aware and child oriented in all phases of delivering high-quality child care.

Providing staff training and development is an excellent idea, but it is only the first step. The next step after training and development is to implement what you have learned in the staff training. In this sense, staff development and training is a two-part process: learning and implementation. The California Child Care Program requires all child care providers to have 15 hours of preventative and health safety. In this program they learn how to respond to breathing and cardiac emergencies, first aid and injury prevention, and food preparation and sanitation practices that reduce the spread of infectious diseases. They then implement what they have learned at their child care center.[66] Other professional staff development training is available in technology, early childhood literacy, bullying prevention, discipline and classroom management, differentiation of instruction, response to intervention, safety, and nutrition.

Program Accreditation

In any discussion of quality, the question invariably arises, who determines quality? NAEYC has established a national, voluntary accreditation system to set professional standards for early childhood education programs, and to help families identify high-quality programs. NAEYC accreditation represents the mark of quality in early childhood education. To achieve NAEYC accreditation, early childhood education programs volunteer to be measured against the NAEYC Early Childhood Program Standards. Today, nearly 9,000 NAEYC-accredited early childhood education programs serve families around the nation.[67] Accreditation is administered through NAEYC's National Academy of Early Childhood programs. Its website is listed at the end of this chapter. NAEYC program accreditation standards can be found on the NAEYC website (www.naeyc.org/files/academy/file/OverviewStandards.pdf) and include:

- Standard 1—Relationships
- Standard 2—Curriculum
- Standard 3—Teaching
- Standard 4—Assessment
- Standard 5—Health
- Standard 6—Teachers
- Standard 7—Families
- Standard 8—Community Relationships
- Standard 9—Physical Environment
- Standard 10—Leadership and Management

A center that is NAEYC accredited helps to build a stronger team of teachers, administrators, and families working together to improve quality for children; has improved standards for the overall program; and receive publicity through NAEYC's website. NAEYC-accredited programs are committed to excellence and set forth high standards for quality.[68]

Smart Start: Helping Programs Be Successful.   Smart Start North Carolina is a nationally recognized initiative that helps ensure all children enter school healthy and ready to succeed. Smart Start's vision is to have every child reach their potential and be prepared for success in a global community. Smart Start brings together all the people involved in a young child's life—families, teachers, doctors, caregivers, social workers, and many others—to ensure every child has all they need for healthy growth and development.

Smart Start connects families to physicians, as well as state insurance programs, to keep kids healthy. Smart Start programs help improve parenting skills and teach parents how to effectively read at home with their children. Smart Start connects families to high-quality child care and often helps families pay for this care. Smart Start also improves the quality of child care programs by providing support to improve facilities and staff skills.

Importance of Smart Start.   Experiences during the earliest years literally shape the structure of the brain. Children's healthy growth is directly linked to early childhood experiences. Young children exposed to intense and prolonged stress associated with cyclical or generational poverty, military deployment, sudden parental unemployment, or other conditions require comprehensive intervention to ensure their healthy and productive development.[69] Smart Start is funded through state and private funds. By referring families and communities to the resources they need to support children's growth and development, Smart Start lays the foundation to nurture responsible, productive citizens who will make positive contributions to our society.[70]

Accommodating Diverse Learners

Child care is a critical concern for families and for early childhood professionals. For parents, the quality and security of child care has implications for psychological well-being, management of work/family demands, and continuity of employment.[71] For children, the equality of care has implications for their health, social and physical development, and their education and lifelong success.

Although the use of nonparental care has grown for all socioeconomic groups, the type, quality, and cost burden for parents remain highly stratified along demographic lines.[72] For example, children whose parents are Caucasian, highly educated, and affluent are more likely to be in center-based care arrangements. Children from Hispanic, poorly educated, immigrant, and less affluent families are more likely to be cared for by relatives.[73]

Research clearly shows that caregiver-child warrmth is one of the most important dimensions of a high-quality child care program. What are some things that you will do in your program to help ensure it conveys a feeling of warmth and familiarity for children?

Too often, parents' child care choices are viewed as a single, isolated consumption choice. In reality, parents' child care choices are a part of a dynamic interplay between decisions about employment, child-rearing, and other family values. Therefore, choosing child care is as much a social transaction as it is an economic one.[74] In addition, when selecting child care parents rate warmth of caregivers, utilization of a play-based curriculum, and educational level of caregivers as the most important factors. One challenge of child care is to provide these qualities in a way that responds to families' culture and language.[75]

One of the best ways to do this is by creating a family atmosphere. When you think about it, what intrinsic qualities do families have that you would want for your child to have while you were away at work? Familiarity? Warmth? Kindness?

Familiarity, or the easiness of interaction, is achieved by intimately getting to know your families. Intimacy can be hard to balance with professionalism. Achieve intimacy by asking questions about parents' interests; follow up on how their weekend activities went; and ask in a non-intrusive way about family life. Showing a genuine interest in and concern for parents as individuals goes a long way to create an easy, intimate relationship that leaves parents feeling comfortable and confident about leaving their children with you.

warmth Displaying or exhibiting kindness and genuine affection.

Caregiver **warmth** is more important to parents than the education of the caregiver or even the type of curriculum utilized by the program.[76] A warm environment is achieved through a few simple efforts on your part. Ask for pictures from home of the children with their families, pets, or favorite toys and place them around the room in frames or matted with construction paper. Display pictures of caregivers and children. This contributes to a more family-like, warm atmosphere where caregivers and parents are both honored and the children remain the center of focus. Parents love to see children's artwork and other artifacts. Placing them around the room goes a long way toward creating warmth.

Warmth is also achieved by making the center and children's areas comfortable and inviting. Comfort and approachability should not be sacrificed in the effort to run a clean and efficient caregiving environment. But even in the most sterile of environments, warmth can be achieved by being genuine, kind, interested, and involved.

The Effects of Child Care and Education on Children

Recent research reveals that high-quality early care and education have influences that last over a lifetime. A valuable source of research about child care comes from the Study of Early Child Care and Youth Development (SECCYD) by the National Institute of Child Health and Human Development (NICHD). This is a comprehensive longitudinal study initiated by NICHD designated to answer the many questions about the relationship between child care experiences and characteristics and children's developmental outcomes. The study collected features of child care and the experiences children have in different nonmaternal child care settings. Listed below are some of the study's findings on the use of child care and its effects on children and families. The study results make it clear that professionals must provide high-quality programs and must advocate for that high quality with the public and state legislators. Reflect on what surprises you most as you review the following study results.[77]

Hours in Child Care

- At their first entry into nonmaternal care, children average 29 hours of care per week.
- By twelve months, children in care average 33.9 hours a week of care.

Type of Care

- 44 percent of children receive child care in child care centers and 25 percent in child care homes; 12 percent are cared for by their father or their mother's partner; 10 percent are cared for at home by nannies or babysitters; and 9 percent are cared for by grandparents.

Maternal Attitudes and Child Care

- Mothers who believe their children benefit from their employment tend to place their infants in care earlier and for more hours in center-based child care.
- In contrast, mothers who believe maternal employment carries high risks for their children tend to put their infants in care for fewer hours and are especially likely to rely on the infant's father for child care.

Social, Emotional, Cognitive, and Health-Related Child Outcomes

- Poor-quality child care is related to an increased incidence of insecure infant-mother attachment (the child does not feel safe and will not be as willing to trust his or her parent) at fifteen months, but only when the mother is relatively low in sensitivity and responsiveness.

It is clear that high-quality child care has beneficial outcomes for children and families. You will be involved in advising parents about child care. This research data helps you be informed and knowledgeable. High-quality child care will continue to be important for children's well-being and provide greater social skills, increased academic success, higher self-esteem, and better nutrition and physical health.

Activities for Professional Development

Ethical Dilemma

"The boy who escaped child care."

Rebeka Holly is the lead teacher for a child care program and is responsible for supervising the other child care providers. A few days ago, she was shocked to receive a phone call from the police stating that Bobby Hernandes, one of her children, had "escaped" the child care center; wandered across a busy interstate in 100 degree heat, strolled in and out of an auto shop, took gum and a soft drink from a convenience store, and walked into a nearby restaurant. The story of "the boy who escaped child care" is all over the local news. Rebeka is furious at Stacy Holcomb, the teacher in charge of Bobby's class, for not paying better attention to her class. Unfortunately, the child care center is already under surveillance of the state liscensure board for substandard child-supervision scores.

The director of state licensing's phone is "ringing off the wall" with phone calls and emails, all pouring in to demand Rebeka shut the facility down. Rebeka understands that a huge mistake was made, but she also knows her child care program has the potential to provide high-quality care. She hopes that this situation can be used to spur the center to become a high-quality program. Furthermore, the child care program is in a high-need area serving low-income parents who are just trying to do their best, and she is concerned that closing down their only child care option will hurt their employment and quality of life. Parents are pulling their children from the program. Television channels and local papers are calling for interviews, and now the licensure board is threatening to fire Rebeka because she was supposed to be closely supervising Stacy.

What should Rebeka do? Should she recommend that the child care center fire Stacy? Should Rebeka resign her position to acknowledge her own mistakes? Should she speak to the local news media? Should she hire her own lawyer? Who ultimately is at fault in this situation, Rebeka or Stacy? What would you do if you were Rebeka? What would you do if you were in charge of the state licensing board?

Activities to Apply What You Learned

1. Take photos of a child care program that meets standards of high quality. Be sure to ask permission before taking any photos! Explain how each image illustrates dimensions of quality discussed in the chapter. Post your conclusions to your class website.
2. Make a Venn diagram of three types of child care programs in your area. Compare the similarities and differences of each program and share your findings with your classmates.
3. Observe a classroom and ask permission to take pictures of how providers demonstrate healthy, safe, challenging, and respectful environments for children. Post your pictures on Bebo at www.bebo.com and tag your friends in photos to connect and allow them to express their opinions on your findings.
4. Suppose you were the director of a child care program and the parents of three-year-old Alex, who has Down syndrome, want to enroll him in your child care program. How would you work with Alex's parents? What would you do to prepare yourself for including Alex? The staff? The children? Create a blog based on your experiences about how you can accommodate diverse learners in your classroom and post it to share with classmates.
5. Visit a high-quality child care center. Observe the social, emotional, and cognitive interactions of children. Develop a list of the things you observe that support the program being "high quality." Share your findings with the director of a center.

Linking to Learning

Child Care Bureau
www.acf.dhhs.gov/programs/ccb
Includes information on the Child Care and Development Block Grant, links to other Administration on Children and Families sites, and other information within the Department of Health and Human Services, with links to other related child care sites.

Childcare.gov
www.childcare.gov
A site for parents, child care programs, and early childhood educators; brings all federal agency resources together in one place.

Council for Professional Recognition
www.cdacouncil.org/.
The Council sets the policies and procedures for assessment and credentialing the CDA, publishes the competency standards and other materials, and administers the assessment. It also publishes materials to support professional development activities and administers a military school-age credential.

FIO360
www.fio360.com
FIO360 is an eco–early learning center where children are nurtured and empowered to become well-rounded and promise-filled individuals. Some call this "whole-child development," They call it early education at its finest.

National Association for the Education of Young Children (NAEYC)

www.naeyc.org/accreditation

Provides information about the accreditation process for preschool and child care programs.

National Child Care Information Center

http://nccic.org

Sponsored by the Child Care Bureau, Administration for Children and Families, Department of Health and Human Services; provides a central access point for information on child care and lists the licensure regulations for all fifty states regarding child care, center care, and other kinds of care.

National Resource Center for Health and Safety in Child Care and Early Education

http://nrc.uchsc.edu

Funded by the Maternal and Child Health Bureau of the Department of Health and Human Services; lists the child care licensure regulations for each state. Also has health and safety tips and full-text resources.

PEARSON
myeducationlab

Go to Topic 5 (Program Models) in the MyEducationLab (www.myeducationlab.com) for your course, where you can:

- Find learning outcomes for Program Models along with the national standards that connect to these outcomes.
- Complete Assignments and Activities that can help you more deeply understand the chapter content.
- Apply and practice your understanding of the core teaching skills identified in the chapter with the Building Teaching Skills and Dispositions learning units.
- Check your comprehension on the content covered in the chapter by going to the Study Plan in the Book Resources for your text. Here you will be able to take a chapter quiz, receive feedback on your answers, and then access Review, Practice, and Enrichment activities to enhance your understanding of chapter content.

8

THE FEDERAL GOVERNMENT
Supporting Children's Success

focus questions

1. How has the federal government influenced the field of early childhood education through legislative acts?

2. What are the purposes of federal programs, such as Head Start and Early Head Start, that serve young children and their families?

3. In what other ways does the federal government seek to promote children's success and development?

4. How can you accommodate diverse learners to benefit all children?

naeyc standards

Standard 1. Promoting Child Development and Learning

I use my understanding of young children's characteristics and needs, and of multiple interacting influences on children's development and learning, to create environments that are healthy, respectful, supportive, and challenging for each child.[1]

Standard 2. Building Family and Community Relationships

I know about, understand, and value the importance and complex characteristics of children's families and communities. I use this understanding to create respectful, reciprocal relationships that support and empower families, and to involve all families in their children's development and learning.[2]

Standard 4. Using Developmentally Effective Approaches to Connect with Children and Families

I understand and use positive relationships and supportive interactions as the foundation for my work with young children and families. I know, understand, and use a wide array of developmentally appropriate approaches, instructional strategies, and tools to connect with children and families and positively influence each child's development and learning.[3]

I understand the importance of developmental domains and academic (or content) disciplines in early childhood curriculum. I use my own knowledge and other resources to design, implement, and evaluate meaningful, challenging curricula that promote comprehensive developmental and learning outcomes for every young child.[4]

One of the remarkable political events of the last decade has been the use of early childhood education to achieve federal and state educational goals and to reform education. As a result, more federal and state dollars are being poured into early childhood programs, making this a very exciting and challenging time for all early childhood professionals and their programs. The U.S. Department of Education's Fiscal Year 2010 $46.7 billion budget advances President Obama's agenda to reform the nation's schools.[5] However, with increased federal and state funding come mandates, control, and restructuring. Federal and state laws, regulations, and dollars are changing what early childhood programs look like and how they function. Federally funded programs such as Head Start and Early Head Start are leading the way in changing how the early childhood profession cares for and educates young children.

Federal Legislation and Early Childhood

Federal legislation has had a tremendous influence on the educational process and this will continue into the future. Currently, the Obama administration is committed to providing the support that our youngest children need to prepare to succeed in school and careers. The years before a child enters kindergarten are critical for children's futures; for the workforce; and for the role and place of the U.S. on the global stage. As a result, President Obama continually urges states to impose high standards across all publicly funded early learning settings, develop new programs to improve opportunities and outcomes, engage parents in their child's early learning and development, and improve the early education workforce.[6] As you read this chapter, you will learn how and why federal and state governments are changing the field of early childhood education.

The Economic Opportunity Act of 1964

The **Economic Opportunity Act of 1964 (EOA)** implemented several social programs to promote the health, education, and general welfare of people from low socioeconomic backgrounds. For early childhood education, the EOA provided for the beginning of Head Start in 1965. The EOA was later updated as the Head Start Act of 1981. The passage of the Economic Opportunity Act of 1964 marks the contemporary beginning of federal political and financial support for early childhood education.[7] **Head Start** is one of the longest-running programs to address systemic

Economic Opportunity Act of 1964 Implemented several social programs to promote the health, education, and general welfare of people from low socioeconomic backgrounds.

Head Start One of the longest running programs to address systemic poverty in the United States.

" It will be the goal of this administration to ensure that every child has access to a complete and competitive education—from the day they are born to the day they begin a career. "

PRESIDENT BARACK OBAMA

Early Head Start A federal program serving pregnant women, infants, toddlers, and their families.

poverty in the United States. Its programs include **Early Head Start**; Head Start; Family and Community Partnerships; Migrant and Seasonal Head Start; and American Indian/ Alaska Native Head Start.

Head Start's Purpose

Head Start is a national program that promotes school readiness by enhancing the social and cognitive development of children through the provision of educational, health, nutritional, social, and other services to children and families. The National Head Start program provides grants to local public and private nonprofit and for profit agencies to provide comprehensive child development services to economically disadvantaged children and families, with a special focus on helping preschoolers develop the early reading and math skills they need to be successful in school.[8]

Head Start programs engage parents in their children's learning and help them in making progress toward their educational, literacy, and employment goals. Significant emphasis is placed on the involvement of parents in the administration of local Head Start programs.[9]

The Improving Head Start for School Readiness Act of 2007 reauthorized Head Start through 2012. This act helps more children arrive at kindergarten ready to succeed. The legislation increases teacher qualifications by requiring that 50 percent of Head Start teachers nationwide have a minimum of a baccalaureate degree (B.A. or B.S.) in early childhood education or a related field by 2013. It also requires Head Start programs to develop career ladders and annual professional development plans for full-time staff. Also, it requires that all Head Start programs use research-based practices to support the growth of children's preliteracy and vocabulary skills.

Head Start has always been and remains a program for children of poverty. Although it currently reaches a significant number of poor children, increasing federal support for Head Start will likely increase the number of poor children served. However, we must keep in mind that the federal government is using Head Start to reform all of early childhood education. Federal officials believe that the changes they make in the Head Start curriculum—what and how teachers teach and how Head Start operates—serves as a model for other programs as well.

Elementary and Secondary Education Act

Elementary and Secondary Education Act of 1965 (ESEA) Federal legislation that funds primarily elementary and secondary education.

In 1965, Congress passed the **Elementary and Secondary Education Act (ESEA)**, which serves to more fully fund primary and secondary education by providing funds to help educate children from low-income families. This portion of ESEA is known as **Title I**. Eligibility for Title I funds is based on children's eligibility for free or reduced-price school lunches, which is based on their family's income. Funds are used to provide additional academic support and learning opportunities so that children can master challenging curricula and meet state standards in core academic subjects. For example, funds support extra instruction in reading and mathematics, as well as special preschool, after-school, and summer programs to extend and reinforce the regular school curriculum. More than 54,000 schools use Title I funds and Title I serves more than 20 million children. Therefore, it is likely that you will teach children served by Title I at a Title I school.[10]

Title I Section of the Elementary and Secondary Education Act that provides monies to low-income families.

No Child Left Behind Act of 2001

No Child Left Behind Act (NCLB) Federal law passed in 2001 that has significantly influenced early childhood education.

In 2001 Congress reauthorized the Elementary and Secondary Education Act of 1965 as the **No Child Left Behind Act (NCLB)**. NCLB funds primary and secondary education and is designed to improve student achievement and school performance. The reauthorization of the NCLB has radically and rapidly changed how America conducts its educational business.

NCLB emphasizes state and district accountability, mandates state standards for what children should know and be able to do, puts in place a comprehensive program of testing in grades three to twelve, and encourages schools to use teaching methods that demonstrate their effectiveness in helping children learn.

NCLB targets six fundamental areas:

- The accountability of teachers and schools for children's school achievement.
- An emphasis on literacy and reading and that all children read on or above grade level by third grade.
- Schools and teachers use programs and curriculum that work (based on scientific research).
- Professional staff development of teachers to enhance their abilities to teach all children to achieve high standards.
- The use of educational technology in institutional programs.
- Parent involvement in schools and in decision-making procedures.

NCLB is a significant educational act that will continue to influence what and how you teach for many years to come. The act also influences pre-K education because there is a major emphasis on getting children ready for school. Many federally funded programs now use guidelines mandated in the No Child Left Behind Act to develop goals and objectives for their own programs.

Currently, Congress is in the process of reauthorizing NCLB. The reauthorization may occur in 2011 or later, and will likely include such initiatives as:

- The administration's ongoing commitments to closing the achievement gap between minority and Caucasian students. We have discussed how the persistent achievement gaps across race, culture, socioeconomic backgrounds, and gender keeps America's children from doing their best and being their best. The federal government is determined to prevent and eliminate these gaps.
- Encouraging teacher quality so that all children are taught by high-quality teachers. Currently, many children, especially those in urban schools, have poorly qualified teachers.
- Providing universal, high quality infant, toddler, and pre-kindergarten early childhood programs to all children so they come to school better prepared to learn, with priority consideration given to low-income children and children from diverse backgrounds.
- Adequately funding important children's and educational programs outside of NCLB, including child health and nutrition, Head Start, IDEA, child care, and related programs.

American Recovery and Reinvestment Act of 2009

The **American Recovery and Reinvestment Act of 2009 (ARRA)**, commonly referred to as the "stimulus package," provides funding for early childhood programs and for several programs that benefit young children. The ARRA increased funding is a part of President Obama's Zero-to-Five plan that seeks to reform education by investing quickly in America's youngest children. ARRA is a unique opportunity for school districts and states to improve teaching and learning. The most logical place to start is at the very beginning, in early childhood education. Funds allotted for early childhood education in the ARRA are used in the following ways to help children.[11]

- $2.1 billion for Head Start programs (includes $1.1 billion for Early Head Start and $1 billion for Head Start)
- $2 billion for the Child Care and Development Block Grant designed to assist low-income families, families receiving temporary public assistance, and those transitioning

American Recovery and Reinvestment Act of 2009 (ARRA) Seeks to reform education by investing quickly in America's youngest children. Provides funding for several programs proposed during President Obama's administration that benefit young children.

from public assistance in obtaining child care so they can work or attend training or education

- $14.5 billion for Title I grants to school districts to expand services
- $3 billion for school improvement and construction grants
- $11.3 billion for IDEA Part B state grants for special education
- $500 million for IDEA Part C (infants and families) for special education[12]

Federal Involvement in Literacy Education

A far ranging influence of NCLB is that it has put literacy and reading first in early childhood programs by trying to ensure that every child can read on grade level by the end of third grade. This means that efforts to provide young children with the literacy skills they need begin in Early Head Start and Head Start programs. For example, the Department of Health

FIGURE 8.1

Federal Programs That Support Early Care and Education

We don't really appreciate the extent of federal support and funding for early education until we see a list such as this. Think about what the field of early childhood education would be like without federal dollars!

• Child and Adult Care Food Program (CACFP)	• State and federally funded program that provides funding to licensed child care centers, adult day care centers, and organizations that sponsor day care homes to ensure participants receive nutritionally adequate meals and snacks while in care.
• Child Care and Development Block Grant (CCDBG)	• $2 billion in funding for CCDBG to states to provide eligible low-income families a voucher to enroll their children in child care programs.
• Early Learning Challenge Fund	• $300 million to provide grants to states for the development of state plans and infrastructure to raise the quality of publicly funded early learning programs.
• Early Reading First	• $162.5 million for support to early childhood programs to improve the quality of their early literacy services for preschool-aged children.

• Head Start
  • Early Head Start
  • Migrant and Seasonal Head Start
  • American Indian/Alaska Native
	• $2.1 billion dollars to improve school readiness for disadvantaged students.

• Home Visitation	• $8.6 billion dollars over ten years for new mandatory programs that provide funds to states for evidence-based home visitation programs for low-income families.
• Special Education/ Part C (IDEA) • Special Education/ Preschool Grants (IDEA)	• $11.3 billion in special education state grants in the Recovery Act requires states to provide a free appropriate public education to all children with disabilities. IDEA authorizes grants to states to help pay the additional cost of providing education and services to children with disabilities, ages 3–21.
• Title I	• Provides $14.5 billion dollars to local districts to use Title I Recovery Act funds to establish or expand Title I preschool programs.

Source: U.S Department of Education, www.ed.gov. U.S. Department of Health and Human Services, www.hhs.gov.

and Human Services provides Head Start programs with assistance on ways in which they can better prepare children to be ready for school. Particular emphasis is placed on both child and family literacy so that Head Start children can better develop the skills they need to become life-long readers and parents can better develop the skills they need to improve their own lives and help their children become proficient in reading. Head Start invests considerable resources in early literacy, including providing resources for training and technical assistance to ensure that every Head Start classroom is promoting reading, vocabulary, and language skills.[13]

Every dimension of almost every educational program—public, private, and faith based—is touched in some way by the federal government. Figure 8.1 shows some of the federal programs that help provide funding for early care and education.

The federal legislative and financial influence on early childhood education—indeed, on all of education, from birth through higher education—is vast and significant. You can count on the fact that you, your colleagues, and the children you teach will continue to be under the direction of federal mandates and guidelines. Consequently, you must be aware of the influence of federal and state governments on you and your profession. Additionally, you must be willing to be politically involved in influencing legislation and its implementation in programs and classrooms.

Currently, all early childhood programs, including Head Start, emphasize the development of children's early literacy skills by Involving parents and grandparents. Literacy skills are seen as a key to success in school and life.

Head Start Programs

Head Start (for children three to five years of age) and Early Head Start (for children from birth to three years of age) are comprehensive child development programs that serve children, families, and pregnant women. These programs provide comprehensive health, nutritional, educational, and social services to help children achieve their full potential and succeed in school and life. Currently, the programs serve low-income children and families; thus they are considered **entitlement programs**, which means that children and families who qualify income-wise are entitled to the services. However, only about half of eligible children and families receive these services because of the lack of funding to support full implementation. However, the numbers of children serviced by particular states and regions can be less than the national average.[14]

As public schools provide more kindergarten and preschool programs, Head Start now serves younger children, primarily three- and four-year-olds. Head Start is administered by the Administration for Children and Families (ACF) in the Department of Health and Human Services. Some educators and politicians think Head Start should be administered by the Department of Education. Others disagree. Currently, these two federal agencies collaborate to enhance and expand the Head Start programs to benefit all children from every aspect. Figure 8.2 shows the organizational structure for Head Start and Early Head Start. As you can see, Head Start is comprised of two different kinds of programs on a local level: single purpose agencies such as the local YMCA and community action agencies. Any local public or private nonprofit or local for-profit agency or organization is eligible to apply for funding to establish a Head Start program.[15]

As of 2010 the national Head Start program has an annual budget of more than $7.2 billion and serves some 904,153 low-income children in approximately 49,200 Head Start classrooms. Of these nearly 1 million children, 3 percent are five years old and older; 51 percent are four-year-olds; 36 percent are three-year-olds; and 10 percent are three years old and under. The average cost to educate a child in Head Start is $7,600 annually. Compare this cost to $8700 per child, the price it costs to give a quality preschool education

entitlement programs Programs and services children and families are entitled to because they meet the eligibility criteria for the services.

FIGURE 8.2
**Organizational
Structure of Head Start/
Early Head Start**

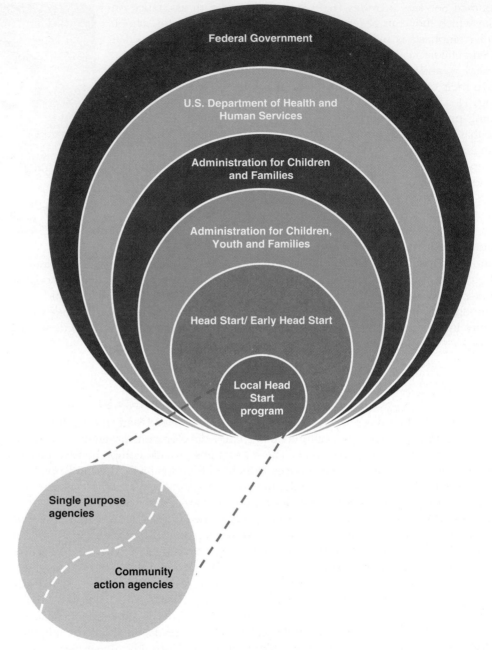

to every three- and four-year old in the nation annually.[16] Head Start has a paid staff of 212,000 and 850,000 volunteers.[17]

However, in President Obama's 2011 budget, the following funds were earmarked: $8.22 billion for Head Start, an increase of $989 million, to serve an estimated 971,000 children, an increase of approximately 66,500 children over fiscal year 2008. Early Head Start will serve approximately 116,00 infants and toddlers in fiscal year 2011, nearly twice as many as were served in fiscal year 2008. The budget also includes $118 million for quality enhancements.[18]

The American Recovery and Reinvestment Act of 2009 (ARRA) also provided an additional $1 billion for Head Start and $1.1 billion for Early Head Start.[19] For example, the building of a new $2.7 million Head Start building in the El Paso (Texas) Head Start program comes from ARRA funds.

The El Paso Head Start program serves 4,600 children and is the third-largest Head Start in the state of Texas. Federal funding helps ensure that children get an early academic boost. It is an example of the federal government helping low-resource and underserved populations.[20]

Head Start Performance Standards

Both Head Start and Early Head Start must comply with federal performance standards, designed to ensure that all children and families receive high-quality services.

The **Head Start Program Performance Standards** play a central role in defining quality services for low-income children and their families. The Performance Standards are the mandatory regulations that programs must implement in order to operate a Head Start and/or Early Head Start program. These standards define the objectives, features, and services of a quality Head Start program; they specify the services that should be delivered to both young children and their families; and they require a group to monitor and enforce quality standards.[21] The framework of the Head Start program includes four cornerstones: child development, family development, community building, and staff development, plus three other areas of importance: administration/management, continuous improvement, and children with disabilities.[22]

Head Start Program Performance Standards Federal guidelines for Head Start and Early Head Start, designed to ensure that all children and families receive high-quality services.

1. ***Child Development:*** Programs must support the physical, social, emotional, cognitive, and language development of each child. Parenting education and the support of a positive parent-child relationship are critical to this cornerstone. The services that programs must provide directly or through referral include:
   - Early education services in a range of developmentally appropriate settings
   - Home visits, especially for families with newborns
   - Parent education and parent–child activities
   - Comprehensive health and mental health services for children
   - High-quality child care services, provided directly or in collaboration with community child care providers

2. ***Family Development:*** Programs must seek to empower families by developing goals for themselves and their children. Staff and parents create individualized family development plans that focus on the children's developmental needs and the family's social and economic needs. Families that are involved in other programs requiring a family service plan will receive a single coordinated plan so that they experience a seamless system of services. The services that programs must provide directly or through referral include:
   - Child development information
   - Comprehensive health and mental health services for family members, including smoking cessation and substance abuse treatment
   - Adult education, literacy, and job skills training to facilitate family self-sufficiency
   - Assistance in obtaining income support, safe housing, or emergency cash
   - Transportation to program services

3. ***Community Building:*** Programs are expected to conduct an assessment of community resources so that they may build a comprehensive network of services and supports for pregnant women and families with young children. The goal of these collaborative relationships is to increase family access to community supports, make the most efficient use of limited resources, and effect system-wide changes to improve the service delivery system for all families in the community.

4. ***Staff Development:*** The success of the Head Start programs rests largely on the quality of the staff. Staff members must have the capacity to develop caring, supportive

relationships with both children and families. Ongoing training, supervision, and mentoring encompasses an interdisciplinary approach and emphasizes relationship building. Staff development is grounded in established "best practices" in the areas of child development, family development, and community building.

5. ***Administration/Management:*** Head Start and Early Head Start programs utilize administration and management practices which uphold the nine principles and four cornerstones mentioned above. An interdisciplinary approach ensures that all staff are trained in the areas of child development, family development, and community building. Staff supervision, with opportunities for feedback and reflection, emphasize relationship building as the foundation for interactions between children, families, and staff members.

6. ***Continuous Improvement:*** Training, monitoring, research, and evaluation enable Early Head Start programs to better meet the needs of young children and families. Ongoing training and technical assistance is provided by the Infant/Family Network and the Early Head Start National Resource Center (EHSNRC).

7. ***Children with Disabilities:*** Early Head Start programs have the responsibility to coordinate with programs providing services in accordance with the Individuals with Disabilities Education Act (IDEA). Children with disabilities are fully included in program activities.

In addition, the Head Start Performance Standards stress that local programs should emphasize the professional development of Head Start teachers and should include reading and math readiness skills in the curriculum. Although the Head Start Bureau provides guidance on meeting the performance standards, local agencies are responsible for designing programs to best meet the needs of their children and families.

Standards of Learning.   Head Start programs implement *standards of learning* in early literacy, language, and numeracy skills. These nine indicators guide teacher planning and act as standards of learning for Head Start children:

1. Develop phonemic, print, and numeracy awareness
2. Understand and use language to communicate for various purposes
3. Understand and use increasingly complex and varied vocabulary
4. Develop and demonstrate an appreciation of books
5. In the case of non–English-background children, progress toward acquisition of the English language
6. Know that the letters of the alphabet are a special category of visual graphics that can be individually named
7. Recognize a word as a unit of print
8. Identify at least ten letters of the alphabet
9. Associate sounds with written words

Implications.   These standards and others embedded in the Head Start performance standards have several implications:

- Today, the Head Start curriculum is more academic.
- Literacy and reading are a priority in Head Start.
- Head Start teachers and programs are more accountable for children's learning.

Child Outcomes Framework.   The Outcomes Framework shown in Figure 8.3 includes the nine indicators of learning as well as many other performance standards that shape the

FIGURE 8.3

Head Start Child Outcomes Framework

DOMAIN	DOMAIN ELEMENT	INDICATORS
Language Development	**Listening and understanding**	• Demonstrates increasing ability to attend to and understand conversations, stories, songs, and poems. • Shows progress in understanding and following simple and multiple-step directions. * **Understands an increasingly complex and varied vocabulary.** * **For non–English-speaking children, progresses in listening to and understanding English.**
	Speaking and communicating	* **Develops increasing abilities to understand and use language to communicate information, experiences, ideas, feelings, opinions, needs, questions, and other varied purposes.** • Progresses in abilities to initiate and respond appropriately in conversation and discussions with peers and adults. * **Uses an increasingly complex and varied spoken vocabulary.** • Progresses in clarity of pronunciation and towards speaking in sentences of increasing length and grammatical complexity. * **For non–English-speaking children, progresses in speaking English.**
Literacy	***Phonological awareness**	• Shows increasing ability to discriminate and identify sounds in spoken language. • Shows growing awareness of beginning and ending sounds of words. • Progresses in recognizing matching sounds and rhymes in familiar words, games, songs, stories and poems. • Shows growing ability to hear and discriminate separate syllables in words. * **Associates sounds with written words,** such as awareness that different words begin with the same sound.
	***Book knowledge and appreciation**	• Shows growing interest and involvement in listening to and discussing a variety of fiction and nonfiction books and poetry. • Shows growing interest in reading-related activities, such as asking to have a favorite book read; choosing to look at books; drawing pictures based on stories; asking to take books home; going to the library; and engaging in pretend-reading with other children. • Demonstrates progress in abilities to retell and dictate stories from books and experiences; to act out stories in dramatic play; and to predict what will happen next in a story. • Progresses in learning how to handle and care for books; knowing to view one page at a time in sequence from front to back; and understanding that a book has a title, author, and illustrator.
	***Print awareness and concepts**	• Shows increasing awareness of print in classroom, home, and community settings. • Develops growing understanding of the different functions of forms of print such as signs, letters, newspapers, lists, messages, and menus. • Demonstrates increasing awareness of concepts of print, such as that reading in English moves from top to bottom and from left to right, that speech can be written down, and that print conveys a message. • Shows progress in recognizing the association between spoken and written words by following print as it is read aloud. * **Recognizes a word as a unit of print,** or awareness that letters are grouped to form words, and that words are separated by spaces.

*Indicates the four specific domain elements and nine indicators that are legislatively mandated.

(continued)

FIGURE 8.3

Continued

DOMAIN	DOMAIN ELEMENT	INDICATORS
Literacy (cont.)	Early writing	• Develops understanding that writing is a way of communicating for a variety of purposes. • Begins to represent stories and experiences through pictures, dictation, and in play. • Experiments with a growing variety of writing tools and materials, such as pencils, crayons, and computers. • Progresses from using scribbles, shapes, or pictures to represent ideas, to using letter-like symbols, to copying or writing familiar words such as one's own name.
	Alphabet knowledge	• Shows progress in associating the names of letters with their shapes and sounds. • Increases in ability to notice the beginning letters in familiar words. * **Identifies at least ten letters of the alphabet, especially those in one's own name.** * **Knows that letters of the alphabet are a special category of visual graphics that can be individually named.**
Mathematics	*Number and operations	• Demonstrates increasing interest in and awareness of numbers and counting as a means for solving problems and determining quantity. • Begins to associate number concepts, vocabulary, quantities, and written numerals in meaningful ways. • Develops increasing ability to count in sequence to ten and beyond. • Begins to make use of one-to-one correspondence in counting objects and matching groups of objects. • Begins to use language to compare numbers of objects with terms such as *more, less, greater than, fewer, equal to.* • Develops increased abilities to combine, separate, and name "how many" concrete objects.
	Geometry and spatial sense	• Begins to recognize, describe, compare, and name common shapes, their parts, and attributes. • Progresses in ability to put together and take apart shapes. • Begins to be able to determine whether two shapes are the same size and shape. • Shows growth in matching, sorting, putting in a series, and regrouping objects according to one or two attributes such as color, shape, or size. • Builds an increasing understanding of directionality, order and positions of objects, and words such as *up, down, over, under, top, bottom, inside, outside, in front*, and *behind.*
	Patterns and measurement	• Enhances abilities to recognize, duplicate, and extend simple patterns using a variety of materials. • Shows increasing abilities to match, sort, put in a series, and regroup objects according to one or two attributes such as shape or size. • Begins to make comparisons between several objects based on a single attribute. • Shows progress in using standard and nonstandard measures for length and area of objects.
Science	Scientific skills and methods	• Begins to use senses and a variety of tools and simple measuring devices to gather information, investigate materials, and observe processes and relationships. • Develops increased ability to observe and discuss common properties, differences, and comparisons among objects and materials. • Begins to participate in simple investigations to test observations, discuss and draw conclusions, and form generalizations. • Develops growing abilities to collect, describe, and record information through a variety of means, including discussion, drawings, maps, and charts. • Begins to describe and discuss predictions, explanations, and generalizations based on past experiences.

FIGURE 8.3

Continued

DOMAIN	DOMAIN ELEMENT	INDICATORS
Science (cont.)	Scientific knowledge	• Expands knowledge of and abilities to observe, describe, and discuss the natural world, materials, living things, and natural processes. • Expands knowledge of and respect for one's body and the environment. • Develops growing awareness of ideas and language related to attributes of time and temperature. • Shows increased awareness and beginning understanding of changes in materials and cause-effect relationships.
Creative Arts	Music	• Participates with increasing interest and enjoyment in a variety of music activities, including listening, singing, finger plays, games, and performances. • Experiments with a variety of musical instruments.
	Art	• Gains ability in using different art media and materials in a variety of ways for creative expression and representation. • Progresses in abilities to create drawings, paintings, models, and other art creations that are more detailed, creative, or realistic. • Develops growing abilities to plan, work independently, and demonstrate care and persistence in a variety of art projects. • Begins to understand and share opinions about artistic products and experiences.
	Movement	• Expresses through movement and dancing what is felt and heard in various musical tempos and styles. • Shows growth in moving in time to different patterns of beat and rhythm in music.
	Dramatic play	• Participates in a variety of dramatic play activities that become more extended and complex. • Shows growing creativity and imagination in using materials and in assuming different roles in dramatic play situations.
Social and Emotional Development	Self-concept	• Begins to develop and express awareness of self in terms of specific abilities, characteristics, and preferences. • Develops growing capacity for independence in a range of activities, routines, and tasks. • Demonstrates growing confidence in a range of abilities and expresses pride in accomplishments.
	Self-control	• Shows progress in expressing feelings, needs, and opinions in difficult situations and conflicts without harming self, others, or property. • Develops growing understanding of how one's actions affect others and begins to accept the consequences of one's actions. • Demonstrates increasing capacity to follow rules and routines and use materials purposefully, safely, and respectfully.
	Cooperation	• Increases abilities to sustain interactions with peers by helping, sharing, and discussion. • Shows increasing abilities to use compromise and discussion in working, playing, and resolving conflicts with peers. • Develops increasing abilities to give and take in interactions, to take turns in games or using materials; and to interact without being overly submissive or directive.

(continued)

FIGURE 8.3

Continued

DOMAIN	DOMAIN ELEMENT	INDICATORS
Social and Emotional Development (cont.)	Social relationships	• Demonstrates increasing comfort in talking with and accepting guidance and directions from a range of familiar adults. • Shows progress in developing friendships with peers. • Progresses in responding sympathetically to peers who are in need, upset, hurt, or angry, and in expressing empathy or caring for others.
	Knowledge of families and communities	• Develops ability to identify personal characteristics including gender and family composition. • Progresses in understanding similarities and respecting differences among people, such as gender, race, special needs, culture, language, and family structures. • Develops growing awareness of jobs and what is required to perform them. • Begins to express and understand concepts and language of geography in the contexts of the classroom, home, and community.
Approaches to Learning	Initiative and curiosity	• Chooses to participate in an increasing variety of tasks and activities. • Develops increased ability to make independent choices. • Approaches tasks and activities with increased flexibility, imagination, and inventiveness. • Grows in eagerness to learn about and discuss a growing range of topics, ideas, and tasks.
	Engagement and persistence	• Grows in abilities to persist in and complete a variety of tasks, activities, projects, and experiences. • Demonstrates increasing ability to set goals and develop and follow through on plans. • Shows growing capacity to maintain concentration over time on a task, question, set of directions, or interactions, despite distractions and interruptions.
	Reasoning and problem solving	• Develops increasing ability to find more than one solution to a question, task, or problem. • Grows in recognizing and solving problems through active exploration, including trial and error, and interactions and discussions with peers and adults. • Develops increasing abilities to classify, compare, and contrast objects, events, and experiences.
Physical Health and Development	Fine-motor skills	• Develops growing strength, dexterity, and control needed to use tools such as scissors, paper punch, stapler, and hammer. • Grows in hand-eye coordination in building with blocks, putting together puzzles, reproducing shapes and patterns, stringing beads, and using scissors. • Progresses in abilities to use writing, drawing, and art tools including pencils, markers, chalk, paint brushes, and various types of technology.
	Gross-motor skills	• Shows increasing levels of proficiency, control, and balance in walking, climbing, running, jumping, hopping, skipping, marching, and galloping. • Demonstrates increasing abilities to coordinate movements in throwing, catching, kicking, bouncing balls, and using the slide and swing.
	Health status and practices	• Progresses in physical growth, strength, stamina, and flexibility. • Participates actively in games, outdoor play, and other forms of exercise that enhance physical fitness. • Shows growing independence in hygiene, nutrition, and personal care when eating, dressing, washing hands, brushing teeth, and toileting. • Builds awareness and ability to follow basic health and safety rules such as fire safety, traffic and pedestrian safety, and responding appropriately to potentially harmful objects, substances, and activities.

Source: Administration for Children and Families, Head Start Bureau, www.hsnrc.org/cdi/child-outcomes.cfm.

Head Start curriculum. (The nine special indicators appear in boldface and are identified with an asterisk.) This outcome framework is important for several reasons:

- It specifies learning outcomes that are essential to children's success in school and life.
- It ensures that all children in Head Start programs work toward the same learning outcomes.
- It impacts what children learn in all preschool programs, not just Head Start.

Program Options

Head Start and Early Head Start programs have the freedom to tailor their programs to meet the needs of the children, families, and communities they serve. To determine strengths and resources, every three years local programs conduct a community survey (the number of families and children living at or below the poverty level; projected benefits of Head Start to meeting social needs of children and families in the community; health status of children and families in the community; etc.) They then design their program options based on these data. There are four Head Start program options:

1. The *center-based option* delivers services to children and families using the center as the base, or core. Center-based programs operate either full-day or half-day for thirty-two to thirty-four weeks a year, the minimum required by the Head Start performance standards, or they operate full-year programs. Center-based staff members make periodic visits to family homes.[23]

2. The *home-based option* uses the family home as the base for providing services. Home visitors work with the parents and children to improve parenting skills and to assist parents in using the home as the child's primary learning environment. Twice a month children and families come together for field trips and classroom experiences to emphasize peer group interaction.[24] The home-based option has these strengths:
   - Parent involvement is the keystone of the program.
   - Geographically isolated families have an invaluable opportunity to be part of a comprehensive child and family program.
   - An individualized family plan is based on both a child and a family assessment.
   - The family plan is facilitated by a home visitor, who is an adult educator with knowledge of and training in all Head Start components.
   - The program includes the entire family.

3. The *combination option* combines the center- and home-based options. The combination options must provide class sessions and home visits that result in an amount of contact with children and families equivalent to the services provided through the center-based program option or home-based option.[25]

4. The *family child care option* includes programs created specifically to meet unique community and family needs. Many parents believe their children benefit from a homelike setting. Head Start agencies have found that family child care is a suitable arrangement when parents are working, in training, or need care for more than one child. The formal recognition of this setting as an option in Head Start is particularly timely given the changing circumstances in many communities where an increased number of families are moving into employment.[26]

The Voice from the Field "Higher Horizons Head Start" provides a good description of a combination program that implements a full-day center-based program for preschool children, as well as home- and center-based services for infants, toddlers, and pregnant women.

Voice from the Field

Higher Horizons Head Start

Higher Horizons operates full-day, full-year Head Start and Early Head Start programs for children from six weeks to five years of age in one of the most culturally diverse communities in the Washington, D.C. metropolitan area. Early Head Start offers home- and center-based services for infants, toddlers, and pregnant women. The Head Start programs offer full-day center-based services for preschool children. Children, families, and staff are representative of the diverse community; over forty-nine of the children speak languages other than English, including Spanish, Creole, Urdu, Somali, Cambodian, Punjabi, and Vietnamese.

Performance Standards

Higher Horizons is guided by Head Start Program Performance Standards. Major elements of the standards include early childhood development and health services, family and community partnerships, staffing, and program design and management. Higher Horizons involves parents and community representatives in all aspects of the program, including policy development, program design, and curriculum and management decisions.

The Head Start Day

A routine day for Head Start children includes transportation pickup from an apartment complex on an agency-owned school bus. Other children are dropped off daily by parents or caregivers. Once children arrive they are observed for general physical and mental health. Any unusual or observable concerns are reported to the health specialist for follow-up with the teacher and parent. Children are engaged in activities throughout the day, with an afternoon rest period. After the rest period, children begin preparing for departure by bus or receive a snack and participate in organized activities.

A typical daily schedule includes:

Arrival: Children are greeted in their home language; personal items (coats/hats) are placed in individual storage areas (cubbies). Teaching staff observe children for health inspections (colds/flu, signs of abuse/neglect, etc).

Breakfast, Cleanup, Toothbrushing

Large Group Time: This is a time when there is group participation. Children and teaching staff make plans for the day; discuss the weather and news; children discuss happenings from home, etc. For example, teaching staff may read a book related to the plans they make and discuss the kites children brought in for "Kite Day". Throughout large group time there are opportunities to build and expand vocabulary. For example, children use the local newspaper to find words that begin with "K" when discussing kites.

Gross Motor Activities—Outdoors/Gym: This is an opportunity for organized activities. Children have balls, hula hoops, obstacle course items, etc. Teaching staff arrange opportunities for children to choose activities to build teams, ensure that all children are actively engaged and encourage physical activity. Children have access to the outdoor play areas with equipment to swing, climb, explore, and run.

Small Group Time—Individualization: Teaching staff work with children individually to develop skills in physical development (putting things together, solving puzzles, making projects with blocks, etc.). Teachers work with children in the art area to compare and match colored pieces of paper and children paint pictures using their imagination as creative thinkers. Children also have access to the dramatic play area and they arrange these items to set up a store. The computer area is available during small group time. Two computers in each classroom support children's development and learning in the areas of problem solving, fine motor control and eye-hand coordination and other activities that help children make the bridge between the concrete and the abstract.

Large Group Time: Children review some of the activities from the small group time. They share their activities. Large group time also provides time for children to plan for the next day and discuss the outcomes of some of the activities they were involved in during small group time. Children may be introduced to music and movement during this time. Songs with lots of repetition, action songs and songs with finger plays are also shared during large group time.

Lunch, Cleanup, Toothbrushing

Rest/Quiet Time

Snack, Parent Pick Up or

Music/Movement/Individualized Work Until Pick Up: Individualized work may include a listening activity with a CD player or MP3 player. Children may select musical instruments to play and small groups of children play in pairs, trios, or large group. Teaching staff ask children to pantomime movements of animals and insects (butterfly, elephant, etc). Individualized work may focus on supporting a child in an area that he/she requires additional support such as vocabulary development, learning mathematical concepts in the block area, and artwork for creativity and self expression.

Mealtime

Meals are served family-style (meaning that children eat together around a table) in each classroom. Children have the opportunity to help with food service, such as table setting and food distribution. Children help themselves to the food offered at breakfast, lunch, and snack. Adults in the classroom sit at each table, sharing the same food the children eat, and utilize this time to encourage

the use of language to discuss both classroom and home activities. The menus are reflective of the diverse population served which includes weekly vegetarian meals. Meal adjustments are made for children with special dietary needs or food allergies. Vegan and vegetarian diets are recognized, soy products are used for children with milk allergies. Special nutrition activities are regularly planned in each classroom. For example, each classroom is assigned a vegetable garden. Children plant vegetables (tomatoes, squash, pumpkins, melons, etc.) each spring of the year and are responsible for watering, feeding, and tending to the growth of the vegetables. Once the vegetables are ready to harvest, they are bought to the classroom for cooking and eating. Children read stories about health food and classrooms are responsible for monthly 'program-wide' nutrition activities. Classrooms select a topic and are responsible for the activity. For example, children visit the local grocery store and select different varieties of apples (Gala, McIntosh, Fuji,

Golden Delicious) to share with the classrooms, and described taste and textures.

The Curriculum

Teachers plan daily activities using *The Creative Curriculum* (www.creativecurriculum.net/) approach to learning for children from infants through the preschool years. This resource based curriculum helps staff plan and provide consistent and responsive care in an environment that starts them on the path to a lifetime of engaged learning. The curriculum for infants and toddlers helps staff build relationships with children by creating meaningful daily routines and experiences that respond to individual children's strengths and interests. The preschool curriculum approach also helps staff successfully plan and implement a content-rich, developmentally appropriate program that supports active learning and promotes children's progress in all developmental areas. For example, in the Cotton Ball Race, children learn to predict the effects of air movement on an object while considering the location of the air source. Children use straws to blow the cotton ball and see how far they can make it travel. They also blow a marble and a magnet to compare and contrast the amount of wind needed and what location they needed to be in to blow the objects to a certain predetermined point.

Parent/Family Involvement

Parents play an active role in collaborating with classroom staff. Staff encourage parents to visit the classrooms and participate in two formal conferences and two home visits during the program year. The information gained during these staff-parent conferences enhances parents' knowledge and understanding of the developmental progress of the children in the program. During parent conferences, staff share that children are able to serve themselves and are independent and can help with simple tasks. Parents are often amazed at the types of items in the classroom found in the home that can be used to support learning. For example, household items can be used for sorting, classification, and counting.

Higher Horizons Head Start continues to focus on developing and implementing quality programs that reflect current research and best practices and promoting the Head Start goal of school readiness for children.

Source: Text and photo contributed by Mary Ann Cornish, Executive Director, Higher Horizons Head Start and Early Head Start, Falls Church, Virginia.

Head Start prides itself on tailoring its programs to the children and families in the local community. In fact, this goal of meeting the needs of families and children at the local level is one of the program's strengths, and one that makes it very popular with parents.

Eligibility for Head Start Services

To be eligible for Head Start services, children must meet age and family-income criteria. Head Start enrolls children ages three to five from low-income families. Income eligibility is determined by whether or not family incomes fall below the official poverty line, which is set annually by the U.S. Department of Health and Human Services. Poverty guidelines for 2010 are shown in Table 8.1.

Ninety percent of Head Start children have to meet the income eligibility criteria. The other 10 percent of enrollment can include children from families that exceed the low-income guidelines. In addition, 10 percent of a program's enrollment must include children with disabilities. Often, the actual enrollment in local programs for children with disabilities surpasses the minimum 10 percent requirement.

Early Head Start

Early Head Start (EHS), launched in 1995, is designed to provide year-round comprehensive child and family development services for low-income pregnant women and families with infants and toddlers ages birth to three years. The purpose of the program is to enhance the physical, social, emotional, and intellectual development of children; support parents' efforts to fulfill their parental roles; and help families move toward self-sufficiency.[27] EHS is also a program for low-income families who meet federal poverty guidelines. It serves about 117,000 infants and toddlers annually with a budget of $1.1 billion.

Head Start's entry into the field of infant and toddler care and education through EHS has achieved many accomplishments.[28]

- EHS now provides services to the long-neglected age groups of infants and toddlers.
- EHS has become a leader in the field of infant and toddler education.
- EHS programs produce statistically significant, positive impacts on standardized measures of children's cognitive, social-emotional, and language development, as well as lower levels of aggressive behavior.[29]
- EHS programs produce significant and positive impacts on the entire family system establishing greater warmth and supportiveness between parent and child, more

TABLE 8.1 2009–2010 Poverty Guidelines for the Forty-Eight Contiguous States and the District of Columbia

Size of Family Unit	Poverty Guidelines
1	$10,830
2	$14,570
3	$18,310
4	$22,050
5	$25,790
6	$29,530
7	$33,270
8	$37,010

Source: U.S. Department of Health and Human Services, 2009 Poverty Guidelines (2009).
http://aspe.hhs.gov/poverty/09poverty.shtml

parent–child play, more stimulating home environments, more daily reading and increased support for language and learning, less spanking by mothers and fathers, more employment hours, and more hours spent in education and job training.

- EHS families who enroll during pregnancy have a greater likelihood of breastfeeding as compared to those not enrolled in EHS, and there are positive impacts on children's cognitive and social-emotional development at 36 months of age.

Through the American Reinvestment and Recovery Act of 2009 (ARRA), the Office of Head Start expanded Early Head Start significantly. With increased funding and support from the federal government, EHS should continue to maintain high-quality services, while evolving programmatically to meet the needs of a diverse population of children and families.[30]

Migrant and Seasonal Head Start Program

A **migrant family** is a family who moves from one geographic location to another within a two-year period for the purpose of engaging in agricultural work. Migrant Head Start provides services tailored to the unique needs of migrant families in some of the most rural areas in America. Services provided to migrant children and their families are identical to those of other Head Start programs, even as they address the unique needs of migrant children and families. **Migrant and Seasonal Head Start** programs emphasize serving infants and toddlers so that they do not have to accompany their parents to the fields or be left with young siblings.

In 1998, seasonal farm workers were added to the population served, and the Migrant and Seasonal Head Start Programs Branch was the result. A **seasonal family** is a family with children who are engaged primarily in seasonal agricultural labor and who have not changed their residence to another geographic location in the preceding two-year period. Migrant Head Start services offer positive, nurturing child development programs for children ages birth to school-entry age. Thirty-five percent of Migrant and Seasonal Head Start's enrollment is composed of infants and toddlers. Programs are center based, full day, and structured to meet local needs.

The Fresno Migrant Head Start program in Fresno, California, provides children with transportation to and from their full-day center-based program. Classroom time includes group time, music, dramatic play, manipulative play, art, food experiences, and more. Each day, children have time to work in a small group with other children and to play outdoors on safe playground equipment. Children receive a nutritious lunch and snack. All children are taught to wash their hands before and brush their teeth after meals, and are encouraged to develop good personal and health habits.[31]

American Indian/Alaska Native Head Start Programs

The American Indian/Alaska Native program of Head Start provides American Indian and Alaska Native children (birth to age five) and their families with comprehensive health, education, nutritional, social, and developmental services designed to promote school readiness.

One such program is the Aleutian Pribilof Islands Association (APIA) Alaska Native Head Start Program in Anchorage, Alaska, which provides a half-day program operating September through May. Currently, it has center-based programs in four locations, which collectively provide education, special needs, mental health, nutrition, and social services to a maximum of 72 children ages three to five and their low-income families. The APIA Head Start encourages parental and family involvement, while embracing a rich Aleut cultural heritage which gives children and families opportunities to learn kayak building, language, dance, basket weaving, bead work with headdresses, regalia sewing, and many more activities.[32]

migrant family A family with school-age children that moves from one geographic location to another to engage in agricultural work.

Migrant and Seasonal Head Start A federal program designed to provide educational and other services to children and families who earn income in agricultural work.

seasonal family A family with children who are engaged primarily in seasonal agricultural labor and who have not changed their residence to another geographic location in the preceding two-year period.

The Migrant and Seasonal and American Indian/Alaska Native Head Start Program branches serve over 58,000 children nationwide.[33]

Education Barriers for Migrant and Seasonal and American Indian/Alaska Native Head Start Programs.   Teachers in the Migrant/Seasonal and American Indian/Alaska Native (AI/AN) Head Start programs struggle with financial, geographic, linguistic, and other barriers on their path to college. Roughly 58 percent of teachers in Head Start programs serving American Indians have at least an associate's degree. For teachers in Migrant or Seasonal Head Start programs, that percentage is 51.2 percent.[34] A federal mandate states that by October 1, 2011, 100 percent of Head Start classrooms must have a teacher with at least an associate's degree in early childhood education or a related field. The American Indian program is about 7,500 teachers short of meeting this requirement.[35]

Colleges and policy makers are working to develop new approaches to distance education, and on providing financial aid to help the teacher population and the children they serve.[36]

Head Start Research

A question that everyone always asks is, "Do Head Start and Early Head Start programs work?" By *work*, people generally mean, "Do these programs deliver the services they are authorized and funded to deliver, and do these services make a difference in the lives of children and families?"

Over the last decade, the federal government has been aggressive in attempting to ensure that the programs it funds provide results. Consequently, we have seen a tremendous increase in federal monies allocated for research of federally funded programs and a corresponding increase in the number of research studies designed to measure the effectiveness of those programs.

The 2010 Head Start Impact Study reveals these results:

- **Program Quality.** On average, Head Start children attend classrooms of good quality, and these classrooms are of higher quality than classrooms in other center-based programs.[37]
- **Head Start Access.** Access to Head Start has positive impacts on children's preschool experiences and school readiness:
  - For the four-year-old group, progress by the end of the Head Start year concentrates on language and literacy, including positive improvements in vocabulary, letter-word identification, spelling, preacademic skills, color identification, letter naming, and parent-reported emergent literacy.
  - For the three-year-old group, benefits include improvements in vocabulary, letter-word identification, preacademic skills, letter naming, elision (phonological processing or understanding letter and word sound), parent-reported emergent literacy, perceptual motor skills and prewriting, and applied problem solving (math).
  - Children attending Head Start show greater cognitive progress than the control group children. Three-year-old children who had attended Head Start demonstrated modest gains in language, literacy, prewriting, and math skills. Four-year-old children demonstrated modest gains in language and literacy skills.[38]
- **Cognitive Impacts.** By the end of first grade, only a single cognitive impact was found for each group. Children who attended Head Start as three- and four-year-old children do significantly better on vocabulary.[39]
- **Socio-Emotional Impacts.** By the end of the first grade, there was some evidence that children who attend Head Start as three-year-olds have closer and more positive relationships with their parents or significant primary adult. Of that same group,

children with special needs showed improvements in the social-emotional domain by the end of first grade. Meanwhile, children who attended Head Start as three-year-olds showed less hyperactive and problem behavior by the end of Head Start, favorable social skills and positive approaches to learning at the end of the age four year, and less hyperactive behavior, increased social skills, and positive approaches to learning by the end of kindergarten.[40]

- **Health Impacts.** Both three- and four-year-old children attending Head Start were more likely to receive access to dental care by the end of their Head Start year and were more likely to have health insurance coverage by the end of their kindergarten year.[41]

- **Parenting Practices.** Parents were less likely to use an authoritarian parenting style with children by the end of the age four year and first grade (see cognitive impacts above). Parents of three-year-old Head Start children were more likely to read to their children during their Head Start year, and more likely to involve them in cultural enrichment activities by the end of Head Start.[42]

While the overall results of the Head Start Impact Study are generally positive, the big issue is the "fade-out" effect of Head Start benefits to children at the end of first grade. The fade-out effect refers to the fact that for some early childhood programs the benefits children receive in a particular program tend to decrease or "fade out" over time, generally after a year or two. So, positive outcomes for children such as enhanced vocabulary, increased reading and math readiness, and increased school readiness skills tend to fade out as children progress through kindergarten and first grade. Many early childhood professionals believe that the causes of the fade-out include a lack of continuity of program services from preschool to kindergarten to first grade; a lack of high-quality teachers who have high achievement standards for all children in kindergarten and first grade; and poor-quality schools. We will hear much about the pros and cons of long-term benefits of Head Start in the years to come.

When children are healthy, they are much more able to benefit from Head Start and other educational programs. Head Start has been a leader in providing for young children's health needs. As a result, other programs such as public school pre-K programs are also providing for children's health needs.

Early Head Start Research Findings.   Findings from a number of research studies conclude that Early Head Start makes a positive difference for children and families in terms of school success, family self-sufficiency, and parental support of child development. Significant benefits of Early Head Start include[43]

- Better vocabulary and improved cognitive and social-emotional development for children
- Lasting positive effects for children
- Improved parenting
- Improved quality among existing providers who partner with Head Start

Concerns with Federal Early Childhood Education Programs.   As with all programs, Head Start has some associated issues of concern. Some of the issues are inherent in what we have discussed so far, and some are making Head Start a center of national attention.

Accountability.   Part of the federal government's ongoing effort to improve Head Start involves making it more accountable for expenditures, children's achievement, and overall program performance. It is likely that Head Start administrators and other personnel will be challenged to enhance performance in all three of these areas. As you might expect, accountability does not come easily for some programs and agencies. As we have discussed, part of the changing educational climate is that the public wants to be assured that programs, especially those serving young children, achieve the goals for which they are funded.

Federal Control and Influence.   One concern about federal legislation, regulations, and funding is that they represent an increasing encroachment of the federal government into state and local educational programs. Historically, the U.S. educational system is based on the idea that states and local communities should develop and implement educational programs and curricula, not the federal government. Opponents of federal control fear that America's highly valued local control is endangered and may even become extinct. With federal funding of any kind brings with it federal control in the form of regulations and guidelines.

Head Start's Influence.   Head Start is big business and serious business. It has a complex operating structure, standards, and regulations. It also has a vast federal bureaucracy of personnel, regional offices, and training centers. Head Start is entrenched in the early childhood field and exerts a powerful influence on how the field functions and operates. In addition, Head Start is supported by the National Head Start Association (NHSA), a powerful, nonprofit lobbying and advocacy agency that serves to protect Head Start and promote its best interests. It wields tremendous power in the halls of Congress.

National Curriculum.   The possibility of a national curriculum is closely associated with federal control and Head Start's influence. Head Start began as, and is based on, local option initiatives; in other words, local Head Start programs have been responsible for developing programs for the people that they represent and serve. Currently, however, an ongoing process of erosion is eating away at the autonomy of local programs to deliver local options within the programs. The push toward common national standards that is currently under way may have some influence on Head Start and all of early childhood education, especially in K–3.

Improving Teacher Quality.   Teacher quality and qualifications are always a predominant issue when Head Start comes up for federal reauthorization every five years. The issue revolves around what percentage of Head Start teachers should have bachelor and associate degrees. Achieving the goal of high-quality personnel will certainly challenge administrators of all Head Start programs. Nonetheless, high-quality teachers and other staff are the heart and soul of any educational program and each child deserves the best teacher possible.

Regardless of the issues associated with Head Start, one thing is certain: Head Start will continue to be an influential program affecting all early childhood programs.

Other Federal Initiatives

National Nutrition Programs

The Family and Nutrition Service (FNS) programs of the U.S. Department of Agriculture provide a national perspective on nutrition and obesity and America's children. Programs like Head Start strive to look at the whole child by not only offering academic progress but also supporting healthy lifestyles. The nutrition component of Head Start focuses on promoting good nutrition and eating habits in children and families.

National School Lunch Program.   The National School Lunch Program is a $9 billion annual federal nutrition program that provides lunch and snacks free or at a reduced rate to the nation's children. This program annually serves 31.2 million students in 101,000 schools.[44]

In Abilene (Texas) Independent School District (ISD), about 60 percent of students qualify for the free or reduced-price meals annually.[45] In 2011, Abilene ISD took advantage of the National School Lunch Program (NSLP) and the opportunities to provide a wider variety of fresh fruits and vegetables, including healthier dessert options such as low-fat pudding, fruit parfaits, and fruit cobblers.

Children from families with incomes below the federal poverty level are eligible for free meals. The U.S. Department of Agriculture's threshold at which children are eligible for free meals and milk and reduced-price meals are obtained by multiplying 2009 federal income poverty guidelines by 1.30 and 1.85, respectively.[46]

Title I Early Childhood Programs

Title I of NCLB provides financial assistance through state educational agencies (SEAs) to local educational agencies (LEAs) and schools with high numbers or percentages of poor children to help ensure that all children meet challenging state academic content and student academic achievement standards.[47] In 2010, the federal government spent almost $13 billion on Title I services.

Federal initiatives like the National School Lunch and Breakfast Programs allow students under the poverty line to have healthy snacks and lunches daily.

Title I focuses on several different objectives, all supporting the goal of giving children a high-quality education:

- Ensuring that high-quality academic assessments, accountability systems, teacher preparation and training, curriculum, and instructional materials are aligned with challenging state academic standards so that students, teachers, parents, and administrators can measure progress against common expectations for student academic achievement

- Meeting the educational needs of low-achieving children in the nation's highest-poverty schools, limited-English-proficient children, migratory children, children with disabilities, Native American children, neglected or delinquent children, and young children in need of reading assistance

- Closing the achievement gap between high- and low-performing children, especially the achievement gaps between minority and nonminority students

- Providing children with an enriched and accelerated educational program, including the use of schoolwide programs or additional services that increase the amount and quality of instructional time

- Elevating the quality of instruction by providing staff in participating schools with substantial opportunities for professional development

- Affording parents substantial and meaningful opportunities to participate in the education of their children

Here are some examples of schools that use Title I Early Childhood Grants to provide more opportunities for their children. Columbia, Missouri, Public Schools offer developmentally appropriate preschool education services to children with developmental needs. Services are provided at no cost to eligible children. The preschool program serves over 500 children, with 17 classrooms located in elementary schools throughout the district. This program is designed to prepare children for successful school entry. Active family involvement is required to help children achieve this success. An early childhood teacher and instructional assistant plan age-appropriate learning experiences to promote development in literacy, communication, decision making, and problem-solving. Teachers follow the HighScope teaching curriculum and a variety of other teaching resources to meet the developmental needs of each child.[48]

Cactus View Elementary in Phoenix, Arizona, offers Title I reading and math services to help struggling students through supplemental instruction and intervention. Karen Owens, Title I Specialist, puts students in small groups (no more than seven students) and provides intense intervention geared to what the students need—whether it be fluency, comprehension, phonemic awareness skills, or a combination of skills. These groups meet four days a week for 30–40 minutes. In the lowest-performing group(s), a reading specialist joins the classroom teacher and provides intervention within the classroom through group work for one hour, four days a week. Each student seen by a reading specialist has his or her progress monitored every two weeks.

Title I funds also helps students struggling with testing. Classes are offered for students who may have test anxiety or trouble understanding testing procedures for the Arizona Instrument to Measure Standards (AIMS). These classes are offered for an hour a day four days a week, for three weeks.[49]

Fatherhood Initiatives

fatherhood initiatives
Various efforts by federal, state, and local agencies to increase and sustain fathers' involvement with their children and families.

The Department of Health and Human Services (DHHS) provides a special **fatherhood initiative** to support and strengthen the roles of fathers in their families. Research consistently shows that when their fathers are involved, children do better academically, socially, and behaviorally.[50] This initiative is guided by the following principles:

- All fathers can be important contributors to the well-being of their children.
- Parents and partners should be involved in raising their children, even when they do not live in the same household.
- The roles fathers play in families are diverse and are related to cultural and community norms.
- Men should receive the education and support necessary to prepare them for the responsibility of parenthood.
- Government can encourage and promote fathers' involvement through its programs and its own workforce policies.

The DHHS emphasis on the important roles of fathers has, in turn, spawned a Head Start Fatherhood Initiative. It is designed to sustain fathers' involvement in their children's lives and, as a result, enhance the development of their children.

Partnerships and Collaboration

All Head Start programs endeavor to build collaborative relationships with local agencies and programs. These collaborative approaches are designed to better serve children and families and to maximize the use of resources. Healthy Beginnings is an example of a collaborative approach.

Healthy Beginnings. Healthy Beginnings provides onsite screening at licensed child care sites in seven counties in the Florida panhandle. Healthy Beginnings collaborates with Head Start's health and nutrition coordinator to form a coalition of health and safety providers. Health care professionals visit each licensed child care center in the seven-county area twice a year in a mobile medical van donated by two local hospitals. Health workers conduct basic screenings for height, weight, general physical health, and oral health.

The program is producing measurable results—approximately 20 percent of children screened for physical health problems and nearly 50 percent of those screened for dental health needs are referred for further services. The response from parents, particularly working parents who have difficulty scheduling routine health care for their children, is overwhelmingly positive.

Voice from the Field

Inclusion and Collaboration

The Head Start program of Upper Des Moines Opportunity, Inc., operates twenty-five fully inclusive preschool classrooms. We have three classrooms specific to toddlers, ages eighteen- to thirty-six months. We also have twenty-two classrooms set up for children ages three to five. Our programs are designated for all children, regardless of race or disability. We use *The Creative Curriculum* as a part of our ongoing instruction and observation of children in the classroom. We also use the *Ages and Stages Questionnaire* for developmental and social-emotional screening for children from birth to five years. In addition, we use Positive Behavior Supports for guiding children's behavior.

Our Head Start programs take pride in the strength of our partnerships with local school districts and other local education agencies. Because of the strength of these relationships we are able to collaborate in program design and offer natural or least-restriction environments to all children.

In Early Head Start, our staff is trained in case management of children with special needs. They take the lead position in coordination of services to our children and their families. These services are provided in the home, in the classroom, or in a child care setting. Support service staff trained in specific areas of early childhood development facilitate our toddler rooms. We use the Child Study model to continually update staff on individual progress, concerns, and needs of our children. We employ many interpreters of different languages as we serve a very diverse population.

Our Head Start classrooms for children ages three to five offer many opportunities for inclusion. In some centers we dually enroll children, allowing them the opportunity to spend half a day in Head Start and the other half in an early childhood special education (ECSE) classroom. We also have classrooms where Head Start teachers and ECSE teachers work side by side, allowing for full-day programming for all children in the least restrictive settings. We operate Head Start classrooms where the lead teacher has a degree in early childhood special education and associate(s) have backgrounds in early childhood, or, the lead teacher has a background in early childhood and associate(s) are qualified to work with children having special needs. Support service staff facilitate all of our classrooms for three- to five-year-olds, and they, too, use the Child Study team approach to communicate the progress, needs, and concerns of all children.

Source: Contributed by Mary Jo Madvig, Early Childhood Program Director, Upper Des Moines Opportunity, Inc., Des Moines, Iowa.

Early Intervention and Preschool Programs for Children with Disabilities (IDEA). Part C of the Individuals with Disabilities Education Improvement Act provides for services to young children ages birth to three years with disabilities and their families to address their needs, concerns, and priorities. Part B of IDEA provides for special education services to children ages three to five years with a disability or delay. The Voice from the Field, "Inclusion and Collaboration," illustrates the operation of a fully inclusive Head Start Program.

Department of Defense Child Care

Military child care is an important part of military families' support network. Just as non-military families depend and rely on quality child care for the successful growth and development of their children, so do military families. The Department of Defense (DoD) has recognized the need to help provide military families with quality and affordable child care and currently oversees nearly 800 Child Development Centers (CDCs) on military installations worldwide. Offering a safe child care environment and meeting professional standards for early childhood education, military child care accommodates the special needs of military families by extending hours to meet the work and deployment needs and schedules of their installation's population.[51]

The National Association of Child Care Resource and Referral Agencies (NACCRRA) is one organization that helps military families find quality child care programs individualized for their family. NACCRRA refers different military child care programs based on whether the parent is active or inactive, location of military installation, and even which war the parent is currently deployed in! For example, Operation

Military families need and rely on quality child care as a part of their support network to ensure their children are getting a quality education while in the care of others.

Sure Start A Department of Defense Education Activity (DoDEA) program based on the Head Start program model for command-sponsored children at overseas installations.

Military Child Care (OMCC) serves military children ages birth to 12 years with families serving in one of six deployments.[52]

These programs offer assistance to military personnel and their families to ensure their children are getting a quality education while they are off facing many challenges for our country.

Sure Start. A Department of Defense Education Activity (DoDEA) program for children at overseas installations, **Sure Start** is based on the Head Start model. The Sure Start program assists qualified preschool-aged children by providing education, health, and social services based on income and need guidelines.[53] Sure Start's comprehensive model, although appropriate for all preschool children, targets preschoolers who are at risk for school failure because of economic circumstance or other health and/or family factors.[54]

Accommodating Diverse Learners

Now that you have read about various Head Start programs, let's further explore the services available for children with disabilities in these programs. Head Start is critical for children with or at risk of developing disabilities because the program emphasizes addressing children's various abilities, learning styles, and conditions. Often, Head Start is the first place a child's disability or developmental delay is identified. This identification can lead to early intervention, which has tremendous benefits for young children and their families. Early intervention can lead to remediation or amelioration of disabilities and reduced special education costs and costs borne by families. Specially trained personnel work collaboratively with community agencies to provide services to children with disabilities.

Head Start has specific guidelines that specify that services provided to children with disabilities must be appropriate and inclusive. Here are some examples you can use in your early childhood classroom to benefit *all* children:

1. Although providing lists of children's therapy schedules is useful for teachers, do not post them because you do not want to publicly identify individual children with disabilities.
2. Encourage independence by providing opportunities for children to try new things. One good approach to get children to try new things is to break down goals into small steps. This is called "chunking" and is very effective.
3. Include *all* students in field trips. Carefully plan your trips to allow each child to benefit from the experience.
4. Just as your classroom has books showing children from many different cultural groups, also include books with pictures that show children with disabilities.
5. Promote acceptance of children with disabilities in all you do and say to your children, parents/families, and the community. Positive attitudes about children and inclusive classrooms begin with you!

Activities for Professional Development

Ethical Dilemma

●●●●●●

"Waste of time?"

Yolanda Gonzales has devoted ten years of teaching in a big city local Head Start program. She is a supporter of Head Start and believes in its mission of helping low-income children and families. She and director Maritza Mouton are concerned that their children are not receiving adequate instruction when their children enter school and that the positive effects of their good efforts will fade out in kindergarten or first grade. Many are placed in a "transitional kindergarten." Yolanda and Maritza believe lowered expectations is one of the reasons for the "fade-out" effect for Head Start children, as shown in the 2010 Head Start Impact Study research (see page 215).

Yolanda and Maritza were invited to the school district's annual administrators' meeting to address the "fade-out" issue in the district. As they made their presentation, they noticed several of the principals chattering among themselves while others showed no interest. When they concluded their presentation, one principal told them not to waste their time, because educators in the district have set beliefs about Head Start children and that Head Start has flaws. Another principal told them, "Head Start needs to really prepare children for kindergarten, instead of babysitting." Yolanda and Maritza were livid about the principals' responses but aren't sure what to do next.

What should Yolanda and Maritza do? Do they continue to press the benefits of Head Start programs and advocate for their children? What actions should they take to ensure that all children are receiving the education it takes to prevent the "fade-out" effect? Should they complain to the superintendent about the principals' attitudes and lack of support? What would you do?

●●●●●●

Activities to Apply What You Learned

1. Research three legislative acts that have changed the face of early childhood education. Create a video podcast about the changes in early childhood due to federal legislation. Encourage a discussion, pro or con, of the federal government's role in early childhood programs.

2. Why do the benefits of Head Start seem to fade out in grade one? Participate in an online discussion that addresses this question. Be sure to consider such things as the way children are taught in kindergarten through first grade. What are some things you would do to help assure that the fade out effect does not happen?

3. Go to YouTube.com and view videos of some of the early childhood educational federal initiatives listed in this chapter. Who are the people advocating for these initiatives? How are they trying to promote awareness of the services and benefits of these programs? Then, create a YouTube video of your own advocating for one of the initiatives or programs described in this chapter.

Linking to Learning

Early Head Start National Resource Center
www.ehsnrc.org/
Created by the U.S. Department of Health and Human Services as a storehouse of early childhood expertise that promotes the building of new knowledge and the sharing of information through several Head Start and Early Head Start affiliates.

Fatherhood Initiative
http://fatherhood.hhs.gov
An overview that presents facts, statistics, and reports of the Department of Health and Human Services' involvement and activities with the Fatherhood Initiative.

National Head Start Association (NHSA)
www.nhsa.org
A nonprofit organization dedicated to meeting and addressing the concerns of the Head Start community.

National Migrant and Seasonal Head Start Association
www.nmshsaonline.org/
A nonprofit organization seeking to advocate for resources, create partnerships, and affect public policy for migrant and seasonal children and their families.

Office of Head Start
www.acf.hhs.gov/programs/ohs/
United States Department of Health and Human Services official website for Head Start contains information on legislation and regulations, program services, and current information and research concerning Head Start.

University of Colorado-Denver: Centers for American Indian and Alaska Native Health-Head Start Research Center
http://aianp.uchsc.edu/headstart/headstart_index.htm
The goals of the American Indian and Alaska Native Head Start Research Center (AIANHSRC) are to operationalize and implement

a research and training agenda for American Indian/Alaska Native (AI/AN) Head Start and Early Head Start Programs.

U.S. Department of Agriculture Food and Nutrition Service
www.fns.usda.gov/cnd/
Information about the U.S. Department of Agriculture's role in providing healthy and nutritious meals for children.

myeducationlab

Go to Topic 3 (Family/Community) in the MyEducationLab (www.myeducationlab.com) for your course, where you can:

- Find learning outcomes for Family/Community along with the national standards that connect to these outcomes.

- Complete Assignments and Activities that can help you more deeply understand the chapter content.
- Apply and practice your understanding of the core teaching skills identified in the chapter with the Building Teaching Skills and Dispositions learning units.
- Check your comprehension on the content covered in the chapter by going to the Study Plan in the Book Resources for your text. Here you will be able to take a chapter quiz, receive feedback on your answers, and then access Review, Practice, and Enrichment activities to enhance your understanding of chapter content.

PART IV

TEACHING TODAY'S YOUNG CHILDREN: LINKING DEVELOPMENT AND LEARNING

9

INFANTS AND TODDLERS
Foundation Years for Learning

naeyc standards

Standard 1. Promoting Child Development and Learning

I use my understanding of young children's characteristics and needs, and of multiple interacting influences on children's development and learning, to create environments that are healthy, respectful, supportive, and challenging for each child.[1]

Standard 4. Using Developmentally Effective Approaches to Connect with Children and Families

I understand and use positive relationships and supportive interactions as the foundation for my work with young children and families. I know, understand, and use a wide array of developmentally appropriate approaches, instructional strategies, and tools to connect with children and families and positively influence each child's development and learning.[2]

Interest in infant and toddler care and education is at an all-time high and will likely continue at this level well into the future. The growing demand for quality infant and toddler programs stems primarily from political and cultural trends. For example, Stephanie and Brent Hill, a young couple in Houston, just had their first baby, Addie, three months ago. Stephanie says, "With the economy the way it is, I just have to work to help keep the family afloat. I need to know she's *really* being cared for." It is also fueled by parents who want their children to have an early start and get off on the right foot so they can be successful in life and work. Raoul Hernandez, dad to two-year-old Daniel, is looking for a program that can help Daniel get a good start. "He's so smart—he's like a sponge. I want to be sure he gets as much as he can right now so that he'll be ready for school in a few years." The popularity of early care and education is also attributable to a changing view of the very young and the discovery that infants are remarkably competent individuals. Let's examine the ways that infants' and toddlers' development and early experiences shape their lives.

What Are Infants and Toddlers Like?

Think for a minute about your experiences with infants. What characteristics stand out most in your mind? Review the developmental profiles of Marla, Antonio, Sam and Kalea in the Portraits of Infants and Toddlers that follow. This chapter will help you understand their development across four domains—social-emotional, cognitive, motor, and adaptive (i.e., daily living). After you read the chapter, reflect on and answer the questions that accompany the portraits.

Have you ever tried to carry on an extended conversation with an infant? They are full of coos, ahas, giggles, smiles, and sparkling eyes! Or have you ever tried to keep up with a toddler? A typical response is, "They are into everything!" The infant and toddler years between birth and age two are full of developmental milestones and significant events. **Infancy**, life's first year, includes the first breath, the first smile, first thoughts, first words, and first steps. During **toddlerhood**—from twelve to twenty-four months—two of the most outstanding developmental milestones are walking and rapid language development. Mobility and language are the cornerstones of autonomy that enable toddlers to become independent. How you, other early childhood professionals, and parents respond to infants' first accomplishments and toddlers' quests for autonomy determines how they grow and master life events.

infancy The first year of life.

toddlerhood Children twelve to twenty-four months.

Understanding Child Development

Understanding the major development processes that characterize the formative years of infants and toddlers helps you fully grasp your roles as educator and nurturer. Here are some important considerations:

- Recognize that infants and toddlers are not the miniature adults pictured in many baby product advertisements; children need many years to develop fully and become independent. This period of dependency and your responses to it are critical for children's development.
- Keep in mind that "normal" growth and development milestones are based on averages, and the average is simply the middle ground of development (e.g., Table 9.1 gives the average heights and weights for infants and toddlers). Know the milestones of different stages of development to assess children's progress or lack of it.

" Babies are not just cute faces but are the greatest learning machines in the universe. "

PATRICIA KUHL
The Scientist in the Crib

portraits of infants and toddlers

MARLA

ANTONIO

	MARLA	ANTONIO
General Description	10 months, Caucasian, Female • Lives with both her mother and father • Expresses her feelings easily and openly • Loves to eat	13 months, Hispanic, Male • Attends child care eight hours a day • Cautious around strangers • Loves to be close to family members
Social-Emotional	• Begins to demonstrate separation anxiety—Marla cries when her mother steps out of the room. • Experiences stranger anxiety— Marla bursts into tears when a stranger peeks into her stroller. • Uses social referencing and strong attachments to primary caregivers to feel secure—Marla looks at her teacher's face to see if a noisy toy is safe. • Expresses a variety of emotions such as anger, sadness, grief, and happiness—Marla frowns when her father says goodbye in the morning, and gives him a joyous smile when he returns.	• Securely attached children explore away from primary caregivers but go to them for comfort and attention—Antonio plays with books, and then he brings one to his teacher. • Continues to experience separation and stranger anxiety—Antonio appears cautious when a stranger enters the room or when mom leaves. • Self-regulation: Uses strategies to calm himself—Antonio reaches for his mom or his bunny when he is tired. • Communicates with and imitates peers—Antonio communicates with peers by smiling, vocalizing, frowning, retreating, giving objects, and taking objects.
Cognitive	• Object permanence—By eight months of age, children begin to look for observed objects that are placed or moved out of sight—When mom put the toy behind her back, Leah crawled around her to retrieve the toy. • Repeats actions that have an effect—Marla pulled the tail of the toy inosaur to hear a song. • Children can begin to learn sign language at approximately eight months and learn to say the words in their language or use sign language for their primary caregivers—Marla explained, "Mama" when her mother entered the room.	• Children often imitate adults to accomplish goals—Antonio tries to get up on the couch after his dad sits down. • Children pretend with objects—Antonio pretends to drink from a toy cup. • Says words and/or uses sign language but still communicates primarily with gestures, body movements, and facial expressions—Antonio and his teacher enjoy a moment as he points at the butterfly. • Understands many more words/phrases than they can say—Antonio claps his hands together when his father sings, "Pat-a-Cake."
Motor	• Sits, at first wobbly, then well, freeing hands to manipulate objects—By eight months of age, Marla sits and hardly ever topples over. • Children learn to move in a variety of ways—Marla creeps on her tummy at seven months, crawls on hands and knees by eight months, and pulls on sturdy objects (such as a coffee table) to stand by ten months. • First uses raking grasp (using all of her fingers), then scissors grasp (using thumb and fingers), and then pincer grasp (using thumb and first finger) to pick up objects. Marla uses a pincer grasp to pick up a Cheerio. • Children bring hands together in midline around eight months of age—Marla banged two objects together.	• Many children begin to walk—Antonio cautiously lets go of the couch and takes his first steps. • Enjoys moving in a variety of ways to explore the environment—Antonio takes a few steps and then crawls on his way to retrieve the ball. • Turns pages of books alone or when read to by an adult—Antonio enjoys sitting in the book area at his school and turning the pages of a book by himself. • Begins to enjoy putting objects into containers—Antonio puts large dominoes in a slot in the lid of a plastic container and later focuses on putting blocks into a basket.
Adaptive (Daily Living)	• Begins to eat solid food when fed by adult—Marla opens her mouth as her mother approaches with a spoonful of soft cereal. She "tells" her mom that she doesn't want any more by turning her head, putting her lips together, or arching back. • Begins to pick up food such as Cheerios with fingers—At nine months Marla seems to delight in picking up Cheerios one by one.	• Likes to hold a spoon while being fed. Some children begin to use a spoon awkwardly to eat—Antonio stabs at his yogurt with his spoon and licks off the yogurt. • Uses pincer grasp (thumb and first finger together) well to pick up small objects and hold a cup with a lid on it—Antonio picks up his sippy cup with both hands and brings it up to his mouth.

SAM

17 months, African American, Male
- Attends a family child-care program
- Likes to play with other children
- Is persistent at solving problems

- Continues to demonstrate strong attachments to primary caregivers. Seeks these adults for enjoyment and security. Sam likes to sit on his teacher's lap as she reads him a story.
- Begins to demonstrate autonomy—Sam protests when his teacher tries to put a bib on him.
- Shows concern for peers when they are hurt or distressed—Sam hands Talia her blanket when she cries.
- Peers take turns during play—Sam and Sandi laugh as they take turns chasing each other.
- Friendships and prosocial behaviors develop as early as one year of age—Sam likes to be with Leah and is upset when she doesn't come to school. He often pats her on the back when she is upset.

- Experiments with strategies to accomplish goals—Sam tries many strategies to get the toy out of the box.
- Directs pretend action to a toy—Sam moves the toy car across the floor and makes car noises.
- Imitates actions after a delay in time—Sam watches a peer kiss a doll and then does the action when he gets home.
- Children say words by eighteen months to inform, reject, request, refuse, and demand—Sam states "eat" emphatically to his teacher. Later he says "no" to refuse a bite of banana.
- Follows two-step directions—Sam's mother tells him to get the ball and take it in the kitchen.

- Children walk, but still may be cautious as they learn to walk on different surfaces—Sam slows down as he begins to walk in the mud.
- Enjoys crawling and walking up steps, placing one foot up and then placing the other foot on that step—Sam went up and down his grandparents' steps, walking up and then crawling backwards down the steps.
- Increased fine motor skills allow children to manipulate more objects—Sam presses on the spot on the bear's foot to hear it sing a song.
- Uses an overhand grasp with utensils and crayons—Sam holds his chalk tightly, with his whole hand over the chalk.

- Children become increasingly independent, wanting to do things all by themselves—Sam likes to take his own socks off but at times he still wants an adult to do it.
- Uses a spoon to feed himself, but spills often as wrist muscles develop—Sam uses a spoon for five minutes and then eats with his hands.

KALEA

22 months, Asian, Female
- Very affectionate with everyone
- Plays well with others and by herself
- Is learning to use words to express feelings, but still "falls apart" when frustrated

---

- Affectionate relationships with primary caregivers help children feel secure. Kalea often runs to her teacher for a hug.
- Self-regulation may be challenging—At times, especially when she's tired, Kalea cries and falls to the floor when frustrated.
- Friendships blossom and conflicts occur as children are learning to express needs and feelings with words—Kalea understands the concept of "mine" and holds her toy tightly when Sam tries to take it.
- Peers interact with words, gestures, imitation, and glee—Kalea and Tamera laugh excitedly as they poke their fingers into their playdough.

- Uses a sequence of pretend actions such as waking a doll, feeding it, and putting it to bed again—Kalea pats her doll, wraps it in a blanket, and sings a few words to it.
- There is often a "language explosion" during this period as children learn to communicate with many words or sign language—To her family's surprise, Kalea seems to learn several new words each day.
- Uses two or more words together—Kalea said to her mother, "More juice, pease."

- Runs with increased coordination—Kalea seems to run energetically everywhere she goes.
- Balance improves and children climb, jump off short objects (such as steps), master sliding down short slides, kick balls, and throw balls with increased ease—Kalea climbs up on a two-foot rock and slides down on her bottom.
- Coordination increases and crayons, paints, using utensils, and playing with zippers become interesting—In the middle of the night, Kalea pulls down the zipper of her sleeper.

- Children put feet into their shoes (or big people's shoes)—Kalea puts her feet into her dad's shoes and joyfully clomps around the living room.
- Chooses which shirt, pants, or socks to wear when adult offers a choice between two—Kalea chooses the red shirt over the blue shirt as her mother holds them out and says, "Which shirt do you want to wear today?"

Source: Contributed by Donna S. Wittmer, former professor of early childhood education at the University of Colorado–Denver. Donna is the author of Focusing on Peers: The Importance of Relationships in the Early Years *(ZERO TO THREE, 2008) and is co-author, with Sandra Petersen, of* Endless Opportunities for Infant and Toddler Curriculum *(Pearson, 2009) and* Infant and Toddler Development and Responsive Program Planning: A Relationship-Based Approach *(Pearson, 2010).*

TABLE 9.1 Average Height and Weight of Infants and Toddlers

Age	Males Height (inches)	Males Weight (pounds)	Females Height (inches)	Females Weight (pounds)
Birth	20.0	8.0	19.5	7.5
3 months	24.0	13.0	23.5	12.5
6 months	26.5	17.5	25.5	16.0
9 months	28.5	20.5	27.5	19.0
1 year	30.0	23.0	29.5	21.0
1½ years	32.5	27.0	33.0	24.5
2 years	34.0	28.0	34.0	26.5
2½ years	36.5	30.0	36.0	28.5
3 years	37.5	31.5	37.5	30.5

Source: National Center for Health Statistics in collaboration with the National Center for Chronic Disease Prevention and Health Promotion (2005), www.cdc.gov/growthcharts.

- Know each child as an individual and what is normal for each child.
- Remember to care for and reach the whole child—the physical, social, emotional, intellectual, and linguistic.
- Take into account gender and socioeconomic, cultural, and family background, including nutritional and health history, to determine what is normal for individual children. Consider that when children are provided with good nutrition, health care, and a warm, loving environment, development tends toward what is normal for each child.

Culture and Child Development

culture A group's way of life, including basic values, beliefs, religion, language, clothing, food, and practices.

Many factors influence how children grow and develop; for example, reflect on the influence of parents, siblings, home, and schools. But what about culture? **Culture** is a group's way of life, including basic values, beliefs, religion, language, clothing, food, and various practices. Child rearing, for instance, is influenced by the culture of a particular group. Think for a minute about how the following routines, which are culturally based, affect children's developmental outcomes:[3]

Bottle or Breast Feeding.   Whether children are held during a feeding, whether they are allowed or encouraged to hold the bottle, what feeding position is used, how frequently they are fed, and whether a bottle is used to induce sleep all depend on a culture's perspective. For example, the United States is predominantly a bottle-feeding culture. Breast feeding is usually done in private because breasts are seen as sexual in nature. But, in many eastern countries, breasts are seen as functional, so there is no shame in being uncovered or in feeding children in public. In still other cultures where religions prohibit the showing of women's bodies, there is a taboo of breast feeding in front of men though not necessarily other women. Similarly, different cultures have different views on promoting babies' independence, which affects breast-feeding practices. In western cultures such as those in western Europe and the United States, babies are often fed at specific intervals to encourage the baby to be self-soothing and independent, whereas in many eastern cultures such as those in some African countries, children are seen as being naturally dependent and in need of care and so are fed on cue in short intervals all day and night. In addition, in the west where many women work outside the home and in the United States where workplaces are not required to provide child care, breast feeding is not an option for many women. Conversely, in many other cultures, it is an accepted practice for nursing mothers to aid one another in feeding their children.

Feeding Solid Foods.   Culture dictates when and which foods are introduced, whether mess and waste are permitted, how much child choice and independence are allowed or encouraged, what utensils are used, and where and when feeding occurs. For example, people in the United States commonly express discomfort about children nursing after they have teeth. The American Academy of Pediatricians recommends that babies be breast-fed a minimum of one year, and the World Health Organization recommends a minimum of two years, but in many cultures, weaning can continue for several years.[4,5] When and how people encourage eating solid foods also differs by cultures. I'm sure you have seen a toddler covered with gooey food from head to toe and waving an unused fork or spoon. In the United States, this behavior might be seen as encouraging the child's independence and sense of self. However, in other areas of the world, especially in places where food may be scarce, such an exhibition might be considered wasteful.

Toileting.   One's culture also determines such child rearing practices as the age toileting begins, whether the goal is independent use of the toilet or reduction in number of diapers needed, how much adult involvement or time is required, how toileting accidents are handled, and whether diapers, training pants, or disposable pants are used. The American Academy of Pediatrics (AAP) states that before children are twelve months of age, they have no control over bladder or bowel movements. In the United States many children start to show signs of being ready to start toilet training between eighteen and twenty-four months of age. The AAP cautions that some children may not be ready until thirty months or older.[6] In the United States it is generally accepted that boys are harder to toilet train than girls and that they shouldn't be toilet trained until they are older. However, in many other cultures, such as China, both girl and boy infants are often toilet trained by seven or eight months old. In other cultures, using diapers is uncommon or even unheard of, while other cultures may view diapers as unsanitary. In the United States, recommended toilet-training methods range between rigid and child-centered while in other countries, toilet training is a more traditional part of culture.

Napping.   How often, how long, and where a child naps; and how much adult assistance and participation are required for a child to fall and stay asleep, also depend on culture. Culture influences sleeping and waking times, including whether sleep is consolidated into a single continuous period and thus is associated with a single specific "bedtime." Whether sleep is confined to nighttime or to private spaces or may occur acceptably in daytime or in public spaces, and whether a child sleeps alone or in groups, varies by culture. In the United States, independence in almost every aspect of life is emphasized and valued, so it is common for babies to sleep alone, often in their own rooms. But other cultures, such as those throughout Asia, South America, and Africa, are more collectivist; they value interaction and aiding one another. As a result, in those cultures, it is uncommon for infants to sleep alone and may even be considered unkind because it causes the children to be unnecessarily lonely. In the United States, it is generally accepted that babies need lots of sleep, but the emphasis is on having babies sleep at regular intervals. Other cultures often promote communal sleeping among all age groups at different times of the day.

Use of Comfort Items.   Whether a child is allowed or encouraged to use a pacifier or thumb, blanket, stuffed animal, or other object to provide comfort, and if so, when, where, and how often the child is allowed to use it, are all culturally connected. Again, the United States emphasizes independence and as a result, it is generally frowned upon for children to be "dependent" on comfort items past a certain age. Usually parents see the age of two or three as the cutoff mark, but parents of children even one year old sometimes want their babies to quit pacifiers "cold turkey." Children often face a great deal of pressure from parents, dentists, pediatricians, and teachers to quit their thumb-sucking and "blankies," but pressure can cause a sense of shame or a reversion to even more reliance on items. Most current practices encourage parents to allow their children to simply "grow out of it." In other countries where poverty is an issue, comfort items may not be available to children at all.

Discipline.   The tone used when a child is disciplined or reprimanded for actions that are not approved of by adults varies; whether or not physical punishment is used varies; and margin for error and how that is tolerated varies from culture to culture. In the United States, the debate still rages about the acceptability of spanking. There are demographics of parents who are more likely to use spanking as discipline. For example, studies find that most parents who spank in the United States tend to have little education, are young parents, are single-parents, and may have significant levels of depression and stress.[7] Spanking is also most commonly used among parents who were spanked themselves and who tend to think, "I was spanked, and I turned out fine." This group of parents are more likely to live in the South and to self-identify as conservative Christians.[8] When asked why they used spanking, this demographic of parents reply that they believe spanking is effective and that the child is to blame for the punished behavior; in other words, they believe that the child "deserved" to be spanked.[9] Interestingly, research shows that African American children are spanked significantly more often than children from Caucasian and Mexican-American families. African American children are also verbally reprimanded more often than their peers at ages two and three.[10] As you can see, there are many factors, including socioeconomic status, marital status, religion, region, and race, that go into discipline decision making. However, these studies on spanking have found that children who were spanked as one-year-olds tend to behave more aggressively at ages two and three, and do not perform as well as other children on a test measuring thinking skills at age three.[11] Some cultures condone only family members punishing or disciplining children, while others who live in more collectivist societies tend to take a more, "it takes a village to raise a child" approach, which allows non-family members to take part in discipline practices.

You need to consider the cultural practices of your families and form close partnerships with family members. It is very likely that you will experience cultural practices that are different from your own, but it is important that you try to understand them and respect them if they are safe, healthy, and developmentally appropriate for the child.

Research and Infant/Toddler Education

For the past decade, brain and child development research have received a lot of attention. Brain research has focused especially on the first three years of life. As we discuss these early years now, let's review some interesting facts about infant and toddler brain development and consider the implications they have for you as a professional.

First, review Figure 9.1, which shows the regions of the brain and their functional processes. The brain is a fascinating and complex organ. Anatomically, the young brain is like the adult brain, except smaller. Whereas the average adult brain weighs approximately 3 pounds, at birth the infant's brain weighs $3/4$ pound; at six months, $1^1/_2$ pounds; and at two years, $2^3/_4$ pounds. So, you can see that during the first two years of life the brain undergoes tremendous physical growth. The brain finishes developing physically at age ten, when it reaches its full adult size.

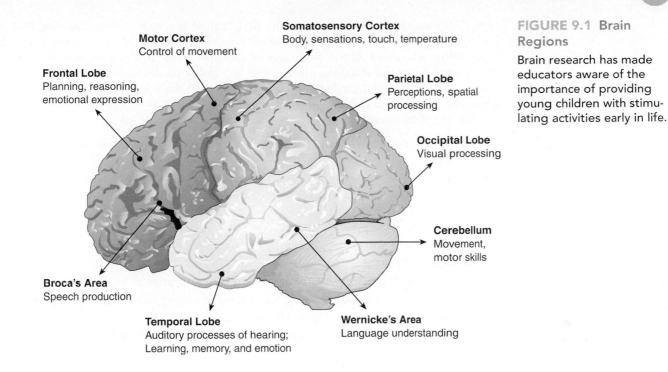

FIGURE 9.1 Brain Regions

Brain research has made educators aware of the importance of providing young children with stimulating activities early in life.

Neural Shearing

At birth the brain has 100 billion neurons, or nerve cells—all the brain cells it will ever have! As parents and other caregivers play with, respond to, interact with, and talk to young children, brain connections develop and learning takes place. As those connections are repeatedly used, they become permanent. In contrast, brain connections that are not used or are used only a little may wither away. This withering away, or elimination, is known as **neural shearing**, or **pruning**. Consequently, children whose parents seldom talk or read to them may have difficulty with language skills later in life. This process helps explain why children who are not reared in language-rich environments may be at risk for academic failure.

neural shearing (pruning) The selective elimination of synapses.

Synaptogenesis

By the time of birth, those billions of neurons will have formed more than 50 trillion connections, or synapses, through a process called **synaptogenesis**, the proliferation of neural connections. This process continues to occur until the age of ten. During just the first month, the brain forms more than 1,000 trillion more synaptic connections between neurons. These connections and neural pathways are essential for brain development, and it is children's experiences that help form these neural connections. Thus infants whose parents or other caregivers talk to them are more likely to develop larger vocabularies; using different words and speaking to infants in complex sentences increase the infants' knowledge of words and their later ability to speak in complex sentences.[12]

synaptogenesis The rapid development of neural connections.

Age-Appropriate Experiences

However, children need not just any experiences but the right experiences at the right times. There are developmental windows of opportunity, or **sensitive periods**, during which it is easier to learn something than it is at another time. For example, the critical

sensitive periods Periods of developmental time during which certain things are learned more easily than at earlier or later times.

period for language development is the first year of life. It is during this time that the auditory pathways for language learning are formed. Beginning at birth, an infant can distinguish the sounds of all the languages of the world. But at about six months, through the process of neural shearing, infants lose the ability to distinguish the sounds of languages they have not heard. By twelve months their auditory maps are pretty well in place.[13] It is literally a case of use it or lose it.

We can draw several conclusions about the brain:

- Babies are born to learn. They are remarkable learning instruments; their brains make them so.
- Children's brain development and their ability to learn throughout life rely on the interplay between nature (genetic inheritance, controlled by 20,000 to 25,000 genes)[14] and nurture (the experiences they have and the environments in which they are reared).
- What happens to children early in life has a long-lasting influence on how they develop and learn.
- Critical periods influence learning positively and negatively.
- The human brain is quite "plastic"; it has the ability to change in response to different kinds of experiences and environments.
- The brain undergoes physiological changes in response to experiences.
- An enriched environment influences brain development.

Based on this information, there has been a rapid evolution of television shows and DVDs designed to make babies smarter by building on the plasticity and the spongy-ness of their brains. But the American Academy of Pediatrics recommends no television time for toddlers younger than two. On average, babies spend 1.2 hours per day watching TV during their first two years of life, and a recent study found that with each additional hour spent in front of a screen, babies at eight to sixteen months learned six to eight fewer vocabulary words than infants who stayed away from videos.[15]

Conversely, another study found that playing and talking with babies is the best way to help them develop. In fact, basic activities like playing with blocks with an eighteen-month-old can improve his or her language skills six months later. To make the most of the amazing abilities of all children, the best thing to do is interact with them, not turn on the television.[16]

Nature and Nurture

So, which of these factors—nature (genetics) or nurture (environment)—plays a larger role? On the one hand, many traits are fully determined by heredity. For example, your eye color is a product of your heredity. Physical height is also largely influenced by heredity—as much as 90 percent. Certainly height can be influenced by nutrition, growth hormones, and other environmental interventions; but by and large, an individual's height is genetically determined. And other traits, such as temperament and shyness, are highly heritable. So we can say that many differences in individuals are due to heredity rather than to environmental factors.

On the other hand, nurture—the environment in which individuals grow and develop—plays an important role in what individuals are and how they behave. For example, the years from birth to age eight are extremely important environmentally, especially for nutrition, stimulation of the brain, affectionate relationships with parents, and opportunities to learn. Think for a moment about other kinds of environmental influence—such as family, school, and friends—that affect development. This would be a good time to review Bronfenbrenner's ecological theory and how interacting

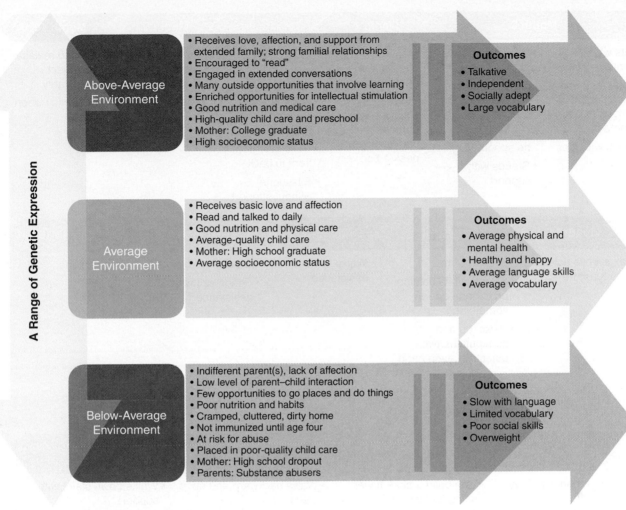

Above-Average Environment
- Receives love, affection, and support from extended family; strong familial relationships
- Encouraged to "read"
- Engaged in extended conversations
- Many outside opportunities that involve learning
- Enriched opportunities for intellectual stimulation
- Good nutrition and medical care
- High-quality child care and preschool
- Mother: College graduate
- High socioeconomic status

Outcomes
- Talkative
- Independent
- Socially adept
- Large vocabulary

Average Environment
- Receives basic love and affection
- Read and talked to daily
- Good nutrition and physical care
- Average-quality child care
- Mother: High school graduate
- Average socioeconomic status

Outcomes
- Average physical and mental health
- Healthy and happy
- Average language skills
- Average vocabulary

Below-Average Environment
- Indifferent parent(s), lack of affection
- Low level of parent–child interaction
- Few opportunities to go places and do things
- Poor nutrition and habits
- Cramped, cluttered, dirty home
- Not immunized until age four
- At risk for abuse
- Placed in poor-quality child care
- Mother: High school dropout
- Parents: Substance abusers

Outcomes
- Slow with language
- Limited vocabulary
- Poor social skills
- Overweight

A Range of Genetic Expression

FIGURE 9.2 The Interplay of Nature and Nurture

environmental influences affect children's development. For children with disabilities who may have limited capability for interacting with their environment, think about the potential impact on their development. For children who are from diverse cultural, linguistic, or socioeconomic backgrounds, think about the potential impact their environments have on their development.

A generation ago, we believed that nature and nurture were competing entities and that one of these was dominant over the other. Today we understand that they are not competing entities; both are necessary for normal development, and it is the interaction between the two that makes children the individuals they are (see Figure 9.2).

Motor Development

What would life be like if you couldn't walk, run, or participate in your favorite activities? Motor skills play an important part in all of life. Even more so for infants and toddlers, motor development is essential because it contributes to their intellectual and skill development. Figure 9.3 lists infant and toddler motor milestones.

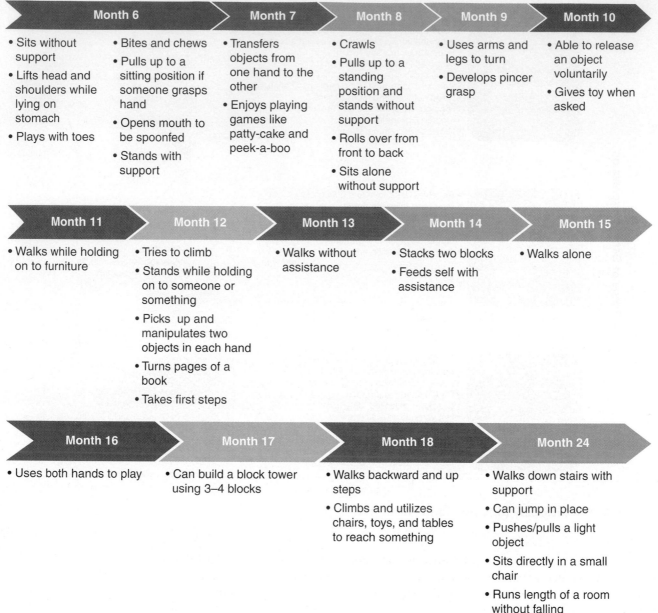

FIGURE 9.3 Infant and Toddler Motor Milestones

Source: Information from Shana R. May, Baby's Developmental Milestones from Birth Until Age 2. Mommyguide.com.

Basic Principles of Motor Development

Human motor development is governed by certain basic principles:

- Motor development is sequential.
- Maturation of the motor system proceeds from gross (large) to fine (small) behaviors. For example, as part of her learning to reach, Maria sweeps toward an object with her whole arm. Over the course of a month, however, as a result of development and

experiences, Maria's gross reaching gives way to specific reaching, and she grasps for particular objects.

- Motor development occurs from *cephalo* to *caudal*—from head to foot (tail). This process is known as **cephalocaudal development**. At birth Maria's head is the most developed part of her body; thereafter, she holds her head erect before she sits, and she sits before she walks.
- Motor development proceeds from the *proximal* (i.e., midline, or central part of the body) to the *distal* (i.e., extremities), known as **proximodistal development**. Thus Maria is able to control her arm movements before she can control her finger movements.

cephalocaudal development
The principle that development proceeds from the head to the toes.

proximodistal development
The principle that development proceeds from the center of the body outward.

Toilet Training

Motor development plays a major role in social and behavioral expectations. For example, toilet training (also called *toilet learning* or *toilet mastery*) is a milestone of the toddler period that often causes a great deal of anxiety for parents, professionals, and toddlers. Many parents want to accomplish toilet training as quickly and efficiently as possible, but frustrations arise when they start too early and expect too much of their children. Because toilet training is largely a matter of physical readiness and cultural acceptance, most child-rearing experts recommend waiting until children are two years old before beginning the training process.

The principle behind toilet training is that parents and teachers can help children develop control over an involuntary response. When an infant's bladder or bowel is full, the urethral or sphincter muscles open; the goal of toilet training is to teach children to control this involuntary reflex and use the toilet when appropriate. Training involves maturational development, timing, patience, modeling, preparing the environment, establishing a routine, and developing a partnership between the child and parents/teachers. Another necessary partnership is that between parents and the professionals who are assisting in toilet training, especially when parents do not know what to do, are hesitant about approaching toilet training, or want to start the training too soon. The key for toilet training is to follow the lead of the child.

Intellectual Development

Reflect on children's cognitive development and remember that a child's first developed schemata, or schemes, are sensorimotor. According to Piaget, infants do not have "thoughts of the mind," or private behaviors. Rather, they come to know their world by acting on it through their senses and motor actions. Piaget said that infants construct (as opposed to absorb) their schemes using reflexive sensorimotor actions.

Assimilation, Accommodation, and Adaptation at Work

Infants begin life with only their billions of neurons and reflexive motor actions to satisfy their biological needs. In response to specific environmental conditions, they modify these reflexive actions through a process of adaptation, which consists of two processes, *assimilation* and *accommodation*. Piaget believed that children are active constructors of intelligence through assimilation (taking in new experiences) and accommodation (changing existing schemes to fit new information). During assimilation children adjust their already-existing schemes to interpret what is going on in their environment. Through accommodation children create new schemes or modify existing schemes to fit with the reality of their environments. Patterns of adaptive behavior initiate more activity, which leads to more adaptive behavior, which, in turn, yields more schemes.

Consider sucking, for example, an innate sensorimotor scheme. Kenny turns his head to the source of nourishment, closes his lips around the nipple, sucks, and swallows. As a result of his experiences and maturation, Kenny adapts or changes this basic sensorimotor scheme of sucking to include both anticipatory sucking movements and nonnutritive sucking, such as sucking a pacifier or a blanket.

Stages of Cognitive Development: Sensorimotor Intelligence

Sensorimotor cognitive development consists of six stages (shown in Figure 9.4 and described here). Let's follow Madeleine through these stages of cognitive development:

Stage 1: Reflexive Action (Birth to One Month).   During this stage Madeleine sucks and grasps everything; she is literally ruled by reflexive actions. Because reflexive responses are undifferentiated, Madeleine responds the same way to everything. But sensorimotor schemes help her learn new ways of interacting with the world, and new ways of interacting promote her cognitive development.

Grasping is a primary infant sensorimotor scheme. At birth the grasping reflex consists of closing the fingers around an object placed in the hand. Through experiences and maturation, this basic reflexive grasping action becomes coordinated with looking, opening the hand, retracting the fingers, and grasping, thus developing from a pure reflexive action to an intentional grasping action. As Madeleine matures in response to experiences, her grasping scheme is combined with the delightful activity of grasping and releasing everything she can get her hands on.

Stage 2: Primary Circular Reactions (One to Four Months).   The milestone of this stage is the modification of the reflexive actions of stage 1. Sensorimotor behaviors not previously

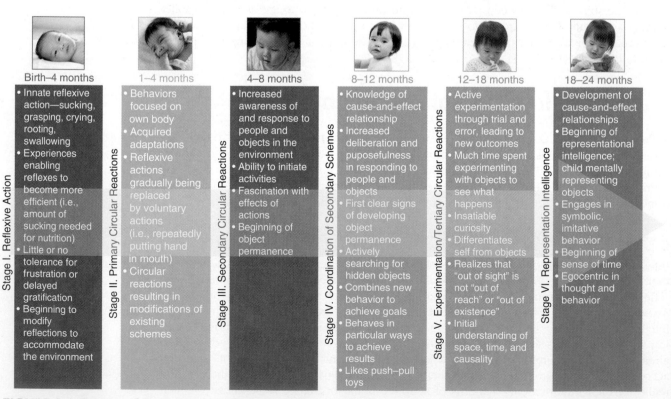

FIGURE 9.4 Stages of Sensorimotor Cognitive Development

present in Madeleine's repertoire of behaviors begin to appear: habitual thumb sucking (indicating hand–mouth coordination), tracking moving objects with the eyes, and moving the head toward sounds (indicating the beginning of recognition of causality). Thus Madeleine starts to direct her own behavior rather than being totally dependent on reflexive actions.

Primary circular reactions also begin during stage 2. In the first few months of life, Madeleine's behaviors—that is, her basic reflexive responses—involve her own body. Piaget called this stage primary. And Madeleine repeats the same behaviors over and over again—for example, constantly putting her hand and thumb to her mouth. Consequently, these actions are called circular reactions. By the end of this stage—at four months—Madeleine will have "practiced" her primary circular reactions hundreds of times, laying the cognitive and behavioral groundwork for the more coordinated and intentional actions of stage 3.

primary circular reactions Repetitive actions that are centered on the infant's own body.

Stage 3: Secondary Circular Reactions (Four to Eight Months).

Secondary circular reactions begin during this stage. This process is characterized by repetitive actions intended to get the same response from an object or person; for example, Madeleine repeatedly shakes a rattle to repeat the sound. Repetitiveness is characteristic of all circular reactions. *Secondary* here means that the reaction is elicited from a source other than the infant. Madeleine interacts with people and objects to make interesting sights, sounds, and events happen and last. Given an object, Madeleine uses all available schemes, such as mouthing, hitting, and banging; if one of these schemes produces an interesting result, she continues to use that scheme to elicit the same response. Imitation becomes increasingly intentional as a means of prolonging interest.

secondary circular reactions Repetitive actions focused on the qualities of objects, such as their shapes, sizes, colors, and noises.

Piaget also referred to this stage of cognitive development as "making interesting things last." Madeleine manipulates objects, demonstrating coordination between vision and tactile senses. She also reproduces events for the purpose of sustaining and repeating acts. The intellectual milestone of this stage is the beginning of **object permanence**. When infants in stages 1 and 2 cannot see an object, it does not exist for them—out of sight, out of mind! During stage 3, however, awareness grows that things that are out of sight continue to exist. Parents and infant/toddler caregivers spend a lot of time playing with their children. One of the fascinating games they play is "find the hidden object." Playing this game is a good way to determine whether or not children have developed the cognitive scheme of object permanence and also gives insight into how children "think."

object permanence The concept that people and objects have an independent existence beyond the child's perception of them.

Stage 4: Coordination of Secondary Schemes (Eight to Twelve Months).

During this stage, "coordination of secondary schemes," Madeleine uses means to attain ends. For instance, she moves objects out of the way (means) to get another object (end). She also begins to search for hidden objects, although not always in the places they were hidden, indicating a growing understanding of object permanence.

Stage 5: Experimentation/Tertiary Circular Reactions (Twelve to Eighteen Months).

This stage, the climax of the sensorimotor period, marks the beginning of truly intelligent behavior. Stage 5 is the *stage of experimentation*. Madeleine's experiments with objects to solve problems are characteristic of intelligence that involves **tertiary circular reactions**; she repeats actions and modifies behaviors over and over to see what will happen. This repetition helps develop understanding of cause-and-effect relationships and leads to the discovery of new relationships through exploration and experimentation.

tertiary circular reactions Modifications that infants make in their behavior to explore the effects of those modifications.

Physically, stage 5 is also the beginning of the toddler stage, with the commencement of walking. Toddlers' physical mobility, combined with their growing ability and desire to experiment with objects, makes for fascinating and often frustrating child rearing. Madeleine is an avid explorer, determined to touch, taste, and feel all she can. Although the term *terrible twos* was once used to describe this stage, professionals now recognize there is nothing terrible about toddlers exploring their environment to develop their intelligence. What is important is that teachers, parents, and others prepare environments for exploration. As

Madeleine's mom describes it, "I keep putting things up higher and higher because her arms seem to be getting longer and longer!" Novelty is interesting for its own sake, and Madeleine experiments in many different ways with a given object. For example, she may use any available item—a wood hammer, a block, a rhythm band instrument—to pound the pegs in a pound-a-peg toy.

Stage 6: Representational Intelligence (Eighteen Months to Two Years). This is the stage of transition from sensorimotor to symbolic thought. **Symbolic representation** occurs when Madeleine can visualize events internally and maintain mental images of objects not present. Representational thought enables Madeleine to solve problems in a sensorimotor way through experimentation and trial and error and predict cause-and-effect relationships more accurately. She also develops the ability to remember, which allows her to try out actions she sees others do. During this stage Madeleine can "think" using mental images and memories, which enable her to engage in pretend activities. Madeleine's representational thought does not necessarily match the real world and its representations, which accounts for her ability to have other objects stand for almost anything: a wooden block is a car; a rag doll is a baby. This type of play, known as **symbolic play**, becomes more elaborate and complex in the preoperational period.

In summary, we need to keep in mind several important concepts regarding infant and toddler development:

- Chronological ages associated with Piaget's stages of cognitive development are approximate; children can do things earlier (and later) than Piaget thought. Focus on children's cognitive behavior, which gives a clearer understanding of their level of development and can guide developmentally appropriate education and caregiving.
- Infants and toddlers do not "think" as adults do; they know their world by acting on it and thus need many opportunities for active involvement.
- Infants and toddlers actively construct their own intelligence. Children's activity with people and objects stimulates them cognitively and leads to the development of mental schemata (schemes).
- At birth infants do not have knowledge of the external world. They cannot differentiate between themselves and the external world. For all practical purposes, they are the world.
- The concept of causality, or cause and effect, does not exist at birth. Infants' and toddlers' concepts of causality begin to evolve only through acting on the environment.
- As infants and toddlers move from one stage of intellectual development to another, later stages evolve from, rather than replace, earlier ones. Schemes developed in stage 1 are incorporated and improved on by the schemes constructed in stage 2, and so forth.

Exploration and experimentation are essential to toddler development and well-being. You can support these developmental processes by creating challenging environments in which toddlers can explore with a wide variety of materials.

symbolic representation The ability to use mental images to stand for something else.

symbolic play The ability of a young child to have an object stand for something else.

Language Development

Language development begins at birth. Indeed, some developmentalists argue that it begins *before* birth. The first cry, the first coo, the first "da-da" and "ma-ma," the first words—all are auditory proof that children are participating in the process of language development. Language helps define us as human and represents one of our most remarkable intellectual accomplishments. But how does the infant go from the first cry to the first word a year later? How does the toddler progress from saying one word to saying several hundred words a year later? Although everyone agrees that children do learn language, not everyone agrees about how. How *does* language development begin? What forces and processes prompt children to participate in one of the uniquely human endeavors?

If you said that parents are forces that encourage children to participate in language development you are absolutely right. We cannot overestimate the role parents play in the language development of their children. Ask yourself these questions:

- What techniques does the parent use to encourage and support the child's literacy development?
- What are some developmentally appropriate ways the parent engages the child?

Theories of Language Acquisition

Just as we use theories to help us explain children's intellectual (Piaget) and social-emotional development (Erikson), so too must we use theories to help explain children's language development. The following are the major ways we explain language development.

Heredity Factors.   Heredity plays a role in language development in a number of ways. For one, humans have the respiratory and laryngeal systems that make rapid and efficient vocal communications possible. For another, the human brain makes language possible. The left hemisphere is the center for speech and phonetic analysis; it is the brain's main language center. But the right hemisphere also plays a role in our understanding of speech intonations, which enables us to distinguish between declarative, imperative, and interrogative sentences. Without these processing systems, language as we know it would be impossible.

Some theorists believe that humans are innately endowed with the ability to produce language. For example, Eric Lenneberg studied innate language acquisition in considerable detail in many different kinds of children, including the deaf. According to Lenneberg, "all the evidence suggests that the capacities for speech production and related aspects of language acquisition develop according to built-in biological schedules."[17] These built-in schedules are similar to sensitive periods.

The idea of the sensitive period of language development also had a particular fascination for Montessori, who believed there were two such sensitive periods. The first begins at birth and lasts for about three years. During this time children unconsciously absorb language from the environment. The second period begins at age three and lasts until about age eight. During this time children are active participants in their language development and learn how to use their power of communication. Milestones of language development are illustrated in Figure 9.5.

Environmental Factors.   Although the ability to acquire language has a biological basis, the content of the language—syntax, grammar, and vocabulary—is acquired from the environment, which includes parents and others as models of language. Development depends on talk between children and adults and between children and children. Optimal language development ultimately depends on interactions with the best possible language models. Thus the biological process may be the same for all children, but the content of their language will differ according to environmental factors. Children in language-impoverished homes will not learn language as well as children reared in linguistically rich environments.

Sequence of Language Development

Regardless of the theory of language development you choose to adopt as your own, the fact remains that children develop language in predictable sequences, and they don't wait for us to tell them what theory to follow in their language development! They are very pragmatic and develop language regardless of our beliefs.

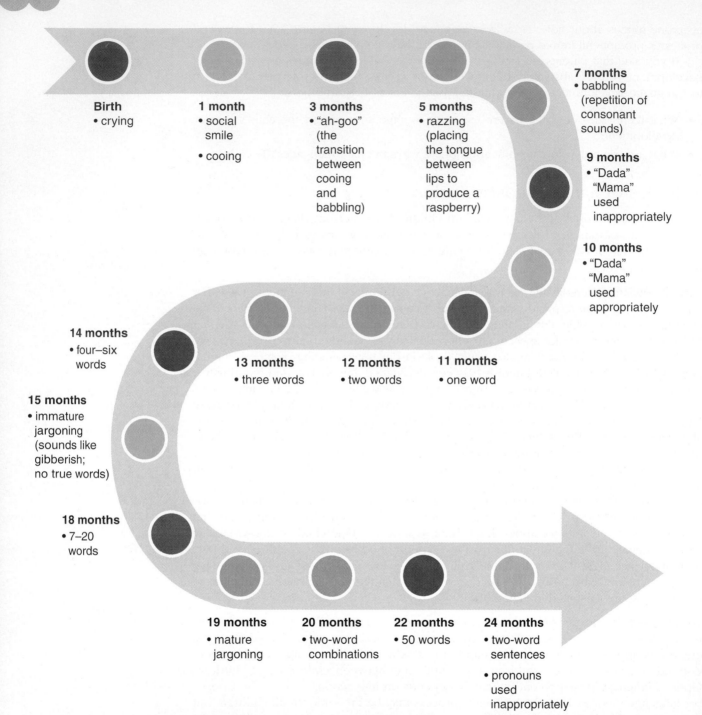

FIGURE 9.5 Language Development in Infants and Toddlers

As you can see in this figure, children's language development is linear and progressive. Each stage builds upon the next. It is important for you to provide rich language opportunities for infants and toddlers so that each individual may progress through each level and gain the language competency he or she needs in order to fulfill his or her full promise of capabilities.

Source: Information from A. J. Capute and P. J. Accardo, "Linguistic and Auditory Milestones During the First Two Years of Life," *Clinical Pediatrics, 17*(11), (November 1978), 848. Used by permission.

Baby Signing. Think of the number of ways you use signs, that is, gestures to communicate a need or emotion. You blow a kiss to convey affection or hold your thumb and little finger to the side of your head to signal that you're talking on your cell phone. I'm sure you can think of many other examples. Now apply this same principle to young children who have needs and wants and emotional feelings long before they learn to talk. As a result, there is a growing movement in support of teaching children to use signs and gestures to communicate desires or signify objects and conditions before they learn language. This is called **baby signing**.

Beginning at about five months, babies can learn signals that stand for something else (e.g., a tap on the mouth for food, squeezing the hand for milk). However, there is no universal agreement about whether to teach babies a common set of signs or to use ones that parents and children themselves make up.

Regardless of the signs used, Linda Acredola and Susan Goodwyn, popularizers of baby signing, identify these benefits:

- Reduces child and parent frustration
- Strengthens the parent–child bond
- Makes learning to talk easier
- Stimulates intellectual development
- Enhances self-esteem
- Provides a window into the child's world[18]

The baby sign for *Mom* (one hand held with all fingers apart and thumb pointing toward mouth).

baby signing Teaching babies to use signs or gestures to communicate a need or emotion.

Children are remarkable communicators without words. When they have attentive parents and caregivers, they become skilled communicators, using gestures, facial expressions, sound intonations, pointing, and reaching to make their desires known and get what they want. Pointing at an object and saying, "Uh-uh-uh" is the same as saying, "I want that rattle" or "Help me get the rattle." Responsive caregivers can respond by saying, "Do you want the rattle? I'll get it for you. Here it is!" Responsiveness is one attribute of attentive caregivers; it is the ability to read children's signs and signals, anticipating their desires even though no words are spoken.

Holophrasic Speech. The ability to communicate progresses from sign language and sounds to the use of single words. Toddlers become skilled at using single words to name objects, to let others know what they want, and to express emotions. One word, in essence, does the work of a whole sentence. These single-word sentences are **holophrases**.

The first words of children are just that, first words. Children talk about people—dada, papa, mama, mummie, and baby (referring to themselves); animals—dog, cat, kitty; vehicles—car, truck, boat, train; toys—ball, block, book, doll; food—juice, milk, cookie, bread, drink; body parts—eye, nose, mouth, ear; clothing and household articles—hat, shoe, spoon, clock; greeting terms—hi, bye, night-night; and a few actions—up, no more, off.

The one-word sentences children use are primarily *referential* (used to label objects, such as "doll") or *expressive* (communicating personal desires or levels of social interaction, such as "bye-bye" and "kiss"). The extent to which children use these two functions of language depends in large measure on caregivers and parents. For example, children's early language use reflects their family's verbal style. Thus how parents speak to their children influences how their children speak.[19]

holophrases The single words children use to refer to what they see, hear, and feel (e.g., *up, doll*).

Motherese or Parentese. Research studies verify that caregivers talk to infants and toddlers differently than adults talk to each other. This distinctive way of adapting

motherese (parentese) The way parents and others speak to young children in a slow, exaggerated way that includes short sentences and repetition of words and phrases.

everyday speech to young children is called **motherese** or **parentese**.[20] Parentese has several characteristics:

- The sentences are short, averaging just over four words per sentence with babies. As children become older, the length of sentences mothers use also becomes longer. Mothers' conversations with their young children are short and sweet.
- The sentences are highly intelligible. When talking to their young children, mothers tend not to slur or mumble their words, perhaps because mothers speak more slowly to their children than they do to adults in normal conversation.
- The sentences are unswervingly well formed—that is, they are grammatical sentences.
- The sentences are mainly imperatives and questions, such as "Give Mommy the ball," and "Do you want more juice?" Since mothers can't exchange a great deal of information with their young children, their utterances direct their children's actions.
- Mothers use sentences in which words like *here, that*, and *there* are used to stand for objects or people: "Here's your bottle," "That's your baby doll," "There's your doggie."

telegraphic speech Two-word sentences that express actions and relationships (e.g., "Milk gone").

- Mothers expand or provide an adult version of their children's communication. When a child points at a baby doll on a chair, the mother may respond by saying, "Yes, the baby doll is on the chair."
- Mothers' sentences involve repetitions: "The ball, bring Mommy the ball. Yes, go get the ball—the ball—go get the ball."

Symbolic Representation. Two significant developmental events occur at about the age of two. First, the development of symbolic representation occurs when something—a mental image, a word—is used to stand for something else not present. Words become signifiers of things—ball, block, blanket. Parents and teachers help children by using the names of things directly ("This is a ball") or indirectly ("Tell me what this is"). They can also use physical labels (*chair*) and use the names of things in conversations with children ("This is a shoe; let's put your shoe on").

The use of words as mental symbols enables children to participate in two processes that are characteristic of the early years: symbolic play and the beginning use of words and sentences to express meanings and make references.

Vocabulary Development. The development of a fifty-word vocabulary and the use of two-word sentences is the second significant achievement that occurs at about age two. This vocabulary development and the ability to combine words mark the beginning of *rapid language development*. Vocabulary development plays a very powerful and significant role in school achievement and life success. Research repeatedly demonstrates that children who come to school with a large vocabulary achieve more than their peers who do not have an expanded vocabulary.[21] Adults are the major source of children's vocabularies.

The process of language development begins at birth—perhaps even before. What are some specific things parents, teachers, and caregivers can do to promote a child's language development?

Telegraphic Speech. You have undoubtedly heard a toddler say something like "Go out" in response to a suggestion such as "Let's go outside." Perhaps you've said, "Is your juice all gone?" and the toddler responded, "All gone." These two-word sentences are called **telegraphic speech**. They are the same kind of sentences you use when you text message; the sentences are primarily made up of nouns and verbs, generally without prepositions, articles, conjunctions, and auxiliary verbs.

Grammatical Morphemes.   There is more to learning language than learning words; there is also the matter of learning grammar. Grammar is the way we change the meanings of sentences and place events and actions in time: past, present, and future tense. Grammatical morphemes are the principal means of changing the meanings of sentences. A *morpheme* is the smallest unit of meaning in a language. It can be a word, such as *no*, or an element of a word, such as *-ed*. A morpheme that can stand alone, such as *child*, is a *free morpheme*. A morpheme that cannot stand alone is a bound morpheme. *Kicked* consists of the free morpheme *kick* and the bound morpheme *-ed*. Morphological rules govern tenses, plurals, and possessives.

The order in which children learn grammatical morphemes is well documented; the pattern of mastery is orderly and consistent. The first morpheme to be mastered is the present progressive ("I drinking"), followed by prepositions (*in* and *on*), plural (*dolls*), past irregular ("toy fell"), possessive ("Sally's doll"), uncontractible verb ("it is"), articles (*a, the*), past regular (*stopped*), third-person regular ("he runs"), uncontractible auxiliary ("I am going"), contractible verb (*that's*), and contractible auxiliary ("I'm going").[22]

Negatives.   If you took a vote on a toddler's favorite word, "No!" would win hands down. When children begin to use negatives, they simply add *no* to the beginning of a word or sentence ("no milk"). As their *no* sentences become longer, they still put *no* first ("*no* put coat on"). Later, they place negatives appropriately between subject and verb ("I no want juice").

When children move beyond the use of the one-word expression "no," negation progresses through a series of meanings. The first meaning conveys nonexistence, such as "no juice" and "no hat," meaning that the juice is all gone and the hat isn't present. The next level of negation is the rejection of something. "No go out" is the rejection of the offer to go outside. Next, the use of *no* progresses to the denial of something the child believes to be untrue. If offered a carrot stick under the pretense that it is candy, the child will reply, "No candy."[23]

By the end of the preschool years, children have mastered most language patterns. Because the basis for language development is these early years, no amount of later remedial training can completely make up for development that should have occurred during this sensitive period of language learning.

Implications for Professionals

A high priority for early childhood professionals is to provide programs that support and facilitate children's language development. You must recognize that when children come from culturally or linguistically diverse backgrounds, certain patterns may emerge as they acquire second language or if they are simultaneously learning two languages, or if they are being reared in a home where no adults speak fluent English; these patterns may mimic speech or language disorders or delays. Another priority is to provide a child–staff ratio that supports language development. For example, in a recent study of the effects of a reduced child–staff ratio on children's development, researchers found that in programs with ratios of 1:4 for infants and 1:6 for toddlers, language proficiency improved dramatically when compared to programs with higher ratios.[24] Figure 9.6 provides guidelines that will help you promote children's language development. For children with disabilities that impact their speech or language acquisition, it is just as important to implement the guidelines presented in Figure 9.6 to promote the development of their language development.

FIGURE 9.6 Guidelines for Promoting Language Development
Providing a language-rich context that supports children's language and literacy is one of the most important things you can do as an early childhood professional.

Treat children as partners in the communication process.

- Many infant behaviors—smiling, cooing, and vocalizing—serve to initiate conversation and professionals should be responsive.

Initiate conversations with infants and toddlers.

- Conversations are the building blocks of language development. Attentive and caring adults are infants' and toddlers' best stimulators of cognitive and language development.

Talk to infants in a soothing, pleasant voice, with frequent eye contact.

- Simplify verbalization—not by using baby talk, but by speaking in an easily understandable way. For example, instead of saying, "We are going to take a walk around the block, so you must put your coat on," you could say, "Let's get coats on."

Use children's names when interacting with them.

- Using children's names personalizes the conversation and builds self-identity.

Use a variety of means to stimulate and promote language development.

- Include reading, stories, singing songs, and listening to music.

Encourage children to converse and share information.

- Provide children with opportunities to talk and interact with adults, other children, and more developed peers.

Help children learn to converse in various settings.

- Take children to different places so they can use their language with a variety of people.

Have children use language in different ways.

- Children need to know how to use language to ask questions, explain their feelings and emotions, tell what they have done, and describe things.

Give children experiences in the language of directions and commands.

- It is important for children to learn that language can be used as a means to an end—a way of attaining a desired goal.

Converse with children about what they are doing and how they are doing it.

- Children learn language through feedback.

Talk to children in the full range of adult language.

- Include past and present tense.

Help children learn the names of people and things.

- Learning names is an important part of vocabulary development. Label things as you interact with children.

Provide many experiences so that children have lots of things to talk about.

- The more experiences children have the more they can talk about. Help expand speaking skills by helping them describe experiences.

Psychosocial and Emotional Development

The first of Erikson's psychosocial stages, *basic trust vs. basic mistrust,* begins at birth and lasts about one-and-a-half to two years. For Erikson basic trust means that "one has learned to rely on the sameness and continuity of the outer providers, but also that one may trust oneself and the capacity of one's organs to cope with urges."[25] Whether children develop a pattern of trust or mistrust depends on the "sensitive care of the baby's individual needs and a firm sense of personal trustworthiness within the trusted frame-work of their culture's life-style."[26]

Basic trust develops when children are reared, cared for, and educated in an environ-ment of love, warmth, and support. An environment of trust reduces the opportunity for conflict between child, parent, and caregiver.

Social Behaviors

Social relationships begin at birth and are evident in the daily interactions between infants, parents, and teachers. Infants are social beings with a repertoire of behaviors they use to initiate and facilitate social interactions. Because *social behaviors* are used by everyone to begin and maintain a relationship with others, healthy social development is essential for young children. Regardless of their temperament, all infants are capable of and benefit from social interactions.

Crying. Crying is a primary social behavior in infancy. It attracts parents or caregivers and promotes a social interaction of some type and duration, depending on the skill and awareness of the caregiver. Crying has a survival value; it alerts caregivers to the presence and needs of the infant. However, merely meeting the basic needs of infants in a perfunc-tory manner is not sufficient to form a firm base for social development. Parents and care-givers must react to infants with enthusiasm, attentiveness, and concern for them as unique persons.

Imitation. Imitation is another social behavior of infants. They have the ability to mimic the facial expressions and gestures of adults. When a mother sticks out her tongue at a baby, after a few repetitions, the baby will also stick out its tongue. This imitative behavior is satisfying to the infant, and the mother is pleased by this interactive game. Since the imi-tative behavior is pleasant for both persons, they continue to interact for the sake of inter-action, which in turn promotes more social interaction. Social relations develop from social interactions, but we must always remember that both occur in a social context, or culture.

Infants and toddlers are on a developmental trajectory. Social behaviors like imitation are positive indications of proper development. However, not all children develop the same way and some may need early intervention to help them on their developmental journey. Read the Voice from the Field on page 246 to learn more about the importance of early intervention.

Attachment and Relationships

Bonding and attachment play major roles in the development of social and emotional relationships. **Bonding** is the process by which parents or teachers become emotionally attached, or bonded, to infants. It is the development of a close, personal, affective rela-tionship. It is a one-way process, which some maintain occurs in the first hours or days after birth. **Attachment**, on the other hand, is the enduring emotional tie between the infant and the parents and other primary caregivers; it is a two-way relationship and often endures over a lifetime.

Attachment behaviors serve the purpose of getting and maintaining proximity; they form the basis for the enduring relationship of attachment. Parent and teacher attachment behaviors include kissing, caressing, holding, touching, embracing, making eye contact, and looking at the face. Infant attachment behaviors include laughing, crying, sucking, making eye contact, babbling, and general body movements. Later, when the infant is developmentally able, attachment behaviors include following, clinging, and calling.

Adult Speech. Adult speech has a special fascination for infants. Interestingly enough, given the choice of listening to music or listening to the human voice, infants prefer the human voice! This preference plays a role in attachment by making the baby more responsive.

bonding A parent's initial emotional tie to an infant.

attachment An emotional tie between a parent/caregiver and an infant that endures over time.

The trajectory of a child's development is evident from birth, although it may take parents and others several months to recognize that the child is not meeting developmental milestones.[27] In still other cases, a child may appear to be meeting developmental milestones and then undergo a developmental delay. Early intervention can make a monumental, even pivotal, difference in helping parents, professionals, and you address developmental issues. **Early intervention** is the term used to describe the developmental services provided by professionals to children and families early in life, usually from birth through age three.[28] These services are designed to prevent or curb developmental problems and to accommodate children's learning as a result of developmental delays. Early intervention is vital during the early years because children learn and develop at the fastest rate during the first few years of life.[29] When a child does not develop typically, this may result in lifelong developmental issues. It's important that children not miss out on the crucial early years of development[30] which set the stage for the rest of their social, emotional, physical, cognitive, and academic development.

Examples of early intervention services include health, educational, and therapeutic services. A service can be as simple as prescribing glasses for a two-year-old; as pivotal as identifying a child who has autism; or as complex as developing a complete physical therapy program for an infant with cerebral palsy. Other early intervention programs also may include occupational therapy, social services, respite care, speech therapy, audiology, counseling and play therapy, nursing services, assistive technology, nutritional planning, vision screening and services, family training and therapy, family support services, and in-home counseling.[31]

Services professionals provide depend on the agency or organization. For example, at ACHIEVA, western Pennsylvania's largest early intervention provider, interventions such as speech therapy, occupational therapy, physical therapy, movement therapy, nutrition therapy, sensory integration (therapy provided for children who do not process sensory input as most children do; e.g., when a soft touch feels like a punch), visual perception, augmentative communication, auditory/verbal and auditory/oral therapy, and cochlear implant support are available for infants and toddlers with hearing loss, speech delays, autism spectrum disorders, fragile X syndrome, Down syndrome, spina bifida, and cerebral palsy[32] Other agencies, on the other hand, provide more specific services and may only target areas of early intervention for specific populations, such as speech pathology for infants and toddlers with cleft palates or occupational therapy for children with sensory processing disorders.

Regardless of the specific intervention, the goal is always the same—to help children achieve the highest possible functioning and interaction at home with their families and in their communities and to provide support and guidance to families.[33]

---

early intervention A system of educational and social services that support families and children's growth and development; for example, Early Head Start.

Infants attend to language patterns they will later imitate in their process of language development; they move their bodies in rhythmic ways in response to the human voice. Babies' body movements and caregiver speech synchronize to each other: Adult speech triggers behavioral responses in the infant, which in turn stimulate responses in the adult, resulting in a "waltz" of attention and attachment. Today, the focus in studying infant social development is on the caregiver-to-infant relationship, not on the individuals as separate entities.[34]

Multiple Attachments. Increased use of child care programs inevitably raises questions about infant attachment. Parents are concerned that their children will not attach to them. Worse yet, they fear that their baby will develop an attachment with the caregiver rather than with them. However, children can attach to more than one person, and there can be more than one attachment at a time. Infants attach to parents, or to the primary caregiver, as well as to others—child care providers, siblings, and parents, resulting in a hierarchy of attachments in which the latter attachments are not of equal value. Infants show a preference for the primary caregiver, usually the mother.

Parents should not only engage in attachment behaviors with their infants, but they should also select child care programs that employ caregivers who understand the importance of the caregiver's role and function in attachment. High-quality child care programs help mothers maintain their primary attachments to their infants in many ways. The staff keeps parents well informed about infants' accomplishments, but parents are allowed to "discover" and participate in infants' developmental milestones. A teacher, for example, might tell a mother that today her son showed signs of wanting to take his first step by himself. The teacher thereby allows the mother to be the first person to experience the joy of this accomplishment. The mother might then report to the center that her son took his first step at home the night before.

The Quality of Attachment.   The quality of infant–parent attachment varies according to the relationship that exists between them. A primary method of assessing the quality of parent–child attachment is the Strange Situation, an observational measure developed by Mary Ainsworth (1913–1999) to assess whether infants are securely attached to their care-givers. The testing episodes consist of observing and recording children's reactions to several events: a novel situation, separation from their mothers, reunion with their moth-ers, and reactions to a stranger. Based on their reactions and behaviors in these situations, children are described as being securely or insecurely attached, as detailed in Figure 9.7.

The importance of knowing and recognizing different classifications of attachment is that you can inform parents and help them engage in the specific behaviors that will pro-mote the growth of secure attachments.

Fathers and Attachment.   Fathers—and their roles in families—are a prominent part of early childhood education today. Many fathers have played important roles in child rear-ing and have engaged in shared and participatory parenting. Currently, there is an increased emphasis on ways to encourage fathers to become even more involved in their families and in child rearing.

Fathers who feed, diaper, bathe, and engage in other caregiving activities demon-strate increased attachment behaviors, such as holding, talking, and looking.[35] Early childhood educators can encourage fathers to participate in all facets of caregiving and can conduct training programs that will help fathers gain the skills and confidence needed to assume their rightful places as coparents in rearing responsible children.

Secure Attachment	Avoidant Attachment	Resistant Attachment	Disorganized Attachment
• Secure infants use family members as a secure base from which to explore their environments and play with toys. • When separated from a parent, they may or may not cry, but when the family member returns, these infants actively seek the member and engage in positive interaction. • About 65 percent of infants are securely attached.	• Avoidant infants are unresponsive/avoidant to family members and are not distressed when family members leave the room. • Avoidant infants generally do not establish contact with a returning family member and may even avoid him or her. • About 20 percent of infants demonstrate avoidant attachment.	• Resistant infants seek closeness to family members and may even cling to them, frequently failing to explore. • When family members leave, these infants are distressed and on the parent's return may demonstrate clinginess, or they may show resistive behavior and anger, including hitting and pushing. These infants are not easily comforted by a parent. • About 10 to 15 percent of infants demonstrate resistant attachment.	• Disorganized infants demonstrate disorganized behavior. • They look away from parents and approach them with little or no emotion. • About 5 percent of children demonstrate disorganized attachment.

FIGURE 9.7 Individual Differences in Attachment

Source: Based on Mary Ainsworth, *Patterns of Attachment: A Psychological Study of the Strange Situation* (Hillsdale, NJ: Lawrence Erlbaum, 1978). Photos by Fotolia, LLC – Royalty Free.

Temperament and Personality Development

temperament A child's general style of behavior.

Children are born with individual behavioral characteristics, which, when considered as a collective whole, constitute **temperament**. This temperament, or essentially what children are like, helps determine the development of their personalities. Personalities develop as a result of the interplay between these particular characteristics and the environment.

There are nine characteristics of temperament: level and extent of motor activity; rhythm and regularity of functions such as eating, sleeping, regulation, and wakefulness; degree of acceptance or rejection of a new person or experience; adaptability to changes in the environment; sensitivity to stimuli; intensity or energy level of responses; general mood (e.g., pleasant or cranky, friendly or unfriendly); distractibility from an activity; and attention span and persistence in an activity. Based on these nine temperament characteristics clustered together, there are three classifications of children: the *easy child*, the *slow-to-warm-up child*, and the *difficult child* (see Figure 9.8).[36]

I cannot overemphasize, particularly in child care programs, the importance of developing a match between children's temperament and the caregiver's child-rearing style. As the parenting process extends beyond the natural parents to include all those who care for and provide services to infants, it is reasonable to expect that all who are a part of this parenting cluster will accommodate their behavior to take infants' basic temperaments into account.

Infant and Toddler Mental Health

infant/toddler mental health The overall health and well-being of young children in the context of family, school, and community relationships.

The early childhood profession has always emphasized the importance of providing for children's social and emotional development. One of the benefits of recent research into the importance of early learning is the rediscovery that emotions and mental health play a powerful role in influencing development, especially cognitive development and learning. **Infant/toddler mental health** is a state of emotional and social competence in young

FIGURE 9.8 Children's Temperaments

Reflect on each of these three temperaments, and provide examples of how each could affect the outcome of children's development.

Source: Based on A. Thomas, S. Chess, and H. Birch, "The Origin of Personality," *Scientific American 23* (1970): 102–109.

Easy Children
- Few problems in care and training
- Positive mood
- Regular body functions
- Low to moderate intensity of reaction
- Adaptability and positive approach to new situations

Slow-To-Warm-Up Children
- Low activity level
- Slow to adapt
- Withdraw from new stimuli
- Negative mood
- Low intensity of response

Difficult Children
- Irregular body functions
- Tense reactions
- Withdraw from new stimuli
- Slow to adapt to change
- Negative mood

children who are developing appropriately within the interrelated contexts of biology, relationships, and culture.[37] Think of your own emotions and the ways they influence your daily well-being and approaches to learning. If you are mad or angry right now, your attention is focused elsewhere, and these words don't carry the importance they would if you were happy, focused, and attentive. Now think about many of the stressful and traumatic events that affect children each day and the negative impacts these have on their lives.

There is growing attention focused on ensuring that all young children are reared and educated in environments that will ensure their optimum mental health and well-being, and their growth and development to their fullest potential. Figure 9.9 illustrates some risk factors and potential causes of poor mental health in children; the associated outcomes; and some remedies available to early childhood professionals, community services providers, mental health experts, and others.

Growth of the Infant Mental Health Movement.   The infant mental health movement represents a new direction in early childhood education; efforts are under way to make mental health a central part of infant/toddler care and education.

There are a number of reasons for the growth of the infant mental health movement:

- A growing realization that we must provide for the whole child.
- Brain research findings about how important relationships are in the growth and development of young children.
- The understanding that high-quality early environments and nurturing relationships are essential for children's optimal development.

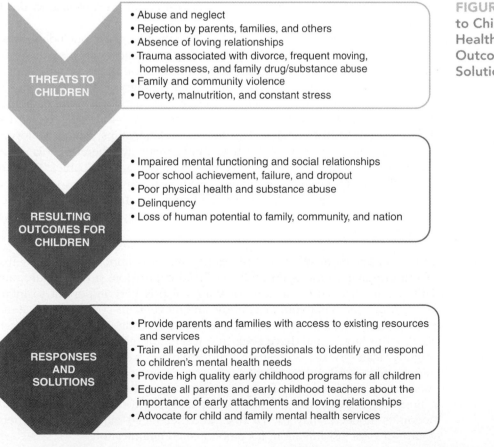

FIGURE 9.9 Threats to Children's Mental Health, Resulting Outcomes, and Solutions

THREATS TO CHILDREN
- Abuse and neglect
- Rejection by parents, families, and others
- Absence of loving relationships
- Trauma associated with divorce, frequent moving, homelessness, and family drug/substance abuse
- Family and community violence
- Poverty, malnutrition, and constant stress

RESULTING OUTCOMES FOR CHILDREN
- Impaired mental functioning and social relationships
- Poor school achievement, failure, and dropout
- Poor physical health and substance abuse
- Delinquency
- Loss of human potential to family, community, and nation

RESPONSES AND SOLUTIONS
- Provide parents and families with access to existing resources and services
- Train all early childhood professionals to identify and respond to children's mental health needs
- Provide high quality early childhood programs for all children
- Educate all parents and early childhood teachers about the importance of early attachments and loving relationships
- Advocate for child and family mental health services

continuity of care The ongoing nurturing relationship between a child and his or her caregiver.

- Renewed interest in how children are affected by multiple risk factors in their lives, including maternal depression, abusive home environments, absence of fathers from the home, parent and teacher stress, and the lack of **continuity of care** (the ongoing nurturing relationship between a child and his or her caregiver) in homes and child care programs.

The field of early childhood is now witnessing burgeoning initiatives designed to strengthen attachments between parents and children and between caregivers/teachers and children and to provide continuity of care for infants and toddlers. Some approaches to promoting continuity of care include the following:

- Screening teachers prior to hiring to determine their beliefs about the importance of relationships and the best ways to provide for them.
- Having infants and toddlers and their caregivers choose each other to arrive at a best fit.
- Having caregivers stay with the same children for several years.
- Providing help and support to grandparents who become the primary caregivers of infants and toddlers.

Emotional Sensitivity.   New research finds that the brains of infants as young as seven months old demonstrate a sensitivity to the human voice and to emotions communicated through the voice that is remarkably similar to what is observed in the brains of adults. The researchers used near-infrared spectroscopy to investigate at what point during development regions in the temporal cortex become specifically sensitive to the human voice. These specific cortical regions play a key role in processing spoken language in adults. Researchers observed that seven-month-olds but not four-month-olds showed adultlike increased responses in the temporal cortex in response to the human voice when compared to nonvocal sounds.[38]

In humans, sensitivity to the rhythm of spoken language, including stress and intonation, is crucial for social communication. The researchers observed that a voice-sensitive region in the right temporal cortex showed increased activity when seven-month-old infants listened to words spoken with emotional (angry or happy) prosody.[39]

This means that infants pick up the emotional "vibes" around them, even if they don't understand the what or why of the emotions—they still *feel* it. This can affect the development of the child's attachments, relationships, language development, self-regulation, and temperament positively and negatively. Therefore it is important for you to be mindful of the tone of voice you use with and around babies. Remember to speak to infants kindly, happily, positively, enthusiastically, gently, soothingly, or excitedly. Avoid sounding annoyed, angry, sad, irritated, and frustrated—if you sound negative, the children will intuit this, and it may affect how they feel, not just in that moment, but about you too!

Emotional Communication.   At the same time, it is important to know that 55 percent of our communication is through our facial expression, body posture, and gestures.[40] This means that while the tone of your voice is very important to infants, it is also vitally important what your face, body, and movements communicate. It may be hard to believe that infants are that attuned to emotions, but simply think for a moment of a six-month-old you may have seen in a restaurant, grocery store, or park. If you smile brightly, lean forward interestedly, and wave, the baby will probably look at you for a minute, then break into a bright smile, coo, or even reach for you. But if you frown or sneer at, ignore, lean away from, or lower your eyebrows at the baby, the baby may try a hesitant smile at you, but when that doesn't produce a smile in return, the baby becomes agitated, may cry or fuss, and her facial expression will begin to mirror yours—it's not just imitation, it's emotional communication!

Quality Infant and Toddler Programs and Environments

Consider the importance of a holistic approach to caring for infants and toddlers. Think about the interplay between emotional health and attachment, between the environment and motor development, and between language development and emotional sensitivity. My goal for you after reading this chapter is to never again think "He's just a baby—he doesn't understand (need, want, or feel) . . ." As a result, it should be clear how important quality infant and toddler programs are for all children.

Developmentally Appropriate Programs

All early childhood professionals who provide care for infants and toddlers—indeed, for all children—must understand and recognize the process of developmental appropriateness, which provides a solid foundation for any program. The NAEYC states that early childhood professionals must also understand the importance of providing programs for infants and toddlers that are different from programs for older children. NAEYC discusses the necessity of providing unique programming for infants and toddlers. Developmentally appropriate programs for children from birth to age three are distinctly different from all other types of programs—they are not a scaled-down version of a good program for preschool children. These program differences are determined by the unique characteristics and needs of children during the first three years:

- Changes take place far more rapidly in infancy than during any other period in life.
- During infancy, as at every other age, all areas of development—cognitive, social, emotional, and physical—are intertwined.
- Infants are totally dependent on adults to meet their needs.
- Very young children are especially vulnerable to adversity because they are less able to cope actively with discomfort and stress.[41]

Infants and toddlers learn through their own experiences, trial and error, repetition, imitation, and identification. Adults guide and encourage this learning by ensuring that the environment is safe and emotionally supportive. An appropriate program for children younger than three invites play, active exploration, and movement. It provides a broad array of stimulating experiences within a reliable framework of routines and protection from excessive stress. Relationships with people are emphasized as an essential contribution to the quality of children's experiences.[42]

Providing different programs of activities for infants and toddlers first involves helping parents and other professionals recognize that infants, as a group, are different from toddlers and need programs, curricula, and facilities specifically designed for them. They need developmentally appropriate curricula.

It is also important to match caregivers with children of different ages. Not everyone is emotionally or professionally suited to provide care for infants and toddlers. Both groups need adults who can respond to their particular needs and developmental characteristics. Infants need especially nurturing professionals; toddlers, in contrast, need adults who can tolerate and allow for their emerging autonomy and independence.

Curricula for Infants and Toddlers

Curricula for infants and toddlers consist of all the activities and experiences they are involved in while under the direction of professionals: feeding, washing, diapering/toileting, playing, learning, and having stimulating interactions, outings, being involved with others, having conversations, and participating in stimulating cognitive and language

Voice from the Field

How to Plan a Curriculum for Infants and Toddlers: Day to Day the Relationship Way

Talitha (nine months old) leans against her teacher while laughing and giving her a quick hug.

Marcus (thirteen months old) figures out how to make music with a small drum.

Kareem (eighteen months old) climbs into a teacher's lap with a book in his hand.

Tanya (twenty-four months old) splashes water with her peers in a small water table.

All of these fortunate infants and toddlers have something in common. They attend programs in which teachers know how to plan a curriculum that is responsive and promotes relationships.

What Is an Infant and Toddler Curriculum?

A curriculum for infants and toddlers includes everything that they experience (from their perspective) from the moment they enter the program until they leave to go home. Every experience makes an impression on how children view themselves, others, and the world. Caring teachers plan a curriculum that is (a) relationship based and (b) responsive to infants' and toddlers' needs, interests, and developmental levels as well their families' goals for their children.

Why Are Relationships Important in Curriculum?

A relationship is a bond of caring between two people that develops over time. In a relationship-based program, teachers support all the relationships that are key to children's development—parent–child, teacher–child, teacher–family, and child–child relationships. Children need these sustaining, caring relationships to provide them a sense of self-worth, trust in the positive intentions of others, and motivation to explore and learn. To thrive, they need protection, affection, and opportunities to learn.

How Can You Plan and Implement a Responsive Curriculum?

In a responsive curriculum, teachers interact with children and plan day to day the relationship way. Teachers make daily and weekly changes in the environment and in their interactions in response to each child's needs, interests, goals, and exploration of concepts. How do you do this? First, you *respect*, then you *reflect*, and then you *relate*.

STEP 1

Respect

- *Respect infants and toddlers as competent, and honor their individual differences.* Recognize that infants and toddlers are active learners and thinkers who are using many different strategies to figure out how things work. In an emotionally supportive environment, they become problem solvers, make good choices, and care about others. Respect that children are unique human beings with different styles (e.g., some eat fast and others slow), different interests, and one-of-a-kind personalities. "Each child is valued as a child, not just for what adults want the child to become."[*]

- *Respect that children will be motivated to learn if you provide a responsive environment.* It should engage them and appeal to a variety of ages, cultures, and individual needs. Provide opportunities for children to choose from such things as blocks, creative materials, sensory experiences, manipulatives, books, dramatic play, and active play opportunities.

- *Respect that play is the way that infants and toddlers learn.* When infants and toddlers aren't sleeping or eating, they should be playing with toys, people, and objects. As they make choices, infants and toddlers focus on their important goals for learning and nurturing—opening and closing a door on a toy, filling a hole on the playground, playing with a friend, turning a page in a book, putting objects in containers, or climbing on a teacher's lap for a hug. As they play, they explore concepts such as how objects fit into various spaces, cause and effect, object permanence, how to comfort another child, or what they can do with different sizes of paper (e.g., crumple, stack, make into a ball, color on it, cover up toys). Children will pursue their goals in an emotionally supportive and physically interesting environment. For example, a child who feels secure might work for long periods of time on figuring out how to stack blocks. Anything that infants and toddlers decide to do in an interesting and relationship-based program supports their learning in all domains of development— emotional, social, cognitive, language, and motor. Nurturing and responsive adults stay close by, support children's play, and meet their emotional needs by using all of the strategies described in the next sections.

STEP **2** Reflect

- *Reflect with families to learn about each child's unique interests, explorations, and culture.* If you are open and interested, families will share with you new words that their children are saying, their latest physical accomplishments, blossoming interests, how they celebrate holidays, or what they want for their children.

- *Reflect through observing children.* Each day observe children to know them well. Each teacher in the room should choose a few children to focus on each week and then take pictures or write notes to capture children's needs, interests, goals, and strategies. You can use an observation and planning guide such as the one shown here to capture your observations. Also, a developmental checklist such as the Ounce[†] allows you to capture the sequence and quality of a child's development over time and then use the information for responsive planning.

- *Reflect on your observations at least weekly with other teachers and often with families.*
  - What is the child trying to do, and how is the child trying to do it?
  - What is the child learning? (Not "what am I teaching?") What concepts (e.g., space, time, social interactions, expressing emotions, ways to open containers) is the child exploring?
  - What is the child telling you he or she needs? (More positive attention, more affection, new strategies to use when another child takes a toy, more room to learn to walk?)
  - What is new in the child's development? For example, is he or she learning to climb or jump, comfort peers, use two words together, or ask questions?

Individual Child Planning Guide

Child's Name: _____

Plans for Week of (Date): _____

Person(s) Completing the Guide: _____

Respect: Child's Emotions, Effort, Goals, Learning, and Relationships

Write an observation or use a photograph or other documentation here—date all notes:

Reflect	Relate
Date all notes: *What am I doing?*	What will you do to support my development and learning?
How am I feeling?	*Responsive Interactions and Building Relationships*
What am I learning? • Emotional: • Social with Peers: • Cognitive: • Language: • Motor:	*Environment, Toys, Materials, and Experiences*

Source: Adapted from D. S. Wittmer and S. H. Petersen (2006), *Infant and Toddler Development and Responsive Program Planning*, p. 267. Upper Saddle River, NJ: Merrill/Prentice Hall.

(continued)

Relate

- *Relate to children by providing the basics—moment-to-moment responsive adult interactions.* Infants and toddlers need to feel that you really care about them.
  - Comfort distressed children.
  - Respond to children's cues and signals—for example, a frown that indicates discomfort, a cry that indicates distress, a plop in the lap with a book that means "Please read to me," sounds that indicate concentration and enjoyment, and words that communicate.
  - Talk responsively with children, abundantly describe your own and the children's actions, provide reasons and explanations, and engage in cooing, babbling, and word conversations.
  - Sing, read, play with children, and respond in nurturing ways to children's need for sleep, food, and comfort.
  - Guide children to learn how to be prosocial by noticing when they are kind, modeling helpfulness, and demonstrating how to care for others.
  - Be open and receptive to what each child is learning in the moment, and follow each child's lead during play.
  - Encourage the children to experiment and problem solve.
  - When a child becomes frustrated, scaffold learning and motivation by helping just enough to support the child's learning *how* to do the task.
  - Remember that sometimes you facilitate children's concentration and peer play by sitting near and observing with engaged interest.
- *Relate during routines.* Consider routines such as diapering/toilet learning, feeding/group eating, and nurturing to sleep as central parts of the curriculum for infants and toddlers. Use these times to support children's emotional development and other learning. Talk to children to help them learn language, show affection to help them build a sense of self-worth, and respond to their cues of hunger and tiredness to help them learn to trust themselves and others.
- *Relate by using the observations and reflections to make changes*—day-to-day and week-to-week—in your interactions, the environment, opportunities, and routines.
  - Plan new ways to support healthy relationships between teachers, children, peers, and families. For example, to help a child who has started to bite peers, plan for a teacher to stay near to help the child learn new behaviors to get needs met.
  - While much of the environment and materials stay the same for the children's sense of security and stability, choose a few new songs to sing, books, toys, changes in the environment, and new opportunities (e.g., art and sensory materials, puzzles, manipulatives, large-motor equipment) based on the children's interests and learning. Continue reading favorite books and singing familiar songs while introducing a few new ones each week.

In the following two examples, teachers use the **respect-reflect-relate model** to plan a responsive, relationship-based curriculum. They trust that each child is expressing a need or conveying an interest. They communicate with families, observe the child, reflect on their observations, and then relate by planning changes in the environment, opportunities for the child, and moment-to-moment responsive interactions to build healthy relationships.

> *Tommy (twelve months old) was dumping toys out of containers. His teacher observed the dumping and asked, What is he trying to do? How is he trying to do it? What is he learning? What does he need? She asked Tommy's mother how Tommy was playing with his toys at home. Tommy's teacher decided that he was interested in how a container can be full one minute and then empty the next. She provided more containers full of safe objects that Tommy could dump. Soon he also began to fill the containers as he explored different strategies for how objects fit into different spaces.*
>
> *Another teacher observed Latisha (fifteen months old). She seemed to need to stay near the teacher lately. Her teacher discussed this with Latisha's parents and the other teachers in the room. They decided together that Latisha desired to be near her teacher for protection, affection, and encouragement. Her teacher decided to sit with Latisha more often, give her positive attention, and encourage other children to join them in play.*

These teachers were being responsive to Tommy's and Latisha's relationship and learning needs, interests, and developmental changes. When teachers plan the curriculum in a responsive, relationship-based way, infants' and toddlers' motivation to learn and love gets stronger with each caring moment.

....

Source: Contributed by Donna S. Wittmer and Sandra H. Petersen, authors of Infant and Toddler Development and Responsive Program Planning: A Relationship-Based Approach, *2nd ed. (Upper Saddle River, NJ: Pearson, 2010). Donna was a professor of early childhood education at the University of Colorado-Denver. Sandy works for Zero to Three with the National Infant Toddler Child Care Initiative and Early Head Start and is also an instructor for WestEd Laboratories with the Program for Infant and Toddler Caregivers (PITC).*

*R. N. Emde and J. K. Hewitt, Infancy to Early Childhood: Genetic and Environmental Influences on Developmental Change *(Denver, CO: Oxford University Press, 2001), viii.*

†TKW Consulting, Ounce Scale, www.tkwconsulting.com/ounce.htm.

experiences. Caregivers must plan the curriculum so that all activities are developmentally appropriate. However, not everyone agrees that planning for infants and toddlers should be such a linear process. Some think that planning should be more circular, that is, based on responses to child and teacher interactions. I believe planning is a combination of linear, circular, and relational processes. The Voice from the Field "How to Plan a Curriculum for Infants and Toddlers" is a Competency Builder that shows you how to plan a curriculum that promotes relationships and responds to children's needs and interests.

respect-reflect-relate model A responsive curriculum for infants and toddlers in which teachers show respect for children, reflect on what children need, and relate to them by providing appropriate care and education.

Preparing Environments to Support Infant and Toddler Development

Research studies repeatedly show that children who are reared, cared for, and taught in environments that are enriched are healthier, happier, and more achievement oriented than children who are not raised in such environments.[43] Environments for infants and toddlers should be inviting, comfortable, healthy, safe, supportive, challenging, and respectful. You must plan in order to create environments with these features.

Looking at and observing environments will help you think about what you can include in your environments for infants and toddlers. Also, as you plan, think about how you can make the environment as homelike as possible. Infants and toddlers like and need environments that are cozy, warm, and safe places to be. You can customize your children's homelike environment with curtains, family pictures on the walls, a couch, and so forth. Make sure that your home away from home includes objects from children's cultures.

Provide for Health and Safety. Safe environments are essential for infants, toddlers, teachers, and families. Here are some guidelines for providing safe environments for infants and toddlers—and for all children:

- Areas used for diapering and toileting are separate from areas used for cooking, eating, and children's activities.
- Mattresses used for infants are firm; avoid soft bedding, such as comforters, pillows, fluffy blankets, or stuffed toys.
- All infant and toddler toys are made of nontoxic materials and sanitized regularly, and are safe, durable, and in good condition.
- All electrical outlets accessible to children are covered and maintained to prevent shock.
- All required policies and plans of action for health emergencies requiring rapid response (such as choking or asthma attacks) are posted.
- Locations and telephone numbers of emergency response systems, and posted and up-to-date family contact information and consent for emergency care, are readily available.
- Playground equipment and surfaces are maintained to avoid injury to children.
- Teachers, staff, volunteers, and children wash their hands with soap and running water after diapering and toilet use, before and after food-related preparation or activity, after hands have become contaminated with blood or other body fluids, after handling pets or other animals, before and after giving medications, before and after bandaging a wound, and after assisting a child with toilet use.
- Staff and volunteers wear nonporous gloves when in contact with blood or other visibly bloody body fluids.

- Spilled body fluids are immediately cleaned up and disinfected according to professionally established guidelines. Tools and equipment used to clean spills are promptly disinfected, and blood-contaminated materials are disposed of in a plastic bag with a secure tie.[44]

Support Developmental Needs.   Supportive environments enable infants to develop basic trust and toddlers to develop **autonomy**. An Erikson concept, autonomy occurs as toddlers mature physically and mentally and want to do things by themselves with no outside help. Infant care should be loving and responsive to their needs. The trusting infant can depend on others to meet his or her needs. Toddlers want to do things for themselves and be independent. We know through research that children's emotional, physical, and intellectual experiences in the first three years of life are vital in laying the foundation for the future, so you should seek to support their developmental needs in these ways:

autonomy An Erikson concept that says as toddlers mature physically and mentally, they want to do things by themselves with no outside help.

- Respond immediately to an infant's expressions of need or discomfort; soothe and comfort the child. Meet infants' and toddlers' needs in warm, sensitive ways.
- Provide for their choices while taking into account their temperament, emotions, and individuality.
- Express love and be affectionate to your children. Toddlers may need extra or continual confirmation that they are loved and that trusted adults are there for them. Tell them, "I love you!"
- Give infants and toddlers your undivided attention—respond to their actions. Be alert to the baby's cues that he or she is ready to interact or play, or that he or she needs a break from activity.
- Create a stable, nurturing environment that is consistent. Make an extra effort to maintain schedules that are in synch with the baby's rhythms.
- Provide appropriate stimulation and freedom for a child to explore and master new experiences.
- Encourage families to have their infants and toddlers receive regular health checkups because illness and hospitalization often threaten a toddler's developing autonomy.
- Talk and read to children constantly. Engage them in conversations, comment on what they are doing using rich language and feeling words, and explain their surroundings to them.
- Encourage mastery of self-help skills and socialization, but support children's reliance on security objects such as a pacifier, blanket, or favorite stuffed animal and other successful self-coping strategies as they are needed.
- Validate all expressions of emotions and teach appropriate behaviors in high-emotion situations.[45]
- Treat each child as special and important.

Provide Challenging Environments.   A challenging environment is one in which infants and toddlers can explore and interact with a wide variety of materials. It is important for you to provide all children with developmentally appropriate challenges. Challenging curriculum enables children to go from their present levels of development and learning to higher levels. Providing an enriched environment is a powerful way to promote infants' and toddlers' overall development. Here are some things you can do to enrich environments for infants and toddlers:

- Include a wide variety of multisensory, visual, auditory, and tactile materials and activities to support all areas of development—physical, social, emotional, and linguistic. For example:
  - Hold, play with, and be responsive to infants and toddlers—you are the best toy a child has.

- Provide mirrors for infants and toddlers to look at themselves and others. Talk with the children about how they look. Encourage them to laugh and smile at themselves, you, and others.
- Provide visually interesting things for children to look at—mobiles, pictures, murals and so on.
- Provide toys and objects that children can manipulate—feel, suck, and grasp.
- Provide objects and containers that children can use to put in or dump out.
- Provide responsive toys that make sounds, pop up, and so on, as children manipulate or act on them.
- Include materials for large and small muscles for reaching, grasping, kicking, pulling up, holding on, walking, and so forth.

- Enable children to be actively involved. An essential component of a challenging but appropriate environment is that it encourages active involvement. Active involvement is at the heart of constructivist approaches to early childhood education. So, providing opportunities for infants and toddlers to be active supports their learning and provides them with feelings of accomplishment and achievement. You should:
  - Take infants and toddlers on walks so they can observe nature and people.
  - Provide safe floor space indoors and grassy areas outdoors so children can explore and move freely.
  - Allow infants and toddlers to crawl, pull up, walk, move freely, and safely explore.
  - Provide activities based on children's interests and abilities—a key to responsive and relational caregiving.
  - Provide low open shelves that allow children to see and select their own materials.
- The environment should promote language all of the time. Provide for a full range of language and literacy development.
  - Read, read, and read to infants and toddlers. Read aloud with enthusiasm, which shows children how much you love to read.
  - Read from all kinds of books—stories, poems, and so on.
  - Provide books (washable, cloth, etc.) for children to "read," handle, manipulate, and mouth.
  - Sing for and with children. Play a wide variety of music. Sing while changing diapers and other teacher–child activities.
  - Talk, talk, talk—use the guidelines for supporting literacy in Figure 9.6.
- Provide for children's health needs.
  - Consider massage or touch therapy as a way of getting in touch with your infants and toddlers and as a way of providing for relaxation and muscle stimulation.
  - Serve child-size portions at mealtimes and let them ask for more.

Promote Respectful Social Development and Interactions. Social interactions involve how children interact and get along with other children, their teachers, and others; they also include how teachers relate to, and get along with, the children they care for and other children. Here are some things you can do to promote respectful social development and interactions:

- Play games and engage in activities that include small groups of children.
- Play with toys that involve more than one child. For example, use a wagon and let one child pull another.
- Allow and encourage infants and toddlers to make choices. You can do this by asking them questions that encourage choice making. For example, "Can I help you dry

As an infant/toddler caregiver, you must respond to and interact with infants and toddlers in responsive ways that support their mental, physical, language, and social development.

your hands? Or can you do it by yourself?" or "You get to decide." Encourage autonomy with statements such as "That is something you can do."

- Give infants and toddlers the time they need and want to engage in an activity. Some infants and toddlers complete activities quickly; others need more time.
- Provide opportunities for infants and toddlers to engage in activities with others.
- Provide for friendship-making opportunities:
  - Provide for parallel play. Parellel play is when two children sit next to each other while they play, but may not necessarily interact. Donna Wittmer, author of *Focusing on Peers: The Importance of Relationships in the Early Years*, says "Kids move from parallel play to parallel aware play. They'll look over at their buddy, smile, and even imitate him by stacking blocks the same way." This is a sign toddlers are becoming more social and building skills that lead to friendships.
- Group children with familiar faces so that they can form recognition and comfort with their peers.
- Schedule play opportunities at a time of day that is not right before nap time, eating times, or go-home time—all times of the day that infants and toddlers are likely to be more fussy or irritable. Help situations stay meltdown free by enabling children to put their best foot forward.
- Model collaborative play such as helping one toddler roll a ball to another toddler. Provide lots of encouragement and positive feedback to encourage sharing and kindness.
- Be observant and on guard for the need to step in to prevent mishaps or meltdowns, but don't intervene too soon. Let children grow in independence as they are able.
- Label emotions to develop mutual empathy. For example, if Jack takes Emily's truck away, say quietly to Jack, "Look, Emily's crying. She feels sad that you took her truck. She'll feel happy if you give it back." If you need to, you can help Jack give the truck back by guiding his hands, then help him ask for a turn (be sure that he gets a turn soon to encourage him to share in the future!).[45]

Accommodating Diverse Learners

self-regulation A child's ability to gain control of bodily functions, manage emotions, maintain focus and attention, and integrate cognitive, physical, and social-emotional abilities.

Meet Gabby, a two-month-old Caucasian infant. She is new to your care and you are beginning to build a relationship with her. Like all babies, Gabby must begin to learn how to self-regulate. **Self-regulation** is a child's ability to gain control of bodily functions, manage emotions, maintain focus and attention, and integrate cognitive, physical, and social-emotional abilities. The growth of self-regulation is a developmental milestone across early childhood that begins in infancy that influences all aspects of behavior.[46] Babies must learn to increasingly self-regulate and control their emotions over time. Responsive caregivers act as helpers, external regulators, who help babies learn to gain self-control. Therefore, when you care for Gabby, you act as an extension of, or as a support for, her internal ability to regulate.

Several factors influence a baby's ability to move from external to internal self-regulation. Temperament is one factor. Temperament traits like mood, irritability, and adaptability affect a baby's capacity for emotional regulation. **Goodness of fit**—how well a teacher recognizes and responds or adapts to a child's temperament—also affects the learning of self-regulation. You develop a goodness of fit by working with babies' temperaments, not against them. You can work to lessen or soften some of the difficult features of temperament, and you can emphasize the strengths of temperament, but you can't change an infant's temperament! This means that you make changes in your own style of relating and change the environment to work with the baby's temperament.[47]

Granted, it is taxing to care for a baby who fusses non-stop or who sleeps for only an hour here and there; or a toddler who bites; or who constantly throws tantrums. Negative behaviors give you cues and clues that the infant or toddler is having difficulty with self-regulation. You help Gabby learn self-regulation when you provide her with manageable challenges that are part of everyday life, like waiting to be fed or self-soothing into sleep. When you offer manageable challenges while providing external support, you help Gabby and all babies build self-regulation and personal responsibility.[48]

Here are some strategies you can use to help Gabby and other infants and toddlers develop self-regulation.

goodness of fit How well a teacher recognizes and responds or adapts to a child's temperament—also affects the learning of self-regulation.

- Build a close relationship with Gabby. This helps her regulate her emotions and actions because she learns to trust you to fulfill her needs. She can rely on you for consistent care and constant attention. As a result, Gabby gradually learns to quiet and control herself. To build close relationships:[49]
  - *Observe closely and respond.* Babies always give you cues to let you know when they are ready to play or when they are tired, hungry, or full. Be aware of and accepting of individual differences reflected in each baby's needs. For example, when Gabby is two months old, she cries loudly when she is hungry; if you respond promptly so that she does not become distressed, she will learn to trust you. Then, by the time she is four months old, she will be able to only whimper to cue you to her needs.[50]
  - *Provide structure and predictability.* Babies need consistent caregivers who provide continuity of care. You strengthen your relationship with Gabby as she trusts the continuity of your relationship with her. For example, if you follow a regular sleep schedule each day, Gabby will feel safe because she learns what to expect.[51]
  - *Show empathy and caring.* When caregivers identify children's needs and respond to them as significant, infants and toddlers feel good about themselves and are better able to handle their emotions. When Gabby reaches eight months of age and cries when her mother leaves in the morning, you can use a soft, soothing voice to empathize and reassure her, "It's so hard for you. I know you feel so sad." You can hold her and rub her back to offer empathy and strengthen your relationship with her.[52]
  - *Define age-appropriate limits.* Help Gabby know what is expected. When she is a ten-month-old, you can tell her, "No biting. That hurts me." As Gabby grows, be consistent in expressing expectations and setting rules or consequences. The goal is to guide children and set limits so that they feel supported and valued, not judged and rejected. When Gabby grows into a curious toddler and wants to explore, you can verbalize and model limits. Tell her, "Wait for me, Gabby. We go out together," as you take her hand and help her open the door.[53]
- Play! When you play with babies and toddlers, you help them learn to find answers to problems and also help them develop the attention they need to attend to tasks.[54] To help Gabby develop self-regulation through play:
  - *Model language.* Early on, Gabby won't have many words, so you should describe what she is doing and what you and she are doing together. This responsive

approach helps Gabby build understanding between her actions and words. Soon Gabby will be talking! She will also begin to use "self-talk" to help her control her own behavior. As her language and emotional development progresses, you can encourage Gabby to use her words to express her feelings and thoughts rather than immediately acting on her impulses.[55]

- *Be a consultant.* As children begin to pretend, their play scripts are very straightforward and uncomplicated. When Gabby is younger, her pretend script may consist of using a brush to brush her own hair. When you take part in her play, you can help her grow her script by showing her how to brush the hair of a doll and your own hair. When you insert new roles or ideas into pretend situations and toys, Gabby learns to apply her behavior to the new scenario, which increases her self-regulation.[56]

Helping Gabby and other babies develop self-regulation helps them grow into a child ready for school and for life. As a result, Gabby will be able to understand what teachers and others ask of her in given situations, monitor her own behavior to see if it matches, and maintain or change what she is doing based on her evaluation of the behavior.

Activities for Professional Development

Ethical Dilemma

"Postpartum mom?"

Carlie is an infant and toddler caregiver at an early learning center. She has always enjoyed caring for Jacob, a happy-go-lucky two-year-old, and interacting with his mother, Amanda. Amanda just started bringing her new baby, Adam, to the early learning center, and Carlie has noticed that Amanda is often out of sorts, disheveled, short tempered, and that she often looks dejected, and her voice and affect are mostly flat. Amanda is so different from the way she was before she gave birth that Carlie is concerned. One day when Amanda picked up Jacob and Adam, Carlie was shocked to see Amanda give Adam a shake when he wouldn't stop crying. Before she can say anything, the family is out the door. Carlie thinks Amanda might have postpartum depression, and she's concerned for Adam and Jacob.

What should Carlie do? Should she consult a supervisor or call Amanda's husband and share her concerns? Should Carlie alert Child Protective Services? Should Carlie talk to Amanda, or wait for more evidence that the children are in danger before she makes a decision? What do you think Carlie should do?

Activities to Apply What You Learned

1. Visit a parenting blog or Web page and peruse the posts. What are parents saying about their infants and toddlers? What are their questions, concerns, and delights? How does this give you a picture of what infants and toddlers are like? Post your findings on your online journal.

2. Conduct an Internet search of scientific magazines, teacher magazines, and newspapers for the latest brain research relating to infants and toddlers.

3. Observe a program that provides care for infants and toddlers. Is the curriculum developmentally appropriate? Explain what you liked most and least about the program. What suggestions would you make for improving the curriculum?

4. Which stage of sensorimotor cognitive development do you think is most important in an infant/toddler's development and why? Post your opinion in a Facebook note and tag your friends to start a friendly debate.

5. Select five books for infants and five for toddlers. Tell why you selected each and give examples for how you would use them in your infant/toddler program.

6. Make a list of five caregiver–infant/toddler relationships that you think are essential to their education and development. For example, one relationship might be "responding appropriately to infants' cries and sounds."

7. Make a list of the ways curricula for infants and toddlers influence the environment and vice versa. Then do research on the Internet of infant/toddler programs in your area. Pay attention to what their websites say about curricula, environments, and caregivers. Make a list of pros and cons of what you find.

8. How might a child's temperament affect how you care for him or her? Are there some behaviors that are difficult for

you to empathize with or understand? Write a paragraph about how you will provide for goodness of fit between yourself and your charges when you come up against infants/toddlers with temperaments you find challenging.

Linking to Learning

Brain Development in Infants and Toddlers: Information for Parents and Caregivers

www.nccic.org/poptopics/brain.html

Provides an overview of resources available concerning the brain.

Early Brain Development: What Parents and Caregivers Need to Know

www.educarer.org/brain.htm

Presents facts about early brain development that parents and educators need to know.

Zero to Three

www.zerotothree.org

Concentrates exclusively on the miraculous first years of life, the critical period when a child undergoes the greatest human growth and development. Seeks to develop a solid intellectual, emotional, and social foundation for young children.

PEARSON
myeducationlab

Go to Topics 2 (Child Development/Theories) and 4 (Observation/Assessment) in the MyEducationLab (www.myeducationlab.com) for your course, where you can:

- Find learning outcomes for Child Development/Theories along with the national standards that connect to these outcomes.
- Complete Assignments and Activities that can help you more deeply understand the chapter content.
- Apply and practice your understanding of the core teaching skills identified in the chapter with the Building Teaching Skills and Dispositions learning units.
- Hear viewpoints of experts in the field in Professional Perspectives.
- Check your comprehension on the content covered in the chapter by going to the Study Plan in the Book Resources for your text. Here you will be able to take a chapter quiz, receive feedback on your answers, and then access Review, Practice, and Enrichment activities to enhance your understanding of chapter content.

10

THE PRESCHOOL YEARS
Getting Ready for School and Life

naeyc standards

Standard 1. Promoting Child Development and Learning

I use my understanding of young children's characteristics and needs, and of multiple interacting influences on children's development and learning, to create environments that are healthy, respectful, supportive, and challenging for each child.[1]

Standard 4. Using Developmentally Effective Approaches to Connect with Children and Families

I understand and use positive relationships and supportive interactions as the foundation for my work with young children and families. I know, understand, and use a wide array of developmentally appropriate approaches, instructional strategies, and tools to connect with children and families and positively influence each child's development and learning.[2]

I understand the importance of developmental domains and academic (or content) disciplines in early childhood curriculum. I use my knowledge and other resources to design, implement, and evaluate meaningful, challenging curricula that promote comprehensive developmental and learning outcomes for every young child.[3]

The road to success in school and life begins long before kindergarten and first grade. This is why early childhood teachers, parents, and society view the preschool years as a cornerstone of success. As a result, the **preschool years** are playing a more important role in the educational process than they have at any other time in history, and they will continue to be the focus of public attention and financial support.

preschool years The period from three to five years of age, before children enter kindergarten and when many children attend preschool programs.

Why Are Preschools So Popular?

Preschools are programs for three- to five-year-old children before they enter kindergarten. Today, child care beginning at six weeks is commonplace for children of working parents, and many children are in a school of some kind as early as age two or three. About 47 percent of three-year-old children and 74 percent of four-year-old children are enrolled in a public or private preschool program.[4] Reasons for the popularity of preschool programs are many and varied.

Working Parents

Working parents believe the public schools hold the solution to their child care needs so they advocate (rather strongly) for public schools to provide preschool programs. Some parents cannot afford quality child care; they believe preschools, furnished at the public's expense, are a reasonable, cost-efficient way to meet their child care needs. The alignment of the public schools with early childhood programs is becoming increasingly popular. Some think it makes sense to put the responsibility for educating and caring for all of the nation's children under the sponsorship of one agency—the public schools.

For their part, public school teachers and the unions that represent them are anxious to bring early childhood programs under the umbrella of the public schools. Public school teachers see their involvement as a step toward bringing higher-quality programs to more children. The unions see preschool teachers as another source of growing membership.[5]

Highly Educated Workforce

A more highly educated workforce will increase economic growth.[6] Business leaders see early education as one way of developing highly skilled and more productive workers.[7] Many preschool programs include work-related skills and behavior in their curriculum. For example, approaches to learning or dispositions for learning are important preschool goals. Approaches to learning such as self-regulation and understanding, accepting, and following rules and routines are essential workplace behaviors. We discuss approaches to

> "Even as we invest in early childhood education, let's raise the bar for early learning programs that are falling short, to ensure that children are better prepared for success by the time they enter kindergarten."
>
> **PRESIDENT BARACK OBAMA**

learning again on page 273. Likewise, being literate begins in the early years and literacy is an essential workforce skill. Research supports the importance of preschool early literacy learning as a basis for successful reading.[8] Learning to read is a high priority for our nation's schools. It makes sense to lay the foundation for reading as early as possible in the preschool years.

Equal Opportunity

Many believe that early public schooling, especially for children from low-income families, is necessary if the United States is to promote equal opportunity for all. They argue that low-income children begin school already far behind their more fortunate middle-class counterparts and that the best way to keep them from falling hopelessly behind is for them to begin school earlier. Extensive research shows that investing in our children is important, and not as expensive as some people believe.[9]

Cost Effective

High-quality early education benefits children of all social and economic groups. It helps prepare young children to succeed in school and become better citizens; they earn more money, pay more taxes, and commit fewer crimes.[10] Quality early childhood programs help prevent and reduce behavioral and social problems, such as substance abuse and school dropout. Research supports the effectiveness of this early intervention approach.[11] Advocacy exists for publicly supported and financed preschools as a means of helping ensure that all children and their families, regardless of socioeconomic background, receive the benefits of attending high-quality preschool programs.

Publicly supported and financed preschools are one means of ensuring that no children are excluded from the known benefits of quality preschool programs. Given that more than 14 million, or 19 percent, of American children live in families with incomes below the federal poverty level—$22,050 a year for a family of four—early intervention programs are essential for them. In addition, research shows that, on average, families need an income of about twice that level to cover basic expenses. Unfortunately, 41 percent of the nation's children live in low-income families, which attests to the importance of and need for affordable quality preschool programs because of the influence they have for positive social change in children's lives.[12]

Eager to Learn

Three- and four-year-old children are ready, eager, and able to learn. Recognizing the strong connection between a child's early development and success later in life, states are funding preschool programs for four- and even three-year-olds.[13] The National Research Council concluded in its study *Eager to Learn: Educating Our Preschoolers* that the last thirty years of child development research demonstrate that "two- to five-year-old children are more capable learners than had been imagined, and that their acquisition of linguistic, mathematical, and other skills relevant to school readiness is influenced (and can be improved) by their educational and developmental experiences during those years.[14]

Early Intervention

For children with disabilities or delays, preschool programs also offer opportunities for early intervention. For example, Montgomery County Public Schools in Rockville, Maryland, implemented its Preschool Education Program (PEP) to address the needs of children ages three to five years with developmental delays or disabilities. All children in PEP have an Individualized Education Program (IEP) with learning goals and objectives based on needs identified through assessment and testing. The goals and objectives guide teachers as they support children's improvement and progress. Most children have delays in more than one area and receive services for speech/language, occupational, and/or physical therapy.[15]

What Are Preschoolers Like?

Today's preschoolers are not like the children of previous decades. Many have already attended one, two, or three years of child care or school. They have watched hundreds of hours of television, and many are technologically sophisticated. Many have also experienced the trauma of family divorce or the psychological effects of abuse. Many have experienced the glitz and glamour of boutique birthday parties or hardships of living below the poverty level. Both collectively and individually, the experiential backgrounds of today's preschoolers are quite different from those of previous generations.

I have stressed the individuality of each child while at the same time understanding the commonalities of developmental processes for all children. Within this context of individuality and developmental commonalities, introduce yourself to four preschoolers in the "Portraits of Preschoolers" at the end of this chapter. While reading this chapter, think about the characteristics and needs of these preschoolers and how you would teach them if they were in your classroom.

Physical and Motor Development

Understanding preschoolers' physical and motor development enables you to understand why active learning is so important. One noticeable difference between preschoolers and infants and toddlers is that preschoolers have lost most of their baby fat and taken on a leaner, lankier look. This slimming down and increasing motor coordination enables them to participate with more confidence in the locomotor activities so necessary during this stage of growth and development. Both girls and boys continue to grow several inches per year throughout the preschool years. Table 10.1 shows the average height and weight for preschoolers.

Preschool children are learning to use and test their bodies. It is a time to learn what they can do individually and how they can do it. Locomotion plays a large role in motor and skill development; it includes activities of moving the body through space—walking, running, hopping, jumping, rolling, dancing, climbing, and leaping. Preschoolers use these activities to investigate and explore the relationships among themselves, space, and objects in space.

TABLE 10.1 Average Height and Weight of Preschoolers

| Age | Males | | Females | |
	Height (inches)	Weight (pounds)	Height (inches)	Weight (pounds)
3 years	37.5	32.0	37.0	31.0
3½ years	39.0	34.0	38.5	32.5
4 years	40.0	36.0	40.0	35.0
4½ years	41.5	38.0	41.0	38.0
5 years	43.0	40.5	42.5	40.0

Source: National Center for Health Statistics in collaboration with the National Center for Chronic Disease Prevention and Health Promotion (2000), www.cdc.gov/growthcharts.

Preschoolers also like to participate in fine-motor activities such as drawing, coloring, painting, cutting, and pasting. They need programs that provide action and play, supported by proper nutrition and healthy habits of plentiful rest and good hygiene.

Social-Emotional Development

A major responsibility of preschool teachers is to promote and support children's social-emotional development. Positive social-emotional development enables children to learn better and to succeed in all school and life activities. During the preschool years (ages three to five), children are in Erikson's psychosocial development stage of initiative versus guilt. During this stage, children are fully involved in locomotive activities and the enjoyment of doing things. They are very active and want to plan and be involved in activities. They want to move and be active. You can help support children's initiative in these ways:

- *Give children freedom to explore.* Lisa Frank, in her Bright Futures Pre-K classroom, has students try anything from yoga to sign language. Lisa always makes it an enjoyable experience. For example, she transformed her classroom into a magical ocean experience, complete with blue cling wrap and sea creature stickers on the window, an ocean sound CD during naptime, and an edible ocean made of blueberry Jell-O and Swedish fish.[16]

- *Provide projects and activities that enable children to discover and experiment.* Science means success for Wendy Butler-Boyensen's children at EWEB Child Development center. She motivates her young students by exploring different scientific themes each month, from hiking through local wetlands to studying the solar system.[17]

- *Encourage and support children's attempts to plan, make things, and be involved.* Carla Lyles of Chicago, Illinois, listens, observes, and engages her students in conversations to determine their interests. For example, when her children expressed interest in building houses, she took them on a construction-site field trip to explore the renovation of homes in their community. The class created a book filled with photos and captions from their excursion, and even enjoyed an onsite school visit by the backhoe driver they befriended on their trip.[18]

self-regulation The ability of preschool children to control their emotions and behaviors, to delay gratification, and to build positive social relations with each other.

executive function See self-regulation.

Self-Regulation. During the preschool years, children are learning **self-regulation**, also referred to as **executive function**. Self-regulation is the ability to plan, initiate, and complete an activity; control emotions and behaviors; delay gratification; maintain attention; respond to feedback; and build positive social relations with others.[19] Teaching self-regulation is a major teacher task during the preschool years. The following guidelines will enable you to teach self-regulation so preschool children can guide their own behavior:

- *Provide a variety of learning experiences.* Young children are very good at creating diversion when none is available. Often teachers think they cannot provide interesting learning experiences until children are "under control," when, in fact, the real problem is that children may be out of control because they have nothing interesting to do!

- *Arrange the environment to help children do their best.* Make sure activities are arranged so there is enough space for them and so they are protected from the traffic of other children.

- *Get to know each child.* Establish relationships with parents, and support children's strengths as well as their needs. As you get to know each child, you can begin to tailor activities to their specific needs. Christine Lyall of Culver City Schools at the Office of Child Development tailors activities to her students' needs by being sensitive to their various learning styles. For example, she accommodates mathematical–logical intelligence by using hands-on materials and rhythmic patterning activities, which she makes herself. Christine attends to children's musical–rhythmic intelligence by composing her own songs about concepts the class is learning and the children are captivated! She also addresses the often under-recognized bodily–kinestheic intelligences of her students by incorporating dance and movement into learning strategies.[20]

- *Set clear guidelines for what is and is not appropriate behavior.* Guide behavior with rational explanations in a climate of mutual respect and caring.

- *Work with children to establish a few simple group rules.* Some appropriate rules: take care of other people; take care of yourself; and take care of the classroom. Teach and reinforce these rules continuously throughout the school year.

- *Use the child's home language as often as possible.* Make every effort to show children you support their culture and respect their language. For example, preschool teacher Trudy George uses children's home language through her "World Day" activity. Her students are taught greetings in different languages (e.g., "Hola," "Adiós") and read stories about children from different nations.

- *Coach children to verbally express their feelings.* Help children use either their home language or English, and model how to solve social problems with others using words. For many children, this will mean providing appropriate words and offering possible solutions and guidance when these problems arise.

- *Model self-control by using self-talk.* "Oh, I can't get this lid off the paint. I am feeling frustrated [take a deep breath]. Now I'll try again."[21]

Cognitive Development

Preschoolers are in the preoperational stage of intellectual development. Characteristics of the preoperational stage are (1) children grow in their ability to use symbols, including language; (2) children are not capable of operational thinking (an **operation** is a reversible mental action), which explains why Piaget named this stage preoperational; (3) children center on one thought or idea, often to the exclusion of other thoughts; (4) children are unable to conserve; and (5) children are egocentric.

Preoperational characteristics have particular implications for teachers. Here are some ways you can promote preschool children's cognitive development:

operation A reversible mental action.

- *Provide concrete materials to help children see and experience concepts and processes.* Children learn from touching and experimenting with actual objects, as well as from pictures, stories, and media. When you read stories about fruit and nutrition, bring in a collection of apples for children to touch, feel, smell, taste, classify, manipulate, and explore. Collections also offer children an ideal way to learn the names of things, classify, count, and describe.

- *Use hands-on activities that give children opportunities for active involvement in their learning.* Encourage children to manipulate and interact with the world around them so they can construct concepts about relationships, attributes, and processes. Through exploration, preoperational children begin to collect and organize data about the objects they manipulate. For example, when children engage in water play with funnels and cups, they learn about concepts such as measurement, volume, sink/float, bubbles and the prism, evaporation, and saturation.

- *Give children many and varied experiences.* Diverse activities and play environments lend themselves to teaching different skills, concepts, and processes. Children should spend time daily in both indoor and outdoor activities. Give consideration to the types of activities that facilitate large- and fine-motor, social, emotional, and cognitive development. For example, outdoor play activities and games such as climbing, throwing and catching balls, and riding tricycles enhance large-motor development; fine-motor activities include using scissors, stringing beads, coloring, writing, and completing simple puzzles.

Indoor and outdoor play contributes to children's cognitive development. Preschool teachers can help children learn many concepts as they participate with children in play—both indoors and outdoors. What are some concepts these children are learning through their involvement in play?

- *Scaffold appropriate tasks and behaviors.* Preoperational children learn to a great extent through modeling. For example, children should see you and other adults reading and writing daily. Provide opportunities for children to view brief demonstrations by peers or professionals on possible ways to use materials. For example, after children have spent time in free exploration with blocks and math manipulatives, you can show children patterning techniques and strategies they may want to experiment with in their own play.

- *Provide a literacy-rich environment to stimulate interest in and development of language and literacy.* Display class stories and dictations, children's writing, and charts of familiar songs and fingerplays. Have a variety of literature for students to read, including books, magazines, and newspapers. Make sure paper and writing utensils are abundant to motivate children in all kinds of writing. Daily literacy activities should include opportunities for shared, guided, and independent reading and writing; singing songs and fingerplays; and creative dramatics. In addition, read to children every day.

- *Allow children periods of uninterrupted time to engage in self-chosen projects.* Children benefit more from a few extended blocks of time that provide for in-depth involvement in meaningful projects than they do from frequent, brief periods of time.

Language Development

Preschool children's language skills grow and develop rapidly. Vocabulary and sentence length increase as children continue to master syntax and grammar. During their third year or earlier, children add helping verbs and negatives to their vocabulary; for example, "No touch" or "I don't want milk." Sentences also become longer and more complex. During the fourth and fifth years, children use noun or subject clauses, conjunctions, and prepositions to complete their sentences. "No" is a common part of preschool children's language. This is a sign of children's desire for independence and autonomy. Preschoolers want to do things for themselves!

During the preschool years, children's language development is diverse and comprehensive and constitutes a truly impressive range of learning. Even more impressive is the fact that children learn intuitively, without a great deal of instruction, the rules of language that apply to the words and phrases they use. You can use many of the language practices recommended for infants and toddlers with preschoolers as well.

School Readiness and Young Children

School readiness is a major topic of discussion about preschool and kindergarten programs. The early childhood profession is reexamining readiness, its many interpretations, and the various ways the concept is applied to educational practices.

For most parents, *school readiness* means that their children have the knowledge and abilities necessary for success in kindergarten. But what does readiness for kindergarten really include?

Readiness is no longer seen as consisting solely of a predetermined set of specific capabilities children must attain before entering kindergarten. Furthermore, the responsibility for children's early learning and development is no longer placed solely on the child or the parents but is seen as a shared responsibility among children, parents, families, early childhood professionals, communities, states, and the nation. Regardless of the child or family's diversity or background (culture, language, socioeconomic status, disability, etc.), readiness remains a shared responsibility.

For example, states are taking the initiative to ensure preschool children are ready for kindergarten. Texas School Ready! is a program that certifies preschool education classrooms that effectively prepare their students for kindergarten. Based on children's assessment scores as they enter kindergarten, the preschools they attended are—or are not—certified. This certification system is an incentive for all preschools to prepare their children for kindergarten.

School Readiness

Some early childhood professionals and many parents believe that time cures all things, including a child's lack of school readiness. They think that as time passes and as children grow and develop physically and cognitively they become ready to achieve. This belief is manifested in school admissions policies advocating that children remain out of school for a year if they are found not ready by a school readiness test.

Assuming that passage of time brings about readiness is similar to the concept of unfolding, popularized by Froebel. Unfolding implies that development is inevitable and certain and a child's optimum degree of development is determined by heredity and a biological clock. Froebel likened children to plants and parents and teachers to gardeners, whose task is to nurture and care for children so they can mature according to their genetic inheritance and maturational timetable. The concept of unfolding continues to be a powerful force in early childhood education; it is based on the belief that maturation is predictable, patterned, and orderly.

However, although much of child development does occur in predictable ways, it is not the same for all children. Some children may have delayed development and, for others, their development may be advanced. In addition, teachers and parents cannot and should not simply wait for children to develop or acquire age-appropriate skills and behaviors. Creating rich and supportive environments helps ensure that all children will develop to their appropriate levels.

Readiness for Learning

As the United States moves closer to universal preschool with all three- to five-year-old children attending public-supported early childhood programs, readiness issues take on greater importance and significance. Preschool is the portal to kindergarten and the process of schooling through grade twelve and beyond. Preschool experiences and success set the trajectory for how well children achieve in kindergarten and beyond. This reality helps explain why early childhood educators are so interested in and concerned about preschool readiness skills and behaviors.

Unfortunately, America's children enter preschool programs at uneven levels of preparedness and readiness for learning what the public schools expect of them. Socioeconomic background, culture, language, and maternal education all contribute to children's readiness for leaning. In fact, significant learning and educational and preparedness gaps exist at children's entry to preschool.[22] Many children enter preschool well prepared to learn what is necessary for entry into kindergarten as depicted in Figure 10.1. On the other hand, many children will struggle to learn essential readiness skills and behaviors and will continue to fall behind their more advantaged peers. In order to help level the

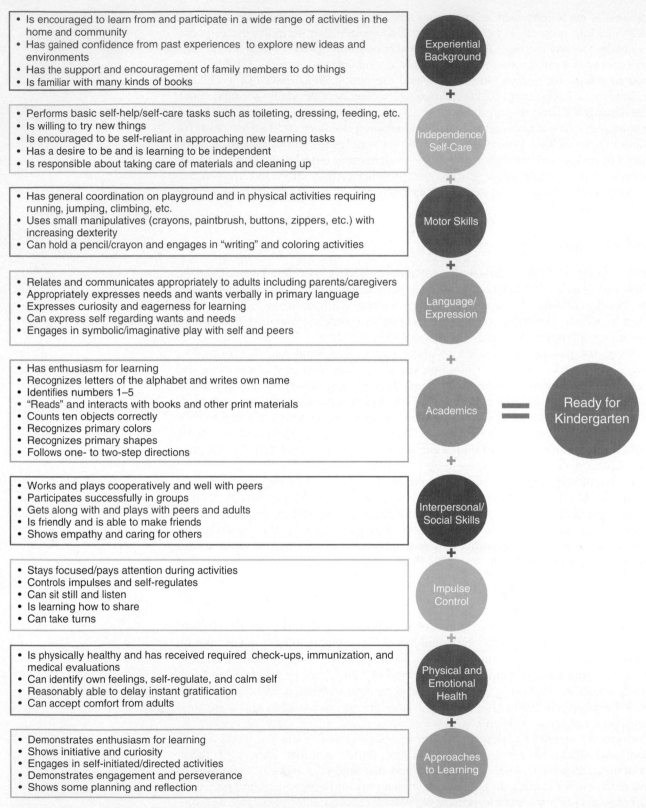

- Is encouraged to learn from and participate in a wide range of activities in the home and community
- Has gained confidence from past experiences to explore new ideas and environments
- Has the support and encouragement of family members to do things
- Is familiar with many kinds of books

Experiential Background

+

- Performs basic self-help/self-care tasks such as toileting, dressing, feeding, etc.
- Is willing to try new things
- Is encouraged to be self-reliant in approaching new learning tasks
- Has a desire to be and is learning to be independent
- Is responsible about taking care of materials and cleaning up

Independence/ Self-Care

+

- Has general coordination on playground and in physical activities requiring running, jumping, climbing, etc.
- Uses small manipulatives (crayons, paintbrush, buttons, zippers, etc.) with increasing dexterity
- Can hold a pencil/crayon and engages in "writing" and coloring activities

Motor Skills

+

- Relates and communicates appropriately to adults including parents/caregivers
- Appropriately expresses needs and wants verbally in primary language
- Expresses curiosity and eagerness for learning
- Can express self regarding wants and needs
- Engages in symbolic/imaginative play with self and peers

Language/ Expression

+

- Has enthusiasm for learning
- Recognizes letters of the alphabet and writes own name
- Identifies numbers 1–5
- "Reads" and interacts with books and other print materials
- Counts ten objects correctly
- Recognizes primary colors
- Recognizes primary shapes
- Follows one- to two-step directions

Academics = Ready for Kindergarten

+

- Works and plays cooperatively and well with peers
- Participates successfully in groups
- Gets along with and plays with peers and adults
- Is friendly and is able to make friends
- Shows empathy and caring for others

Interpersonal/ Social Skills

+

- Stays focused/pays attention during activities
- Controls impulses and self-regulates
- Can sit still and listen
- Is learning how to share
- Can take turns

Impulse Control

+

- Is physically healthy and has received required check-ups, immunization, and medical evaluations
- Can identify own feelings, self-regulate, and calm self
- Reasonably able to delay instant gratification
- Can accept comfort from adults

Physical and Emotional Health

+

- Demonstrates enthusiasm for learning
- Shows initiative and curiosity
- Engages in self-initiated/directed activities
- Demonstrates engagement and perseverance
- Shows some planning and reflection

Approaches to Learning

FIGURE 10.1 Building Blocks of Kindergarten Readiness

Source: Some of the readiness skills in Figure 10.1 are from the Kindergarten Observation Form, developed by Applied Survey Research. Used with permission.

playing field of preschool education and to ensure that all children learn essential knowledge, skills, and behaviors, all fifty states and the District of Columbia have identified Early Learning Guidelines (ELGs) to guide teachers and programs. For example, the Florida Voluntary Prekindergarten (VPK) Education Standards cover these areas:

- Physical Health
- Approaches to Learning
- Social and Emotional Development
- Language and Communication
- Emergent Literacy
- Mathematical and Scientific Thinking
- Social Studies and the Arts
- Motor Development[23]

You must be very familiar with your state's ELGs and use them as you plan and teach. Consider the readiness skills of language and social expression, which we discussed earlier, and independence, impulse control, interpersonal skills, experiential background, motor skills, academics, approaches to learning, and physical and mental health. All are important and necessary for a successful school experience. Even with individual states identifying important readiness skills, the level of preparedness varies dramatically from child to child, particularly children who are from diverse backgrounds. Some of this unevenness of preparedness may be based on the way the cultural background views the skill (as more or less important) or may be based on the (perhaps limited) capabilities of the child due to a disability or delay. Figure 10.1 shows important factors for kindergarten readiness. These are some of the things children should know and be able to do before they enter kindergarten.

Independence.   Independence means the ability to work alone on a task, take care of oneself, and initiate projects without always being told what to do. Independence also includes mastery of self-help skills, including, but not limited to, dressing skills, health skills (toileting, hand washing, using a tissue, and brushing teeth), and eating skills (using utensils and napkins, serving oneself, and cleaning up).

Impulse Control.   **Impulse control**, or the ability to resist or moderate one's immediate reactions, urges, and desires, relates to self-regulation, which we discussed earlier. Controlling impulses includes working cooperatively with others; not hitting other children or interfering with their work; developing an attention span that permits involvement in learning activities for a reasonable length of time; and being able to stay seated for a while. Children who are not able to control their impulses are frequently labeled hyperactive or learning disabled.

impulse control See self-regulation.

Interpersonal Skills.   Interpersonal skills include getting along and working with peers, teachers, and other adults. Asked why they want their children to attend preschool, parents frequently respond, "to learn how to get along with others." One interpersonal skill children are encouraged to develop is "sharing with others." Every preschool program is an experience of participating in a community of learners in which children have the opportunity to interact with others to become successful in a group setting. Interpersonal skills include working cooperatively with others, learning and using basic manners, and, most important, learning how to learn from and with others. Collaboration is a valuable skill and asset.

Experiential Background.   Experiential background is important to readiness because experiences are the building blocks of knowledge, the raw materials of cognitive development. Children must go places—the grocery store, the library, the zoo—and they must be involved in activities—creating things, painting, coloring, experimenting, and discovering. Children can build only on the background of information they bring to a new experience.

Varied experiences are the context in which children learn new words, and the number and kinds of words children know are major predictors of later school success. Again, the unevenness of experiences before and during children's preschool enrollment is a major contributor to the school preparedness gap.

Physical and Mental/Emotional Health.   Children must have good nutritional and physical habits that enable them to participate fully in and profit from any program. They must also have positive, nurturing environments and caring professionals to help them develop a self-image for achievement. Today, more attention than ever is paid to children's physical and mental health and nutrition. Likewise, the curriculum at all levels includes activities for promoting wellness and healthy living.

Increasingly, early childhood professionals are taking into account children's emotional development as an important factor in school readiness. A major reason for this new attention is that research clearly shows that young children with aggressive and disruptive behaviors are much less likely to do well in school.[24] Here are several ways you can support children's mental/emotional health:

- Observe children, listen to them, and note typical and atypical behavior.
- Use modeling, role play, and group discussion to help children learn appropriate behavior.
- Devote class time to instructing children how to identify and label feelings and how to appropriately communicate with others about emotions and how to resolve disputes with peers (e.g., using words instead of fists).
- Help parents gain the parenting skills they need to help their children. Surprisingly, increasing numbers of parents lack the parenting skills necessary for rearing children in the twenty-first century. Helping parents improves children's emotional and behavioral outcomes and enables families to provide sensitive, responsive care. In addition, good parenting techniques help curtail families' use of inconsistent and harsh discipline practices.

Dimensions of Readiness

Readiness for life and learning begins at birth and is affected and influenced by many factors. Here are some things to keep in mind about the many dimensions of readiness:

- *Readiness is never ending.*   Readiness is a continuum throughout life—the next life-event is always just ahead, and the experiences children have today prepare them for the experiences of tomorrow.
- *All children are always ready for some kind of learning.*   Children always need the experiences that promote learning and get them ready for the next step. The kind and quality of experiences children have—or don't have—influence their readiness for learning.
- *Schools and teachers are responsible for the education of each child.*   Today, teachers don't play the blame game. They recognize that readiness is the responsibility of all. Schools should get ready for children and offer a curriculum and climate that allow for a full range of learning.
- *Readiness is individualized.*   Three-, four-, and five-year-old children exhibit a range of abilities. Although all children are ready for learning, not all children are ready for learning the same thing at the same time, or in the same way.
- *Readiness is a function of culture.*   You have to be sensitive to the fact that different cultures have different values regarding the purpose of school, the process of schooling, children's roles in the schooling process, and the roles of the family and culture in promoting readiness.

- *Readiness is a function of family income, maternal education, and parenting practices.*[25] Helping families get their children ready for school is as important as getting the children themselves ready for school.
- *Readiness involves the whole child*—physical well-being, positive social and emotional development, language development, cognitive development, and enthusiasm for learning.

Approaches to Learning. **Approaches to learning** are the inclinations, dispositions, and learning styles necessary to interact effectively with the learning environment. Children will need to utilize approaches to learning if they are to be ready to move on to kindergarten.

> Four-year-old Louis is hard at work completing a puzzle. The puzzle, given to him by his teacher, is a little harder than the ones he has worked on before. He picks up a puzzle piece and looks at the puzzle, trying to decide where it might go. He tries it one way. It doesn't fit. He turns it around and tries again. Success! He has been working at the puzzle for a long time. His teacher comments, "Louis, you worked so hard to finish that puzzle."[26]

Louis demonstrated that he has certain dispositions that will serve him well when he enters kindergarten. He's able to persist with a task, try something different when what he first tried did not work, and has the self-control necessary to pay attention. These dispositions are part of approaches to learning. Approaches to learning include:

1. **Curiosity/initiative.** The child chooses to engage and participate in a variety of new and challenging activities.
2. **Persistence.** The child is able to persist in and complete a variety of tasks and activities.
3. **Attention.** The child demonstrates increased attentiveness during teacher-directed activities.
4. **Self-direction.** The child is able to set goals, make choices, and manage time and effort with increased independence.
5. **Problem solving.** The child is able to solve problems in a number of ways, including finding more than one solution, exploration, and interactions with peers.
6. **Creativity.** The child is able to approach tasks with increased flexibility, imagination, and inventiveness.[27]

approaches to learning
How children react to and engage in learning and activities associated with school.

Play and Preschool Children

Montessori thought of play as children's work and the home and preschool as workplaces where learning occurs through play. This comparison conveys the total absorption, dedication, energy, and focus children demonstrate through their play activities. They engage in play naturally and enjoy it; they do not select play activities because they intentionally set out to learn. They do not choose to put blocks in order from small to large because they want to learn how to seriate, nor do they build an incline because they want to learn the concept of *down* or the principles of gravity. However, the learning outcomes of such play are obvious.

Children's play is full of opportunities for learning, but there is no guarantee that children will learn through play all they need to know when they need to know it. Providing opportunities for children to choose among well-planned, varied learning activities enhances the probability that they will learn what they need to know through play.

Montessori said that play is children's work. The children in this picture are actively involved in building and constructing. Why is this type of activity an important part of the play process? What are some concepts these children are learning?

Purposes of Play

Children learn many things through play. Play activities are essential for their development across all developmental domains—the physical, social-emotional, cognitive, and linguistic. Play enables children to accomplish many things:

- Develop social skills
- Develop physical skills
- Develop literacy skills
- Practice language processes
- Enhance self-esteem
- Achieve knowledge, skills, and behaviors
- Learn concepts
- Prepare for adult life and roles (e.g., learn how to become independent, make decisions, and cooperate/collaborate with others)
- Master life situations

Value of Play: Literacy

Early childhood educators have long recognized the value of play for social, emotional, and physical development. Recently, however, play has achieved greater importance as a medium for literacy development. It is now recognized that literacy develops in meaningful, functional social settings rather than as a set of abstract skills taught in formal pencil-and-paper settings.

Enhancing Literacy.   Literacy development involves a child's active engagement in cooperation and collaboration with peers; it builds on what the child already knows. Play provides this setting. During observation of children at play, especially in free-choice, cooperative play periods, you can note the functional uses of literacy that children incorporate into their play themes. When the environment is appropriately prepared with literacy materials in play areas, children engage in reading and writing activities in collaboration with other children.

To demonstrate how play in an appropriate setting can nurture literacy development, consider the following classroom setting in which the teacher has designed a veterinarian's office to go along with a class study on animals, focusing in particular on pets.

The dramatic play area is designed with a waiting room, including chairs; a table filled with magazines, books, and pamphlets about pet care; posters about pets; office hour notices; a No Smoking sign; and a sign advising visitors to check in with the nurse when arriving. On the nurse's desk are patient forms on clipboards, a telephone, an address and telephone book, appointment cards, and a calendar. The office contains patient folders, prescription pads, white coats, masks, gloves, a toy doctor's kit, and stuffed animals for patients.

Scaffolding Literacy Activities.   The teacher, Betty Meyers, guides students in using the various materials in the veterinarian's office during free-play time. For example, she reminds the children to read important information they find in the waiting area, to fill out forms about their pets' needs, to ask the nurse for appointment times, or to have the doctor write out appropriate treatments or prescriptions. In addition to giving support, Betty also models behaviors by participating in the play center with the children when she first introduces materials.

Materials and Settings.   When selecting settings to promote literacy in play, choose those that are familiar to children and relate them to themes. Suggestions for literacy materials and settings for the dramatic play areas include the following:

- A fast-food restaurant, ice cream store, or bakery includes menus, order pads, a cash register, specials for the day, recipes, and lists of flavors or products.
- A supermarket or local grocery store can include labeled shelves and sections, food containers, pricing labels, cash registers, telephones, shopping receipts, checkbooks, coupons, and promotional flyers.
- A post office to mail children's letters needs paper, envelopes, address books, pens, pencils, stamps, cash registers, and labeled mailboxes. A mail carrier hat and bag are important for children who deliver the mail, and they need to identify and read names and addresses.
- A gas station and car repair shop, designed in the block area, can have toy cars and trucks, receipts for sales, road maps for help with directions to different destinations, automotive tools and auto repair manuals for fixing cars and trucks, posters that advertise automobile equipment, and empty cans of different products typically found in service stations.[28]

Kinds of Play

Children engage in many kinds of play: social, cognitive, informal, sociodramatic, outdoor, and rough-and-tumble.

Social Play.   Much of children's play occurs with or in the presence of other children. **Social play** occurs when children play with each other in groups. Mildred Parten, a children's play researcher, developed the most comprehensive description and classification of the types of social play. These are:

social play Play of children with others and in groups.

- *Unoccupied play:*   The child does not play with anything or anyone; the child merely stands or sits without doing anything observable.
- *Solitary play:*   Although involved in play, the child plays alone, seemingly unaware of other children.
- *Onlooker play:*   The child watches and observes the play of other children; the center of interest is others' play.
- *Parallel play:*   The child plays alone, but in ways and with toys or other materials similar to the play of other children.
- *Associative play:*   Children interact with each other, perhaps by asking questions or sharing materials, but do not play together.
- *Cooperative play:*   Children actively play together often as a result of the organization of the teacher.[29]

Social play supports many important functions. It provides the means for children to interact with others and learn many social skills. Play provides a context in which children learn how to compromise ("OK, I'll be the baby first, and you can be the mommy"), learn to be flexible, resolve conflicts, and continue the process of learning who they are. Children also learn what skills they have, such as those relating to leadership. In addition, social play provides a vehicle for practicing and developing literacy skills; children have others with whom to practice language and learn. And social play helps children learn impulse control; they realize they cannot always do whatever they want. Finally, social play negates isolation and helps children learn how to have the social interactions so vital to successful living.

Cognitive Play.   Froebel, Montessori, and Piaget all recognized the cognitive value of play. Froebel through his gifts and occupations and Montessori through her sensory materials saw children's active participation with concrete materials as a direct link to knowledge and development. Piaget's theory influences contemporary thinking about the cognitive basis for play; from a Piagetian perspective, play is literally cognitive development.

informal (free) play Play in which children play in activities of interest to them.

Informal Play. Proponents of learning through **informal play**, or **free play**, activities maintain that learning is best when it occurs spontaneously in an environment that contains people and materials with which children can interact. Learning materials may be grouped in centers—a kitchen center, a dress-up center, a block center, a music and art center, a water or sand area, and an outdoor climbing area—usually with items such as tricycles and wagons that are good for promoting large-muscle development.

The atmosphere of this kind of preschool setting tends to approximate a home setting, in which learning is informal, unstructured, and unpressured. Talk and interactions with adults are spontaneous. Play and learning episodes are generally determined by the interests of the children and, to some extent, teachers, based on what they think is best for children. The expected learning outcomes are socialization, emotional development, self-control, and acclimation to a school setting.

In a quality program of free play both indoors and outdoors, teachers are active participants. Sometimes they observe, sometimes they play with the children, sometimes they help the children, but they never intrude or impose. When well managed, the free-play format enables children to learn many things as they interact with interesting activities, materials, and people in their environment.

sociodramatic play Play involving realistic activities and events.

fantasy play Play involving unrealistic notions and superheroes.

Dramatic Play. Dramatic, or pretend, play allows children to participate vicariously in a wide range of activities associated with family living, society, and cultural heritage. Dramatic play is generally of two kinds: **Sociodramatic play** usually involves everyday realistic activities and events, whereas **fantasy play** typically involves fairy-tale and superhero play. Dramatic play centers often include areas such as housekeeping, dress-up, occupations, dolls, school, and other situations that follow children's interests. Skillful teachers think of many ways to expand children's interests and then replace old centers with new ones. For example, after a visit to the police station, a housekeeping center might be replaced with an occupations center.

In sociodramatic play, children have an opportunity to express themselves, assume different roles, and interact with their peers. Sociodramatic play centers thus act as a nonsexist and multicultural arena in which all children are equal.

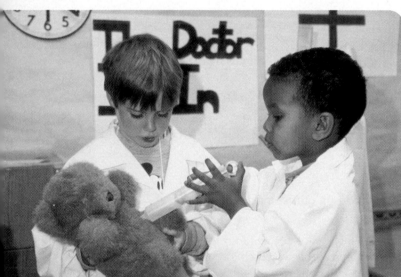

Dramatic play promotes children's understanding of concepts and processes. Here, play allows children to explore their feelings and ideas about medical practitioners and medical settings.

Outdoor Play. Children's outside play is just as important as their inside play. Children need to relieve stress and tension through play, and outdoor activities provide this opportunity. However, plan for what children will do and what equipment will be available; outdoor play is not an opportunity for children to run wild.

Children at the Grove School planted over twenty different types of vegetable and herb seeds in the planting beds. Rain barrel water and compost and worm bin fertilizer help children nurture a healthy harvest ready for sampling and donating! The outdoor play area also includes turf grass, shaded areas, a greenhouse, and an outdoor classroom sand pit with water.[30]

Outdoor environments and activities promote large- and small-muscle development and body coordination as well as language development, social interaction, and creativity for all children. Plan to make your playground a learning environment.

Many teachers also enjoy bringing the indoor learning environment outdoors, using easels, play dough, or dramatic play props to further enhance learning opportunities. In addition, taking a group of children outdoors for story or music time, sitting in the shade of a tree, brings a fresh perspective to daily group activities. As with indoor activities, provisions for outdoor play involve planning, supervising, and helping children be responsible for their behavior.

Adapting Outdoor Play for Children with Disabilities. Here are some ways you can adapt your outdoor space to accommodate children with disabilities.

- Position a child with physical challenges to achieve maximum range of motion, muscle control and visual contact with materials and other children. A child might need to lie on his or her side or use a bolster to access materials and interact with other children during activities such as gardening and painting.
- Furnish specifically adapted play and recreation equipment when necessary. This might include modified swings, tricycles, and tables to accommodate independent participation in activities.
- Encourage the children to use their own means of getting around—whether a wheelchair, walker, or scooter—to participate in the activities and games of other children.
- For a child with limited use of hands and upper body, provide activities for the lower body and feet, such as foot painting, splashing in a wading pool, digging in the garden or sand, and kicking a ball.
- For a child with limited use of feet, legs, and lower body, provide activities such as painting, water table, sandbox, and gardening, which the child can do independently and successfully with the upper body. Always ensure correct positioning of the child's torso.
- Increase the width of balance beams and modify slippery surfaces to support better balance.
- Use softer balls (e.g., foam balls) or lightweight objects to facilitate throwing and catching when a child lacks strength or endurance.
- Use large balls (e.g., beach balls) and other large objects to make catching easier for a child who is unable to grasp smaller objects.[31]

Rough-and-Tumble Play. All children, to a greater or lesser degree, engage in rough-and-tumble play. One theory says that children play because they are biologically programmed to do so; that is, it is part of children's genetic heritage to engage in play activities. Indeed, there is a parallel between children's rough-and-tumble play and behaviors in the animal kingdom—for example, run-and-chase activities and pretend fighting. Rough-and-tumble play activities enable children to learn how to lead and follow, develop physical skills, interact with other children in different ways, and grow in their abilities to be part of a larger group.

Teachers' Roles in Promoting Play

You are the key to promoting meaningful play in early childhood programs. What you do and your attitudes toward play determine the quality of the preschool environment and play events. For example, the accompanying Voice from the Field, "Using Blocks to Help Preschoolers Build Mathematical Skills," demonstrates how you can use block play to help children meet preschool math standards.

Voice from the Field

Using Blocks to Help Preschoolers Build Mathematical Skills

Froebel, the father of kindergarten, introduced blocks to the early childhood curriculum with his creation of gifts. Froebel created these gifts to facilitate children's creativity and provide opportunities for them to construct geometric forms. Enabling children to explore and experiment with blocks provides them with several opportunities to develop the foundation for mathematical concepts related to algebra, geometry, and measurement.

When reflecting on how to create opportunities for children to use blocks, consider the following ideas prior to using these materials.

1. Develop a Variety of Learning Opportunities for Children to Use Blocks

Offer young children different types of learning opportunities to use blocks that will foster their development of mathematical concepts.

- Give children time to explore freely with blocks during center time or other times in the day. Providing opportunities for free play allows children to develop various intuitive geometric concepts and problem-solving skills.

- Informally guide children during these experiences to help them connect prior learning experiences or deepen their understanding of a concept. Ask children questions to provoke mathematical conversations. For example, when a child sorts blocks into different groups, ask the child about these groupings with questions such as:
  - Why did you put these blocks together?
  - What other blocks could you put into this group?
- Use the blocks in the classroom to introduce or review mathematical concepts such as counting or identifying various shapes.

2. Provide Children with a Variety of Different Types of Blocks to Explore

Incorporate a variety of manipulatives—including different types of blocks—for young children to use in your preschool classroom. Providing these materials will allow children to explore mathematical concepts such as sorting, patterns, measurement, and geometry. The accompanying table lists some of the common types of blocks used in preschool classrooms and some of the possible mathematical concepts children might develop when using these materials.

Type of Block	Mathematical Concepts	Examples
Building/architect blocks	Patterns, sorting, geometry, measurement, spatial relationships, counting	Children will build various structures with these materials. Consider playing an "I Spy" type of game where children find different shapes in their creations.
Pattern blocks	Patterns, sorting, geometry, measurement, spatial relationships, counting	Children can practice creating patterns with these blocks or creating "new" shapes.
Snap cubes	Patterns, sorting, measurement, counting	Children can use blocks to determine the length/width of various objects in the room.

Type of Block	Mathematical Concepts	Examples
Color tiles	Patterns, sorting, measurement, counting	Children might use these blocks to measure objects in the classroom or to start thinking about how many color tiles might cover a certain object in the classroom (area).
Tangrams	Patterns, sorting, geometry, measurement, spatial relationships, counting	Provide children with opportunities to create "new" shapes with tangrams. Children can trace the perimeter of these designs and have friends try to create their new shapes.
Three-dimensional geometric models	Patterns, sorting, geometry, measurement, counting	These solids not only provide examples of various three-dimensional shapes, but also allow children different types of materials to sort.
Color cubes	Patterns, sorting, measurement, counting	Children can use these cubes to start understanding the concept of capacity. For instance, have children explore how many cubes different objects in the classroom can hold.
Attribute blocks	Patterns, sorting, geometry, measurement, counting	Children can practice sorting these blocks into various groups. Allow children to develop groups and labels instead of telling them to sort by color or by shape. Children will develop groupings that are more interesting with this flexibility.

(continued)

3. Ask Children a Variety of Questions

It is important for you to ask students thought-provoking questions that will allow them to explore a variety of mathematical concepts. Asking children questions about their block structures not only provides them with the opportunity to engage in mathematical conversations about their work, but also gives you the occasion to explore children's mathematical knowledge. For example, if a preschooler made a pattern like this with pattern blocks, you might ask the following questions:

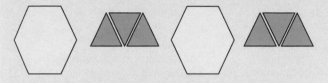

- Tell me about your creation. What did you make? (Give the child an opportunity to use her words to describe the blocks.)
- What type of pattern did you make?
- If I wanted to add to your pattern, what blocks would I have to use?
- Is there a block that looks the same as the three green triangles?

As you ask these questions, encourage children to use their own words to describe their work. Also, verify your understanding of the child's descriptions. For example:

Ms. Jones: What type of pattern did you make?
Alicia: We used one yellow block and then three green blocks.
Ms. Jones: So you used one yellow hexagon and three green triangles, and then another yellow hexagon and three green triangles?
Mason and Alicia: Yes.

Providing children with opportunities to explore and construct with blocks helps lay the foundation for future mathematical success. These experiences not only allow children to deepen their understanding of algebra, geometry, and measurement, but they also offer children opportunities to practice their problem-solving skills. In addition, children will engage in meaningful mathematical conversations with their peers and their teacher.

Source: Contributed by Elisabeth Johnston, doctoral candidate at the University of North Texas. Her current research relates to young children's mathematical development. Elisabeth taught second grade at a gifted and talented magnet school for six years in Texas, where she was responsible for teaching math to a diverse range of second graders. Photos: iStockphoto.com, p. 278 (second from top, bottom); David Mager/Pearson Learning Photo Studio, p. 279 (second from top); Tom Ridley © Dorling Kindersley, p. 279 (third from top); Stockxpert/Jupiter Unlimited, p. 278 (top), p. 279 (second from bottom, bottom); Lori Whitley/Merrill, p. 279 (top).

As far as possible, implement the curriculum through play. Integrate specific learning activities with play to achieve specific learning outcomes. Play activities should match children's developmental needs and be free of gender and cultural stereotypes. Be clear about curriculum concepts and ideas you want children to learn through play.

Providing a safe and healthy environment is an important role that applies to the playground as well as to inside facilities. Outdoor areas should be safe for children to play in. Usually, states and cities have regulations requiring a playground to be fenced and have a source of drinking water, a minimum number of square feet of play area for each child, and equipment that is in good repair. Careful child supervision is a cornerstone of playground safety.

Play is an important part of children's lives and the early childhood curriculum. You and others need to honor, support, and provide many opportunities for children to play.

The New Preschool Curriculum: Guidelines and Goals

guidelines (standards)
Preschool statements of what children should know and be able to do.

Increasingly, the responsibility for setting the preschool curriculum is being taken over by state departments of education through **guidelines** (or **standards**) statements of what students should know and be able to do. Typically preschool standards are called guidelines because states do not require preschool attendance. Now would be a good time to access your state's preschool guidelines. Keep these in mind as you prepare preschool curricula and lesson plans. The Voice from the Field "Planning and Teaching: Lesson Plans for Preschoolers" on pages 282–283 is a Competency Builder. Read how Shannon Keller uses her state's Preschool Guidelines to plan for her preschoolers.

Preschool Goals

As preschool programs have grown in number and popularity over the last decade, they have also changed in purpose. Traditional purposes of preschool are to socialize children; enhance their social-emotional development; and prepare them for kindergarten and first grade. A second purpose of preschools is to teach basic academic skills related to literacy, math, and science. In addition, preschools are now promoted as places to accomplish numerous goals:

- *Support and develop children's innate capacity for learning.*   Preschool programs seek to develop in children an interest in and love of learning as early in life as possible. Brain research clearly shows that birth to age five is a critical time for learning.[32]
- *Deliver a full range of health, social, economic, and academic services to children and families.*   Indeed, family well-being is considered a justification for operating preschools; in fact, increasingly, preschool education is seen as a family affair.
- *Closing achievement gaps.*   Closing the *achievement gap* that exists between white and African American and Hispanic students is a high priority for America and the early childhood profession. In fact, the achievement gap may be a *preparation gap*. Many children enter kindergarten without the skills they need—from identifying colors to not being able to sit still. They have a hard time playing the game of catch-up.[33]
- *Educate children for the global world of tomorrow.*   The United States wants to continue to be a world leader. A well-educated workforce helps achieve this goal and the preparation of a well-educated workforce begins in preschool.[34]

Given the popularity of and reasons for preschools, it is little wonder that the preschool years are playing a larger role in early childhood education and will continue to do so.

Appropriate Preschool Goals

All programs should have goals to guide activities and to provide a base for teaching methodologies. Without goals it is easy to end up teaching just about anything. The goals of preschools vary by state and individual programs. Your state preschool guidelines are the starting place for preschool goals. Here are essential goals that apply to all preschool programs.

Social and Interpersonal Skills.   Human beings are social, and much of students' learning involves social interactions such as:

- Getting along with other children and adults and developing good relationships with teachers
- Helping others and developing caring attitudes
- Playing and working cooperatively
- Following classroom rules

Self-Help and Intrapersonal Skills.   Children must learn how to manage their behavior and their affairs:

- Taking care of personal needs, such as dressing (e.g., tying, buttoning, zipping) and knowing what clothes to wear
- Eating skills (e.g., using utensils, napkins, and a cup or glass; setting a table)
- Health skills (e.g., how to wash and bathe, how to brush one's teeth)
- Grooming skills (e.g., combing hair, cleaning nails)

Voice from the Field

Planning and Teaching: Lesson Plans for Preschoolers

Planning for teaching is a lot like planning for a trip: there are certain essential steps you should follow if you want children to learn new things and for them and you to have a good time!

- Identifying goals and objectives for teaching and learning is like identifying your destination (e.g., New York City).
- Selecting the methods you will use is like deciding how you are going to get to New York—by car, bus, train, or plane.
- Selecting the materials you will need is similar to selecting what you will need on your trip—clothing, suitcase, tickets, maps.
- Selecting specific activities is like selecting what you will do when you get to New York—walk in Central Park, visit Chinatown, zip to the top of the Empire State Building.
- Evaluation and assessment come into play after you have taught your lesson, just as you would assess whether you had a good time on your trip.

Here are four steps to follow:

STEP 1 Identify the Goals and Objectives of Your Lesson

You may find goals and objectives already selected for you in state or local standards.

Your lesson will need to address all of the goals in an integrated way. Remember, however, that although state standards set goals, you have the creativity to teach your way using your professional knowledge, talents, and abilities.

STEP 2 Select the Materials You Will Need

Compile a list of materials that you will need to execute the activity. Are the materials safe and developmentally appropriate?

STEP 3 Select Activities and Adapt Them for Individual Needs

As you develop activities, keep in mind children's prior knowledge, their cultural backgrounds, and their individual and collective interests, and use them as a basis for your activities.

STEP 4 Assessment/Evaluation

Determine how you will assess what your children learned. Relate your assessment to the standards and your lesson plan objectives. Here is how Shannon Keller plans for her preschool children. Notice how Shannon achieves the four steps discussed above.

It all "Quacks" up
(2- to 3-day lesson on addition)

Teach to your state's standards

- **IDENTIFY GOALS AND OBJECTIVES**

  2008 Texas Prekindergarten Guidelines V.A. 8: Child uses concrete models or makes verbal word problems for adding up to five objects

  Focus:
  The teacher will model for students how to join objects together. The students will then practice joining (adding) objects together and create their own verbal word problem regarding addition by stating "2 ducks and 1 more duck makes 3 ducks."

Academics. As academics play a more central role in preschool curriculum, some key areas of knowledge include these:

- Names, addresses, and phone numbers (including their own)
- Colors, sizes, shapes, and positions such as *under*, *over*, and *around*
- Numbers and prewriting skills, shape identification, letter recognition, sounds, and rhyming
- Simple sentence structure
- Simple addition and subtraction
- Ways to handle a book[35]

- **SELECT THE MATERIALS YOU WILL NEED**

  Materials:

  - *Little Quack* by Lauren Thompson (published by Simon & Schuster)
  - 5 rubber ducks
  - 5 duck erasers (counters) for each pair of students
  - 1 pond story mat (1/2 sheet of blue construction paper) for each pair of students

Use concrete materials to facilitate learning

- **SELECT THE ACTIVITIES AND ADAPT THEM FOR INDIVIDUAL NEEDS**

  Vocabulary:

  join—to put objects together
  adding—joining quantities

  Activity:

  The teacher will share the story *Little Quack* with students. After reading the story the teacher chooses five students to help her retell the story and to model how to join objects together using rubber ducks. The teacher groups students into pairs. The teacher will give each student pair a pond story mat and five duck counters. The teacher retells the story of *Little Quack* while students act the story out on the pond story mat. The teacher checks for understanding and knowledge using the questions below. Student pairs will be encouraged to create a story problem for joining. Allow student pairs to share their problems and continue with questioning.

- **ASSESSMENT/EVALUATION**

  Quality Questions:

  Use Bloom's Taxonomy as a basis for questions

  - **Knowledge:** What kind of animal is Little Quack?
  - **Comprehension:** What happened to the ducks in the story?
  - **Application:** Did Little Quack and his brothers and sisters jump in the pond at the same time? Can you show how the ducks got in the pond?
  - **Analysis:** Why do you think the group of ducks in the pond grew bigger?
  - **Synthesis:** What would have happened to the number of ducks in the pond if Little Quack didn't join his brothers and sisters?
  - **Evaluation:** What did you like about this book and activity? Why?
  - **Evaluation Option**: Informally assess student's knowledge of joining objects together (addition) by having students illustrate the problem they created on a piece of paper. Look to see if students were able to draw a picture of two groups of objects and a picture of both groups joined into one large group. This form of evaluation allows the teacher the opportunity to see which students understand the concept of joining objects.

Source: Contributed by Shannon Keller, former preschool and kindergarten teacher at Curtsinger Elementary, Frisco, Texas. Shannon now teaches third grade.

Character Education.   Many schools and school districts identify, with parents' help, the character traits they want all students to demonstrate. Children need multiple opportunities to learn about and demonstrate character traits such as positive mental attitude, persistence, respect for others, cooperation, honesty, trustworthiness, and sensitivity.

Kim Gorka develops community-mindedness in her young children at Children's Palace Preschool and Childcare. "We do a different theme every week and in July we have volunteerism. Everyone brings in a wrapped gift for 'a friend we don't know,' and we give all the presents to New Horizons Shelter and Women's Center," Gorka said. "I just love that—it's one of the best things we do, teaching them the joys of not getting anything out of it except the feeling of being a good person."[36]

Music and the Arts.   Brain research supports the use of music and the arts to encourage learning in all areas. Preschoolers can learn about music and the arts in many ways:

- Varied materials (e.g., crayons, paint, clay, markers) to create original work
- Different colors, surface textures, and shapes to create form and meaning
- Art as a form of self-expression
- Music activities, including varieties of simple songs and movement to various tempos
- Dramatic play with others

For example, Love A Lot Preschool in New York City offers music and piano classes for their students. Music and movement classes for preschools provide an outlet for creative energy in which the children learn to read music through individual and group lessons and sing songs and finger plays.[37]

Wellness and Healthy Living.   When children are not healthy, they cannot achieve their best. Helping children learn healthy habits will help them do well in school. Healthy habits include the following:

- Good nutritional practices, including a balanced menu and essential nutrients
- Trying new foods
- Management of personal belongings such as keeping track of one's possessions
- Ability to dress oneself appropriately
- Personal hygiene, such as washing one's hands and wiping one's nose

For example, Nobel Learning Communities' preschools throughout the nation have implemented the "New Physical Education" early childhood program, which emphasizes physical activity, teaching good nutrition, reducing health risks, and introducing movement into the early stages of development. The "New PE" classes are more inclusive, active, and fun than traditional physical education programs and engage students through the use of energetic music, toys, and bright colors.[38]

Literacy in the Preschool

Emergent literacy means children's communication skills are in an emerging state—in the process of developing.[39] Teachers and parents can support emergent literacy in preschool children by not only reading to them, but also reading with them and encouraging their participation in the process of reading. One of the ways to support children's involvement is by supporting and encouraging their **modes of response**, the various ways they respond to learning, activities, and materials.

Elisabeth Epstein reads a book on seals to her children and then engages them in activities such as jumping like seals, pretend swimming, drawing pictures of seals, and comparing what seals eat to what other animals eat.

Emergent literacy also involves writing. Remember it was Montessori who said that writing comes before reading. For many children, writing becomes a pathway, a stepping stone, a scaffold for emerging into reading.

Language.   Language is the most important readiness skill. Children need language skills for success in both school and life. Important language skills include *receptive language*, such as listening to the teacher and following directions; *expressive language*,

---

emergent literacy
Children's communication skills are in an emerging state—in the process of developing.

modes of response The various ways children respond to books and conversations.

We want children to be involved in child-initiated and active learning. These children wanted to make pudding after the teacher read *Geronimo Stilton's Cookbook*. What are some things children can learn by making and eating pudding?

demonstrated in the ability to talk fluently and articulately with teachers and peers, to express oneself in the language of the school, and to communicate needs and ideas; and *symbolic language*, knowing the names of people, places, and things, as well as words for concepts and adjectives and prepositions. Knowledge of the letters of the alphabet and vocabulary are two of the most important factors in being able to read.[40] These crucial readiness skills are especially critical for children from linguistically diverse backgrounds and for children with disabilities or delays in speech and/or language.

Conventional Literacy Skills.   **Conventional literacy skills** refer to such skills as decoding (turning written words into spoken words), oral reading fluency, reading comprehension, writing, and spelling. The use of these skills is evident within all literacy practices, and they are readily recognizable as being necessary or useful components of literacy.[41]

Conventional reading and writing skills developed in the years from birth to age five have a clear and consistently strong relationship with later conventional literacy skills. Six variables have medium to large predictive relationships with later measures of literacy development.[42] These are:

- **Alphabetic knowledge (AK)**: Knowledge of the names and sounds associated with printed letters.
- **Phonological awareness (PA)**: The ability to detect, manipulate, or analyze the auditory aspects of spoken language (including the ability to distinguish or segment words, syllables, or phonemes), independent of meaning.
- **Rapid automatic naming (RAN) of letters or digits**: The ability to rapidly name a sequence of random letters or digits.
- **Rapid automatic naming (RAN) of objects or colors**: The ability to rapidly name a sequence of repeating random sets of pictures of objects (e.g., "car," "tree," "house," "man") or colors.
- **Writing or writing name**: The ability to write letters in isolation on request or to write one's own name.
- **Phonological memory (PM)**: The ability to remember spoken information for a short period of time.[43]

An additional five early literacy skills are also important and show a moderate relation to later literacy success. These include:[44]

- Concepts about print: knowledge of print conventions (e.g., left-right, front-back) and concepts (book cover, author, text)
- Print knowledge: a combination of elements of AK, concepts about print, and early decoding
- Reading readiness: usually a combination of AK, concepts of print, vocabulary, memory, and PA
- Oral language: the ability to produce or comprehend spoken language, including vocabulary and grammar
- Visual processing: the ability to match or discriminate visually presented symbols.

Supporting English Language Learners' Language and Literacy Skills.   Greater numbers of children of immigrants are entering preschools today. Here are some things you can do to support English Language Learners (ELLs) in five important literacy domains. As you review these activities, consider how you can apply them to your classroom teaching.

   Alphabet Knowledge: *Activities that target letter recognition*: Comparing alphabets or writing systems in other languages
   - Take an alphabet walk around the school, and look for letters in the environment.
   - Place children in groups of four or five, and have them use their bodies to form letters.

conventional literacy skills Skills such as decoding (turning written words into spoken words), oral reading fluency, reading comprehension, writing, and spelling.

alphabetic knowledge (AK) Knowledge of the names and sounds associated with printed letters.

phonological awareness (PA) The ability to detect, manipulate, or analyze the auditory aspects of spoken language (including the ability to distinguish or segment words, syllables, or phonemes), independent of meaning.

rapid automatic naming (RAN) of letters or digits The ability to rapidly name a sequence of random letters or digits.

rapid automatic naming (RAN) of objects or colors The ability to rapidly name a sequence of repeating random sets of pictures or objects (e.g., "car," "tree," "house," "man") or colors.

writing or writing name The ability to write letters in isolation on request or to write one's own name.

phonological memory (PM) The ability to remember spoken information for a short period of time.

- Divide the class in half, and give one half lowercase letter cards and the other half matching uppercase cards. Have the children find their matches.
- Teach Spanish-speaking students a song of the English alphabet.[45]

Phonological Awareness: *Activities that emphasize the sounds that make up words:* Presenting the sounds of other languages to make words
- Word-to-word matching: Do *pen* and *pipe* begin with the same sound?
- Sound isolation: What is the first sound in *rose?*
- Odd word out: Which word starts with a different sound—*bag, nine, beach, bike?*[46]

book and print concepts Activities that show how books look and how they work.

Book and Print Concepts: *Activities that show how books look and how they work:* Show how books have covers and front and back pages. Show that words make up letters.
- Leave multiple pieces of familiar text posted in the room at children's eye level, available for them to be read independently.
- Use magnetic letters, word tiles, and name cards to emphasize similarities and differences between words and letters.[47]

vocabulary knowledge Activities that emphasize words and their meanings.

Vocabulary Knowledge: *Activities that emphasize words and their meaning:* Emphasizing that there are words in other languages that mean the same things as words in English
- Give each student a card with one word on it, and have them form two circles, one inside the other. When the teacher calls out "inside" or "outside," the students in that circle show their cards to the students in front of or behind them, who must come up with the definitions. The circles then rotate to make new partners.[48]

discourse skills Activities that encourage telling stories and explaining how the world works.

Discourse Skills: *Activities that encourage telling stories, explaining how the world works, building a fantasy world using English:* Demonstrating that other languages have similar forms although they may seem a bit different
- Discuss the storyline of short DVDs, and point out characters, scenes, and time changes; review the story periodically.
- Play guessing games like I Spy, and have students give specific clues about a hidden object or picture.[49]

The Daily Schedule

What should a preschool day be like? Although a daily schedule depends on many things—your philosophy, the needs of children, parents' beliefs, and state and local standards—the following suggestions illustrate what you can do on a typical preschool day. Because an important preschool trend is toward full-day and full-year programs, this preschool schedule is for a whole-day program as shown in Figure 10.2.

Opening Activities. As children enter, greet each individually. Daily personal greetings make children feel important, build a positive attitude toward school, and provide an opportunity for them to practice language skills. Greetings also give you a chance to check each child's health and emotional status. Greeting time is a nice opportunity to incorporate "greetings from around the world," which could reflect the diversity of children and families in the program.

Children usually do not arrive all at one time, so the first arrivals need something to do while others are arriving:

- Offer free selection of activities or let children self-select from a limited range of quiet activities (such as puzzles, journals to write in, or markers to color with).

Schedule

Time	Activity	Notes
8:00	Opening Activities	Peg boards, puzzles, coloring, reading, journal writing, etc.
8:45	Group Meeting	Circle time, group singing, planning, sharing, announcements, etc.
9:30	Learning Centers	Reading center, math center, science center, civics center, history center, etc.
10:30	Bathroom/ Wash Hands	Self-help skills, toileting, hand washing, etc.
10:45	Snack	Nutritious, encourages independence (i.e., self-serving, self-prepared, etc.)
11:15	Outside Time	Climbing, jumping, swinging, throwing, kicking, pretending, etc.
12:00	Bathroom	Teach health, self-help, and intrapersonal skills, but children can use restroom at any time
12:15	Lunch Time	Meal served family style: teachers and children eat together. Use time to relax, build relationships, engage in conversation, etc.
1:00	Relaxation and / or Nap Time	Rest, quiet time, coloring, listening to music on headphones, self-soothing and relaxation techniques, breathing exercises, teacher-read story time, read to self, etc.
2:45	Centers/ Projects	Art activities, drama activities, music activities, cooking, project approach (see Ch. 5) holiday activities, work projects, collecting activities, field trips, etc.
3:15	Group Time	Listening and attention skills, discuss the day, discuss learning, evaluate performance and behavior, etc.
3:30	Good-Bye Time	Classroom clean up, self-directed activities as parents arrive (i.e., coloring, reading, etc.)
4:00	Close	

FIGURE 10.2 Sample of a Daily Schedule

- Organize arrival time by having children use an assignment board to help them make choices. Limit the available choices, and have children practice concepts such as colors and shapes and recognition of their names. Stand beside the assignment board when children come, and tell each child what the choices are.
- Hand children their name tags and help them put them on the board. Later, children can find their own tags and put them up. Include each child's picture on the name tag.

Morning Meeting/Planning.   After all children have arrived, plan together and talk about the day ahead, helping children think about what they plan to learn during the day. This is also the time for announcements, sharing, and group songs. Songs from other languages and cultures can easily be incorporated here. Songs using sign language can be incorporated for children with hearing impairments.

Learning Centers.   After the group time, children are free to go to one of various learning centers, organized and designed to teach concepts. Table 10.2 lists types of learning centers you can use and the concepts each is intended to teach. Learning centers should include items that are culturally relevant and reflective of a diversity of cultures.

TABLE 10.2 Types of Classroom Learning Centers

Theme-Based Centers	Concepts
Use theme centers as an extension of classroom themes: • Space • Dinosaurs • The Ocean • All About Me • My Family Generally a classroom theme lasts for one to two weeks and occasionally longer. Children can use theme centers for varying amounts of time from fifteen to thirty minutes and during their free time.	• Use language skills, participate in sociodramatic play, and verbalize. • Identify role(s) as a family member. • Cooperate with others in joint activities. • Learn how to cooperate and practice good habits of daily living such as sharing, taking turns, and following rules.

Subject Centers	Concepts
• *Literacy/Language:* Be sure to change books frequently. Add ten new books every two to three weeks. The goal is to have preschoolers familiar with at least 100 books. Also include books from all genres: picture books, fiction, science, and so on.	• Verbalize; listen; understand directions; how to use books; colors, size, shapes, and names; print and book knowledge; vocabulary development; print awareness.
• *Writing:* Provide various and plentiful materials for writing: paper, blank books, folded paper, envelopes, markers, pencils, and so forth. Every center should have materials for writing.	• Learn alphabet, word knowledge, that words have meaning, that words make sentences, and so forth. • Learn that writing has many useful purposes, and that written words convey meaning.
• *Math:* Provide plastic number tiles, math cards, pegboards. There should be many concrete materials to promote hands-on experiences. The math center should also have picture books about math and stories involving math.	• Understand meanings of whole numbers. • Recognize the number of objects in small groups without counting and by counting. • Understand that number words refer to quantity. • Use one-to-one correspondence to solve problems by matching sets and comparing number amounts and in counting objects to ten and beyond. • Understand that the last word stated in counting tells "how many." Count to determine number amounts and compare quantities (using language such as "more than" and "less than"). • Order sets by the number of objects in them. • Find shapes in the environment and describe them. • Build pictures and designs by combining two- and three-dimensional shapes. • Solve problems such as deciding which piece will fit into a space in a puzzle. • Discuss the relative positions of objects with vocabulary such as "above," "below," and "next to." • Identify objects as "the same" or "different," and "more" or "less," on the basis of attributes that can be measured. • Measure attributes such as length and weight. Make comparisons of objects based on length, weight, etc.

(continued)

TABLE 10.2 Types of Classroom Learning Centers (*Continued*)

Subject Centers	Concepts
• *Science:* Provide books on science; provide materials for observing, for discovering relationships, and for learning about nature, plants, animals, and the environment.	• Develop skills in observation, size, shape, color, whole/part, figure/ground, spatial relations, classifying, graphing, problem-solving skills. • Learn how to observe, make comparisons, classify, and problem-solve. • Investigate and explore.
• *Life Science:* Provide various plants and animals, terrariums, and habitats.	• Understand plant and animal care and habitats.
• *Art/Music/Creative Expression:* Provide materials for painting, coloring, drawing, cutting, pasting. Engage children in activities involving singing and movement. Provide puppets and puppet theater to encourage dramatic and creative expression.	• Listen to a wide range of musical styles. • Learn color relationships and combinations. • Engage in creative expression, aesthetic appreciation, satisfaction. • Create representations of homes and places in the community. • Participate in group singing, finger-plays, and rhythm.

Activity Centers	Concepts
• *Construction/Blocks:* Provide a variety of different kinds of blocks.	• Describe size, shape, length, seriation, spatial relationships. • Develop problem-solving skills.
• *Woodworking:* Make real tools and building materials available. Be sure to provide goggles and other precautions for children's safety.	• Learn to follow directions; learn how to use real tools; learn about planning and the construction process. • Discover whole/part relationships.
• *Dramatic Play:* Provide various materials and props for home activities, including a child-size stove, table, chairs, refrigerator, sink, etc. Provide clothing, hats, and shoes, as well as outfits and props from many occupations such as nurse/doctor, firefighter, construction worker.	• Learn language skills, sociodramatic play, functions, processes, social skills. • Engage in pretend and imaginary play. • Learn roles and responsibilities of community workers.
• *Water/Sand Play*	• Learn what floats; investigate capacity; compare volume. • Develop social skills and responsibility (i.e., cleanup).

Technology Centers	Concepts
• *Computer/Technology:* Provide computers, printer, scanner, digital camera, video camera. A computer center can have one or more workstations or can have one or more laptops or handheld devices.	• Learn socialization, keyboarding, how technology can solve problems. • Learn basic technology skills. • Write (using e-mail, word processing). • Use technology to learn basic math and language skills. • Use technology to play games.

Bathroom/Hand Washing.   Before any activity in which food is handled, prepared, or eaten, children should wash and dry their hands. Instructing children in proper hand washing procedures can prevent the spread of illness and form healthy lifelong habits. Frequent hand washing has a major role in the prevention of diseases.

Snacks.   Provide a nutritionally sound and culturally relevant snack that the children can serve (and often prepare) themselves. You will need to find out whether any children have food allergies, such as to peanuts, which can cause serious health risks. More programs at all levels emphasize healthy and organic snacks. For example, Crawmer's

Critterz Preschool believes "nutrition provided without additives, chemicals, and coloring benefits children as they grow and strive to be the best they can be! Meals that are made from whole foods, not premade or frozen, provide our students with extra nutrition that students with packed meals just miss out on. We pride ourselves on cooking tasty meals from scratch that our kids just love."[50]

Outdoor Activity/Play/Walking.   Help children practice climbing, jumping, swinging, throwing, and using body control. Incorporate walking trips and other events into outdoor play. Outdoor play is becoming a much more important part of the preschool curriculum and program.

Bathroom/Toileting.   Bathroom/toileting times offer opportunities to teach health, self-help, and intrapersonal skills. Children should also be allowed to use the bathroom whenever necessary.

Lunch.   Lunch should be a relaxing time, and the meal should be served family style, with professionals and children eating together. Children should set their own tables and decorate them with place mats and flowers they can make in the art center or as a special project. Children should be involved in cleaning up after meals and snacks. On the other hand, in many programs, preschool children go to the school cafeteria for their lunch. Children at the Albany California Children's Center receive a hot family-style lunch, such as spaghetti or teriyaki chicken, made fresh daily from their in-house kitchen.[51] Try to make this a relaxing experience also.

Relaxation.   After lunch, children should have a chance to relax, perhaps to the accompaniment of teacher-read stories, CDs, and music. This is an ideal time to teach children breathing exercises and relaxation techniques.

Rest Time.   Give children who want or need to rest an opportunity to do so. Provide quiet activities for children who do not need to or cannot sleep on a particular day. Don't force children to sleep or lie on a cot or blanket if they cannot sleep or have outgrown their need for an afternoon nap.

Centers or Special Projects.   Engage children in center activities or projects. (Projects can also be conducted in the morning, when some may be more appropriate, such as cooking something for a snack or lunch.) Projects can include holiday activities, collecting things, art activities, and field trips.

Group Time.   End the day with a group meeting to review the day's activities. Such a meeting develops listening and attention skills, promotes oral communication, stresses that learning is important, and helps children evaluate their performance and behavior.

Helping Preschoolers Make Successful Transitions

transition A passage from one learning setting, grade, or program to another.

A **transition** is a passage from one learning setting, grade, program, or experience to another. Young children face many such transitions in their lives. The transition from preschool to kindergarten can influence positively or negatively children's attitudes toward school and learning. You can help ensure that the transition is a happy and rewarding experience. Children with special needs who are making a transition from a special program to a mainstreamed classroom need extra attention and support.

Increasingly large amounts of public funds are now dedicated to educating young children with the intent of boosting their chances for success in elementary school and beyond. Preschool learning environments are quite different from traditional elementary school classroom settings and it is imperative children establish competencies critical to children's school success and achievement.[52]

Preschool and kindergarten staff can collaborate and work out a transitional plan. Continuity between programs is important for social, emotional, and educational reasons. Children should see their new setting as an exciting place where they will be happy and successful. You can suggest that kindergarten teachers make booklets about their programs, including photographs of the kindergarten children, letters from them, and pictures of kindergarten activities. You can then place these booklets in your reading center, where your preschool children can read about the programs they will attend. Below you will read how teachers help transition their preschoolers into kindergarten.

It is also important to prepare children and their parents as much as possible for what to expect in the new setting:

- Educate and prepare children ahead of time for any new situation. Children can practice certain routines as they will do them when they enter their new school or grade. For example, Amy Christensen helps transition four-year-old preschoolers into kindergarten as the "Begindergarten" teacher at Gertie Belle Rodgers Elementary in Mitchell, South Dakota. She teaches a half-day morning transition class in the elementary school which allows four-year-olds to become acquainted with the school and experiment and explore as they meet new friends. Amy writes a weekly newsletter for parents which gives details of the week and recaps children's accomplishments. For example, students read about Yao Ming, the Chinese professional basketball player, and his talent in basketball. They brainstormed about what their special talents are. The children were very creative and drew a page for a class book to be displayed at their end-of-the-year program.[53]

- Alert parents to new and different standards, dress, behavior, and parent–teacher interactions. Preschool professionals, in cooperation with kindergarten teachers, should share curriculum materials with parents so they can be familiar with what their children will learn.

- Let parents know ahead of time what their children will need in the new program (e.g., lunch box, change of clothing).

- Provide parents of children with special needs and bilingual parents with additional help and support during the transition.

- Offer parents and children an opportunity to visit the new program. Children will better understand its physical, curricular, and affective climates if they visit in advance. Teachers can incorporate methods they observed into their own program that will help children adjust to the new settings. For example, students attending Kokomo (Indiana) Center Schools are "gearing up" for kindergarten. At the annual "Ready, Set, GO!!! Kindergarten Round-Up," future kindergartners and their parents receive registration information, are introduced to available resources, and "race" to activities that are a great preview of the kindergarten year.[54]

- Exchange class visits between preschool and kindergarten programs. Class visits are an excellent way to have preschool children learn about the classrooms they will attend as kindergartners. Having kindergarten children visit the preschool and tell preschoolers about kindergarten provides a sense of security and anticipation.

- Hold a "kindergarten day" for preschoolers in which they attend kindergarten for a day. This program can include such things as riding the bus, having lunch, and participating in kindergarten activities.

The nature, extent, creativity, and effectiveness of transitional experiences for children, parents, and staff will be limited only by the commitment of all involved. If professionals are interested in providing good preschools, kindergartens, and primary schools, we will include transitional experiences in the curricula of all preschool programs.

Accommodating Diverse Learners

typically developing The majority of developmental milestones at the time when most young children achieve them without deficits in social or communication areas.

Meet Han Ling. Preschool is her first opportunity to go to school. Han Ling is **typically developing** (meaning that she reaches the majority of developmental milestones at the appropriate time and does not have deficits in social areas) and enjoys coloring, story time and playing on the swing set outside. In preschool, Han Ling must learn the rules of a more structured environment, such as sitting for longer periods of time, and she must learn pre-math and language skills. With so much to teach her, it is easy to forget that Han Ling's first job as a preschool-aged child is play. Play is the true language of children. It is how they learn social norms, hone peer interactions, express their emotions, engage in their environment, and learn problem solving. However, play does not always erupt spontaneously, so here are some tips to encourage Han Ling in play:

- Provide different play opportunities by arranging your room in centers. Block centers with blocks of varying weights and sizes, dramatic play centers with dress-up clothes, home centers with pretend food and cooking appliances, and manipulative centers with toys like dolls, action figures, or cars are just a few examples of centers that elicit play.

- Change out your centers as you rotate your units. For example, if you are in a transportation unit, put toy boats, bicycles, cars, trucks, and trains in the manipulative center. Your students will begin to act out and internalize the information you've given them in their play.

- Start a rotation of three or four children grouped by their personalities, strengths, and weakness for each center. Don't put students in a center by themselves. Play is a wonderful opportunity to help Han Ling learn social skills and problem solving, which is much more difficult to do solo. It is natural and acceptable for centers and the children in them to occasionally blend into one another.
  - When children repeatedly combine, like the block center with the manipulative center or the home center and the dress-up center, go ahead and combine them. This may make your groups larger but also more vibrant and conducive to greater social skill building.
  - Move children into different groups. You may not find the perfect group for every child right away.

- Play! For most children, play comes naturally, but for some, especially if they are unfamiliar with the toys, the other children, have high anxiety, or if they are developmentally delayed, may not readily engage in play. You notice that Han Ling seems unsure and doesn't participate very much. To start:
  - Choose similar or complementary toys. If Han Ling has a mommy doll, you pick up the daddy doll and the baby doll. Once you show interest, Han Ling will likely take the initiative and tell you what part to play or what to say. Let her lead you and don't ask too many direct questions.
  - If Han Ling does not take the initiative in play, you can ask for directions in a roundabout way, saying, "Hmm, I'm not sure which one to be, the dad or the baby . . ." She will likely take the lead and tell you what role to take.
  - To begin a play sequence, start with a scenario that Han Ling will be familiar with, like fixing breakfast or going to the grocery store. Once she is on familiar

ground, Han Ling may become more directive and steer the pretending in other directions.

- Use play as an opportunity to observe your students. Through their play, they are communicating to you their strengths and weaknesses, their home lives, relationships, fears and insecurities, as well as greatest joys and interests. Use this information to become a better teacher for them.

- Remember that play is a way children "work things out," explore, and communicate. So, if Han Ling uses language or acts out behavior that is overly aggressive or abusive, make a note of the situation, time, and date. Report it to the school counselor and your principal. Ask them whether you should notify the family or Child Protective Services. Play can be an adventure for both Han Ling and for you. If you accommodate play in your classroom, both you and your students will learn a lot and enjoy the school day.

The Future of Preschool

The further growth of public preschools for three- and four-year-old children is inevitable. Growth to the point that all children are included will take decades, but it will happen. Most likely, the public schools will increasingly focus more on programs for four-year-old children and then, over time, include three-year-olds. A logical outgrowth of this long-term trend will be for the public schools to provide services for even younger children and their families.

One thing is certain: Preschool as it was known a decade ago is not the same today, and ten years from now it will again be different. Your challenge is to develop your professional skills so you can assume a leadership role in the development of quality universal preschool programs.

Universal Preschool

When you think of the idea of universal preschool, what comes to mind? Universal preschool means different things to different people. For some it means free and required for *all*, for others it means free and accessible for *all*, for some it means voluntary and free for some children, and for others it means accessible for some with pay. For purposes of our discussion, universal means free and accessible for *all*. Ned Barholt, former chairman and CEO of Agilent Technologies, says:

> The practical first step is to get three- and four-year-olds from low-income families into better preschools. It is possible to envision a future in which every child starts kindergarten ready to learn and thirteen years later walks across the stage to accept a diploma. If we succeed, all our children will have the support and tools to achieve their dreams. Universal preschool would give all kids a chance to succeed."

Universal preschool is fast becoming a program whose time has come, and it is now a permanent part of the American public school system. While not all children have free access to public school, I predict they will in the next ten years—unless there is another Great Recession. Preschool is the beginning of public schooling. Research is clear that universal preschool benefits *all* children. Of course, it will take many more years before every four-year-old in every state has the opportunity for a free public preschool education.

Investing in High-Quality Preschool Programs

One of the ongoing issues of federal, state, and local governments is whether they are or are not going to invest funds for early childhood programs. When there is not enough money to fund all priorities, which is always the case, different constituencies compete for funding, and questions of priority abound. Do we fund juvenile justice programs, jails, senior health care, or preschools? Numerous research studies show that investing in high-quality preschool programs has short- and long-term educational and monetary benefits. You can use these data as you advocate for investing in young children. Below is research about the value and benefits of investing in high-quality preschool programs.

Perry Preschool Project[55]

- For every dollar spent, $12.90 was saved in tax dollars.
- Sixty-six percent of the program group graduated from high school on time, compared to forty-five percent of the control group.
- The program's group suffered only half as many arrests as the control group.

Chicago Child–Parent Center Program[56]

- For every dollar invested in the program, $7.10 was returned.
- Participants had a 51 percent reduction in child maltreatment.
- Participants had a 41 percent reduction in special education placement.

New Jersey Abbott Preschool Program[57]

- Increased receptive vocabulary scores by an additional four months, a particularly significant finding since this measure is strongly predictive of general cognitive abilities.
- Increased scores on measures of early math skills by 24 percent over the course of the year.
- Increased print awareness scores by 61 percent over the course of the year. Children who attended the program know more letters, more letter-sound associations, and are more familiar with words and book concepts at entry to kindergarten.

Los Angeles Universal Preschool[58]

- The percentage of children scoring near proficient on social and emotional skills needed to do well in kindergarten increased 72 percent.
- English Language Learners (ELLs) who scored significantly lower than their non–English learner peers closed the gap in skills such as demonstrating proficiency in using crayons, washing hands, controlling impulses, expressing needs, counting to ten, and recognizing letters of the alphabet, as well as shapes and colors.
- In general skills, such as writing their first names, recognizing rhyming words, and using books, ELLs' gains exceeded those made by non–English learners.

Portraits of Children

Now that you have learned about effective programs, this is a good time for you to think more about the children you will be helping to transition to kindergarten. Read, review, and reflect on the "Portraits of Preschoolers" on pages 296. As you answer the questions about developmentally appropriate practice, think how you would meet the needs of each of these children in your classroom.

Activities for Professional Development

Ethical Dilemma

"I think we should do something!"

Kindergarten teacher Michelle Ripkin teaches in a small east-coast state that has not offered a public preschool program. Michelle, a strong advocate for early education, was ecstatic when she heard that her state finally was going to provide support for pre-kindergarten education. However, in the days following the initial announcement, Michelle was very disappointed to learn that the state was planning to fund only five pilot pre-kindergarten classrooms and they would serve only about seventy-five four-year-old children. Michelle was so upset by the news, she scheduled a meeting with Stephanie Bottoms, her elementary principal. "Stephanie, how can the state legislature be so short-sighted? We know the advantages of high-quality preschool programs for young children! Why can't our state do its part and provide proper funding! I'm tired of all of these excuses about no money because of hard times and the recession! I think we should do something! Why don't we contact our state representatives and put some pressure on them to provide more funding?" Stephanie was not pleased with Michelle's suggestions. "Now Michelle, we have to take a step at a time. We should be happy with the funding we get. Let's not do anything to embarrass ourselves or the politicians who are providing the funding!"

What should Michelle do? Should she visit her state representatives and share her opinions with them? Should she take Stephanie's advice and keep quiet? Should she take a more proactive approach and contact the local teachers' union and get them involved? Or, should Michelle take another course of action? What should Michelle do?

Activities to Apply What You Learned

1. Create a survey for parents and preschool staff. Ask them why preschool programs are important to them and what they think are the benefits to children and families. E-mail your survey to three preschool programs in your area and preschools in other states. Post the results on your early childhood education discussion board and ask your classmates to comment on the results of your survey.

2. Choose a domain of development: physical, cognitive, social-emotional, or language. Create a list of activities in different preschool environments that stimulate growth and maturity in that domain. Share this information with your classmates on your blog.

3. Create a theme you can incorporate into your classroom (e.g., springtime, holidays, etc.) How can you use the theme to develop activities that are full of rich learning to support ELLs' literacy development?

4. You have been invited to speak at the meeting of the local NAEYC affiliate on the topic "School Readiness: What Teachers and Parents Can Do." Develop your presentation outline using these questions: What is readiness? Why is children's readiness for school important? What should be critical features of a preschool that is "getting children ready for school"? What are five key skills and behaviors a child should have on entering kindergarten? Post your outline on your Facebook page or show on your class blog.

5. Go online and research the outdoor facilities of preschool programs. Also look at the outdoor play designs of commercial playground companies. List five things that you find new and interesting. Share this information on your blog.

6. Based on material presented in this chapter, develop a set of ten guidelines for ensuring that preschool programs are developmentally appropriate. Visit a local preschool. Look at the environment, curriculum, and teaching practices. Are there any things that are exceptional? Any things that can be improved? Write a 200-word reflection about developmentally appropriate practice in the preschool. Share this with your classmates and ask for comments.

7. Create an event for a preschool class to help them transition into kindergarten. Develop five transition activities for children and families. Who will you collaborate with to ensure parents and families receive information to support their children's success in kindergarten?

8. After reviewing all the information in the chapter, create a 3- to 5-minute video podcast answering the question, "In ten years, the future of preschool will be _____." Discuss what changes you think will take place in preschools and where you would like to be in the early education profession in ten years.

Linking to Learning

International Association for the Child's Right to Play
www.ipausa.org

An interdisciplinary organization affiliated with IPA (founded in Denmark in 1961), with membership open to all professionals working for or with children. Includes a position statement on the need for recess in elementary schools and resources on playground games and activities.

Pre-K Now
www.preknow.org

A website dedicated to the advancement of high-quality, voluntary pre-kindergarten for all preschool-age children. It is a public education and advocacy campaign that features up-to-date information on the reform of education for young children.

Preschool Teacher
www.preschoolbystormie.com

A website dedicated to pre-K teachers. A place to share classroom ideas.

CAIDEN

GABRIELA

	CAIDEN	GABRIELA
General Description	Three Years, Caucasian, Male • Outgoing, amiable, patient • Has traveled extensively with family • Only child, professional household: mother—master's degree, father—doctorate	Three Years, Hispanic, Female • Studious, friendly, nurturing • Loves to interact with books • Lives with mother, father, and younger sister
Social-Emotional	• Is beginning to interact with others voluntarily • Takes turns when asked to and is supported • Engages in solitary dramatic play • Reacts physically when upset	• Remains very self-centered (mine, mine, mine!) • Enjoys helping with simple household tasks • Is developing her sense of humor and enjoys being silly and making others laugh • Makes choices between two things
Cognitive	• Enjoys naming many concrete items, especially animals • Counts up to at least 3 consistently • Identifies 900 to 1,000 words • Understands and expresses similarities and differences	• Carries out two related directions • Enjoys repetitive stories • Sings simple songs • Draws a person with at least three parts
Motor	• Large muscle skills are much more highly developed than small muscle skills • Alternates feet when walking, running, and ascending, but not descending, stairs • Moves with music but not necessarily with the beat • Can roll a ball toward a specific target	• Makes marks on paper: circles, crosses, rectangles, etc. • Stacks up to seven blocks to build a tower • Is a messy eater; uses both hands and utensils • Pedals a tricycle
Adaptive (Daily Living)	• Puts on shoes himself; needs assistance with most fasteners • Effectively indicates wants and needs • Washes his own hands when asked to do so • Sleeps through most nights without wetting the bed but still has occasional accidents	• Recognizes community environments (McDonald's, Wal-mart) • Is beginning to follow common routines independently • Hangs up her own coat or backpack on a hook • Often forgets rules and must be reminded daily

Source: Contributed by Barb Tingle, kindergarten teacher at Sahuarita Primary School, Tuscon, Arizona, 2009 Freeport-McMoRan Sahuarita District Teacher of the Year, 2008 Wal-Mart Regional Teacher of the Year, and 2010 AZ Educational Foundation Ambassador for Excellence; and Deborah Palmer, director of Shepherd's Fold Preschool, NACCP Director of the Year.

Developmentally Appropriate Questions

1. Three-year-old Caiden reacts physically when upset. Four-year-old Preston throws temper tantrums over minor frustrations. What are some things that you can do to teach self-regulation and emotional control with your preschoolers? What is some information that you can share with parents to help them develop their children's self-regulation?

2. Three-year-old Gabriela "remains very self-centered." Is this typical behavior development for a three-year-old? Which of Piaget's stages of cognitive development is she in?

PRESTON

GRISELDA

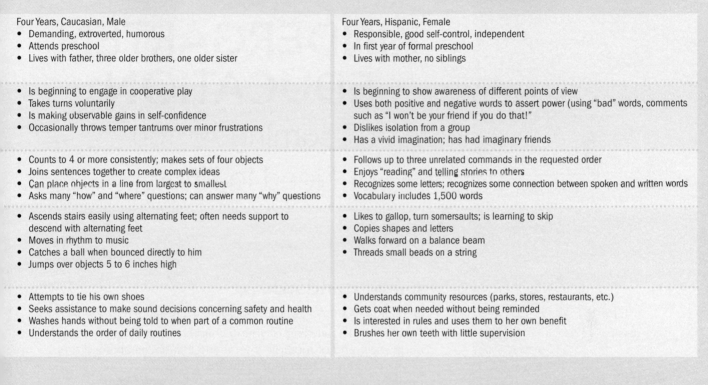

PRESTON	GRISELDA
Four Years, Caucasian, Male	Four Years, Hispanic, Female
• Demanding, extroverted, humorous	• Responsible, good self-control, independent
• Attends preschool	• In first year of formal preschool
• Lives with father, three older brothers, one older sister	• Lives with mother, no siblings
• Is beginning to engage in cooperative play	• Is beginning to show awareness of different points of view
• Takes turns voluntarily	• Uses both positive and negative words to assert power (using "bad" words, comments such as "I won't be your friend if you do that!")
• Is making observable gains in self-confidence	• Dislikes isolation from a group
• Occasionally throws temper tantrums over minor frustrations	• Has a vivid imagination; has had imaginary friends
• Counts to 4 or more consistently; makes sets of four objects	• Follows up to three unrelated commands in the requested order
• Joins sentences together to create complex ideas	• Enjoys "reading" and telling stories to others
• Can place objects in a line from largest to smallest	• Recognizes some letters; recognizes some connection between spoken and written words
• Asks many "how" and "where" questions; can answer many "why" questions	• Vocabulary includes 1,500 words
• Ascends stairs easily using alternating feet; often needs support to descend with alternating feet	• Likes to gallop, turn somersaults; is learning to skip
• Moves in rhythm to music	• Copies shapes and letters
• Catches a ball when bounced directly to him	• Walks forward on a balance beam
• Jumps over objects 5 to 6 inches high	• Threads small beads on a string
• Attempts to tie his own shoes	• Understands community resources (parks, stores, restaurants, etc.)
• Seeks assistance to make sound decisions concerning safety and health	• Gets coat when needed without being reminded
• Washes hands without being told to when part of a common routine	• Is interested in rules and uses them to her own benefit
• Understands the order of daily routines	• Brushes her own teeth with little supervision

3. Gabriela eats with her hands. Is this appropriate three-year-old behavior? What can you do to encourage and support children's appropriate eating habits?

4. Four-year-old Griselda uses words to assert power over others. What would you do to help Griselda and other children in your program get along and work peacefully with each other?

5. Four-year-old Griselda has a 1,500-word vocabulary and three-year-old Caiden has a 1,000-word vocabulary. Is this vocabulary development appropriate for three- and four-year-old children? What would you do to promote preschool children's vocabulary development?

• Hear viewpoints of experts in the field in Professional Perspectives.

• Check your comprehension on the content covered in the chapter by going to the Study Plan in the Book Resources for your text. Here you will be able to take a chapter quiz, receive feedback on your answers, and then access Review, Practice, and Enrichment activities to enhance your understanding of chapter content.

11

KINDERGARTEN EDUCATION
Learning All You Need to Know

naeyc standards

Standard 1. Promoting Child Development and Learning

I use my understanding of young children's characteristics and needs, and of multiple interacting influences on children's development and learning, to create environments that are healthy, respectful, supportive, and challenging for each child.[1]

Standard 3. Observing, Documenting, and Assessing to Support Young Children and Families

I know about and understand the goals, benefits, and uses of assessment. I know about and use systematic observations, documentation, and other effective assessment strategies in a responsible way, in partnership with families and other professionals, to positively influence the development of every child.[2]

Standard 4. Using Developmentally Effective Approaches to Connect with Children and Families

I understand and use positive relationships and supportive interactions as the foundation for my work with young children and families. I know, understand, and use a wide array of developmentally appropriate approaches, instructional strategies, and tools to connect with children and families and positively influence each child's development and learning.[3]

Standard 5. Using Content Knowledge to Build Meaningful Curriculum

I understand the importance of developmental domains and academic (or content) disciplines in early childhood curriculum. I use my knowledge and other resources to design, implement, and evaluate meaningful, challenging curricula that promote comprehensive developmental and learning outcomes for every young child.[4]

As we begin our discussion of kindergarten children and programs, perhaps you are thinking back to your kindergarten or pre–first-grade school experiences. I am sure you have many pleasant memories that include your teachers and classmates, as well as what you learned and how you learned it. It is good that you have these fond memories, but we can't use just memories to build our understanding of what today's high-quality kindergartens are and should be like.

Kindergarten Today

The kindergarten is in an ongoing transitional stage from a program that previously focused primarily on social and emotional development to one that emphasizes academics, especially early literacy, math and science, and activities that prepare children to think and problem-solve. These changes represent a transformation of great magnitude and will continue to have a lasting impact on the kindergarten curriculum and the education of young children.

The Changing Kindergarten

The kindergarten classroom of today is very different from the kindergarten of yesterday and it requires a different kind of teacher. Elizabeth Plotkin, a Teacher of the Year, expresses it this way: "My goal as a teacher is to provide opportunities for children to make positive memories in the school environment; build a foundation of finding joy in learning; and to claim each day as a chance to be the change in a child's life." Elizabeth believes that making connections between children's lives and the curriculum creates engaged learners.[5] Kindergarten teacher of the year Abby Lowe says one of the most rewarding things about being a teacher is watching her students grow. She wants her students to always feel smart and have a love for school.[6]

Kindergarten teachers adjust in response to changes in kindergarten education. Here are some of the ways kindergarten is evolving and the reasons why:

- *Longer school days and the transition from half-day to full-day programs.* National Education Association (NEA) President Dennis Van Roekel says, "Full-day

> " Success will require preparing every child, everywhere in this county, to out-compete any worker anywhere in the world because we know that those students who are getting the best education are going to be able to compete. "
>
> **PRESIDENT BARACK OBAMA**

kindergarten provides our youngest students more time to explore, learn, and grow in an engaging and supportive environment."[7] Today, 72 percent of kindergarten children are enrolled in full-day programs.[8] For their part, parents feel that their children benefit by being in a classroom environment and away from home for longer periods during the day. For example, Amy Hartley, a kindergarten parent, believes that attending full-day kindergarten benefited her two oldest children, and sees similar results in her kindergartner. "They learn social skills, and how to get along with others. There are so many requirements in kindergarten; it's nice that they can spend the morning on academics and the afternoon on some of the other activities."[9]

Reasons for longer school days and full-day kindergarten programs:

Easier transition and flexibility.

- Helps children adapt to the demands of longer school days in the primary grades.
- Provides more flexibility and more time for children to participate in activities and projects.

Helps children develop academically and socially.

- Enables children with developmental delays and those at risk for school problems to have more time to complete projects and more time for socialization with peers and teachers.
- Gives teachers more time to plan curriculum, incorporate a greater number of activities into the school year, and offer more in-depth coverage of each standard.[10]

Provides greater progress in literacy, math, social skills, and science.

Emphasizes academics, especially reading, math, and science:

- State and district standards that specify what children should know and be able to do.
- Better-prepared kindergartners are more prepared for the primary grades.[11]

More testing.

- The accountability of teachers and schools for children's achievement.
- Helps children avoid school grade failures.
- Teachers use tests and assessments to plan instruction and promote achievement.[12]

The almost universal goal of having all children reading well by entry into first grade.

- Recognition that literacy and reading are pathways to success in school and life. Learning to read is a basic right for all children.[13]

If you want to gain a good picture of what is expected of kindergarten children today, now would be a good time to review the kindergarten standards for your state. Be sure to review their depth and breadth across all of the content areas.

The Escalated Curriculum.   After reviewing state kindergarten standards, you may be thinking, "Wow, a lot of what they're doing in kindergarten I did in first grade!" and you are right.

A number of reasons account for the escalated curriculum. First, beginning in the 1990s, there has been a decided emphasis on academics in U.S. education, particularly early childhood education. Second, some parents believe an academic approach to learning is the best way for their children to succeed in school and the work world. Third, the standards, testing, and high-quality education reform movement encourages greater emphasis on academics. Fourth, the federal government sees kindergarten and the primary grades as important to the national goal of being a world leader. The federal government also believes that learning twenty-first century work skills begins in kindergarten and before.

These higher expectations for kindergarten children are not necessarily bad. However, achieving them in developmentally appropriate ways is one of the major challenges facing you and early childhood professionals today.

Who Attends Kindergarten?

Froebel's kindergarten was for children three to seven years of age. In the United States, kindergarten is for five- and six-year-old children before they enter first grade. The age at which children enter kindergarten differs from state to state and district to district. Many parents and professionals support an older rather than a younger kindergarten entrance age because they think older children are more ready for kindergarten and will learn better. Consequently, it is not uncommon to have children in kindergarten who are seven by the end of the year. In the past, children had to be five years of age prior to December 31 for kindergarten admission; today the trend is toward an older admission age. For example, Maryland children must now be five by September 1 rather than the previous date of December 31.[14] Current legislative practices indicate that states and school districts will continue to push back the kindergarten entrance age so that kindergarten children will continue to be "older."

Redshirting.   You may have heard of the practice of **redshirting** college football players—that is, holding a player out a year for him to grow and mature. The theory is that the extra year will produce a better football player. The same practice applies to kindergarten children with about 9 percent of children entering kindergarten being academically redshirted—held out of school for a year.[15] Parents and administrators who practice redshirting think that the extra year gives children an opportunity to mature intellectually, socially, and physically. Redshirting might have some benefit for children who are immature and whose birthdates fall close to the cut-off for school entrance. One parent says, "I think my son should be held back to give him time to mature more socially and academically."[16] Some affluent parents redshirt their sons in particular because they want them to be the oldest members of the kindergarten class. They reason that their children will be class leaders, will get more attention from the teachers, and will have another year under their belts, all the better to handle the increasing demands of the kindergarten curriculum.

Research and Redshirting.   An analysis of research data regarding children's achievement in reading and math found that redshirted children have slightly higher reading knowledge and skills at the end of first grade than children who started kindergarten on time. In mathematics, however, redshirted children's scores were somewhat behind those of children who had started kindergarten on time. Research also suggests that children who are older than their peers score higher on achievement tests and are less likely to repeat a grade or to be diagnosed with learning disabilities than younger students in the same class.[17]

Rather than the constant juggling of entrance ages, what is needed are early childhood programs designed to serve the needs of all children, regardless of the ages at which they enter school. At the heart of this issue is disagreement about whether developmental maturation or school experiences are the more potent factor in children's achievement. Research studies comparing age and school effects suggest that academic achievement is closely tied with age.[18] Also, for children who are not ready for kindergarten or who find kindergarten too challenging, there are other kinds of programs.

Today, kindergarten is a universal part of schooling, enrolling children from different cultures and socio-economic backgrounds and, subsequently, different life experiences. What are some things you can do to ensure that kindergarten experiences meet the unique needs of each child?

redshirting The practice of postponing the entrance into kindergarten of age-eligible children to allow extra time for social-emotional, intellectual, or physical growth.

Alternative Kindergarten Programs

Given the changing kindergarten curriculum; the almost universal nature of kindergarten; and the prevalence of a variety of abilities and disabilities, it is not surprising that some children are not ready for many of the kindergarten demands placed on them. As a result, teachers and schools have developed alternative kindergarten programs.

developmental kindergarten (DK)
A kindergarten designed to provide children with additional time for maturation and physical, social, emotional, and intellectual development.

Developmental Kindergarten.   The **developmental kindergarten (DK)** is a prekindergarten for kindergarten-age children who are developmentally or behaviorally delayed; it is viewed as one means of helping them succeed in school. School districts have specific criteria for placing children in developmental kindergartens:

- Kindergarten-eligible children are given a kindergarten screening test to identify those who have special learning or behavioral needs. Some states, such as Massachusetts, require that all children take a screening test prior to kindergarten enrollment.[19]

- Pre-kindergarten children are given a readiness test, such as the Kindergarten Readiness Test (KRT),[20] to help determine their readiness for regular kindergarten. (The placement of children in any program should not be made solely on the basis and results of one test, an issue we discuss in more detail later in this chapter.)

- Parents and preschool teachers who believe that children are not ready for kindergarten consult the school district and/or their local school about the placement of individual children.

For example, the Troy Michigan District has a DK program that provides meaningful and challenging experiences that build on children's prior knowledge. Their integrated program of teacher-directed and child-initiated learning allows children many opportunities to manipulate materials, explore and discover ideas, interact with others, and develop at their own unique rate. This program fosters the development of a positive self-image and enhances children's growth toward their individual potential.[21]

transition kindergarten
A kindergarten designed to serve children who may be old enough to go to first grade but are not quite ready to handle all of its expectations.

Transition Kindergarten.   A **transition kindergarten** is designed to give children the time they need to achieve what is required for entry into first grade. These children are really getting two years to achieve what others would normally achieve in one. A transition class is different from a nongraded program in that the transition class consists of children of the same age, whereas the nongraded classroom has children of different ages.

The concept of transition classes implies, and practice should involve, linear progression that promotes ongoing achievement and success. Children are placed in a transition kindergarten so they can continue to progress at their own pace. The curriculum, materials, and teaching practices should be appropriate for each child's developmental age or level.

Proponents of transitional programs identify these benefits:

- Promotes success, whereas retention is a regressive practice that promotes failure
- Provides for children's developmental abilities
- Enables children to be with other children of the same developmental age
- Provides an appropriate learning environment
- Puts children's needs ahead of the desire to place them in a particular grade
- Provides additional time for children to integrate learning—often referred to as the **gift of time**

gift of time The practice of giving children more time in a program or at home to develop physically, emotionally, socially, and cognitively as preparation for kindergarten.

Students at Honor Roll Elementary School who attend transitional kindergarten (TK) classes engage in a well-integrated, nurturing environment that focuses on socialization and active learning. Teachers work with children so they are able to complete their work independently, read and write, and discover their five senses. Academic skills are further developed through phonics-based reading, hands-on math activities, spelling, and simple grammar. Music, art, and physical play are also important parts in the TK curriculum.[22]

Mixed-Age/Multiage Grouping.   **Mixed-age grouping** provides another approach to meeting the individual and collective needs of children. In a multiage group, there is a diversity of abilities, at least a two-year span in children's ages, and the same teacher. Multiage groups:

- Provide materials and activities for a wider range of children's abilities
- Create a feeling of community and belonging; most mixed-age groups have a feeling of family because children spend at least two years in the group
- Support children's social development by providing a broader range of children to associate with; older children act as teachers, tutors, and mentors; younger children are able to model the academic and social skills of their older class members
- Provide for a continuous progression of learning

Today more teachers and schools are using multi-age grouping to support kindergarten learning. "By grouping students by ability rather than age, we're better able to respond to the student's needs," Principal Dawn Gonzales says. "Research shows that multiage classrooms can be beneficial to academic achievement." Collaboration and friendships across all age groups are gained, creating a unique community. Older students have an opportunity to become role models and to reinforce their own understanding through teaching. Younger students get to preview concepts they'll study later.[23]

Looping.   **Looping** occurs when a teacher spends two or more years with the same group of same-age children. In other words, a teacher involved in looping begins teaching a group of kindergartners and then teaches the same group as first graders and perhaps as second graders. Another teacher might do the same with second, third, and fourth graders. Kindergarten teacher Carla Rodriguez lists these advantages of looping:

- Teachers, students, and parents develop a deep relationship because of the longer amount of time together.
- Teachers understand the children's family dynamics and the expectations of the parents.
- Teachers develop a deeper understanding of children's learning styles.
- The second year around the students are already familiar with classroom procedures and expectations. Furthermore, the teacher already knows the needs of the students and can jump right in.[24]

Retention.   Along with the benefits of early education and **universal kindergarten** come other issues as well. One of these is retention. Children who are retained, instead of participating in kindergarten graduation ceremonies with their classmates, are destined to spend another year in kindergarten. Many of these children are retained, or failed, because teachers judge them to be immature, or they fail to measure up to the district's or teachers' standards for promotion to first grade.

Across our country, 10 to 30 percent of children are retained in kindergarten.[25] These children are failing kindergarten because they are presumably not ready for the demands of first grade. Yet the early years of schooling are crucial in determining the child's long-term attitudes toward self, teachers, and learning. Children who emerge from the early years feeling good about themselves, respecting teachers, and enjoying

---

mixed-age grouping
Students in two or three grade levels combined in one classroom with one teacher.

looping A single-graded class of children staying with the same teacher for two or more years.

universal kindergarten The availability of publicly funded kindergarten to all children.

Children are born to learn. Learning is not something children get ready for but is a continuous process. What factors do you think are critical for children's readiness to learn?

learning will regard education as exciting and as a positive challenge. On the other hand, children who leave the early years of schooling feeling badly about themselves, with a low regard for teachers, and turned off to learning may find recess the best part of the school day.[26]

Do children do better the second time around? Despite our intuitive feelings that children who are retained will do better, research evidence is unequivocally contrary to that notion: children *do not* do better the second time around. In fact, studies show that children do worse and that retention causes children to drop out.[27]

Environments for Kindergartners

NAEYC Standard 1 at the beginning of this chapter identifies one of your professional roles as being able to create environments that are healthy, respectful, supportive, and challenging for each child and create a setting for positive learning experiences.

The Healthy Environment

A healthy setting is important for all children. A safe, clean, well-maintained classroom with a positive atmosphere and social climate increases student and staff self-esteem and student achievement.[28] A healthy environment includes having children practice healthy habits. In Arlington, Virginia schools have installed hand sanitizer dispensers in all classrooms and have large supplies of gel available. "Now when children come in from recess or go to lunch without time for a restroom break, they get a squirt of the gel," says principal Lolli Laws. Principal Karen Hodges has her children sing the ABC song while they wash their hands, because washing hands for the time it takes to sing the song is long enough to kill the germs.[29]

A healthy environment also includes a relaxed and happy eating environment. Areas should be disinfected properly before eating. Substantial research clearly indicates that a healthy diet and environment contribute to children's overall health and well-being.[30]

Healthy Foods.   Since 2004, the federal government has required that every school district participating in the national school lunch and breakfast program develop a wellness plan to help children eat healthier foods.[31] Schools now include more fruits, vegetables, and whole grains on lunch trays. Connecticut schools prohibit the sale of soda and other sugary drinks, and deep fryers are disappearing from school cafeterias nationwide. Many schools have already banned junk food in vending machines, and even classroom birthday parties are under attack.[32] Alternative healthy foods that parents can bring are sealed yogurts, bagels, and fruits.[33] At Louisa May Alcott Elementary School in Chicago, children eat home-cooked breakfast and lunch made mainly from locally farmed products. Lunches include meals such as baked penne with Italian chicken sausage, ratatouille, and rosemary-roasted potatoes.[34]

Organic Foods.   Growing and eating organic foods is part of the greening of America and its schools. Creating lesson plans about organic foods, the benefits of organic food, and organic agriculture enables children to be familiar with organic products. If there's an organic farm near the school, a field trip is a good way to really teach children about organic farming. You can also talk about the environmental impact of choosing organic products and ways children can talk to their parents (or even to the school cafeteria staff) about using more organic products. If there is space, starting a classroom organic garden is a wonderful way for children to take home lessons about organic foods. Students can research organic gardening methods on the Internet or in books; start a classroom compost pile; and take care of their plants using organic methods.[35] Casa dei Bambini Montessori School in Santa Maria, California has an organic snack menu:

Beverages

Organic carrot juice, water, organic rice milk

Monday

Organic whole grain crackers with organic hummus

Organic persimmons and apples

Tuesday

Organic vegan blueberry muffins

Dried apricots and cranberries

Wednesday

Organic granola bars with sunflower butter and flax

Various fruits

Thursday

Soy and regular organic yogurt

Organic whole grain crackers

Various fruit

Friday

Quesadillas with organic cheese and blue corn tortillas

Organic vegetables and vegan ranch dips[36]

The Respectful Environment

A **respectful environment** is one in which teachers show respect for children, colleagues, and families. In addition, children are respectful of adults and peers.[37] This psychologically friendly environment contributes to a respectful environment and includes the attitudes, feelings and values of the school and community.

In a respectful classroom, teachers treat children courteously, talk with them about in- and out-of-school activities and events, and show a genuine concern for them as individuals with specific needs. Unfortunately, not all children get the respect they need and want at home or at school. Some children, especially children with behavior and attention problems, can be subjected to verbal abuse by teachers and children.[38] This is one reason why your respectful classroom means so much to each child.

respectful environments
Environments that show respect for each individual child and for their culture, home language, individual abilities or disabilities, family context, and community.

The Supportive Environment

A **supportive environment** creates a climate where children can do their best work. Teachers have high expectations and students are expected to succeed. [39] The supportive environment consists of the immediate physical surroundings, social relationships, and cultural settings in which children function and interact. To help create a supportive social environment, *all* children of all cultures, genders, socioeconomic levels, and backgrounds are valued and included in all activities. In addition, a supportive kindergarten environment:

- *Meets children's safety needs.* Children feel safe and secure socially and emotionally. They have teachers who care about and help them.
- *Has a balance between teacher-initiated and child-initiated activities.* Children should be able choose to do things that they consider challenging and also things they do very well.

supportive environments
Environments in which professionals believe each child can learn, and that help children understand and make meaning of their experiences.

- *Provides a classroom arrangement and materials for active learning.* In a supportive environment, children are listening to stories, telling stories, dictating stories, looking at and reading books independently, singing, relating events that happened outside school, and talking, talking, talking. Children are also using computers interactively with appropriate games and tasks, solving puzzles, counting napkins to put on the table to match the number of children, and measuring heights and weights. In other words, the teachers, the classroom arrangement, and the materials support children's active learning.

- *Is a place that emphasizes social and emotional development as well as academic achievement.* Generally, age is the only criterion that determines whether a child may enroll in kindergarten. This means that some children come to kindergarten emotionally immature and more than a little self-centered. However, in any group of 5-year-olds, there are children who function more like 4-year-olds and others who are like 6-year-olds. And overall development isn't the only type of difference that exists. Some children are sociable, while others do not get along well with their peers.

- *Have a well-trained teacher in charge.* Training for kindergarten teachers has steadily become more rigorous over the past few decades. In addition, children who have highly trained and qualified teachers do better academically.[40]

A curriculum that helps children feel good about themselves also helps them become aware that other children also have needs and rights. In a good kindergarten environment children learn to wait, to share, to take turns, and to help others as they also gain confidence in their own abilities and self-worth.[41]

The Challenging Environment

A challenging learning environment provides curricula that are neither too easy nor too hard. Teachers adjust learning levels to children's abilities while also making it possible for children to meet state and local expectations. Challenging environments match children's abilities and achievement levels so they are successful. A challenging kindergarten classroom is responsive to children's cultures and socioeconomic backgrounds. In these types of environments, teachers are attentive to individual students and provide them with one-on-one attention and instruction.

In challenging environments teachers assess children's learning on a daily basis to inform instructional decisions and provide the necessary assistance. Challenging learning environments that encourage the active involvement of students can sometimes be difficult for teachers to create. The following are some suggestions for how you can create a challenging environment:

- Be knowledgeable about children's academic, social, and cultural backgrounds.
- Meet each child at his or her developmental level, foster that stage, and scaffold him or her to the next level.
- Use diverse and appropriate teaching approaches to provide meaningful learning opportunities for each child.
- Differentiate instruction and activities.
- Engage children in projects and small group activities, while also enabling children to do their best work.
- Use technology to focus on academics and cognitive learning and to engage children.
- Interact with children in ways that help them to think and problem-solve at their own levels.[42]

The Physical Environment

Environments that support learning are essential if we want *all* kindergarten children to be successful.

Classroom Arrangement and Organization.   The classroom is organized to promote interaction and learning. Desks, tables, and workstations are clustered together; work areas have a variety of learning materials to encourage group projects, experiments, and creative activities.

A high-quality kindergarten classroom is one in which children feel at home. You should collaborate with your children to personalize your classroom. Using plants, rugs, beanbag chairs, and pillows can make the classroom homelike and cozy. Prominently displayed artifacts give children a sense of pride and ownership. Here are some things you can do to provide a high-quality physical environment for kindergarten:

- Provide many materials that support children learning to read and write such as paper, pencils, crayons, and all kinds of books.
- Organize children into groups of different sizes and ability levels. This provides for social interaction and cooperative learning and encourages children to help others (scaffolding).
- Use a variety of different instructional approaches, such as small groups, large groups, seat work, center time, free activity choice time, individual one-on-one work with children, and free play time.
- Arrange your classroom so that it supports district and state learning standards. For example, to meet reading content standards, make books easily accessible to students. Also, make sure the classroom has a comfortable area for group and individual reading times.
- Adapt your classroom arrangement so it meets the learning and social needs of your children. For example, set aside time for children to work in groups, assign group projects, and assign projects that include different cultures.
- Make supplies and learning materials accessible to children. Store them on open shelves with labels (using pictures and words).

Environments that are healthy, respectful, supportive, and challenging create the kindergarten stage on which children and teacher collaborate for success.

What Are Kindergarten Children Like?

Kindergartners have similar developmental, physical, and behavioral characteristics that characterize them as kindergartners—children ages five to six. Yet, at the same time, they have characteristics that make them unique individuals. To sample this uniqueness, review the four portraits of kindergarten children on pages 308–309, and respond to the accompanying questions.

Physical Development

Kindergarten children have a lot of energy, and they want to use it in physical activities such as running, climbing, and jumping. Their desire to be involved in physical activity makes kindergarten an ideal time to involve children in projects of building—for example, making **learning centers** resemble a store, post office, or veterinary office.

From ages five to seven, children's average weight and height approximate each other. For example, at six years, boys, on average, weigh 46 pounds and are 45 inches tall; girls,

learning centers Areas of the classroom set up to promote student-centered, hands-on, active learning, organized around student interests, themes, and academic subjects.

portraits of kindergartners

	MADISON	**DION** 
General Description	Five Years, Caucasian, Female • Consistently cheerful and enthusiastic • Did not attend child care or preschool • Lives with mom, dad, and older brother	Five Years, African American, Male • Very energetic and excitable • Attended preschool • No siblings in the single-parent home
Social-Emotional	• Often prefers to play with others rather than playing by herself • Responds to reasoning; asks serious questions, and wants to be taken seriously • Often feels sympathetic to others and understands and enjoys both giving and receiving • Attempts to organize other children and toys for pretend play	• Can take turns and share, but doesn't always want to • Plays contentedly and independently without constant supervision • Has a good sense of humor, and enjoys sharing jokes and laughter with adults • Is often embarrassed by his own mistakes, wants to fit in and learn the rules; seeks approval of adults
Cognitive	• Understands that stories have a beginning, middle, and end; is able to remember stories and repeat them • Asks higher-level questions (e.g., asks, "What would happen if the bus was late?") • Sequences three or more events chronologically • Relies heavily on hands-on experiences to support abstract thinking and learning	• Can concentrate on a single task for 15 minutes or more at a time • Is interested in cause and effect; wants to know more about how and why things in his world work and happen • Asks more analytical questions and weighs the choices available to him • Is project minded; likes to plan buildings, act out scenarios, and create drawings related to his play
Motor	• Is able to skip, run, gallop, hop, tumble and run on tiptoe • Has not yet established a definite right or left-hand dominance • Uses her fingers flexibly to control writing and painting tools, to dress and undress dolls and to manage zippers and buttons; uses drawing and painting tools with efficiency and is skillful at coloring within the lines of a picture • Demonstrates clear contrasts between slow and fast movement while moving and enjoys games of chasing and fleeing (e.g., "tag")	• Throws ball overhead; catches bounced balls • Displays high energy levels; he finds inactivity difficult, seeks active games, and enjoys climbing, sliding, swinging, and dancing • Is interested in performing tricks like standing on his head, performing dance steps, and enjoys practicing complex body coordination skills like swimming and riding bicycles • Can walk down stairs, alternating feet without using a handrail
Adaptive (Daily Living)	• Shows and acts on an awareness of personal hygiene needs (e.g., cleans up or grooms when appropriate or necessary) • Can usually determine when she must seek help from a peer or adult to solve a problem or complete a task • Can think of and try out possible solutions to problems and can use varied and flexible approaches to solve longer-term or more abstract challenges • Follows basic health and safety rules within her everyday environment.	• Manages mealtime tools and skills independently (carries lunch tray, opens milk carton, uses fork, spoon, and napkin) • Dresses himself independently and generally chooses appropriate clothing; sometimes needs help with zippers or buttons, experiments with tying shoes • Is able to say his name, address, age, and birthday • Organizes and maintains his own possessions at school (backpack, jacket, water bottle, cubby)

Source: Contributed by Barb Tingle, kindergarten teacher at Sahuarita Primary School, Tuscon, Arizona, 2009 Freeport-McMoRan Sahuarita District Teacher of the Year, 2008 Wal-Mart Regional Teacher of the Year, and 2010 AZ Educational Foundation Ambassador for Excellence; and Deborah Palmer, director of Shepherd's Fold Preschool, NACCP Director of the Year.

Developmentally Appropriate Questions

1. Consider the fact that both Madison and Dion are young kindergartners. Do their profiles reveal causes or concerns?

2. Dion finds "inactivity difficult." What implication does this have for how you teach him?

3. Do you think that because Madison did not attend preschool, this has or will influence her kindergarten performance?

4. Dion comes from a single-parent home. Will this influence how you teach him? How you relate to his mother and family?

ANDREW

Six Years, Caucasian, Male
- Outgoing and active
- Interested in science-related topics
- Oldest of four children in the home

- Likes to create rules for games and expects peers to follow them
- Questions authority out of a greater sense of independence (i.e., "Why should I do it?")
- Enjoys role playing fantasy situations in which he has no actual experience (e.g., piloting a helicopter), often creating scripts to guide play
- Expresses needs and wants effectively, but sometimes still impulsively

- Identifies many letters and letter sounds and is interested in learning to read
- Can concentrate on a single task for 20 minutes or more at a time
- Likes to play simple board games
- Is developing phonological awareness, playing orally with sounds and words, which supports his beginning reading skills

- Catches a gently thrown ball consistently, kicks a stationary ball from a run, dribbles a ball with hands and feet
- Enjoys testing muscle strength and skills in comparison to those of peers
- Pours from a small pitcher into a glass without spilling
- Has established right hand dominance

- Can usually zip and button clothing independently; can tie shoes with some proficiency
- Assists with classroom clean-up using a broom and dustpan
- Brushes his teeth with minimal assistance and supervision
- Is independent with all toileting needs

EMMA

Six Years, Hispanic, Female
- Shy and quiet
- Lives in a bilingual home
- Has an older, younger, and twin sister

- Is interested in procedures, rules and rituals
- Is increasingly aware that others sometimes have feelings different from her own
- Will play in a mixed-gender group, but prefers to play with girls
- Often chooses friends based on shared activities and immediate environment rather than shared interests

- Knows the difference between left and right
- Understands the difference between even and odd numbers; can complete simple addition and subtraction problems
- Is interested and eager to expand her vocabulary—about 3,000 new words this year
- Draws people with details, often including eyelashes, eyebrows, hair and clothing accessories

- Uses simple combinations of movements such as running and kicking a ball or jumping and twisting
- Can move in time with music or a beat, varying movement with fast and slow beats
- Has fairly good control of pencils, crayons, and scissors; can cut on a straight or curved line
- Skillfully uses a computer mouse and many keyboard controls

- Folds and puts away some of her own clean laundry
- Brushes her own hair; needs help with ponytails and braids
- Prepares her own PBJ sandwiches
- Is learning to use proper etiquette to answer the telephone

5. What features of Andrew's profile impress you the most? How would you accommodate Andrew's impulsivity in your classroom?

6. Do you think that the fact that Andrew is the oldest of four siblings influences his behavior? How?

7. Why do you think Emma prefers to play with girls? Is this a problem?

8. Do you think Emma's and Andrew's development is "normal" for kindergarten? Is there anything in their profile that you would consider a red flag? What are two things you would do to teach to Emma's strengths? To Andrew's?

TABLE 11.1 Average Height and Weight of Kindergartners

	Boys		Girls	
Age	Height (inches)	Weight (pounds)	Height (inches)	Weight (pounds)
5 years	43	40.5	42.25	40
6 years	45.25	45.5	45.25	44
7 years	48	50	47.75	50
8 years	50.5	56	50.25	56

Note: Remember that averages are just that—averages. Children are different because of their individual differences. Ongoing growth and development tend to accentuate these differences.

Source: Adapted from 2000 CDC Growth Charts: United States, National Center for Health Statistics; accessed May 10, 2010 at www.cdc.gov/growthcharts.

on average, weigh about 44 pounds and are 45 inches tall. At age seven, both boys and girls weigh, on average, 50 pounds and are about 48 inches tall (see Table 11.1).

Social-Emotional Development

Kindergarten children ages five to six are in Erikson's industry vs. inferiority stage of social-emotional development. During this stage they are continuing to learn to regulate their emotions and social interactions. Here are some things you can do to promote kindergartners' positive social-emotional development:

- Provide opportunities for children to be physically and mentally involved in problem solving and social activities with peers and adults. For example, by playing simple games like Tic-Tac-Toe, Connect Four, and Chutes and Ladders, children are challenged to think strategically to win games, while at the same time having fun while learning.[43]

- Give children opportunities to be leaders in projects and activities. Teacher Alice Hays gives every child in her class a job—from cleaning up to organizing learning centers to being classroom manager. She rotates these jobs on a weekly basis so that all children have a chance to be leaders.

- Teach and role-model how to make and keep friends. For example, you can have children work in many different kinds of groups to promote friendships. Group work also demonstrates the importance of working together to achieve a common goal.[44]

- Model positive social and emotional responses. Read stories and discuss feelings such as anger, happiness, guilt, and pride. For example, when you understand that a child's challenging behavior is caused by problems at home, you can show greater concern and empathy and are better able to help children learn appropriate behaviors.[45]

- State your expectations for appropriate behavior and discuss them with your children. For example, Glenwood Elementary School in Chapel Hill, North Carolina, sets clear expectations for student behavior in the classroom, and in shared areas such as the gym, cafeteria, and playground. They have a positive school climate that encourages children to meet and exceed expectations and to excel academically and socially. The school places signs in different locations that explain how students are expected to behave. Each teacher has a system for rewarding students as they meet classroom expectations. Teachers also explain to their children what each expectation means and what it looks like when performed correctly.[46]

Most kindergarten children, especially those who have attended preschool, are very confident and eager to be involved, and they want to and can accept a great deal of responsibility. They like going places and doing things, such as working on projects, experimenting, and working with others. Socially, kindergarten children are both solitary and independent workers and, at the same time, desire to work cooperatively with others. They want to be industrious and successful. Their combination of a can-do attitude and their cooperation and responsibility make them a delight to teach and work with. Kindergarten Teacher of the Year Barb Tingle "enjoys working with her kids." Her classroom culture is based on growth and success. Barb strives to become an expert in both her children's strengths and weaknesses and from there she designs a classroom that fosters success for all students. She believes that everyone is a teacher, and everyone is a student.[47]

Cognitive and Language Development

Kindergarten children are in a period of rapid intellectual and language growth. They have a tremendous capacity to learn words and like the challenge of doing so. This helps explain their love of big words and their ability to say and use them. This is nowhere more apparent than in their fondness for dinosaurs and words such as *brontosaurus*. Kindergarten children like and need to be involved in many language activities.

Additionally, kindergartners like to talk. You should encourage their desire to be verbal by providing many opportunities to engage in various language activities such as singing, telling stories, drama, reciting poetry, and using tongue twisters. You will find a good website for tongue twisters at the end of this chapter. You can also read to children so they discover the joys of hearing stories, learning about words, and using their imaginations.[48]

The Kindergarten Curriculum

The kindergarten curriculum includes activities that support children emotionally, socially, and academically in literacy and reading, mathematics, science, social studies, and the arts. As a future teacher, you should implement curriculum and instructional activities by considering five-, six-, and seven-year-olds' developmental capabilities and their desire to play as they learn.

Literacy, Reading, and Kindergarten Children

Literacy education is discussed in virtually all educational circles, and early childhood professionals spend a lot of time in preparation for how to promote it. Literacy achievement is one of the main objectives of many kindergarten and primary programs. *Literacy* means the ability to read, write, speak, and listen, with an emphasis on reading and writing well, within the context of one's cultural and social setting.

Literacy education is a hot topic for several reasons:

First, too many children and adults cannot read. Twenty percent of Americans are functionally illiterate and read below a fifth-grade level. Forty-two million American adults can't read at all. The number of American adults classified as functionally illiterate increases by about 2.25 million each year.[49]

Second, conventional reading and writing skills developed in the years from birth to age five have a clear and consistently strong relationship with later conventional literacy skills.[50]

Third, businesses and industry are concerned about how unprepared the nation's workforce is to meet the demands of the workplace. Critics of the educational establishment

literacy education
Teaching that focuses on reading, writing, speaking, and listening.

maintain that many high school graduates do not have the basic literacy skills required for today's high-tech jobs.[51] Therefore, schools, especially in the early grades, are feeling the pressure to adopt measures that will give future citizens the skills they will need for productive work and create a stronger foundation for school and life success.[52] (See the chapter opening quotation of President Obama).

Fourth, state governments are at the forefront of making sure all children learn to read well and that they read on level by third grade. Not surprisingly, then, the goals for kindergarten learning are higher than they were in the past.[53]

Emergent Literacy.   The literacy terms in Figure 11.1 will prove helpful in our discussion of literacy.

Emergent literacy is used to explain and describe the process of how children interact with books and with writing even though they cannot read in a conventional sense.[54] This process begins at birth and continues throughout preschool, kindergarten, and the primary grades. Children's emergent literacy activities include reading from pictures, writing while scribbling, and dictating stories to teachers.

Emergent literacy emphasizes using environmental and social contexts to support and extend children's reading and writing. Children want to make sense of what they read and write. The meaningful part of reading and writing occurs when children talk to

FIGURE 11.1

Reading/Literacy Instructional Terminology

Alphabet knowledge The knowledge that letters have names and shapes and letters can represent sounds in language.

Example: Children recognize and name the letters of the alphabet.

Alphabetic principle Awareness that each speech sound or phoneme in a language has its own distinctive graphic representation and an understanding that letters go together in patterns to represent sounds.

Example: Letters and letter patterns represent sounds of the language. Introduce just letters that are used a lot such as M, A, T, S, P, and H. Teach consonants first for sound–letter relationships.

Comprehension In reading, the basic understanding of the words and the content or meaning contained within printed material.

Example: Keisha is able to retell the story. Mario is able to tell who the main character is.

Decoding Identifying words through context and phonics.

Example: James can figure out how to read a word he does not know by using his knowledge of letters and sounds. Also, he uses context clues (information from pictures and the sentence before and the sentence after a word) to decode it. He looked at the picture with a "pile" of wood to figure out *pile,* a word he did not know.

Orthographic awareness The ability to analyze visually the appearance and structure of words.

Example: Ben knows the word *man* and uses that knowledge to read the word *fan.*

Phoneme The smallest unit of speech that makes a difference to meaning.

Example: The word *pig* has three phonemes, /p/ /i/ /g/.

Phonemic awareness The ability to notice, think about, and work with the individual sounds in spoken words.

Example: Alex can identify the words in a set that begin with the same sound: *boy, big, bike.*

Phonics The learning of alphabetic principles of language and knowledge of letter–sound relationships.

Example: Children learn to associate letters with the phonemes (basic speech sounds) to help break the alphabetic code.

Phonological awareness The ability to manipulate language at the levels of syllables, rhymes, and individual speech sounds.

Example: Maria can distinguish words that rhyme from those that don't rhyme. Whitney can match words that sound alike. Caroline can segment words into sounds. Angie can blend sounds into words.

Print awareness The recognition of conventions and characteristics of a written language.

Example: Mario pretends to read a bedtime story to his teddy bear. Also, he recognizes the Kentucky Fried Chicken sign on his way to school.

each other, write letters, and read good literature or have it read to them. All of this occurs within a print-rich environment, one in which children see others read, make lists, and use language and the written word to achieve goals.

Reading to and with children is an excellent way to scaffold their learning and to invite them into processes and activities that support their literacy development. In emergent literacy, becoming literate is viewed as a natural process; reading and writing are processes that children participate in naturally, long before they come to school. No doubt you have participated with or know of toddlers and preschoolers who are literate in many ways. They "read" all kinds of signs (Taco Bell) and labels (Campbell's soup) and "write" with and on anything and everything.

English Language Learners.   With the increasing demands for accountability and high academic achievement for all students, educational policy makers are increasing their attention to young children (ages three to eight) from non-English-speaking backgrounds.[55] Children who speak a language other than English in the home and are not fully fluent in English are considered English language learners (ELLs). All children can benefit cognitively, linguistically, and culturally from learning more than one language. Research suggests that young ELL children are quite capable of learning subject matter in two languages. The rate of growth of ELLs in America's school systems over the past decade is dramatic, with some southern states experiencing 300 to 400 percent increases. In some parts of the country, more than 50 percent of the kindergarten population comes from non-English-speaking homes. As a group, ELL students struggle to become fluent in English, lag well behind in terms of academic achievement, and have dropout rates almost twice those of native English speakers.[56] This is why today, beginning in kindergarten and before, educators place a premium helping ELLs learn English and become successful in school.

Approaches to Literacy and Reading for Young Children.   Literacy and reading are certainly worthy national and educational goals, not only for young children but for everyone. However, how best to promote literacy has always been a controversial topic. Here are some approaches to reading instruction that are incorporated into basic reading programs today.

Whole Word.   One of the most popular methods used for literacy and reading development is the *sight word approach* (also called *whole word* or *look-say*), in which children learn whole words (e.g., *cat, bat, sat*) and develop a sight vocabulary that enables them to begin reading and writing. Visual–spatial learners in particular do well with a whole word approach. Here are some things you can do to teach children to read with a whole word approach:

- Label things in their classrooms (e.g., door, bookcase, desk) as a means of teaching sight vocabulary.
- Create a **word wall**. Word walls are a collection of words displayed on a wall or other display place in the classroom designed to promote literacy learning. Words for the word wall come from stories, sight vocabulary lists, and children's writing.
- Create an **interactive word wall**. Interactive word walls enhance vocabulary learning as children interactively engage in activities structured around words on the word wall. In addition, children can take the words off the wall and use them to help with

Reading plays an important role in the kindergarten curriculum. Provide your children many opportunities to read different kinds of books, including nonfiction literature such as science, math, and alphabet books, fairy tales, biographies, cookbooks, and newspaper and magazine articles.

word wall A collection of words displayed on a wall or another display place in the classroom designed to promote literacy learning.

interactive word wall A collection of frequently used words in the classroom that children use to make sentences or use in other classroom literacy activities.

their spelling. Kindergarten teacher Mandy Richmond plays Twenty Questions with her children. She picks a word from the interactive word wall and the children ask twenty questions to help discover the secret word![57]

• Use picture dictionaries and other dictionaries. Children love to look up words and this supports their research skills.

• Have children match words to pictures and objects. This is one approach used in Montessori programs.

• Have children make their own books and keep journals. They can use whole words to write stories, poems, and such. Each child can have his or her own word box/file to keep words for reading and writing. Each time a child learns/uses a new word, he or she can put that word in the file.[58]

The emergent literacy and reading models view reading and written language acquisition as a continuum of development. Think of children as being on a continuous journey toward full literacy development.

A good source of sight words is the Dolch Sight Words, a list of 220 words children need for reading fluency. Many of the 220 words cannot be sounded out and must be learned by sight.[59] Its website is listed at the end of this chapter.

Phonics.   Another popular approach to literacy and reading is *phonics instruction,* which stresses letter–sound correspondence. By learning these connections, children are able to combine sounds into words (*C-A-T*). The proponents of phonics instruction argue that letter–sound correspondence enables children to make automatic connections between words and sounds and, as a result, to sound out words and read them on their own.[60]

From the 1950s until the present time, there has been much debate about which of these two approaches to literacy development—phonics or whole word—is better. Today, there is a decided reemphasis on the use of phonics instruction. One reason is that research evidence suggests that phonics instruction enables children to become proficient readers.[61]

Language Experience.   Another method of literacy and reading development, the *language experience approach,* follows the philosophy and suggestions inherent in progressive education philosophy. This approach is child centered and maintains that literacy education should be meaningful to children, growing out of experiences that are interesting to them. Using children's own experiences for instructional purposes is a key element in such child-centered approaches. Many teachers transcribe children's dictated experience stories and use them as a basis for writing and for reading instruction.

whole-language approach Philosophy of literacy development that advocates the use of all dimensions of language—reading, writing, listening, and speaking—to help children become motivated to read and write.

Whole Language.   The **whole-language approach** to literacy development advocates using all aspects of language—reading, writing, listening, and speaking—as the basis for developing literacy. Children learn about reading and writing by speaking and listening; they learn to read by writing, and they learn to write by reading. Other characteristics of the whole-language approach:

• Spending time on the processes of reading and writing is an important part of learning to read. Consequently, from the moment they enter the learning setting, children are involved in literacy activities—that is, being read to; "reading" books, pamphlets, and magazines; scribbling; "writing" notes; and so forth.

• The whole word approach is an important part of the whole-language approach.

• Reading, writing, speaking, and listening are taught as an integrated whole, rather than in isolation.

• Writing begins early; children are writing from the time they enter the program.

- Whole language is literature based. Children learn words by reading them and having teachers read to and with them. Also, children's written materials are used as reading materials.

Balanced Approach. As with most things, a balanced approach is generally the best, and many early childhood advocates encourage literacy approaches that provide a balance across all of the methods for teaching children literacy and reading in a print-rich environment. A print-rich environment includes labeling; bulletin boards with children's journals, stories, and such; word walls; a wide variety of books and magazines across all genres; the use of technology to support literacy development and reading; literacy stations (centers); a classroom library; and materials for writing.

Other features of a balanced approach include:

- Intentional instruction in the skills necessary for learning to read: phonics, word recognition, and so forth
- Reading workshops—a process of involving students in reading
- Writing workshops—a teaching technique that makes writing an integrated part of the reading process[62]
- Shared reading (see below)
- Guided reading—a teacher-directed approach that helps all children learn essential reading skills

A primary goal of kindergarten education is for children to learn how to read. Thus, teachers must instruct, support, and guide them in learning what is necessary to be successful in school and life.

Shared Reading. Because children love books and reading, shared reading is a good way for you to capitalize on this interest and help them learn to read. **Shared reading** is a means of introducing children to reading, using favorite books, rhymes, and poems. Teachers model reading for the students by reading aloud a book or other text and ultimately inviting students to join in.

Shared reading builds on children's natural desire to read and reread favorite books. The repeated reading of books over several days, weeks, or months deepens children's understanding of them because each time the reading is for a different purpose: to extend, refine, or deepen children's abilities to read and construct meaning.

Shared reading is especially good for English language learners (ELLs) because it helps make the written language comprehensible and improves English proficiency. The shared reading routine requires that you have on hand a big-book form of the book to be read, as well as multiple little-book copies for individual student re-reading later. For example if you used the children's classic, *If You Give a Pig a Pancake* by Laura Numeroff, (or any other popular children's book), you would follow these three steps:

Step 1. *Introduce the book.* Gather the children where they can all see the big book.

- Show and discuss the book cover: read the title, author, illustrator, and other appropriate book features.
- Discuss some of the pages in the book, but don't give away the entire story.
- Invite children to predict what they think will happen in the book. If they have difficulty, model thinking aloud to show them how you would predict. Record their predictions on a chart for later reference.

Step 2. *Read and respond to the book.* Read the book aloud to the children, holding it so they can see each page. As you read, run your hand or a pointer under each line of print to help children develop a sense of left-to-right orientation, speech-to-print match, and other concepts of print. If some children wish to join in, encourage them to do so.

shared reading A teaching method in which the teacher and children read together from text that is visible to all.

As you read, you may stop briefly to discuss the story or to respond to reactions, but progress through the entire book rather quickly to give children a complete sense of the story. At the conclusion of the reading, encourage children to respond, using 5W questions (who, what, when, where, why) such as these:

- Were your predictions right?
- What did you like best in this story?
- What was your favorite part?
- What made you happy (or sad)?
- Who was your favorite character? Why?
- When did the story take place?
- Why did the pig want a pancake?
- Where did the pig eat the pancake?

Then return to the book, rereading the story and inviting children to read along. Many will feel comfortable doing this right away, but others may not join in until another day. After the second reading, many children will say, "Let's read it again"—especially for books, songs, or rhymes that are lots of fun. Under most circumstances, when children are excited and want to reread, you *should* reread.

After you have read the book again, have children respond, using activities such as these:

- Talk with a friend about a favorite part.
- Retell the story to a partner.
- Draw a picture about the story and write a word or a sentence about it.
- Draw and write about a favorite character.
- Write a list of favorite characters.

Help children become comfortable with making decisions by initially giving them only a couple of choices.

Step 3.   *Extend the book.*   You may want to wait until children have read a book several times before extending it, or you may wait unit they have read several books within a thematic unit and combine them for extension activities. Although each repeated reading may seem to be just for fun, each should have a particular focus. You might first invite children to recall what the title was and what the book was about, prompting and supporting them if necessary.

Then tell the children why they are rereading the book, using statements such as the following:

- "As we reread this book, let's think about who the important characters are" (comprehension).
- "In our story today, notice how the author repeats lines over and over" (exploring language).
- "Today, as we reread one of our favorite stories, look for places to use phonics skills we have been learning" (decoding).[63]

Using the 5E Model to Plan Lessons.   Part of your role as a kindergarten teacher is to write lesson plans, either individually or as a team member. Some school districts have prepared lesson plans that you will be required to use. Other districts may ask you to prepare lesson plans a week or two in advance. Whatever the case may be, a good lesson plan helps you be an effective teacher.

The 5E Model is a valuable approach to lesson planning. There are regional and even district differences in curriculum, but the use of 5E Model lessons is effective for any classroom, anywhere, for several reasons. First, these lessons are research based, and enhance both teacher and student performance. Second, the 5E Model encourages and supports active learning and is constructivist in its approach and design. Third, the lessons are designed to develop knowledge while at the same time forming collaborative relationships between children and between children and teachers. Fourth, these lessons lend themselves easily to differentiation among various types of learners, allowing students to progress through varying levels of Bloom's Taxonomy of Inquiry. Finally, they are layered (structured to build on prior knowledge) to ensure that all learners are successful.

The 5E Model emphasizes the five Es:

- **Engage**
- **Explore**
- **Explain**
- **Extend**
- **Evaluate**

The 5E Model lesson plan on pages 318–319 is an excellent example of the 5E approach.

Writing Workshop. Writing workshops help children gain skills and confidence they need to be good writers. Kindergarten teacher Lauren Gonzales uses writing workshops in her class. Lauren starts with "Kid Writing," a process using inventive spelling, in which children write words any way they want, regardless of spelling. Lauren then moves on to phonetic spelling. She then teaches children what she calls "Star Writing," in which the children learn how to:

- Write and spell sight words correctly
- Use spaces
- Use capital letters when needed
- Use correct punctuation

When Lauren thinks her children are ready she then uses the Six-Trait Writing Method.[64] (See the 5E Model lesson plan.) The six traits include:

- *Ideas:* Have children include ideas (people I know, things I do, things I have, places I go). More ideas lead to better writing.
- *Organization:* Have children look at the structure of their writing (beginning, middle, and end).
- *Voice:* Encourage children to find their writer's voice and write to their audience (a note to mom would be in a more informal voice than a story the child writes about her dog to read to the class).
- *Word Choice:* Have children use word walls and encourage them to think about their word choice.
- *Sentence Fluency:* Teach children to check for smooth writing and varied sentence structure (Are my sentences easy to understand?).
- *Conventions:* Have children check their work for mechanics of writing (punctuation, capitalization, grammar, paragraphing, etc.).[65]

Reader's Workshop. Duval County Florida schools conduct reader's workshops by immersing children in rich literature and mini-lessons that teach that reading is fun and exciting. In their workshops they use books with great stories and identifiable characters, settings, sequenced events, problems, and solutions. Haley Alverado's reading workshop classes look at four important components:

- *Connecting:* Haley begins the lesson by connecting yesterday's lesson with today's lesson. The previous day's lesson focused on *Goldilocks and the Three Bears*, and

Lesson Title: Pumpkin Venn Diagram

Time Frame for Lesson: Two days in October

    Day 1—Read story and complete Venn diagram
    Day 2—Journal-writing activity

Standards: Texas Essential Knowledge and Skills (TEKS):

(English Language Arts—Reading/Comprehension of Literary Text/Theme and Genre)

Include appropriate state/ district standards for kindergarten

- K.6A Identify elements of a story including setting, character, and key events.
- K.8A Retell a main event from a story read aloud.
- K.8B Describe characters in a story and the reasons for their actions.
- K.10B Retell important facts in a text, heard or read. (Writing/Writing Process)
- K.13A Plan a first draft by generating ideas for writing through class discussion (with adult assistance).
- K.13E Share writing with others (with adult assistance).
- K.14A Dictate or write sentences to tell a story and put the sentences in chronological sequence.

Materials: Copy of the book, *The Biggest Pumpkin Ever* by Steven Kroll and illustrated by Jeni Bassett; a large piece of butcher paper; markers; student journals or writing paper; pencils; and crayons.

Targeted Vocabulary: Venn diagram; fertilizer/fertilized; manure; enormous; and admire.

Lesson Procedure:

Step 1—Engage: Introduce children in the text. Read *The Biggest Pumpkin Ever* by Steven Kroll.

Step 2—Explore: Have children raise their hands to do an open retell of the story. (An open retell is an opportunity for students to take turns telling the events of the story.)[1] Have them try to sequence the events of the story as each student raises his/her hand to volunteer a response. Ask, "What happened first? What did Desmond do to care for the pumpkin? What happened next?"

Step 3—Explain: The learner will compare and contrast the two main characters in the story, Desmond and Clayton, using a Venn diagram. Explain that today we are going to make a Venn diagram and that a Venn diagram is an illustration of how two things are alike and how they are different. Practice making a Venn diagram on the white board together as a class, comparing two other things such as apples and oranges, dogs and cats, and so on.

Step 4—Extend: Using the butcher paper, draw two large intersecting circles, and draw features on them to resemble two large pumpkins. At the top of one pumpkin, write <u>Clayton</u>. At the top of the other pumpkin write <u>Desmond</u>.

Questions to ask:

- What did each mouse do to take care of the pumpkin?
- What did Clayton and Desmond want to do with their pumpkins?
- Where did each mouse live?
- Who else helped to care for the pumpkin?
- What happened to the pumpkin at the end of the story?

Include the 5W questions: Who? What? Why? Where? When?

As children begin to answer these questions and discuss similarities and differences, the teacher writes sentences to fill in the Venn diagram based on their comments. If there is something specific to Clayton, write it on the pumpkin on the left. If it is specific to Desmond, then write it on the pumpkin on the right. If there is something that they both have in common, write it in the space where both pumpkins intersect. Once the Venn diagram is complete, encourage students to discuss among themselves what they can observe from the Venn diagram.

Step 5—Evaluate:

Integrate reading and writing

Once students have completed the Venn diagram, have them do a writing activity about pumpkins. They may discuss in a small group or with a partner how to grow a pumpkin. They will then write a story about "How to Grow a Pumpkin." This may be done on writing paper or in writing journals. This is an excellent time for differentiation of strategies to be used.[2] In evaluating the stories, a teacher may do so through informal observation by having the students read their entries to him or her. Or a more formal evaluation may be performed by using a rubric. The rubric should include rating the writer as "emerging," "developing," or "proficient" in the areas of ideas, organization, voice, word choice, sentence fluency, and conventions (this is commonly referred to as the Six-Trait Writing Method). This lesson also lends itself well to extension through science and social studies.[3] The student writing sample meets the expectations defined in the rubric. The student performed the task with little to no help from the teacher.

Today is Wednesday. I will plant a seed. What will it be? I will water it. It grew (growed) and grew until it was the biggest pumpkin in the world! We are getting ready for Halloween. I like pumpkins.

Source: Lynne B. Rhodes, team leader and kindergarten teacher, Curtsinger Elementary School, Frisco, Texas. Photos by Jenny Clemens (p. 318, top) and Lynne B. Rhodes (pp. 318, bottom, and 319).

[1]*One way to ensure that every student has an opportunity to share is to write their names on craft sticks. Teacher takes turns drawing a stick out of a cup and calling on that student to speak. This is a fair and unbiased technique.*

[2]*Suggestions for differentiating among various levels of learners: The high-level ability learner may independently write in his/her journal with no help from the teacher. The average learner may need help sounding out words. The lower-level learner may need to dictate sentences to the teacher and then copy them over.*

[3]*In an authentic kindergarten classroom, you could also do different 5E lessons focusing on science and/or math. In science, students could carve a pumpkin and plant the seeds and observe them as they grow. In math, they could weigh a pumpkin, measure it, count the seeds, and so forth.*

today's lesson focuses on a nonfiction book. The class then begins by drawing a chart comparing all the nonfiction features to the fictional story, *Goldilocks and the Three Bears*.

- *Teaching:* In the teaching component Haley teaches children some of the features that are in the nonfiction text versus their previous readings. She lists things such as
  - Has real pictures
  - Teaches things that we did not know before
  - Has captions and fun facts
- *Active Involvement:* In this part of the workshop Haley has groups discuss things that they noticed in the nonfiction book. She adds additional features the children noticed.
- *Linking:* To link the lesson to independent reading, Haley gives each child a sticky note to place on any page that they find any of the non-fiction text features listed.[66]

Math in the Kindergarten.   In today's kindergarten classroom, math, along with reading, plays a very prominent role. If you were to glimpse a kindergarten classroom, you might see groups and individual children engaged in such activities as graphing data from their observations and experiments; writing in their math journals; counting, sorting, and comparing concrete objects and keeping records of their work; making decisions about how to earn and spend money; working on computer math games and lessons; reading books about math; and engaged in math center activities. Kindergartners are active learners and like to learn with concrete materials in hands-on, "minds-on" active learning.

Your teaching of mathematics in kindergarten should be in alignment with the National Council of Teachers of Mathematics (NCTM) curriculum focal points. Curriculum focal points are important mathematical topics for each grade level, from pre-kindergarten through grade twelve. The integration of your math curriculum with the curriculum focal points should promote these five processes: problem solving; reasoning; communication; making connections; and designing and analyzing representations.[67]

Review now the NCTM kindergarten curriculum focal points in Figure 11.2. Note how the focus in kindergarten on mathematics is in the areas of number and operations, geometry, and measurement.

State standards, which come in part from NCTM standards, primarily determine the subject matter content or "what gets taught" in the kindergarten. Take the kindergarten mathematics content standards for California, for example. They specify that students should understand small numbers, quantities, and simple shapes in their everyday environment and be able to count, compare, describe and sort objects, and develop a sense of properties and patterns. The standards describe the level at which students do these tasks so it is clear, for example, that a kindergartner should be able to "Compare two or more sets of objects (up to ten objects in each group) and identify which set is equal to, more than, or less than the other."[68]

How teachers teach math content to kindergartners is quite often left up to them, although in some school districts, teachers have to use and follow school district lesson plans. The primary reason more districts are using "scripted" lesson plans is because they want to ensure that all children are learning what the standards call for.

Science in the Kindergarten

Science plays an increasingly important role in the kindergarten curriculum. If our children are to develop a love of science and the ability to think and express themselves scientifically, they need to learn about scientific concepts, methods, and attitudes while they are young.

FIGURE 11.2

NCTM's Curriculum Focal Points of Kindergarten

The set of three curriculum focal points and related connections for mathematics in kindergarten follow. These topics are the recommended content emphases for this grade level. It is essential that these focal points be addressed in contexts that promote problem solving, reasoning, communication, making connections, and designing and analyzing representations.

Kindergarten Curriculum Focal Points	Connections to the Focal Points
Number and Operations: Representing, comparing, and ordering whole numbers and joining and separating sets Children use numbers, including written numerals, to represent quantities and to solve quantitative problems, such as counting objects in a set, creating a set with a given number of objects, comparing and ordering sets or numerals by using both cardinal and ordinal meanings, and modeling simple joining and separating situations with objects. They choose, combine, and apply effective strategies for answering quantitative questions, including quickly recognizing the number in a small set, counting and producing sets of given sizes, counting the number in combined sets, and counting backward.	**Data Analysis:** Children sort objects and use one or more attributes to solve problems. For example, they might sort solids that roll easily from those that do not. Or they might collect data and use counting to answer such questions as, "What is our favorite snack?" They re-sort objects by using new attributes (e.g., after sorting solids according to which ones roll, they might re-sort the solids according to which ones stack easily).
Geometry: Describing shapes and space Children interpret the physical world with geometric ideas (e.g., shape, orientation, spatial relations) and describe it with corresponding vocabulary. They identify, name, and describe a variety of shapes, such as squares, triangles, circles, rectangles, (regular) hexagons, and (isosceles) trapezoids presented in a variety of ways (e.g., with different sizes or orientations), as well as such three-dimensional shapes as spheres, cubes, and cylinders. They use basic shapes and spatial reasoning to model objects in their environment and to construct more complex shapes.	**Geometry:** Children integrate their understandings of geometry, measurement, and number. For example, they understand, discuss, and create simple navigational directions (e.g., "Walk forward ten steps, turn right, and walk forward five steps").
Measurement: Ordering objects by measurable attributes Children use measurable attributes, such as length or weight, to solve problems by comparing and ordering objects. They compare the lengths of two objects both directly (by comparing them with each other) and indirectly (by comparing both with a third object), and they order several objects according to length.	**Algebra:** Children identify, duplicate, and extend simple number patterns and sequential and growing patterns (e.g., patterns made with shapes) as preparation for creating rules that describe relationships.

Source: Reprinted with permission from *Curriculum Focal Points for Prekindergarten Through Grade 8 Mathematics: A Quest for Coherence,* copyright 2006 by the National Council of Teachers of Mathematics. All rights reserved. The complete document may be viewed at www.nctm.org/focalpoints.

This gives them a foundation for future work in the sciences, math, language, and the arts. One of the most effective ways for young children to learn about science is through first-hand authentic objects and real specimens.[69] The accompanying Voice from the Field, "How to Integrate Science and Literacy in Kindergarten," provides you with important guidelines for how to make sure your children are scientifically literate. Pay particular attention to the 5E Model for lesson planning.

Why Is Teaching Science in Kindergarten Important?   Science is assuming a more important role in kindergarten for these reasons:

- Science is an ideal vehicle for developing children's questioning minds about the natural world.

Voice from the Field

How to Integrate Science and Literacy in Kindergarten

Lightning is flashing and thunder is rolling in my bilingual kindergarten classroom. The children are trying to say how the storm is scaring them. But they don't know how to describe what's going on. They can only say that there's a lot of rain and wind. They've never heard the words for thunder or lightning—in either Spanish or English! Since many of these children are performing at high levels in other areas, this underdevelopment of oral language in science is amazing. No wonder we see such high failure rates in state science test scores!

If our children are to develop a love of science and the ability to think and express themselves scientifically, they need to learn about scientific concepts, methods, and attitudes while they are young. This gives them a foundation for future work in the sciences, math, language, and the arts.

Kindergartners Can Act Like Scientists

Teaching children what a scientist is and what scientists do is fundamental to science education. Scientists observe with their five senses (sight, touch, taste, smell, and hearing). They draw what they see, write about their observations, classify, ask questions, make predictions, create models, design experiments, count accurately, test their hypotheses, repeat their experiments, and keep on trying. Children learn this scientific method and practice it from pre-kindergarten to grade twelve. Use the following information to help you plan ways to integrate science.

ELEMENT 1 Plan an Activity and Address Standards

Always plan activities that provide opportunities to *engage, explore, explain, elaborate,* and *evaluate*—the 5E Model. Central to teaching science is developing scientific concepts and methodology rather than merely studying some favorite topic or, worse yet, displaying some dramatic effect, such as a foaming "volcano." State and district standards will have science learning objectives. Plan activities as you consider the standards.

Example: Use "Planting Pumpkin Seeds" (a small part of an ongoing unit) to teach the following objectives as stated in the *Texas Essential Knowledge & Skills* publication:

- Students will ask questions about organisms, objects, and events.
- Students will plan and conduct simple descriptive investigations and communicate their findings.

ELEMENT 2 Include Hands-On Experiences

Because children come from diverse backgrounds, they may not all have experience with a particular topic. To level the playing field, begin every science unit with an activity that *engages* the students with a shared, hands-on experience.

Example: Bring a real pumpkin to the classroom and let the children touch it. Ask them to describe it and encourage them to ask questions.

Teacher:	"What do you notice about the pumpkin?"
Jonathan:	"It's orange."
Sara:	"It's like a ball."
Carolina:	"It has brown spots on it."
Anthony:	"It has lines on it."
Edward:	"It's big."
Teacher:	"What do you wonder about the pumpkin?"
Kevin:	"Is it real?"
Carolina:	"Are there seeds inside?"
Daniela:	"Will it get bigger?"
Pedro:	"Is it heavy?"

ELEMENT 3 Incorporate Writing and Drawing

- Model writing for the class by recording on a chart what children say about the pumpkin.
- Encourage interactive writing. With guidance from the teacher, children take turns with a marker on

- Implementing the National Science Education Standards helps students take their place in a scientifically literate society.
- When children explore science they acquire oral and written language for scientific expression—and learn to read in new contexts.
- Science teaches children to appreciate the diversity of life and its interconnectedness.
- When children learn about nature they respect and care for our planet and its natural resources.

a large piece of paper writing their observations as a group and using invented spelling.
- Teach children to make direct observations by individually drawing only what they see—in their science journals or on recording sheets.
- Depending on the children's developmental levels, they will either write about their observations, or you will record their observations.

ELEMENT 4 Incorporate Literature

- Incorporate both nonfiction and fiction materials for read-alouds, free reading, and research: *Apples and Pumpkins* (Rockwell, Anne), *Calabazas/Pumpkins* (Berger, Melvin & Gilda), *From Seed to Plant* (Fowler, Allan), *From Seed to Pumpkin* (Pfeffer, Wendy), *Pumpkin Jack* (Hubbell, Will), *Pumpkin, Pumpkin* (Titherington, Jeanne), and *Too Many Pumpkins* (White, Linda). Also, choose nonfiction books with photos (including children if possible): *Perfect Pumpkins* (Bauer, Jeff) and *Pumpkin Circle* (Levenson, George) (Spanish version: *El círculo de las calabazas*) are two examples.
- Use charts of songs and poems for shared reading to teach scientific vocabulary and concepts.
- Explain science text features such as table of contents, diagram labels, glossary, and index.

ELEMENT 5 Ask Questions to Promote Student-Designed Experiments

- Start children wondering. Model asking testable questions for the children:

  "What would happen if we watered these seeds?"
  "What would happen if we didn't water some others?"
  "What would happen if these seeds got a lot of light?"
  "What would happen if these seeds got a little light?"

- Ask: "Which of these would grow faster and how could we find out?"

- Now say:

  "Let's put three seeds in each cup with some soil."
  "We'll put one cup where it will get a lot of light and water the seeds."
  "We'll put one cup where it will get a lot of light and not water the seeds."
  "We'll put one cup where it will get a little bit of light and water the seeds."
  "We'll put one cup where it will get a little bit of light and not water the seeds."

- Prompt the class to make predictions and record their answers.

  Brandon: "I think the seeds will grow in three days."
  Samantha: "I think the seeds will grow in five days."

- The children will check the seeds every day and record the results in their science journals.
- Use plastic connecting cubes or some other nonstandard unit of measure such as paper clips to determine which plants are growing faster.
- Discuss the results.

Additional Strategies

Go into depth with a few topics rather than scratching the surface of many. Place additional materials in the science center for the children to explore and extend their studies of seeds, plants, and life cycles. Some examples are a tray with paper, crayons, and rubbing plates of leaves; field identification guides of leaves, trees, and other plants; seeds for sorting and sorting sheets; rubber stamps of the life cycle of a plant for the children to use to sequence the life cycle of a plant; and plant puzzles.

Source: Contributed by Lori D. Cadwallader, bilingual kindergarten teacher and Denton (Texas) ISD Teacher of the Year. She is an authorized International Baccalaureate World School staff development trainer for "SALSA" (Science and Literacy Saturday Academy) and "The Nature of Science."

- Learning scientific methods teaches children to view themselves as scientists.
- Exciting lessons in science can foster a lifelong love for the subject.[70]

Scaffolding with Science.   Science offers many wonderful opportunities to apply Vygotsky's ideas, especially scaffolding. For example, in meeting the science content standard *science as inquiry*, a problem-solving chart like that shown in Figure 11.3 can help you not only teach

FIGURE 11.3

A Sample Problem-Solving Chart

① Identify Problem	② Preview Solution	③ Assemble Resources
What kind of soil will a bean seed grow in: soil from outside our classroom, humus, sand, water, rocks, or clay?	We think that a bean seed will grow best in humus because it has nutrients in it.	We need soil from outside our classroom, humus, sand, water, rocks, clay, see-through cups, beans, and a well-lit place in our classroom.
④ Analyze Resources & Plans	⑤ Select Plan & Begin Doing It	⑥ Monitor the Process
We need to make sure each cup gets the same amount of light. We need to make sure we use the same amount of planting material.	Each group of four students needs to plan the experiment and do it.	What is happening to the seeds? After four days? After eight days? Why is this happening?

Source: *Launching Learners in Science, PreK–5* by K. C. Williams and G. E. Veomett. Copyright 2007 by Sage Publications Inc. Reproduced with permission of Sage Publications Inc. via Copyright Clearance Center.

science as inquiry but also help your students learn the process of scientific inquiry in their study of plants and how they grow.

Social Studies in Kindergarten

In kindergarten, the social sciences most often included are history, geography, economics, and civics.[71] For each of these disciplines you will want to include knowledge, concepts, and themes. Your teaching of the social studies should be content based and child centered, and you will want to make sure you consult your state's content standards for social studies.

Historically, social studies in the kindergarten focused on the **expanding horizons approach** (or *expanding environments approach*) for sequencing and selecting content. In this approach children are at the center of the expanding horizons and at each grade level are immersed in a widening environment.

Today's teaching of the social studies is also designed to provide children with content knowledge and skills from the four social sciences. You will want to make sure you provide children with authentic content and activities that help them learn knowledge, apply knowledge, and engage in critical thinking.

Ideas for Teaching Social Studies.   The following are some ideas you can use to help you teach the social studies content standards of your state and school district:

- *Geography.* Emily Thompson teaches her kindergarten class about different cultures by placing a ribbon on a world map with the United States on one end and the other end on the country they are studying. Emily discusses with her students the different modes of transportation that are available for travel to the country. Children place pictures on the map above that country pertaining to the culture there. Emily then instructs the children to draw a picture, write a story, or create a poem to put on the map as well.

expanding horizons approach Also called the *expanding environments approach*, an approach to teaching social studies where the student is at the center of the expanding horizons and initial units, and at each grade level is exposed to an ever-widening environment.

- *Economics.* Latonya Carter teaches her children about assembly lines through the use of creative arts. She draws a picture of a stick figure person using a different color crayon for each line drawn. After displaying the drawing on the wall, she then separates her class into small groups and gives each group member a different color crayon and one piece of paper per group. The piece of paper is passed down the line of students, and each student draws one line with their crayon matching Latonya's drawing. The class then discusses the importance of assembly lines, why each member must do his or her part, and the different products made on assembly lines.

- *Civics.* Brandon Phillips has his kindergarten children make a U.S. flag collage using large paper, magazines, crayons, scissors, and glue. He then discusses with the class that the flag is a national symbol, explains what the stars and stripes stand for, and discusses the role national symbols play in society. Children then tell Brandon where they've seen the American flag flown, and he makes a list of these places on chart paper. After the discussion, students individually draw pictures of other flags they have seen.

- *History.* Madelyn Hubbard teaches her kindergarten children about ancient cultures through photographs and online reproductions of wall paintings from ancient civilizations that illustrate life as it was lived in ancient times. She then asks the students to give her ideas about which animals lived at that time, which animals the people hunted, and what games the people played. Madelyn then has her students illustrate a picture of a day in their lives. The pictures include scenes such as driving to school, reading in class, recess, lunch, and playing with pets or siblings at home. After their drawings are complete, Madelyn hangs the students' pictures next to the pictures of the ancient civilization. The class then holds a discussion about the similarities and differences in the ancient civilizations and their own.

Arts in Kindergarten

Teaching the arts in kindergarten consists of knowledge, skills, and concepts from these four areas: music, art, dance, and theater. Unfortunately the arts in the curriculum are not as highly valued as they should be. You can, however, teach the arts "across the curriculum" by integrating them with reading, math and science. All integration of the arts depends on these factors: time, opportunity, and materials.

Time.   Finding time to teach the arts is often a problem because of the emphasis on reading/literacy and math in the primary grades. Solve the problem by integrating the arts into your already scheduled time for teaching reading/literacy, math, science, and social studies. The following are ideas for integrating the arts into each of these areas:

Reading /Literacy.   Students can act out the stories of their favorite book, thereby engaging in drama; students can illustrate a story that they or the class have written.

Math.   Students can use art materials to make charts and graphs, and to design and make different kinds of shapes. Students can also develop rules to describe the relationship of one shape to another; for example, "You can put two right triangles together to make a rectangle."

Science.   Children can use their artistic skills to draw and paint various examples of the life cycle of butterflies or write and produce a public service announcement on the importance of personal health in the kindergarten classroom.

Social Studies.   Students can learn about and sing many of the songs popular in their state's history; students can learn the folk dances of various cultural groups in their state.

Opportunity.   The opportunities to teach the arts during the school year are endless. Consider the events that children are already experiencing in their everyday lives in their community. Was there a fire nearby? Is there a construction project? Did a storm pass through town? Did the zoo expand? Capitalize on such opportunities by weaving artistic elements such as puppetry, stories, drawing, or model building into the content areas. For example, in discussing the collapse of a bridge as the result of a flood, one teacher read the story *The Three Billy Goats Gruff*, and children made paper masks to depict the goats and built a bridge out of blocks and other found materials. Students clamored for a starring role as the troll. Every thematic unit provides opportunities for all of the arts, and children should be encouraged to explore ways to express ideas from the thematic units in an artistic way.

Materials.   Materials are just as important as time and opportunity. Materials include all of the materials related to the visual arts—paints, crayons, markers, brushes, and so on— as well as materials necessary for music and dance. For example, you can provide materials such as DVDs of folk dances, popular songs, and sing-along tunes. To encourage theater expression, children need props: clothes, hats, puppets, and plenty of materials such as cardboard boxes, glue, and tape for making their own stage settings and backgrounds. Keep in mind that the *process* of exploring the creative arts is more important than the finished *product*. Children are learning to enjoy learning when teachers respect the *process* of learning. You can create an arts center in which you have materials—paper, chalk, paintbrushes, pencils, and so on, with which children can represent the results of their scientific experiments, graph their math data, and illustrate their creative stories, poetry, and personal journals.

Developmentally Appropriate Practice

Throughout this book I emphasize that in all things early childhood professionals do for and with children, their efforts should be *developmentally appropriate*. Developmentally appropriate practice involves teaching and learning that is in accordance with children's physical, cognitive, social, linguistic, cultural, and gender development. Professionals help children learn and develop in ways that are compatible with their ages and who they are as individuals; that is, respecting their background of experiences and culture.

Talking about developmentally appropriate practice is one thing; actually doing it is another. Here are some things you can do to make your kindergarten program developmentally appropriate and help children learn:

- Make learning meaningful to children by relating it to what they already know. For example, last week Blanca Davis and her children planted seeds and watched them sprout and grow. They talked about what plants need to grow and why some of their plants died. Yesterday, when the class pet, Fishey, died, Blanca took the opportunity to extend their discussion about living things and death. She selected two special books, *Goodbye Mousie* and *Jasper's Day,* to read to the children.
- Individualize your curriculum as much as possible to account for the needs of all children of all diversities of abilities and backgrounds. All children do not learn the same way, nor are they interested in learning the same things as everyone else all the time.
- Make learning physically and mentally active. Children should be actively involved in learning activities—building, making, experimenting, investigating, and working collaboratively with their peers.
- Involve children in *hands-on* activities with concrete objects and manipulatives. Emphasize real-life activities as opposed to workbook and worksheet activities.

Remember, developmentally appropriate practice begins with you.

Accommodating Diverse Learners

Now that you have read about changes and issues in kindergartens today, let's focus our attention on the transition to kindergarten for children with disabilities. Most parents of typically developing children feel positive about their child's transition to kindergarten, but they nonetheless remain anxious about this major entry point into the world of school. Parents of children with disabilities share these worries with other parents and also have practical questions related to how, where, when, and who will provide their children's services. For the many parents who have worked hard to establish support systems in their preschools, the thought of starting all over again from scratch can seem daunting. The Individuals with Disabilities Education Act (IDEA) clearly articulates the importance of transitions for children with disabilities from early intervention programs to early childhood special education and inclusive kindergarten classrooms.

You can help facilitate all children's transitions to kindergarten by making a conscious effort to think about the acronym SCHOOL:

S: *Start early.*   Schools must carefully bridge the distance between a play-based curriculum and the increasing academic demands of kindergarten. It is not unreasonable to start the transition process a full year to year and a half before kindergarten begins. For example, in the fall of a child's last year of preschool, teachers at the child's current school should contact the kindergarten to schedule times to meet and visit each program.

C: *Collaborative team approach.*   Planning and making decisions with a collaborative team should involve families, preschool teachers, kindergarten teachers, school administrators, and any related service providers that the child sees (e.g., occupational therapists, physical therapists). For example, the team may observe several schools and choose the one that best meets the needs of the child.

H: *Honor active involvement of families.*   This may include teaching parents about the school and kindergarten and addressing their questions and concerns about how specialized services will be provided for their children. For example, parents may want to meet with the therapists or visit the school with their child prior to the beginning of school.

O: *Observe current and future schools.*   Observe at the preschool and have the teachers and families observe at the kindergarten prior to the start of the kindergarten year. This will allow you to identify the needs and strengths of the child and prepare for any modifications or accommodations. For example, you may observe that the classroom arrangement of the preschool is easily replicated and meets the needs of *all* children.

O: *Outline goals and anticipated outcomes.*   Work as a team to develop the goals and outcomes in the child's Individualized Education Program. This may not be necessary for every child, but *all* children need goals and outcomes to ensure an optimal kindergarten experience. For example, a common kindergarten goal is following rules, routines, and directions. This can then include modifications or adaptations for children who need them.

L: *Listen and learn.*   The child's previous teachers, therapists, and parents have a wealth of child-specific, relevant information that includes strategies or adaptations that have previously been successful. Having a collaborative dialogue also allows you to share the services and supports available at your school. For example, a parent might tell you that a child uses modified scissors when cutting or enjoys social praise.

Activities for Professional Development

Ethical Dilemma

"Full-day kindergarten poses a problem."

In your state, full-day kindergarten is supposed to be offered by every public school starting in the fall of 2012. Although it is a statewide mandate for all school districts in your state, it may or may not happen in your district. District officials are saying that because of the poor economy they are unable to afford to add the teachers and classrooms necessary to make the change from the traditional half-day schedule to a full-day schedule.

Sarah Collins is a kindergarten teacher and a strong advocate for full-day kindergarten. When Sarah heard the news about the delay, she scheduled a meeting with Paul Gardner, the district superintendent, to discuss her concerns about the delay of full-day kindergarten. During their conversation the superintendent said, "A lot of research shows that full-day kindergarten is very beneficial to kids, but there are a lot of districts like us who will have to wait until we find the money to make this happen." Based on her discussion with the superintendent, Sarah is very doubtful that the district will take any action to ensure that full-day kindergarten happens in the fall.

What should Sarah do? Should she keep quiet and say nothing? Or should she talk with the board of education and present her case? Does Sarah ask the president of the local teachers' union to call a special meeting so she can persuade them to take action? Or should Sarah choose another course of action? What should Sarah do? What would you do?

Activities to Apply What You Learned

1. Kindergarten goals today are higher than they were in the past. Discuss with classmates your opinion on kindergarten in the past versus kindergarten today. Update your status on Facebook to see what your friends say.
2. Think about ways you can make your kindergarten classroom environments healthy, respectful, supportive, and challenging. Look for teachers' blogs to see how they make changes to their classroom environments to support these four areas.
3. Go online and research ways you can promote physical, social-emotional, and cognitive development for kindergartners. Identify five of your most important findings and share them by posting links on www.bebo.com.
4. Think about ways kindergarten teachers have used technology to help children learn the curriculum. How can you integrate technology in your classroom to help children learn math, science, reading/literacy and social studies? Demonstrate to your colleagues how you would use this type of technology.
5. How can you make children's transitions from early childhood special education programs to kindergarten easier? Conduct an online interview on Skype with a special education teacher to get his or her advice. Share these suggestions with your peers in a blog, online, or in a discussion.

Linking to Learning

Dolch Sight Words
www.dolchsightwords.org
Dedicated to providing various educational activities to teach reading, including teachers teaching their students and parents teaching their children.

Kindergarten Connection
www.kconnect.com
Dedicated to providing valuable resources to primary teachers; offers new hints, tips, and information each week.

Indian Child
www.indianchild.com
This website provides various resources for parents and teachers. They offer tongue twisters, short stories, optical illusions, and other educational supplements for children.

National Kindergarten Alliance
www.nkateach.org
The result of a summit of leaders from various kindergarten associations, organizations, and interest groups that met in January 2000. A national organization that serves kindergarten teachers throughout the United States.

Susan Elizabeth Blow and History of the Kindergarten
www.froebelweb.org/images/blow.html
Outlines Blow's contributions to the development of the kindergarten and provides many links to Froebel and interesting kindergarten topics.

PEARSON
myeducationlab

Go to Topics 2 (Child Development /Theories) and 8 (DAP/Teaching Strategies) in the MyEducationLab (www.myeducationlab.com) for your course, where you can:

- Find learning outcomes for Child Development/Theories and DAP/Teaching Strategies along with the national standards that connect to these outcomes.
- Complete Assignments and Activities that can help you more deeply understand the chapter content.
- Apply and practice your understanding of the core teaching skills identified in the chapter with the Building Teaching Skills and Dispositions learning units.

- Hear viewpoints of experts in the field in Professional Perspectives.
- Check your comprehension on the content covered in the chapter by going to the Study Plan in the Book Resources for your text. Here you will be able to take a chapter quiz, receive feedback on your answers, and then access Review, Practice, and Enrichment activities to enhance your understanding of chapter content.

12

THE PRIMARY GRADES

Preparation for Lifelong Success

naeyc standards

Standard 4. Using Developmentally Effective Approaches to Connect with Children and Families

I understand and use positive relationships and supportive interactions as the foundation for my work with young children and families. I know, understand, and use a wide array of developmentally appropriate approaches, instructional strategies, and tools to connect with children and families and positively influence each child's development and learning.[1]

Standard 5. Using Content Knowledge to Build Meaningful Curriculum

I understand the importance of developmental domains and academic (or content) disciplines in early childhood curriculum. I use my knowledge and other resources to design, implement, and evaluate meaningful, challenging curricula that promote comprehensive developmental and learning outcomes for every young child.[2]

Teaching in Grades One to Three

Reform continues sweeping across the educational landscape. Nowhere is this more evident than in grades one to three. Changes include how schools operate and are organized, how teachers teach, how children are evaluated, and how schools involve and relate to parents and the community. State governments are specifying curriculum and testing agendas. Accountability and collaboration are in; schooling as usual is out.

The Primary Grades and Contemporary Schooling

Nancy Berry, a first grade teacher in Fort Walton Beach, Florida, and an All-USA Today teacher, welcomes kids from diverse backgrounds and learning styles to "Berryland USA: A Place Where Children Love to Learn." Her classroom is alive with hermit crabs and oysters, uncaged caterpillars, chrysalises and butterflies. Nancy accepts students unconditionally and treats them as if they are smart to make learning a self-fulfilling prophecy. She reassures kids that she made mistakes as a child as a personal example to encourage them to read, write, organize thoughts, and make decisions at a higher level. Nancy uses singing, moving, reading, experiencing, applying, and writing to reach all types of learners. "I don't teach to a test," she says. "I teach to life."[3]

Elizabeth Parker, a second grade teacher and a Milken Family Foundation National Educator Award winner is recognized by supervisors and colleagues as an outstanding literacy educator. According to her principal, "Beth is a teacher leader who constantly researches best teaching practices to better help her students achieve academic success in her classroom and to assist fellow teachers with curriculum and instructional questions." Parker's creative, well-planned, motivating lessons and excellent classroom management skills have helped most of her students read above grade level. Parker's students have also experienced significant gains in math, with many scoring above the district average.[4,5]

Valorie Lewis, a third grade USA Today Teacher, shares her story of overcoming poverty, teasing, and low expectations with her rural Oklahoma students to inspire them to believe in themselves, and believes "there is no such thing as a child without the potential for success." Valorie holds weekly "Community Circle" community meetings in which her students share thoughts and feelings and learn empathy. She fosters an environment where students respect and value others by having kids draw names each week and fill out "Positive Comment Cards" about that person each day to share with the class. Valorie uses multisensory lessons such as cooking to reach all students. She developed a daily review program to practice basic skills and Third Grade Brain Olympics, used in other classes and schools.[6]

As we begin our discussion of living and learning in grades one to three, it will be helpful to look at the nature of primary grades today.

Diversity.   Schools and classrooms are more diverse than ever before. This means you will be teaching children from different cultures and backgrounds, and you will have to take those differences into account in your planning and teaching. In addition to cultural and linguistic differences, diversity is also reflected in socioeconomic status and diversity of physical, cognitive, social, emotional, adaptive, and communication abilities.

> " I am committed to making STEM more accessible to all students—from the kindergartener asking "Why?" to the high school student whose work in original research or sustainability practices might lead to the solutions to problems impacting our nation. "
>
> **JENNIFER HARPER-TAYLOR**
> Siemens Foundation president

Achievement.   The achievement of all students is a high priority locally and nationally. Schools and teachers place a premium on closing the achievement gap that exists between races and socioeconomic levels. In an era in which the American Recovery and Investment Act of 2009 holds them to higher standards of achievement, high-quality teachers are dedicated to ensuring that each child learns.

Testing.   Testing is a part of contemporary school culture. You will be involved in helping students learn appropriate grade-level content so they can pass local, state, and national tests. In addition, you will use test data as a basis for planning.

Standards.   The curriculum of schools is commonly aligned with local, state, and national standards. As a result, you will teach content designed to help students learn what state standards specify within the parameters of national standards. You won't always get to teach exactly what you want to teach, when you want to teach it, and how you want to teach it. However, good teachers always find ways to include in the curriculum what they believe is important and developmentally appropriate. Teaching to the standards does not have to be dull and boring; you can make learning interesting and relevant to your students' lives.

Megan Marie Allen, the 2010 Florida Teacher of the Year, says this about standards and teaching: "We need to work together as states creating focused, unified common standards and smarter assessments so teachers will have more pointed focuses for instruction. Within common standards we need to remember our children and keep standards high enough to prepare them for global success. If we work as a community of advocates, helping our children succeed and putting our students' needs first, then our students, the souls of our communities, will fulfill their dreams and achieve success."[7]

Academics.   The contemporary curriculum in grades one to three is heavy on reading, math, and science. There is also an emphasis on the arts, social studies, character education, and health and wellness through physical education. Many of these other areas, however, are integrated with the basic curriculum.

The primary grades of today are not the same as they were when you were there. Changing times and children demand different approaches. You and other early childhood professionals must look at the education of children in grades one to three with new eyes and a fresh approach.

What Are Children in Grades One to Three Like?

This text stresses the uniqueness and individuality of children, who also share common characteristics. Those common characteristics guide our practice of teaching, but we must always account for individual needs. All children are unique.

How are children of today different from the children of yesterday?

- Children of today are smarter than children of previous generations: average intelligence test scores have increased about three points over each decade.[8] There are a number of reasons for this: better health and nutrition, better-educated parents, better schooling, and access to and involvement with technology, such as computers, electronic games, learning systems, and television.

- Many children bring to school a vast background of experiences that contribute to their knowledge and ability to learn.

- However, many children do *not* have a rich background separate from school experiences, and an increasing number are living in poverty. Today, 21.3 percent of children under age six and 35.7 of children under the age of eighteen live in poverty and come to school unprepared.[9]

- More children are from diverse racial, cultural, and socioeconomic backgrounds. In many communities and schools, children from minority backgrounds make up the majority. Many children from diverse populations come to school with health, home, and learning challenges.

Now let's take a look on pages 334–335 at six typically developing children who are in classrooms today. After you review and reflect on the Portraits of First, Second, and Third Graders, answer the questions that accompany them.

Physical Development

Two words describe the physical growth of primary-age children: *slow* and *steady*. Children at this age do not make the rapid and obvious height and weight gains of infants, toddlers, and preschoolers. Instead, they experience continual growth, develop increasing control over their bodies, and explore the things they are able to do. Primary children are building on the development of their earlier years.

From ages seven to eight, children's average weight and height approximate each other, as shown in Table 12.1. The weight of boys and girls tends to be the same until after age nine, when girls begin to pull ahead of boys in both height and weight. However, wide variations appear in both individual rates of growth and development and in the sizes of children. These differences in physical appearance result from genetic and cultural factors, nutritional intake and habits, health care, and experiential background.

Motor Development

Six-year-old children are in the initiative stage of psychosocial development; seven- and eight-year-old children are in the industry stage. Thus, not only are children intuitively driven to initiate activities, but they are also learning to be competent and productive individuals. The primary years are a time to use and test developing motor skills. Children at this age should be actively involved in activities that enable them to use their bodies to learn and develop feelings of accomplishment and competence. Children's growing confidence and physical skills are reflected in games involving running, chasing, and their enthusiasm in organized sports of all kinds. A nearly universal characteristic of children in this period is their almost constant physical activity.

Differences between boys' and girls' motor skills during the primary years are minimal—their abilities are about equal. Teachers therefore should not use gender as a basis for

TABLE 12.1 Average Height and Weight for First- to Third-Grade Children

Conduct your own survey of the height and weight of primary-age children. Compare your findings with this table. What conclusions can you draw?

| Age | Males | | Females | |
	Height (inches)	Weight (pounds)	Height (inches)	Weight (pounds)
6 years	45.25	45.50	42.25	44.00
7 years	48.00	50.00	47.75	50.00
8 years	50.50	56.00	50.25	56.00
9 years	52.25	62.00	52.50	64.00

Source: Adapted from National Center for Health Statistics in collaboration with the National Center for Chronic Disease Prevention and Health Promotion (2004), www.cdc.gov/growthcharts.

	RAY	**VALERIE**	**SAM**
General Description	Six year old African American, male • Humorous, active • Interested in art and nature • Lives with both parents and older sister	Seven year old biracial Japanese American, female • Outgoing and confident • Laughs and talks loudly to friends • Only child of older parents	Eight year old Caucasian, male • Sensitive, easily distracted • Interested in science and animals • Lives with both parents and has two older brothers
Social-Emotional	• Seeks attention and reassurance; unable to sit still listening to a story or to other children • Feels he has no friends (new this year) • Unaware of many classmates' names (together 6 months) • Worries about coming to school	• Eagerly volunteers and shares thoughts with the class • Enjoys interacting with boys more than girls in class and recess • Loves to read alone absorbed in a book • Aware of others' special needs but laughs at their mistakes	• Unable to keep focused on oral instructions • Takes frequent "mental" mind trips • Quick to cry when he makes mistakes • Worries about being wrong
Cognitive	• Writes on topics using pre-phonetic and phonetic spelling • Receives supplemental reading support to help with decoding • Literal comprehension is easier than inferences; can identify main idea • Able to solve simple math problems and count to 20; more complex problems are difficult • Reverses some numbers and letters	• Reads above grade level for rate and accuracy • Comprehension skills above grade level; able to think more critically about story elements • Writes on topic and generates own ideas; uses spelling rules and knowledge of word parts to spell correctly • Able to solve simple multiplication and division problems • Explains strategies used in completing complex story problems; shows flexible thinking by solving problems more than one way	• Writes slowly in all subjects • Writes in short sentences with little detail • Literal comprehension easier than inferences, but identifies main idea • Able to solve math problems that involve borrowing and carrying correctly with numbers in the 100s • Processes answers slowly
Motor	• Balances and walks heel-toe • Runs and leaps from one object to another • Uses a mixture of capitals and lowercase letters • Creative, colorful and detailed drawings	• Likes soccer and T-ball • Good computer skills, beginning to use home-row hand position • Ties own shoes • Handwriting legible with good size and spacing	• Awkward gait • Slow moving • Very small printing • Immature drawings
Adaptive (Daily Living)	• Seeks help from adults when unsure of what to do; needs immediate response • Uses restroom alone but has had some accidents • Comes prepared with materials and knows where things go • Hair uncombed daily; needs help with shoes, zippers etc.	• Raises hand when she has an answer to share or question to ask • Aware of family members' roles and relationships/history • Loves her family and expresses appreciation for what they do for her • Organized and ready to learn each day	• Doesn't seek help from adults when unsure of what to do • Uses restroom to escape work • Comes prepared with materials and knows where things go

Source: The first grade portraits are based on information from Cathy Dugovich (Lakeridge Elementary, Mercer Island, Washington), the second grade portraits are based on information from Barbara Tivnan (Lakeridge Elementary, Mercer Island, Washington); Rayna Freedman (Jordan/Jackson Elementary School, Mansfield, Massachusetts) contributed the third grade portraits.

Developmentally Appropriate Questions

1. Why do you think Valerie is more interested in interacting with boys than girls? Do you think this is "normal" developmental behavior? What would you do if Valerie were in your class?

2. Why do you think Valerie laughs at children who have special needs? What would you do to promote acceptance of and understanding of special needs?

ADANA	WILL	MAYA

ADANA	WILL	MAYA
Eight year old Columbian American, female • Quiet • Obedient • Lives with both parents and has one older sister	Nine year old Caucasian, male • Opinionated and energetic • Youngest of three children (older brother and sister)	Nine year old Caucasian, female • Loves art, music, and drama • Youngest of two children (has an older brother who is gifted)
• Likes to sit in the back or side when in the group to avoid participating • Has one good friend • Avoids social actions with her peers • At times moody but can't explain why	• Often is at the side of a classmate who is upset, trying to make him or her feel better, but has trouble articulating his own feelings to adults • Plays with all classmates regardless of gender or ethnicity, but gets along better with girls • Questions authority when he does not agree with decisions being made • Would rather work in a group than independently	• Is aware of others' feelings and is empathetic towards them • Expresses ideas clearly and likes to be the leader in a group • Asks questions in order to understand social situations and be a better problem solver • Likes being part of a group but often enjoys a quiet moment to herself
• Highly capable • Reads all the time when work is finished • Rarely asks for help • Completes more complex addition and subtraction story problems correctly • Able to explain her math strategies clearly and accurately (often using complex thinking) • Selects harder spelling words to learn	• Can concentrate on a single task for 5–10 minutes and benefits from teacher check-ins to make sure he is on task and understands directions • Benefits from concepts being modeled and then guided practice before being able to work independently on an assignment • Can complete one by two digit multiplication problems but might need a visual of the process before beginning • Can remember things that occur personally to him in vivid detail and has his own perception of events	• Can concentrate on a single task for thirty minutes or more • Enjoys reading above grade level books (can read up through sixth-grade level with understanding). • Can complete two by two digit multiplication problems • Enjoys learning new things and facing challenges in her academic work
• Loves to swim and dance • Loves drawing and coloring pictures using markers, colored pencils • Handwriting legible with good size and spacing	• Can sit up straight but has difficulty sitting in one place for lengthy periods of time; needs to lean over or move frequently • Can grasp a pencil, but he has trouble forming print letters; benefits from extra time to do so or lined paper for support • Uses simple combinations of movements such as running or jumping • Skillfully uses an iPod Touch	• Can balance on one foot with ease • Has fantastic hand-eye coordination • Can grasp a pencil and write in cursive or print neatly • Skillfully uses a computer mouse and keyboard controls
• Has to be reminded to go to bathroom • Keeps a disorganized desk • Needs reminders to hand in homework	• Enjoys helping to clean the classroom and puts back his materials where they belong • Has a great sense of humor and seeks to please others • Is unaware that sometimes what he says might offend others and often needs his conversations explained to him so he can see this • Benefits from a consistent schedule	• Independent with getting materials but often needs reminders to put materials away or to organize her desk • Polite and gracious when talking to people and is a good listener • Is flexible with routines and schedules • Has a positive attitude about learning and life, enjoys creative experiences

3. Sam is unable to stay focused on oral instructions. What could you do to help Sam be more focused?

4. Why do you think Adana wants to avoid participating in activities with others? What can you do to encourage Adana to participate?

5. Why do you think Will tends to question authority when he disagrees with a decision? Do you think this is a positive or negative attribute? What can you do to help Will?

6. Sam uses the restroom to escape work. What are some possible reasons for this? How could you help Sam?

determining involvement in activities. On the contrary, we should promote *all* children's involvement in age-appropriate activities.

During the primary years we see evidence of continuing refinement of fine-motor skills in children's mastery of many tasks they previously could not do or could do only with difficulty. They are now able to dress themselves relatively easily and attend to most of their personal needs. They are also more proficient at school tasks that require fine-motor skills such as writing, making artwork, and using computers and other technology. In addition, primary children want to and are able to engage in real-life activities; they want the real thing. This makes teaching them easier and more fun because many activities have real-life applications.

Social Development

middle childhood Describes children in Erikson's industry versus inferiority stage of social-emotional development, ages six to nine years, during which time they gain confidence and ego satisfaction from completing demanding tasks.

mastery-oriented attributions Attributions that include effort (industriousness), paying attention, determination, and perseverance.

learned helplessness A condition that can develop when children perceive that they are not doing as well as they can or as well as their peers, lose confidence in their abilities and achievement, and then attribute their failures to a lack of ability. These children are passive and have learned to feel they are helpless.

Children in grades one to three (ages six through nine) are in Erikson's industry vs. inferiority stage of social-emotional development. They are in **middle childhood**, a time when they gain confidence and ego satisfaction from completing demanding tasks. Children want to act responsibly and are quite capable of achieving demanding tasks and accomplishments. Children take a lot of pride in doing well. All of this reflects the industry side of social-emotional development.

Children during this stage are at varying levels of academic achievement. Those who are high in academic self-esteem credit their success to such **mastery-oriented attributions** as trying hard (industriousness), paying attention, determination, and stick-to-itiveness. If they have difficulty with a task, they believe that by trying harder they will succeed.[10]

At the same time, children in this stage compare their abilities and accomplishments with their peers. When they perceive they are not doing as well as they can or as well as their peers, they may lose confidence in their abilities and achievement. This is the inferiority side of this stage of social-emotional development. Some children develop **learned helplessness**, a condition in which children attribute their failures to a lack of ability. You, the teacher, can be helpful and supportive of children, providing them with tasks they can accomplish and encouraging them to do their best.

Here are some things you can do to accomplish this goal:

- Provide activities children can reasonably accomplish so they can experience the satisfaction that comes from a job well done.
- Apply Gardner's theory of multiple intelligences to your teaching, which will encourage children to excel at things they are good at. All children develop skills and abilities in particular areas. Build a classroom environment that enables children to be competent in their particular intelligence and learning style.
- Be supportive and encouraging of children's efforts. For example, "See what you can do when you really try!"

Emotional Development

Think for a moment about how important emotions are in your life and how emotions influence what and how you learn. When you are happy, life goes well! When you are sad, it is harder to be enthusiastic about doing what you have to do. The children you teach are no different. Emotions are an important part of children's everyday lives.[11] One of your responsibilities is to help them develop positive emotions and express their emotions in healthy ways.

The following activities give you specific ideas for how to support the positive social-emotional development of children in the industry vs. inferiority stage of development:

1. *Use literature to discuss emotions.* Children in grades one to three like to talk about their emotions and the emotions of characters in literature.[12] They are able to make inferences about characters' emotional states and discuss how they are or are not

appropriate to the story. They can then relate these emotional states to their own lives and to events at home and in the classroom. Some good books to use to discuss emotional states include these:

- *How Are You Peeling? Foods with Moods* by Saxton Freymann and Joost Elffers offers brief text and photographs of carvings made from vegetables that introduce the world of emotions by presenting leading questions such as "Are you feeling angry?"
- *Today I Feel Silly: And Other Moods That Make My Day* by Jamie Lee Curtis follows a little girl with curly red hair through thirteen different moods including silly, grumpy, mean, excited, and confused.
- *When Sophie Gets Angry . . . Really, Really Angry* by Molly Bang conveys young Sophie's anger when her mother allows her younger sister to play with her stuffed gorilla, the eventual calm she feels after running outside and crying, and the calm and relaxed return home.

2. *Encourage children to express their emotions.* Beginning and ending the day with class meeting discussions is a good way to help children express their thoughts and feelings. This provides children a safe and secure outlet to say how they felt about their day.
3. *Write about feelings.* Give children opportunities to keep journals in which they can write about home, life, and classroom events and how they feel about them. One teacher has her children keep several journals; they share one only with her and they share another with their classmates if they choose.

   Figure 12.1 shows a journal entry seven-year-old Maddie wrote in reaction to her feelings about the main character in a book she read. Maddie will decide if she wants to share her thoughts about the book with her teacher and classmates. In this journal entry, pay particular attention to several things. First, note Maddie's invented spelling, which enables her to be a writer and express her thoughts. She is well on her way to mastering the writing and reading processes. Second, note how sensitive she is to others. Maddie is developing the capacity for empathy—being able to identify with the feelings of others.
4. *Provide opportunities for play.* Play is a powerful outlet for releasing energy and expressing emotional states. Through fantasy and superhero play, children can express feelings and try out their growing range of emotions.

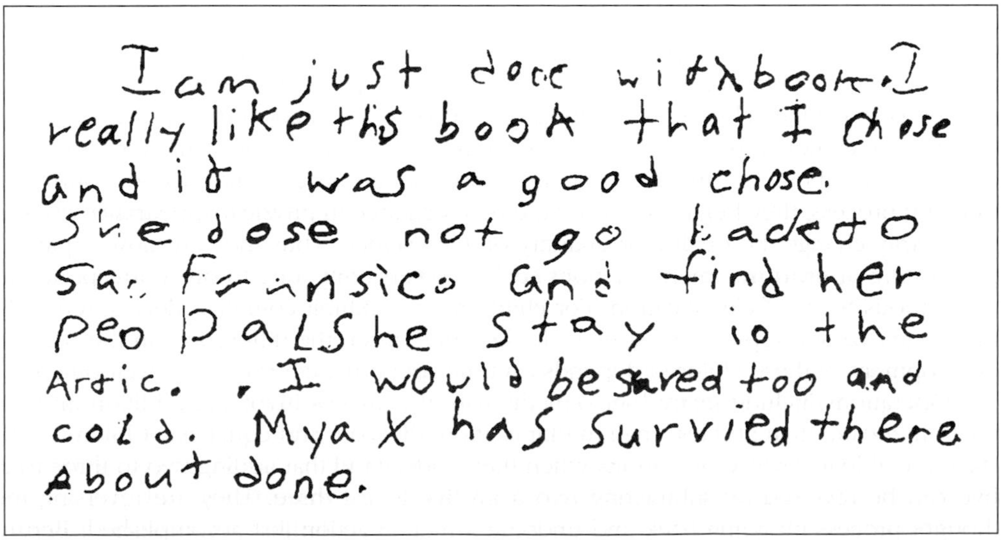
I am just done witx book. I really like this book that I chose and it was a good chose. She dose not go back to San Fransico and find her peopal She stay io the Artic. I would be scared too and cold. Mya X has survied there About done.

FIGURE 12.1 A Seven-Year-Old's Journal Entry: A Response to Literature

instrumental-relativist orientation The second stage of preconventional moral development, when children's actions are motivated by satisfaction of their needs.

bring pleasure. In stage 2, the **instrumental-relativist orientation** stage, children's actions are motivated by satisfaction of needs. Consequently, interpersonal relations have their basis in mutual convenience based on need satisfaction ("You scratch my back; I'll scratch yours").

Just as Piaget's cognitive stages are fixed and invariant for all children, so too are Kohlberg's moral levels. All individuals move through the process of moral development beginning at level 1 and progress from there. No level can be skipped, but each individual does not necessarily achieve every level. Just as intellectual development may become fixed at a particular level of development, so may an individual become fixed at any one of the moral levels.

Implications for Teachers. All of these theories have implications for primary-grade classroom practice. Here are some things you can do:

- Like and respect *all* children from all cultures and diverse backgrounds.
- Create a classroom climate to support individual values. Be willing to deal with the varied issues, morals, and value systems children bring to school.
- Give children opportunities to interact with peers, children of different age groups and cultures, and adults in order to move to higher levels of moral functioning.
- Provide opportunities for children to make moral decisions and judgments and discuss the results of their decision making. Responsibility comes from being given opportunities to be responsible.

Teachers of primary students look for opportunities every day to present moral values and decisions. Examples can come from stories or from discussions about heroes in the community. Children's out-of-classroom experiences can also prompt discussions of moral values. What is most important with any approach is that students have many chances to actually *practice* their moral decision making. Knowing children's stages of moral development will help you guide them in this important area.

Character Education. Moral development is closely aligned with character education, which is rapidly becoming a part of many early childhood classrooms across the United States. Whereas everyone believes that children have to learn how to count, growing numbers of individuals also believe that schools have to teach children *what* counts. As character education is becoming a higher priority, curricula designed to teach specific character traits are now commonplace. In fact, the early childhood curriculum now consists of the six Rs: *r*eading, *wr*iting, *ar*ithmetic, *r*easoning, *r*espect, and *r*esponsibility.

Herrington Elementary School provides another example of ways to promote healthy, happy children in a school environment. Herrington is a school that seeks to promote community and working together to prevent bullying and hate. Herrington, a pre-K to grade five urban public school located in Pontiac, Michigan, has an enrollment of over 400 students. Community is very important at Herrington, and the community presence is strong in the neighborhood and in the school. Each morning, all students eat breakfast together and then participate with teachers, support staff, and custodians in *harambee*, a Swahili term for "gathering" that means a call to unity for collective work. Throughout the school day, students are given opportunities to reflect on the golden rule and the community's values and to learn conflict resolution skills. Leading the district in scores and attendance rates, Herrington works hard to be a leader in the community. Character education ties the school's efforts together and provides the basis for unity. Herrington's lesson is clear: promoting community involvement, unity, character education and conflict resolution promotes healthy children, families, schools, and test scores!

All character education programs seek to teach a set of traditional core values that will result in civic virtue and moral character, including honesty, kindness, respect, responsibility, tolerance for diversity, racial harmony, and good citizenship. Efforts to promote character qualities and values are evident in school and statewide efforts. For example, all school districts in the state of Georgia are required to implement a comprehensive character education program for all children. Some of the traits included are honesty, fairness, responsibility for others, kindness, cooperation, self-control, and self-respect.[17]

So that children can broaden their perceptions, help them understand that their world is larger than their immediate neighborhood. You can do this through many activities:

- Read books that teach character traits, often referring to the list of traits adopted by your school system.
- Use the special kids sections of the *Times News* (Character Counts and the Kids Scoop pages) to understand the importance of good character skills.
- Use visitors and artifacts from other states and countries to help students compare where they live with other areas so that they can appreciate the similarities and differences, eliminate prejudice, and accept cultural differences.
- Study the traditions of other cultures and have international tasting parties with food, games, folktales, or stories about the cultures.
- Write letters to soldiers for several holidays, including Veterans Day.
- Make encouragement cards and small gifts for the cafeteria and maintenance workers and staff.
- Write to other classes and school groups to express gratitude and encouragement when they have performed for your school.[18]

Character education is rapidly becoming a part of many early childhood classrooms across the United States. What characteristics do you think are important to teach children so that they develop positive morals and character skills?

Primary Education Today

In the last five years, the educational spotlight has cast its beam on the primary grades, where the academic rubber really hits the road. Grades one to three are more academically challenging and rigorous now than they have ever been. Politicians and educational reformers use the third grade as the demarcation for standards of achievement and grade promotion or retention. The federal government talks about all children being able to read on grade level by grade three. Thus, even though all teachers pre-K through third grade are responsible for ensuring that all children achieve this goal, it is in the third grade that this goal is measured and decisions are made about whether children will be promoted or retained. One of your major challenges of teaching in grades one to three will be to ensure that all of your children learn and achieve so that they can be promoted with their peers.

State Standards

Review again our discussion of state and national standards and the ways they are changing teaching and learning in all grades. All fifty states have statewide academic standards, and all have some kind of test to measure how well students are learning and, in many cases, how well students and schools are meeting the standards. Standards are not only changing what students learn but are also changing how teachers teach. Let's look at some of the changes standards are making.

Teacher Roles.   Standards have transformed (some would say reformed) teaching from an input model to an output model. As a result, teachers are no longer able to say, "I taught Mario the use of structural cues to decode words." Now the questions are, "Is Mario able to use and apply decoding skills?" and "Will Mario do well on decoding skills on the state test?" Good teachers have good ideas about what and how to teach, and they always will. However, the time and opportunity to act on those good ideas are reduced by increasing requirements to teach to the standards and teach so that students will master the standards.

Curriculum Alignment.   Increasing student achievement is at the center of the standards movement. Policy makers and educators view standards, tests, and teaching alignment as a viable and practical way to help ensure student achievement. **Alignment** is the arrangement of standards, curriculum, and tests so that they complement one another. In other words, the curriculum should be based on what the standards say students should know and be able to do; tests should measure what the standards indicate. **Curriculum alignment** is the process of making sure that what is taught—the content of the curriculum—matches what the standards say students should know and be able to do.

alignment The arrangement of standards, curriculum, and tests so they are in agreement.

curriculum alignment The process of making sure that what is taught matches the standards.

Data-Driven Instruction of the Outcomes of Standards and Testing.   Accountability initiatives, including No Child Left Behind, have brought about a shift in focus from covering subject matter to meeting the needs of each student. There is only one way to determine whether or not the needs of the students are being met: through an ongoing analysis of data collected from assessing children. In **data-driven instruction**, teaching decisions are based on the analysis of assessment data to make decisions about how to best meet the instructional needs of each child. To use data-driven instruction, start by analyzing existing data on each student from their cumulative record files to get a general profile of each student. Then align objectives to assessments by planning collaboratively with your grade-level colleagues to determine when you will be teaching district and state standards and how you will assess each standard. Next, gather data by using formal assessments, informal assessments, and technology. After gathering data, use it to guide your next steps in the instructional process. Which students are ready to move on? Which students need remediation? Which students need enrichment? Just remember that making data-based decisions to guide instruction is an ongoing process. You should be constantly assessing, analyzing, and adjusting throughout the school year.[19]

data-driven instruction The analysis of assessment data to make decisions about how best to meet the instructional needs of each child.

Teaching Practices

A lot of change has occurred in the primary grades, with more on the way. One of the more dramatic changes is the integration of early childhood education and special education. As a result, instructional practices are blending and those used by special educators are now routinely used in all primary grade programs.

Another dramatic change is the widespread use of technology to facilitate teaching and learning. Students routinely have access to and use a wide variety of technological devices. Increasingly content comes from the Internet. Classrooms and whole school districts do use textbooks, but increasing numbers are electronic textbooks.[20]

intentional teaching Developing plans, selecting instructional strategies, and teaching to promote learning.

Intentional teaching.   **Intentional teaching** is the process of teaching children the skills they need for success. Letter grades and report cards are still very popular, although narrative reports (in which professionals describe and report on student achievement), checklists (which describe the competencies students have demonstrated), parent conferences, portfolios containing samples of children's work, and other tools for reporting achievement are being used to supplement letter grades.

Response to Instruction/Response to Intervention (RTI).   Response to Instruction/Intervention (RTI) is a multi-tiered approach to the early identification and support of students with learning and behavior needs. It is the opposite of the "wait to fail approach." RTI seeks to prevent academic failure through early intervention; frequent assessment; and increasingly intense

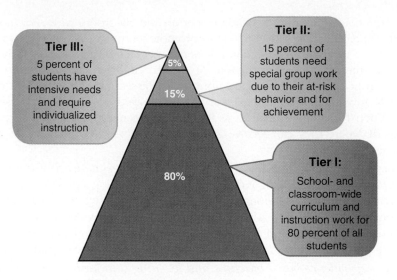

FIGURE 12.2 The Three Tiers of Continuous Intervention/Instruction

Through RTI, teachers and schools provide ongoing assessments and instructional processes to assure that each child is successful.

instructional interventions/processes for children who continue to have difficulty. These are the essential components of RTI.

- *Early intervention is essential for enhancing the child's success.* RTI is founded in the principle that too little too late is an inadequate approach to education. Instead, early intervention is considered the best chance of promoting children's success academically, developmentally, socially, and emotionally. If a child's difficulty is caught early enough and treated with the appropriate level of intensity, RTI can be essential in enhancing success.

- *Use of multiple tiers of interventions.* RTI uses a three-tiered approach to providing instruction and intervention as shown in Figure 12.2, "The Three Tiers of Continuous Intervention/Instruction." Children advance through the three tiers based on their level of responsiveness to instruction or intervention. The less responsive a child is to instruction/intervention, the more intense the intervention/instruction becomes as shown in Figure 12.3. Tier I consists of generalized, evidence-based core curricula and

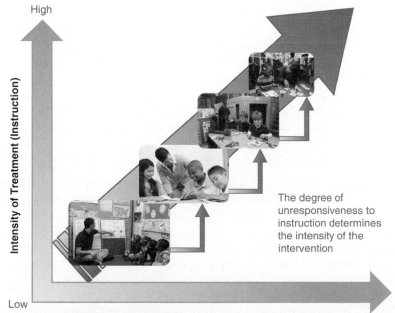

FIGURE 12.3 The RTI Model at Work

Through ongoing assessment, teachers match instructional practices to their students' learning needs, helping each child to achieve.

instruction that is provided to children school- and classroom-wide. For most children (about 80 percent), Tier I is sufficient to promote learning. However, for 15 percent of students, the generalized curriculum does not meet all of their needs, so they advance to Tier II intervention or instruction. At Tier II, children receive a more intensified instruction because they show through ongoing assessment that they are not making adequate growth. In Tier II, children have increased opportunity to practice Tier I skills. When Tier II is insufficient, as it is for 5 percent of students, children move on to Tier III where they can receive more individualized and focused intervention to meet Tier I benchmarks.

- *Problem-solving approach to determine most appropriate level of intervention for individual students.*[21]   Teachers take a problem-solving approach to determining the tier in which a child belongs. If a child is unresponsive to Tier I instruction and intervention, then the child advances to Tier II, which provides more intense instruction and intervention. If Tier II is not adequately meeting students' needs, the teacher solves the problem by providing Tier III instruction and intervention.

- *Reliance on evidence-based practices and learning standards guide instruction and the use of intentional teaching methods that include embedded and explicit instruction at all tiers.*[22]   RTI is meant to help children reach education standards through the use of evidence-based practices. Some evidenced-based practices include intentional teaching methods such as embedded and explicit instruction. Under No Child Left Behind, teachers must use curriculum and instructional methods that are based on research to ensure children's academic success. RTI seeks to infuse each tier of intervention/instruction with evidence-based practices.

- *Use of monitoring to determine if students are making progress using multi-dimensional, authentic assessments that can identify the child's strengths and needs over time.*[23] Throughout the instruction, students are assessed for their learning and level of achievement. The data from these assessments are then used when determining which students need closer monitoring or intervention. Decisions regarding students' instructional needs are based on multiple assessment data taken over time. Authentic assessments, not just screening tools and standardized tests, should be used to make decisions regarding student's needs.

- *Holistic view of child development.*[24]   RTI takes a holistic view of children as the approach to providing intervention/instruction. The holistic view of children takes into account social development, linguistic/literacy development, emotional development, cognitive development, physical and motor development, and other aspects such as character education, gender education, culture, artistic, and socioeconomic context.

- *The critical contributions of parents and families to the success of the child.*[25]   RTI recognizes that parents and families are critical to the overall success of the child. Without continuing support of families at home, RTI may have limited success in school. Families help reinforce and expand on what children learn at school, and teachers work to keep parents and families aware and informed of their children's successes, progress, and difficulties at each tier of instruction.

RTI and ELLs.   As you can see from the many elements of RTI, it lends itself to being successful for a range of students, from children with disabilities to children struggling in an academic area to English language learners (ELLs). In fact, a recent study has found that RTI helps children who are ELLs make positive gains. In Chula Vista, California, the school district uses RTI to target children who are ELLs. They have seen a dramatic increase in test scores in reading and mathematics as a result. The district's superintendent John Nelson said RTI works because it changes teachers' thinking from "I taught it and it's their fault if they got it or not," to "I need to keep teaching it and support students."[26]

The RTI approach is also useful in helping to make sure that children who don't know English aren't prematurely referred for special education evaluation, which raises the risk of mistaking a language barrier for a disability. Instead, RTI permits teachers to determine what kind of instruction a child needs on an individual level and to build on what the child can already do. This equals catching children before they fall.[27]

Differentiated Instruction. **Differentiated instruction** is an approach to teaching and learning for students of differing abilities in the same class—and all classrooms have differing abilities. The intent of differentiating instruction is to maximize each student's growth and individual success; meet each student where he or she is; and assist the child in the learning process.

There is no single set of strategies that constitutes differentiated instruction. Instead, the practice rests on principles that require teachers to continuously assess students and adjust instruction accordingly. In a class where the teacher differentiates instruction, he or she frequently rotates students into small groups based on demonstrated knowledge, interest, and/or learning style preferences. The teacher then targets instruction to the needs of each group with the aim of moving all students toward high levels of achievement. A differentiated classroom is a dynamic environment where students move in and out of learning groups based on achievement data, interests, and learning styles.

When you give directions in a differentiated classroom, start class with a small task, such as a review question or skill practice, and then meet with one small group at a time to provide specific directions for each group. Also, write out directions for each group. Have the directions on the group's table or cluster at the beginning of the class or include the directions at a learning center or with a packet of learning materials that the students select. Then, use group lessons, activities, or graphic organizers to introduce concepts to the entire class before expecting small groups to work independently with a new concept or skill.

Extended time. Another practice that is influencing teaching today in the primary grades is the advent of extended time. Reports find that schools that expand their academic days or years in an effort to improve student performance are effective. Schools that extend time on average extend their time by 25 percent, which amounts to three more years of academics over the span of a student's education. Extended-time schools tend to serve a greater proportion of racial minorities and low-income children than other schools.[28]

Curriculum Content Areas

In the primary grades, curriculum content areas take on greater emphasis. Children are not as concrete or literal, and the possibilities for new learning experiences and challenging children are endless.

Reading and Language Arts in the Primary Grades

Just like preschool and kindergarten programs, today's primary grades emphasize literacy development, vocabulary, and reading. In fact, this emphasis is apparent in all the elementary grades, from pre-K to six. Parents and society want children who can speak, write, and read well.

Literacy and Reading. I cannot overstate the importance of children's learning to read on grade level by the end of grade three. Here is what the Annie E. Casey Foundation has to say about why reading by the end of third grade is important:

> Millions of American children reach fourth grade without learning to read proficiently. The shortfall is especially pronounced among low-income children: Of the fourth graders who took the National Assessment of Educational Progress (NAEP) reading tests in 2009, 83 percent of children from low-income families—and 85 percent of low-income students who attend high-poverty schools—failed to reach the "proficient" level in reading. Reading proficiently by the end of third grade is a crucial marker in a child's educational

differentiated instruction
An approach that enables teachers to plan strategically to meet the needs of every student in order to teach to the needs of each child and allow for diversity in the classroom.

One of the best ways for children to develop language proficiency is for them to read, read, read. In the process, children develop a love of reading and reading becomes an important part of their daily lives.

development. Failure to read proficiently is linked to higher rates of school dropout, which suppress individual learning potential as well as the nation's competitiveness and general productivity.[29]

To teach literacy effectively, you will need to align your teaching with state standards. Connections with others, especially families, are important in making literacy meaningful for children; recall Bronfenbrenner's theory about ecological systems and the significance of the home–school connection.

Guided Reading. Guided reading is designed to help children develop and use strategies of independent reading. During guided reading, children read texts that are at their developmentally appropriate reading level and have a minimum of new things to learn. The children read in small groups (usually five to eight) with their teacher.

Guided reading is beneficial for all students. For the more advanced readers, guided reading is a great way to introduce and practice skills that their peers may not be ready for. Guided reading offers struggling readers a safe setting for the extra support they need to master skills at a comfortable pace. When you teach guided reading in small groups, you can reinforce skills as many times as needed for the students to achieve mastery. The children are not pressured from the feeling that they are the only ones "not getting it."[30]

Guided reading is also very beneficial to teachers. Small group instruction allows teachers to pinpoint the strengths and weaknesses of individual students. It is an easy way for teachers to differentiate instruction, which makes it much easier to teach all students on their current level. Guided reading is also a great time to level the students or group children with the same reading level, because it gives a great deal of information about which reading strategies the students are using, as well as showing the progress each student has made.[31] Following are some guidelines for implementing guided reading:

- Frequency: You should teach guided reading every day. Guided reading sessions are short; fifteen minutes per group works well. Meeting with struggling readers daily is essential to their progress and success. Students reading on grade level should meet at least three times a week. Advanced readers need to meet at least once or twice a week as time permits.[32]

- Content: Since time is limited, guided reading activities are short and simple, yet they are quite effective due to the individualized instruction. Guided reading gives students time to practice the skill with the support of the teacher. Afterwards, students can apply the skills they learned as they play a learning game, use a book to go on a word hunt, or read leveled books (e.g., books targeted to a specific reading level). Provide constant support, take notes on student progress, and document the teaching strategies you use. These notes are very helpful because you can refer to them daily to plan future lessons or regroup the students based on their needs.[33]

- Materials: Use book bags and browsing boxes. Book bag books are leveled books that students read during Self-Selected Reading (SSR), throughout the day, and at home. These book bags often hang on the back of student's chairs. The students choose the books for their book bags based on their individual interests from browsing boxes that are set up within reach of the students throughout the classroom. Browsing boxes are set up according to reading level to provide students with a wide array of reading choice and to also ensure that students are reading books that are just right for their reading level. You can also keep books used in guided reading in the book bags and let students take them home for practice. Here are some other suggested materials for guided reading:

- Dry erase boards/markers
- Magnetic letters
- Index cards
- Teacher-made skill practice games (Concentration, I Spy, etc.)
- Pencils/sticky notes
- Leveled books[34]

- Grouping: When you set up guided reading groups, give much thought and serious consideration to how to group the students based on ongoing assessment of their reading skills. Regroup students who have similar needs. As students master the skills practiced, they should then be regrouped. Students generally do not know what group they are in because the groups change constantly. It is easiest to call individual students to the reading table for instruction rather than naming each group, due to the constant regrouping that should be happening and to protect the self-esteem of each student.[35]

- Management: How can you manage guided reading and centers simultaneously? Students are in literacy centers. You must use good classroom management skills. Explicitly teach center expectations, activities, and routines and have children practice them for several weeks before you begin guided reading. Monitor, praise good choices, and give consequences when needed for reinforcement. When you implement guided reading, children know well the central expectations and procedures. However, consistently reinforce procedures, rules, and expectations before, during, and after guided reading.[36]

Literacy Circles. A new trend in teaching reading in the primary grades is the use of literacy circles. **Literacy circles** are discussion groups in which children meet regularly to talk about books. Literacy circles are rarely the sole form of teaching reading but are a part of a balanced literacy program. As such, literacy circles are intended to act as a context in which children apply reading and writing skills. Groups are determined by book choice and are reader response centered, meaning that discussion and conversation focus on what the readers thought and felt while reading the book. Literacy circles are structured so as to foster independence, responsibility, and reading ownership. As such, literature circles are guided primarily by student insight and questions. As a result, literacy circles are flexible and fluid; they never look the same twice. To read how to implement literacy circles in your classrooms, read third grade teacher Candice Bookman's Voice from the Field on pages 348–349.

literacy circles Discussion groups in which children meet regularly to talk about books.

RTI and Reading. Despite the many advances and new trends in teaching children to read, some still struggle. The Institute of Education Sciences (IES) addresses the challenge of reducing the number of children who struggle and ultimately fail to learn to read well by recommending the use of RTI. The IES recommends using these five steps:[37]

1. Screen all students for potential reading problems and regularly monitor the progress of students who are at elevated risk for developing reading disabilities.
   - Accurately identify children at risk.
   - Use benchmarks or growth rates to identify children at varying risks for developing reading disabilities.
2. Provide differentiated reading instruction for all students based on assessments of current reading levels.
   - Provide differentiated instruction to students at varied reading levels for part of the day.
   - Differentiate instruction—including varying time, content, degree of support and scaffolding—based on students' skills.

Voice from the Field

How to Use Literature Circles in the Elementary Grades

I can't imagine teaching without literature circles. There are just a few things that I think are important for any teacher willing to give literature circles a try.

STEP 1 — Have a Good, Strong Classroom Management System in Place

Students must know your expectations, and that if they don't make good choices for their behavior and use their time wisely, they will have an immediate consequence. I teach my expectations and we practice together for the first six weeks of school. Each day I ask the children to tell me what is important to remember about literature circles, and we discuss their responses as a class. We practice the entire routine including where to get their literature tub (see below), what to do in their literature circles, and what to do when time is up. We practice each specific expectation I have for them. As the students go to literature circles, I actively monitor each group. I listen to their discussions, watch for off-task behavior, compliment good group work, give reminders or consequences when appropriate, and help with their activities when needed. I provide constant support until the students feel comfortable with the entire literature routine.

STEP 2 — Hold Students Accountable for Their Learning

This ensures that the time provided for literature circles is not wasted. Students know they will turn in their activities weekly and they will receive a grade. If the students do not work well together, it will be reflected in their grade. Students should have everything they need when they get to their literature circle so there is less of a chance for disruption such as wandering around the room or engaging in off-task behavior. I provide a tub for each group that holds their books, folders with the activities for the week, a dictionary, pencils, and so forth. If the children need anything different in a given week, for whatever reason, I provide it in the tub. Also, I let the students know in advance that things will be a little bit different that week.

STEP 3 — Give Each Group Member a Job

Each child has a responsibility for the week. Make sure that each member knows what the jobs are. I put a laminated list of jobs and descriptions in each group's folder. Since it is laminated, I write a student's name next to each job with a VCV marker, and then just erase it and rotate names weekly. In my class, the jobs during literature circles are as follows:

Material Manager: This child is responsible for picking up and putting away the tubs, passing out books and activities, and making sure they are put in the folders when completed. If there is anything missing from a tub for any reason, the material manager takes care of it.

Recorder: This child is responsible for writing down the ideas their group comes up with after the reading and group discussion. I often provide question stems to monitor comprehension. When I do not give them questions, the recorder is responsible for asking good thought-provoking

3. Provide intensive, systematic instruction on up to three fundamental reading skills in small groups to students who score below benchmark scores on universal screening.
   - Use curriculum that addresses the components of reading instruction (comprehension, fluency, phonemic awareness, phonics, and vocabulary) and relate to students' needs and developmental levels.
   - Implement this program 3 to 5 times a week for 20–40 minutes.

4. Monitor the progress of Tier II students at least once a month. Determine whether students still require intervention. If so, design a Tier III intervention plan.
   - Monitor progress of Tier II students on a regular basis (at least eight times during the school year).
   - While providing Tier II instruction, monitor data to identify students who need additional instruction.

5. Provide intensive instruction on a daily basis that promotes the various components of reading to students who continue to show minimal progress after small group instruction.
   - Implement concentrated instruction that is focused on a small but targeted set of reading skills.

questions and recording the responses of their group members. (This takes quite a bit of practice.) I expect the responses to be text dependent so children must back up the question with a page number and proof from the text.

Word Wizard: This child is responsible for using the dictionary to look up and write the definition of any unfamiliar word encountered in their reading. Sometimes I make some suggestions of words that they may need to look up.

Illustrator: This child is responsible for drawing pictures of scenes from the book that go along with their learning. I may ask the children to find a part of the book they thought was funny, a turning point, a particular point of view, and so forth.

Graphic Organizer: This child is responsible for completing a graphic organizer to help the group comprehend what they are reading. These are sometimes story maps, Venn diagrams, T-charts, bubble maps, and such.

Teacher: I also have responsibilities during literature circles. While children work in their groups, I pull small groups of children for guided reading. I help them in areas of weakness, which may include phonics or comprehension skills. I have one group that I meet with daily to work on phonics skills. The other groups work on identifying the main idea, writing summaries, making inferences, understanding the author's purpose, and so forth.

STEP 4 Group Students in Different Ways

You can change groups when they are done with particular books and are ready to begin new ones. Comprehension skills and reading abilities will vary, but you can handle them in different ways. If you want skill levels to be close in each group, choose books with similar reading levels. One group may be reading chapter books, while another group is reading trade books on their level. The activities you give to each group will reflect what they are reading. If you want mixed-ability groups, partner children with different abilities.

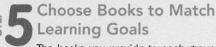

STEP 5 Choose Books to Match Learning Goals

The books you provide to each group depend on the skill level of each group member. You can use literature circles for novel studies, and integrate content areas with nonfiction reading materials. When I have a mixed-ability group, I provide that group with different books on a particular topic written on different reading levels. Currently I have a group reading about the solar system. I have provided them with six books, all on different reading levels. Each book contains different information and my low-level reader has at least one book on his independent reading level.

The Value of Literature Circles

Literature circles are a great way to provide differentiated instruction to my class. They allow me to integrate reading with science and social studies as well as writing. When appropriate, I integrate English and grammar skills. Literature circles allow the class to learn practically every skill we learn in third grade in approximately 45 minutes, while simultaneously giving me the flexibility to meet with students in small groups every day.

Source: Contributed by Candice M. Bookman, first grade teacher, Lawrence Elementary School, Mesquite Independent School District, Mesquite, Texas.

- Adjust the overall speed of the lesson. Some students may require a slower pace in order to gain comprehension.
- Plan and individualize Tier III instruction.
- Ensure that Tier III students master a reading skill or strategy before moving on.

Children's Literature.   One of the best ways to engage and encourage readers is through literature that appeals to them. For children, this means that literature needs to connect with them on their individual and developmental levels. The development of literature directed at children is at an all time high and there are various trends in children's literature that are aimed at creating a contemporary base of readers. Take, for example, *Harry Potter* and the *Percy Jackson and the Olympians* series, which use different and new ways to tell a story; the plots are non-linear, and they create or explain characters in new ways.[38] They use fantasy, magic, and mythology to appeal to and engage children, often creating lifelong readers. Underneath the contemporary trappings, they have themes that are classic and enduring. Themes such as a sense of belonging, a belief in hope for the future, the importance of relationships, and the importance of courage, will always appeal to children.[39] You can use classic and contemporary books in your teaching to engage and appeal to young readers. Some new books you might try are:

- *Just Grace Walks the Dog* by Charise Mericle Harper. Third grader Grace is determined to have a pet, so she embarks on an adventure with her cardboard dog to prove to her parents that she is responsible and dependable enough to get a real dog.
- *Herbie Jones Sails Into Second Grade* by Suzy Kline. Herbie and his new friend Raymond start the first day of second grade with lots of fears and a teacher that takes them on adventures.
- *More Stories Huey Tells* by Ann Cameron. One of the five stories in this book is about Huey, a good problem solver, and when Huey and his older brother Julian get worried about their father's smoking, they find a way to work together to help him quit.
- *Lizzie Logan, Second Banana* by Eileen Spinelli. Lizzie's mom and her new dad are having a baby and Lizzie is worried her new dad will love the new brother more than her, so she signs up for a beauty contest and learns about families and love in the process.
- *PeeWee's Tale* by Johanna Hurwitz. Nine-year-old Robbie's mother doesn't like Robbie's guinea pig, PeeWee, so she has her husband set PeeWee loose in Central Park. PeeWee is lost in the wild environment until he makes a new friend who passes on a few survival strategies. PeeWee returns the favor by warning his friend about the city's plan to cut down the tree that she lives in.

Math in the Primary Grades

School districts all across the United States are emphasizing mathematics. Just as reading receives a great deal of national attention, the same is true of math. Because the twenty-first century requires a workforce that is competent and comfortable with math, math is at the top of the national policy agenda as part of the movement to improve children in the United States' technical and scientific competency.[40]

Today's new math, sometimes referred to as the *new-new math*, emphasizes hands-on activities, problem solving, group work and teamwork, application and use of mathematical ideas and principles to real-life events, daily use of mathematics, and an understanding of and use of math understandings and competencies. The *new-new math* seeks to have students be creative users of math in life and workplace settings and also includes the ability to recall addition sums and multiplication products quickly.

The ten standards of the National Council of Teachers of Mathematics (NCTM) identify these understandings and competencies such as number and operations, algebra, geometry, measurement, data analysis and probability, problem solving, reasoning and proof, communication, connection, and representation.[41]

Your teaching of math in the primary grades will also most likely align with the NCTM's Curriculum Focal Points, which outline important mathematical topics for each grade level. Three of these Focal Points are shown in Figure 12.4.

Children from Low-Income Families and Math. Despite the efforts of standardizing math in the primary grades, children in general and children who have low socioeconomic backgrounds in particular continue to lag in performance.[42] All young children have the capability to learn and become proficient in math, but a lack of mathematical opportunities in early childhood settings and everyday experiences at home and in the community dampens this potential. There are two areas of math that are very important for children to learn early: numbers (including wholes, operations, and relations), and geometry (including spatial thinking and measuring).[43] Other math skills include classification, pattern skills, and problem solving.

It is important to realize that not every child acquires mathematical understanding at the same time, the same pace, or through the same modality. As a result, mathematics teaching needs to be across the spectrum, just like literacy. For example, embed math

Focal Point	Understanding the Focal Point	Applying the Focal Point
Numbers and Operations	Children develop an understanding of the base-ten numeration system and place-value concepts (at least to 1,000). Their understanding of base-ten numeration includes ideas of counting in units and multiples of hundreds, tens, and ones, as well as a grasp of number relationships, which they demonstrate in a variety of ways, including comparing and ordering numbers. They understand multi-digit numbers in terms of place value, recognize that place-value notation is shorthand for the sums of multiples of powers of 10 (e.g., 853 as 8 hundreds + 5 tens + 3 ones).	Children use place value and properties of operations to create equivalent representations of given numbers (such as 35 represented by 35 ones, 3 tens and 5 ones, or 2 tens and 15 ones) and to write, compare, and order multi-digit numbers. They use these ideas to compose and decompose multi-digit numbers. Children add and subtract to solve a variety of problems, including applications involving measurement, geometry, and data, as well as non-routine problems. In preparation for grade 3, they solve problems involving multiplicative situations, developing initial understandings of multiplication as repeated addition.
Number Operations and Algebra	Children use their understanding of addition to develop quick recall of basic addition facts and related subtraction facts. They solve arithmetic problems by applying their understanding of models of addition and subtraction (such as combining or separating sets or using number lines), relationships and properties of number (such as place value), and properties of addition (commutatively and associatively). Children develop, discuss, and use efficient, accurate, and generalizable methods to add and subtract multi-digit whole numbers. They select and apply appropriate methods to estimate sums and differences or calculate them mentally, depending on the context and numbers involved. They develop fluency with efficient procedures, including standard algorithms, for adding and subtracting whole numbers, understand why the procedures work (on the basis of place value and properties of operations), and use them to solve problems.	Children use number patterns to extend their knowledge of properties of numbers and operations. For example, when skip counting, they build foundations for understanding multiples and factors.
Measurement	Children develop an understanding of the meaning and processes of measurement, including such underlying concepts as partitioning (the mental activity of slicing the length of an object into equal-sized units) and transitivity (e.g., if object A is longer than object B and object B is longer than object C, then object A is longer than object C). They understand linear measure as an iteration of units and use rulers and other measurement tools with that understanding. They understand the need for equal-length units, the use of standard units of measure (centimeter and inch), and the inverse relationship between the size of a unit and the number of units used in a particular measurement (e.g., children recognize that the smaller the unit, the more iterations they need to cover a given length).	Children estimate, measure, and compute lengths as they solve problems involving data, space, and movement through space. By composing and decomposing two-dimensional shapes (intentionally substituting arrangements of smaller shapes for larger shapes or substituting larger shapes for many smaller shapes), they use geometric knowledge and spatial reasoning to develop foundations for understanding area, fractions, and proportions.

FIGURE 12.4 Curriculum Focal Points for Grade 2

into everyday routines. When math becomes a part of everyday routines, as children explore their environment, they acquire basic math skills and concepts. Their school lives will involve the use of numerous math concepts on a daily basis. When you teach math to children early, and across many environments, in a developmentally appropriate fashion, they acquire the skills they need to be successful!

Planning for Math. Helping children be successful includes planning for their learning. However, this means that you must be flexible and willing to try a variety of teaching techniques if you want your children to achieve meaningful mathematical learning. By presenting mathematical concepts orally, visually, and kinesthetically, each child can move the information into long-term memory in a manner that works best for him or her. One way to appeal to different learning modalities is to integrate literature with mathematics. In order to meet the child's individual needs, you should incorporate tactile, auditory, and visual learning experiences. Using children's literature to help them make sense of math

Lesson Title: Measuring Temperature

Time Frame for Lesson: Two days

Day 1—**E**ngage, **E**xplore, and **E**xplain
Day 2—**E**laborate and **E**valuate

> *Include state and local standards as a basis for planning.*

Standards: Texas Essential Knowledge and Skills (TEKS)

12.A Use a thermometer to measure temperature

Materials: 4–5 thermometers that measure in degrees Fahrenheit and degrees Celsius; clipboards; notebook paper; thermometer models; Temperature Recording Sheet (1 per student)

Temperature Recording Sheet

Fahrenheit vs. Celsius

	Fahrenheit	Celsius
Freezing Point	32°F	0°C
Boiling Point	212°F	100°C

Inside	Outside

Investigation

	Fahrenheit	Celsius
Inside		
Outside		

What is the difference in temperature in degrees Fahrenheit?

_____

What is the difference in temperature in degrees Celsius?

_____

---

gives them a meaningful context for math concepts. It also helps math become relevant, familiar, and interesting. Just as importantly, it relates children's prior knowledge or experiences to math, motivates students to explore, and supports memorization. Another way to appeal to different learning modalities in math is to use manipulatives. When children can count beans, coins, and pattern blocks, they are able to understand concepts more readily, which boosts self-esteem and confidence in their math capabilities. The Lesson Plan "Math 5E Model Lesson—Measuring Temperature" shows you how to create and implement a mathematics lesson plan for measuring temperature.

How Math Is Taught in Other Countries.   Recently, there has been a lot of press about how the United States' performance in mathematics compares to that of other countries.[44] When

DAY 1

Engage: Walk students outside to feel the temperature. Come back inside and ask them how the temperature inside the classroom compares to the temperature outside. Which is warmer? How do they know? What would we use to measure accurately?

Explore: Divide the class into four or five groups. Give each group a thermometer to inspect. Students should make a list of observations about the thermometer on their notebook paper (examples: there is red liquid inside, there are numbers increasing on the sides, etc.). Then they should try to find the temperature of the classroom in degrees Fahrenheit and degrees Celsius.

Explain: Show a model of three thermometers with different scales. One thermometer measures degrees by a scale of one degree, another by two degrees, another by five degrees. Ask the students if they can spot the difference. Explain that a scale on the thermometer helps us know how to measure temperature. It is essential to determine the scale before measuring the temperature. Demonstrate how to look at the top of the mercury to find the exact temperature using the scale.

Give each student a copy of the "Fahrenheit vs. Celsius" table (see temperature recording sheet). Explain that we use degrees Fahrenheit in the United States, but other parts of the world use degrees Celsius. We can compare the two using these charts. Ask students, "What do you think will happen to water when the temperature reaches the freezing point?" (It will freeze, creating ice or snow). Ask students, "What do you think will happen to water when the temperature reaches the boiling point?" (It will evaporate, creating steam).

Measure the temperature of the classroom again together in degrees Fahrenheit and degrees Celsius and record on the recording sheet. Make sure students are using the correct scale based on the thermometers they are using.

Notice how a twenty-first century skill engages students and gets them to think about and act like scientists.

Group work encourages collaboration!

Notice how the teacher poses questions to promote critical thinking— another 21st Century skill

DAY 2

Elaborate: Take students outside again with clipboards and the temperature recording sheet to measure and record the temperature in degrees Fahrenheit and Celsius.

Students then complete the blank thermometers on the recording sheet by choosing and creating the scales and shading to show the correct temperature.

Evaluate: Give students a temperature assessment that asks them to name the temperature on thermometers with varying scales and temperatures. Give immediate feedback and correction.

Differentiate for lower-level learners: Allow students to use a multiplication chart or number line to be able to correctly determine and create the scales on the thermometers.

Extend for gifted and talented learners: Students measure and record the temperature outside for a two-week period (same time, same location). They document their results using a bar graph so that the different days can be compared. Is the temperature increasing or decreasing over time? Were there any other factors that could affect the temperature (rain, etc.)?

Teaching and assessing is a constant cycle.

Always identify ways to differentiate for all levels of learners.

Source: Text and photo contributed by Angela Livengood, third grade teacher, Curtsinger Elementary School.

it comes to math, students from many countries in Asia continue to outperform students in the United States. U.S. students' lack of math achievement raises concerns about the United States' international competitive abilities. However, it also gives us an opportunity to look at how math is taught in other countries, which may help you teach math more effectively.

Hong Kong Math. Take, for example, Hong Kong's math instruction. A recent study found that although Massachusetts is the highest-ranking state in the United States in terms of math scores, Hong Kong children outscore Massachusetts' children. Why do 40 percent of Hong Kong's third grade test-takers score at advanced levels but only 22 percent of third graders in Massachusetts and just 10 percent of third graders across the United States?[45]

There are several reasons why. One main reason is that in the United States, third grade math tests are "high-stakes." There is a lot of pressure on children to perform and on teachers to teach to the test. However, in Hong Kong, similar tests are not for achievement-accountability purposes; instead they are for basic assessment and are used by teachers to shape lessons.[46]

Another difference in math between our countries is that Hong Kong uses a broader range of questions that ask children to build their responses using mathematical concepts, rather than bubble in multiple-choice answers. The Hong Kong model is more complex; demands a higher level of thinking; requires the use and comprehension of knowledge rather than memory recall; and uses more multiple-stepped problems that apply to everyday situations. Hong Kong tests follow this instructional model whereas tests in the United States are usually multiple-choice and emphasize memorization. This tells us two things: third graders are capable of a higher level of thinking and expectations; and children in the United States are being taught to a lower level of thinking in order to achieve in accountability testing.[47]

Japan, South Korea, and Singapore employ mathematics teaching methods similar to those of Hong Kong.[48] Read on to learn more about Singapore's specific approach to teaching math and its growing popularity in the United States.

Singapore Math.   The Singapore method is becoming more popular based on scores from the Trends in International Mathematics and Science Study, which shows Singapore is at the top of the world in mathematics scores. Singamore math programs have a consistent and strong emphasis on problem solving and model drawing, with a focus on in-depth understanding. The Singapore framework states, "Mathematical problem solving is central to mathematics learning. It involves the acquisition and application of mathematics concepts and skills in a wide range of situations, including non-routine, open-ended and real-world problems.[49,50] Figure 12.5 shows sample problems from the Singapore Mathematics model.

Singapore math features problems that often are more complex than what American textbooks contain. It demands deep mastery of a few math concepts, rather than an overview of many different ideas. It aims to give students a basic understanding of how math works, rather than a simple rote system for finding answers. Complex word problems are the norm in the Singapore textbooks, but students begin with very simple problems that follow a well-articulated scope and sequence. The Singapore method takes seriously the proposition that the purpose of math is to solve complex problems. As students develop confidence, they tackle more complicated problems, including non-routine ones. Then, children are expected to discuss their math problems. By sharing and discussing their solution methods, students develop metacognitive processes, or the awareness and understanding about one's own reasoning and thinking. They also have to listen to others and learn to understand others' ways of thinking.[51, 52]

As you can see, there are many different ways to approach teaching mathematics in the primary grades. It is up to you to find what works best for your students.

Science in the Primary Grades

When teaching science in the primary grades, you must be aware of the National Science Content Standards of the Center for Science, Mathematics, and Engineering.

> The NSES Science Teaching Standards encourage teachers to plan an inquiry-based science program for their students; guide and facilitate learning; engage in ongoing assessment of their teaching and of student learning; design and manage learning environments that provide students with the time, space, and resources needed for learning science; develop communities of science learners that reflect the intellectual rigor of scientific inquiry and the attitudes and social values conducive to science learning; and actively participate in the ongoing planning and development of the school science program.[53]

Today's science teaching is *inquiry based;* that is, it is all about helping children learn to solve problems. **Inquiry learning** is the involvement of children in activities and processes

inquiry learning
Involvement of children in activities and processes that lead to learning.

Samples of Typical Singapore Math Problems

A part-whole model problem

Mrs. Tan bought a box of pens for $12 and a book for $15. She paid with a $50 bill. How much change should she get?

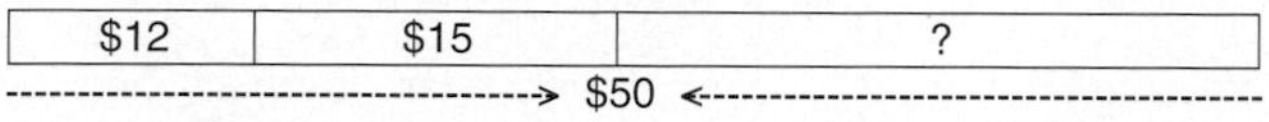

$12	$15	?

```
<-------------------------------------> $50 <------------------------------------->
```

$12 + $15 = $27

$50 − $27 = $23

Mrs. Tan should get $23 as change.

A comparison model problem

There are 3 baskets: A, B, and C. Basket A contains 4 times more apples than Basket C. Basket B contains 16 fewer apples than Basket A. Basket C contains half as many apples as in Basket B. Find the amount of apples in each basket.

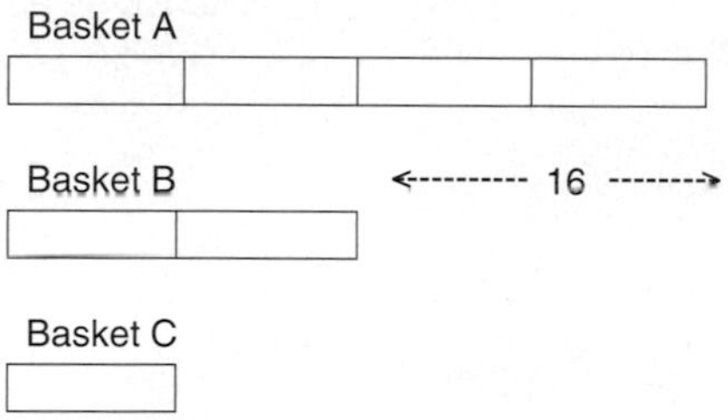

Basket A

Basket B   <--------- 16 ------->

Basket C

2 units--> 16   Therefore,
1 unit --> 8   Basket A has 32 apples.
4 units--> 32   Basket B has 16 apples.
                            Basket C has 8 apples.

FIGURE 12.5 Singapore Math Problems

Source: Berinderjeet Kaur, National Institute of Education, Singapore; accessed May 24, 2010, from http://home.sandiego.edu/~pmyers/singapore/Kaur_method_of-model.pdf.

that lead to learning. The process of inquiry involves (1) posing questions; (2) observing; (3) reading and researching for a purpose; (4) proposing solutions and making predictions; and (5) gathering information and interpreting it. As you can see from Figure 12.6, the science curriculum heavily emphasizes inquiry-based learning in all content areas.

Linda Rasmussen is a third grade teacher. Linda's classroom environment encompasses the world of nature. Third graders use binoculars to watch bird stations outside their classroom. They examine insect eggs, learn about bugs, snakes, and butterflies, and become aware and respectful of the outside world. Classroom writing assignments combine research and observation. Scientists visit the classroom and students are treated to visits to San Diego's natural habitats.[54]

Science Technology Engineering Math (STEM).   We have discussed before the emphasis on science, technology, engineering, and mathematics (STEM). Ever since the Soviet Union launched Sputnik satellites in 1957, the United States has focused on the improvement of science education. This emphasis intensified recently because the Programme for International Student Assessment (PISA) comparison found that American students ranked twenty-first out of thirty in science literacy among students from developed countries, and twenty-fifth out of thirty in math literacy.[55]

As a result, in January 2010, President Obama announced more than $250 million in private investments to help attract and prepare new teachers for science, technology, engineering, and mathematics, and to help improve instruction in those areas by practicing teachers as a part of his "Educate to Innovate" campaign.[56] The initiative is important because, as President Obama said, "Our future depends on reaffirming America's role as

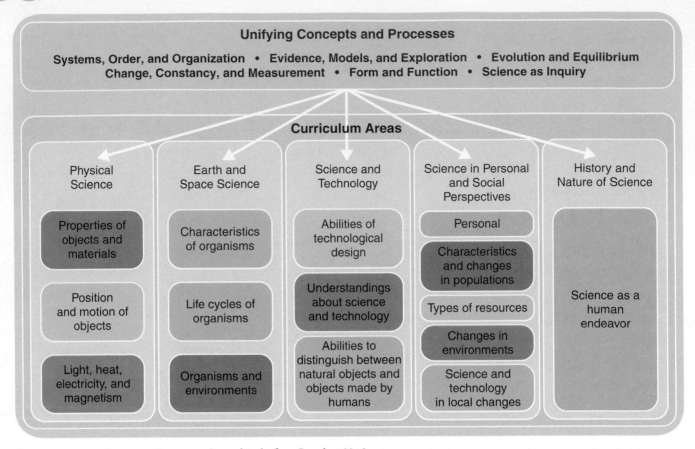

Unifying Concepts and Processes

Systems, Order, and Organization • Evidence, Models, and Exploration • Evolution and Equilibrium
Change, Constancy, and Measurement • Form and Function • Science as Inquiry

Curriculum Areas

Physical Science	Earth and Space Science	Science and Technology	Science in Personal and Social Perspectives	History and Nature of Science
Properties of objects and materials	Characteristics of organisms	Abilities of technological design	Personal	Science as a human endeavor
Position and motion of objects	Life cycles of organisms	Understandings about science and technology	Characteristics and changes in populations	
Light, heat, electricity, and magnetism	Organisms and environments	Abilities to distinguish between natural objects and objects made by humans	Types of resources	
			Changes in environments	
			Science and technology in local changes	

FIGURE 12.6 Science Content Standards for Grades K–4

Source: Data from National Science Education Standards (1996), Center for Science, Mathematics, and Engineering Education. Copyright 2000 National Academy of Science.

the world's engine of scientific discovery and technology innovation, and that leadership tomorrow depends on how we educate our students today, especially in math, science, technology, and engineering."[57]

STEM in the Classroom.   So, what are some ways you can integrate STEM into your teaching? Robotics offers a rich tool for engaging teachers and young children in STEM. Robotics provides opportunities for active design of meaningful projects and constructive thinking in order to explore, play, and develop new concepts and ways of thinking. Robotics is a tool for fostering children's interest in science and technology. For example, LEGO® *Education WeDo*™ for children seven to eleven years of age redefines classroom robotics, making it possible for children to build and program their own solutions.

Technological activities should address students' developmental characteristics. They should include students' natural curiosity and inventive thinking skills. For example, children should be given ample opportunities to explore wheels, axles, levers, gears, pulleys, and cams by playing with a variety of toys and construction kits that include these mechanisms. Children are fascinated with building and with taking things apart to see how they work. They engineer informally all the time. By encouraging these explorations in elementary school, we can keep these interests alive. Describing their activities as "engineering" when they are engaged in the natural design process helps children develop positive associations with engineering, and increases students' awareness of and access to scientific and technical careers. The number of American citizens pursuing engineering is decreasing. Early introduction to engineering can encourage many capable students, especially girls and minorities, to consider it as a career and enroll in the necessary science and math courses in high school.

Social Studies in the Primary Grades

Social studies are the integrated study of the social sciences and humanities to promote civic competence. The primary purpose of social studies is to help young people develop the ability to make informed and reasoned decisions for the public good as citizens of a culturally diverse, democratic society in an interdependent world.[58]

Teaching social studies is an important part of your responsibility as an early childhood teacher. While teachers devote a lot of instructional time to literacy/reading and math, you need not neglect the social studies. You can integrate social studies content with reading and math, so that children are reading and engaged in math processes "across the curriculum." Be sure you are familiar with your state standards for the grade level you are teaching in order to incorporate them into your planning and teaching. Here are some ideas for incorporating social studies into your curriculum.

LEGO® robotic engineering kits are an excellent way to introduce children to concepts of engineering at an early age. In addition, you can provide many other opportunities for children to learn basic engineering concepts, such as gears, wheels, pulleys, levers, and axles.

Culture. The best place to begin teaching about culture is with you and your students. At the beginning of the school year, third grade teacher Alessia Rossi shares information about her Italian background with her students by showing where her ancestors came from. She uses social studies tools such as maps and globes to help her students put Italy in the world geographic context. She invites members of the local Italian Sons and Daughters of America (ISDA) to share Italian culture and heritage. She introduces Italian words and ties these to the reading lessons. She has books about the Italian culture in the reading center and DVDs with Italian songs and dances. In the process of Alessia's sharing, her students feel comfortable and start to share their cultures and backgrounds. At the end of the school year, the class hosts a Cultural Heritage Festival.

Time, Continuity, and Change. Just as culture is all around us, so we are surrounded by time, continuity, and change. Second grade teacher Kelie Shipley involved her students in a community history project in which her students research not only the history of their town, but also how the town is changing and why. In the course of the research, the children discovered that on one of the dedication plaques, the name of the person for whom their school is named was misspelled. They wrote letters to school and city officials, resulting in a new plaque. At the new dedication, relatives of the school's namesake came and talked about what school was like when they were in the second grade.

People, Places, and Environment. Your local museums, art institutes, and historical centers are wonderful resources for involving your students in learning about people, places, and the environment. For example, the Allen Memorial Art Museum in Oberlin, Ohio, collaborates with the Asian Art/Educational Outreach Funding Initiative of the Freeman Foundation and has developed Asian art educational programming for children and teachers. One of the lessons involves children ages five to eight in *gyotaku,* the Japanese art of fish painting, and *haiku,* a form of Japanese poetry.

Individual Development and Identity. First grade teacher Ashley Gotkins incorporates the North Carolina Grade One Social Studies Standards into her teaching. They focus on neighborhoods and communities around the world. Ashley, whose grandmother was

1/16 Cherokee, uses her cultural heritage to teach about Native Americans and the Cherokee tribes. She builds her Native American lessons around these North Carolina Standards:[59]

- Describe the roles of individuals in the family.
- Identify various groups to which individuals and families belong.
- Compare and contrast similarities and differences among individuals and families.
- Explore the benefits of diversity in the United States.

Individuals, Groups, and Institutions.   On the first day of school, first grade teacher Tanika Ramsey holds a "morning meeting" in which all of the children introduce themselves. Then she talks about families, and what a family is. The children brainstorm about what things they can do to live peacefully in their classroom family. In the following days, Tanika expands the discussion to include what children can do to live harmoniously in the school. The children discuss school rules, interview administrators, staff, and other teachers and develop a "blueprint for school living." They share their blueprint with other kindergarten classes.

Power, Authority, and Governance.   Classroom living requires a lot of compromises and getting along with others. Second grade teacher Jacki Aochi believes she should share her "power" with children and can accomplish this goal by teaching her children how to resolve conflicts. In addition, Jacki conducts a morning meeting which consists of three parts. Each part takes about five minutes:

- *Announcements*: Both she and the students make announcements related to classroom and school events and activities as well as life events such as birthdays, sporting events, and family activities.

Having children map their community and compare it with maps of other communities around the world using Google Earth is an excellent way to involve students in understanding global similarities and differences.

- *Concerns*: The children discuss events inside and outside of the classroom and suggest resolutions for how they and others can turn the concern into a positive situation.
- *Being a Good Citizen*: Children have an opportunity to state what they are going to do during the day or week to be good citizens in the classroom, school, home, and community.

Production, Distribution, and Consumption.   Matt Blair teaches his third graders about the production, distribution, and consumption of consumer products by creating, selling, and distributing handmade cards. The children design and illustrate get well, birthday, and thank you cards and provide original verses and sentiments. They also package, sell, and distribute their cards. As part of the project, children visit design studios and printers and consult with marketing executives of local businesses. All proceeds from the sales of the cards go to a community charity selected by the children.

Science, Technology, and Society.   Second grade teacher Beverly Huang integrates her teaching of science, technology, and society with the teaching of the scientific method. (Review our earlier discussion in this chapter.) She involves the children in a project in which they survey their homes and community to determine the ways in which computers influence how people live and work. The children post their own research questions, develop their surveys—both online and hard copy versions—analyze their data, draw conclusions, write their results in their science journals, and publish the results in their school newspaper.

Global Connections.   Melissa Gloria's students are third graders whose first language is primarily English, but they are learning Spanish as a second language. They are studying world cultures and use ePal Global Community (www.epals.com) to exchange letters, postcards, photographs, and journal entries via e-mail with their electronic pals in Ecuador. They collaborate by exchanging information about culture, history, and so on.

Civic Ideals and Practices.   First grade teacher Gretchen Reich uses the local community to teach civic pride. Her students engage in a project of learning about community agencies and how they help others. The students select agencies they would like to know more about, such as the Salvation Army, and invite agency members to their classroom to talk about what they do. As a result of their community civic involvement, the children decided to collect pennies to support the Salvation Army Red Kettle drive. In six weeks, the children raised $50. Also, once a month, the children bake cookies and take them to homes for senior citizens. Last month, in addition to baking cookies, the children also made cards and visited the Jewish Home for the Aged.

Expressive Arts in the Primary Grades

In the primary grades, the creative arts most often included in the curriculum are music, theater, dance, and the visual arts. For each of these disciplines you will want to include content knowledge, skills, concepts, and themes in your students' learning experiences. As specified by your state standards, your teaching of the arts should be content based and child centered. Make sure you consult your state's content standards for the arts.

Ideas for Teaching Creative Arts.   You will want to make sure children are provided with authentic content and engaged in activities that help them learn and apply knowledge of the arts.

Dancing to Music.   Tiffany Dwyer encourages her students to appreciate and examine different styles of music as well as create dance presentations that are specifically related to the music. She plays music and asks her students to listen to it carefully and think about what it is about and how it makes them feel. She plays the music again and asks her students to move to the music. If the music is fast, she encourages them to move fast. At the same time, she asks her students to show her how the music makes them feel: happy, sad, and so forth.[60]

New Topics and Curriculum in the Primary Grades

Curriculum changes are due in part to the influences of world events, politics, and new research and knowledge. Here are some recent additions to curriculum in the primary grades.

Fiscal Education.   The financial recession of 2008–2010 has had a great impact on the U.S. economy and education today. As a result, the Department of Education is determined to educate children in fiscal matters. This includes knowing how to manage money.

The Department of Education released a report that identifies different options for incorporating financial education into schools. Some of these options are including financial education in standards set by state school boards; incorporating financial concepts into material on states' tests; urging textbook publishers to include more financial education content; incorporating financial education materials into classroom lessons; and training teachers on the importance of financial education.[61]

Teacher Janice Belcuore integrates money concepts into her second grade class throughout the school year. Students alternate classroom jobs, such as door holder, line leader, and paper passer, at regular intervals. Some jobs earn more than others—just like in the real world. Students get paid for their "jobs" twice a month, but they are required to pay rent—for their desks and chairs—save a certain amount each month, and keep a checkbook. A vital component of Janice's fiscal education is the checkbook because her students must enter their paycheck, deduct rent and debits, and save for expensive purchases—in other words, they must continuously use addition, subtraction, and carrying over in the real world. At the end of every month, children have the opportunity to "shop" with their money, and like the real world, they can go into debt, too! Missing homework assignments or inappropriate behavior costs Janice's students. In addition, each student completes a year-end fiscal report which includes comparing their spending and checks and balances with an adult family member. Janice's fiscal education is hands on, real-world oriented, and meets state standards for math concepts. She hopes that these lessons will translate into lifelong learning about fiscal responsibility, which will impact how they behave in the global market.[62]

Bullying Education.   Bullying at all levels of education is a serious problem, but bullying in the primary grades has recently received a lot of national attention. Nine out of every ten elementary students are bullied by their peers.[63] Both the bullies and the bullied suffer higher levels of depression and other mental health problems throughout their lives than those who are neither perpetrators nor victims.[64] And recently, news broadcasts across the country have shown us that victims are paying the ultimate price of bullying. In Baltimore an eight-year-old third grader attempted to kill herself by jumping out a window.[65] In Chicago, a seven-year-old and a ten-year-old boy hanged themselves. In Texas, a nine-year-old boy hanged himself in the nurse's office.[66] This is a reality that must be faced by early childhood professionals. Suicide in response to bullying does not just occur in high school; it's happening in the first, second, and third grades too!

In response to the escalating awareness of bullying, schools are implementing anti-bully campaigns. Character education is also used to decrease bullying. Positive prevention programs focus on the power of words and how to use them positively rather than negatively. Such programs not only prevent bullying, they promote character, citizenship, and diversity. The positive approach focuses on solutions to bullying by instilling positive character traits through character education rather than punishing negative behavior. This approach shows us that approaching bullying from a positive perspective, based on increasing positive traits in children rather than focusing on the negative and punishing behaviors, is a powerful way to address bullying.[67] Schools using the positive approach, rather than a punitive approach to bullying, see amazing results. For example, national averages saw kindness, tolerance, and cooperation increase by 60 percent; name-calling decrease by 53 percent; bus discipline and distraction incidents decrease by 60 percent; and classroom distraction minutes decrease by 55 percent, extending available teaching time up to three weeks.

Twenty-First Century Skills.   Our world is being transformed by technological advances, the "knowledge revolution," a global economy, and environmental changes.[68] Education has to keep up so that our children can be successful in the global community. To compete successfully for tomorrow's jobs, today's students need to learn to be future leaders who can think creatively, work collaboratively, use technology to solve problems effectively and peaceably, and take initiative. This means integrating the use of twenty-first century skills in every subject and at every grade to encourage students to learn the skills for the future even as they learn the content. Gerald Chertavian, chair of a twenty-first century skills task force, says, "Today's employers have been clear that basic skills just aren't enough to be successful in today's high-technology, fast-moving global economy anymore."[69]

Twenty-first century learning skills include:

- Information and communication skills such as media literacy, information literacy, and information and communication technology literacy.

- Thinking and problem-solving skills such as critical thinking and systems thinking, problem identification formulation and solution, creativity, and intellectual curiosity.
- Interpersonal and self-directional skills such as flexibility and adaptability; initiative and self-direction; social and cross-cultural skills; productivity and accountability; leadership and responsibility.[70]

You will need to teach twenty-first century skills in a twenty-first century context. You can create the appropriate context by making content relevant to students' lives. You also create context by bringing the world into the classroom and taking the students out into the world. Also, be sure to incorporate twenty-first century content such as global awareness, financial, economic, and business literacy, civic literacy, and health literacy.[71]

Language Immersion.   We live in a global economy and our children are not just citizens of their local communities; they are global citizens. As a result, they need twenty-first century language skills. Many schools take a language immersion approach. They introduce language and culture as early as possible during children's sensitive period for language development. English and the immersion language—often Spanish or Mandarin Chinese—are taught simultaneously for everyone, not just English language learners. The language immersion movement is catching on. In the past decade, the number of children taking Mandarin has jumped from 5,000 to 60,000 because immersion programs have been proven to provide cognitive benefits such as flexible and creative thinking.[72]

Spanish-English Immersion.   In Salt Lake City, Horizon Elementary school has a Spanish–English immersion program for first graders. Every day, the first graders spend half the day speaking only English and the other half speaking only Spanish. In just two weeks, native English speaking children are already speaking Spanish with some fluency and native Spanish speaking children are already speaking English. Spanish teacher Tristin West says, "Dual language immersion is not about learning to conjugate verbs or memorizing the names of colors. It's about simply submerging children in Spanish as if they were at a Spanish language school in the heart of Madrid." She goes on to say that she teaches her six-year-olds in Spanish using a lot of gestures, dancing, singing, and kinesthetic movement because children are tactile learners and the "movement helps the learning stick." The Spanish–English immersion program is equally beneficial for both native English and Spanish-speaking children. For children who are native English speakers, the program opens the world of language to them and will help them become highly marketable professionals in the future; for native Spanish speakers, the same goes, but there are added benefits. Children who learn in both their native language and in English don't lose their native tongue and they also achieve far and above in testing situations in comparison to their peers who do not benefit from the same program.[73]

The Family Approach.   Studies show that family engagement makes a big difference in teaching and student achievement, especially among children who come from low socioeconomic families. Reach out any way you can: web pages, e-mail, blogs, parent consultations, and family meetings. One way to emphasize family in the classroom is to make it a part of the curriculum. Include family members in the classroom by having them be "guest teachers" on topics they are passionate about or are learned in. For example, have a lawyer mother volunteer to teach a unit on the law and justice in social studies; have a doctor grandfather teach a lesson on anatomy, cells, or chemistry in science; have a musician father teach about song writing and personal expression; have a mechanic uncle teach a lesson about cars and how engines work in science and math units. The possibilities are endless. Each year you have a new crop of relatives with a diverse array of backgrounds and professions that you can tap to increase familial involvement and real-world applicability in the classroom.

Voice from the Field

The Secret Agents of Jordan/Jackson Elementary School

I don't teach a class of third graders—I lead a group of Secret Agents. The Secret Agency has changed my life. Setting it up has given me a unique opportunity to get to know all my students and their families on an individual basis and it gives me the freedom to push my students and myself to meet our potential. The Secret Agency is a way of life.

Getting the Agency off the Ground

I begin the Agency each year in August when I send students and their families a letter explaining they are now members of the student Secret Agent force. In the letter I tell them what to expect for the year and that everything we do ties into the year-long theme of investigative learning. On the first day of school, students receive their Agent numbers.

The process for assigning Agent numbers is similar to that of Harry Potter and the sorting hat. The number chooses them. Students pick a popsicle stick out of a mug, and whatever number is on that stick becomes their Agent number. As their leader, I learn not only their names, but also their Agent numbers. Children take ownership and pride in their number. Over the years students come back and ask me if I remember their number, and of course I do! Several have even used their numbers on their athletic jerseys. I am always Agent 24 because I always have at least twenty-five students in my class. This way they know I am a part of their group. I am not just their teacher, I am a fellow Agent. When we line up by number, I can stand in line with them because I am a part of their Agency.

Throughout the year, we Agents are held to a moral code based on the four pillars of our classroom: expectations, respect, responsibility, and imagination.

Expectations

Using the Secret Agent approach led to me to give up control and put the power of learning in the hands of these young Agents. Doing so allows them to see me, as head of the Secret Agent force, as an active learner and investigator of my world.

In that way, I am an example of what I expect of them as learners and as individuals. I let them know that the word "can't" is removed from an Agent's vocabulary. They know that Agents are expected to always try their best and ask questions when they do not understand something.

Respect

The Agents become a catalyst for change in many ways, including participating in community service projects with the local food pantry. Students also know I expect courtesy. They learn the importance of listening to speakers; responding when someone is speaking; and looking someone in the eye. Phrases like "please," "thank you," and "may I" are mandatory when addressing a member of our community. Most important, we hold a high regard for other's thinking and we celebrate mistakes. Respect is something one earns in our Agency, and I make it my mission for all the Agents to successfully earn respect in our classroom.

Responsibility

The Agents are required to take responsibility for their own learning. They teach at the SMART board and run Web pages on our

---

Bring families into the school. Encouraging families to volunteer in all aspects of school life is helpful. Grandparents, parents, aunts, uncles, brothers, and sisters can all volunteer in the library, cafeteria, and classroom. Using volunteers has the dual benefit of involving families in their children's educational lives as well as demonstrating acceptance and promotion of diversity. Another great way of emphasizing family in the school is for you, the teacher, to get out of the school. Teachers like third grade teacher Rayna Freedman (see the Voice from the Field on pages 362–363) and first and second grade teacher Joe Dorn make it a point to attend their students' family events, baseball games, chess tournaments, and whatever other extracurricular activities their children and their families are interested in.[74] This increases the link between schools and families and fortifies family-school-child relationships.

classroom website. They coach each other through difficult tasks. They build their classroom community. They blog, create PowerPoint projects, have extra math homework, and question the world around them. Agents run their own student-led conference and develop twenty-first century learning skills.

Imagination

I dissolve the walls of the classroom and show my students there are no limits to what they can accomplish. I guide them along an educational journey through the wonders of childhood and set them on a path to become lifelong learners. Breaking boundaries through the power of imagination helps these global learners become global leaders of tomorrow.

Connecting Agents and Their Families to Learning

I send a monthly e-letter home to update families on classroom activities. We include all Agents and families in our classroom activities because the involvement of families is critical to the success of our classroom. Parents run math explorations, science experiments, listen to student book or multimedia presentations, or read to us. As a result, students understand that their families, teacher, and they are part of one team and we all grow as scholars and individuals.

Connecting Agent 24 to Families

In order to get to know the whole child, I attend one out-of-school event for each Agent if he or she will have me. Spending time with my students makes them feel important and special. They know I really care about them and want to see them succeed in all that they do. A calendar sits on my desk and students can fill in their events. I ask for at least a week's notice. Sporting events, dance recitals, dinners, birthday parties, play dates, plays, and black belt celebrations are just a few of the things I have been privileged to attend. Doing this has allowed me to experience the life of my students and get to know them in deeper more meaningful ways.

Agents are also invited to stay after school on Mondays and Wednesdays for Homework Club. This is a place for them to get work done and make social connections with other Agents. Agent alumni and siblings are also welcomed and encouraged to attend.

We also do a birthday book celebration instead of a birthday party. Agents sit in a seat of honor and open up a wrapped book from home. They read to us for 15 minutes and then donate their book to the classroom library. I put an honor plate in it so they can come back year after year to find their book. It is the gift that keeps on giving, and the experience shows us how we are all readers.

An Agency with Meaning

Everything—all class assignments, project-based learning activities, parent events, individual lessons, and how they are differentiated—throughout the school year has meaning and can be connected back to students' daily lives. At the end of the year we have a Secret Agent ceremony. Each student gets a Secret Agent t-shirt with his or her number on the back. I share a tale of where I envision each Agent to be in 30 years. They pledge to hold the high ideals of being a Secret Agent as they matriculate. Finally, each Agent signs a special book pledging themselves to their academic career. That book currently has ten years of signatures. Each one is doing great things, whether it's in the language or performing arts, math, technology, sciences, athletics, or social studies. Parents often e-mail me, sharing their child's accomplishments. I started a Facebook group for Secret Agents and their parents to share their lives with other Agents and make new connections or revisit old friends.

Being a Secret Agent unlocks a door and invites students into a world where the impossible becomes possible. It puts students in charge of their learning and shapes them into members of society who are not afraid to challenge boundaries and strive for excellence. With a clear vision and a little creativity all you need is a mug and some popsicle sticks to make a huge difference in the life of a child and his or her family.

Source: Contributed by Rayna Freedman, Teacher of Honor for Kappa Delta Pi, recipient of Apple School Night Award and the CLC Innovative Curriculum Project Grant, and finalist for North Attleboro Chamber of Commerce Teacher of the Year (2009); published in The Record, New Teacher Advocate, *and* Education World. *Photo by Nancy True.*

Accommodating Diverse Learners

All early childhood teachers are inclusion classroom teachers at one time or another in their careers. Inclusion is defined as educating children with and without disabilities in the same classroom. The Division for Early Childhood (DEC) of the Council for Exceptional Children (CEC) and the National Association for the Education of Young Children (NAEYC) have identified inclusion as the preferred service delivery option for young children with special needs. However, there is no agreed-on model for developing and delivering these services. A classroom template for inclusion is not available, but it is essential that you believe that preparing all children to function in society is best achieved by creating environments for children whose diversity includes varying abilities and disabilities and backgrounds.

The following are some ways you can create, implement, evaluate, and modify your classroom to create optimal learning conditions for all students:

- *Classroom schedule:* A consistent schedule helps students feel secure and adds to the predictability of the environment. A visual schedule reviewed orally every day benefits all children. In addition, some students will need their own individual schedules, particularly if their day includes therapists who assist them.

- *Routines:* Routines for different times of the day and scheduling a particular activity at the same time every day or on the same day every week is beneficial for students who need the stability of knowing what their day involves.

- *Transitions:* Develop transition strategies that support smooth transitions between activities. Use verbal cues (e.g., 5 minutes before clean-up), visual cues (e.g., picture schedules), auditory cues (e.g., timers), and praise after successful transitions.

- *Classroom curriculum:* An appropriate classroom curriculum includes activities that you can modify and adapt to meet the needs of each child.

- *Classroom management:* You must support and encourage appropriate behavior, prevent inappropriate behavior, and guide or redirect misbehavior when it does occur. In the inclusive classroom, you can achieve this goal by creating a positive management plan that addresses skill deficits. A **skill deficit** is the inability to perform a skill because the child does not possess the skill. For example, a child with a disability may have a social skill deficit associated with making friends and gaining popularity. Motivational deficits involve the unwillingness or lack of cooperation of children to perform a skill they possess, either entirely or at an appropriate level. For example, some children may be reluctant or hesitant to engage in an activity because of their disability. In contrast, some children may lack motivational self-control and be aggressive and intrusive in their behavior.

- *Rules:* State rules positively; limit their number; and make sure they are observable and measurable. Ensure that children's rules don't involve academic or homework issues that can unfairly impact students with disabilities or who are linguistically diverse.

- *Physical arrangement:* The four-desk cluster provides the most opportunities for students with disabilities to be included in the classroom. You can efficiently move from child to child, and at the same time the children support socialization, cooperation, and group work.

- *Grouping:* Grouping in the inclusive classroom is an excellent way to differentiate instruction in order to meet each child's needs. Appropriate assessment enables you to form appropriate groups.

skill deficit When a child has not learned how to perform a particular skill or behavior.

Activities for Professional Development

Ethical Dilemma

"Caught in the middle."

Julia Le is a second grade teacher. One day, she, her colleagues, and her students are stunned to learn that, Greg, a nine-year-old third grader, just committed suicide at school. The whole school community is shocked and grieving. Julia's students pepper her with tearful questions. "Why did he do it? How did he do it? Where will he go? But why?" Julia struggles to answer their questions. When Julia goes to her teaching mentor for advice on how best to help her students through this terrible time, her mentor empathizes but says, "It's not really your job to answer questions like that. That's what school counselors are for. If they keep asking you questions, just send them to the counselor." In addition, the principal tells Julia, "It's inappropriate for eight-year-olds to be talking about suicide." Julia just doesn't feel right about it. She did some research and found that the

American Hospice Foundation (AHF) explains that the best policy is to tell children the truth and provide reassurance because fantasy is often more frightening than facts.[75] The AHF recommends that adults should give simple, honest, and age-appropriate explanations about loss or death.[76] Julia is caught between her school's "gag order" and her own sense of right and wrong.

What should Julia do? How should she answer her students' questions? How should Julia balance her own feelings and grieving with those of her students? What would you do? Would you abide by the school's and your mentor's advice, or would you follow your feeling?

Activities to Apply What You Learned

1. Make a list of the ways education in the primary grades is different now from how it was when you were in elementary school. What things have stayed the same? What changes do you find the most surprising? Write a 200-word reflection and share with your classmates.

2. Skype with a local elementary school teacher and ask him/her about the developmental changes he/she observes in his/her classroom. Which changes are the most obvious and which are more subtle? Share your experience with your classmates.

3. Conduct an internet search of several leading newspapers such as the *New York Times,* the *Boston Globe,* and *USA Today.* What current events are influencing the field of education? Next, peruse your local newspaper. How are current events influencing education on a local level? Post your findings in your blog.

4. Identify five character traits to teach in your second grade classroom and explain why you think they are essential in a Facebook note and tag your friends.

5. How will you accommodate diverse learners in your inclusive classroom? Choose from the following differences that influence learning: ADHD, economic disadvantages, autism, or visual impairments. Give three examples of how you will accommodate the child.

Linking to Learning

A to Z Teacher Stuff
www.atozteacherstuff.com/
Created for teachers by a teacher; designed to help teachers find online lesson plans and resources quickly and easily. Offers ideas on thematic units and lesson plans and contains a large collection of printable worksheets and pages.

CHARACTER COUNTS! National Homepage
www.charactercounts.org/
A nonprofit, nonpartisan, nonsectarian coalition of schools, communities, and nonprofit organizations working to advance character education by teaching the six pillars of character.

Scholastic Teachers
http://teacher.scholastic.com/
Contains great resources for building student success, including lesson plans, activities, reproducibles, and thematic units. Also provides time-saving teacher tools, such as Standards Match, which lets you easily locate classroom resources aligned to your state standards.

myeducationlab

Go to Topics 2 (Child Development/Theories) and 7 (Curriculum/Content Areas) in the MyEducationLab (www.myeducationlab.com) for your course, where you can:

- Find learning outcomes for Child Development/Theories and Curriculum/Content Areas along with the national standards that connect to these outcomes.
- Complete Assignments and Activities that can help you more deeply understand the chapter content.
- Apply and practice your understanding of the core teaching skills identified in the chapter with the Building Teaching Skills and Dispositions learning units.
- Examine challenging situations and cases presented in the IRIS Center Resources.
- Check your comprehension on the content covered in the chapter by going to the Study Plan in the Book Resources for your text. Here you will be able to take a chapter quiz, receive feedback on your answers, and then access Review, Practice, and Enrichment activities to enhance your understanding of chapter content.

13

TECHNOLOGY AND YOUNG CHILDREN
Education for the Information Age

naeyc standards

Standard 4. Using Developmentally Effective Approaches to Connect with Children and Families

I understand and use positive relationships and supportive interactions as the foundation for my work with young children and families. I know, understand, and use a wide array of developmentally appropriate approaches, instructional strategies, and tools to connect with children and families and positively influence each child's development and learning.[1]

Standard 5. Using Content Knowledge to Build Meaningful Curriculum

I understand the importance of developmental domains and academic (or content) disciplines in early childhood curriculum. I use my knowledge and other resources to design, implement, and evaluate meaningful, challenging curricula that promote comprehensive developmental and learning outcomes for every young child.[2]

You need go no further than the daily newspaper (online, of course!) to see how technology is changing the face of education as we know it. Third grade teacher of the year Joy Jenkins is a model of the technological twenty-first century classroom. She uses iPods and computers to teach her children lessons. Joy has her children listen to lessons of cursive handwriting on the iPod. She records her voice so that children can hear her teach the lesson. The iPod Touch gives children visualization of the letters. Joy uses computers to teach lessons about twenty-first century public issues such as bullying. She allows her students to record their own stories and illustrate them with Kid Pix. Joys feels that "technology has transformed my teaching, the kids, and how we look at school."[3] Technological devices are increasingly powerful learning aids that enable collaboration, communication, and learning. The use of technology has and will continue to change the way children learn and the way you teach.[4]

Children of the Net Generation

Children today are technologically oriented. They are the net generation, and their growth, development, and learning are intimately tied to large doses of television, videos, electronic games, and computers in the home and shopping centers. American children spend 7.5 hours a day absorbing and creating media.[5] Today, more and more students have laptop and handheld computers that they easily carry back and forth between home and school. Three-year-olds Emma and Emily Slinger have been immersed in technology since they were six months old. They love to explore the latest games, flip through photos, and watch YouTube videos while waiting at a restaurant, having their hair done, or between ballet and French lessons. Emma and Emily belong to a generation with ever-present handheld and networked technology.[6]

Young children do not remember a time without the constant connectivity technology brings. Here are some distinct traits that identify the iGeneration:

- Ability to multitask. Many children text and talk at the same time![7]
- Introduced to technology at a young age. Three-year-old Darci has a collection of cell phones. Four are nonworking phones from her family members, while others are plastic.[8]
- Urgent need for instant gratification. Children are so anxious to respond to text messages in class that they forget that cell phones are banned in the classroom.[9]
- Using technology to create a wide range for content.[10] The iPod touch is a learning device that allows children to download applications that help them read, do math, tell time, write, and so on.[11]

Technology is a growing part of the world of young children. It has a great deal to offer, and there is much that young children can learn via technology in all domains—cognitive, social, emotional, and linguistic. Software is designed for children as young as nine months; it is often referred to as *lapware* because children are held in their parents' laps to use it, and it is intended to be used by parents and children together.

You will find many software programs for the very young such as Jumpstart Baby and Reader Rabbit Playtime for Baby aimed specifically at children ages one to three. Jumpstart Baby leads children through eight activities, including woodblock puzzles and nursery rhyme sing-a-longs. Reader

> " To me, technology should be infused in everything we do. "
>
> **ARNE DUNCAN**
> U.S. Secretary of Education

Programs such as JumpStart Baby are very popular with parents of infants and toddlers. They provide many opportunities for parents to interact with their children and they promote and support learning and involvement.

technology The application of tools and information used to support learning.

technological literacy The ability to understand and apply technological devices to reading and writing.

Rabbit Playtime for Baby allows young children to explore colors, shapes, songs, animals, letters, and numbers. There are also software programs for toddlers, such as Reader Rabbit Toddler and Reader Rabbit Playtime for Baby and Toddler.

Today, handheld and networked devices are tools for expression and connection. For children born in the past decade, the transformative potential of technology is just beginning to be felt.[12]

Technology: A Definition

Technology is the application of tools and information that is used to support learning. With this definition, technology goes far beyond computers and video games. However, the most common use of the term refers to electronic and digital applications—in other words, devices you can plug in. Such tools commonly found in early childhood programs include handheld computers, televisions, video cameras, iPhones, iPods, iPads, digital cameras, and many types of assistive technology. As an early childhood professional, you must plan to use the full range of technology applicable to your classroom, learning centers, and activities.

Technological Literacy

Technology is changing and, in the process, changes what the goals of education are, what it means to be educated, and what literacy means. Literacy now has added dimensions: students not only have to read, write, listen, and speak—skills fundamental to participation in a democratic society—but also have to use technology to be truly literate. In society **technological literacy**, the ability to understand and apply technology to reading and writing, is becoming as important as the traditional components of literacy—reading, writing, speaking, and listening.

Digital Literacy

Young children become immersed in digital media opportunities and develop digital literacy, the ability to use digital media for speaking, listening, reading, and writing purposes.[13] Digital literacy includes not only traditional emergent literacy skills like reading and writing, but also the psychomotor skills needed for keyboarding and cell phone use and the problem-solving skills needed for navigating search engines such as Google and using iPhone applications. As literacy skills develop, so do skills in digital literacy, especially as young children become more comfortable using digital media as tools.[14] Digital literacy also includes writing electronically and sending text material such as messages, stories, and such.

In today's world children have multiple opportunities to observe, explore, play with, and learn from digital media such as television, DVDs, MP3s, iTouch, iPhones, computers, video games, cell phones, and smart toys. These learning opportunities come at a particularly critical period in development as their brains are remarkably active making and reinforcing connections with almost every experience. This is a time of discovery and exploration during which children are developing a natural sense of wonder and joy about their world, as well as a time when their emergent literacy skills are beginning to develop based on their experiences and neural circuitry.[15]

Technology and Social Collaboration

Social collaboration is important for young children. They rely on and seek out the involvement of peers, siblings, parents and teachers. Almost all digital games designed for three- to five-year-old children can claim to support collaboration and social interactions, which as Vygotsky's theory suggests, leads to cognitive development. Beyond computer games, however, collaboration and social interaction are abundant in technologies—smart phones, blogs, instant messaging (IM), Flickr, MySpace, Facebook, Skype, YouTube, iChat, and so on. All of these allow young children to observe literacy skills at work within the social interaction of same age and older peers. The effects of these observations on emerging literacy skills have a tremendous impact on young children's development and learning.[16] Collaborative technology use motivates children to be active and involved learners.

The following is an example of how technology impacts children's day-to-day activities: As a group of kindergarten children gets off the bus, Charlie spots a bird high in a tree. Running inside, the children tell their teacher in excited voices: "There's an owl in the tree." Armed with digital cameras, they run back outside with their teacher, who identifies the bird as a red-tailed hawk. Students capture the hawk digitally. One student excitedly asks, "Can I Google *red-tailed hawk*?" The student shares his findings with his classmates via a large-screen projector. Using word processing software, the children create stories and illustrate them with Kid Pix. Some e-mail their stories to their parents. The teacher organizes the class to create a torn-paper collage of the red-tailed hawk, which is framed and displayed in the classroom.[17]

Supporting Children's Technology Use

In Lina Miller's kindergarten classroom at Great Oaks Elementary in Round Rock, Texas, the children sit on the floor watching for their voice and animal pictures to pop up on the television screen. They created Voice Threads (a program in which several people at once can converse and comment on an uploaded page, PowerPoint, photo, Word document, or video using typing or voice recordings). The students use the Internet to research an animal, and then use the computer to draw an animal. Afterwards, they use the computer again to record short story voice-overs. Lina's class is Internet savvy.[18]

Young children's constant involvement with technology has a number of implications for you as an early childhood teacher:

- Build on the out-of-school technology experiences children bring to your classroom. Partner children who are more technologically adept with students who can benefit from one-on-one help. For example, you can partner children who can collaborate and help each other strengthen technological and reading, writing and math skills.[19]

- Provide enriched technology experiences for all students while ensuring that those students who lack technology competence receive appropriate assistance. For example, you can use the Apple iPad to provide multiple methods of engagement, presentation, and expression. The iPad has multiple universal designs for learning features that enable children to receive technological assistance such as the screen reader for those visually impaired; mono audio feature for the hearing impaired; and zoom, closed captioning, and color configuration tools.[20]

- Involve parents in classroom programs of technology and enrichment. Parents can help you teach technology skills and can extend in-school technology learning at home. For example, the Peters Township School District in Pennsylvania encourages parents to use teachers' websites to access handouts and audio files to assist children while they do homework. The school district has an integrated school system that allows parents to access student schedules and grades, and it also periodically sends e-mail blasts with any new or important information regarding the school.[21]

Integrating technology into your teaching is a powerful way to enrich and extend learning. Third graders at Oswalt Elementary School in Walnut, California, use iTouches to make math lessons fun. They compete to see how quickly they can solve math problems on the iTouch. Third grade teacher Beatrice Azanza believes using iTouches motivates and excites students about mathematics! [22]

Above all, you can be an enthusiastic supporter and user of technology and ensure that each child has high-quality technology experiences. The Voice from the Field "How to Use Technology as a Scaffolding Tool in the Preschool Classroom" on pages 372–373 is also a Competency Builder that helps you introduce technology to young children as a means for acquiring literacy skills.

Children are more likely to retain concepts and ideas through interaction with technology.[23] Technology in the classroom enhances learning in the following ways:

- Technology motivates young children and contributes to their cognitive and social development.
- Technology enhances self concept and children's attitudes toward learning.
- Children show increased levels of spoken communication and cooperation when using technology.
- Children share leadership roles and initiate interactions more frequently. They engage in turn taking and peer collaboration.
- Children tend to narrate what they are doing at the computer as they type text or move objects around on the screen.

Technology and Special Childhood Populations

Technology has a profound effect on children with special needs, including very young children and students with disabilities. In today's rapidly developing technological world, technology is helping to bridge gaps between children's differences at rates many never dreamed possible.

The field of early childhood education is undergoing dramatic changes through its integration with the field of special education. As a result, early childhood professionals use assistive technology to help children and their families. According to Public Law 100–407, the Technology-Related Assistance for Individuals with Disabilities Act of 1988 (Tech Act), **assistive technology** is "any item, device, or piece of equipment, or product system, whether acquired commercially off the shelf, modified, or customized, that is used to increase, maintain, or improve functional abilities of individuals with disabilities."[24]

assistive technology Any device used to promote the learning of children with disabilities.

Assistive technology covers a wide range of products and applications, from simple devices such as adaptive spoons and switch-adapted battery-operated toys to complex devices such as computerized environmental control systems. This range in technology that is available to children with disabilities is generally described as low-tech to high-tech.

Assistive technology can work wonders for children with disabilities and really involve them in lessons and classroom activities.

Uses of Assistive Technology

Assistive technology is particularly important for students with disabilities who depend on technology to help them communicate, learn, and be mobile. For example, for students with vision impairments, closed-circuit television can be used to enlarge print, a Braille printer can convert words to Braille, and audiotaped instructional materials help children so that they are able to hear. Closed-captioned television and FM amplification systems can assist students who are deaf or hard of hearing. Touch-screen computers, augmentative communication boards, and voice synthesizers can assist students with limited mobility or with disabilities that make communication difficult. Kindergarten teacher Cynthia Cregier uses an assitive technology communication program called TeachTown to teach children computer lessons. Cynthia also uses the system to show parents their children's progress.[25]

Technology helps children with vision impairments see and children with physical disabilities read and write. It helps children who are developmentally delayed learn the skills they need to achieve at appropriate levels and enables other children with disabilities to substitute one ability for another and receive the special training they need. In addition, computer-assisted instruction provides software tools for teaching students at all ability levels, including programmed instruction for students with specific learning disabilities. The Center for Best Practices in Early Childhood, featured in the Voice from the Field: How to Use Technology as a Scaffolding Tool in the Preschool Classroom on pages 372–373 has been instrumental in promoting assistive technology and facilitating its use.

Opportunities for using many forms of assistive technology are available to even very young children, from birth to age three. Some of these include powered mobility, myoelectric prostheses, and communication devices. Infants as young as three months interact with computers; eighteen-month-old children have drive-powered mobility devices and use myoelectric hands, and two-year-olds talk via speech synthesizers.

Assistive Technology and Literacy. Assistive technology can be included as an important tool in your work with children with special needs. One of your students with special needs may have trouble holding a pencil. Putting a pencil grip on her pencil makes it easier for her to hold it. The pencil grip is an example of low-tech assistive technology.

Dictionary skills are an important part of language and literacy. If a student has trouble holding and handling a dictionary, an assistive technology solution would be to use an electronic dictionary on the Internet, which also has voice pronunciation. As this textbook has stressed, literacy development and learning to read are given a high priority in all early childhood grades, from pre-K to grade three. Children with special needs can learn to read with the help of assistive technology.[26]

Benefits of Assistive Technology

Technology permits children with special needs to use and enjoy knowledge, skills, and behaviors that might otherwise be inaccessible to them. In this way, technology empowers children with special needs; it enables them to exercise control over their lives and conditions of their learning. It enables them to do things previously thought impossible.

In addition, technology changes people's attitudes about children with disabilities. For example, some may view children with disabilities as unable to participate fully in regular classrooms; however, they may now recognize that instead of being segregated in separate programs, these children can be fully included in the regular classroom with technology.

Below are examples of assistive technology that will help you expand your vision of how technology can support, extend, and enrich children's learning.

Touch Windows 17. Touch Windows 17 is a touch screen which attaches to the computer monitor and allows children to touch the screen directly rather than using a mouse. It can be used on a flat surface, such as a wheelchair tray, and is scratch resistant and resistant to breaking.

Voice from the Field

How to Use Technology as a Scaffolding Tool in the Preschool Classroom

Technology is an exciting tool to help children acquire early literacy skills. Teachers and families with young children have access to cameras, printers, scanners, and software that were once only the tools of media production specialists. With this technology, the possibilities for personalizing activities for literacy scaffolds are endless.* However, knowing how to apply the technology to the preschool curriculum remains a barrier for many professionals. Successful use begins with knowing what equipment to buy.

STEP 1 Select the Equipment

Several pieces of equipment are useful in creating literacy materials and activities.

- **Digital camera** This versatile piece of equipment comes in a variety of models with different features. An inexpensive camera may work just as well as a special model designed for children. There are a number of features to consider:
  - Resolution—the sharpness of the pictures expressed in pixels (the higher the resolution, the better the picture)
  - Optical zoom—magnifies the images using a multifocal-length lens
  - Image capacity—memory capability for images shot at high resolution
  - Expansion slot for memory card
  - LCD display for children to review pictures

- **Digital video camera** This tool documents events in the classroom.
  - Models vary in features, such as zoom, image editing, battery life, and storage capacity.
  - A tripod is recommended for children to ease use and avoid accidents.
- **Printer and scanner**
  - A color printer is essential for book making and literacy material creation.
  - Scanners transfer children's writing samples and artwork into digital format.
  - Printers with scanning capability are suitable for classroom use.
- **Microscope**
  - ProScope (by Bodelin) allows children to magnify specimens, like butterflies or beetles, and view them on the monitor screen.
  - Images can be captured and put into a book or slide show format.
- **PDA (personal digital assistant)** These handheld devices usually include a date book, address book, task list, memo pad, clock, and calculator software. Newer models also have color screens and audio capabilities, enabling them to show multimedia content. Many can also access the Internet.
  - This important documentation tool records children's progress.
  - Children's work is captured in photo form.
  - Software application is key to use with children's portfolio items.
  - Newer versions of these devices with large screens are used by young children as small communication devices.

STEP 2 Learn to Use the Equipment

Most equipment is fairly user friendly, requiring very little, if any, instruction to operate.

- Become familiar with all options and test with chosen application.
- Make sure equipment is easy for children to use.
- Adapt the equipment, if necessary.

Manufacturers have tutorials you can download from their website. Online training sites, found through an Internet search, also offer tips and training on using a device.

STEP 3 Choose the Software

Before choosing software, decide on the literacy activity:

- For creating simple books or class slide shows, a photo-management type of program can be used—such as iPhoto, Kodak EasyShare, or Photo Kit Junior (APTE).
- For interactive books, authoring software is best—such as Classroom Suite (IntelliTools), Pixie (Tech4Learning), or even Microsoft Word.

You can also investigate other photo management and authoring software. Free software applications, such as those available through Google, can also be appropriate for creating books and editing pictures as a collaborative activity for and with young children.

STEP 4 Create Literacy Activities for the Children

By creating their own electronic books, children learn many print concepts, including reading text left to right and top to bottom, separating words with a space, and learning that words have meaning. Books can be created from customized templates or through child-friendly features in software.

- **Electronic book templates**
  - Children can create a book about themselves or they can base it on a field trip, class project, favorite book, and so forth.
  - Teachers can make templates with authoring software.
  - Children can add their own pictures, voices, and text.
  - Page-turning buttons in the bottom corners of each page allow children to navigate forward and backward through the book.
- **Child-created books** Children in preschool classes can learn to use digital cameras, download pictures to the computer, and use software to create books. When using this technology with children, attach a long strap to the camera so that children can put it around their necks to make sure they don't drop the camera.
  - Explain how to plug the camera in to the computer and download the pictures.
  - Show children how to use the photo management application. If needed, prepare photos and import them into the program ahead of time.
  - Teach children how to enter text and sounds into the program.
  - Encourage children to work in small groups to benefit from cooperative play.

STEP 5 Document the Learning

- **Daily documentation** Many teachers choose to take digital photos in the classroom on an ongoing basis. You can immediately share pictures of children's construction, artwork, or play activities. In addition, you can share the images with the class as a review of the week's activities and projects.
- **Wall displays** Displaying digital pictures in a hallway or on a classroom wall gives children documentation of events and an opportunity to review and revisit. Children's language skills may be sparked as they review the pictures. They may also dictate a narrative about the pictures and events.
- **Portfolios** You can save digital photos, scanned photos, writing samples, and artwork in a child's individual electronic portfolio file. At the end of the year, you can copy the images for families or create an electronic book or movie about each child. Families can also create their own books during a workshop at the end of the year. With simple instructions and a template they can choose the images to place in their children's books. You can then burn the creation on a CD or DVD for families to keep.

Source: Text contributed by Linda Robinson, Assistant Director, Center for Best Practices in Early Childhood, Western Illinois University, Macomb, Illinois. The Center (www.wiu.edu/thecenter/) provides technology and assistive technology training, curricula, and online information to educators and families of young children. Photos contributed by Carolina Beach Elementary School.

*L. Robinson, "Technology as a Scaffold for Emergent Literacy: Interactive Storybooks for Toddlers," Young Children 58, No. 6 (2003): 42–48.

BigKeys Keyboard.   BigKeys keyboard is an assistive technology in the form of a keyboard that has keys four times bigger than standard keyboard keys. It arranges letters in alphabetical order to assist young children and generates only one letter, regardless of how long a key is pressed. The BigKeys also accommodates children who cannot press down two or more keys simultaneously.

Big Red Switch.   Big Red Switch is a large, colorful switch to turn devices on and off. It is five-inches in diameter with a surface that is easy to see and activate. It also has an audible click to help children make the cause-and-effect link.

QuickTalker7.   QuickTalker7 is an augmenative communication device that gives children a voice! It allows them to communicate by pressing on pictures.

Talk Pad.   Talk Pad is a portable communication device that is designed to be used by children who need assistance with speech. It uses an electronic chip that records the voice and allows children with language limitations to be active participants in everyday activities.

All-Turn-It Spinner.   An inclusion learning tool, All-Turn-It Spinner allows all children to participate in lessons on numbers, colors, shapes, matching, and sequencing. It is a spinner that is controlled by a switch for easy manipulating and has optional educational overlays, stickers, and books that can be purchased separately.

Tack-Tiles Braille Systems.   Tack-Tiles Braille Systems are Braille literacy teaching toys for all ages. It has LEGO®-type blocks that form Braille codes, which can be put on a board or magnetized for use on file cabinets or refrigerators. The system is durable and tolerant of sudden jarring movements. It is available in several codes, including five languages, mathematics, and music notation.

Aurora.   Aurora is a device that works with the Windows operating system to help people with learning disabilities, including dyslexia, to write and spell better. It speeds up typing by predicting words. It reads back what is typed and reads text from applications for those with reading difficulties. Aurora also helps people with physical disabilities to communicate and allows phrases to be organized into categories for quick conversation.

There is an assistive technology to meet the needs of almost any child with a disability. You will want to be diligent in ensuring your children have appropriate technology to help them to achieve at their highest levels.

Implementing Technology in Early Childhood Education Programs

Integrating technology into educational curriculum provides students with additional tools to enhance their learning. Technology in the classroom can help students become capable users, information seekers, problem solvers and decision makers.[27]

STEM

STEM refers to the areas of science, technology, engineering, and mathematics. STEM initiatives started as a way to promote education in these related areas so that students would be prepared to study STEM fields in college and pursue STEM-related careers. Schools with a strong emphasis on STEM education often integrate science, technology, engineering, and mathematics into the entire curriculum. Workforce projections for 2014 by the U.S. Department of Labor show that fifteen of the twenty fastest growing occupations require significant science or mathematics training to successfully compete for a job.[28] According to the U.S. Bureau of Labor Statistics, professional information technology careers will increase well into the future.[29] However, as jobs requiring a solid background in science, technology, engineering, and mathematics are growing, more students are choosing not to major in these areas. In Virginia, Prince William County offers programs designed to challenge and motivate students in science and math through hands-on discovery and exploration, while also developing critical thinking skills.[30] Scales Technology Academy (STA), in Tempe, Arizona, provides one-to-one laptops for all students from kindergarten through fifth grade and focuses on a high-technology curriculum.[31] STA is one of several schools that appeal to parents' preferences while integrating technology into the curriculum and providing a balance between core knowledge and twenty-first century skills. Teachers empower students to be independent learners, critical thinkers, and problem-solvers. Teachers use interactive whiteboards, document cameras, and audio enhancements. The entire school campus features wireless Internet, promoting anytime, anywhere learning for all students.[32]

Assistive technology enables children with disabilities to participate in regular classrooms and to learn skills and behaviors not previously thought possible. What are some examples of assistive technologies that would enable this child and others with disabilities to learn?

On a given school day, students benefitting from an education that integrates not only science and math, but also engineering and technology into the learning process may collaborate on an interactive whiteboard, use simulation programs to graph data from class projects, use handheld devices to collect and analyze data on local community environmental problems, and use technology to understand the basic physics of music. For example, the Southeast Elementary School has a LEAP program for third graders that teaches students the engineering aspect of STEM using science. In this program, students use the engineering design processes to imagine, plan, create, and improve science projects. As the year progresses the class explores sounds and other engineering content that apply to their state standards.[33] This helps to promote enthusiasm in the field of engineering and also enhance the knowledge of our next generation of engineers and inventors. Students need an education with a solid foundation in STEM areas so that they are prepared to both work and live in the twenty-first century.

Integrating Technology in Your Program

Technology is such a fact of life in classrooms today, you will want to integrate technology into all of your instructional activities. Cathy Faris, Instructional Technology Coach, and Karla Burkholder, Director of Instructional Technology at Northwest Independent School District in Forth Worth, Texas, provide these ideas for how you can integrate technology into your instruction:

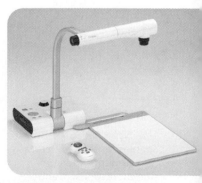

- In pre-K, you can display children's books on a document camera and the students can circle characters or settings in the story. A document camera (also known as an image presenter, visual presenter, digital visualizer, or docucam) is a real-time image-capturing device that displays an object to a large audience. It magnifies and projects the images of actual, three-dimensional objects onto a big screen.

- In kindergarten, students use multimedia software to create a slide show that demonstrates their knowledge of phonemes. The students may choose pictures from a gallery to match the sound that the teacher assigns and then creates a slide show either as a group or individual project. Children save the slide show as a podcast to post to the teacher's website synced to an iPod.

What are some ways you could use a document camera in your teaching?

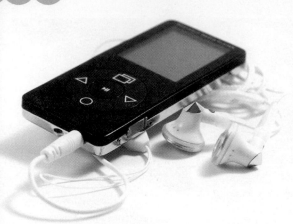

MP3 players and iPods enable children to participate in a wide range of activities and to learn basic knowledge and skills.

- First grade students place their shared writing on a document camera then use an interactive whiteboard or wireless chalkboard to highlight, circle, or make notes of important components in the writing sample.

- Second grade students use a digital video camera to record their participation in a science inquiry lesson. The children save the video to classroom computers for later review and study.

- Third grade students research a project on the Internet. They create a slide show to display their information. They also create a movie from the slide show pictures by saving photos and placing them into movie editing software. They save the movie as a podcast and place it on the teacher's website.

- In science, students use a document camera to focus in on insects, plants, rocks, minerals, and such. As the object becomes enlarged the students can see its properties. This gives the students an opportunity to experience science in a way that they normally would not.

- Scientific probes enable students to measure temperature, sound, and light. They graph the data and display for discussion and then a print the reports.

- Blogs allow students to share information, opinions, and experiences with other students via the Internet.

- Student response systems (clickers), such as the CPSPulse™, enable teachers to capture real-time assessment data to gauge student comprehension and identify individual learning needs and differentiate instruction.[34] This device is similar to polling the audience of a TV game show. In addition, teachers are able to document a student's progress over time.[35]

Of course not all children have the same access to technology, so making sure they have this access is an important factor when designing a classroom environment and planning curricula that promote learning.

The INTERWRITEMOBI enables teachers to interact with students, monitor student responses, and support student-centered learning.

Using SMART Boards in the Classroom.   Students today are digital natives. They were born into a digital world where the Web, podcast and Google are basic vocabulary words. They expect and require a high level of engagement in their learning. They read, write, and think differently than students did just ten years ago. They think digitally. We must keep pace with technological changes, such as Web 2.0 applications like wikis, blogs, and other social networking sites, in order to keep up with our students. We also must integrate technology tools such as interactive whiteboards, document cameras, webcams and other technology in our classrooms and curriculum.

An interactive whiteboard such as the one marketed by Smart Technologies (the SMART Board) is one of the most valuable teaching and learning tools in the early childhood classroom. It will revolutionize the way you teach! The SMART Board projects a computer image onto a touch-sensitive whiteboard. You can write with digital ink with pen tools or with your finger! Teachers and students use their finger or hand as they would a mouse to drag and drop objects or click just as they would using a mouse. Content displayed on the SMART Board becomes interactive so that students can move objects, click links, write on Web pages, and more. When young children interact with the whiteboard it engages them visually, kinesthetically, and aurally.

Here are some real classroom examples of SMART Board integration, suggested by Pamela Beard, ESL specialist at Forest Ridge Elementary in College Station, Texas:

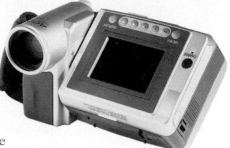

Math

- Students move images of red or green apples to construct a graph of their favorite kind of apple.
- Kindergarteners practice completing patterns using various clip art and the "infinite cloning" tool. This tool enables children to pull multiple copies of a single clip such as a red or blue bear, moving each one independently.
- Flash files include dice that roll when children click on them, a hundreds chart that they click to reveal patterns, a movable protractor, and more.

Writing

- Children do interactive writing, sharing digital ink pens to compose a journal entry. Teachers can change handwritten text into typed text for the children to read.

Reading

- Children highlight sight words using digital ink or move words into sentences using a poem for shared reading.
- Children sort words by long or short vowel sounds by physically moving them into a column chart.

Handwriting

- The whiteboard enables children to experiment with handwriting as they trace letters with larger gross motor strokes on a vertical surface.
- Children watch a quick animation of pen strokes needed to form a letter before they use the pen to practice on their own.

Science

- Movable models such as frog dissection or the water cycle make science interactive.
- Children record with an attached document camera and the teacher can circle or use a spotlight tool to call attention to the results as they are replayed on the big screen.

Social Studies

- Teachers use the "Smart Capture" tool to digitally cut out pictures of historical characters to use as puppets for retelling the Thanksgiving story.[36]

With SMART Boards, you can have at your fingertips charts, journals, and models for instant display. Imagine your kindergarten class where students learn letters for the first time and are introduced to the letter "K" seeing various fonts of it on one slide; practicing it on a handwriting line; sorting pictures of things that start with that letter from things that don't; watching a five-minute videocast of Sesame Street's clips of that letter; and finally putting it all in context by reading poetry focused on that specific letter. You can do it all by simply making a few clicks at the SMART Board![37]

Using iPods in the Classroom. The iPod is a tremendously useful, versatile, and easily accessible tool. iPods are used to increase fluency with English Language Learners (ELLs), as a remediation resource with at-risk students, for ongoing longitudinal assessments, and for data-driving instruction. The following are ways kindergarten teacher Andrea Spillet-Mauer uses an iPod with her English language learners.

Developing Fluency. Fluency, the smoothness and ease of speaking, is a critical attribute in learning English. English language learners need to practice this, as much as possible, during the school day. To meet this need, use an iPod Learning Center, which can be as simple as a table supplied with iPod docks where students go to hear English, speak English, read English, and write English.[38]

Camcorders and flip cameras enable you to capture important learning events, document individual and small projects, and reinforce student skills. They also enable children to actively participate as researchers and authors.

Student Response Systems, also known as Classroom Performance Systems, and "clickers" are an ideal way to get students actively involved in their learning.

You can also use iPods to teach to standards. One of the California kindergarten standards is to be able to audibly recite poems, rhymes, and songs without missing a word. With this in mind, each month give students the responsibility for learning a selection of songs, poems, rhymes, and chants. Record yourself reciting poems, rhymes, songs, and chants, which the children listen to and learn on their iPods. By using iPods individually, students have the time they need to hear and practice with correct English modeling. Have a chart that always accompanies the material. This enables the children to have a visual picture of what they are learning. A class of thirty-one five- to six-year-olds is very active and the iPod Learning Center provides students the opportunity to explore learning materials in an easy and accessible way.[39]

Data-Driven Instruction.   In addition to using the iPod as a teaching tool, you can also use it as a way to assess students' progress and drive teaching instruction. One of the language arts kindergarten standards is to retell stories. Have the students who did not initially meet this particular kindergarten benchmark retell the story of "The Three Bears." Record the students by using the iPod. Later, you can listen to the students retell their version of the story and evaluate many things such as their use of pronouns and how they use present and past tense. With this information, you are able to create appropriate lessons and offer students opportunities to work on these concepts with each other.[40]

You will find that iPods are a wonderful learning tool for you and your children. As you plan how you will use iPods in your classroom, think across the curriculum and discover how you can also use iPods to integrate all content areas in your teaching.[41]

Blogging in the Classroom.   I'm sure that in your life, you are involved in many kinds of technology. I'll bet some of you are bloggers! You can use technology to your advantage in your classroom by creating your own blog and getting your children blogging. For those of you who don't blog, a blog is a Web publishing tool that allows you to self-publish commentary in a journal format, while adding artwork and links to other blogs or websites.

Why Blog?   Blogs are used to motivate children and give them authentic reasons to write. We have talked about authentic assessment and authentic environments. Authentic also applies to children applying what they learn to real-life activities and events and using the real world as a source of ideas.

Third grade teacher Todd Wasil has three main goals for his classroom blog:

- To keep students and parents updated on daily homework, weekly curriculum, and events
- To allow students and parents to access information that will help them succeed in the third grade
- To give students and parents a chance to express their ideas and comment on weekly posts[42]

Here is an excerpt from Kathy Cassidy's blog at the beginning of a new school year:

> Our first day of grade one: What an exciting day! In between sorting supplies and meeting new friends, we took some time to talk about what things we might learn this year and what goals we might make for the year. To help us think about what we might learn, we talked via Skype to some "experts" about what they learned in grade one. We talked to Cindi Crandall, a grade one teacher in California, and to Rodney Turner's grade four class in Glendale, Arizona.[43]

Here is an excerpt from Ashley Hix's blog for her first grade class:

> First graders are continuing to learn every day and I am amazed at their progress since the beginning of the year! This week we have had several end-of-the-year assessments and I have seen remarkable growth! I am so proud of them . . . In science students are keeping track of the plants we are growing in our room by writing in a science journal. We planted green beans and peas. The class makes one journal entry a week by writing a sentence to describe what is happening. Students enjoy coming in each morning to see if anything has changed.[44]

Meeting Learners' Individual Needs with Technology.   All technology in your classroom should meet children's individual needs. Take children's individual differences into account when deciding how best to involve them in learning activities. Some children will need more help and encouragement; others will naturally want to be more involved. Individual children will have different needs, interests, and abilities and, therefore, will use computers in different ways.

Promoting Meaningful Learning with Technology.   Many school districts have specific approaches and goals of using technology in classrooms. For example, Trussville School District in Alabama provides development training for teachers on how to integrate Web technologies into their curriculum.[45] The Northwest Independent School District provides all their staff "just-in-time training" by sending technology experts into the classroom to help teachers use technology to teach young children.[46]

Higher-Order Learning.   Technology can support and facilitate critical educational and cognitive processes, such as cooperative learning, group and individual problem solving, critical thinking, reflective practices, analysis, inquiry, process writing, and public speaking. Kindergarten teacher Jennifer Fredrick uses "Kidspiration" to help her children learn. Kidspiration develops thinking, literacy, and numerical skills using visual learning techniques. It strengthens word recognition, vocabulary, comprehension, and written expression.[47]

Technology and Curriculum Integration.   Technology should be integrated as fully as possible into the early childhood curriculum and learning environment so that its use can help promote learning and achieve positive outcomes for *all* children. For example, the Salem-Keizer District uses an iPod touch to conduct elementary reading assessments. Traditionally, students would read a book aloud to a teacher, but now the teacher can follow along on the iPod touch and mark common mistakes while reading. After teachers give the assessments they then sync the assessment data to district computers through wireless connections.[48]

For some children with disabilities, computers and other technology are the only means they have for communicating and socializing with peers and adults. Here are some things you can do to help these children communicate and socialize:

- Have children work on projects together in pairs or small groups. Make sure the computer has several chairs to encourage children to work together. Learning through technology is not inherently a solitary activity. You can find many ways to make it a cooperative and social learning experience.

- Provide children with opportunities to talk about their technology projects. Part of social development includes learning to talk confidently, explain, and share information with others.

- Encourage children to explore adult roles related to technology, such as newscaster, weather forecaster, and photographer. Invite adults from the community to share with children how they use technology in their careers. Invite a television crew to show children how they broadcast from community locations.

- Read stories about technology and encourage children to talk about technology in their lives and the lives of their families.

The Voice from the Field "Carolina Beach Elementary: Technology Across the Curriculum" on page 380 provides ways to integrate technology into reading, science, math and language.

Supervision of Children's Internet Use

Parents and teachers face a technological challenge in trying to separate the good from the bad on the Internet. One approach is to monitor constantly what their children

Voice from the Field

Carolina Beach Elementary: Technology Across the Curriculum

Preparing students to participate productively in a digital world is an important educational goal. Finding ways to achieve this goal is the challenge of all educators. Children, teachers, and schools all across the country are in different stages of using technology to facilitate and support teaching and learning. Many schools have progressed from simply teaching technology to integrating technology across the curriculum. As a result, teachers don't spend a lot of time teaching specific technology skills; rather, they integrate the technology skills into their curriculum.

Carolina Beach Elementary School provides good examples of how teachers integrate technology in all curriculum areas. They use technology to teach skills and concepts related to the content areas (e.g., math, science, literacy) and knowledge and skills specified by North Carolina State Standards. Here are some examples of how technology is integrated into teaching lessons:

Kindergarten

- *Science:* Classify Animals: Children use interactive whiteboards to place animals into a Venn Diagram.
- *Language Arts:* Children access Education City, a Web-based program aligned with the North Carolina Standard Course of Study, to learn about sound and letter recognition.
- *Math:* Children use an interactive whiteboard to create patterns.

First Grade

- *Social Studies:* Children use Google Earth, an online resource, to virtually visit a location they've been learning about.

- *Science:* In Kid Pix, children create a Venn diagram to teach, compare, and contrast environments of animals. With labels *land, water*, and *both*, children stamp animals in the correct area.
- *Language Arts:* Children use the word processing software Scholastic Keys Max Write to write their core words. Several software programs give children the individual help they need with blends, rhyming words, and beginning and ending sounds.
- *Math:* Children use a software program called Scholastic Keys Max Data to create spreadsheets with data from tracking weather for a week.

Second Grade

- *Language Arts:* Children use AlphaSmarts to create stories.
- *Science:* Children use a WebQuest on weather. Children create a picture with a sentence about each season during the year. At the end of the year they create a multimedia presentation in Scholastic Keys Max Show.
- *Social Studies and Language Arts:* Children create a classroom book on community workers. Using a word-processing program, children write about their community workers and import a graphic on the subject for the book.
- Children search an Accelerated Reader database for books on their level.

Teachers at Carolina Beach are enthusiastic about utilizing technology resources. For example, technology facilitator Gina Graziani says, "The technology resources in the classroom provide the teachers with tools to differentiate, engage their students, and track data to better design instruction. We hope to prepare our students to collaborate, connect, and compete with their global peers."

....

Source: Text and photo contributed by Gina Graziani, a technology assistant and webmaster at Carolina Beach Elementary School in Carolina Beach, North Carolina.

access. However, for most parents, this is an impractical solution. Another approach is to use a filter, a computer program that denies access to sites parents specify as inappropriate. One such program, Net Nanny (see website in the Linking to Learning section at the end of the chapter) blocks access to chat rooms, stops instant messages, blocks violent games, and has the capability to filter Facebook usage.

At Stephens Elementary School in Madison, Wisconsin, students use the Internet to support and extend learning within the classroom. All school computers are fully networked. Laser printers, digital cameras, and scanners are available and all students receive keyboarding instruction in the third, fourth, and fifth grade classes. Each classroom has at least two computers, with additional computers housed in the school computer lab. Students may use the Internet with parent permission and teacher supervision. The district has a filtering program and staff must understand Internet safety and security. The district has strict restrictions on the websites the students go to and ensure that they avoid sexually obscene and social sites.[49]

Angel Oak Elementary School in Johns Island, South Carolina, has similar policies. They believe that security on any computer system is a high priority, especially when the system involves children. Teachers inform students that the use of the Internet is a privilege, not a right, and inappropriate use will result in the cancellation of the privilege and alternative assignments. If parents are uncomfortable with the option of their children accessing the Internet, the student(s) may be assigned to a different activity when classmates are using the Internet. Children can't simply "surf" the Internet. Students must have a topic, or subject, to be researched; and it must be directly related to a given assignment from one or more teachers. Adult supervision is required while any student is using the Internet.[50]

The Children's Online Privacy Act is designed to ensure the privacy rights of children and protect them from unscrupulous individuals and companies. The act requires Web operators to secure parental permission before they receive children's e-mail or home addresses. Congress also passed the Child Online Protection Act, which calls for commercial website operators who offer harmful material to check the IDs of visitors. It is likely that Congress will continue to legislate ways to protect children ages twelve and under from the danger of the Internet.

Parents and Technology

Technology has changed the way early childhood professionals teach and the way children learn. It should come as no surprise that it has also changed parents' roles. With the help of technology, parents now have more resources for participating in, supervising, and directing their children's education. They also have more opportunities to be involved in school activities and monitor children's school programs.

Technology and Parent Participation

Even though parenting may seem like a full-time proposition, many parents also have demanding work schedules, and many work two jobs to make ends meet. Juggling the demands of parenting and work causes anxiety and concern about parenting and about children's school achievement. Parents' questions and concerns often exceed the capability of teachers and school personnel to respond within the time constraints of the school day. In addition, many parents have difficulty getting to the school for parent conferences, programs, and assistance.

Technology such as e-mail offers new ways to exchange or gain information and to get help and assistance. Other uses of technology to increase parent involvement include school websites, teacher and classroom websites, and phone conferencing. Some teachers use their websites to regularly post pictures of students doing everyday activities in class. In Florida, the Polk County School District uses an online instructional system to help parents as well as students develop critical technology literacy. Parents are encouraged to participate in after-school programs and in family technology nights to become more familiar with technology.[51]

Another good way to involve parents and families is through a school/teacher/classroom website. For example, third grade teacher Doug DeCamilla at Sanders Elementary School uses a classroom website to share classroom correspondence. He provides a link for students who are absent to get the class materials. Doug also provides a parent section that contains non-curriculum-related links to parent organizations and general parenting information. Additional sections provide resources for holidays, safe Internet searches, computers in the classroom, kids' sites, and so forth.[52]

Using technology to document children's learning is an excellent way to have an ongoing record of children's achievement. It also provides an opportunity for children to make books about their progress to electronically share with family, friends, and relatives.

Technology allows children to explore different worlds, access resources, and engage in learning activities on their own. How can you use computers and other technology to appropriately support children's learning?

Accommodating Diverse Learners

Now that you have read about technology and assistive technology in the early childhood classroom, let's review a common low-tech option often used in early childhood classrooms to help children acquire a way to communicate. Picture Exchange Communication System (PECS) is an augmentative/alternative communication system.[53] PECS is exactly what the name implies. Children using PECS learn to exchange a picture of a desired item to communicate. This is particularly useful for children with no verbal skills or limited verbal communication because the child learns to initiate interactions spontaneously and to make requests using pictures. These pictures can be photographs, line drawings, commercially prepared (e.g., Boardmaker) or teacher-made pictures. Your knowledge of PECS will enhance your ability as a teacher of *all* students within your classroom. Young children of *all* abilities can use pictures as an easy, inexpensive form of assistive technology. Let's meet a child using PECS and see how you can integrate communication goals of using PECs into your curriculum and classroom.

Eliana is a four-year-old girl with autism. She is nonverbal and spends the majority of her day in an inclusive classroom. Her teachers are using PECS to help her learn to communicate her needs, wants, and emotions. She is currently working on Goal 4 and as her communication increases, her inappropriate behaviors are decreasing.

Goal 1: The Physical Exchange

Using a highly preferred item, Eliana will pick up the picture, reach toward another person, and give the picture to the individual. This may be done during art time, when the picture of crayons is placed on the box of crayons and Eliana has to give the picture to the teacher.

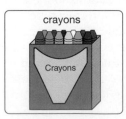

Goal 2: Expanding Spontaneity

Eliana will go to her communication board/book and pick up the picture and then go to a teacher and give him or her the picture. For example, at snack time, Eliana will pick a picture of a preferred snack and find an adult she can give the picture to.

Goal 3: Picture Discrimination

Eliana will go to her communication board/book and pick out a picture from an array and then go to an individual and give him or her the picture. For example, during center time, Eliana will choose what center she wants to go to.

 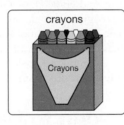 

Goal 4: Sentence Structure

Now that Eliana can quickly and easily choose between pictures, the teacher creates pictures of multiword phrases (e.g., I want . . .) and Eliana can use them to combine a picture for "I want" with a picture of the preferred items.

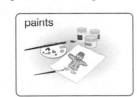

Goal 5: Responsive and Spontaneous Commenting

Using pictures for "I see," "I hear," "I feel," and so on, Eliana will be taught to comment on her environment, express her likes and dislikes, and expand her communication.

As you can see, the pictures do not need to be elaborate or require the use of extensive art skills! Any teacher can use readily available pictures to assist all children in the class in communicating.

Activities for Professional Development

Ethical Dilemma

"It's unfair!"

Attempting to use social networking tools, read blogs, or see multimedia presentations on a classroom computer is generally restricted, but not in the Sunny-Vale School District. Teachers teach lessons using YouTube videos and film trailers, Internet chats with peers across the globe, blogs, and online search engines such as Google. Amy Vandermall has a student, Andy, whose mother greatly restricts what her son can access on websites. She is constantly having to check with Andy's mother to ensure Andy can be a part of her lessons. Sometimes she has to create entirely new lessons just for Andy because his mother feels so strongly about his Internet use. It is not only exhausting and frustrating for Amy; Amy is concerned that Andy is missing out on learning important skills he will need for his future. She is sure Andy feels left out and some of his classmates are starting to tease him for being a "mama's boy."

Amy talked to her principal, Destinee Davis, about her concerns. Amy says, "It's just unfair to Andy! And, frankly, it's unfair to me, too!" Destinee replied, "Twenty-first century children today are highly technological. Andy needs those skills just to keep up." She advised Amy to explain to Andy's mother that the teachers at their school teach digital citizenship and appropriate ways of using everything that is on the Internet. They are educating students and teachers on how to navigate the Internet's vast resources responsibly, safely, and productively. Andy's mother is still skeptical, and the ongoing stress of negotiating the issue has strained the parent–teacher relationship.

Do you agree with Principal Davis? Should Amy continue to argue for the use of Internet? Should she call for a parent conference with Andy's mother? How should Amy rescue the parent–teacher relationship? What should Amy do? What would you do if you were Amy?

Activities to Apply What You Learned

1. Go to www.youtube.com and search for teachers who teach using technology. Take note of the different techniques and technology they use. Give five examples of how you can use technology in your classroom.

2. Contact an occupational therapist in a school district near you and ask him or her for an online interview with you on Skype to discuss the best uses of assistive technology. Make a list of all of the technology recommendations provided by the therapist.

3. If you taught in a first grade classroom, what technology would you put on your "wish list" to help you implement technology into your teaching and children's learning? Go online and research what types of technology first grade teachers use. Share your list with colleagues and ask for their comments.

4. Review the ways that several parents participate in, supervise, and direct their children's technological education. Think of ways you can help parents stay informed about technology and ways that they can be involved in their children's technological world. Share your findings with colleagues in an online discussion.

5. Sit in on a second grade class. Observe how children learn using technology in the classroom. Think about some of the ways you can use technology to accommodate diverse learners. Share your observations and suggestions with a second grade teacher and ask for comments. Write a 200-word message to your classmates about what you learned.

Linking to Learning

AbleNet
www.ablenetinc.com

They have helped millions of children with a variety of disabilities to discover the joy of playing with battery-operated and electronic toys. The Big Red Switch has allowed countless persons with disabilities to access the world around them at the slightest touch of a button.

Aurora Systems
www.aurora-systems.com

They provide assistive technology for children with learning disabilities and dyslexia, and support augmentative communication.

BigKeys
www.bigkeys.com

BigKeys offers keyboards for those that need larger keys in order to locate and operate the keys.

Net Nanny
www.netnanny.com/

Internet filtering software that delivers family-safe computing solutions for the home, library, education, government, and small/medium business markets.

Tack Tiles
www.tack-tiles.com

Tack Tiles Braille System is a sophisticated teaching tool for all ages based on LEGO®-type blocks. These Braille blocks provide a smoother, shorter, more interesting path to Braille literacy.

PEARSON
myeducationlab

Go to Topic 7 (Curriculum/Content Areas) in the MyEducationLab (www.myeducationlab.com) for your course, where you can:

- Find learning outcomes for Curriculum/Content Areas along with the national standards that connect to these outcomes.
- Complete Assignments and Activities that can help you more deeply understand the chapter content.
- Apply and practice your understanding of the core teaching skills identified in the chapter with the Building Teaching Skills and Dispositions learning units.

- Examine challenging situations and cases presented in the IRIS Center Resources.
- Check your comprehension on the content covered in the chapter by going to the Study Plan in the Book Resources for your text. Here you will be able to take a chapter quiz, receive feedback on your answers, and then access Review, Practice, and Enrichment activities to enhance your understanding of chapter content.

PART V

MEETING THE SPECIAL NEEDS OF YOUNG CHILDREN

14

GUIDING CHILDREN
Helping Children Become Responsible

naeyc standards

Standard 1. Promoting Child Development and Learning

I use my understanding of young children's characteristics and needs, and of multiple interacting influences on children's development and learning, to create environments that are healthy, respectful, supportive, and challenging for each child.[1]

Standard 4. Using Developmentally Effective Approaches to Connect with Children and Families

I understand and use positive relationships and supportive interactions as the foundation for my work with young children and families. I know, understand, and use a wide array of developmentally appropriate approaches, instructional strategies, and tools to connect with children and families and positively influence each child's development and learning.[2]

What Is Behavior Guidance?

Guiding children's behavior is a process of helping them build positive behaviors through **behavior guidance**, a process by which all children learn to control and direct their behavior and become independent and self-reliant. Behavior guidance is a process of helping children develop skills useful over a lifetime.

As you work with young children, one of your goals will be to help them become independent and able to regulate or govern their own behavior. **Self-regulation** is the ability to plan, initiate, and complete an activity; control emotions and behaviors; delay gratification; maintain attention; respond to feedback, and build positive social relations with others.[3]

Over the last few years, a new buzz phrase, **executive function**, is used by scholars and scientists who study early childhood development. It refers to the ability of children to order their thoughts, process information in a coherent way, hold relevant details in short-term memory, and avoid distractions and focus on the task at hand.[4]

The ability of young children to control their emotional and cognitive impulses is a strong indicator of short- and long-term success—academic and lifetime. According to some research, self-regulation predicts academic achievement more reliably than I.Q. tests.[5] In a national survey, 46 percent of kindergarten teachers said that at least half the kids in their classes had problems following directions.[6] In a Head Start study, teachers reported more than a quarter of their students exhibited self-control-related negative behaviors. It is estimated that more than five thousand children are expelled from pre-K programs annually, because teachers feel unable to control them.[7]

Three teacher behaviors are essential for promoting self-regulation in children:

1. Use of reasoning, verbal rationales, and explanations to guide behavior.
2. Gradually relinquishing control and encouraging children to be independent.
3. Creating a warm environment to support positive emotional growth.

The Importance of Guiding Children's Behavior

As an early childhood professional, you will assume major responsibility for guiding children's behavior in up-close and personal ways. You will spend many hours with young children as a parent/family surrogate. As a result, you need to know how to best guide children's behavior and help them become responsible. There are a number of reasons why guiding children's behavior is important.

Academics. Helping children learn to guide and be responsible for their own behavior is as important as helping them learn to read and write. Think for a moment about how many times you have said or have heard others say, "If only the children would behave, I could teach them something!" or "This student won't learn!" Appropriate behavior and achievement are interconnected; you can't have one without the other. Consequently, one of your primary roles as an early childhood teacher is to help children learn the knowledge, skills, and behaviors necessary to help them act responsibly.

Lifelong Success. Helping children learn to act responsibly and guide their behavior lays the foundation for lifelong responsible and productive living. As early childhood educators, we believe that the early years are the formative years.

behavior guidance The processes by which children are helped to identify appropriate behaviors and use them.

self-regulation (executive function) The ability to keep track of and control one's behavior.

executive function *see* **self-regulation.**

> "Children need structure, routine, and discipline, but at the same time they need to be loved and nurtured."
>
> **ROSEMARY LAMKIN**
> retired kindergarten teacher in Hamilton Township School District, Hamilton, New Jersey

Thus what we teach children about responsible living, how we guide them, and what skills we help them learn will last a lifetime.

Preventing Future Delinquency Problems.   The roots of delinquent and deviant behavior form in the early years. From research we know what behaviors lead to future problems. For example, some characteristics of preschool children are precursors of adolescent behavior problems and delinquency—disruptive behavior, overactive and intense behavior, irritability, noncompliance, and intensity in social interactions.[8] Involving parents and other family members in school-based programs and activities helps prevent many behavioral problems that are the basis for school failure.

Civility.   The public is increasingly concerned about the erosion of civility and what it perceives as a general breakdown of personal responsibility for bad behavior.[9] One reason the public funds an educational system is to help keep society strong and healthy. Parents and the public look to early childhood professionals to help children learn to live cooperatively and civilly in a democratic society. Getting along with others and guiding one's behavior are culturally and socially meaningful accomplishments. Society wants educators to prepare responsible children for responsible democratic living.

Guiding Behavior in a Community of Learners

Think for a moment of the early childhood classes you have taught, volunteered in or observed. In some of the classes children were actively involved in meaningful activities based on state and district standards. In other classrooms, the children and teachers seemed disorganized with little real learning occurring. What makes the difference? A community of learners, a well-organized classroom, and a well-thought-out and implemented plan for guiding children's behavior and learning.

The Community of Learners

Classrooms are and should be a community of learners in which children of all ages take shared responsibility for the physical, social, and learning environments. You, the teacher, must help children develop the behaviors for living and learning in the classroom.

A learning community is child centered. All that you do in classrooms should focus on children's growth and development as persons and as learners. The practices you use and teach for guiding children's behavior are for their benefit.

As a result of our guiding children's behavior—and helping them guide their own behavior—children should be successful, confident, responsible, and contributors to the learning community.

Democratic Living.   In our efforts to help prepare all children to live effectively and productively in a democracy, we place increasing emphasis on providing them experiences that enable them to productively live and learn in democratic school and classroom communities. The idea of teaching democratic living through classrooms that are miniature democracies is not new. John Dewey was an advocate of this approach and championed democratic classrooms as a way of promoting democratic living.[10] However, running a democratic classroom is easier said than done. It requires a confident professional who believes it is worth the effort.

Key Foundational Practices.   Learning communities are grounded in key foundational practices, including morning meetings, respect for children, character education, and teaching civility.

Morning Meetings.   You can promote cooperative living in which children help each other direct their behavior. Children are born seeking social interactions, and social relations are necessary for children's learning and development. Children's natural social groups and play groups are ideal and natural settings in which to help children assist each other in learning new behaviors and being responsible for their own behavior. The classroom as a whole is an important social group. Peers help each other learn. A good way to provide children time and opportunity to talk about behavior and classroom problems is through a morning class meeting.

Classroom meetings in which teachers and children talk serve many useful functions. They talk about expected behaviors from day to day ("When we are done playing with toys, what do we do with them?"), review with children what they did in a particular center or situation, and help them anticipate what they will do in future situations ("Tomorrow morning when we visit the Senior Citizen Center . . . "). In all these situations, children are cooperatively engaged in thinking about, talking about, and learning how to engage in appropriate behavior.

In addition, you can initiate, support, and foster a cooperative, collaborative learning community in the classroom in which children are involved in developing and setting guidelines and devising classroom and, by extension, individual norms of behavior. Teachers assist children but do not do things for them, and they ask questions that make children think about their behavior—how it influences the class, themselves, and others. This process of cooperative living occurs daily. Discussions grow out of existing problems, and guidance is provided based on the needs of children and the classroom. An excellent resource for learning about class meetings and how to conduct them is an NAEYC resource book, *Class Meetings: Young Children Solving Problems Together* by Emily Vance and Patricia Jimenez Weaver.

Respect for Children.   Throughout this text I have repeatedly emphasized the necessity for honoring and respecting children as human beings. When children are respected and honored they are much more likely to engage in behavior that is respectful and honorable.

Democratic learning environments require that students develop responsibility for their own behaviors and learning, that classrooms operate as communities, and that all children are respected and respectful of others.

Character Education.   Promoting character education continues to grow as a means of promoting fundamental behaviors that early childhood teachers and society believe are essential for living in a democratic society. For example, teachers and their students at Broad Street School learn just how far a simple act of kindness can go. The Caught Caring event is a program sponsored by the school's Character Education Committee, which aims to instill in students good citizenship and civility. Third grader Angela Oleto is viewed by her peers as a comforter. She says, "When children in my class are sad, I give them a pat on the back and say nice things about them."[11]

Teaching Civility.   Civil behavior and ways to promote it are of growing interest at all levels of society. The specific teaching of **civil behavior**—how to treat others well and in turn be treated well—is seen as essential for living well in contemporary society. At a minimum, civil behavior includes manners, respect, and the ability to get along with people of all races, cultures, and socioeconomic backgrounds.

civil behavior Polite, courteous, and respectful behavior.

A Social Constructivist Approach to Guiding Children

Piaget's and Vygotsky's theories support a social constructivist approach to learning and behavior. Teachers who embrace a **social constructivist approach** believe that children construct, or build, their behavior as a result of learning from past experiences

social constructivist approach Approaches to teaching that emphasize the social context of learning and behavior.

and from making decisions that lead to responsible behavior. The teacher's primary role in the constructivist approach is to guide children in constructing their behavior and using it in socially appropriate and productive ways. This process begins in homes and classrooms.

We can now apply *scaffolding* and the *zone of proximal development* (ZPD), two concepts you can use to guide children's behavior. We also add two other constructivist essentials: **adult–child discourse** and **private speech**, or *self-talk*. The central belief that the development of a child's knowledge and behavior occurs in the context of social relations with adults and peers is foundational to Vygotskian and constructivist theory. This means that learning and development are socially mediated as children interact with more competent peers and adults. Thus, as children gain the ability to master language and appropriate social relations, they are able to intentionally regulate their behavior. Below are ways you can guide children's behavior using scaffolding, zone of proximal development, adult-child discourse, and private speech.

Guiding Behavior in the Zone of Proximal Development

The ZPD is the cognitive and developmental space created when a child is in social interaction with a more competent or knowledgeable person. Teachers take children with the behavioral and social skills they have and guide them to increasingly higher levels of responsible behavior and social interactions. Even though we often think that guiding behavior is a one-on-one activity, your role in guiding behavior also includes large and small groups. Figure 14.1, "The Zone of Proximal Development Applied to Guiding Behavior," illustrates again the ZPD and suggests how to guide children's behavior within it. Problem solving is part of what guiding behavior is all about.

Using our knowledge of Vygotsky's theories, we can develop some strategies to guide children's behavior. Here are some things you can do:

- Guide problem solving

  "Tanya, what are some things you can do to help you remember to put the books away?"

  "Harry, you and Juana want to use the easel at the same time. What are some ways you can both use it?"

- Ask questions that help children arrive at their own solutions

  "Jesse, you can't use both toys at the same time. Which one do you want to use first?"

  "Mary, here is an idea that might help you get to the block corner. Ask Amy, 'Would you please move over a little so I can get to the blocks?'"

- Model appropriate skills

  Practice social skills and manners (e.g., say please and thank you).

  Listen attentively to children and encourage listening. For example, "Rodney has something he wants to tell us; let's listen to what he has to say."

In the short term, telling children what to do may seem like the easiest and most efficient way to manage classroom behavior. However, in the long run, it robs them of growth-producing opportunities to develop skills that will help them guide their behavior throughout their lives. Using strategies such as those just listed is essential and should become a routine part of your classroom life.

Guiding Behavior with Scaffolding.   One of the facts of teaching is that you are the leader in the classroom. Children look to you to develop and maintain appropriate expectations and also to help them practice good behavior. You can use scaffolding to guide children's behavior in the ZPD. Recall that scaffolding involves informal methods such as conversations, questions, modeling, guiding, and supporting to help children learn concepts, knowledge, and skills that they might not learn by themselves. When

---

adult–child discourse The talk between an adult and a child, which includes adult suggestions about behavior and problem solving.

private speech Self-directed speech that children use to plan and guide their behavior.

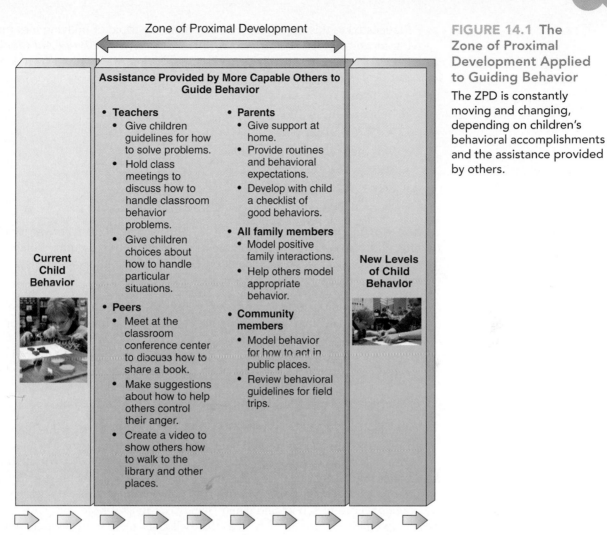

Zone of Proximal Development

Assistance Provided by More Capable Others to Guide Behavior

Current Child Behavior

- **Teachers**
  - Give children guidelines for how to solve problems.
  - Hold class meetings to discuss how to handle classroom behavior problems.
  - Give children choices about how to handle particular situations.
- **Peers**
  - Meet at the classroom conference center to discuss how to share a book.
  - Make suggestions about how to help others control their anger.
  - Create a video to show others how to walk to the library and other places.

- **Parents**
  - Give support at home.
  - Provide routines and behavioral expectations.
  - Develop with child a checklist of good behaviors.
- **All family members**
  - Model positive family interactions.
  - Help others model appropriate behavior.
- **Community members**
  - Model behavior for how to act in public places.
  - Review behavioral guidelines for field trips.

New Levels of Child Behavior

FIGURE 14.1 The Zone of Proximal Development Applied to Guiding Behavior
The ZPD is constantly moving and changing, depending on children's behavioral accomplishments and the assistance provided by others.

more competent others provide help (think: you!), children are able to accomplish what they would not have been able to do on their own. In other words, children are capable of far more competent behavior and achievement if they receive guidance and support from you and other teachers.

Class Discussion. You can use class discussion as an appropriate context for scaffolding. Here are some strategies you can use to give students guidance on how to guide their behavior during classroom discussions:

- Everyone listens to everyone's ideas.
- Children who don't understand something can ask others to repeat what they said.
- All children get a chance to participate; you may direct and facilitate the conversation to ensure that all children are involved.
- Encourage children to state their thoughts clearly.
- At the conclusion of the discussion, children summarize what was discussed.
- You and/or children write down the main points from the discussion. For example, at the beginning of the school year, in her first grade classroom, Frances Corella observes what she believes are some early warning signs of bullying. Some children are engaging in rude behavior and there is mild shoving by some of the bigger boys.

Frances takes this opportunity to introduce the topic of bullying into the class morning meeting. Over several meetings, Frances reads *The Band-Aid Chicken* by Becky Rangel Henton. As the children discuss bullying, they write down some ways they can deal with bullies:

- Walk away.
- Tell a teacher.
- Ask a friend for help.
- Tell the bully "Leave me alone!"
- Walk with a friend.
- Stand up for yourself.
- Don't fight the bully. You might lose or get in trouble too.

Adult–Child Discourse. The scaffolding script that follows is illustrative of adult–child discourse. It is an example of a learning conversation, which invites student participation. This discourse centers on how student authors should act while they are sharing their stories:

Teacher:	Maybe we should now think about how to behave as the author during author's chair. What do authors do? Who can remember? Tina, would you like to start?
Tina:	The author sits in the author's chair and speaks loud and clear.
Isabel:	The author should not fool around, like making faces or having outside conversations.
Shauna:	The author should not be shy and should be brave and confident.

The teacher continues to invite students to participate using this type of scaffolding. A list of responsibilities is created and used in subsequent lessons.[12]

You will want to conduct similar discourses with children as you help them develop their skills and behavior. Discourse can also involve talking about how children might solve problems, interact and cooperate with others, understand norms of social conduct, and act on values related to school and family living. You must initiate and guide these discourses and help children learn the new skills that will assist them in developing self-regulation.

Private Speech and Self-Guided Behavior. Jennifer, a four-year-old preschooler, is busily engrossed in putting a puzzle together. As she searches for a puzzle piece, she asks herself out loud, "Which piece comes next?" I'm sure you have heard children talk to themselves. More than likely, you have talked to yourself! Private speech, or self-talk, is commonplace among young children.

Private speech plays an important role in problem solving and self-regulation of behavior. Children use it to transfer problem-solving knowledge and responsibility from adults to themselves:

> When adults use questions and strategies to guide children and to help them discover solutions, they elevate language to the status of a primary problem-solving tool. This use of language by adults leads children to use speech to solve problems. Research reveals that the relation of private speech to children's behavior is consistent with the assumption that self-guiding utterances help bring action under the control of thought.[13]

Ten Steps to Guiding Behavior

So, thinking about and learning how to guide children's behavior within a constructivist framework enables you to apply the following ten standards as you teach young children. The goal of most parents and early childhood professionals is to have children behave in socially acceptable and appropriate ways that contribute to and promote life in a democratic society. You should view children's behavior as a process of learning by doing—with guidance. Children cannot learn to develop appropriate behavior and be responsible by themselves; they must be shown and taught through precept and example. But just as no one learns to ride a bicycle by reading a book on the subject, children do not learn to guide themselves by only being told what to do. They need opportunities to develop, practice, and perfect their abilities to control and guide their own behavior. At the same time they need the guidance, help, support, and encouragement of you, parents, and early childhood professionals. Effective guidance of children's behavior consists of the following ten essential steps.

Step One: Arrange and Modify the Environment

Environment plays a key role in children's ability to guide their behavior. For example, arrange your classroom so that children can get and return their own papers and materials, use learning centers, and have time to work on individual projects.

In child care centers, early childhood classrooms, and family day care homes, early childhood professionals arrange the environment so that it supports the purposes of the program and makes appropriate behavior possible. Room arrangement is crucial to guiding children's behavior; appropriate arrangements signal to children that they are expected to be responsible for their own behavior. And, it is much more pleasant to live and work in an attractive and aesthetically pleasing classroom or center. We all want a nice environment—children should have one, too.

Here are some guidelines to reflect on and help you arrange your classroom to assist children in guiding their own behavior:

- Have an open area in which you and your children can meet as a whole group for morning meetings, etc. Starting and ending the day with a class meeting allows children to discuss their behavior and plan for how they can do a better job.
- Make center areas well defined and accessible to all children. Make center boundaries low enough so that you and others can see over them for proper supervision and observation.
- Provide for all kinds of activities, both quiet and loud. Try to locate quiet areas together (e.g., reading area and puzzle area) and loud centers together (e.g., woodworking and blocks).
- Have appropriate and abundant materials for children's use, and locate them so that children can easily have access to them. Having to ask for materials promotes dependency and leads to behavior problems.
- Make materials easy to store and put away. A general rule of thumb is that there should be a place for everything, and everything should be in its place when not in use.
- Provide children with guidelines on how to use centers and materials. Time spent on teaching and reviewing guidelines and procedures is time well spent.

The Supportive Classroom.   Arrange the physical setting into a **supportive classroom**, conducive to the behaviors you want to teach. If you want to encourage independent

Parents and early childhood professionals have an obligation to help children learn appropriate behavior by guiding their actions and modeling correct behaviors. What role does setting rules play in guiding behavior?

supportive classroom
Physical arrangement of the classroom so that it is conducive to the behaviors taught.

work, provide places and time for children to work alone. Disruptive behavior is often encouraged by classroom arrangements that force children to walk over or through other children to get to equipment or materials.

The Encouraging Classroom.   Your classroom should be a place where children can do their best work and be on their best behavior. It should be a rewarding place. The following are components of an **encouraging classroom**:

- Opportunities for children to display their work
- Opportunities for freedom of movement (within guidelines)
- Opportunities for independent work
- A variety of workstations and materials based on children's interests

The Positive Classroom.   Your classroom should also be a place where children can receive positive energy and love. The following are characteristics of a **positive classroom**:

- Emphasize community and a culture of caring.
- Set high, yet clear and achievable expectations.
- Display consistent behavior.
- Develop open communication among all children and adults.
- Be an efficacious teacher, one who believes children can and will learn and teach accordingly.
- Obtain sufficient materials to support learning activities.
- Establish and maintain routines.
- Plan for a daily balance between cooperation and independent learning.
- Observe children learning, reflect on how each learns best, and identify trouble areas.

Time and Transitions.   Time, generally more important to adults than to children, plays a major role in every program. The following guidelines relate to time and its use:

- *Do not waste children's time.*   Children should be involved in interesting, meaningful activities from the moment they enter the center, classroom, or family day care home. Keep children productively engaged throughout the day.
- *Do not make children wait.*   When children have to wait for materials or their turn, provide them with something else to do, such as listening to a story or playing in the block center. Problems can occur when children have to wait because they like to be busy and involved.
- *Allow transition time.*   Transitions are times when children move from one activity to another. They should be as smooth as possible and as fun as possible. In one program, teachers sing "It's Cleanup Time!" as a transition from one activity to cleanup and then to another activity.
- *Provide time for rest, relaxation, and pleasure.*   At Jefferson Elementary, the first and third graders practice yoga several times a week with their teachers. Max, a third grade student, says, "The thing I like about yoga is you can concentrate more, and you will get better grades." Sydney likes yoga "because it relaxes you and makes you smarter." Alejandro says, "I like the tree (pose) the best because I never give up. It makes me relax. Yoga is a good exercise for everyone in the classroom."[14]

Step Two: Establish Appropriate Expectations

Expectations set the boundaries for desired behavior. They are the guideposts children use in learning to direct their own behavior. When children know what adults expect, they can better achieve those expectations.

---

encouraging classroom
A classroom environment that rewards student accomplishment and independence.

positive classroom
A classroom environment that promotes appropriate behavior and success.

Setting appropriate expectations for children means you must first decide what behaviors are appropriate. Up to a point, the more we expect of children, the more and better they achieve. Generally, we expect too little of most children. However, having expectations for children is not enough. You have to help children know and understand what the expectations are and then help them meet these expectations. Some children need little help; others need demonstrations, explanations, encouragement, and support as they learn.

Set Limits.   Setting limits is closely associated with establishing expectations and relates to defining unacceptable behavior. For example, knocking over a block tower built by someone else and running in the classroom are generally considered unacceptable behaviors. Setting clear limits has several benefits. They help you clarify in your own mind what you believe is unacceptable, based on your knowledge of child development, children, their families, and their culture. Clear limits help prevent inconsistency and help children act with confidence because they know which behaviors are acceptable. Limits provide children with security; children want and need limits. Remember, as children grow and mature, the limits change and are adjusted to developmental levels, programmatic considerations, and life situations.

Develop Classroom Rules.   Although I like to talk about and think in terms of expectations and limits, other early childhood professionals think and talk about rules. Here are some guidelines about rules:

Plan classroom rules from the first day of class. As the year goes on, you can involve children in establishing other classroom rules, but in the beginning, children want and need to know what they can and cannot do. For example, rules might relate to changing small groups and following bathroom routines. Whatever rules you establish, they should be fair, reasonable, and appropriate to the children's age and maturity. And, you should keep rules to a minimum—the fewer the better.

Remind children of the rules and encourage them to conform to them. Later, review the rules, and have the children evaluate their behavior against the rules. Children are able to become responsible for their own behavior in a positive, accepting atmosphere where they know what the expectations are.

Second grade teacher Sherlyn Luetta at Upper Peninsula Elementary School in Michigan have established the following classroom expectations for her children:

1. We always be polite to everyone.
2. We will make good use of our time.
3. We will always do our BEST work.
4. We will be kind to everyone.

Setting and establishing classroom rules is an important part of having a classroom that supports learning. Involving students in the setting of classroom rules is a good idea.

Step Three: Model Appropriate Behavior

We have all heard the maxim "Telling is not teaching." Nevertheless, we tend to teach by giving instructions, and, of course, children do need instructions. Teachers soon realize, however, that actions speak louder than words.

Children see and remember how other people act. After observing another person, a child tries out a new behavior. If this new action brings a reward of some kind, the child repeats it. Proponents of the modeling approach to learning believe that most behavior people exhibit is learned from the behavior of a model(s). They think children tend to model behavior that brings rewards from teachers, parents, and peers.

The classroom environment is one of the most important factors that enable children to develop and use appropriate behavior. The classroom should belong to children, and their ownership and pride in it makes it more likely they will act responsibly.

You can use the following techniques to help children learn through modeling:

- *Show*. For example, show children where the block corner is and how and where the blocks are stored.
- *Demonstrate*. Perform a task while students watch. For example, demonstrate the proper way to put the blocks away and store them. An extension of this technique is to have children practice the demonstration while you supervise. Also have a child demonstrate to other children while you supervise.
- *Model*. Modeling occurs when you practice the behavior you expect of the children. For example, model and demonstrate social and group-living behaviors, using simple courtesies ("Please," "Thank you," "You're welcome") and practicing cooperation, sharing, and respect for others. You can call children's attention to desired behaviors when another child models it.

- *Supervise*. Supervision is a process of reviewing, maintaining standards, and following up. If children are not performing the desired behavior, you need to review the behavior. You must be consistent in your expectations: Children will learn that they do not have to put away their blocks if you allow them not to do it even once. Remember, you are responsible for setting up the environment that enables children's learning to take place.

Do not encourage children's misbehavior; frequently, teachers see too much and ignore too little. Ignoring inappropriate behavior is probably one of the most overlooked strategies for managing an effective learning setting and guiding children's behavior. Ironically, some teachers feel guilty when they use this strategy; they believe that ignoring undesirable behaviors is not good teaching. Certainly, ignoring must be combined with positive discipline and teaching, but if you focus on building responsible behavior, there will be less need to solve behavior problems.

For example, if Charlie jumps up during circle time and grabs a book from the book rack to get attention, you don't want to reinforce his inappropriate behavior by giving him that attention. Instead, you might ignore his behavior while at the same time praising other children for sitting quietly and listening to you read the story. After several days of this strategy, Charlie will probably stay in the circle, at which point you can praise and encourage him for sitting and listening to the story as the other children are. Ignoring *can* work!

Teaching peace, cooperative learning and conflict resolution are important parts of helping children guide their behavior. The Voice from the Field, "Teaching Peace and Conflict Resolution in the Classroom," provides you with many practical ideas and activities for promoting peaceful living in your classroom.

Step Four: Guide the Whole Child

Children are not one- or two-dimensional persons. Children are a unified whole. There is much discussion today about teaching the whole child—physically, socially, emotionally, cognitively, linguistically, and spiritually. The same applies to guiding behavior of the whole child. This renewed interest in the whole child reflects the profession's ongoing dedication to developmentally appropriate practice. The Association for Supervision and Curriculum Development (ASCD) leads a national effort to include the whole child in all

FIGURE 14.2 Guiding the Whole Child

A key to guiding the behavior of the whole child is to guide his or her behavior across all developmental domains.

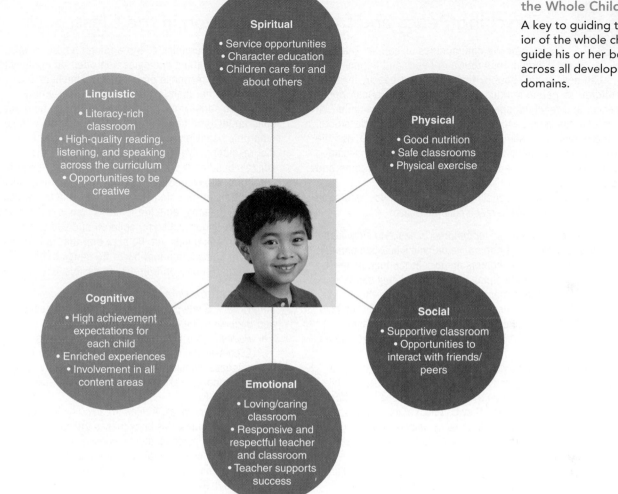

instructional programs and practices. Their website is listed at the end of the chapter in the Linking to Learning section. Figure 14.2 shows the various dimensions involved in guiding children in and across all domains. As you work with your children, reflect on how you can promote their positive development in all dimensions.

Step Five: Know and Use Developmentally Appropriate Practice

Knowing child development is the cornerstone of developmentally appropriate practice. You cannot guide the whole child if you do not know and understand where he or she is developmentally. Children cannot behave well when adults expect too much or too little of them based on their development or when parents expect them to behave in ways inappropriate for them as individuals. A key for guiding children's behavior is to *really know what each child is like.* This is the real meaning of developmentally appropriate practice. You will want to study children's development and observe children's behavior to learn what is appropriate for all children and individual children based on their needs, gender, socioeconomic backgrounds, individual disposition, and culture.

Voice from the Field

Teaching Peace and Conflict Resolution in the Classroom

Classrooms are communities of learners. Teachers and children need to live in peace and harmony. You can achieve this goal by teaching about peace, engaging children in peace-making activities, reading books about peace, and teaching specific skills for conflict resolution. In addition, teaching peace begins in the home and classroom, but expands to the school, the community, the nation, and the world. Teaching about other cultures of the world is included in a curriculum that encourages peaceful classrooms and relationships.

Here are some specific classroom conflict resolution strategies you can use to teach children peace:

- *Provide opportunities for children to help and show kindness to others.* Cooperative programs between primary classes and senior centers are excellent opportunities to practice kind and helping behaviors. Children can bake cookies and take them to the senior centers where they read to and with the senior citizens. The possibilities here are endless for showing acts of kindness and sharing.
- *Conduct classroom routines and activities so they are as free of conflict as possible.* Provide opportunities for children to work together and practice skills of cooperative living. Design learning centers and activities so children are able to share and work cooperatively. Children are great teachers and they can help others learn. Also, children learn leadership roles by helping others. Children helping others can cross over grade levels—third graders can help kindergartners, and so on.
- *When real conflicts occur, provide practice in conflict resolution.* These skills include talking through

problems, compromising, and apologizing. But a word of caution regarding apologies: Too often an apology is a perfunctory response on the part of teachers and children. Rather than just offering the often-empty words "I'm sorry," it is far more meaningful to help one child understand how another is feeling. To encourage empathic behavior, you can provide examples of conflict resolution: "Vanessa, please don't knock over Lucila's building, because she worked hard to build it"; "Brandon, what's another way that you can tell Monica she's sitting in your chair—instead of hitting her, which hurts?" A meeting table in the classroom is a great way to provide opportunities for children and you to sit down and talk things out. Be sure that the "talking out" results in a resolution for how to do things better, for improved attitudes, and for new behaviors.

- *Read stories to children that exemplify prosocial behaviors.* Some good books for promoting peace and understanding are:
  - *Peace Begins With You* by Katharine Scholes. Expresses the different definitions and dimensions of peace culminating with the responsibility of each individual to make the choice to be a peacemaker (ages 4–8).
  - *Somewhere Today: A Book of Peace* by Shelley Moore Thomas. This book makes the concept of non-violence a personal thing by describing recent events like violence in schools and communities and shows how we all can become a part of promoting peace (ages 4–8).

Step Six: Meet Children's Needs

Part of knowing children is knowing their needs. Can you really expect a child to sit quietly and pay attention if he is hungry? Can you expect appropriate social interactions from a child if she never learned to trust? Abraham Maslow believed that human growth and development is oriented toward **self-actualization**, the striving to realize one's potential. Maslow felt that humans are internally motivated by five basic needs that constitute a hierarchy of motivating behaviors, progressing from physical needs to self-fulfillment. Maslow's hierarchy moves through physical needs, safety and security needs, belonging and affection needs, and self-esteem needs, culminating in self-actualization.

self-actualization An inherent tendency to reach one's true potential.

Physical Needs. Children's abilities to guide their behavior depend in part on how well their physical needs are met. Children do their best in school, for example, when they are well nourished. Thus parents should provide for their children's nutritional needs by giving them breakfast, and early childhood professionals should stress its benefits. For example, the brain needs protein and water to function well. Consequently,

- *Planting Trees in Kenya: The Story of Wangari Maathai* by Claire A. Nivola. Tells the story of environmentalist Wangari Maathai, the first woman from Africa to win a Nobel Peace Prize, for her direct response to the devastated natural resources and poverty caused by the deforestation of her homeland (ages 5–8).
- *I Have a Dream* by Kathleen A. Wilson. Gives children the opportunity to experience Martin Luther King Jr.'s speech through the eyes of fifteen African American artists. Each artist depicts a portion of the story of the civil rights movement (ages 4–8).
- *The Colors of Us* by Karen Katz. Lena discovers that she and her friends and neighbors are all beautiful shades of brown. "I am the color of cinnamon. Mom says she could eat me up," says Lena. Then she sees everyone else in terms of delicious foods. Different ethnicities celebrate the color of their skin and the different shades of brown (ages 4–8).
- *Encourage children to do something else.* Teach children that one strategy for reducing conflict is to walk away and get involved in another activity. Children can learn that they do not always have to play with a toy someone else is playing with. They can get involved in another activity with a different toy; they can do something else now and play with the toy later. Chances are, however, that by getting involved in another activity, they will forget about the toy they were ready to fight for.
- *Have children take turns.* Taking turns is a good way for children to learn that they cannot always be first, have their own way, or do a prized activity. Taking turns brings equality and fairness to interpersonal relations. Also, devise ways to involve all children. For example, put every child's name on a popsicle stick and you can pull a name to see who goes next.
- *Teach children to share.* Sharing is good behavior to promote in any setting. Children have to be taught how to share and how to behave when others do not share. You can help children to select another toy rather than hitting or grabbing. But keep in mind that during the early years, children are egocentric, and acts of sharing are likely to be motivated by expectations of a reward or approval, such as being thought of as a good boy or girl.
- *Have children ask for help.* Encourage children to ask others for help for solving problems. Many teachers have a rule that before children come to them for help, students should ask their peers for help. Teacher Lisa Bailey has this rule: "One, two, three—ask three before me." When given opportunities, children are good at solving problems and helping other children. Helping promotes collaboration and encourages compromise and problem solving.
- *Involved parents are part of the peace and conflict resolution processes.* Counsel and work with parents to encourage them to limit or eliminate children's exposure to violence. Suggest that they regulate or eliminate watching violence on television, attending R-rated movies, playing video games with violent content, and buying CDs with objectionable lyrics. Also, share with your families your expectations for peaceful living in your classroom. Share with parents activities you use to help children peacefully resolve conflicts. In addition, you can ask parents for their help and ideas in helping their children learn and live in peace.

many teachers allow children to have water bottles at their desks and to have frequent nutritional snacks.

In addition, the quality of the environment is important. Children cannot be expected to behave appropriately if classrooms are dark and noisy and smell of stale air. And children need adequate rest to do and be their best. The ideal amount of rest is an individual matter, but preschoolers need between eleven and thirteen hours of sleep, while young school-age children need ten to eleven hours of sleep each night.[15] A tired child cannot meet many of the expectations of schooling.

Safety and Security Needs. Children can't learn in fear. They should not have to fear their parents or teachers and should feel comfortable and secure at home and at school. Asking or forcing children to do school tasks for which they do not have the skills makes them feel insecure, and children who are afraid or insecure become tense. Consider also the dangers many urban children face—such as crime, drugs, or homelessness—or the emotional toll on children who constantly live in an atmosphere of domestic violence.

Part of guiding children's behavior includes providing safe and secure communities, neighborhoods, homes, schools, and classrooms.

Need for Belonging and Affection. Children need the sense of belonging that comes from being given jobs to do, having responsibilities, and helping make classroom decisions. Love and affection needs are satisfied when parents hold, hug, and kiss their children and tell them, "I love you." Teachers meet children's affectional needs when they smile, speak pleasantly, are kind and gentle, treat children with courtesy and respect, and genuinely value each child. An excellent way to show respect and affection for children and demonstrate their belonging is for you to personally greet them when they come into your classroom. A personal greeting helps children feel wanted and secure and promotes feelings of self-worth. In fact, all early childhood programs should begin with this daily validation of each child.

Need for Self-Esteem. Children who view themselves as worthy, responsible, and competent act in accordance with these feelings. Children's views of themselves come primarily from parents and early childhood professionals. The foundations for self-esteem are success and achievement. Consequently, it is up to you to give all children opportunities for success.

Self-Actualization. Children want to use their talents and abilities to do things on their own and be independent. Professionals and parents can help young children become independent by helping them learn to dress themselves, go to the restroom by themselves, and take care of their environment. Adults can also help children set achievement and behavior goals ("Tell me what you are going to build with your blocks") and encourage them to evaluate their behavior ("Let's talk about how you helped with cleanup after free play.").

These categories highlight children's basic needs professionals and parents must consider when guiding children and helping them develop responsibility for their behavior.

locus of control The source of control over personal behavior, either internal or external.

Step Seven: Help Children Build New Behaviors

When guiding children, it is important for you to realize that it is not enough to model behaviors or state expectations. You cannot expect children to come up with appropriate behaviors on their own. You must be prepared to help children build new behaviors to replace malfunctioning or maladaptive behaviors that are getting in the way of their learning.

Inner control helps children work independently, which is an important social and behavioral skill necessary for ongoing school achievement.

Internal Control. Helping children build new behaviors means that you help them learn that they are primarily responsible for their own behavior and that the pleasures and rewards for appropriate behavior are internal, coming from within them, as opposed to always coming from outside (i.e., from the approval and praise of others). We refer to this concept as **locus of control**—the source or place of control. The preferred and recommended locus of control for young and old alike is internal. However, young children with disabilities often develop an *external* locus of control as the adults in their environment "overhelp" them with difficulties they experience as a result of their disability. Additionally, children without disabilities may also have difficulty with internal control. To avoid the development of an external locus of control in children with and without disabilities, foster an attitude of capability and independence.

Teacher-Child Relations in Guiding Behavior. Think for a minute about your social relations with others. How others treat you affects you emotionally, physically, and cognitively. The same is true for the children you teach. How you relate to them really matters and affects how well they achieve, as well as how well they do and behave. What are teacher behaviors that really matter in preventing children's behavior problems? Consider these:

- Responding to children in a timely fashion
- Anticipating student needs and emotions
- Giving frequent feedback
- Providing strong supports for children's academic and social competence in the classroom setting

Researchers have found that the extent to which children can access the instructional and socialization resources of the classroom environment may be, in part, predicated on teacher–child interactions: "The association between the quality of early teacher–child relationships and later school performance can be both strong and persistent. The association is apparent in both academic and social spheres of school performance."[16]

In addition, teacher–child closeness, such as having an affectionate and warm relationship, can reduce the tendency for aggressive behavior. "Closer teacher–child relationships may provide young children with resources (e.g., emotional security, guidance, and aid) that facilitate an 'approach' orientation—as opposed to an 'avoidant' or 'resistant' stance—toward the interpersonal and scholastic demands of the classroom and school."[17] The implication for you and other early childhood professionals is that you need to really care for your children and develop strong and affectionate relationships with them.[18]

The Voice from the Field, "How to Guide Children to Help Ensure Their Success," on page 404 is a Competency Builder that guides you through steps to help children build more socially appropriate behaviors.

Step Eight: Empower Children

Helping children build new behaviors creates a sense of responsibility and self-confidence. As children are given responsibility, they develop greater self-direction, which means that you can guide them at the next level in their ZPD. Without responsibilities children are bored and frustrated and become discipline problems—the very opposite of what we intend.

To reiterate, guiding behavior is not about compliance and control. And, it is not a matter of getting children to please adults with remarks such as, "Show me how perfect you can be," "Don't embarrass me in front of others," "I want to see nice groups," or "I'm waiting for quiet." Instead, it is important to instill in children a sense of independence and responsibility for their *own* behavior. For example, you might say, "Jasmine, you worked a long time cutting out the flower you drew. You kept working on it until you were finished. Would you like some tape to hang it up?"

You can do a number of things to empower children:

- *Give children responsibilities.* All children, from an early age, should have responsibilities—that is, tasks that are theirs to do and for which they are accountable. Being responsible for completing tasks—doing such things as putting toys and learning materials away—promotes a positive sense of self-worth and conveys to children that people in a community of learning have responsibilities for making the community work well.

- *Give children choices.* Life is full of choices—some require thought and deliberation; others are automatic, based on previous behavior. But every time you make a decision, you are being responsible and exercising your right to decide. Children like to have choices, and choices help them become independent, confident, and self-disciplined. Making choices is a key to developing responsible behavior and inner control; it lays

Voice from the Field

How to Guide Children to Help Ensure Their Success

Kenneth entered the kindergarten classroom on the first day of the school year, trailing several feet behind his mom, who appeared to be unaware of his presence. She called out a greeting to another mom, and the two of them had an extended discussion about events in the neighborhood. Kenneth glanced around the room and headed purposefully toward the housekeeping center, where he grabbed a baby doll, threw it out of the doll bed, and then ran to the block box and grabbed a large block in each hand. At this point I deflected his trail of destruction and redirected his progress. "Good morning, welcome to my class. My name is Ms. Cheryl. What's your name?" The whirlwind stopped briefly to mumble a response that I could not understand and glared at me in open hostility. "Let's go talk to Mom," I suggested, touching his shoulder and directing him toward his mom.

Understanding Behavior

In our opening scenario, what important facts should we as educators recognize as signals that Kenneth has some behaviors that require adjustment to ensure his success in school?

- He seems unaware of the expected protocol for entering a classroom.
- His mother's apparent lack of interest in her child's behavior could be an indicator that Kenneth does not expect the adults around him to be involved with his activities.
- He may have been in an atmosphere that requires very little from him when it comes to following rules and, as indicated by his hostility, may see adult intervention as only restrictive rather than supportive and nurturing.
- Kenneth may even have an undiagnosed speech problem that prohibits adults and other children from understanding his needs. If adults in his world have failed to observe and interact with him, he is also probably lacking in basic language skills and vocabulary, which would limit his understanding.
- He appears to deal with his world in a very physical manner.

Behaviors Necessary for Success in School

Behavior #1: Recognition of authority—Kenneth was not even aware that an adult was in charge of the classroom.
Behavior #2: Trust in adults—The process of building trust is lengthy, but Kenneth needs to learn to see adults as nurturing and supportive.
Behavior #3: Use of verbal skills rather than physical reactions—If Kenneth is lacking in language, his teacher can help provide language experiences: defining words, explaining everything in detail, showing and describing pictures, reading books aloud, helping with activities, and talk, talk, talking.

STEP 1 Plan

Plan what activities you will offer your children. What part of the day will I use for centers? How can I show my students the best ways to use materials? Where will your children keep their belongings?

STEP 2 Be Explicit

Be sure that all of your children fully understand the classroom expectations. For example, I give my children opportunities to practice how we are to walk in the hallways, play on the playground, eat in the cafeteria, and move about the classroom. Many behaviors that inhibit success in school occur because students are not made aware of appropriate and inappropriate school procedures.

STEP 3 Model Behavior

Model appropriate behaviors and use sociodramatic play to give children an opportunity to "act out" inappropriate behaviors. Lead a class discussion on appropriate versus inappropriate behaviors and allow children to discuss how they feel. Teach children how to handle these issues through conflict resolution methods. Remember, it takes numerous rounds of modeling and role playing to make an impact on behavior that has been ingrained for five years at home and is still the norm when students return home.

STEP 4 Develop Classroom Rules

Our classroom rules are as follows:

1. We listen to each other.
2. We use our hands for helping, not hurting.
3. We use caring language.
4. We care about each other's feelings.
5. We are responsible for what we say and do.

STEP 5 Reinforce

Helping children learn to guide their own behavior takes consistent reteaching and reinforcement. Encourage students to deal with their conflicts appropriately by providing an area for students to talk away from the group. For example, when two students are having a problem with a toy, in a calm voice intervene by asking the students, "Would you two like to go to the discussion area and talk about your feelings?" Spend time daily stating expectations so students get the practice they need to internalize appropriate behaviors.

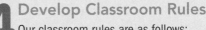

Source: Contributed by Cheryl Doyle, National Board Certified preschool teacher, Miami, Florida.

the foundation for decision making later. Here are some guidelines for giving children choices:

- Give children choices only when there are valid choices to make. When it comes time to clean up the classroom, don't let children choose whether they want to participate. Instead, let them choose between collecting the scissors or the crayons.
- Help children make choices. Instead of "What would you like to do today?" say, "Sarah, you have a choice between working in the woodworking center or the computer center. Which would you like to do?"
- *Help children succeed.* Children want to be successful, and you can help them in their efforts. For example, you can arrange the environment and make opportunities available for children to be able to do things. Successful accomplishments are a major ingredient of positive behavior.

Step Nine: Use Praise and Encouragement

When you have done a good job, you want to be told you have done a good job! Children are the same way. Children want to receive feedback in the form of praise and encouragement and they want to feel good about their accomplishments.

With the blending of early childhood and special education, more teachers are incorporating praise in their repertoire of teaching strategies. Many special education practices are based on reinforcing appropriate behavior through praise and rewards. The Accommodating Diverse Learners section at the end of this chapter illustrates the use of different types of reinforcement to encourage children's efforts and promote their success. However, simply telling a child "Good!" or "Fantastic job!" doesn't really give her the feedback she needs in order to learn from her accomplishments and have ideas for how she can do even better. Using encouragement is a much better approach.

Encouragement versus Praise. Think about when somebody says to you, "Good job!" You know what they are referring to but you don't know any of the specifics of the "good job." Perhaps you wanted more feedback on how you could do even better, or, you wanted feedback about what part of your accomplishments were good and what part you might improve. The same is true for children. Encouragement provides children opportunities for improving and growing. When we encourage children, we provide them with greater levels of self-motivation and with suggestions for how they can develop new skills and behaviors.

Here are some other reasons why you should use encouragement:

- *Encouragement acknowledges the child's effort.* For example, kindergarten teacher Rebecca Winston does not generalize the work of her children by saying that it is "good" or "great." She points out David's accomplishment in creating purple when combining blue and red and Maya's curving brush strokes in her painting.
- *Encouragement recognizes the child's success.* Rebecca recognizes her children are unique and have individual accomplishments she needs to acknowledge. She says, "David, your painting is very colorful. You used lots of reds and blues. You actually made the color purple, here. Do you see it?" "Maya, your bird is ready to fly! You used curved lines to make wings look real! You are very skilled at making curves and circles."
- *Encouragement helps children self-evaluate their efforts.* When teachers provide children with feedback about what they are doing, children learn to self-evaluate their efforts and successes without comparing their efforts with others. David can now try to see what other colors he can mix together to make new colors! Maya can try to create new drawing designs, such as zigzags or wavy lines!

Step Ten: Develop a Partnership with Parents, Families, and Others

Involving parents and families is a wonderful way to gain invaluable insights about children's behavior. You and parents must be partners and work cooperatively in guiding children's behaviors.

Know Your Children. An important rule in guiding behavior is to *know your children*. A good way to learn about the children you care for and teach is through home visits. If you do not have an opportunity to visit the home, a parent conference, e-mails, and phone calls are other ways you can collaborate to get the information you and they need. Either way, gather information concerning the child's health history and interests; the child's attitude toward schooling; the parents' educational expectations for the child; the school support available in the home (e.g., books, places to study); home conditions that would support or hinder school achievement (such as where the child sleeps); parents' attitudes toward schooling and discipline; parents' support of the child (e.g., encouragement to do well); parents' interests and abilities; and parents' desire to become involved in the school.

Involve Parents. A visit or conference also offers an opportunity for you to share ideas with parents. For example, express your desire for children to do well in school; encourage parents to take part in school and classroom programs; suggest ways parents can help children learn; describe some of the school programs; give information about school events, projects, and meetings; and explain your belief about discipline. Many teachers also include this information on their class or school websites.

Develop Your Philosophy. A good way to clarify your beliefs is to develop a philosophy about what you believe concerning child rearing, guidance, and children. Now would be a good time to list three or four of your main ideas for guiding children's behavior. Knowing what behaviors you want to support in children also helps you determine what is developmentally appropriate for your children. In addition, knowing what you believe makes it easier for you to share with parents, help them guide their children's behavior at home, and counsel them about discipline.

Physical Punishment

Is it possible to guide children's behavior without physical punishment? More and more, early childhood professionals agree that it is. Whether parents and professionals should spank or paddle as a means of guiding behavior is an age-old controversy. Some parents spank their children, following a "No!" with a slap on the hand or a spank on the bottom; some base their use of physical punishment on their religious beliefs. However, spanking is now mostly considered an inappropriate form of guidance. Thirty-one states have legislatively prohibited corporal punishment in schools.[19] The American Academy of Pediatrics strongly opposes striking a child for any reason. If a spanking is spontaneous, parents should later explain calmly why they did it, the specific behavior that provoked it, and how angry they felt. They also might apologize to their child for their loss of control.[20]

There are several problems with spanking and other forms of physical punishment. First, physical punishment is generally ineffective in building behavior in children; it does not show them what to do or provide them with alternative ways of behaving. Second, adults who use physical punishment are modeling physical aggression, saying, in effect, that it is permissible to use aggression in interpersonal relationships. Children who are spanked are thus more likely to use aggression with their peers.[21] Third, spanking and physical punishment increase the risk of physical injury to the child. Because spanking can be an emotionally charged situation, the spanker can become too aggressive, overdo the punishment, and hit the child in vulnerable places. Fourth, parents, caregivers, and teachers are children's sources of security. Physical punishment erodes the sense of security that children must have to function confidently in their daily lives.

In the long run, parents and early childhood professionals determine children's behavior. Thus, in guiding the behavior of children entrusted to their care, professionals and others must select procedures that are appropriate to their own philosophies and to children's particular needs. The best advice regarding physical punishment is to avoid it and use nonviolent means for guiding children's behavior. Helping children develop an internal system of control benefits them more than a system that relies on external control and authoritarianism. Developing self-regulation in children should be a primary goal of all professionals.

Accommodating Diverse Learners

Many young children exhibit problem behaviors in early childhood, and for most children these behaviors are transient or respond well to developmentally appropriate management techniques. In this chapter you have learned about some of these techniques. Unfortunately, some students do not respond to guidance strategies and require additional assistance. Positive reinforcement can be used for *all* children and *increases* the occurrence of appropriate behavior. Positive reinforcement is different from rewards. You can give rewards to children when they engage in desirable behavior, but if the reward does not lead to an increase in positive behavior, it is not actually a positive reinforcer. Here are some different types of positive reinforcement that you can use in your classroom.

Tangible Reinforcement

Tangible reinforcers are edible or material objects a child wants, such as stickers, stamps, or certificates. A child's positive behavior is reinforced by access to these items that may not be related to the specific behavior. For example, a child who sits appropriately during circle time may be given a sticker.

Activity-Based Reinforcement

Activity-based reinforcement is access to fun or preferred activities that can reinforce a child's behavior. For example, allowing a child to have free time in the puzzle center if he finishes seat work is an activity-based reinforcement.

Token Reinforcement

Token reinforcement gives children points or tokens for appropriate behavior. These rewards have little value in themselves but can be exchanged for something the child wants. For example, giving children tickets that they can exchange for free time or trips to the "treasure chest" is a common token reinforcement system.

Social Reinforcement

Social reinforcement is given out by teachers who express praise and approval for appropriate behavior. They may be verbal, "good job!" written with a smiley face, or expressions such as a smile, a pat on the back, or a wink.

Natural Reinforcement

Natural reinforcement results directly from the child's behavior. For example, a child is struggling to open her juice. The child says "help," and an adult helps the child. The opening (of and getting the juice) is reinforcing. This successful interaction increases the likelihood that the child will *ask* for help in the future, rather than requesting assistance in a more inappropriate manner.

The goal is for children to behave appropriately with natural or social reinforcement. Meeting the needs of *all* children requires knowledge of different types of reinforcement to tailor your interventions to the individual needs of each child.

Activities for Professional Development

Ethical Dilemma

"Just give him a good whack."

The school principal has just assigned six-year-old Eduardo to Kim Valerio's kindergarten class. Eduardo acts out, hits other children, and screams when he doesn't get his own way. In a team meeting, Kim asks for ideas on how to help guide Eduardo's behavior. One of her colleagues suggests that when Eduardo hits another child, Kim should "just give him a good whack on the bottom, and he'll soon get the message not to hit others." Kim learned in her early childhood classes at the university that physical punishment promotes aggressive behaviors in children. She is appalled that another teacher would recommend a "good whack" for any child.

How should Kim handle her disagreement? Should she suggest that giving a child a good whack is professionally, developmentally, and culturally inappropriate? Or should Kim talk with her colleagues after the meeting and share her views that she doesn't think physical punishment is a way to guide children's behavior? Should she report her colleague to the central administration because the state prohibits physical punishment? Or should she pursue another course of action? What would you do?

Activities to Apply What You Learned

1. Develop your plan for guiding children's behavior in your classroom. In your plan discuss how guiding behavior can have an impact on academics, lifelong success, and future delinquency. Create a wiki so that you can share your plan with your classmates. Ask them for feedback.

2. Think about ways that you can help develop behaviors for living and learning in the classroom. In a journal, write two examples of how you would encourage and promote development of behaviors in your program or classroom of first, second, and third graders. Go to TeacherTube and find ways that other teachers develop positive behavior.

3. Blog about how you can use the social constructivist approach to guide children. Include the importance of scaffolding, the zone of proximal development, adult child discourse, and private speech. Also, tell how you will incorporate these topics in your lessons.

4. In this chapter you learned ten steps for guiding children's behavior. Although they are all important, rank-order the ten in importance to you. Your first choice will be 1, your second, 2, and so on. Compare this list with your peers. What are some reasons for your difference of opinions?

5. Research Internet sources devoted to physical punishment. Determine the various methods of physical punishment. Consult a mentor, and ask for specific examples for how they deal with punishment. Do you agree with the methods recommended? What implications does your research have for your role as a teacher of young children?

6. Refer back to the chapter discussion about ways you can reward children for their behavior. How will you use tangible, activity-based, token, social, and natural reinforcement in your class room? Go online and research behavior modification techniques. Which do you find most effective? Start a chat room discussion and discuss your results with your peers.

Linking to Learning

Association for Supervision and Curriculum Development
www.ascd.org
Professional educational leadership organization dedicated to advancing best practices and policies for teachers and students.

Center for Effective Discipline
www.stophitting.com
A nonprofit organization that provides educational information to the public on the effects of corporal punishment and on alternatives to its use.

University of Arkansas Division of Agriculture: Guiding Children Successfully
www.arfamilies.org/child_care/gcs/educational_guides.htm
Provides information, organized into different programs, on how to successfully guide children.

Virginia Cooperative Extension
www.ext.vt.edu
Shows several commonsense strategies for effectively guiding the behavior of young children so they can make positive choices, learn problem-solving skills, and learn respect and responsibility.

PEARSON
myeducationlab

Go to Topic 9 (Guiding Children) in the MyEducationLab (www.myeducationlab.com) for your course, where you can:

- Find learning outcomes for Guiding Children along with the national standards that connect to these outcomes.

- Complete Assignments and Activities that can help you more deeply understand the chapter content.
- Apply and practice your understanding of the core teaching skills identified in the chapter with the Building Teaching Skills and Dispositions learning units.
- Check your comprehension on the content covered in the chapter by going to the Study Plan in the Book Resources for your text. Here you will be able to take a chapter quiz, receive feedback on your answers, and then access Review, Practice, and Enrichment activities to enhance your understanding of chapter content.

15

MULTICULTURALISM
Education for Living in a Diverse Society

naeyc standards

Standard 1. Promoting Child Development and Learning

I use my understanding of young children's characteristics and needs, and of multiple interacting influences on children's development and learning, to create environments that are healthy, respectful, supportive, and challenging for each child.[1]

Standard 2. Building Family and Community Relationships

I know about, understand, and value the importance and complex characteristics of children's families and communities. I use this understanding to create respectful, reciprocal relationships that support and empower families, and to involve all families in their children's development and learning.[2]

America the Multicultural

The population of the United States is changing and will continue to change. It will continue to become more and more diverse. In fact, by 2025, 21 percent of the population will be Hispanic. In addition, the United States will become even more of a nation of blended races. Projections are that by 2050, 21 percent of the population will be of mixed ancestry.[3] For example, today marriages are more mixed than ever, with the Caucasian–Hispanic combination being the most common.[4]

The Cultures of Our Children

In schools all across America, a very diverse population of immigrant children from other countries such as Mexico, El Salvador, Venezuela, Vietnam, Sierra Leone, and Pakistan are in our nation's schools. They are learning the content of schooling and they are learning to speak English. Today, there are 5.1 million English language learners (ELLs) in our nation's schools.[5] Sixty-four percent of children at Edison Elementary School in Long Beach, California, are ELLs. Edison won a top national urban education award for achieving impressive results with large numbers of ELL children. Teachers at Edison use academic vocabulary lessons that support children in their learning. These lessons enable children to actively participate in content-rich discussions to ensure that they learn vocabulary terms and English.[6]

Routh Roach Elementary of Garland Independent School District in Garland, Texas, has an academic track record of student success with language minority students whose number one language is Spanish. In 2006 Routh Roach was named a National NCLB Blue Ribbon School. Each year the school receives exemplary status ratings by the Texas Education Agency with most of the bilingual fifth grade students achieving commended on TAKS Reading, Math, and Science. Most students test in Spanish. The late-exit bilingual program supports Spanish literacy being developed before introducing English literacy, with substantial support in the students' first language, Spanish, in the early grades and continued Spanish support through fifth grade. The program design was developed based on a synthesis of studies examining long-term language minority student data on academic achievement. Longitudinal data of the Roach students has them excelling in English throughout the remainder of their formal education with national test scores equal to or excelling the native English-speaking students. Students are not introduced to English phonemes or syntax until fourth grade. The school has a substantial collection of library books in Spanish with formal academic Spanish being an integral part of the program. Transition of literacy skills from Spanish to English begins when the individual students ask the librarian if they can read library books in English, which usually occurs in the third grade. Formal English literacy is presented in fourth grade and continues in fifth grade. The program design of teaching the Spanish-speaking students literacy skills in Spanish in the early grades is the foundation of the successful Routh Roach program. Students master on-grade level skills in Spanish while being taught to speak English.[7]

Southside Elementary School in Miami, Florida, follows right behind Routh Roach, with a student population of fifty-six percent ELLs. At Southside, principals and teachers tell students they "are the smartest kids in Miami" and the children prove it! Teachers provide lessons that require students to explain, analyze, compare, and construct information. For

> "We must be aware of students' needs, and provide assistance that will ensure gains in academics and language fluency."
>
> **THELMA MELENDEZ DE SANTA ANA**
> Assistant Secretary for Elementary and Secondary Education

Voice from the Field

The PANDA Project: Mandarin Language Learning

Fallbrook Union Elementary

The Fallbrook Union Elementary School District (FUESD)'s student population is comprised of 33 percent English language learners and 58.4 percent students qualifying for the free or reduced-price lunches. Two schools are located on Camp Pendleton Marine Base and many of our students come from active duty military families.

PANDA (Promoting and Nurturing Dynamic Academics)

Prior to the advancement of this program, there were no foreign language programs offered at the elementary level in the school district. Parents consistently expressed great interest in the development of the PANDA Project and we received more than 700 parent requests seeking placement in the program for their children.

Mandarin Chinese

Prior to offering the Mandarin learning opportunity, the district actively sought to educate parents and community members regarding the benefits to students in learning Mandarin Chinese. Mandarin is a tonal, character-based language, which is very different from English (an alphabetic Latin-based language). Mandarin Chinese is a tonal language with words created using just 23 beginning sounds (called initials), and 32 ended sounds (called finals). Initial and ending sounds are combined to create words, but in addition to initials and finals, Mandarin incorporates five different tones that vary the meaning of the words when spoken aloud.

Mandarin Chinese is a challenging second language to learn and students need many opportunities to hear and speak the new language to reap the full benefits. In order for children to get those enriched opportunities, classroom instructional strategies reflect best practices and offer students a variety of learning supports such as visuals, manipulatives, cooperative learning, the integration of technology, and Total Physical Response (TPR). TPR is a means of pairing auditory teaching practices (like discussions or talking) with other sensory input (such as physical movement) to reinforce the learning. With TPR, students respond physically to the words of the teacher. The activity may be a simple game such

example, students dissect, weigh, and compare pig hearts while learning about the circulatory system.[8] The PANDA (Promoting and Nurturing Dynamic Academics) Project in the Fallbrook Union Elementary School District (California) is yet another approach to language, literacy, and culture. You can read about the PANDA Project in the accompanying Voice from the Field.

Minorities—The Emerging Majority. Presently, minorities make up nearly half of the children born in the United States.[9] Demographers expect 2011 will be the "tipping point" when more minority babies are born than Caucasian children.[10] In addition, several states including California, Hawaii, New Mexico, and Texas, are minority majority states. For example, in Texas, only 32 percent of the kindergarten children are Caucasian.[11]

When we think of minority children and families, we might tend to think of African-Americans and Hispanics. Yet minority children of all cultures attend our nation's schools. For example, Minnesota is the home to the largest number of Somali immigrants in the United States.[12] The United States is also home to 535,000 Haitian immigrants with the majority residing in Florida and New York.[13]

The great diversity of young children in American schools creates interesting challenges for you and all early childhood educators. Not only do children speak languages other than English, they also behave differently based on cultural customs and values, and they come from varied socioeconomic backgrounds, and with different life experiences. Yet early childhood professionals must prepare *all* children to live happily and productively in our society. Assistant Secretary for Elementary and

as "Simon Says," or creating hand gestures to accompany different tones and words. All of these methods encourage a high level of student engagement and motivation to learn. For example, teacher Grace Cox employs a variety of teaching strategies, including TPR, modeling, and realia to help students comprehend and retain lesson vocabulary. She uses a modified version of "There Was an Old Lady Who Swallowed a Fly" taught entirely in Mandarin Chinese using the best practices described above. Her students were engaged, motivated, and highly successful!

Professional development for teachers and administration has been critical as we established our program. Additionally, our district established a collaborative partnership with the Confucius Institute of San Diego State University in order to link our program directly with important resources, such as experts in Chinese culture, language, and instruction, as well as "sister schools" in China. The establishment of sister schools provides students with real-life opportunities to engage with Chinese-speaking peers and authentically implement acquired Mandarin language skills.

Benefits of PANDA

Mandarin elicits right-brain activity, as opposed to English, which elicits more left-brain activity. Therefore, learning Mandarin in addition to English encourages more brain activity in both hemispheres, which improves global thinking and relating. For struggling students, Mandarin can be an instructional pathway to increase motivation and provide opportunities to develop mental flexibility. Further, PANDA provides students with challenging and rigorous programs that will prepare them with critical skills needed to be professionally competitive in the twenty-first century. In addition, the U.S. Department of Education identifies Mandarin as a U.S. government priority language and supports programs like ours that provide students with early opportunities to develop Mandarin language skills which will later support the attainment of advanced Mandarin fluency. FUESD also believes the rigor of learning Mandarin provides gifted and talented students the opportunity to participate in a challenging and engaging program which will supply important language skills they can carry with them into their future endeavors at both the college and professional levels.

Source: Text contributed by Stacey Larson-Everson, Director of State and Federal Programs, Fallbrook Union Elementary School District, Fallbrook, California.

Secondary Education, Thelma Melendez, feels, "Every child in this nation is entitled to a quality public education, regardless of their race, creed, zip code, or first language." She believes that education is the one and only way to make real the promise of the American Dream.[14]

These demographics about our nation's children and their families have tremendous implications for your professional practice. More students will require special education, bilingual education, and other special services. Issues of culture and diversity will continue to shape curriculum and instructional practices. In part, how you respond to the diverse makeup and needs of your children will determine how well they fulfill their responsibilities as citizens in the years to come. The strategies and solutions for achieving this goal are not always easy, but they require our utmost attention and dedication.

Developing Your Cultural Competence

As classrooms across America become more diverse, it is important for you to develop the cultural competence you need to effectively teach your students. **Cultural competence** is the ability to interact effectively with children, families, and colleagues of different cultures, as well as an awareness of cultural differences and cultural values.[15] You practice cultural competence by treating everyone with respect, learning about other cultures, and incorporating cultural dimensions into all aspects of your teaching. In addition, you become culturally competent by creating strong home–school relationships: keeping in touch with parents and families, learning about and understanding their hopes and goals for their

cultural competence The ability and confidence to interact effectively with children, families, and colleagues of different cultures.

The diversity of today's society is clearly evident in many classrooms. Teachers must teach lessons that are multicultural to help enrich children's learning experiences.

multicultural awareness
Developing in all children an appreciation and understanding of other people's cultures, socioeconomic status, and gender, including their own.

multicultural infusion
Making multiculturalism an explicit part of curriculum and programs.

children, and involving them in your classroom and school. Patricia Edwards, the Assistant Secretary for Elementary and Secondary Education, says, "Teachers need to learn the cultural background of their students. This country is very diverse, but we don't have a lot of diverse teachers. People from all over the world come to America, but teachers are unaware of what they need to do to become literate."[16]

Multicultural Awareness

Culturally competent teachers promote and track multicultural awareness in their classrooms. **Multicultural awareness** is developing in all children an appreciation and understanding of other people's cultures, socioeconomic status, and gender, including their own.[17]

Bringing multicultural awareness to your classroom does not mean teaching about certain cultures to the exclusion of others. Rather, multicultural awareness activities focus on diverse cultures while making children aware of the content, nature, and richness of their own. Learning about other cultures while also learning about their own culture enables children to integrate commonalities and appreciate differences without inferring inferiority or superiority of one culture over another.

Promoting multicultural awareness in an early childhood program has implications far beyond the program itself. Culture influences and affects work habits, interpersonal relations, and a child's general outlook on life. You must take these multicultural influences into consideration when designing curriculum and instructional processes for young and impressionable children.

Teaching and Multicultural Infusion

One way to positively change the lives of children and their families is to infuse multiculturalism into early childhood activities and practices. **Multicultural infusion** means that multicultural education permeates the entire curriculum. From a larger perspective, infusion strategies ensure that multiculturalism becomes an essential part of your classroom. Here are some ways you can achieve multicultural infusion.

Foster Cultural Awareness

It is important to teach children about other cultures, including their own. A lack of understanding about cultural differences leads to intolerance, suspicion, and even violence. Researchers believe that children are aware of racial differences by the time they are in preschool. They also believe that by age twelve, most children have developed an image of most racial and ethnic groups in America.[18] Educating children early is a good way to equip them with the knowledge they need before they conform to racial stereotypes. As we say in early childhood, it is more effective to prevent than to remediate.

Assess Your Attitudes Toward Children.   In your teaching of young children it is important that you assess your attitude toward children and their families to ensure you are multiculturally sensitive and aware. Answer these questions:

- Do you believe that *all* children can and will learn?
- Are you willing to spend the time and effort necessary to help each child learn?

- Are you willing to teach children individually according to their cultural and individual learning styles?
- Do you have high expectations for *all* children regardless of their race, socioeconomic status, or gender?
- Are you willing to work with the parents and families of your children to learn more about their culture, educational values, and lifestyle preferences?

As you reflect on these questions, you may find some areas in which you need more information and help from colleagues and mentors. What is important is that you are willing to enhance your cultural competence, learn, change, and become the teacher all children need and deserve.

Develop Awareness.   Keep in mind that you are the key to a multicultural classroom. You need to integrate different cultures and populations throughout the school year and throughout the curriculum. It is not enough to celebrate African-American culture in February and Hispanic culture in September; to study women's contributions with Women's History Month in March or be attentive to disabilities in Disabilities Awareness Month in October. In fact, doing so reinforces that these populations are on the fringe or the exception to the "norm." Instead, integrate the contributions and impacts of all cultures, genders, and abilities throughout the curriculum as a part of your everyday teaching and approach to interacting. The following guidelines will help you gain multicultural competence and develop your own awareness and the awareness of your students:

- *Recognize that all children are unique.*   They all have special talents, abilities, and styles of learning and relating to others. Provide opportunities for children to be different and use their abilities. For example, kindergarten teacher Alma Brooks teaches a lesson that allows children to see the physical differences in one another. In this lesson she has the children paint pictures of themselves, and write down what makes their physical characteristics and talents or special abilities different from others. At the end of the lesson they all gather around and sing about their personal unique characteristics to emphasize that each person is different yet special.[19]
- *Get to know, appreciate, and respect the cultural backgrounds of all your children.*   Visit families and community neighborhoods to learn more about cultures, religions, and ways of life. For example, kindergarten teacher Ally Smith knows that in D'hjira's culture people rarely wear shoes all the time, so she allows him to take off his shoes and socks during naptime.[20]
- *Infuse your children's cultures into your lesson planning and teaching.*   Use all subject areas—math, science, language arts, literacy, music, art, and social studies—to relate culture to your children. For example, third grade teacher William Rodriguez teaches a Spanish language lesson by introducing a balero. A balero is a traditional Mexican toy that resembles a cup and ball. While children play with the balero, William introduces Spanish words, and numbers. As the children continue to play the game they are surrounded with the Spanish language while also having fun learning a Spanish game.[21]
- *Use children's interests and experiences to form a basis for planning lessons and developing activities.*   This approach helps students feel good about their backgrounds, cultures, families, and experiences. Also, when children relate what they are doing in the classroom to the rest of their daily lives their learning is more meaningful. For example, third grade teacher Carol Read noticed that her children are fascinated and interested in insects, so she decided to do a lesson on silkworms. In this lesson she discusses what the silkworm eats, allows students to observe silkworms, and brings the lesson to a close by allowing children to draw

and label the body parts of a silkworm. She also uses this opportunity to discuss and teach the Chinese culture.[22]

- *Use authentic situations to provide for cultural learning and understanding.* For example, a field trip to a culturally diverse neighborhood of your city or town provides children an opportunity to understand *firsthand* many of the details about how people conduct their daily lives. Such an experience provides wonderful opportunities for involving children in writing, cooking, reading, and dramatic play activities. What about setting up a market in the classroom? Second grade teacher of the year Jamee Miller generates new ways to expose her children to life beyond their neighborhoods through online exploration and digital field trips. Recently her class experienced St. Augustine, Florida. Jamee spent weekends taking pictures and compiling them to create a virtual world for her children to experience. Such activities allow her children to prepare to live and work in diverse communities without going outside the classroom![23]

- *Use authentic assessment activities to fully assess children's learning and growth.* You will want to assess students within a cultural framework—this is a part of your implementing the Whole Child approach and is essential to developmentally appropriate practice. Portfolios are ideal means for children to learn and grow in a culturally sensitive, unbiased environment by allowing them to self-evaluate their work and progress while honoring and respecting their culture. For example, Madison, Connecticut, third grade teacher Sandra Brand allows her students to do student-led conferences using self portfolios to review their progress and assignments through the school year with their parents. If students have missing or incomplete assignments then they explain why the work is incomplete or missing during the conference and their plans to plan to keep from failing to complete other assignments.[24]

Early childhood educators must consider the diverse characteristics of students—including gender, ethnicity, race, and socioeconomic factors—when planning learning opportunities for their classes. What are some ways diversity can enrich the curriculum?

- *Be a role model by accepting, appreciating, and respecting other languages and cultures.* It is important to communicate and demonstrate that uniqueness and diversity are positive. For example, third grader A'ishah wears a hijab or head scarf (concealing hair, ears, and neck) to school. Her classmates understand and respect her Muslim culture and practices. Second grader Rajiv eats foods that look and smell different from most of the other children in the classroom. During lunch the children in class learn about the different foods he eats instead of thinking he is "weird" or different.[25]

- *Be knowledgeable about, proud of, and secure in your own culture.* Children will ask about you, and you should share your background with them. For example, kindergarten teacher Danasha Johnson shares her culture and experiences throughout the school year. She uses lessons and activities that discuss and explain the African-American culture. Danasha discusses famous African-American activists and those that have paved the way for equality for all races. Most important of all, she shares herself with her children. She invites other teachers to share their cultures with her class and uses this information to inform her lessons. In doing so, she models for her students that you can be both aware and proud of your own culture and still be accepting and sensitive to other cultures.

- *Collaborate with your school administrators and colleagues to promote cultural awareness.* Remember, it takes a school for multicultural infusion to really be effective. For example, at Alain Locke Elementary School in Philadelphia, Pennsylvania, faculty and staff hold a culture day in which the children are encouraged to wear clothing of their culture, make a flag of their country, and share information about their culture.[26]

Select Appropriate Instructional Materials.   In addition to assessing your own attitudes and infusing personal sensitivity into the multicultural classroom, you also need to carefully consider and select appropriate instructional materials to support multicultural infusion.

Multicultural Literature.   Choose literature that emphasizes people's habits, customs, and general living and working behaviors. This approach stresses similarities and differences regarding how children and families live their *whole* lives and avoids merely noting differences or teaching only about habits and customs. Multicultural literature today is more representative of various cultural groups and provides authentic language experiences for young children. It is written by authors from particular cultures and contains true-to-life stories and culturally authentic writing styles. The following are some examples of the rich selection of literature available and authentic literature themes represented in cultures around the world.

- *Forgotten or Unknown Princesses* by Philippe Lechermeier and Rebecca Dautremer: A story of unique princesses that all have their own positive and negative attributes.
- *The Best Mariachi in the World* by J. D. Smith: A tale about finding one's own talent.
- *Teo in the Snow* by Violeta Denou: A story about Teo and his friends who go on a winter excursion in the mountain and do not always make safe choices in the pursuit of having fun.
- *Leon and Bob* by Simon James: A story about a boy whose father is away in the army and his imaginary friend who is his confidant and playmate.
- *Oh No!* by Rotraut Susanne Berner: A story about a hen who complains about everything, her friend who has a solution to every complaint, and their discovery that things are not always black and white.
- *Hush!* by Minfong Ho: A Thai lullaby about a mother who begs a mosquito, water buffalo, and other animals to let her baby sleep.
- *Nine-in-One Grr! Grr!* by Blia Xiong: A folktale from the Hmong people of Laos that answers questions in a beautiful, clever fashion.

Thematic Teaching.   Early childhood professionals often use thematic units to strengthen children's understanding of themselves, their culture, and the cultures of others. Thematic units are lessons based on groups of topics that are designed around activities and cover several areas of the curriculum.[27] Thematic choices from a variety of cultures help children identify cultural similarities and encourage understanding and tolerance. Consider the following suggestions of themes:

- *Getting to know myself, getting to know others.*   Kindergarten teacher Maci Daniels uses a toilet tissue activity to familiarize her children with one another. In this activity Maci passes a roll of toilet tissue and tells students to take as many sheets as they like, without explanation as to what they will do with it. Once everyone has chosen their toilet tissue squares, Maci explains that the number of squares represents the number of things that each child must tell about themselves. This allows everyone to introduce themselves and get to know fun facts about their peers.[28]
- *What is special about you and me?*   Second grade teacher Nicky Gunther has her children interview each other, taking note of the one special characteristic, interest, or hobby each student wants to be recognized for. She allows the children to read one

another's lists after they have interviewed each other. Nicky then instructs the children to place their papers face down. At the end of the lesson Nicky calls out the special characteristics of each student to see if the children can guess each others' talents and special abilities.[29]

- *Growing up in the city.*   Second grade teacher Candice Mason has a lesson in which her children illustrate on a square piece of paper what their city or neighborhood looks like. In their drawings children draw the buildings that surround them, houses, trees or anything significant about their city. Once each child finishes drawing their city, Candice and the children combine the square pieces and make a mural.[30]

- *Growing up in my country.*   Third grade teacher Timothy Reynolds gives his students one 8 × 11-inch piece of paper to illustrate their country of origin. On this page they include a picture and a short description of their country's beliefs and traditions. He also asks that they include flags and symbols that reflect their country. After they are all done, Timothy compiles each page and makes a class scrapbook for everyone to review.[31] For children born in the United States, Timothy explains that even though they are born here, they each have their own experiences, cultures, and traditions in this country. He asks them to write about their families' and communities' traditions, symbols, and beliefs and assures his students that it is OK if each of their papers looks differently even though they are from the same country.

- *Tell me about Africa (South America, China, etc.)*   Third grade teacher Kathy Lynn has her children learn firsthand about other cultures by setting them up with pen pals in different countries. Children in her classroom write to third graders in Uganda about their traditions, cultural etiquette, foods, etc.[32] Second grade teacher Donald Marcel uses the online pen pal service ePal to collaborate with art students in the Caribbean. His students post their artwork on the ePal portal and also get the opportunity to view Caribbean artwork as well.[33] You will want to review your school's policy on using services such as ePal.

Teach Your State and Local Standards.   State standards cover all subjects and content areas. While your particular state may not specifically have a set of standards relating to multicultural awareness and infusion, more than likely the content standards do. For example, in the California English Language Arts Standards first graders "identify how language uses reflect region and cultures." They also have to compare and contrast different versions of the same stories that reflect different cultures.[34] In the Florida Social Studies Content Standards second graders must "compare the cultures of Native American tribes from various geographic regions of the United States."[35] So your state standards will provide you many opportunities to infuse culture into all you teach.

Multicultural Accomplishments.   Add to classroom activities, as appropriate, the accomplishments of people from different cultural groups, women of all cultures, and individuals with disabilities. The following criteria are most important when picking materials for use in a multicultural curriculum for early childhood programs:

- Represent people of all cultures fairly and accurately.
- Represent people of diverse ethnic groups and people with exceptionalities.
- Be sure that historic information is accurate and nondiscriminatory.
- Be sure that materials do not include stereotypical roles or language.
- Ensure gender equity—that is, boys and girls must be represented equally and in nonstereotypical roles.

Avoid Sexism and Gender-Role Stereotyping.   Current interest in multiculturalism in general and nondiscrimination in particular raises concern about sexism and gender-role stereotyping. **Sexism** is "the collection of attitudes, beliefs, and behaviors which result from the assumption that one sex is superior. *In the context of schools,* the term refers to

sexism Prejudice or discrimination based on sex.

the collection of structures, policies, practices, and activities that overtly or covertly prescribe the development of girls and boys and prepare them for traditional sex roles."[36]

Title IX of the Education Amendments Act of 1972, as amended by Public Law 93–568, prohibits such discrimination in the schools: "No person in the United States shall, on the basis of sex, be excluded from participation in, be denied the benefits of, or be subjected to discrimination under any education program or activity receiving Federal financial assistance."[37] For example, the Mason Elementary School in Duluth, Georgia, encourages and supports girls and boys to participate in sports, choir, band, and extracurricular clubs. Their sports club is open to children who would like to play basketball, football, Frisbee, or soccer. Their coaches' goal is to make the most positive contribution possible to the physical, emotional, and social well-being of students. In the choir and band, children learn and perform a wide variety of musical styles to gain a better understanding of the elements of choral music. They also have a broadcast club, Junior Beta Club (academic honor society), academic achievement club, and health club.[38]

You and other early childhood professionals need to be concerned about the roots of sexism and **sexual harassment** and realize that these practices have their beginnings in children's early years in homes, centers, and preschools. You must constantly examine personal and programmatic practices, evaluate materials, and work with parents to eliminate sexism and ensure that no child is shortchanged in any way.

sexual harassment
Unwelcome sexual behavior and talk.

You can provide children with an open framework in which they can develop their gender roles. The following are some suggestions for avoiding gender stereotypes:

- *Provide opportunities for all children to experience the activities, materials, toys, and emotions traditionally associated with both sexes.* Give boys as well as girls opportunities to experience tenderness, affection, and the warmth of close parent–child and teacher–pupil relationships. Conversely, girls as well as boys should be able to behave energetically, get dirty, and participate in what are typically considered male activities, such as woodworking and block building.

- *Become conscious of words that promote sexism.* In a lesson on community helpers, taught in most preschool and kindergarten programs at one time or another, many words carry a sexist connotation. *Fireman, policeman,* and *mailman,* for example, are all masculine terms; nonsexist terms are *firefighter, police officer,* and *mail carrier.* Examine all your curricular materials and teaching practices to determine how you can make them free of sexist language.

- *Determine what physical arrangements in the classroom promote or encourage gender-role stereotyping.* Are boys encouraged to use the block area more than girls? Are girls encouraged to use the quiet areas more than boys? Do children hang their coats separately—a place for boys and a place for girls? All children should have equal access to all learning areas of the classroom; no area should be reserved exclusively for one sex. In addition, examine any activity or practice that promotes segregation of children by gender or culture. Cooperative learning activities and group work provide ways to ensure that children of both sexes work together.

- *Examine your behavior to see whether you are encouraging gender stereotypes.* Do you tell girls they cannot empty wastebaskets but they can water the plants? Do you tell boys they should not play with dolls? Do you say that boys aren't supposed to cry? Do you reward only the girls who are always passive, well behaved, and well mannered? Follow these guidelines in your teaching:
  - Give all children a chance to respond to questions. Research consistently shows that teachers do not wait long enough after they ask a question for most children, especially girls, to respond. Therefore, quick responders—usually boys—answer most of the questions. By waiting longer, you will be able to encourage more girls to answer.[39]
  - Help all children become independent and do things for themselves. Discourage behaviors and attitudes that promote helplessness and dependency.

- Use portfolios, teacher observations, and other authentic means of assessing children's progress to provide bias-free assessment. Involving children in the evaluation of their own efforts is also a good way of promoting children's positive images of themselves.

- *Encourage children to dress in ways that lead to full participation in all activities.* Children should be encouraged to dress so they will be able to participate in a range of both indoor and outdoor activities. This is an area in which you may be able to help parents by discussing how dressing children appropriately can contribute to more effective participation. However, you have to work within what different cultures believe and practice about personal attire.

As you collaborate with parents, be sure to discuss appropriate attire for all children that makes it possible for them to engage in a wide variety of indoor and outdoor activities. Your goal is to make sure that both genders are clothed so that they can participate freely in all activities.

Implement an Antibias Curriculum and Activities.   The goal of an *antibias curriculum* is to help children learn to be accepting of others, regardless of race, ethnicity, gender, sexual orientation, socioeconomic status, or disability. Children participating in an antibias curriculum become comfortable with diversity and learn to stand up for themselves and others in the face of injustice. Additionally, in such a supportive, open-minded environment, children learn to construct a knowledgeable, confident self-identity.

Young children are constantly learning about differences and need a sensitive teacher to help them form positive, unbiased perceptions about differences among people. As children color pictures of themselves, for example, you may hear a comment such as, "Your skin is white and my skin is brown." You may be tempted, in the name of equality, to respond, "It doesn't matter what color we are—we are all people." Although this remark does not sound harmful, it fails to help children develop positive feelings about themselves. A more appropriate response might be, "Amanda, your skin is a beautiful dark brown, which is just right for you; Christina, your skin is a beautiful light tan, which is just right for you." A response such as this positively acknowledges each child's different skin color, which is an important step in developing a positive self-concept.

Through the sensitive guidance of caring teachers, children learn to speak up for themselves and others. By living and learning in an accepting environment, children find that they have the ability to change intolerable situations and can have a positive impact on the future. This is part of what empowerment is all about, and it begins in the home and in early childhood programs. An antibias curriculum should start in early childhood and continue throughout the school years. The book *Anti-Bias Education for Young Children and Ourselves* by Louise Derman-Sparks and Julie Olsen Edwards will help you learn more about anti-bias education.

Promote and Use Conflict-Resolution Strategies and Peaceful Living

We all live in a world of conflict. Television and other media bombard us with images of violence, crime, and international and personal conflict. Unfortunately, many children live in homes where conflict and disharmony are a way of life rather than an exception. Increasingly, early childhood professionals are challenged to help children resolve conflicts in peaceful ways. *Conflict-resolution strategies* help children learn how to solve problems, disagree in appropriate ways, negotiate, and live in harmony with others.

Your goal is to have children reach mutually agreeable solutions to problems without the use of power (e.g., fighting, hitting, pushing, or verbal taunts or threats). The following no-lose method of conflict resolution helps you achieve your goal:

1. Identify and define the conflict in a nonaccusatory way ("Vinnie and Rachael, you have a problem—you both want the green paint").

2. Encourage children to help in solving behavior problems ("Let's think of how to solve this problem").

3. Brainstorm solutions with children; accept a variety of solutions, and avoid evaluating them ("Yes, you could both use the same paint cup. . . . You could take turns").

4. Discuss with children each solution, and discuss the pros and the cons ("Vinnie, that's a good idea—putting paint in the two paper cups so that both you and Rachael can use the green paint at the same time, thank you.").

5. Put the plan into action ("See whether the two of you can get the green paint into the paper cups without help").

6. Follow up to evaluate how well the solution worked (After a few minutes, "Looks like your idea of how to solve your green paint problem really worked!").[40]

The Voice from the Field, "How to Create Classroom Environments That Support Peaceful Living and Learning," is a Competency Builder that will help you develop learning environments that support children's learning.

Welcome Parent and Community Involvement

As we have noted earlier, as an early childhood professional, you will work with children and families of diverse cultural backgrounds. You will need to learn about their cultural backgrounds so that you can respond appropriately to their needs. Let's take a look at the culture of some families who are of Hispanic descent and its implications for parent and family involvement.

Within the Hispanic culture, particularly families from Latin American countries, there is belief in the authority of the school and teachers. In many of these Latin American countries it is considered rude for a parent to intrude in the life of the school. Parents believe it is the school's job to educate and the parent's job to nurture and that the two jobs do not mix. A child who is well educated is one who has learned moral and ethical behavior.

Hispanics tend to have strong family ties, believe in family loyalty, and have a collective orientation that supports community life; they have been found to be field dependent (i.e., learning best in group and highly organized environments) and sensitive to nonverbal indicators of feeling.[41] These traits are represented by an emphasis on warm, personalized styles of interaction, a relaxed sense of time, and a need for an informal atmosphere for communication. Given these preferences, a culture clash may result when Hispanic students and parents are confronted with the typical task-oriented style of most American teachers.

Although an understanding of the general cultural characteristics of Hispanics is helpful, it is important not to overgeneralize. Each family and child is unique, and care should be taken not to assume values and beliefs just because a family speaks Spanish and is from Latin America. It is important that teachers take time to discover the particular values, beliefs, and practices of families in the classroom.

You, the child's teacher, are the person in your school whom Hispanic families will most likely trust the most. Consequently, you play an important role in the empowerment of children and parents. You can serve as a contact point, parent colleague, and a confidant.[42]

Use the following guidelines to involve Hispanic parents:

- *Use a personal touch.* It is crucial to use face-to-face communication in the Hispanic parents' primary language when first making contact. It may even take several personal meetings before the parents gain sufficient trust to participate actively. Home visits are a particularly good way to begin to develop rapport.

Voice from the Field

How to Create Classroom Environments That Support Peaceful Living and Learning

"Establishing lasting peace is the work of education; all politics can do is keep us out of war."

—*Maria Montessori*

Peaceful living begins with peaceful homes, peaceful classrooms, and peaceful communities. Today's children are surrounded by violence, aggression, and uncivil behavior. Many children live in violent homes, are victims of abuse, and are constantly bombarded with violence on television and other media. In 2008, 1 in 136 children were neglected, 1 in 601 children were victims of physical abuse, 1 in 1,064 were victims of sexual abuse, 1 in 1,333 were victims of emotional abuse, and 1 in 5 children were maltreated in some way.* We know that it is much more difficult to remediate than it is to prevent. Consequently, creating peaceful classrooms that promote peaceful and respectful living and learning will go a long way to keep children from developing aggressive behaviors that lead to violence and wasted lives.

You and every early childhood professional have to lead the way in creating environments for young children that will help them live peaceful lives and that will help them learn and grow to be peaceful in all of their relationships with others.

STRATEGY 1 Create a Classroom Environment That Supports Peaceful Living

To create a classroom environment that supports peaceful living, include these dimensions:

- Create an environment that is warm, welcoming, and productive; supports a home-like atmosphere; that is attractive and in which children feel comfortable and welcomed. Such an atmosphere has a calming influence on children and supports peaceful living.
- Use a "peace table," a place you and the children can sit to talk things over and talk about behavior and share thoughts and feelings about themselves and others. A peace table gives children a chance to develop classroom strategies for how to give and receive respect and do their best work.
- A peaceful environment is a well-organized environment. Arrange your learning environment so that children can help each other and work collaboratively together. Create your environment so children have free access to a wide range of learning materials that support their

learning. When children know where things belong and when they are able to help care for and maintain the classroom, they develop a sense of ownership and feel a responsibility for living with others in the classroom.
- Support children's independent learning and industriousness. Children like to be active and busy and, when they are, there are fewer problems and more positive involvement and behavior.
- Be at your classroom door every morning. Greet each child with a smile, a handshake, and words of welcome and encouragement.
- Reduce clutter. Environments for young children should be as organized as possible and lack clutter. Cluttered and chaotic environments create a sense of anxiety and promote aggression. Closely examine your classroom to make sure that it is well-organized, uncluttered, and is an inviting and pleasant place to live and learn for you and your children.

Picture yourself in this classroom. You are discussing peaceful living with your students. What are some behaviors you would suggest to your students for living peacefully in their classroom?

STRATEGY 2 Collaborate with Parents

- Make parents your partners in peace. Invite parents into your classroom so they can see how you promote peaceful living and learning.
- Give parents tips and ideas for how they can create peaceful environments at home.
- Ask parents for their ideas for how to make your classroom a place of peace and learning.

- *Provide bilingual support.* All communication with Hispanic parents, written and oral, must be provided in Spanish and English. In addition, many programs report that having bicultural and bilingual staff helps promote trust.[43]
- *Use nonjudgmental communication.* To gain the trust and confidence of Hispanic parents, avoid making them feel that they are to blame for something or are doing something wrong. Support parents for their strengths.

STRATEGY 3 — Teach and Practice Peaceful Dispositions

Dispositions are frequent and voluntary habits of thinking and doing.[†] They are "habits of the mind." Childhood dispositions that support peaceful living include:

- Cooperation
- Friendliness
- Respectfulness
- Kindness
- Thoughtful behavior
- Helpfulness
- Empathy

There are many opportunities to conduct activities related to peaceful living. Here children are sharing their ideas for how to live peacefully with all children regardless of socioeconomic background and culture. What are some activities you could incorporate in your classroom for peaceful living with children from all cultures?

STRATEGY 4 — Integrate Peace into Your Curriculum

- Teach responsible and peaceful living. Give children many opportunities to be responsible and show that they are capable of responsible living by helping others and by being in charge of their own learning.
- In your morning meeting, talk about the dispositions that support peaceful living.
- Have children talk and write about qualities of life in a peaceful classroom. Talk about current events that relate

to violence and what children think are solutions to violence.

- Create a chart of behaviors that support peaceful learning. Review the chart in class meetings. Send the chart home to parents. Discuss topics such as: "How do you want to be treated?"
- Read books about peaceful living. Constantly be on the lookout for books about peaceful living. For example, the Jane Addams Peace Association (Jane Addams won the Nobel Peace Prize in 1931 and was the first woman to do so) annually gives awards to children's books that promote peace and peaceful living. The 2010 Children's Book Award winner, *Nasreen's Secret School: A True Story from Afghanistan,* is a wonderful book about the importance of education.[‡] When selecting books of any kind to include in your classroom, library, and learning centers, make sure the topics are appropriate for your children and their individual cultures and that they represent a wide array of topics.
- Have children role-play peaceful living and act out and demonstrate appropriate classroom behaviors that support peaceful attitudes and behaviors.

STRATEGY 5 — Model Peaceful Living

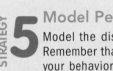

Model the dispositions you want children to learn. Remember that children are always watching you and your behaviors. Children learn very quickly how you react to certain situations. Therefore, you must practice dispositions of cooperation, friendliness, and respectfulness. If you want children to work cooperatively with each other, then they should see you working cooperatively with them, your colleagues, and with their parents.

---

*CDC. Child Maltreatment 2008. U.S. Department of Health and Human Services, 2008. Accessed November 4, 2010, from www.acf.hhs.gov/programs/cb/pubs/cm08/cm08.pdf.

[†]Early Childhood Learning and Knowledge Center, "Why Children's Dispositions Should Matter." Accessed November 4, 2010, from http://eclkc.ohs.acf.hhs.gov/hslc/ecdh/eecd/Domains%20of%20Child%20Development/Science/WhyChildrensDi.htm.

[‡]Jane Addams Peace Organization, "About the Children's Books." Accessed November 4, 2010, from www.janeaddamspeace.org/.

Photos by Hope Madden/Merrill.

- *Address real concerns.* To keep Hispanic parents actively engaged, make plans that respond to a real need or concern. Communicate clearly what parents will get out of each meeting and how the meeting will help them in their role as parents.
- *Participate in staff development focused on Hispanic culture.* Understand the key features of Hispanic culture and its impact on students' behavior and learning styles.

Everyone has the obligation to learn as much about children, their culture, and their backgrounds as possible.

- *Facilitate community connections.* As we have said, early childhood is a family affair and many Hispanic families may benefit from family literacy programs, vocational training, ESL programs, improved medical and dental services, and other community-based social services. Your school or early childhood program can serve as a resource and referral agency to support the overall strength and stability of the families.

Keep in mind that while the above suggestions support Hispanic parent and family involvement, you can apply similar processes to involve parents of all cultures.

Teaching English Language Learners

Most people assume that children who do not speak English when they enter school will learn English in the schools. Some people interpret this to mean that a child's native language (often referred to as the *home language*)—whether Spanish, French, Italian, Chinese, Tagalog, or any of the other languages, will naturally be suppressed. Title III—the English Language Acquisition, Language Enhancement, and Academic Achievement Act—of 2002 under NCLB neither prohibits nor promotes bilingual instruction.[44]

One of the greatest reasons for interest in teaching ELLs is the sheer number of students who speak a language other than English. Districts across the nation serve over 5 million ELLs. Spanish is the native language spoken by the largest number of ELL students.[45] However, there are districts that serve other predominant native languages. This suggests that some languages are concentrated within particular districts more than others. The National Clearinghouse for English Learning Acquisition indicates that in Texas, Asian languages are the next most frequently spoken language.[46]

Programs for Students with Limited English Proficiency

Early childhood teachers and schools have a range of programs and instructional responses to meet the needs of English language learners. These include:

Two-Way Bilingual: About half of students are native English speakers; the other half are English language learners from the same language group. Instruction is in both languages. The goal is to develop strong skills and proficiency in both languages.

Maintenance Bilingual: Most students are English language learners and are from the same language background. They receive significant amounts of instruction in their native language. The goal is to be academically proficient in both languages.

Transitional: In this program there is a rapid shift toward using English only. Students are transitioned into English-speaking classrooms with their peers as soon as possible. The goal is to learn English without delaying other academic core content.

Heritage Language Program: This program targets non-English-speakers with weak literacy skills in their home language. In this program content is taught in both languages and the goal is to learn literacy in two languages.

English as a Second Language (ESL): Students receive specified periods of instruction aimed at the development of English language skills, with a primary focus on grammar, vocabulary, and communication rather than academic content areas. Academic content is addressed through mainstream instruction, where no special assistance is provided. The goal of the program is to learn the English language fluently.

Structured English Immersion: Students are limited English proficient, usually from different language backgrounds. Instruction is in English, with an adjustment made to the level of English so that subject matter is more easily understood. Typically, there is no native language support.

Pull-Out English: Students leave the mainstream classroom part of the day to receive ESL instruction that focuses on grammar, vocabulary, and communication skills. No academic content is discussed.

Push-In ESL: Students are served in a mainstream classroom and receive instruction in English with some native support if needed. The ESL teacher is used to provide clarification, translation, and ESL strategies to help the child learn.[47]

Accommodating Diverse Learners

As I have discussed before, there is a risk that children who are English language learners can be disproportionately placed in special education programs and classes. This often occurs because of a child's race, ethnicity, gender, language proficiency, and/or family income. As a result, students may not receive services, or they may receive services that do not meet their needs because they are misclassified or inappropriately labeled. In that event, a child's placement in special education classes can actually become a form of discrimination. As a teacher of the next generation, you will want to ensure that each child receives the best education and the right kind of services and accommodation so that they can be successful.

Meet Rolo and Anh. They are both English Language Learners. Both are bright, friendly, and respectful second graders. But in the classroom, they both are having difficulties learning. Rolo works hard, but he just can't seem to get the knack for reading. Anh's teacher has to frequently get her attention because she stares off into space. Both Rolo and Anh struggle to recall information they have already learned. As they fall farther and farther behind their English-speaking classmates, Rolo and Ahn get more frustrated and more downhearted.

It is often very difficult to determine if a child's issues are language-acquisition related or learning disability related because many indicators of learning disabilities are also indicators of the language learning process. For example, lack of attention, difficulty interpreting verbal messages, difficulty retrieving stored information, and difficulty sequencing and organizing information are hallmarks of learning disabilities and also of problems in language acquisition.[48] For this reason, Rolo and Anh have very similar classroom behaviors and both have been referred for special education services. But do they both have learning disabilities? Are their classroom problems actually language learning issues?

To determine if special education services are the right accommodation for both Rolo and Ahn, remember the acronym STOP and carefully consider the following before you decide to refer Rolo and Anh, or any other ELL child, to special education or special language attention support:

Sustain a classroom climate that supports the wide range of individual and family differences described in this chapter. Providing a wide range of instructional activities and individualizing attention and instruction may be exactly what each child needs to succeed.

Try reasonable accommodations and modifications within your classroom that can improve the academic, social, and emotional skills of students and make special education unnecessary. Response to intervention (RTI), a data-based process and a diagnostic tool, is a method of academic intervention designed to provide early, effective assistance to children who are having difficulty learning.

Organize a pre-referral team within your school or utilize one in existence. This may be called the Child Study Team, Student Intervention Team, Teacher Support Team, or Student Success Team. Regardless of its name, the purpose of the team is to identify, implement, evaluate, and document strategies in the general classroom prior to referral to special education.

Proficiency in English should be evaluated and not just assumed. Students who have been identified as Limited English Proficient should be evaluated and partake in the pre-referral process in their native language prior to referral to special education.

Activities for Professional Development

Ethical Dilemma

"Should I protest?"

Third grade teacher Denise Garza loves teaching in Upper Falls School District, which is 65% Hispanic. Many of her children are immigrant children and she suspects that some come from illegal immigrant families. Recently, Denise's state passed a law that authorizes state police to arrest anyone who they reasonably suspect is an illegal immigrant. Many of the administrators and teachers at her school have publicly voiced their support of the law. Denise is fearful for many of her families and children. Denise opposes the law so much that she is prepared to join a protest march next week at the state capital. "I am afraid the law encourages racial profiling and may lead to deportation and separation of children from their families." However, Denise is fearful that if her principal and other school administrators find out about her opposition to the law and her planned participation in the protest she may be viewed as a radical and trouble maker. When Denise shares her feelings with her best friend and colleague, Mia, she advises Denise to "Keep your mouth shut! Don't make waves! You've got too much to lose!"

What should Denise do? Should she keep her mouth shut? Or should she publicly state her opinions and take part in the planned protest? What would you advise Denise to do?

Activities to Apply What You Learned

1. Think about ways that you can help your students be more aware of the various cultures in the classroom. Go online and find ways teachers of the year foster cultural awareness. Share what you learned by posting the link on Facebook.
2. Stories and literacy play an important role in transmitting to children information about themselves and what to expect in life.
   a. Review the multicultural books suggested in this chapter. Provide several suggestions for how you would use them in your classroom.
   b. Identify five children's books that you think would be good to use with children, and indicate why you think

so. Post your suggestions online and ask your colleagues for feedback. Also, post your suggestions for how to use the books suggested in this chapter on a discussion board.
3. Review and reflect on the types of programs for ELLs discussed in this chapter. Create a chart with the similarities and differences of each program. Post this chart on a bulletin board for your peers to review. Ask for their comments.
4. How can you use the acronym STOP (discussed in the chapter) to help accommodate your diverse learners? What other methods can you think of that will ensure that young children from diverse backgrounds are not disproportionately placed in special education programs and classes? Start an online blog to see what others around the world think.

Linking to Learning

Colorín Colorado
www.colorincolorado.org/
A free web-based service that provides information, activities and advice for educators and Spanish-speaking families of English language learners (ELLs).

National Association for Bilingual Education
www.nabe.org/
The only national professional organization devoted to representing bilingual learners and bilingual education professionals.

National Association for Multicultural Education (NAME)
www.nameorg.org/
Brings together individuals and groups with interests in multicultural education from all levels and disciples of education. Has six points of consensus regarding multicultural education that are central to NAME's philosophy and serve as NAME's goals.

National Clearinghouse for English Language Acquisition and Language Instruction Educational Programs
www.ncela.gwu.edu/
Funded by the U.S. Department of Education to collect, analyze, and disseminate information relating to the effective education of linguistically and culturally diverse learners in the United States.

Go to Topic 10 (Cultural & Linguistic Diversity) in the MyEducationLab (www.myeducationlab.com) for your course, where you can:

• Find learning outcomes for Cultural & Linguistic Diversity along with the national standards that connect to these outcomes.

- Complete Assignments and Activities that can help you more deeply understand the chapter content.
- Apply and practice your understanding of the core teaching skills identified in the chapter with the Building Teaching Skills and Dispositions learning units.
- Access video clips of CCSSO National Teachers of the Year award winners responding to the question, "Why Do I Teach?" in the Teacher Talk section.

- Hear viewpoints of experts in the field in Professional Perspectives.
- Check your comprehension on the content covered in the chapter by going to the Study Plan in the Book Resources for your text. Here you will be able to take a chapter quiz, receive feedback on your answers, and then access Review, Practice, and Enrichment activities to enhance your understanding of chapter content.

CHILDREN WITH DIVERSE NEEDS
Appropriate Education for All

naeyc standards

Standard 1: Promoting Child Development and Learning

I use my understanding of young children's characteristics and needs, and of multiple interacting influences on children's development and learning, to create environments that are healthy, respectful, supportive, and challenging for all children.[1]

Standard 2: Building Family and Community Relationships

I know about, understand, and value the importance and complex characteristics of children's families and communities. I use this understanding to create respectful, reciprocal relationships that support and empower families, and to involve all families in their children's development and learning.[2]

Standard 4: Using Developmentally Effective Approaches to Connect with Children and Families

I understand and use positive relationships and supportive interactions as the foundation for my work with young children and families. I know, understand, and use a wide array of developmentally appropriate approaches, instructional strategies, and tools to connect with children and families and positively influence each child's developmental learning.[3]

Children with special needs are in every program, school, and classroom in the United States. As an early childhood professional, you will teach students who have a variety of special needs. These children may come from low-income families, various racial and ethnic groups, and may have exceptional abilities or disabilities. In fact, some students may have more than one exceptionality; they may be **twice exceptional**. For example, students may be gifted and also have a learning disability.

Students with special needs are often discriminated against because of their disability, socioeconomic background, language, ethnicity, or gender. You will be challenged to provide for *all* your students an education that is appropriate for their physical, intellectual, social, and emotional abilities and to help them achieve their best. To meet the challenge, you should learn as much as you can about the special needs of children and collaborate with other professionals to identify and develop teaching strategies, programs, and curricula for them. Most of all, you need to be a strong advocate for meeting each child's individual needs.

twice exceptional
Students with dual exceptionalities.

Children with Disabilities

Children with special needs and their families absolutely must have the education and services that will help them realize their potential. You will be a part of the process of seeing that they receive such services. Unfortunately, quite often children with disabilities are not provided appropriate services and fail to reach their full potential. Figure 16.1 shows various statistics about disabilities that you may find troubling. This is one reason for laws to help ensure that children have special education and related services and that schools and teachers have high expectations for them. As we will discuss, the federal government has passed many laws protecting and promoting the rights and needs of children with disabilities. One of the most important of these federal laws is the Individuals with Disabilities Education Improvement Act of 2004 (IDEA).

As with many special areas, the field of special education has a unique vocabulary and terminology. The glossary in Figure 16.2 helps you understand these terms as you read the chapter and as you work with children and families. As the fields of early childhood and special education continue to slowly integrate and blend, early childhood educators must learn more about the field of early childhood special education and the terminology associated with it.

Individuals with Disabilities Education Act (IDEA)
A federal act providing a free and appropriate public education to youth between ages three and twenty-one with disabilities.

children with disabilities
IDEA defines children with disabilities as those children with mental retardation, hearing impairments (including deafness), speech or language impairments, visual impairments (including blindness), serious emotional disturbance, orthopedic impairments, autism, developmental delays, traumatic brain injury, other health impairments, or specific learning disabilities, and who, by reason thereof, need special education and related services.

Individuals with Disabilities Education Act (IDEA)

The purpose of the **Individuals with Disabilities Education Act (IDEA)** is to ensure that all children with disabilities have available to them

> a free appropriate public education which emphasizes special education and related services designed to meet their unique needs, to assure that the rights of the disabled children and their parents or guardians are protected, to assist states and localities to provide for the education of all disabled children, and to assess and assure the effectiveness of efforts to educate disabled children.[4]

IDEA defines **children with disabilities** as those children with mental retardation, hearing impairments (including deafness); speech or language impairments; visual impairments (including blindness); serious emotional disturbance; orthopedic impairments; autism; developmental delays;

> " I'm asking all of us to redouble our efforts and redouble our supports. High expectations must be the norm, not the exception. "
>
> Secretary of Education Arne Duncan

FIGURE 16.1 **Children with Disabilities: Facts, Figures, and Questions**

Early intervention is mandated in IDEA, Part C, for infants and toddlers with disabilities who are under the age of three. Disabilities include diagnosed developmental delays and physical or mental conditions that have a high probability of resulting in developmental delay, as well as other at-risk conditions at the state's discretion.

Source: U.S. Department of Education, Office of Special Education and Rehabilitative Services, Office of Special Education Programs, *28th Annual Report to Congress on the Implementation of the Individuals with Disabilities Education Act, 2006*, vol. 1, Washington, D.C., 2009.

58 percent of children receiving early intervention transitioned to kindergarten "very easily"	60 percent of children who received early intervention services communicated their needs well	7.9 percent of children receiving special education services have emotional disturbances	African American students are 2.8 times more likely to receive special education and related services for mental retardation than all other racial/ethnic groups combined and 2.2 times more likely for emotional disturbance
American Indian/Alaskan Natives (ages 6–21) account for 13.7 percent of students receiving special education services for autism and developmental delays	Hispanic preschoolers represent 20 percent of the general population but are less likely to be served under Part B of IDEA than children of all other racial/ethnic groups combined	44 percent of American Indian/Alaska Native children with disabilities drop out of high school, nearly double the dropout rate of Caucasians with disabilities	African American students (ages 6–21) represent only 14.8 percent of the general population but comprise 44.8 percent of students with specific learning disabilities

Questions
- Are Hispanics with disabilities overrepresented or underrepresented in these data? Why might this occur?
- Why do you think African American students are overrepresented in the population of students with disabilities? What other statistic helps explain this?
- What is the primary developmental delay with children in early intervention?
- Why is early intervention important for success in school?

traumatic brain injury; other health impairments; or specific learning disabilities and who, by reason thereof, need special education and related services.[5]

About 10 to 12 percent of the nation's students have some type of disability.[6] Table 16.1 lists the number of persons from ages three to twenty-one with disabilities in the various categories covered under IDEA. IDEA applies to infants and toddlers (ages zero to three) and students (age three through twenty-one). Infants and toddlers have needs unlike those of older children. IDEA consists of four parts, but the parts of most interest to you are Part B and Part C, which are age specific.

IDEA, Part B. Part B of IDEA is the foundation upon which all special education and related services rests.[7] Part B benefits students who are ages three through twenty-one. Part B details the general purposes of IDEA and how IDEA defines important terms; state and local education agency eligibility for funding; evaluation; procedural safeguards designed to protect children and their families' rights; conflict resolution; enforcement and use of funds; and grants for preschool programs. Most important to you, however, Part B describes free and appropriate public education, the least restrictive environment, and the individual education programs.[8]

IDEA, Part C. Part C is designed to provide early intervention to benefit any child under age three who needs services because of developmental delays. However, Part C gives states discretion whether to serve infants and toddlers in progams. Part C also gives each

FIGURE 16.2

Glossary

Children with disabilities: The expression that replaces former terms such as *handicapped.* To avoid labeling children, do not use the phrase *disabled children.*

Coteaching: The process by which a regular classroom professional and a special educator or a person trained in exceptional student education team-teach a group of regular and mainstreamed children in the same classroom.

Differentiated instruction: An approach to teaching and learning for students of differing abilities in the same class. The intent of differentiating instruction is to maximize each student's growth and individual success, meet each student where he or she is, and assist the child in the learning process.

Disability: A physical or mental impairment that substantially limits one or more major life activities.

Early intervention: Providing services to children and families as early in the child's life as possible in order to prevent or help with one or more special needs.

Embedded instruction: Instruction that is included as an integral part of normal classroom routines, often using naturalistic teaching strategies.

Exceptional student education: Replaces the term *special education;* refers to the education of children with special needs.

Integration: A generic term that refers to educating children with disabilities along with typically developing children. Such education can occur in mainstream, reverse mainstream, and full-inclusion programs.

Least restrictive environment (LRE): Students who have disabilities must, to the maximum extent appropriate, be educated with students who do not have disabilities, with access to the same curriculum and classroom activities.

Mainstreaming: The social and educational integration of children with special needs into the general instructional process, usually a regular classroom program.

Normalized setting: A place that is normal, or best, for the child.

Reverse mainstreaming: The process by which typically developing children are placed in programs for children with disabilities, who are in the majority.

---

state the option of serving at-risk toddlers. These are children who would be at risk of experiencing a substantial developmental delay if they did not receive early intervention services.[9]

The Seven Principles of IDEA.   IDEA has established seven basic principles to follow as you provide education and other services to children with special needs:

1. *Zero reject*: IDEA calls for educating all children and excluding none from an education. Before IDEA many children were excluded from educational programs or were denied an education.

2. *Nondiscriminatory evaluation*: A fair evaluation is required to determine whether a student has a disability and, if so, what the student's education should consist of.

3. *Multidisciplinary assessment*: In this team approach, a group of people use various methods of evaluation to ensure that a child's needs and program are not determined by one test or one person.

TABLE 16.1 Individuals Age Three to Twenty-One Served by IDEA

Type of Disability	Number Served
Specific learning disabilities	2,633,740
Speech or language impairments	1,482,540
Mental retardation	510,710
Emotional disturbance	444,663
Multiple disabilities	139,667
Hearing impairments	79,930
Orthopedic impairments	67,999
Other health impairments	647,745
Visual impairments	29,675
Autism	297,739
Deafness/blindness	1,578
Traumatic brain injury	24,767
Developmental delay	358,450
Total	6,718,203

Source: U.S. Department of Education, Office of Special Education Programs, Data Analysis System (DANS), OMB #1820-0043: "Children with Disabilities Receiving Special Education Under Part B of the Individuals with Disabilities Education Act," 1998–2007. Data updated as of July 15, 2008; accessed May 21, 2010.

free and appropriate public education (FAPE) Education suited to children's age, maturity, condition of disability, past achievements, and parental expectations.

least restrictive environment (LRE) Placement that meets the needs of students who are disabled in as regular a setting as possible.

4. *Appropriate education*: IDEA provides a **free and appropriate public education (FAPE)** for all students between the ages of three and twenty-one. *Appropriate* means that children must receive an education suited to their age, maturity, condition of disability, past achievements, and parental expectations.

5. *Least restrictive placement/environment*: Students with disabilities must, to the maximum extent appropriate for each one, be educated with students who do not have disabilities. The **least restrictive environment (LRE)** is not necessarily the regular classroom.

6. *Procedural due process*: IDEA provides schools and parents with ways to resolve their differences by mediation or by having hearings before impartial hearing officers or judges.

7. *Parent and student participation*: IDEA specifies a process of shared decision making whereby educators, parents, and students collaborate in deciding the student's educational plan.

Referral, Assessment, and Placement.   Under IDEA educators must follow certain procedures in developing a special plan for each child. Referral of the student for exceptional student services can be made by anyone, including a teacher, parent, doctor, or other professional. The referral is usually followed by a comprehensive individual assessment to determine whether the child possesses a disability and is eligible for services. In order for testing to occur, parents or guardians must give their consent.

If a child is eligible for exceptional student services, the child study team meets to develop an individualized education program (IEP) for the child (see Figure 16.3). Essentially, the IEP is a contract or agreement that specifies the school's plan for providing the child with FAPE and services. The child study team includes a parent or parent representative, the student when appropriate, a special education teacher, a regular education teacher, a representative of the school district, and a principal, assistant principal, or coordinator of exceptional student services. The IEP must be reviewed annually and revised as appropriate. The child study team is also responsible for dismissing students

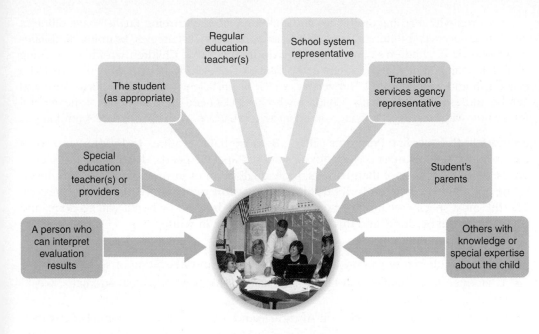

FIGURE 16.3 IEP Team

An IEP team member can fill more than one of the team positions if properly qualified and designated. For example, the school system representative may also be the person who can interpret the child's evaluation results.

Source: US Department of Education, Building the Legacy: IDEA 2004, Statute TITLE I/B/614/d/1/B, accessed June 1, 2010, from http://idea.ed.gov/explore/view/p/%2Croot%2Cstatute%2CI%2CB%2C614%2Cd%2C1%2CB%2C. Photo by Lori Whitley/Merrill.

from exceptional student education services when they are able to function in the regular classroom without the services.

English Language Learners and Referral, Assessment, and Placement. The question of referral, assessment, and placement has always been a tricky one when it comes to children who are English language learners (ELLs). Data show that there is an overrepresentation of minorities in special education. The ELL population is both overrepresented and underrepresented in special education. Children who are ELLs are frequently inappropriately referred for special education services based on tests that actually measure their language acquisition rather than their learning abilities. Also recall from Figure 16.1 that Hispanic children constitute 20 percent of the general population but receive special education services less than all other racial and ethnic groups combined.[10] Therefore, ELLs often have the problem of actually having a learning disability that goes undiagnosed and unaccommodated based on the belief that language is the issue. Additionally, children who are ELLs may in fact be referred to special education but still not receive appropriate or adequate services because of a lack of bilingual special education teachers.[11]

Indicators of Learning Disabilities. Distinguishing between incomplete second-language acquisition and a learning disability is a difficult but vitally important task. Many indicators of learning disabilities are also indicators of the language learning process. For example, lack of attention, difficulty interpreting verbal messages, difficulty retrieving stored information, and difficulty sequencing and organizing information are hallmarks of both learning disabilities and language acquisition. As a result, many argue that the only way a language disability can reliably be distinguished from second-language acquisition is to do a complete assessment in both languages. If problems are apparent only in the second language, it is probably a language acquisition issue; if they are present in both languages, it is a learning disability. However, this approach assumes that ELLs have acquired a solid foundation of language skills in their native language. What about the students who don't have a learning disability but were disadvantaged in their native language and now are expected to perform in a second language?[12] The implications are challenging because these children are at such a great risk for failure.

Children with learning disabilities and children who are learning English have different needs that necessitate different interventions and educational strategies. Learning disabilities occur outside of children's control and they do not go away. Children who have learning disabilities can and need to be taught compensatory strategies to help them persevere, to be successful and well-educated. Conversely, a lack of proficiency in English has a cause and can be addressed educationally. Children who are ELLs need large amounts of meaningful interaction with academic language, in interactive situations, with appropriate scaffolding.[13]

Individualized Education Programs (IEPs). Because IDEA requires **individualization of instruction**, schools must provide for all students' specific needs, disabilities, and preferences, as well as those of their parents. Individualization of instruction also means developing and implementing an **individualized education program (IEP)** for each student. The IEP must specify what will be done for the child, how and when it will be done, and by whom it will be done, and this information must be in writing.

IEPs have several purposes. They:

- Protect children and parents by ensuring planning and delivering of services.
- Guarantee that children will have plans tailored to their individual strengths, weaknesses, and learning styles.
- Help professionals and other instructional and administrative personnel focus their teaching and resources on children's specific needs, promoting the best use of everyone's time, efforts, and talents.
- Help ensure that children with disabilities receive a range of services from other agencies if needed, and must specify how a child's total needs will be met.
- Clarify and refine decisions about what is best for children, where they should be placed, and how they should be taught and helped.
- Ensure that children will not be categorized or labeled without discussion of their unique needs.
- Require review on at least an annual basis, encouraging professionals to consider how and what children have learned, determine whether what was prescribed was effective, and prescribe new or modified strategies.

In developing the IEP, a person trained in diagnosing disabling conditions, such as a school psychologist, must be involved, as well as a classroom professional, the parent, and, when appropriate, the child. Because so many classrooms of today are inclusive, more than likely you will have children with disabilities in your classroom. This means you will participate in the development of an IEP.

Individualized Family Service Plans. The process of helping children ages zero to three with disabilities begins with referral and assessment and results in the development of an **individualized family service plan (IFSP)**, which is designed to help families reach the goals they have for themselves and their children. IDEA Part C provides funds for infants and toddlers to receive early intervention services through the IFSP, which includes the following:

- Multidisciplinary assessment developed by a multidisciplinary team and the parents.
- Planned services to meet developmental needs, including, as necessary, special education, speech and language pathology and audiology, occupational therapy, physical therapy, psychological services, parent and family training and counseling services, transition services, medical diagnostic services, and health services.
- Supporting information—a statement of the child's present levels of development; a statement of the family's strengths and needs in regard to enhancing the child's development; a statement of major expected outcomes for the child and family; the criteria, procedures, and timelines for determining progress; the specific early intervention services necessary to meet the unique needs of the child and family; the projected

individualization of instruction Providing for students' specific needs, disabilities, and preferences.

Individualized education program (IEP) A plan for meeting an exceptional learner's educational needs, specifying goals, objectives, services, and procedures for evaluating progress.

individualized family service plan (IFSP) A plan designed to help families reach their goals for themselves and their children, with varied support services.

dates for initiation of services; the name of the case manager; and transition procedures from the early intervention program into a preschool program.

An IFSP requires an integrated, team approach to intervention. A **transdisciplinary team model** is one method of integrating information and skills across professional disciplines. In this model all team members (including the family) teach, learn, and work together to accomplish a mutually agreed-on set of intervention outcomes. With a transdisciplinary model, one or a few people are primary implementers of the program; other team members provide ongoing direct or indirect services. For example, an occupational therapist might observe a toddler during meals and then recommend to the parent how to physically assist the child.

Benefits of Family-Centered Services.   Services that can be provided through the IFSP include, but are not limited to, assistive technology devices and services; audiology; family training; counseling; home visits; health services; medical services for diagnosis or evaluation; nursing services; nutrition services; occupational therapy; phsyical therapy; psychological services; service coordination; social work services; special instruction; speech-language pathology; transportation and related costs; and vision services. Family-centered services are an important component of early childhood programming now, and they will become even more important. Programs that embrace and utilize family-centered services achieve some important improvements in child developmental and social adjustment outcomes; decrease parental stress as a result of accessing needed services for their children and themselves; and recognize the family's role as decision maker and partner in the early intervention process.

Inclusion.   IDEA requires that schools meet the needs of students with disabilities as much as possible in the general education classroom. Teachers use a variety of adaptations to ensure that all students, regardless of abilities, have equal access to a quality education. **Adaptive education** is aimed at providing learning experiences that help each student achieve desired educational goals. Education is adaptive when schools modify learning environments to respond effectively to student differences and to enhance an individual's ability to succeed in such environments. Gayle Solis Zavala, the 2009 National Special Education Teacher of the Year, is constantly finding ways to improve her students' receptive and expressive language through multisensory activities. To appeal to both children with physical and cognitive disabilities and their nondisabled peers, she draws on board games, gardens, digital cameras, and puppetry. Her students have performed in a local arts festival, which helps them embrace different cultures and languages. Gayle has also developed school-wide projects to teach her students entrepreneurship, respect, and other important life skills; these projects have included a pickle sale and an indoor plant care service.[14] You can read more about Gayle in the Voice from the Field, "Special Children Need Extra-Special Touch" on pages 436–437.

The Full Inclusion Debate.   Inclusion supports the right of all students to participate in natural environments. **Full inclusion** means that students with disabilities receive the services and support appropriate to their individual needs entirely in their natural environments such as general classrooms, playgrounds, family care centers, and child care centers. **Partial inclusion** means that students receive part of their instruction in the general classroom and the other part in pull-out classrooms, or resource rooms, where they work individually or in small groups with special education teachers.

Full inclusion receives a lot of attention and is the subject of great national debate for several reasons:

- Court decisions and state and federal laws mandate, support, and encourage full inclusion; many of them relate to basic civil rights. For example, in the 1992 case *Oberti v. Board of Education of the Borough of Clementon School District*, the judge ruled that

transdisciplinary team model Professionals from various disciplines working together to integrate instructional strategies and therapy and to evaluate the effectiveness of their individual roles.

adaptive education Modifications in any classroom, program, environment, or curriculum that help students achieve desired educational goals.

full inclusion An approach whereby students with disabilities receive all instruction and support services in a general classroom.

partial inclusion An approach whereby students with disabilities receive some instruction in a general classroom and some in a specialized setting.

Voice from the Field

Special Children Need Extra-Special Touch

Little faces pressed against the school bus window, kindergarten students arrive on their first day of school. After warm welcomes from their teacher, the next task of the day is lining up. Lining up? Where? What for? Why can't I be the first one? Do I have to carry this backpack all by myself?

The seasoned teacher knows that she must count heads at least three times before she reaches the cafeteria door for breakfast and politely bids farewell to parents, grandparents, or big brothers or sisters who may be lingering close by the class.

A Warm Welcome

I want to emphasize the importance of the warm welcome each day. A handshake or friendly pat on the back is a personal gesture that lets the students know they are important and you are glad to see them.

Support Independence

Call this first day of school "Independence Day." Students with disabilities just as students without disabilities find themselves facing this day with many of the same feelings and anxieties. Students with disabilities, however, especially students with English as a second language, may oftentimes have little or no way to communicate their needs or feelings. They may walk or dash away or squat down refusing to move in fear of what is waiting ahead.

Entering the cafeteria is like entering another world altogether, where once again they will be asked to wait in a line, but this time there are choices to make, a cashier to greet, a table that stretches for miles to sit at, and food wrapped in plastic bags and cartons to figure out how to open.

The waiting in line part is something even adults will have to learn to do the rest of our lives, and hopefully without bothering the person in front of us. The choices for breakfast, and later for lunch, are eventually communicated by the students in a way that begins to give them independence and a communicative voice (i.e., pointing, verbalizing part or all of a word, sign language, or picture communication board). The same will be expected of the student as he or she encounters the cashier or other friendly staff. Cafeteria staff give students numbers to use whenever they get breakfast or lunch. Students carry their number with them to key in on what looks like a debit card machine. The seasoned teacher will consult with the cafeteria staff ahead of time to gain support and their patience in allowing the students to use this important functional and practical opportunity to learn numbers and add another independent skill. For those students in which cognitive and/or physical limitation is a challenge, a communication board or simple one-message voice output device could be used to convey any needed communicative message.

Scaffold

Scaffolding as a teaching strategy is needed when orienting and teaching students with disabilities during the early childhood years. As students are learning to sign, verbalize, and select what they want to say on their picture board, the teacher or staff may need to model or provide assistance to help the student learn a more independent response. Continuing on

---

Rafael, an eight-year-old child with Down syndrome, should not have to earn his way into an integrated classroom but had a right to be there from the beginning.

- Some teachers feel they do not have the training or support necessary to provide for the disabilities of children in full-inclusion classrooms. These teachers believe they cannot provide for children with disabilities even with the assistance of aides and special support services.
- Some parents of children with disabilities are dissatisfied with separate programs, which they view as a form of segregation. They want their children to have the academic and social benefits of attending general education classrooms.

Early childhood educators are very much involved in making inclusion work. In order for inclusion to be a reality in your classroom, there are a number of things of which you should be aware. There are both pros and cons associated with inclusive classrooms.

The Pros of Teaching in an Inclusive Classroom. These are just some of the positive aspects associated with an inclusive classroom:

- Provides a full range of educational services in the most natural and appropriate setting for children with disabilities.

with the cafeteria scenario, the adult's first reaction may be to open up the student's juice carton or wipe their soiled mouth or clothing. But if the students are to learn to take care of themselves, they need to repeatedly practice these self-help skills. The reward is evident as the students finally open their own carton and wave their hands in the air with delight and look to their teacher for encouragement.

Encourage

Speaking of encouragement, you will find that this is one of the biggest teaching tools in managing behavior.

"I like the way Jesús is staying in line. Great job, Jesús!"

"I like the way Ashley is keeping her hand to herself (gesturing with folded arms or hands in pocket)."

"Look how nicely Antwan said 'Thank you' to Ms. Vargas. Nice words, Antwan."

The students are always watching to see what gets teachers' and staffs' attentions. It is always more beneficial to voice more positive praise, especially with the most challenging students.

Develop a Social Contract

Once the first day of school gets going, establishing a written social contract (pictures can be added to cue understanding) between the students and the teaching staff is essential. Even if students are nonverbal or have limited communication skills, teachers can model appropriate choices on positive social interaction, use picture prompts, or capture the targeted behavior when

it happens to add to the social contract. Allowing students to participate in creating the social contract is another example of giving them independence and self advocacy. Some of the social contract behaviors could be:

- Listen quietly to one another
- Use nice words with each other
- Make eye contact
- Use humor (have fun) but don't be hurtful (make fun of one another)

A second contract is also an important opportunity to emphasize to paraprofessionals, volunteers, or other classroom personnel how the climate of the classroom should be. Everyone signs the contract and we review it at least once a day to maintain its importance.

There will be times, of course, when the class may get loud or students are not where they are supposed to be in the room. For this reason it is helpful to establish a gesture and/or chant to get the group back together or back on focus. This can be a hand held up by the teacher which signals quiet and/or line up (i.e., if on the playground), a series of claps, which the students can echo, or a chant (i.e., "1-2-3, All eyes on Mrs. Z" chanted by teacher; "4-5-6, Our eyes are fixed" chanted by students.)

Establishing independence, opportunities to communicate, and a safe, nurturing climate is a recipe for success with all children.

....

Source: Contributed by Gayle Solis Zavala, 2009 CEC Teacher of the Year.

- Provides ongoing opportunities for socialization among regularly developing children and children with disabilities; allows all children to learn new social skills; and provides opportunities for all children to form meaningful friendships with a wide range of peers.
- Enables all children to learn about and value diversity and to develop moral and ethical principles.

The Cons of Teaching in an Inclusive Classroom. Here are some of the negative aspects associated with full inclusion:

- The regular classroom may need to be redesigned to accommodate children with special needs, and classroom resources and size may be inadequate to accommodate all children.
- Children may receive less one-on-one attention.
- Inclusion increases responsibilities, planning time, and workload for teachers, and teachers may need specialized training to teach children with disabilities.
- Regular education teachers may be resistant to ideas and practices associated with inclusive education.

Voice from the Field

How to Teach in an Inclusive Classroom

Effective teaching in inclusive classrooms requires many competencies. Listed here are important guidelines to help you understand what you will need to know and do to become a competent and compassionate teacher in an inclusive classroom.

GUIDELINE 1 Understand Students and Their Needs

- Learn the characteristics of students with special needs
- Learn about legislation affecting students with special needs
- Become comfortable with students with special needs
- Learn about and use assistive and educational technologies

GUIDELINE 2 Develop Skill in Instructional Techniques

- Modify instruction for students with special needs
- Use a variety of instructional styles and media and increase the range of learning behaviors

- Individualize instruction and integrate the curriculum
- Provide instruction for students of all ability levels
- Modify assessment techniques for students with special needs

GUIDELINE 3 Manage the Classroom Environment

- Physically adapt the learning environment to accommodate students with special needs
- Foster social acceptance of students with special needs
- Provide inclusion in varied student groupings
- Use peer tutoring
- Guide and manage the behavior of all students
- Motivate all students

GUIDELINE 4 Collaborate with Other Professionals and Parents

- Work closely with special educators and other specialists
- Work with and involve parents
- Participate in planning and implementing IEPs

Clearly, teaching in an inclusive classroom presents many challenges. The Voice from the Field, "How to Teach in an Inclusive Classroom," is a Competency Builder that should help you successfully meet these challenges.

The Need for a Continuum of Services. The policy of the Council for Exceptional Children (CEC), a professional organization of special educators, is as follows:

> CEC believes that a continuum of services must be available for all children, youth, and young adults. CEC also believes that the concept of inclusion is a meaningful goal to be pursued in our schools and communities.[15]

A *continuum of services* implies a full and graduated range of services available for all individuals, from the most restrictive placements to the least. For students with disabilities, a continuum of services would identify institutional placement as the most restrictive and a general education classroom as the least restrictive. Figure 16.4 shows this continuum of services.

There is considerable debate over whether such a continuum is an appropriate policy. Advocates of full inclusion say that the approach works against developing truly inclusive programs. Given the great amount of interest in inclusion, discussion regarding both its appropriateness and the best ways to implement it will likely continue for some time.

Consultation and Collaboration

consultation Seeking advice and information from colleagues.

collaboration Working jointly and cooperatively with other professionals, parents, and administrators.

As an early childhood professional, you will participate in **consultation**, seeking advice and information from colleagues. You will also engage in **collaboration**, working cooperatively with a range of special educators, other professionals, parents, and administrators to provide services to students with disabilities and students at risk. Some of those professionals include the following:

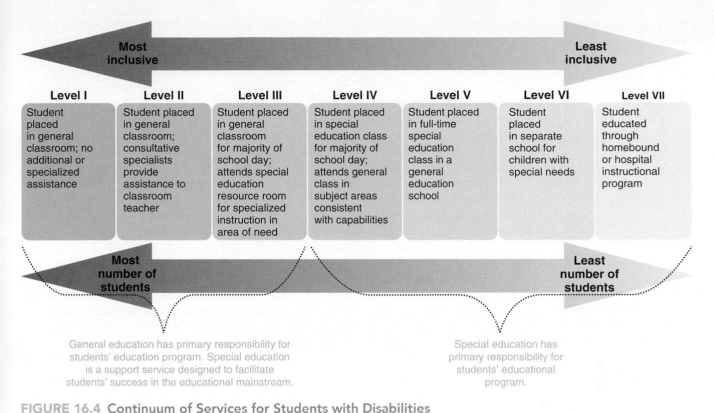

FIGURE 16.4 Continuum of Services for Students with Disabilities

Service options range from the most physically integrated, with the regular classroom teacher meeting most of a child's needs, to the least integrated, a residential setting providing a therapeutic environment.

Source: From Michael L. Hardman et al., *Human Exceptionality: School, Community, and Family*, 8th ed. (Boston: Allyn & Bacon, 2005). Copyright 2005 by Pearson Education. Reprinted by permission of the publisher.

- Diagnosticians, who are trained to test and analyze students' strengths and weaknesses
- Special educators, who are trained to instruct students with special needs
- **Itinerant teachers**, who travel from school to school, providing assistance and teaching students
- **Resource teachers**, who provide assistance with materials, planning, and teaching
- Physical therapists, who treat physical disabilities through nonmedical means
- Occupational therapists, who direct activities that develop muscular control and self-help skills
- Speech and language pathologists, who assess, diagnose, treat, and help prevent speech, language, cognitive communication, voice, swallowing, fluency, and other related disorders

itinerant teachers
Professionals who travel from school to school, providing assistance and teaching students.

resource teachers
Professionals who provide assistance with materials and planning for teachers of exceptional students.

Consultation with experienced teachers, experts in the field of special education, and administrators enables you to see your options more clearly, gain important knowledge and insight, and consider teaching and learning strategies you might not have thought of on your own. With collaboration you will be able to implement those strategies and new approaches with the help and support of others.

With Colleagues. Consulting and collaborating with colleagues, especially special education teachers, is an excellent and even necessary means of understanding students' needs and the best ways to meet those needs. Collaborating with your colleagues is an essential component of successful teaching and learning in an inclusive classroom. As a classroom teacher, you will be expected to provide information and ideas about content knowledge, curriculum objectives, curriculum sequence, and content evaluation. Special education teachers are expected to contribute information about disabilities, learning and motivation strategies that work with students with disabilities, and ideas about how to adapt curriculum to meet students' special needs.

Itinerant Special Educators.   Many school districts use the services of a special education itinerant teacher, who is a valuable resource to you, your students, and their parents. This traveling teacher provides information, assists you in making helpful modifications to the classroom environment, coaches you in some new instructional techniques, and in some cases works directly with the child(ren) for part of each week.

The itinerant teacher gives you and parents information about a child's disability, explains any jargon or medical terms that may be present in evaluation reports, and refers the parents to helpful resources, such as pertinent websites or parent support groups. In addition, the itinerant teacher talks with you about how the physical environment is working for a child with a disability. Is the room fully accessible, is the equipment appropriate, and does the child seem to find all areas of the room inviting? The itinerant teacher may also loan equipment to you and help you provide more visual support for the child, such as a picture-schedule or markings on the floor to indicate where children sit and line up.

embedded instruction
Instruction that is included as an integral part of normal classroom routines.

naturalistic teaching strategies Incorporating instruction into opportunities that occur naturally or routinely in the classroom.

School districts are required to provide specialized instruction to students with disabilities, but the itinerant teacher will look for opportunities for **embedded instruction** that can use **naturalistic teaching strategies**. In these cases, the instruction will blend right into normal classroom routines. For example, if the child has a social objective to greet classmates using their names, a natural opportunity might prompt this behavior with a greeting-song during arrival time or opening-circle time and again when classmates enter an area where the child is working during free-choice time.

In a collaborative teaching experience with an itinerant special education teacher, you can learn a lot and share together the joy of watching young children with special needs succeed in their very own neighborhood schools.[16]

Autism occurs on a spectrum; each child exhibits it uniquely. There is no cure for autism, but early intervention can help with symptoms tremendously and increase the quality of life for the child and their whole family.

With Parents.   The development of an IEP requires that you work closely with parents in developing learning and evaluation goals for students with disabilities. Also, some parents may want to spend time in your classroom to help you meet the needs of their children. All parents have information about their children's needs, growth, and development that will be helpful to you as you plan and teach.

With Paraprofessionals.   You may have one or more full- or part-time paraprofessionals in your classroom, depending on the number of students with disabilities and the nature of their disabilities. Classroom assistants can help you in providing multimodal instruction and assessing students' skills. For example, Megan Molina is a paraprofessional in Wendy Stark's blended classroom. When Wendy is busy handling Brian's meltdown or spending a few extra minutes on making observation assessments for Teneka, Megan keeps the other children on task and helps them complete their lesson. Other times, Megan takes Cho for a walk when she becomes over-stimulated so that she can regroup while Wendy continues teaching the rest of the class. Megan and Wendy spend a lot of time planning and preparing for class together.

With Administrators.   Administrators can help you with the legal, political, and procedural matters of teaching students with special needs in your classroom. Administrators can also help by providing more planning time and opportunities for special education and general education teachers to plan together and by employing a "floating" substitute to aid teachers and increase release time for teacher planning. In addition, in supporting coteaching partnerships, administrators can give you access to a network of other services, information, and resources.

As you read now about children with autism and attention deficient hyperactivity disorders, reflect on how you will consult and collaborate with colleagues and families to meet their needs.

Children with Autism Spectrum Disorders (ASD)

Autism is a complex developmental disability that appears during the first three years of life. It is the result of a neurological disorder that affects the normal functioning of the brain, impacting development in the areas of social interaction and communication skills. Children with autism typically show difficulties in verbal and nonverbal communication, social interactions, joint attention (sharing one's experience or event by following eye gaze, gesturing, or leading), and leisure or play activities. Autism affects each child differently and to varying degrees. Autism is currently diagnosed four times more often in boys than girls, though we do not know why.[17] Its prevalence is not affected by race, region, or socioeconomic status. Since autism was first diagnosed in the United States, the occurrence has climbed to 1 in 100 people across the country and autism diagnoses are increasing at the rate of 10 to 17 percent per year.[18] Autism is the fastest growing serious developmental disability in the United States.[19] More children will be diagnosed with autism in the coming years than children with AIDS, diabetes, and cancer combined. Spectrum delays (another term used to refer to autism and developmental delays) cost the nation more than $60 billion per year, a figure expected to reach $200–400 billion in the next decade,[20] but receives less than 5 percent of the research funding of many less prevalent childhood diseases.[21]

Children with autism typically demonstrate the following characteristics:

- Deficits in receptive and expressive communication skills
- Repetitive or "stereotyped" behaviors[22]
- Difficulty initiating and sustaining symbolic play and social interactions[23]
- Limited interests
- Trouble keeping up with conversations[24]

The cause of autism remains unknown. Dr. Christopher Walsh, chief of genetics at Children's Hospital Boston, remarks that "Almost every kid with autism has their own particular cause of it."[25] However, twin and family studies suggest an underlying genetic vulnerability to autism.[26] Researchers have identified several genes associated with autism and have found anomalies in multiple areas of the brain of people who have autism. Other studies found that people with autism have atypical levels of serotonin or other neurotransmitters in their brains. This suggests that autism results from the interference in typical brain development caused by glitches in the genes that organize brain growth and guide how neurons communicate with one another as the fetus develops in utero.[27] Still other research suggests that in infancy and toddlerhood brain synapses are pruned in such a way as to "turn on or off" the autism gene, indicating that autism is a synaptic disorder.[28] Still other researchers have found that there may be environmental triggers for autism spectrum disorders,[29] but contrary to popular belief, there is no scientific evidence of a relationship between vaccines and autism.[30] It is likely that the cause of spectrum disorders is likely due to a combination of all of these factors. Regardless of the cause, autism is a prevalent presence in American society and will continue to be.

Autism can be diagnosed as early as eighteen months of age, and the earlier children with autism receive intense and consistent intervention, the more likely they are to have positive experiences in the school, the home, and later, occupational realms.[31] There are

autism A developmental disability that typically appears during the first three years of life and is the result of a neurological disorder that affects the normal functioning of the brain, impacting development in the areas of social interaction and communication skills.

applied behavior analysis (ABA) ABA is based on the learning theory of Behaviorism, which states that all behavior is motivated by a purpose and is learned through systematic reinforcement.

play therapy The developmentally appropriate practice and model to incorporate social experiences and enjoyable interactions to enhance a child's pretend skills, joint attention, communication skills, and appropriate behavior.

a number of effective interventions for autism. One is **applied behavior analysis (ABA)**, the theory that behavior rewarded is more likely to be repeated than behavior ignored. To reinforce behavior, ABA therapists initiate a sequence of stimuli, responses, and rewards. For example, an ABA therapist who is working on joint attention with Leland, a child with ASD, will ask Leland to "show me" the red block (stimulus). If Leland points to the red block (response), the ABA therapist gives him an M&M (reward) or another appropriate reward such as a sticker. If Leland does not respond or points to a different colored block, the therapist ignores the behavior and repeats the stimulus.

Play therapy is another effective intervention for children on the autism spectrum. Play therapy uses developmentally appropriate practices and models to incorporate social experiences and enjoyable interactions to enhance a child's pretend skills, joint attention, communication skills, and appropriate behavior. Play therapy can take place individually between a therapist and one child, in a group with other children, or along with the parents. Unlike ABA, play therapy is generally child led.[32] For example, a play therapist working with Kate, who has autism, would use different toys to engage her. Over time, the play therapist would challenge Kate's behaviors and content of play by initiating different play scenarios. The play therapist reflects and comments on Kate's emotions and activities in order to elicit and reward language development, play skills, and relationship development so that Kate can feel understood and valued for who she is.

Music, Art, and Occupational Therapy. Music, art, and occupational therapies are also highly effective interventions for children with autism.[33] Music therapists or art therapists use their respective expressive mediums (musical instruments, singing, painting, clay, etc.) to provide children who have spectrum delays with different means of experiencing relationships, self-expression, and expanding various other skills. These therapies are unique in that they give children with spectrum delays an opportunity to develop skills that have social utility. As a result, children gain in peer interaction, self-esteem, and improve their everyday functioning. Physical and occupational therapists use a more body-centered approach to reach children with developmental delays. By swinging, receiving deep compressions to their body, climbing, and jumping, children's bodies are challenged and made more comfortable, thereby eliciting more language, social reciprocity, and joint attention. These types of therapies can also be done individually, in groups, or with parents to maximize the effects of therapy. For example, an occupational therapist might put Benjamin in a hammock swing and push him in it to stimulate his vestibular needs while engaging him in developmentally appropriate conversation.

Other methods of effective intervention include a highly supportive teaching environment; predictability and routine; family involvement; and working with young children in small teacher-to-child ratios, often one-to-one in the early stages. Later in the chapter we will describe how teachers can accommodate a child with autism disorder through the creation of a *social story*.

Children with Attention Deficit Hyperactivity Disorder

Attention Deficit Hyperactivity Disorder (ADHD) Difficulty with attention and self-control, which leads to problems with learning, social functioning, and behavior that occur in more than one situation and have been present for a significant length of time.

Attention Deficit Hyperactivity Disorder (ADHD) is a neurobehavioral disorder involving the brain that affects emotions, behaviors, and learning. Children with ADHD generally suffer with difficulties in three specific areas: attention, impulse control, and hyperactivity.[34] Research strongly suggests that ADHD is genetic; studies of twins show that almost 80 percent of the influence of ADHD are due to genetic factors.[35] Other causes can be brain injury; environmental exposure, such as lead; alcohol and tobacco use during pregnancy; and premature birth and low birth weight. Despite popular opinion, research does not support the beliefs that ADHD is caused by eating too much candy and sodas, watching too much TV, parenting, or social and environmental factors such as poverty or family chaos. However, many things such as environment and poverty may make ADHD symptoms more prominent and contribute to the failure to resolve it. Still, the evidence is not strong enough to conclude that they are the main causes of ADHD.[36]

To be classified as having ADHD, a student must display for a minimum of six months at least six of the following characteristics to a degree that is maladaptive and inconsistent with developmental level. There are three types of ADHD: predominantly inattentive type, predominantly hyperactive-impulsive type, and combined type.

ADHD, Predominantly Inattentive Type.   Frequently, the term *attention deficit disorder* (ADD) is used to refer to the predominantly inattentive type of ADHD and not the hyperactive component. Children diagnosed with the predomiantly inattentive type of ADHD:

- Are thought of as "spacey" or daydreamers because they often seem to fail to give close attention to details or make careless mistakes in schoolwork and other activities.
- Often have difficulty sustaining attention in tasks or play activities and often don't appear to be listening when spoken to.
- Struggle to follow through on instructions and fail to finish schoolwork, chores, or duties in the workplace (but not as a result of oppositional behavior or failure to understand instructions).
- Have difficulty organizing tasks and activities and so children often avoid, dislike, or are reluctant to engage in tasks, especially when they require sustained effort.
- Frequently lose things necessary for tasks or activities (e.g., toys, school assignments, pencils, books, or tools) and are very often easily distracted by extraneous stimuli.[37]
- Process information more slowly. For example, when given instructions, they seem not to hear you. Children with this type are often thought of as "slow," lazy, or underachievers, when in reality they simply process information differently.[38]

ADHD, Predominantly Hyperactive-Impulsive Type.   Children with the hyperactive-impulsive type tend to exhibit a combination of impulsivity and overactivity. This type is the stereotype of ADHD. Children with predominantly hyperactive-impulsive type:

- Frequently fidget with hands or feet or squirm in their seats. Children may also often leave their seat in the classroom or in other situations in which remaining seated is expected.
- Often run about or climb excessively in situations in which it is inappropriate.
- May have difficulty playing or engaging in leisure activities quietly, are often on the go or act as if driven by a motor, and talk excessively.[39]
- May blurt out statements, opinions, or answers before questions have been completed and have difficulty waiting turns.
- May interrupt or intrude on others (e.g., butt into conversations or games) without intending to be rude or inappropriate.[40]
- Have trouble with personal boundaries (e.g. invade others' space or grab things).[41]

ADHD, Combined Type.   Children who have the combined type of ADHD exhibit both inattentive behaviors and hyperactive and impulsive behaviors. They may not show sufficient symptoms in either category to make a diagnosis of one type or another but do exhibit symtoms in both types enough to interfere with daily life and learning.[42]

ADHD and Gender.   ADHD is diagnosed about three times more often in boys than in girls, though they are no more likely to have it, and conservatively affects eight percent of all students.[43] Boys are more likely to have the hyperactive component, and thus are identified with ADHD more often and more quickly, whereas girls tend to show the symptoms of ADHD in different ways. However, both boys and girls can have any combination of symptoms. Some speculate that the typical hyperactive symptoms of boys disrupt the

All children, but particularly those with learning differences, learn best when they are involved in hands-on activities. Students can be involved in learning to tell time by making a clock face out of a paper plate.

classroom more, and as a result, teachers are more likely to recommend testing and diagnosis.[44] Hallmark symptoms for boys tend to be impulsivity and inability to sit still or concentrate. Researchers speculate that because girls are socialized to please parents and teachers, they are more likely to compensate for their ADHD in behavior-appropriate ways. Symptoms for ADHD in girls are nonstop, uncontrollable talking; friendship difficulties; inordinate messiness; and difficulty paying attention, which may sometimes present as simply "not getting it." Some researchers have found that when these symptoms are identified, teachers tend to see them as evidence of a lack of the girl's academic abilities or intelligence rather than a symptom of a learning and behavior disorder. Some estimate that as many as 50 to 75 percent of girls who have ADHD are not diagnosed.[45] As a result, girls may not get the help they need. In addition, girls are often diagnosed five years later than boys, at around age twelve in comparison to boys at age seven.[46]

The Effects of ADHD.   When ADHD is left untreated, children are more likely than their counterparts who have gotten help for their ADHD or those who don't have ADHD to experience lower educational achievement and are less likely to graduate from high school or college. They are also more inclined to have low self-esteem, antisocial thoughts, a pessimistic outlook on their future, and problems with their romantic relationships and jobs.[47] With the right combination of medication and intervention, children with ADHD have a better chance for a successful academic, personal, and career life. Interventions for ADHD include differentiated academic instruction, behavioral interventions, classroom accommodation, and various medications.[48]

Academic Instruction.   You can apply these principles of effective teaching when you introduce, conduct, and conclude each lesson during the school day.[49]

Introducing Lessons.   When you first introduce lessons, provide students with an advance organizer. Prepare students for the day's lesson by quickly summarizing the order of various activities. Explain, for example, that a review of the previous lesson will be followed by new information and that both group and independent work is expected. Next, review previous lessons on the topic. For example, remind children that yesterday's lesson focused on learning how to regroup in subtraction. Then review several problems before describing the current lesson. Be sure to set learning expectations. State what students are expected to learn during the lesson. For example, explain to students that a language arts lesson will involve reading a story about Paul Bunyan and identifying new vocabulary words in the story. Also, set behavioral expectations. Describe how students are expected to behave during the lesson. For example, tell children that they may talk quietly to their neighbors as they do their seat work or they may raise their hands to get your attention. Also, be sure to identify all materials that the children will need during the lesson, rather than leaving them to figure that out on their own. For example, specify that children need their journals and pencils for journal writing or their crayons, scissors, and colored paper for an art project. Finally, remind students how to obtain help in mastering the lesson. For example, refer children to a particular page in the textbook for guidance on completing a worksheet. Many teachers have the "three students before me" (ask three peers for help before going to the teacher) rule.

Teaching Lessons.   As you teach your lessons be sure to support students' participation in the classroom. Provide students with ADHD with private, discreet cues to stay on task and an advance warning that they will be called on shortly. Avoid bringing attention to differences between students with ADHD and their classmates. At all times avoid the use of sarcasm and criticism. Integrate technology into your lessons. For example, use a document camera to demonstrate how to solve an addition problem requiring regrouping. The students can work on the problem at their desks while you manipulate counters on the projector screen. Be certain to continually check student performance. Question individual students to assess their mastery of the lesson. For example, you can ask students doing seat work (i.e., lessons completed by students at their desks) to demonstrate how they arrived at the answer to a problem, or you can ask individual students to state in their own words how the main character felt at the end of the story. As you perform ongoing student evaluation, identify students who need additional assistance. Watch for signs of a lack of comprehension, such as daydreaming or visual or verbal indications of frustration. Provide these children with extra explanations, or ask another student to serve as a peer tutor for the lesson. At the same time, describe how students can identify and correct their own mistakes. For example, remind students that they should check their calculations in math problems, and reiterate how they can check their calculations. Also, remind them of particularly difficult spelling rules and ways to watch out for easy-to-make errors.

Help Students Focus.   As lessons progress, help students continue to focus. Remind students to keep working and to focus on their assigned task. For example, you can provide follow-up directions or assign learning partners. These practices can be directed at individual children or at the entire class. Follow up directions are effective and take different forms. For example, after giving directions to the class as a whole, provide additional *oral directions* for a child with ADHD. Ask whether the child understood the directions, and then repeat the directions together. Another way to provide follow up direction is in writing. For example, write the page number for an assignment on the chalkboard, and remind the child to look at the board if he or she forgets the assignment.

Organizational Study Skills.   Throughout your lessons, be sure to use cooperative learning strategies. Have students work together in small groups to maximize their own and each others' learning. Use strategies such as **T**hink-**P**air-**S**hare, in which you ask students to think about a topic, pair with a partner to discuss it, and share ideas with the group. Also, individualize instructional practices. For example, use partnered reading activities—pair the child with ADHD with another student who is a strong reader. Have the partners take turns reading orally and listening to each other. You can use scheduled storytelling sessions in which children retell a story that they have recently read. Keep a word bank or dictionary of new or hard-to-read sight-vocabulary words. Encourage computer games for reading comprehension. Schedule computer time for children to have drill-and-practice with sight-vocabulary words. Finally, make available to students a second set of books and other materials that they can use at home.

Time Management.   keep in mind that organization and study-skill strategies are particularly important for children with ADHD. They need to learn and use organization and study skills both throughout lessons and throughout their daily lives. The following list suggests different ways to help your students with ADHD develop and use organizational and study-skill strategies:

- *Assignment notebooks*—Provide the child with ADHD with an assignment notebook to help organize homework and seat work.
- *Color-coded folders*—Provide the child with color-coded folders to help organize assignments for different academic subjects (e.g., reading, mathematics, social science, and science).
- *Homework partner*—Assign the child a partner to help record homework and seat-work in the assignment notebook and to help file worksheets and other papers in the proper folders.

Time management is an essential skill for children with ADHD because they tend to need extra help managing their time. Here are some tips to help students with ADHD learn to manage their time effectively:

- *Use a clock or wristwatch*—Teach the child with ADHD how to read and use a clock or wristwatch to manage time when completing assigned work.

- *Use a calendar*—Teach the child how to read and use a calendar to schedule assignments.
- *Practice sequencing activities*—Provide the child with supervised opportunities to break down an assignment into a sequence of short, interrelated activities.
- *Create a daily activity schedule*—Tape a schedule of planned daily activities on the child's desk.
- Provide parents with time management strategies to use at home.

Behavioral Intervention. The purpose of behavioral intervention in the school setting is to assist students with ADHD in developing the behaviors that are most conducive to their own learning and that of classmates. Well-managed classrooms prevent many disciplinary problems and provide an environment that is most favorable for learning. Consequently, behavioral intervention should be viewed as an opportunity for teaching in the most effective and efficient manner, rather than as an opportunity for punishment.[50]

- *Define the appropriate behavior while giving encouragement.* Make encouragement specific for the positive behavior the student displays; that is, your comments should focus on what the student did right and should include exactly what part(s) of the student's behavior were desirable. Rather than praising a student for not disturbing the class, praise the student for quietly completing a math lesson on time.
- *Give praise immediately.* The sooner approval is given regarding appropriate behavior, the more likely the student is to repeat it.
- *Vary statements of praise.* The comments you use to praise appropriate behavior should vary; when students hear the same praise statement repeated over and over, it may lose its value.
- *Be consistent and sincere with praise.* Appropriate behavior should receive consistent praise. Consistency among teachers is important to avoid confusion on the part of students with ADHD. Similarly, students will notice insincere praise, which will make praise less effective.

Classroom Accommodation. Children with ADHD often have difficulty adjusting to the structured environment of a classroom, determining what is important, and focusing on assigned work. Because they are easily distracted by other children or by nearby activities, many children with ADHD benefit from accommodations that reduce distractions in the classroom environment and help them stay on task.[51]

- *Seat the child near the teacher.* Assign the child with ADHD a seat near your desk or the front of the room. This seating assignment allows you to monitor and reinforce the child's on-task behavior.
- *Seat the child near a student role model.* This arrangement enables children to work cooperatively and to learn from their peers.
- *Provide low-distraction work areas.* As space permits, make available a quiet, distraction-free room or area for quiet study time and test taking. Students should be directed to this area privately and discreetly in order to avoid the appearance of punishment.

Medication. The use of drugs to help children control their behavior is common. Some teachers and other education professionals object to medication for fear that children are overmedicated. However, medications such as Adderall, Concerta, Focalin, and Ritalin can be a vital and effective component in helping children who have ADHD. Each medication affects children differently, and children may need to try different types and at different dosages before a right fit is found. With the right combination of medication, behavioral interventions, and creative teaching, children with ADHD can be successful learners and students, which will set them up for success later in life.

Instructional Strategies for Teaching Children with Disabilities

Sound teaching strategies work well for *all* students, including those with disabilities, but you must plan how to create inclusive teaching environments. There are many strategies that can help make your classroom a true learning environment.

Universal Design.   We have talked about universal design before. **Universal design (UD)** is important to remember in regard to teaching children with disabilities because it describes the adaptation of teaching strategies and technology to make the learning environment, the curriculum, and the instruction processes accessible to each young child— much in the same way that universal design in architecture incorporates curb cuts, automatic doors, ramps, and other accommodations for people with disabilities. Universal design is about ensuring that learning is accessible to all students, and that success and achievement are feasible for students regardless of their differences. Universal design was established in order to integrate a greater number of students with disabilities into general education classroom settings. Universal design is based on two best practices: (1) instruction is developmentally appropriate, and (2) teaching is based on a constructivist approach to learning. Developmentally appropriate practices and constructivist learning are based on the belief that children need multiple means of engagement expression, as well as practical experiences that support what they have learned.

For example, when teachers teach oral language and conversation skills, they use different modes of presenting the material and provide positive reinforcement. Teachers might record children's thoughts and ideas via written language, audio, or video in order to provide alternate ways for children to interact with the material. If the teacher is focusing on writing, he or she would embed writing into a variety of activities across the board, accept all students' attempts, and remain sensitive to the physical demands of writing that may be difficult for some students. He or she would also provide computers and other electronic devices to promote alternate routes to written expressive language.

When it comes to universal design, flexibility is the key. For example, in a lesson on whole numbers and comparing number values according to Indiana's Grade 1 Mathematics academic standards, the teacher would present numbers and value comparison using multiple media, such as oral directions, charts or diagrams, storybooks, blocks, or even cooking activities.[52] The idea is to reach each child at the level he or she understands best. The teacher may introduce the concept of value comparison through graphs and group discussion one day, and then use a cooking experiment to demonstrate the concept practically ("Which is more: two cups of flour, or three cups of water?").

Response to Intervention/Response to Instruction (RTI).   We have talked about response to intervention/instruction before. To recap, **response to intervention/response to instruction (RTI)** is a multi-tier instructional approach to the early identification and support of students with learning and behavior needs. RTI works by efficiently differentiating instruction for all students at their developmental level. Students who are responsive to initial high-quality instruction continue to be taught in the manner that is effective for them. Students who have difficulty, for whatever reason, are engaged in increasingly smaller groups with increasingly need-oriented instruction until they succeed. RTI is successful because it incorporates increasingly intense instruction based on the individual needs of students.

Other Teaching Strategies.   The following ideas will also help you teach children with disabilities and create inclusive settings that enhance the education of *all* students:

* *Accentuate the positive.* One of the most effective strategies is to emphasize what children can do rather than what they cannot do. Children with disabilities have talents and abilities similar to those of other children.

universal design (UD) A broad-spectrum solution that produces buildings, products, and environments that are usable and effective for everyone, not just people with disabilities.

response to intervention/ response to instruction (RTI) A multi-tiered approach to the early identification and support of students with learning and behavior needs.

- *Use appropriate assessment.* Include work samples, cumulative records, and appropriate assessment instruments. Parents and other professionals who have worked with individual children are sources of valuable information and can contribute to accurate and appropriate plans for them. Appropriate assessment includes using culturally sensitive tools and measures.

- *Use concrete examples and materials.*

- *Develop and use multisensory approaches to learning.* Use multisensory learning centers. Multisensory learning centers can assist in meeting diverse needs in an inclusive classroom; they can address various instructional levels with emphasis on visual, auditory, and kinesthetic pathways to learning.

- *Model what children are to do.* Rather than just telling them what to do, have a child who has mastered a certain task or behavior model it for others. Also, ask each child to perform a designated skill or task with supervision. Give corrective feedback. Then let children practice or perform the certain behavior. Later, involve them in their own assessment of that behavior.

- *Make the learning environment a pleasant, rewarding place to be.*

- *Create a dependable classroom schedule.* All children develop a sense of security when daily plans follow a consistent pattern. Children with disabilities in particular benefit from dependable schedules because it provides routine and stability and a sense of control. However, allowing for flexibility is also important.

- *Encourage parents to volunteer at school and to read to their children at home.*

- *Identify appropriate tasks children can accomplish on their own.* Create opportunities for them to become more independent of you and others.

- *Use cooperative learning.* Cooperative learning enables all students to work together to achieve common goals. Cooperative learning has five components:

  - *Positive interdependence.* Group members establish mutual goals, divide the prerequisite tasks, share materials and resources, assume shared roles, and provide feedback to each other.

  - *Face-to-face interaction.* Group members encourage and facilitate each other's efforts to complete tasks through direct communication.

  - *Individual accountability/personal responsibility.* Individual performance is assessed, and results are reported back to both the individual and the group, which holds members accountable for completing their fair share of responsibility.

  - *Interpersonal and small-group skills.* Students are responsible for getting to know and trust each other, communicating accurately and clearly, accepting and supporting each other, and resolving conflicts in a constructive manner.

  - *Group processing.* Group reflection includes describing which contributions of members are helpful or unhelpful in making decisions and which group actions should be continued or changed.

- *Develop a peer buddy system.* In a peer buddy system, classmates serve as friends, guides, or counselors to students who are experiencing problems. Variations are to pair an older student with a younger one who is experiencing a problem or to pair two students who are experiencing similar problems.[53]

Testing Strategies for Children with Disabilities.   We've talked about the difficulty of using tests and assessments with children who have disabilities. We have known for a long time that too many children with disabilities are taking inappropriate state tests that produce results that don't reflect what they really can do. States are responding by providing modified tests. For example, Pennsylvania is field-testing modified tests in math in all districts and is currently field-testing in reading and science in some districts. The modified assessment test is the same as the grade level standard test, but it has a simplified format that administrators and educators hope is accommodating enough that students' performance will more accurately reflect their capabilities and increase the number of children in special education scoring at a proficient level. The push for modified tests comes in part from some schools missing making Adequate Yearly Progress (AYP) as required by NCLB because too many exceptional children do not score at the proficient level. Teachers involved in the modified testing report that the process is much smoother than in previous years and that they believe the results can support the use of the modified tests.[54]

Children Who Are Gifted and Talented

Children identified as gifted and talented receive services through the Jacob K. Javits Gifted and Talented Students Education Act of 1988. This act defines *gifted and talented children* as those who "give evidence of high performance capabilities in areas such as intellectual, creative, artistic, or leadership capacity or in specific academic fields, and who require services or activities not ordinarily provided by the school in order to fully develop such capabilities.[55] The definition distinguishes between *giftedness*, which is characterized by above-average intellectual ability, and *talented*, which refers to individuals who excel in such areas as drama, art, music, athletics, and leadership. Students can have these abilities separately or in combination; for example, a gifted student may also have a learning disability, and a student with an orthopedic disability may also be gifted.

Characteristics of Gifted and Talented.   Figure 16.5 outlines the characteristics displayed in each of the areas of giftedness; you can use these to help identify gifted children in your program. Although children may not display all of the identified markers, the presence of several of them can alert parents and professionals to make appropriate instructional,

Creative Thinking	Visual/Performing Arts	General Intellectual Abilities	Specific Academic Ability	Leadership
• Independent thinker • Exhibits original thinking in oral and written expression • Comes up with several solutions to a given problem • Possesses a sense of humor • Creates and invents • Challenged by creative tasks • Improvises often • Does not mind being different from the crowd	• Outstanding in sense of spatial relationships • Unusual ability in expressing feelings, moods, etc. through dance, music, drama, art, etc. • Good motor coordination • Exhibits coordination • Exhibits creative expression • Desire for producing "own product" (not content with mere copying) • Observant	• Formulates abstractions • Processes information in complex ways • Observant • Excited about new ideas • Enjoys hypothesizing • Learns rapidly • Uses a large vocabulary • Inquisitive • Self-starter	• Good memorization ability • Advanced comprehension • Acquires basic skills knowledge quickly • Widely read in special-interest area • High academic success in special-interest area • Pursues special interests with enthusiasm and vigor	• Assumes responsibility • High expectations for self and others • Fluent, concise self-expression • Foresees consequences and implications of decisions • Good judgment in decision making • Likes structure • Well-liked by peers • Self confident • Organized

FIGURE 16.5 Giftedness

Source: Reprinted by permission from the National Association for Gifted Children (NAGC), Washington, DC. This chart may not be further reproduced without the permission of NAGC.

environmental, and social adjustments. Professionals tend to suggest special programs and sometimes special schools for the gifted and talented, which would seem to be a move away from providing for these children in regular classrooms. Regular classroom teachers can provide for gifted children through enrichment and acceleration. *Enrichment* allows children to pursue topics in greater depth and in different ways than the curriculum specifies. *Acceleration* permits children to progress academically at a quicker pace.

Providing for/Accommodating Gifted and Talented

In regular classrooms teachers can also use parents and resource people to tutor and work in special ways with these children and can provide opportunities for the children to assume leadership responsibilities. For example, children who are gifted and talented may be interested in tutoring other students who need extra practice or help. Tutoring can cut across grade and age levels. Students can also help explain directions and procedures to the class. In addition, teachers can encourage them to use their talents and abilities outside the classroom by becoming involved with other people and agencies.

Teachers can foster creativity through classroom activities that require divergent thinking (e.g., "Let's think of all the different uses for a paper clip"). They must challenge children to think, using higher-order questions that encourage children to explain, apply, analyze, rearrange, and judge. Many schools have resource rooms for gifted and talented students, where children can spend a half day or more every week working with a professional who is interested and trained in working with them. Resource room pullout is the most popular of these methods.

In your work with children who are gifted, the more you can find out about them, the easier it will be for you to meet all of their exceptional needs. For example, one of the things that you will want to know is what motivates your children who are gifted, and how you can take that intrinsic motivation and apply it to your teaching and children's learning. For many children, having the opportunity to use a block of time in any way they would like is a powerful motivating factor.

Gifted and Talented Children with Disabilities.   A word of caution: just like children with disabilities, the gifted and talented labels carry with them systemic societal prejudices. Recall from Figure 16.1 that African American and Native American children are disproportionately identified as learning disabled and Hispanic Americans are underrepresented. Similarly, Caucasians and Asians represent the majority of children labeled as gifted and talented. Take Los Angeles Unified School District as a microcosm of the whole; LA Unified total enrollment includes 8.4 percent Caucasians who make up 23 percent of the children identified as gifted and talented in the district. The disparities between Caucasian Americans and other races and ethnicities are exacerbated in low income and minority-majority schools. Recognizing that economically disadvantaged minority children have just as much potential as high socioeconomic and Caucasian students is vital to ensuring that everyone receives the best education available.[56]

Gifted and Talented Identification.   Children can receive the gifted and talented label through many avenues, but the most popular is generally through IQ testing, which is conducted at the request of teachers and families. Schools with a minority-majority and low socioeconomic populations historically don't receive recommendations for IQ testing through either avenue. Some schools are trying to fight this trend to ensure that all children have an equal opportunity to be seen as gifted and talented. The LA Unified School district now makes IQ testing for all second graders mandatory and has already seen a 9% increase in minority students identified as gifted and talented in just six months. One mother whose son is now recognized as gifted and talented says proudly "now he has something not everybody has and it's going to follow him for the rest of his life. It could expand his life and open doors. It gives him the opportunity to be noticed."[57]

It is important to remember, however, that IQ testing is not the only way to measure giftedness or talent. IQ only measures certain qualities in a certain way. As a result, children who have learning disabilities or are English language learners (ELLs) but may also be gifted and talented may not get the GT label, which can provide motivation, encouragement, and enriched education. As a teacher, you can take the intitiative to reconize many types of intelligences (recall Gardner) and talents such as those described in Figure 16.5. You can play a huge part in securing the best education for all your students when you reconize their gifts!

Children Who Are Abused and Neglected

Many of our views of childhood are highly romanticized. We tend to believe that parents always love their children and enjoy caring for them. We envision family settings full of joy, happiness, and harmony. Unfortunately for many children, their parents, and society, these assumptions are not always true. In fact, the extent of child abuse is far greater than we might imagine. In 2008, an estimated 772,000 children were determined to be victims of abuse or neglect, and an estimated 3.3 million children were referred to Child Protective Services in the United States.[58] Abuse knows no religious, ethnic, age, or economic boundaries. Children of all races and ethnicities can be victims of child abuse. In 2007, nearly one-half of all victims of child abuse and neglect were Caucasian, one-fifth were African American, and one-fifth were Hispanic. Thirty-two percent of the victims of child abuse and neglect are under the age of four. Children whose parents are unemployed are twice as likely to be victims of child abuse and two to three times more likely to suffer from neglect than children whose parents are employed. To that effect, children from low socioeconomic families have more than three times the rate of child abuse and seven times the rate of neglect compared to other children. Additionally, children who live with a single parent who has a live-in partner are eight times more suceptible to abuse and neglect than children who live with their married biological parents.[59]

Children as Property.   Child abuse is not new; it has been documented throughout history. The attitude that children are property partly accounts for this record. Parents have believed, and some still do, that they own their children and can do with them as they please. The extent to which children are abused is difficult to ascertain but is probably much greater than most people realize. Valid statistics are difficult to come by because definitions of child abuse and neglect differ from state to state and reports are categorized differently. Because of the increasing concern over child abuse, social agencies, hospitals, child care centers, and schools are becoming more involved in identification, treatment, and prevention of this national problem.

Public Law 93–247, the Child Abuse Prevention and Treatment Act, defines *child abuse and neglect* as the

> physical or mental injury, sexual abuse, negligent treatment or maltreatment of a child under the age of eighteen by a person who is responsible for the child's welfare under circumstances which indicate that the child's health or welfare is harmed or threatened thereby as determined in accordance with regulations prescribed by the secretary.[60]

In addition, all states have some kind of legal or statutory definition of child abuse and mistreatment, and many define penalties for child abuse.

Definition of Abuse.   As you can see from the Child Abuse and Treatment Act, there are many kinds of child abuse. The general definition of abuse includes physical abuse, neglect, emotional abuse, and sexual abuse. The latest numbers state that 325,000 out of 1.25 million children suffer from physical abuse annually.[61] Physical abuse includes but is not limited to hitting with an open hand, closed fist, or another object (such as a strap or switch); punching; shaking; throwing; kicking; burning; stabbing; drowning; electrocuting; tying up; or choking.[62]

Child Neglect.   Neglect is distressingly common; in fact, of all the types of abuse, neglect is probably the most common. Of the children who suffer from abuse, 61 percent (771,700 children) are specifically victims of neglect, meaning a parent or guardian failed to provide for the child's basic needs. Forms of neglect include educational neglect (360,500 children), physical neglect (295,300 children), and emotional neglect (193,400).[63]

Emotional Abuse.   Just as debilitating as physical abuse and neglect is *emotional abuse*, which occurs when parents, teachers, and others strip children of their self-esteem. Adults take away children's self-esteem by continually criticizing, belittling, screaming and nagging, verbally berating, creating fear, and intentionally and severely limiting opportunities. Because emotional abuse is difficult to define legally and difficult to document, the unfortunate consequence for emotionally abused children is that they are often left in a debilitating environment. Conservatively 148,500 children suffer from emotional abuse.[64]

Sexual Abuse.   Finally, sexual abuse is one of the most inherently deplorable abuses of children. Sexual abuse is far more common than we like to acknowledge, and likely occurs more frequently than we are able to ascertain. In fact, over 30 percent of victims never disclose the experience to anyone. Of the children who do disclose their abuse, either when confronted by an adult or when reporting themselves, 80 percent initially deny abuse or are tentative in disclosing, and of those who do admit their abuse, 75 percent tell someone accidentally or inadvertently. Sadly, more than 20 percent of the children who have admitted they suffered from sexual abuse eventually recant out of shame, guilt, or adult pressure, even though the abuse occurred.[65]

As a result, we can only conservatively estimate that sexual abuse wounds 135,000 children nationwide per year. This means that 1 in 4 girls are sexually abused and 1 in 6 boys are sexually abused. Additionally, 1 in 5 children are solicited sexually while on the Internet.[66] It is a crime that children are often doubted when they report their abuse; people commonly think that they "make it up," but children only falsely report sexual abuse one half percent of the time.[67] If a child tells you she is being abused, believe her!

A misleading myth is that children are abused by strangers. It is overwhelmingly more likely that they are abused by family members or people they know and trust, which contributes to the underreporting of sexual abuse. In fact, 30–40 percent of victims are abused by a family member and at least 50 percent are abused by someone outside of their families whom they know and trust. In addition, around 40 percent of sexually abused children are also abused by older or larger children whom they know and who likely were victims of abuse themselves. As a result, we know that only 10 percent are abused by strangers. These statistics tell us that we cannot and must not assume that our students go home to safe homes—you must be aware and vigilant to the signs of abuse and take steps to protect the children you teach.[68]

Figure 16.6 will help you identify abuse and neglect. Remember that the presence of a single characteristic does not necessarily indicate abuse. You should observe a child's behavior and appearance over a period of time.

Reporting Child Abuse

As a teacher you are a mandatory reporter of child abuse. Other mandatory reporters include physicians, nurses, social workers, counselors, and psychologists. Each state has its own procedures and set of policies for reporting child abuse. It can be intimidating to report abuse, but just remember, 70 percent of child sex offenders have anywhere between one to nine victims and at least 20 percent have 10 to 40 victims; a serial child molester may have as many as 400 victims in his or her lifetime.[69] So when you report abuse of any kind, but particularly sexual abuse, you are not only helping the one child you know about, but many, many others as well. Therefore, you need to

Physical Indicators

- Unexplained bruises and welts
  - On torso, back, buttocks, thighs, or face
  - Appear with regularity after absence, weekend, or vacation
  - Identifiable shape of object used to inflict injury (belt, electrical cord, etc.)
- Unexplained burns
  - On soles of feet, palms, back, buttocks, or head
  - Hot water immersion burns (glove-like, sock-like, or doughnut-shaped burn on buttocks or genitals)
- Unexplained fractures or dislocations
- Bald patches on scalp

Behavioral Indicators

- Child states s/he "deserves" punishment
- Fearful when others cry
- Behavioral extremes (aggressive, withdrawn)
- Frightened of parents or caretakers
- Afraid to go home
- Child reports injury by parents or caretakers
- Inappropriate/immature acting out
- Needy for affection
- Manipulative behaviors to get attention
- Tendency toward superficial relationships
- Unable to focus—daydreaming
- Self abusive behavior or lack of concern for personal safety
- Wary of adult contact

Physical Abuse

Physical Indicators

- Difficulty walking or sitting
- Torn, stained, or bloody undergarments
- Pain, swelling, or itching in genital area
- Pain when urinating
- Vaginal or penile discharge
- Bruises, bleeding, or tears around the genital area
- Sexually transmitted diseases
  - Herpes, crabs, vaginal warts
  - Gonorrhea, syphilis
  - HIV, AIDS
- Excessive masturbation

Behavioral Indicators

- Unwilling to change for gym or participate in physical education activities
- Sexual behavior or knowledge inappropriate to child's age
- Sexual acting out on younger children
- Poor peer relations
- Delinquent or runaway behavior
- Report of sexual assault
- Drastic change in school performance
- Sleep disorders/nightmares
- Eating disorders
- Aggression; withdrawal; fantasy; infantile behavior
- Self abusive behavior or lack of concern for personal safety
- Substance abuse
- Repetitive behaviors (handwashing, pacing, rocking)

Sexual Abuse

Physical Indicators

- Not meeting basic needs (food, shelter, clothing)
- Failure to thrive (underweight, small for age)
- Persistent hunger
- Poor hygiene
- Inappropriate dress for season or weather
- Consistent lack of supervision and emotional care
- Unattended physical problems or medical needs
- Abandonment

Behavioral Indicators

- Begging or stealing food
- Early arrival at or late departure from school
- Frequent visits to the school nurse
- Difficulty with vision or hearing
- Poor coordination
- Often tired or falling asleep in class
- Takes on adult roles and responsibilities
- Substance abuse
- Acting out behavior
- Educational failure
- Child verbalizes lack of caretaking

Neglect

Physical Indicators

- Speech disorders
  - Stuttering
  - Baby talk
  - Unresponsiveness
- Failure to thrive (underweight, small for age)
- Hyperactivity

Behavioral Indicators

- Learning disabilities
- Habits of sucking, biting, rocking
- Sleep disorders
- Poor social skills
- Extreme reactions to common events
- Unusually fearful
- Overly compliant behaviors (unable to set limits)
- Suicidal thoughts or actions
- Self abuse
- Difficulty following rules or directions
- Child expects to fail so does not try

Emotional Abuse

FIGURE 16.6 Indicators of Abuse

Source: Reprinted by permission from "Child Abuse: What Is It? What Can You Do?" Childhelp USA® (2003).

be very familiar with your state and district policies about how to identify child abuse and how to report it.

The following guidelines should govern your response to a child with suspected abuse or neglect:

- *Remain calm.* A child may retract information or stop talking if he or she senses a strong reaction.
- *Believe the child.* Children rarely make up stories about abuse.
- *Listen without passing judgment.* Most children know their abusers and often have conflicted feelings.
- *Tell the child you are glad that he or she told someone.*
- *Assure the child that abuse is not his or her fault.*
- *Do what you can to make certain that the child is safe from further abuse.*
- *Do not investigate the case yourself.* Call the police or the child and family services agency.

How child abuse is reported varies from state to state. In Washington, DC, for example, if child abuse or neglect is suspected, you are to call the reporting hotline immediately at (202) 671-SAFE. To make a report, you would need to provide the following information:

- Name, age, sex, and address of the child who is the subject of the report, names of any siblings and the parent, guardian, or caregiver
- Nature and extent of the abuse or neglect, as you know it (and any previous abuse or neglect)
- Any additional information that may help establish the cause and identity of persons responsible
- Your name, occupation, contact information, and a statement of any actions taken concerning the child

Children Who Are Homeless

While walking down a city street, you may have encountered homeless men and women, but have you seen a homeless child? Homeless children are the neglected, forgotten, often abandoned segment of the growing homeless population in the United States. The National Coalition for the Homeless estimates that there are as many as 1.35 million homeless children, living either with homeless families or on their own. This translates to one out of every 50 of your students being homeless. And sadly, children are the fastest-growing population among the homeless.[70]

The National Center on Family Homelessness reported that some states are faring better than others. Connecticut, New Hampshire, and Hawaii are ranked first, second, and third, respectively, for having the least amount of child homelessness while Arkansas, Georgia, and Texas are ranked forty-eighth, forty-ninth, and fiftieth, respectively, with the highest level of child homelessness.[71] In some cities, the rates are even worse; in Minneapolis, 1 in 10 children are currently homeless.[72] The majority of children who are homeless are between the ages of birth and thirteen, the very group of children you will be teaching.[73]

Child Outcome of Being Homeless. Homelessness has long-lasting and devastating effects upon children. They have at least twice as much traumatic stress, overall health problems, and emotional disturbances than do children who are not homeless. Many do not know where they will be sleeping at night, what they will get to eat the next day, or even if they will get to eat at all. Homeless children are more likely to suffer from nightmares, be teased by classmates, and have trouble staying awake during the day. As you can imagine, homelessness and its ramifications drastically affect not only children's personal and developmental well-being, but their school performance as well. Homeless children are less likely to graduate and thus are more likely to perpetuate the homeless cycle. School is difficult for children who are homeless. They exhibit such problem behaviors as short attention spans, weak impulse control, withdrawal, aggression, speech delays, and regressive behavior. They are at greater risk for health problems, and if they do enter school, they face many problems related to previous school experience (e.g., grade failure) and attendance (e.g., long trips to attend school). Grades and academic success suffer, and as a result, so does their self-esteem. Homelessness results in developmental delays and contributes to higher levels of adult homelessness.[74] Fortunately, more agencies are now responding to the unique needs of homeless children and their families.

Public Law 107–110, the McKinney-Vento Homeless Assistance Act of 2001, provides that "each State educational agency shall assure that each child of a homeless individual and each homeless youth has access to the same free, appropriate public education, including a public preschool education, as provided to other children and youth."[75]

Combating Homelessness.   The new federal stimulus plan has allocated an unprecedented $70 million to aid homeless students, but with over 15,000 school districts nationwide, there is still not enough money to go around.[76] Some school districts have aggressively taken on this epidemic to combat homelessness. Here are some things that they have done:

- Nationwide, the McKinney-Vento Homeless Assistance Act requires school districts to establish "liaisons" between children who are homeless and their schools. In Richmond, California, an organization named Families in Transition (FIT) uses liaisons to identify and aid children who are homeless. FIT not only builds community ties, but also monitors homeless children's school attendance and grades.

- In Albuquerque, New Mexico, the school districts utilize liaisons to gain grant funding and to implement summer school programs, career programs, biweekly free tutoring, support groups, and free food programs for children who are homeless.[77]

- In Minneapolis, Minnesota, the school districts (MPS) have taken steps to ensure that homeless students can stay enrolled in one school continuously by providing free transportation, whether by taxi, bus, or school bus, regardless of the pick-up or drop-off site. The schools train staff to recognize the signs of children who are between homes so that they can get them help. MPS also provides brand new back-packs and school supplies for homeless children, as well as allocating a certain amount of their funding to keep homeless children involved in extracurricular activities like sports, dance, music, and art.[78]

Your Role.   Regardless of where you teach and your district's policies, there are things you can do in your classroom and your community to aid children who are homeless:

- Challenge your own conception of homelessness. Regardless of your beliefs about adults who are homeless and accompanying stereotypes, children are not responsible for their families' poverty or home situations. Treat students and their families who are having economic difficulties respectfully and professionally, with empathy and an open mind.

- Know the signs of homelessness. See Figure 16.7 (page 456) for indicators of homelessness.

- Once you've identified children in your classroom who are homeless or are at risk to become so, you should:
  - Stop teasing and bullying of children who are homeless.
  - Be careful of the language you use. If organizing outreach efforts in your classroom for homelessness, such as canned food drives and clothing drives, refer to circumstances in respectful and neutral ways.
  - Don't single out children who are homeless.
  - Encourage children who are homeless in tasks that they enjoy and excel in to build their self-esteem.
  - Make school feel safe, inviting, and consistent. To do so, maintain a routine, assure and reassure children when they are in doubt or afraid, and be available to listen to and encourage them. Provide them with a means to be expressive.

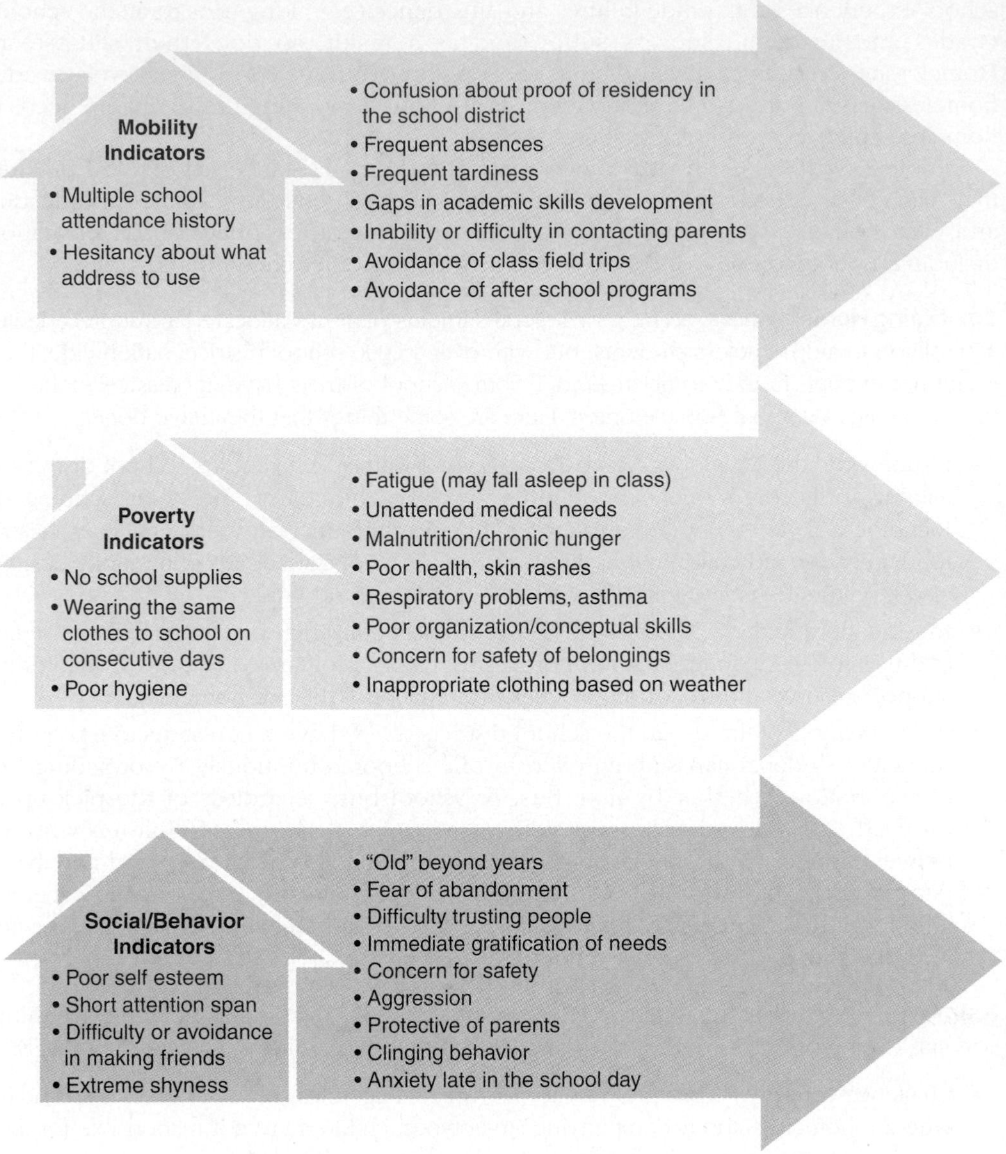

FIGURE 16.7 Indicators of Homelessness

Source: National Center for Homeless Education, www.serve.org/nche.

Mobility Indicators

- Multiple school attendance history
- Hesitancy about what address to use
- Confusion about proof of residency in the school district
- Frequent absences
- Frequent tardiness
- Gaps in academic skills development
- Inability or difficulty in contacting parents
- Avoidance of class field trips
- Avoidance of after school programs

Poverty Indicators

- No school supplies
- Wearing the same clothes to school on consecutive days
- Poor hygiene
- Fatigue (may fall asleep in class)
- Unattended medical needs
- Malnutrition/chronic hunger
- Poor health, skin rashes
- Respiratory problems, asthma
- Poor organization/conceptual skills
- Concern for safety of belongings
- Inappropriate clothing based on weather

Social/Behavior Indicators

- Poor self esteem
- Short attention span
- Difficulty or avoidance in making friends
- Extreme shyness
- "Old" beyond years
- Fear of abandonment
- Difficulty trusting people
- Immediate gratification of needs
- Concern for safety
- Aggression
- Protective of parents
- Clinging behavior
- Anxiety late in the school day

- Encourage children who are homeless to utilize the school counselor so that their emotional and developmental needs are met.
- In and out of the classroom setting, respect children and their families' privacy and wishes. Some parents and/or children do not want to be identified as homeless because of the stereotypes and stigmas attached. If a child does not wish to be identified as homeless, refrain from doing so to protect his or her privacy. Discuss with parents their wishes and how best to get them the help they need.[79]
- Be an advocate. If one does not already exist in your school, work to establish a task force that incorporates social workers, school counselors, principals, teachers, parents, community members, and local businesses. Homelessness does not just affect one or two of us; when it affects our children, it affects us all. Follow Minneapolis's and Albuquerque's lead and encourage your task force to implement similar strategies. Be both creative and practical in order to build on these examples. Work with national and local groups to obtain funds and resources for your students who are homeless.

Accommodating Diverse Learners

Meet Sean: He has just turned four years old and was diagnosed with **autism spectrum disorder**, a neurological developmental disorder characterized by a deficit in communication and social interactions as well as by the presence of restricted and repetitive behaviors. Sean is very attached to routine and although his **receptive language** skills appear to be typical—he can understand spoken, written, or visual communication—he has difficulty expressing himself. In addition, Sean's social interactions with peers are often contentious or stilted because he has difficulty diverting from his own plans or adapting to his peers' perspective. How will you accommodate Sean in your classroom? One way you can help Sean acclimate to your classroom rules and routines is for you to write a **social story** for him. A social story is a personalized, detailed, and simple script that breaks down behavior and provides rules and directions. Social stories can range from drawings featuring stick figures, to computer images, or even better, to digital photos featuring Sean. To write a social story, follow these steps:

Step 1. Identify a behavior or activity you want Sean to comply with. You can use social stories to modify any kind of behavior, from toileting to peer interactions to transitions. However, each social story should focus on one thing at a time. For example, Sean is having difficulty transitioning from his mother's car to your classroom and the morning routine. Before writing the social story, observe Sean and talk with his parents to learn why the home-to-school transition is difficult for him. Is he concerned that his mother won't come back for him? Does Sean understand what will happen next? Are all transitions a source of worry for him? You will use this information to write Sean's social story.

Step 2. Write on the first page: "This is Sean." Use a picture of Sean. You can draw it and label it or use an actual photo. The photo should depict a part of Sean's life he will recognize. If he brings a Spider-Man action figure to school every day, have Spider-Man in the picture.

Step 3. Write on the second page: "On Monday morning, Sean gets into Mommy's car to come to school." Include a photo of Sean getting into his mother's car.

autism spectrum disorder A neurological developmental disorder characterized by a deficit in communication and social interactions, as well as by the presence of restricted and repetitive behaviors.

receptive language An individual whose skills appear to be typical but who has difficulty expressing himself; interactions with peers are often contentious or stilted because of the difficulty of diverting from his own plans or adapting to his peers' perspective.

social story A personalized, detailed, and simple script that breaks down behavior and provides rules and directions.

This is Sean.

On Monday morning, Sean gets into Mommy's car to come to school.

Always use the child's own language. Sean calls his mother "Mommy," so you use the word "Mommy." Keep in mind that different cultures use different words for parents. For example, Ali, whose parents are from Pakistan, calls his father "Abba." Contact Sean's parents and ask them questions about the words he uses. For Sean, using his language makes the story more real, more personal, and reinforces the importance of communication.

Step 4.   Provide routines. Children with autism tend to like routines because they provide predictability. Sean's mother shares with you that if she takes a different route to school Sean has a meltdown. As a result, driving to school can be a daily trauma.

Step 5.   On the third page write: "Sometimes Mommy drives one way to school. If Mommy drives a new way to school, I will be safe. Mommy will keep Sean safe. If I feel worried, I can say, 'I am safe and I am still going to school' or 'It's OK if Mommy goes a different way. I am still going to school.'" Use a picture of Sean giving the "OK" or "thumbs-up" sign inside a car.

Step 6.   Write on the fourth page: "When Sean gets to school, he can say, 'Bye Mommy! See you soon!'" Use a picture of Sean with a big smile on his face waving good-bye. Social stories are a behavior model and a linguistic script, so

Sean's job is to go to school.

Good Morning Class!

Sean can say, "Hi, (teacher's name)."

whenever you use them be sure to model the behavior you wish to reinforce. If Sean is very attuned to time, instead of saying "See you soon," you can include the time his mother will return, saying "See you in three hours at twelve o'clock!" Use a picture of his mother next to a picture of a clock showing the correct time on the same page.

Step 7. Write on the fifth page: "Sean's job is to go to school. Sean can say, 'Hi, (teacher's name).'" Take a picture of yourself and insert it here.

Sean can hang his backpack on his hook.

Now it's time to sit down.

When I sit down, I can say, "Hi, Johnny!"

Step 8. If Sean's next step in the routine is to hang up his backpack, give him instructions for hanging up his backpack. On the sixth page write: "Sean can hang his backpack on his hook. Now it is time to sit down." Use a picture of his hook with an arrow pointing to the next task of sitting down.

Step 9. If Sean does not know how to greet his classmates, it is important to provide him with the steps and the words to do so. On the seventh page write: "When I sit down, I can say 'Hi, Johnny!'" Use a picture of his classmates waving or giving high fives.

Step 10. Follow the same steps to make pages for Tuesday, Wednesday, Thursday, and Friday.

Social stories focus on the behavior you want Sean to use, not on negative behavior. Once you have written the social story, set aside time during the day to read it with Sean. Tell him that you made this very special book just for him. The first day, read it several times. You should read a social story as if it were a picture book with all the inflection and emotion you wish to model. Have Sean practice saying the words with you. Make a copy and send it home with Sean. Ask his parents to read it at home a few times but especially before bedtime and right before he leaves for school in the morning. On the drive over, have Sean's mother let him hold the book and read it to himself. The first few days you use the new story, read it with him as he gets out of the car. Eventually Sean will not need this added support.

Activities for Professional Development

Ethical Dilemma

"They don't need to know everything."

Emma is a first-year teacher and participating in her first team meeting relating to the referral, assessment, and placement process for one of your students. She wants to make sure that seven-year-old Krystal gets all of the services she deserves. During the meeting Emma asks the district supervisor of special education services whether Krystal's parents have been notified about today's meeting and given an opportunity to participate in the meeting. The supervisor's comment is, "Oh, let's not worry about that now. Parents don't need to know everything! We can get a lot of this done and just tell them what we are going to do." Under IDEA, parents are entitled to be members of any group that makes decisions about the educational placement of their child.

What should Emma do? How can she be the best advocate for Krystal? Does she tell the district supervisor what rights parents have, or does she keep quiet and say nothing until she has time to think about what she should do, or does she select some other course of action?

Activities to Apply What You Learned

1. Write a 200-word essay, pro or con, about your beliefs for including students with disabilities in national and district tests. Post your essay on your class's discussion board.

2. What are some ways that you will encourage gifted and talented learners? Skype with local teachers and ask them how they balance the diverse needs of their classrooms.

3. Get in touch with a local play therapist and e-mail him or her about how best to help a child in your classroom who has been sexually abused.

4. Conduct an Internet search to discover the state of homeless children in your area. Are you surprised by how many (or how few) there are? Why or why not? Collaborate with your classmates and develop a plan for how to raise awareness in your school district about homelessness. Post your plan on Facebook and ask for community help.

5. Create a social story to address an issue (other than transitioning) that children with autism typically have, using the steps and techniques described in this chapter. Compile the social stories of your classmates into a booklet and make copies so you all have a set of social stories for your future classrooms.

Linking to Learning

Council for Exceptional Children
www.cec.sped.org/
Publishes extremely up-to-date news regarding education-related legislation; contains numerous links to other sites.

Council for Learning Disabilities
www.cldinternational.org
An international organization of and for professionals who represent diverse disciplines and who are committed to enhancing the education and life span development of individuals with learning disabilities. Establishes standards of excellence and promotes innovative strategies for research and practice through interdisciplinary collegiality, collaboration, and advocacy.

National Association for the Education of Homeless Children and Youth (NAEHCY)
www.naehcy.org/
A professional organization specifically dedicated to homeless education. Established to ensure research-based strategies for effective approaches

to the problems faced by homeless children, youth, and families. Has created guidelines, goals, and objectives that outline strategies for dealing with government agencies and designing effective programs.

National Dissemination Center for Children with Disabilities
www.nichcy.org/
National information and referral center that provides information on disabilities and disability-related issues for families, educators, and other professionals.

Office of Special Education and Rehabilitation Services
www.ed.gov/about/offices/list/osers/index.html?src-mr
Supports programs that assist in educating children with special needs, provides for the rehabilitation of youth and adults with disabilities, and supports research to improve the lives of individuals with disabilities.

Prevent Child Abuse America (PCA)
www.preventchildabuse.org/
A volunteer organization of concerned citizens that works with community, state, and national groups to expand and disseminate knowledge about child abuse prevention.

Teaching Children with Attention Deficit Hyperactivity Disorder
www.ed.gov/teachers/needs/speced/adhd/adhd-resource-pt2.doc
Provides many excellent ideas and specific strategies for teaching students with ADHD.

U.S. Department of Health & Human Services Administration for Children & Families
www.childwelfare.gov
Helps coordinate and develop programs and policies concerning child abuse and neglect.

myeducationlab

Go to Topic 11 (Special Needs/Inclusion) in the MyEducationLab (www.myeducationlab.com) for your course, where you can:

- Find learning outcomes for Special Needs/Inclusion along with the national standards that connect to these outcomes.
- Complete Assignments and Activities that can help you more deeply understand the chapter content.
- Apply and practice your understanding of the core teaching skills identified in the chapter with the Building Teaching Skills and Dispositions learning units.
- Examine challenging situations and cases presented in the IRIS Center Resources.
- Check your comprehension on the content covered in the chapter by going to the Study Plan in the Book Resources for your text. Here you will be able to take a chapter quiz, receive feedback on your answers, and then access Review, Practice, and Enrichment activities to enhance your understanding of chapter content.

17

PARENT, FAMILY, AND COMMUNITY INVOLVEMENT

Building Partnerships for Success

naeyc standards

Standard 2. Building Family and Community Relationships

I know about, understand, and value the importance and complex characteristics of children's families and communities. I use this understanding to create respectful, reciprocal relationships that support and empower families, and to involve all families in their children's development and learning.[1]

Standard 3. Observing, Documenting, and Assessing to Support Young Children and Families

I know about and understand the goals, benefits, and uses of assessment. I know about and use systematic observations, documentation, and other effective assessment strategies in a responsible way, in partnership with families and other professionals, to positively influence the development of every child.[2]

Kindergarten teacher Susan Baldino is a firm believer that by involving parents in their children's education, parents and children will partner together for a more successful learning experience. Baldino sends school-to-home and home-to-school logs to her students' homes on a weekly basis and produces DVDs of class activities for the parents to use at home. She also coordinates and plans Family Science Nights for parents to get involved in the science curriculum and to support the school curriculum.[3]

Schools and Parent/Family Partnerships

One thing we can say with certainty about the educational landscape today is that parents, families, and communities are as much a part of the educational process as are children, teachers, and staff.[4] At no other time in U.S. educational history has support for family and community involvement in schools and programs been so high. All concerned view the involvement of families and communities as critical for individual student success, for the success of school reform efforts, and for preparing a more highly educated workforce. In fact, the public believes that parents are one of the keys to moving the public schools forward.[5] Parent and family involvement is also tied to children's school performance and success. When parents increase involvement in elementary schools by increasing visits to the schools and encouraging educational progress at home:

- Children's problem behaviors—both aggressive and disruptive, as well as anxiety and depression—decrease.
- Children's pro-social skills, such as cooperation and self-control, improve.[6]

Reasons for Parent/Family Involvement. Schooling used to consist mostly of teaching children social and basic academic skills. But as society has changed, so has the content of schooling. Early childhood programs have assumed many parental functions and responsibilities and now also help parents and families with educational and social issues that affect them and their children in their daily lives.

Political and social forces have strengthened relationships between families and schools. The accountability and reform movements of the past and present have convinced families that they should no longer be kept out of their children's schools. They have become more militant in their demand for quality education, and schools and other agencies have responded by seeking ways to involve families in their quest for quality. Education professionals and families now realize that mutual cooperation is in everyone's best interest. Schools are working with parents and families to develop programs to help them and their children reach their full potential.

For example, Porterdale Elementary School's Parent University plans several programs for parents with the goal to increase parental involvement. Parents participate in programs such as Make and Take Math, Reading Make and Take, and Reading Camp-In, where children and families listen to guest speakers read books from different genres. Porterdale's Parent University also sponsors Computer Night for parents, where they learn more about computer safety and etiquette and technology-based learning programs and gather information to help their children learn at home.[7]

As society changes, the problems and issues facing children and their families change. So too, new technological

> "We can spend any amount of money on remediation for children, but we must realize that what children need is prevention. That means working with them at the earliest ages and including their parents."
>
> **MARIA PIÑÓN**
> 2009 Toyota Family Literacy Teacher of the Year

Active involvement is important in children's lives. What can you do to ensure families stay involved?

ways of communicating have changed and are changing how families communicate and interact. Just as families use the Internet, smart phones, texting, and instant messaging to keep in touch with each other, you will have to employ these same methods to communicate and involve parents. We discuss this in more detail later in the chapter.

Family Changes

We have discussed how our traditional understanding of what constitutes a family has changed and is changing. The family of today is not the family of yesterday, nor will the family of today be the family of tomorrow. Many children live with stepparents and have stepsiblings and half-siblings. Families are more diverse with divorce, separation, non-marriages, international adoptions, and foster parenting. Families have single moms and dads, and boyfriends and girlfriends who choose not to get married. Extended families include aunts, uncles, cousins, and others.

We have spent the previous chapters discussing how to meet the needs of *all* children in today's early childhood education and care settings. In this chapter, we emphasize involving *all* families in school and community programs to help all children be successful. In the following sections, you will read about different family compositions and tips for involving all children and their families in school.

Single-Parent Families

The two main reasons for the changing American family are divorce and single parenthood.[8] Depending on where you teach, as many as 50 percent of your children could be from single-parent families. Nationally, 26.3 percent of children in the United States live in single-parent families. More couples are choosing to bear children without getting married; there are an estimated 13.7 million single parents in the United States who have custody of 21.8 million children. In 2009, 41 percent of all births were to single women and most single parents with primary custody are women (82.6 percent).[9] About a quarter of single-parent family households live at or below poverty level.[10] This trend in childbearing and parenting will continue and it has tremendous implications for you and how you involve single-parent families.

Tips for Involving Single Parents.   With the above facts in mind, here are some things you can do to ensure that you involve single-parent families:

- *Accommodate family schedules by arranging conferences and events at other times—perhaps early morning, noon, late afternoon, or early evening.*   Some employers, sensitive to these needs, give release time to participate in school functions, but others do not. In addition, talk with your school administration about going to families, rather than having families always come to you and other teachers.

- *Remember, single parents have a limited amount of time to spend on involvement with their children's school and with their children at home.*   When you talk with single-parent families, make sure that (a) the meeting starts on time, (b) you have a list of items to discuss, (c) you have sample materials available to illustrate all points, (d) you make specific suggestions relative to one-parent environments, and (e) the meeting ends on time. Because one-parent families are more likely to need child care assistance to attend meetings, plan for child care for every parent meeting or activity.

- *Suggest some ways single parents can make their time with their children meaningful.* As an early childhood teacher, you are expected to assist parents by providing them information to help their children in the best ways possible. For example, if a child has trouble following directions, show families how to use home situations to help in this area. Suggest that children can learn to follow directions by assigning responsibilities such as helping with errands, meal preparation, or housework.

    For example, Sharon Parker is a library volunteer and a Parent Teacher Organization (PTO) board member at Marion Elementary School. "Although I am a single parent with a full-time career, I make time to improve the lives of our students by helping to make our library and PTO the best it can be." Parker has helped keep the school library going through some difficult times. She also helps meet community needs, such as opening the free Good Samaritan Medical Clinic for low-income citizens and providing heating assistance to those in need.[11]

- *Get to know families' lifestyles and living conditions.* From a professional standpoint, you want to be able to provide families with valid and reliable information based on their situations and circumstances. For instance, you can recommend that every child have a quiet place to study; but this may be an impossible demand for some households. Visit some of the homes in your community before you set meeting times; decide what family involvement activities to implement; and determine what you will ask of families during the year. All early childhood professionals need to keep in mind the condition of the home environment when they request that children bring certain items to school or carry out certain tasks at home. And, when asking for parents' help, be sensitive to their talents and time constraints.

- *Help develop support groups for single-parent families within your school, such as discussion groups and classes on parenting.* Be sure to consider the needs and abilities of single-parent families in your family involvement activities and programs. After all, single-parent families may represent the majority of families in your classroom.

- *Offer non-traditional opportunities for single parents to volunteer time or services to the school.* For example Huitzilin Mata, a father of two sons who attend Adelante Dual Language Academy in San Jose, California, collaborates with the school in order to plant a small garden on the school grounds and teach students about vegetables, farming, and plant care.[12]

Fathers

More fathers are involved in parenting responsibilities today than ever before; in fact, more than one-fifth of preschool children are cared for by their fathers while their mothers work outside the home.[13] Fathers head 17.4 percent of single-parent families.[14] In addition, half of all U.S. children won't live with their fathers for part of their childhoods.[15] Nonetheless, many of these "non-resident" dads want to be and are involved with their children. The implication is clear: early childhood professionals must make special efforts to involve all fathers in their programs.

More professionals now recognize that fathering and mothering are complementary processes. Many fathers are competent caregivers, directly supervising children, helping set the tone for family life, providing stability in a relationship, supporting a mother's parenting role and career goals, and representing a masculine role model for the children. And, more fathers are turning to professionals for support and advice. Organizations like the National

Fatherhood Initiative (NFI) offer resources and tips for fathers and an online community where fathers can voice their concerns and seek help. The National Fatherhood Initiative also offers school-based programming and school-based organizations to build a foundation for father involvement. By encouraging father involvement, schools reap the benefits of safer, healthier communities, and a richer educational experience for children. When dads are involved, children get higher grades, have fewer behavioral problems, and are more likely to stay in school.[16]

There are many styles of fathering. Some fathers are at home while their spouses work; some are frequently absent because their work requires travel; some have primary custody of their children; some are single; some dominate home life and are controlling; some are passive and exert little influence in the home; some take little interest in their homes and families; some are surrogate parents; some are equal partners with their spouses in raising their children. There are as many kinds of fathering as there are fathers!

Ideas for Involving Fathers.   Regardless of the roles fathers play, make special efforts to involve them. Here are some father-friendly ideas you can use to encourage their involvement:

- *Invite fathers to your class or program.*   Make sure they are included in all your parent/family initiatives.
- *Make fathers feel welcome in your program.*   For example, kindergarten students at Palm Pointe Elementary celebrated Father's Day with their dads by participating in "Donuts with Dad." Students presented their dads with arts and crafts to show appreciation for all fathers.
- *Send a simple survey home to fathers.*   Ask them how they would like to be involved in their children's education. Keep in mind the six types of parent/family involvement shown in Figure 17.2 on page 478, which we will discuss later in the chapter.
- *Provide special fatherhood and parenting classes for fathers.*   For example, the Colorado Fatherhood Initiative has helped Keith Lewis become a father to his seven-year-old son. "I feel like I have a better understanding about being a better man and a father," Lewis said. "The program helped shape me and move me. It will do the same thing for any father, seventeen or forty-five. We can all learn a thing or two from being better fathers." The Colorado Fatherhood Initiative supports fatherhood programs statewide such as Abusive Men Exploring New Directions (AMEND), Special Needs Dadvocate, and Los Padres Fatherhood Program.[17]
- *Have fathers invite other fathers to be involved.*   Fathers may think no other fathers are involved until they themselves get involved. For example, the Bellow Spring Elementary School offers the Watch D.O.G.S. (Dads of Great Students), a program that encourages fathers, grandfathers, uncles, and other father figures to spend time at the school monitoring lunch and recess and helping in the classroom. "It is a very big deal when your dad is a watch dog," said Chris Polimeni, a father who has a daughter in the second grade and a son in kindergarten. Principal Jacqueline Klamerus says, "The children take tremendous pride . . . having their dads spend the day with them."[18]
- *Include books and other literature about dads in your classroom library.*   Two good books are:
  - *My Father Knows the Names of Things* by Jane Yolen. A child celebrates his father's expertise. Not only does dad know "a dozen . . . words for night," he knows about soaps, dinosaurs, bugs, and flowers.[19]
  - *My Father is Taller Than a Tree* by Joseph Bruiac. Thirteen unique father-and-son pairs who come from diverse backgrounds and live in different places. Even though the dads are not all the same, their relationships show us an important truth: Even the simplest and most familiar activities become special when dads and kids do them together.[20]

Multigenerational Families

In January 2009, the nation and the world watched the new, *multigenerational* First Family move into the White House. President Barack Obama, the First Lady, their two daughters, and the First Grandmother, Marian Robinson, represent an emerging trend in today's families. **Multigenerational families** are those in which three or more generations share a common housing unit.[21] Multigenerational households are making a significant comeback due to the effects of the Great Recession on families and as demographic shifts change how families live.

Grandparents as Parents.   More children than ever are living with their grandparents. Reasons for this increase include parental drug use, divorce, mental and physical illness, abandonment, teenage pregnancy, child abuse and neglect, incarceration, and death. One in eight twenty-two- to twenty-nine-year-olds say that because of the Great Recession, they have boomeranged back to live with their parents after being on their own.[22] A record 49 million Americans, or 16.1 percent of the total U.S. population, live in a family household that contains at least two adult generations or a grandparent and at least one other generation.[23]

Many children today are *skipped-generation children*, meaning that neither of their parents is living with them and they are living with grandparents or in some other living arrangement. There are about 640,000 skipped generation grandfamilies in the United States, all with one or more children under eighteen. The number of children in these **grandfamilies** (another term for children living with their grandparents) remains constant at about 1 million.[24] Grandparents in these skipped-generation households have all of the parenting responsibilities of parents—providing for their grandchildren's basic needs and care, as well as making sure that they do well in school. As a result, these grandparents need your support and educational assistance.

Ideas for Involving Grandparents.   You can literally help them learn to parent all over again, keeping in mind that they are rearing their grandchildren in a whole different generation from the one in which they reared their children. Here are some things to do:

- Provide refresher parenting courses to help grandparents understand how children and schooling have changed since they reared their children.
- Link grandparents to support groups, such as Raising Our Children's Children (ROCC) and the AARP Grandparent Information Center.
- Offer grandparents opportunities to engage with children academically and socially. Many universities offer Grandparent University where grandparents can relive memories of being at a university and their grandchildren can experience what college has to offer—dorm life, food, and classes. For example, children or grandchildren of Oklahoma State University (OSU) alumni are invited to OSU's Grandparent University summer program. Students choose from the fourteen majors available including architecture, broadcasting, and horticulture, and also stay in dorms, attend classes in their major and participate in campus activities.[25]

Many grandparents who are raising grandchildren live in poverty. For them, many teachers turn to the community for help. For example, children in Bejae Keil's kindergarten class at King Academy are all fortunate enough to have "Grandma" Velma Turner,

multigenerational families Living arrangements in which three or more generations share a common housing unit.

grandfamilies Children living with their grandparents.

Grandparents acting as parents for their grandchildren are a growing reality in the United States today. What are some things you can do to ensure that grandparents will have the educational assistance and support they need so that their grandchildren will be successful in school?

a volunteer through the Visiting Nurse Services of Iowa's Foster Grandparent Program. She has spent the past three years volunteering as a foster grandparent around Des Moines, working with students in several public schools. Turner has young grandchildren and great-grandchildren of her own, but she said she finds the time to spend at the school because she loves kids. "Oh, yes, they keep you young," she said. "I have a real love of children. What people don't realize is that they're good for me, just as I can help them." Turner helped organize a midday class picnic for the children, many of whom had never eaten a picnic lunch.[26]

Linguistically Diverse Parents and Families

linguistically diverse parents Individuals whose English proficiency is minimal and who lack a comprehensive knowledge of the norms and social systems in the United States.

Linguistically diverse parents are individuals whose English proficiency is minimal and who may lack a deep knowledge of the norms and social systems in the United States. Linguistically diverse families often face language and cultural barriers that greatly hamper their ability to become actively involved in their children's education, although many have a great desire and willingness to participate.

Because the culture of linguistically diverse families often differs from that of the majority in a community, those who seek a truly collaborative involvement must take into account the cultural features that inhibit collaboration. Styles of child rearing and family organization, attitudes toward schooling, organizations around which families center their lives, life goals and values, political influences, and methods of communication within the cultural group all have implications for parent participation.

Linguistically diverse families often lack information about the U.S. educational system—including basic school philosophy, practices, and structure—which can result in misconceptions, fear, and a general reluctance to become involved. Furthermore, the U.S. educational system may be quite different from the ones these families are used to. In fact, they may have been taught to avoid active involvement in the educational process, preferring to leave all decisions concerning their children's education to professionals.

The U.S. ideal of a community-controlled and community-supported educational system must be explained to families from cultures in which this concept is not so highly valued. The traditional roles of children, teachers, and administrators in the United States also have to be explained. Many families need to learn to assume their roles and obligations associated with their children's schooling.

Janet Gonzalez-Mena provides the following culturally sensitive suggestions:[27]

- *Know what each parent in your program wants for his or her child.* Find out families' goals. What are their caregiving practices? What concerns do they have about their child? Encourage parents to talk about all of this; to ask questions; and to be honest with you about their goals for their children.
- *Become clear about your own values and goals.* Know what you believe about children and your goals for them. Have a bottom line, but leave space above it to be flexible. When you are clear, you are less likely to present a defensive stance in the face of conflict.
- *Build relationships.* Relationships enhance your chances for conflict management or resolution. Be patient. Building relationships takes time, but it enhances communications and understandings. You'll communicate better if you have a relationship, and you'll have a relationship if you learn to communicate!
- *Become an effective cross-cultural communicator.* It is possible to learn communication skills—what is your communication style? Learn about communication styles

that are different from your own. What you think a person means may not be what he or she *really* means. Do not make assumptions. Listen carefully. Ask for clarification. Find ways to test for understanding.

- *Use a problem-solving rather than a power approach to conflicts.* Be flexible—negotiate when possible. Look at your willingness to share power. Is it a control issue you are dealing with?
- *Commit yourself to education.* Educate yourself and your families. Sometimes lack of information or understanding of each other's perspective is what keeps the conflict going.

Teenage Parents

At one time most teenage parents were married, but today the majority are not; and they come from culturally and linguistically diverse backgrounds. Despite society's advances over the last few decades, for teen moms, not much has changed. Two-thirds of teenage mothers live in poverty; less than 50 percent graduate high school; and only 2 percent of girls who are moms by the age of eighteen will graduate college by the age of thirty.[28] Further, more teenage mothers are choosing to raise their children with assistance from their mothers and grandmothers. Regardless of their living arrangements, teenage parents have the following needs:

- *Support in their role as parents.* Support can include information about child-rearing practices and child development and help in implementing the information in their interactions with their children. Teen Parents of Lubbock (Texas) enrolls young mothers age twelve to twenty-one in weekly education meetings and monthly social activities or playdates with their mentor moms. The program enables teenagers to meet other young mothers like themselves and be in a support network that keeps them focused on school while raising their children.[29]
- *Support in their continuing development as adolescents and young adults.* Remember that younger teenage parents are really children themselves. They need assistance in meeting their own developmental needs, as well as those of their children.
- *Help with completing their education.* Some early childhood programs provide parenting courses as well as classes designed to help teenage parents complete requirements for a high school diploma. Remember that a critical influence on children's development and achievement is the mother's education level. For example, the Tupelo (Mississippi) School District offers the Link Centre, a high school advancement academy for teenage mothers so they can continue their education while receiving additional help not received in a traditional classroom, like parenting skills.[30]

As early childhood programs enroll more children of teenage families, they must seek ways to creatively and sensitively involve these families.

Lesbian, Gay, Bisexual and Transgender (LGBT) Families

More than likely you will have in your classroom children from lesbian, gay, bisexual, and transgendered (LGBT) families. Here are some important facts and figures you need to consider as you seek to involve and embrace all parents and families:

- Being raised in LGBT families does not impact normal childhood development. Studies show that the sexual orientation of a parent is irrelevant to the development of a child's mental health, social development, sexual orientation, and to the quality of the parent–child relationship.[31] Children raised in lesbian households are psycho-logically well-adjusted and have fewer behavioral problems than their peers raised in heterosexual households. Children from lesbian families rate higher in social, aca-demic and total competence. They also show lower rates in social, rule-breaking, aggressive problem behavior.[32]

- LGBT parents are more likely to be involved in their children's education; are more involved in school activities; and are more likely to report more consistent communi-cation with school personnel than their heterosexual counterparts.[33]

- LGBT parents suffer from various types of exclusion from their school communities, such as being excluded or prevented from fully participating in school activities and events; being excluded by school policies and procedures; and being ignored and feeling invisible. LGBT parents report mistreatment from other parents in the school community and from their children's peers at school.[34]

- Children may be stigmatized because of their parents' sexuality and be victims of teasing and bullying. Studies provide mixed results on whether children from LGBT families suffer from more teasing and bullying than peers from heterosexual families. However, data show that about 45 percent of LGBT parents are either African American or Latino. This is important because it is possible that there is a greater degree of stigmatization of homosexuality in minority groups.[35]

- LGBT families are raising 4 percent of all adopted children in the United States.[36] Adopted children with same-sex parents are more likely to be foreign-born.[37] These children may face not only prejudices about their country of origin but also the prej-udices against the sexual orientation of their families.

So what does this mean for you? Children in your classroom are your students regard-less of their parents' sexual orientation and your own personal beliefs. They deserve the best you can give them. All parents deserve to be and should be involved. One mother said, "I want my sons' school environment to give them the opportunity to learn without harassment. And, I want to be a welcomed and integral part of my children's educational experience as they grow."[38] However, you may face some obstacles to successfully involving LGBT families from other parents, staff members, and community members. Perhaps your own prejudices may get in the way of your ability to provide all children with an equal and quality education. Here is what you can do:

All parents deserve to be and should be involved in their children's education. What can you do to help LGBT families get involved in their children's education?

- Be aware of your own beliefs and how they may impact your teaching and treatment of others. Treat each family member and child equally with dignity, respect, and honor. Under no circumstances should you participate in making disparaging, derogatory, or negative remarks to or about LGBT parents to other teachers, parents, students, or community members.

- Collaborate with other staff members to arrange for a uni-form response to teasing and bullying. Teachers and administrators should be a united front against discrimina-tion and bullying to better support each child's education and sense of belonging.

- Studies show that LGBT parents whose children's schools have a comprehensive safe-school policy that protects students from bullying and harassment report the lowest level of mistreatment. A comprehensive curriculum based on diversity acceptance is also helpful.[39] Work with your colleagues and school district administrators to support and use a comprehensive approach to exploring and welcoming diverse families.

- Invite and encourage LGBT families to attend school functions, volunteer, and participate in classroom activities as you do other families. Let them know you value and desire their input, presence, and participation. Make it clear that your classroom is a friendly, accepting, equalizing place by having classroom decorations reflect the diversity of all families, from bi-racial to LGBT to single parents.

- Be sure to include both parents in the parent-family relationship, not just the biological parent (if the child is not adopted). Encourage both parents' participation and input.

Military Families

You may have heard the phrase, "When one member joins, the whole family serves," when it comes to service members and their families.[40] This could not be more true today with the United States at war in several countries. Children are profoundly impacted by their families' involvement in military service. At the present time, there are over 250,000 servicemen and servicewomen away from home on active duty, so it is likely that you will have a child of a military family in your classroom.[41] Today's service families are unique in that they face a lifestyle that is often in upheaval and results in increased family separations due to frequent deployment, recalls to active duty, and relocations. These are highly stressful and challenging times for service families.[42] Here are some suggestions for how you can support children of military families.

- *Help children keep in contact with families.*   Offer opportunities for children to write letters, e-mail or talk to their parent on the phone. As a project for your students, you can honor your military parents by sending them a class package with a special gift, video, or letter. Many faith-based veterans groups and other community agencies will pay the postage for packages and letters for service personnel. For example, Cindy Bost of Youngsville, Pennsylvania started Pennies for Postage to help families and organizations pay for postage to send care packages to service members overseas. Cindy started with bake sales and donation buckets in stores around town, but now some local organizations are on board.[43] You can also help kids keep a journal, scrapbook, or photo album of daily events to share with their mom or dad when they return.

- *Get in touch with other military families in your school and community.*   The Department of Defense has the Sure Start program, which operates Child Development Programs (CDP) and the Department of Defense Educational Activities (DoDEA). CDP provides child care and before- and after-school care for children six weeks to fourteen years old. DoDEA provides free, public education to all children in grades K–12, plus selected preschool-aged children who have disabilities.[44] Through these programs, you can help children in your class make contact with other children whose parents are on active military duty and give them a forum to talk about their thoughts and feelings.

- *Collaborate with the community to gain access to programs that support military families.*   The Armed Services YMCA's Operation Hero holds biweekly meetings where children come together to work on various projects designed to increase their ability to adapt to making changes in schools and new friends. Such support groups offer many outlets for children and families to form new relationships, establish ties in a new place, and feel comfortable in a school. Frequently relocating is difficult for children; Mikayla Bonner says, "The challenges are different with trying to fit in with your new environment and trying to be yourself and make friends at the same time."[45] Imagine having to do that several times a year! So, if a military support group for families and children does not exist in your school or community, you can help organize one.

- *Understand and spot academic and behavior cues early.* Children may experience a decline in classroom performance while a parent is on active military duty; it may be hard for them to focus with so much to be worried about.[46] Be understanding and supportive; provide a listening ear to your children with deployed family members. Provide extra tutoring and other opportunities for children to learn and practice academics to help keep them on track.

- *Encourage parents to limit the amount of television children watch.* Young children should not watch war-related coverage without adult supervision. Children's fears and worries for their family members can lead to negative emotions, such as depression, anxiety, or aggression.[47] Provide a nurturing relationship and classroom. Sadly, children do know about and are harmed by war and violence. You can produce an antidote for fear and violence by providing a positive and nurturing class and school environment.

Prison/Incarcerated Families

In the United States, 1 in every 31 adults (3.2 percent) are in jail or prison, probation, or on parole.[48] This means that at least 1.7 million minor children in the U.S. have a parent in prison, about a quarter of whom are under age five.[49] Ninety-two percent of incarcerated parents are fathers. The number of children with a father in prison grew by 77 percent from 1991 through mid-2007.[50] In addition, children with an incarcerated parent are two to three times more likely to engage in delinquent behavior.[51]

With these alarming statistics, community programs are taking an active role in preventing juvenile delinquency as well as giving children an opportunity to see their incarcerated parents. Get On The Bus, a Los Angeles-based nonprofit organization founded by Sister Suszanne Jabro, brings children and their guardians/caregivers from throughout the state of California to visit their mothers and fathers in prison every year around Mother's and Father's Day. Get On The Bus is a project of the Center of Restorative Justice. Maria Costanzo Palmer, program director, says that every child has a right to see, talk to, and touch their parents. In May 2010, Get On The Bus took 70 busloads of children from every major city in California to three women's prisons and four men's prisons. Maria says that for many children, this is the only way that they get to visit their parents, many of whom are incarcerated over 300 miles away. Kids on the bus learn that they are not alone and are not the only children with a parent in prison. Maria has this advice for you as a classroom teacher:[52]

- Be aware that you may have children whose parents are in prison in your classroom. Being aware of the fact that many children have incarcerated parents is the first step to helping them.

- Not all children of incarcerated parents know that their mother or father is in prison. Many families are careful of what they say about where the mother or father is, so approach each family carefully and get to know their needs. Ask them how you can help them.

- Let children know that they are loved by you and others. Remember, all children need affection and the security of knowing you care.[53]

Implications of Changing Family Patterns

Given the changes in families today, here are some things you can do to help parents:

- *Provide support services for parents and their children.* Support can range from being a listening ear to organizing support groups and seminars on single parenting. You can help families link up with other agencies and groups, such as Big Brothers and Big Sisters and Families without Partners. Through newsletters and flyers, e-mails, Web pages, and texting you can offer families specific advice on how to help children become independent and how to meet the demands of living in single-parent families, stepfamilies, and other family configurations.

- *Avoid criticism and being judgmental toward parents.* Examine your attitudes toward family patterns and remember there is no right family pattern in which all children should be reared. Be careful not to criticize parents for the jobs they are doing. Parents may not have enough time to spend with their children or know how to discipline them. Regardless of their circumstances, families need help, not criticism.

- *Offer educational experiences for parents and their children to participate in.* Offer experiences children might not otherwise have because of their family organization. For example, outdoor activities such as fishing trips and sports events can be interesting and enriching learning experiences for children who may not have such opportunities.

  Parents and students at Lura A. White Elementary School participated in the annual "Books and Beyond," a national program that promotes student reading outside of school and the involvement of parents in their children's reading. Awards were given to teachers and parents who made the program a success and also students who read the most books. All participants and their families enjoyed a school-wide barbeque. Kindergarten students read 6,720 books; first graders read 7,895 books; second graders read 5,635 books; and third graders read 8,116 books.[54]

- *Be sensitive to the needs of the families in your classroom.* Avoid having children make presents for both parents when it is inappropriate to do so or awarding prizes for bringing both parents to meetings. Replace such terms as *broken home* with *single-parent family*. Be sensitive to the realities of children's home lives. For instance, when a teacher sent a field trip permission form home with children and told them to have their mothers or fathers sign it, one child said, "I don't have a father. If my mother can't sign it, can the man she sleeps with sign it?" Clarify with families how they would like specific situations handled; for example, ask whether you should send notices of school events and in what language and to both parents.

- *Seek professional development training.* Request professional development training to help you work with families. Professional development programs can provide information about referral agencies, guidance techniques, and child abuse identification and prevention. You need to be alert to all kinds of child abuse, including mental, physical, and sexual abuse.

There are unlimited possibilities for a meaningful program of family involvement. Families can make a significant difference in their children's education, and with your assistance they can join teachers and schools in a productive partnership. The following Voice from the Field, "How to Create a Parent-Friendly School," is a Competency Builder that shares effective strategies you can use to create a parent-friendly school.

As you think about how you will involve parents and families, reflect on the powerful influences families have in children's lives. It is in the context of the family unit that children learn about morality and character—essential developmental dimensions of their lives.

Voice from the Field

How to Create a Parent-Friendly School

Parent and community involvement makes the difference between schools being a place to go and a place to learn. "Our PTA brings the school community together and encourages student involvement in affective and academic areas," says Dr. Jesse D. Baker, principal of Stadium Drive Elementary School of the Arts in Lake Orion, Michigan. He cites events such as mother–son dances, daddy–daughter outings, family swim night at the local high school, and a parent-directed spirit week and fun run as examples of parent involvement. In addition, it is usual to have one or two parent volunteers in each classroom on most days. "When parents are welcomed and their decisions are respected, their involvement increases," says Baker.

Parent-friendly schools and programs do not just happen. They require hard work and dedication by everyone involved. Here are some ideas from Stadium Drive Elementary School that you can use to make your classroom and school more parent friendly:

STRATEGY 1 Show That You Care

Develop a compassionate culture toward students, families, and the community in general.

- Send flowers and letters and make telephone calls and visits to ill children or their families to show the extent of the staff's commitment to families.
- Welcome new families and encourage them to become involved.
- Encourage teachers to stand at their classroom doors each morning and greet youngsters as they enter.
- Organize a schoolwide effort to help a community member cope with a life-threatening condition. At Stadium Drive Elementary, students collect money. However, donations of food, offers of transportation, or care for children are other excellent ways to show you care.
- Collect canned goods for needy families at holiday times and throughout the year.
- Collect donations for victims of natural disasters.
- Conduct a coats-for-kids drive before cold weather sets in.
- Reward students' caring behaviors. Stadium Drive Elementary has a Pause to Recognize program that acknowledges caring and respectful behavior.

- Create a scholarship fund. Staff members at Stadium Drive each pay a dollar on Fridays for the privilege of wearing blue jeans, thus creating a scholarship fund for a graduating senior alumnus.

STRATEGY 2 Communicate Frequently with Parents and the Community

Through multiple media, highlight the school's philosophy and activities that support that philosophy. "Communication is key to maintaining a nurturing culture between staff and families," says Jan Seeds, PTA president. Parents at Stadium Drive, named a parent-friendly school by *Parent Magazine,* stay connected with the school through regular communication.

- Make a calendar of school events available on public access cable and the school's website.
- Publish a weekly newsletter in paper and electronic form.
- Ask the PTA to produce a student directory of addresses and phone numbers.
- Call or e-mail parents to update them on classroom activities.

STRATEGY 3 Solicit Feedback from Parents

Gather data from parents and the community regarding their needs and perceptions. Then use the data to set school goals. Gather written comments of parents regarding school climate. When requesting a teacher, one parent at Stadium Drive wrote, "My daughter was in her class last year. Through the different class volunteering I did, I was able to see how she managed her classroom and taught the children, and I was very impressed. Her attentiveness and compassion really helped bring out the best in children." Ask for opinions and suggestions.

STRATEGY 4 Unite Parents and Staff in a Common Goal

Meeting the educational needs of all students should be everyone's top priority. Stadium Drive maintains a positive bond among all stakeholders and establishes school priorities as a result of formal and informal information gleaned from student, parent, and staff surveys.

- Provide funds for field trips and for visiting artists, musicians, dancers, and actors to come to your school to work with students. The PTA at Stadium Drive is responsible for this area.
- Extend the parent–teacher partnership whenever possible. At Stadium Drive's Curriculum Night, teachers explain grade-level curriculum and address specific issues. Fall and spring conferences update parents on their children's progress.

STRATEGY 5 Create Community Partnerships

Cooperative relationships can showcase school efforts and involve businesses in school activities. Partnerships beyond the Stadium Drive school walls exist with both businesses and civic organizations.

- Establish mutually beneficial relationships with local businesses. For example, students can make deposits at school to their bank savings account. Or a local art shop can frame—at no cost—student artwork going to state competition.
- Display student art and written work at local businesses and restaurants.
- Invite community artists, musicians, and journalists to judge student entries in competitions.
- Host senior citizens as special guests at school activities, recitals, concerts, and performances.
- Work with local charities. At Stadium Drive, staff and students work with the local Lions Club in an adopt-a-family program, with each classroom providing wrapped presents for a needy family during winter holidays.

STRATEGY 6 Connect Parents and Students with the School

Programs and services that benefit and involve families can strengthen and unify the school community.

- Recruit parents at the beginning of the year, and then call them to volunteer for classroom help, special projects, and field trip chaperones, as well as in your school art room or media center. Stadium Drive uses this approach, and the growth in their volunteerism over the past six years has been significant—from 975 to nearly 5,000 volunteer hours.

- Tap into students from middle school and high school; they are often willing volunteers. At Stadium Drive these older students volunteered more than 600 hours last year.
- Thank all volunteers at the end of the year. For example, have a volunteer tea or picnic.
- Include nonacademic services for students and families, such as a school social worker, a county nurse, and special education ancillary staff.
- Offer counseling on child rearing, grief management, and conflict resolution.
- Recommend strategies for handling trauma, disruptive behavior, poor student choices, and psychological issues.
- Make referrals to outside agencies for child abuse, drug abuse, alcoholism, or domestic violence.
- Support students and parents with information and training on health issues.

STRATEGY 7 Consider Family Needs

Make meeting times, child care arrangements, and other activities user friendly.

- Provide scholarships to aid students who would be otherwise unable to attend camp or field trips.
- Schedule PTA meetings, parent–teacher conferences, and personal contacts in the evening, before school, or immediately after school. Provide free child care.
- Encourage staff to meet at times convenient to parents.
- Provide before- and after-school child care and enrichment programs, such as cooking, dance, crafts, tumbling, magic, play-building, cartooning, art, and computer applications.
- Make school facilities available after hours to parents and the groups to which they belong for scouting, martial arts training, sports, home designing, or other community interests.
- Use the educational resources of the school and community to extend learning opportunities for families. For example, students at Stadium Drive design Web pages to exhibit classroom activities, and their concerts and musical productions are broadcast on local cable.
- Provide a parent section in the library for materials on child growth and parenting.

Source: Contributed by Dr. Jesse D. Baker, principal, Stadium Drive Elementary School, Lake Orion, Michigan.

Education as a Family Affair

family involvement The participation of parents and other family members in all areas of their children's education and development, based on the premise that parents are the primary influence in children's lives.

Family involvement is a process of helping families use their abilities to benefit themselves, their children, and the early childhood program. Families, children, and the program are all part of the process, and you must work with and through families if you want to be successful.

Education starts in the home, and what happens there profoundly affects the trajectory of development and learning. The greater the family's involvement in children's learning, the more likely it is that students will receive a high-quality education.

The central role families play in children's education is a reality that teachers and schools must address as they make plans for reforming schools and increasing student achievement. Many immigrant groups, such as Mexicans and Hmong, place a great value on the roles and responsibilities of the extended family in child rearing and education.

Partnering with parents is a process whose time has come, and the benefits far outweigh any inconveniences or barriers that may stand in the way of bringing schools and parents together. As an early childhood teacher, you must nurture and develop your partnerships with families. Figure 17.1 "Guidelines for Involving Parents and Families" shows you seven guidelines that can help you effectively involve parents and families.

Activities to Encourage Parent/Family Involvement

As you think about your role in parent and family involvement, think about what activities you will use to engage parents and families in their child's learning. Note the support systems that encourage family involvement. For example, car pools and child care encourage family involvement because families may not be able to attend programs and become involved if they do not have child care for their children or a means of getting to the program in the first place. Child care makes their participation possible and more enjoyable.

The following activities provide for significant family involvement; they are organized according to the Six Types of Parent/Family Involvement shown in Figure 17.2 on page 478. These types of parent/family involvement constitute a comprehensive approach to your work with parents. A worthy professional goal would be for you to try to have some of your parents involved in all six of these types of parent involvement through the school year.

Type 1: Parenting Knowledge and Skills

- *Workshops*—Introduce families to the school's policies, procedures, and programs. Most families want to know what is going on in the school and would do a better job of parenting and educating if they knew how.
- *Adult education classes*—Provide families with opportunities to learn about a range of subjects.
- *Training programs*—Give parents and other family members skills as classroom aides, club and activity sponsors, curriculum planners, and policy decision makers. When parents and other family members are viewed as experts, empowerment results.
- *Classroom and center activities*—Although not all families can be directly involved in classroom activities, encourage those who can. But remember that those who are involved must have guidance, direction, and training. Involving parents and others as paid aides can be an excellent way to provide both employment and training. Many programs, such as Head Start, actively support such a policy.
- *Libraries and materials centers*—Families benefit from books and other articles relating to parenting. Some programs furnish resource areas with comfortable chairs to encourage families to use these materials.

Type 2: Communicating Between Home and School

- *Performances and plays*—These, especially ones in which children have a part, tend to bring families to school; however, the purpose of children's performances should not be solely to get families involved.

1 Welcome families in your classroom and build relationships with them	• **Strategies:** • Conduct home visits. Visiting a few of your students' homes can yield helpful information on the specific needs of your classroom. • Call parents and introduce yourself. • Offer to e-mail parents and answer their questions about their children and the school. • Have a notice board with updated information for families.
2 Find out what goals parents have for their children	• **Strategies:** • Use goals for your classroom, school, parents, and state in your planning. • Request to know more information about the child and send home your state standards on the first day of school. • Cooperatively set goals with parents to encourage children's success when you conference with parents. • Encourage children to set high goals for their learning and share their goals with parents. • Foster the belief that all families want the best for their children.
3 Learn how to best communicate with families according to their cultural and language preferences	• **Strategies:** • Actively involve diverse backgrounds and promote multiculturalism in your classroom. • Overcome any cultural features that can inhibit collaboration. • Ask parents their involvement preferences—before or after school, during the day, field trips, Saturdays, and so on. • Send home information that translates the diverse languages of your classroom.
4 Support families in their roles as the first teachers of their children	• **Strategies:** • Use the telephone and e-mail to let parents know about student progress. • Hold family-teacher conferences several times throughout the school year to discuss children's successes and strengths. • Share information, materials, help with parenting issues, and be available to answer questions for parents. • Let parents know you are always available and willing to help.
5 Provide frequent, open communication and feedback on student progress	• **Strategies:** • Use technology-based resources (Gradespeed, etc.) to keep parents up-to-date on their child's academic and behavioral progress. • Keep parents up-to-date with their child's academic and behavioral reports, report cards, and progress reports. • Know the method of communication your students' parents and families prefer.
6 Support fathers in their role as parents	• **Strategies:** • Encourage fathers to read, play games, and help their children with homework and class projects. • Inform fathers that volunteering at school can enhance their children's learning. • Offer events and programs that will allow fathers to feel needed in your classroom.
7 Encourage families to be mentors, classroom aides, tutors, and homework helpers	• **Strategies:** • Communicate guidelines for helping students prepare for tests. • Let parents know what needs you have and invite them to help. • Offer opportunities where parents can assist with classroom events, field trips, planning, and so forth. • Encourage families to designate time for homework and other academic needs.

FIGURE 17.1 Seven Guidelines for Involving Parents and Families

FIGURE 17.2 Six Types of Parent/ Family Involvement

Source: *School, Family and Community Partnerships: Your Handbook for Action* by Joyce Epstein. Copyright 2008 by SAGE PUBLICATIONS INC BOOKS. Reproduced with permission of SAGE PUBLICATIONS INC BOOKS in the formats textbook and other book via Copyright Clearance Center. Photo © Blend Images/Alamy.

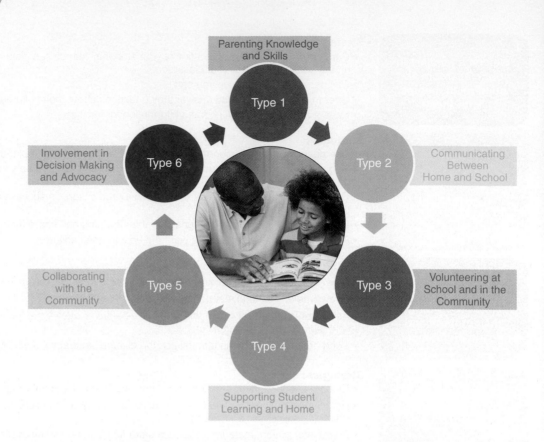

- *Telephone hotlines*—When staffed by families, they can help allay fears and provide information relating to child abuse, communicable diseases, and special events. Hotlines answered by a knowledgeable parent or family member, even if only during certain hours of the week, provide other parents and family members with a means of getting advice and help. Telephone networks or phone trees are also used to help children and parents with homework and to monitor latchkey children.
- *Newsletters*—When planned with parents' help, newsletters are an excellent way to keep families informed about program events, activities, and curriculum information. Newsletters in parents' native languages help keep language-minority families informed.
- *Home learning materials and activities*—Putting out a monthly calendar of activities to be done at home is one good way to keep families involved in their children's learning.
- *IEPs for children with special needs*—Involvement in writing an IEP is not only a legal requirement but also an excellent learning experience and an effective communication tool.

Type 3: Volunteering at School and in the Community

- *Service exchanges*—When operated by early childhood programs and other agencies, exchanges can help families with their need for services. For example, one parent might provide child care in her home in exchange for having her washing machine repaired. The possibilities for such exchanges are endless.
- *Welcoming committees*—A good way to involve families in any program is to have other families contact them when their children first join a program.

Type 4: Supporting Student Learning at Home

- *Books and other materials for home use*—Provide these for parents to read to their children.

- *Suggestions for parents*—Provide parents with tips on how to help their children with homework.
- *A website for parents*—This can inform them about the activities of your classroom. Give suggestions on how parents can extend and enrich classroom projects and activities at home.
- *A home learning kit*—This can consist of activities and materials (books, activity packets, etc.). Send such kits home with children.

Type 5: Collaborating with the Community

- *Family nights, cultural dinners, carnivals, and potluck dinners*—Such events bring families and the community to the school in nonthreatening, social ways.
- *Parent support groups*—Parents need support in their roles. Support groups can provide parenting information, community agency information, and speakers.

Type 6: Involvement in Decision Making and Advocacy

- *Fairs and bazaars*—Involve families in many aspects of the decision making process. Allow and encourage input in regards to fund-raising, planning, and so forth.
- *Hiring and policy making*—Parents and community members can and should serve on committees that hire staff and set policy.
- *Curriculum development and review*—Parents' involvement in curriculum planning helps them learn about and understand what constitutes a quality program and what is involved in a developmentally appropriate curriculum. When families know about the curriculum, they are more supportive of it.

Family-Centered Programs

Family-centered programs focus on meeting the needs of children through the family unit, whatever that unit may be. To most effectively meet the needs of children, early childhood teachers must also meet the needs of family members and the family unit. When planning for the specific needs of students with disabilities, family involvement is critical. **Family-centered teaching** makes sense for a number of reasons. First, the family unit has the major responsibility for meeting children's needs; and the family system is a powerful determiner of developmental processes, for both better and worse. Helping family members improve their roles benefits children and consequently promotes their success in school.

family-centered teaching Instruction that focuses on meeting the needs of students through the family unit.

Second, family issues and problems must be addressed to really help children. For instance, helping parents gain access to adequate and affordable health care increases the chances that the whole family, including the children, will be healthy. For example, California Healthy Families is a statewide program that provides access to health, dental, and vision coverage to uninsured children and families who do not qualify for no-cost Medi-Cal.[55]

Third, teachers can do many things concurrently with children and their families that benefit both. Literacy is a good example. Adopting a family approach to literacy means helping parents learn the importance of literacy and of reading to their children to help ensure literacy development.

The Riverside Parent Academy

The family approach to literacy can be seen in the Riverside Parent Academy. The Riverside Parent Academy originated through a collaborative effort between the school and the Miami-Dade County Public Schools (Florida) division of Community Services. Historically, Riverside Elementary has supported parental involvement through several family literacy initiatives including *Los Padres Aprenden Juntos*, funded by the State of Florida Governor's Literacy grant, the federal *Even Start* family literacy program, the *Children's Trust* grant and the Toyota Family Literacy grant and the Barbara Bush Family Literacy grant.

The Riverside Parent Academy is held in a re-locatable building across the street from the main campus where adult ESOL classes are provided daily for parents by certified adult education teachers. Child care for children up through five years old is provided by Child Development Associate (CDA) certified employees for parents attending ESOL classes. Parent workshops are conducted on a regular basis by district staff from the Parent Academy, the Bilingual Department, Title I, and school-site staff and other community agencies. Workshop topics range from navigating the local school district, immigration issues, prevention of drug abuse, parenting skills, homework help, and HIV/AIDS. Parents from the community use the computer lab, check out books from the library, and pick up information from the Parent Resource Center in the Riverside Parent Academy.

The relationship between Parent Academy staff and school-site staff is very collaborative. All staff members work together to involve parents in the educational process of their children. Riverside teachers understand the importance of the relationship of the school, parents, and children. Parents are encouraged to continue the process of teaching and learning with their children at home. Children are encouraged in school and at home to take ownership of their learning. It has enriched the teaching and learning environment in school and promoted student achievement.

The Healthy Families Program

The Healthy Families Program in Cape May County in New Jersey, provides comprehensive in-home services to at-risk families and their children from birth to five. Parents learn about infant sleeping patterns, the dangers of smoking around a newborn, nutrition, and breastfeeding, and meet in a support group once a month.

Families are referred from county agencies but participation is voluntary. A case manager works with each family for up to three years to ensure support for both the parent and child. Chapter representatives visit mothers for about an hour each week to teach them how to play with their children and to encourage learning about normal growth and development. Peggy Smith, program manager for Healthy Families says, "We have to interact with the families (while the child is) at a young age because there's a lot to learn." About 115 local families receive assistance in Cape May County.[56]

Figure 17.3 helps you to understand more about the outcomes and benefits of family-centered teaching.

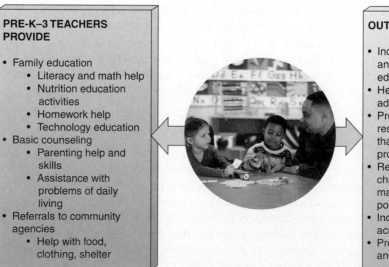

PRE-K–3 TEACHERS PROVIDE	OUTCOMES/BENEFITS

• Family education
  • Literacy and math help
  • Nutrition education activities
  • Homework help
  • Technology education
• Basic counseling
  • Parenting help and skills
  • Assistance with problems of daily living
• Referrals to community agencies
  • Help with food, clothing, shelter
	• Increase knowledge, skills, and understanding of education process
	• Help families and children address and solve problems
	• Provide greater range of resources and more experts than school alone can provide
	• Relieve families and children/youth of stress to make learning more possible
	• Increase student achievement
	• Promote school retention and prevent dropout

FIGURE 17.3 Family-Centered Teaching

AVANCE.   One example of a parenting program is AVANCE (from the Spanish word for "advance" or "progress"), which serves the needs of the hardest-to-reach, primarily Hispanic, families. Founded in Texas, the organization focuses on teaching parents of children from birth through three years of age the skills parents need to nurture children to success in school and life. AVANCE provides a comprehensive parenting education program, including a twenty-seven lesson/nine-month bilingual curriculum. While parents attend the once-a-week, three-hour parenting program—incorporating lessons in child growth and development, toy making, and family support—AVANCE provides transportation and quality developmental care for their children. AVANCE also includes a home visiting component, offers special programs for fathers, and provides literacy training.[57]

AVANCE programs are duplicated in many communities. For example the AVANCE-Dallas (Texas) partnership with United Way offers the Born Learning class to prepare young children for kindergarten and connect low-income parents with resources such as emergency financial assistance for food. Parents like Analise Guerrero are learning new ways to bond with their children. "They're teaching me new ways to connect with my kids."[58]

Home Visits

Home visits are becoming more commonplace for early childhood professionals. Teachers who do home visiting should be trained prior to going on the visits. Plan now for how you will visit in the homes of your children's families.

A home visiting program can show that the school is willing to go more than halfway to involve parents in their children's education. Home visits also help teachers demonstrate their interest in students' families and understand their students better by seeing them in their home environment.

These visits should not replace parent–teacher conferences or be used to discuss children's progress. When completed early, before any school problems arise, visits avoid putting parents on the defensive and signal that you are eager to work with them. Teachers who make home visits say that visits build stronger relationships with parents and children and improve attendance and achievement.[59]

Planning and Scheduling.   Administrators and teachers must be willing to participate in a home visiting program and be involved in planning it. These suggestions help achieve that goal.

Many early childhood teachers conduct home visits to help parents learn how to support their children's learning at home. What useful information can parents provide you about children's learning, experience, and growth and development?

- Teachers' schedules must be adjusted so that they have the necessary time to make home visits.
- Home visits should be scheduled before school begins or early in the school year. Some schools schedule home visits in the afternoon right after school. Others have found that early evening is more convenient for parents. A mix of times may be needed to reach all families.
- Teachers should be given flexibility to schedule their visits during a targeted time period.
- Teachers of siblings may want to visit these children's homes together but should take care not to overwhelm parents.
- Some schools work with community groups (e.g., boys' and girls' clubs, housing complexes, 4-H, Y's, and community centers) to schedule visits in neutral but convenient places.

Making Parents Feel Comfortable.   Here are some useful tips to make your home visits productive for families and for you.

- Send a letter or e-mail parents explaining that you and other teachers want to make informal visits to all students' homes. Include a form that parents can mail back to accept or decline the visit and to request that a translator accompany you.
- State clearly that the intent of this fifteen- to thirty-minute visit is to introduce yourself to parents and family members, and not to discuss the child's progress.
- Suggest that families think about special things their children would want to share with the teacher.
- Calm parents' worries. One school included a note to parents that said, "No preparation is required. In fact, our own homes need to be vacuumed, and all of us are on diets!" This touch of humor and casualness helps set a friendly and informal tone.
- A phone call or e-mail to parents who have not responded to your letter can explain your plan for home visits and reassure parents that it is to get acquainted and not to evaluate students or parents.
- Enlist community groups, religious organizations, and businesses to help publicize the home visits.

Family Conferences

Significant parent involvement occurs through well-planned and well-conducted conferences between families and early childhood professionals, informally referred to as **parent–teacher conferences** or **family–teacher conferences**. Such conferences are often the first contact many families have with a school and are critical both from a public relations point of view and as a vehicle for helping families and professionals accomplish their goals. The following guidelines will help you prepare for and conduct successful conferences:

- *Plan ahead.* Be sure of the reason for the conference. What do you want to accomplish? List the points you want to cover and think about what you are going to say.
- *Get to know the parents.* This is not wasted time; the more effectively you establish rapport with a parent, the more you will accomplish in the long run.
- *Avoid an authoritative atmosphere.* Do not sit behind your desk while the parent sits in a child's chair. Treat parents and others like the adults they are.
- *Communicate at the parent's level.* Use words, phrases, and explanations that parents understand and are familiar with. Avoid jargon or complicated explanations, and speak in your natural, conversational style.
- *Accentuate the positive.* Make every effort to show and tell parents what the child is doing well. When you deal with problems, put them in the proper perspective: identify what the child is able to do; what the goals and purposes of the learning program are; what specific skills or concepts you are trying to get the child to learn; and what problems the child is having in achieving. Most important, explain what you plan to do to help the child achieve and what specific role the parents can play in meeting achievement goals.
- *Give families a chance to talk.* You will not learn much about them if you do all the talking, so encourage families to talk.
- *Learn to listen.* An active listener holds eye contact, uses body language such as head nodding and hand gestures, does not interrupt, avoids arguing, paraphrases as a way of clarifying ideas, and keeps the conversation on track.
- *Follow up.* Ask the parent for a definite time for the next conference as you are concluding the current one. Another conference is the best method of solidifying gains and extending support, but other acceptable means of follow-up are telephone calls, written reports, notes sent with children, and brief visits to the home. Even though

parent–teacher conferences or **family–teacher conferences** Meetings between parents and early childhood professionals to inform the parents of the child's progress and allow them to actively participate in the educational process.

these types of contacts may appear casual, they should be planned for and conducted as seriously as any regular parent–professional conference. No matter which approach you choose, family-teacher conferences have many benefits:

- Families see that you genuinely care about their children.
- Family members can clarify problems, issues, advice, and directions.
- Parents, family members, and children are encouraged to continue to do their best.
- Conferences offer opportunities to extend classroom learning to the home.
- You can extend programs initiated to help families or formulate new plans.

- *Develop an action plan.* Never leave the parent with a sense of frustration, unsure of what you will be doing or what they are to do. Every communication with families should end on a positive note, so that everyone knows what is to be done and how.

Children and Conferences.   A frequently asked question is, "Should children be present at parent–teacher conferences?" The answer is, "Yes, of course, if it is appropriate for them to be present." In most instances, it is appropriate and offers a number of benefits:

- Children have much to contribute. They can talk about their progress and behavior, offer suggestions for improvement and enrichment, and discuss their interests.
- The locus of control is centered in the child. Children learn that they have a voice and that others think their opinions are important.
- Children's self-esteem is enhanced because they are viewed as an important part of the conference and because a major purpose of the conference is to help them and their families.
- Children become more involved in their classroom and education. Students take pride not only in their own accomplishments and their ability to share them, but also in the opportunity to help each other prepare for their conferences. A team spirit—a sense of community—can emerge and benefit everyone involved.[60]
- Children learn that education is a cooperative process between home and school.

As you reflect on the ways you can communicate with children and their families, also think about ways you can involve them in your classroom. Read the Voice from the Field "How to Communicate with Families" to get a better understanding of the importance of communicating with families and ways you can involve them.

Involving Families Electronically

The Internet provides another way for you to reach out to parents and keep them informed and involved. For example, teachers use the Internet to post calendars, newsletters, discussion topics, assignments, assessment tools, spelling lists, and tips. Here are some ways you can electronically connect with families:

- *E-mail.*   E-mail is fast, convenient, and for many families is the preferred mode of communication. E-mail can increase communication between families and teachers, and between faculty and outside personnel involved in working with individual students.
- *Teacher website.*   Most school districts have a website that provides general information about the district and individual schools. Many teachers have their own classroom website as well. Web pages are excellent ways to give parents and community members general information and let them virtually experience school and classroom events and accomplishments. For example, through the Internet, you can access many teachers' websites. Now would be a good time for you to do this.

Marci McGowan, first grade teacher at H. W. Mountz Elementary School, uses her classroom website as an interactive tool to connect with families outside of the classroom. She displays photos of student work and projects, access to other colleagues' teacher websites for resources and information, and educational books and activities students can

Voice from the Field

Communicate with Families

The Wellspring Cape Ann Families Mentor Program

The Wellspring Cape Ann Families Mentor Program in Gloucester, Massachusetts, offers support to stressed and isolated parents in need of a connection, such as a single father who is adjusting to raising a child alone; a mother in need of support as she provides loving structure and encouragement to her young children; a family who recently moved to the area with few connections and needs help connecting to the community; or a mother in need of a supportive friendship to develop her interests. Wellspring Cape Ann Coordinator Cindy O'Donnell says, "Parents have returned to tell us that our friendship helped them to build confidence, explore opportunities, and more fully enjoy their relationship with their children."

Family/Parent Mentor

The Parent Mentor Program partners parents with trained volunteers who meet with them on a weekly basis for a full year. The program's principal belief is "growth happens in the context of relationships." Through relationships, change is possible as demonstrated by this participant: "Before meeting my Parent Mentor, I felt as if I had no hope of having a meaningful future. I have gained the self-confidence to believe I can achieve what I set out to do, and not give up just because I hit a bump in the road. My parent mentor has been a great mentor and friend, and is a positive role model for any woman going through major life changes."

Parent Mentors are the supportive family member or knowledgeable friend many wish they had when difficulties arise in parenthood. They bond, support, and help with figuring out what individuals need as a parent and a person. One parent comments, "If I need a second opinion, and if I need someone to just be there for me, I know I can count on my Parent Mentor!"

Benefits of Working with Community Agencies

As a teacher, you will experience numerous benefits when you collaborate with community agencies that work with parents and families.

- Teachers are often the first people to notice families in need of support. Connecting with community agencies allows you to refer families for support when family difficulties are too big for you to handle alone. For example, teachers notice

---

work on during the summer break. Most importantly, Marci's teaching philosophy is located on her website to guide and direct her teaching of young children. She also writes a letter to the children at the beginning of the year introducing herself, explaining what supplies to bring, and when and where to meet her on the first day of school.[61]

- *Twitter.* Twitter, a social-networking website delivering short (140 characters or less), text-based posts, is useful on many levels. Teachers can use Twitter to send out homework so that parents are automatically updated. Parents can follow teachers and see what their children are up to from any computer (from work, home, coffee shops) at any time of the day. Twitter can also bring students into contact with their community on a local and global level. Students in two Maine elementary schools have been exchanging messages through Twitter. Teachers say the exercise was initiated to help students develop their writing skills by composing messages that must be 140 characters or less.[62]

- *Video chat.* Teachers can use free video chat providers such as Skype or Gmail to hold convenient conferences with parents. If a parent is away on a business trip or can't get away from the office, with the click of a button the parent can take part in a conference with teachers and other parents on their lunch break. In Olathe, Kansas, teachers use Skype to allow both students and their families to attend parent–teacher conferences.[63]

- *Teacher–parent blog.* Teachers can use a blog to connect with students and their families. Blogs can feature lesson summaries, concept introduction and exploration, and classroom notes, reminders, and news. Parents can leave comments, be more informed, and communicate with other parents in the class. "I can whip out something in maybe five minutes and immediately post it," says Melanie Sullivan, a third grade teacher in Needham, Massachusetts. Sullivan started her first classroom blog last school year with her first grade class. "Parents just want to know what's going on. The more they know, the more they understand where you're coming from and what you're

when children in class have significant changes in behavior, look lifeless in class, and talk about stressful things at home as part of classroom sharing. Those may be signs of family stress that require professional intervention.

- Agencies provide an array of services that can help support families. Children whose parents receive support have less stress at home and are more able to learn in school. This makes your job easier and allows you to be more effective. For example, supportive relationships can help parents become more confident in raising children. We have seen parents learn concrete parenting skills, like teaching their children bedtime routines. Children who go to bed around the same time every night are more rested and are better able to learn in school.

- Community agency members can help you work with families to strengthen communication connections between home and school. Parent mentors have helped parents communicate with school personnel by listening to parent concerns, discussing and reframing problems, and helping set up a conversation with the teacher to discuss problems.

- Agency members are often aware of tangible resources to help families in need. For example, they can help connect you with a free new coat for a child who does not have one or help connect families with counseling services to cope with stressful financial situations at home.

Developing Teacher–Community Agency Connections

There are a variety ways you can connect to community agencies:

Step 1: Find out what the procedure is in your school for referring families to community agencies. Some community agencies may work directly with the school psychologist or counselor. Bring concerns about families to the appropriate school personnel who will then make the referral.

Step 2: Contact the agency over the phone or in person. Establish a positive working relationship with a specific person at the agency that you can easily make referrals to and, at the same time trust that your family's needs will be met. Agency staff change frequently and you want to make sure that the parents you refer for support actually find help. If possible have parents sign a release so you can talk about your concerns with the agency.

Step 3: Make good referrals. If you are referring a parent to a voluntary program make sure the parent is aware of the program and wants the support it offers.

Step 4: Keep in touch with the agency by checking in and providing feedback, especially if you notice positive changes in the child, parent, and family. Agencies like to receive feedback to know how their program is working.

trying to accomplish in your room." Parents concur. One Needham parent said the blog gave her something to talk about with her first grade son: "Instead of saying 'what did you learn today' I say, 'you know, I heard that your first grade class got some chicks,' and he would get so excited about the subject matter, he would start blabbering on."[64]

- *Facebook.* You can use Facebook to invite parents of your students to be your friends on the website. This instant line of communication allows you to post photos and videos of what children are doing in class, instant message parents, create classroom events, and give quick status updates on what children are working on or assignments that are due.

Here are some guidelines to follow when you communicate with families electronically:

- Check with your school or program technology coordinator for guidelines and policies for Web page development and communicating electronically with parents.

- Remember that not all parents are connected to the Internet. There is still a "digital divide" in the United States; low-income parents and minorities are less likely to have Internet access. Consider how to provide families without Internet access the same information you provide to families who have Internet service.

- Observe all the rules of politeness and courtesy that you would in a face-to-face conversation.

- Observe all the rules of courteous Internet conversations. For example, don't use all capital letters (this is similar to SHOUTING).

- Remember that just like handwritten notes, electronic mail can be saved. In addition, electronic notes are much more easily transferred.

- Be straightforward and concise in your electronic conversations.

- Establish ground rules ahead of time about what you will and will not discuss electronically.

Community Involvement

Early childhood professionals realize that neither they alone nor the limited resources of their programs are sufficient to meet the needs of many children and families. Consequently, professionals are seeking ways to link families to community services and resources. For example, if a child needs clothing, a professional who is aware of community resources might contact the local Salvation Army for assistance.

Using the community in your teaching is a wonderful way to help children and families come into contact with others and to tap into valuable social and educational services. Reflect on what people and organizations in your community you would use to help teach children the importance and value of the community in which they live.

Community Resources

The community offers a vital and rich array of resources to help you meet the needs of parents and children. Following are suggested actions you can take to learn to use your community in your teaching:

- *Know your students and their needs.* Through observations, conferences with parents, and discussions with students, you can identify barriers to children's learning and discover what kind of help to seek.
- *Know your community.* Walk or drive around the community. Ask a parent to give you a tour to help familiarize you with agencies and individuals. Read the local newspaper, and attend community events and activities.
- *Ask for help and support from parents and the community.* Keep in mind that many parents will not be involved unless you personally ask them. The only encouragement many individuals and local businesses need is your invitation.
- *Develop a directory of community agencies.* Consult the business pages of local phone books, contact local chambers of commerce, and ask parents what agencies are helpful to them.
- *Compile a list of people who are willing to come to your classroom to speak to or work with your students.* You can start by asking parents to volunteer and to give suggestions and recommendations of others.
- *Get involved with community-based agencies.* For example, the Oakland Parents Literacy Project provides essential services to children and families. It is an extension of the region's social services network and provides free dinners for parents and children. Participation has grown dramatically, often hosting as many as five hundred people. "The recession has caught up with the program. The poor are poorer, and instead of moms and babies, we see entire families now."[65] Each Wednesday night, the program holds reading events at three school locations. Parents and their children are invited for a two-hour session that includes dinner—Domino's Pizza provides cut-rate prices to the group and donates fruits and vegetables. There is reading by a guest and a free show— a clown, juggler, puppeteer, or magician to make the night complete. Every child who attends is given a book to take home. "Typically, we see about ten thousand people every school year," says Denise Geer, the group's executive director. The goal of the program is to visit every Oakland elementary school during the school year.[66]

School–Business Involvement

One good way to build social capital in the community is through school–business involvement. More early childhood programs are developing this link as a means of strengthening their programs and helping children and families. For their part, businesses are anxious to develop the connection in order to help schools better educate children. It connects them with the community, expands their basis of business, and gives them an opportunity to give back.

The challenge to early childhood professionals is quite clear: Merely seeking ways to involve parents in school activities is no longer a sufficient program of parent involvement. Today, the challenge is to make families the focus of our involvement activities so that their lives and their children's lives are made better. Anything less will not help families and children access and benefit from the opportunities of the twenty-first century.

Schools and businesses all over the country have come to the same conclusion and have partnered together to help both the schools and the local businesses build involvement and community. For example, the Durham, North Carolina school district sponsors an annual information session for realtors with the Durham Regional Association of Realtors. At this annual event, area real estate professionals learn all about Durham public schools to help them respond to requests from parents who are moving to Durham.[67]

In Salem, Oregon, the *Keizertimes,* a weekly newspaper, offers a free quarter-page of space in the weekly publication for Keizer Elementary School and Gubser Elementary School to promote events and general communications. This space in the weekly paper helps foster a cooperative relationship between the schools and the Keizer community. The *Keizertimes* also provides a quarter of a page in which student reporters write articles that are published monthly. The publisher of the paper sends students e-mails to remind them of their deadline dates and makes school visits to third grade reporters to talk with them about what makes a good reporter.[68]

Partnerships between schools and local businesses range from the simple and informal to highly structured and professional. Partnerships are often managed by teachers. A partnership can be between a single class, the entire school, or even just a few students and a local business or community organization. Community partners range from large corporations to smaller local businesses such as an independently owned pharmacy, the local branch of the YMCA, or a neighborhood grocery store. For example, some partnerships help schools promote a green agenda. Corinne Dowst, head of fundraising for the Parent Teacher Association at Henniker Community School in Henniker, New Hampshire, was looking for new fundraising ideas when she saw an ad for Greenraising, a company that sells eco-friendly products. The school organized a spring sale around Earth Day, and circulated copies of the Greenraising catalog, which features such products as recycled gift-wrap paper and reusable water bottles. The result was the school's most successful fund-raiser in nearly three years, grossing about $2,500. Greenraising has helped about 500 schools and nonprofits raise money.[69]

Parents, Children, and School Absenteeism

We talk about children in the classrooms as though they were just a natural part of the process of education. We take it for granted that children will be in our classroom every day for us to teach! But what if there were no children? For many children, this is exactly the problem: They are not in school! And as you are probably thinking right now, if children are not in the classroom they are not learning. This is exactly right!

While chronic absence (missing 10 percent of the school year) is not a problem everywhere, it can reach surprisingly high levels even in the early grades. Nationwide, nearly 10 percent of kindergartners and first graders are chronically absent. In some communities, chronic early absence can affect 25 percent of all children in kindergarten through third grade across the entire district. Within particular schools in the same district, chronic early absence can range from less than 1 percent to more than 50 percent.[70] Here is what research on children's absenteeism concludes:

Chronic Absence Adversely Impacts Student Performance. This is especially true for children living in poverty. All children, regardless of socioeconomic background, do

Targeted

Coordinate public agency and, if needed, legal response for families in crisis.

Provide early outreach to families with poor attendance and (as appropriate) case management to address social, medical, economics and academic needs.

Offer incentives for attendance to all children.

Encourage families to help each other attend school.

Educate parents about the importance of attendance.

Engage families of all backgrounds in their children's education.

Offer high-quality education responsive to diverse learning needs.

Ensure access to preventive health care, especially as children enter school.

Prepare children for school through quality early care and education experiences.

Universal

FIGURE 17.4 Strategies to Address Absenteeism in Early Childhood Programs

Schools and community agencies can provide universal strategies, programs for all parents and families, and targeted programs aimed at chronically absent children and families. Incentives for attendance can include such things as food (e.g., a pizza party), books, field trips, and such.

Source: National Center for Children in Poverty, *Present, Engaged, and Accounted For: The Critical Importance of Addressing Chronic Absence in the Early Grades*, 2008. Used with permission.

worse academically in first grade if they are chronically absent in kindergarten. Chronic absence in kindergarten especially affects reading performance for Hispanic first graders. Among poor children, chronic absence in kindergarten predicts the lowest levels of educational achievement at the end of the fifth grade.[71]

So, you are probably thinking that one solution to chronic absenteeism is to get children in school. This is exactly right. Achieving the goal of reducing chronic absenteeism and having children in school requires collaboration between teachers, schools, families, and communities. You can implement some strategies universally, such as engaging all families from all backgrounds in education, but depending on the seriousness of the child's absenteeism and the factors contributing to his or her school absence, you may need to implement a more targeted approach to encourage school participation. Such targeted assistance ranges from offering incentives to attend school, such as field trips, to contacting truancy officers. Figure 17.4 outlines strategies that schools and communities can follow in efforts to reduce and eliminate absenteeism.

Accommodating Diverse Learners

Now that you have read about the different ways to involve parents and bolster home–school collaboration, let's discuss some requirements for working with parents when the child has a disability. The Individuals with Disabilities Education Act (2004) supports the belief that the education of children with disabilities is made more effective by strengthening the role of parents in the special education process. IDEA requires that parents participate in each step of the special education process and ensures this by giving parents the following protections:

- *The right to give informed written consent and the right to confidentiality.* Parents must give written permission before their child is evaluated, before services begin or are changed, and before information about their child is shared with anyone else.

- *The right to receive written prior notice.* Parents must receive written notice before any evaluations or assessments can take place and before each meeting to review the Individualized Family Service Plan (IFSP) or Individualized Education Program (IEP).

- *The right to a coordinated IFSP or IEP.* A written plan is developed by a team of professionals and the parents to develop goals for the child and services that will best help reach those goals. This plan also describes when, where, and how services will be delivered.

- *The right to receive services in natural environments and in the least restrictive environment.* Services are focused on the family's and child's daily routines and designed to be carried out within regular activities. The IFSP/IEP team must provide written justification if services are provided anywhere other than the natural environment or least restrictive environment.

- *The right to review records.* Parents may inspect, review, and receive a copy of their child's records.

- *A process to resolve disputes.* Parents who feel their child's rights have been violated may file a written complaint or request mediation or a due process hearing.

Ensuring that children's needs are met and rights are upheld requires a system of communication that is consistent and mutually agreed on. Children's success at home and school is strengthened when this communication is reciprocal and positive. Parents and teachers have knowledge that when shared can benefit *all* children. Sharing back and forth between teachers and families is optimal because each has information the other may not have. The more information families and teachers have, the more they can collaborate to help children. Figure 17.5 shares information that families and teachers can use to effectively collaborate with each other to benefit all children.

Families share information on the child:

- History and development (milestones, medical information, and medication)
- Strengths and weaknesses at home
- Family dynamics that may affect learning and behavior
- Familial expectations
- Academic successes and deficits

Teachers share information on:

- Typical child development and developmental milestones
- The child's strengths and weaknesses at school
- School dynamics that may affect learning and behavior
- Resources available to assist families
- Scope and sequence of curriculum and possible modifications and adaptations

FIGURE 17.5
Information Families and Teachers Use to Benefit Children

Activities for Professional Development

Ethical Dilemma

"That's not in our job description."

First-year teacher Matt Bullock teaches second grade at Willow Bend Elementary in one of the most disadvantaged parts of a large urban school district. Matt is very concerned about some of his children's misbehavior, lack of manners, and overall poor attitude toward learning. When Matt approached his principal, Harry Dimsmoore, for advice about what he can do, Harry told him, "Go get your parents involved! I expect you to get out into the community." Matt wants to help his children but he is taken aback. His teacher education program did not prepare him to be involved in the community. Matt is at a loss for how to begin and approaches his mentor teacher Melisa Dolan for advice. Melisa counsels Matt, "Look, Matt, that's not in our job description. We're teachers, we belong in the classroom. We don't have to take leadership roles in the community and try to change conditions outside of our classroom. You and I didn't go to college to do that kind of thing. Besides, they don't pay us enough to do all that." Matt is confused. He wants to make a difference but isn't sure how to go about it.

What should Matt do? Should Matt attend a seminar on community activism to get the skills he needs to be an effective agent of change in the community? Or should he take Melisa's advice and forget about it? Should Matt just continue to do the best that he can and hope everything turns out all right? Or should Matt write a letter to his alma matter sharing his thoughts about their teaching a course in family-community involvement as part of the teacher education program? What should Matt do?

Activities to Apply What You Learned

1. Create an event in which you increase parental involvement in your school or classroom. Involve an agency in your community that provides resources for parents and families. When you have organized all the details of your event, post your event on your class discussion board and ask for feedback.

2. Choose a demographic from the "Family Changes" section that interests you or you feel you need to learn more about in order to meet the needs of the children in your classroom. Create a PowerPoint presentation documenting research and general information of this particular demographic and its implications for your classroom. Then, create a list of ideas or events that you will use to encourage involvement of this family type in your classroom. Post your ideas to a teacher blog such as TeacherLingo and ask for comments.

3. Choose one type of involvement (e.g., volunteering, learning at home, etc.) from the Six Types of Parent/Family Involvement and develop a plan for parent/family involvement in a grade you plan to teach using the outline below.

   a. Identify overall and specific objectives for your plan.

   b. Using the type of involvement you chose, develop specific activities for involving families and providing services to them.

   c. Explain how you would involve different family types in your event (fathers, single parents, LGBT parents, military families, etc.).

   d. Explain how you will use the community resources in your plan.

   Post your plan on your classroom discussion board and ask for comments from classmates. Critique and offer comments on a classmate's plan for a different type of parent/family involvement.

4. Evaluate social services in your area and find out the particular services they offer to children and families. Compile a binder of resources that are easily accessible to children and families. Put the binder in your professional portfolio for future use.

5. A child in your kindergarten classroom has missed three consecutive days of school. You have decided to call a conference with the child's family to figure out what is going on. What questions would you ask about the child's frequent absences? What would you suggest to ensure the child misses no more days of school? What school or community resources would you involve to ensure the child has success in school? Post your information on your classroom discussion board.

6. Identify resources in your community to help children with disabilities and their families. How would you share this information with parents? How could you help parents access these services? Post this information on your classroom discussion board.

Linking to Learning

AARP
www.aarp.org/relationships/grandparenting/
Provides support and many interesting articles and links for grandparents who are rearing their grandchildren.

AVANCE
www.avance.org

AVANCE is one of the oldest, largest, and most distinguished parenting and early childhood education programs in the country, providing innovative education and family support services to predominantly Hispanic families in low-income, at-risk communities.

Early Childhood Educators' and Family Web Corner
http://users.sgi.net/~cokids/

Provides links to teacher pages, family pages, articles, and staff development resources.

Edvantia
www.edvantia.org/

Offers ways to keep abreast of what's happening with school–community partnerships to address the pressing needs of children and their families.

Family Education Network
www.familyeducation.com

Committed to strengthening and empowering families by providing communities with the counseling, education, resources, information, and training needed to promote a positive and nurturing environment in which to raise children.

National Coalition for Parent Involvement in Education
www.ncpie.org/

Dedicated to developing family–school partnerships throughout America, involving parents and families in their children's lives and fostering relationships among home, school, and community, all of which can enhance the education of our nation's young people.

National Fatherhood Initiative
www.fatherhood.org/

Dedicated to educating and engaging dads. Agency believes that committed fatherhood is the best way to ensure that every child has a happy and secure childhood.

National Parent Teacher Association (PTA)
www.pta.org

Calls for schools to promote partnerships that will increase parent involvement and participation in the social, emotional, and academic growth of children; has voluntary National Standards for Parent/Family Involvement Programs.

National Network of Partnership Schools
www.csos.jhu.edu/p2000/index.htm

NNPS invites schools, districts, states, and organizations to join together and use research-based approaches to organize and sustain excellent programs of family and community involvement that will increase student success in school.

PEARSON
myeducationlab

Go to Topic 3 (Family/Community) in the MyEducationLab (www.myeducationlab.com) for your course, where you can:

- Find learning outcomes for Family/Community along with the national standards that connect to these outcomes.
- Complete Assignments and Activities that can help you more deeply understand the chapter content.
- Apply and practice your understanding of the core teaching skills identified in the chapter with the Building Teaching Skills and Dispositions learning units.
- Check your comprehension on the content covered in the chapter by going to the Study Plan in the Book Resources for your text. Here you will be able to take a chapter quiz, receive feedback on your answers, and then access Review, Practice, and Enrichment activities to enhance your understanding of chapter content.

Appendix A

NAEYC Code of Ethical Conduct and Statement of Commitment

Preamble

NAEYC recognizes those who work with young children face many daily decisions that have moral and ethical implications. The NAEYC Code of Ethical Conduct offers guidelines for responsible behavior and sets forth a common basis for resolving the principal ethical dilemmas encountered in early childhood care and education. The Statement of Commitment is not part of the Code but is a personal acknowledgment of an individual's willingness to embrace the distinctive values and moral obligations of the field of early childhood care and education. The primary focus of the Code is on daily practice with children and their families in programs for children from birth through eight years of age, such as infant/toddler programs, preschool and pre-kindergarten programs, child care centers, hospital and child life settings, family child care homes, kindergartens, and primary classrooms. When the issues involve young children, then these provisions also apply to specialists who do not work directly with children, including program administrators, parent educators, early childhood adult educators, and officials with responsibility for program monitoring and licensing. (Note: See also the "Code of Ethical Conduct: Supplement for Early Childhood Adult Educators," online at www.naeyc.org/about/positions/asp/ethics04.)

Core Values

Standards of ethical behavior in early childhood care and education are based on commitment to the following core values that are deeply rooted in the history of the field of early childhood care and education. We have made a commitment to

- Appreciate childhood as a unique and valuable stage of the human life cycle
- Base our work on knowledge of how children develop and learn
- Appreciate and support the bond between the child and family
- Recognize that children are best understood and supported in the context of family, culture,[1] community, and society

- Respect the dignity, worth, and uniqueness of each individual (child, family member, and colleague)
- Respect diversity in children, families, and colleagues
- Recognize that children and adults achieve their full potential in the context of relationships that are based on trust and respect

Conceptual Framework

The Code sets forth a framework of professional responsibilities in four sections. Each section addresses an area of professional relationships: (1) with children, (2) with families, (3) among colleagues, and (4) with the community and society. Each section includes an introduction to the primary responsibilities of the early childhood practitioner in that context. The introduction is followed by a set of ideals (I) that reflect exemplary professional practice and by a set of principles (P) describing practices that are required, prohibited, or permitted.

The ideals reflect the aspirations of practitioners. The principles guide conduct and assist practitioners in resolving ethical dilemmas.[2] Both ideals and principles are intended to direct practitioners to those questions which, when responsibly answered, can provide the basis for conscientious decision making. While the Code provides specific direction for addressing some ethical dilemmas, many others will require the practitioner to combine the guidance of the Code with professional judgment.

The ideals and principles in this Code present a shared framework of professional responsibility that affirms our commitment to the core values of our field. The Code publicly acknowledges the responsibilities that we in the field have assumed, and in so doing supports ethical behavior in our work. Practitioners who face situations with ethical dimensions are urged to seek guidance in the applicable parts of this Code and in the spirit that informs the whole.

Often "the right answer"—the best ethical course of action to take—is not obvious. There may be no readily apparent, positive way to handle a situation. When one important value contradicts another, we face an ethical dilemma. When we face a dilemma, it is our professional responsibility to consult the Code and all relevant parties to find the most ethical resolution.

---

[1]*Culture* includes ethnicity, racial identity, economic level, family structure, language, and religious and political beliefs, which profoundly influence each child's development and relationship to the world.
[2]There is not necessarily a corresponding principle for each ideal.

Section I: Ethical Responsibilities to Children

Childhood is a unique and valuable stage in the human life cycle. Our paramount responsibility is to provide care and education in settings that are safe, healthy, nurturing, and responsive for each child. We are committed to supporting children's development and learning; respecting individual differences; and helping children learn to live, play, and work cooperatively. We are also committed to promoting children's self-awareness, competence, self-worth, resiliency, and physical well-being.

Ideals

I-1.1—To be familiar with the knowledge base of early childhood care and education and to stay informed through continuing education and training.

I-1.2—To base program practices upon current knowledge and research in the field of early childhood education, child development, and related disciplines, as well as on particular knowledge of each child.

I-1.3—To recognize and respect the unique qualities, abilities, and potential of each child.

I-1.4—To appreciate the vulnerability of children and their dependence on adults.

I-1.5—To create and maintain safe and healthy settings that foster children's social, emotional, cognitive, and physical development and that respect their dignity and their contributions.

I-1.6—To use assessment instruments and strategies that are appropriate for the children to be assessed, that are used only for the purposes for which they were designed, and that have the potential to benefit children.

I-1.7—To use assessment information to understand and support children's development and learning, to support instruction, and to identify children who may need additional services.

I-1.8—To support the right of each child to play and learn in an inclusive environment that meets the needs of children with and without disabilities.

I-1.9—To advocate for and ensure that all children, including those with special needs, have access to the support services needed to be successful.

I-1.10—To ensure that each child's culture, language, ethnicity, and family structure are recognized and valued in the program.

I-1.11—To provide all children with experiences in a language that they know, as well as support children in maintaining the use of their home language and in learning English.

I-1.12—To work with families to provide a safe and smooth transition as children and families move from one program to the next.

Principles

P-1.1—Above all, we shall not harm children. We shall not participate in practices that are emotionally damaging, physically harmful, disrespectful, degrading, dangerous, exploitative, or intimidating to children. *This principle has precedence over all others in this Code.*

P-1.2—We shall care for and educate children in positive emotional and social environments that are cognitively stimulating and that support each child's culture, language, ethnicity, and family structure.

P-1.3—We shall not participate in practices that discriminate against children by denying benefits, giving special advantages, or excluding them from programs or activities on the basis of their sex, race, national origin, religious beliefs, medical condition, disability, or the marital status/family structure, sexual orientation, or religious beliefs or other affiliations of their families. (Aspects of this principle do not apply in programs that have a lawful mandate to provide services to a particular population of children.)

P-1.4—We shall involve all those with relevant knowledge (including families and staff) in decisions concerning a child, as appropriate, ensuring confidentiality of sensitive information.

P-1.5—We shall use appropriate assessment systems, which include multiple sources of information, to provide information on children's learning and development.

P-1.6—We shall strive to ensure that decisions such as those related to enrollment, retention, or assignment to special education services will be based on multiple sources of information and will never be based on a single assessment, such as a test score or a single observation.

P-1.7—We shall strive to build individual relationships with each child; make individualized adaptations in teaching strategies, learning environments, and curricula; and consult with the family so that each child benefits from the program. If after such efforts have been exhausted, the current placement does not meet a child's needs, or the child is seriously jeopardizing the ability of other children to benefit from the program, we shall collaborate with the child's family and appropriate specialists to determine the additional services needed and/or the placement option(s) most likely to ensure the child's success. (Aspects of this principle may not apply in programs that have a lawful mandate to provide services to a particular population of children.)

P-1.8—We shall be familiar with the risk factors for and symptoms of child abuse and neglect, including physical, sexual, verbal, and emotional abuse and physical, emotional, educational, and medical neglect. We shall know and follow state laws and community procedures that protect children against abuse and neglect.

P-1.9—When we have reasonable cause to suspect child abuse or neglect, we shall report it to the appropriate community agency and follow up to ensure that appropriate action has been taken. When appropriate, parents or guardians will be informed that the referral will be or has been made.

P-1.10—When another person tells us of his or her suspicion that a child is being abused or neglected, we shall assist that person in taking appropriate action in order to protect the child.

P-1.11—When we become aware of a practice or situation that endangers the health, safety, or well-being of children, we have an ethical responsibility to protect children or inform parents and/or others who can.

Section II: Ethical Responsibilities to Families

Families are of primary importance in children's development. Because the family and the early childhood practitioner have a common interest in the child's well-being, we acknowledge a primary responsibility to bring about communication, cooperation, and collaboration between the home and early childhood program in ways that enhance the child's development.[3]

Ideals

I-2.1—To be familiar with the knowledge base related to working effectively with families and to stay informed through continuing education and training.

I-2.2—To develop relationships of mutual trust and create partnerships with the families we serve.

I-2.3—To welcome all family members and encourage them to participate in the program.

I-2.4—To listen to families, acknowledge and build upon their strengths and competencies, and learn from families as we support them in their task of nurturing children.

I-2.5—To respect the dignity and preferences of each family and to make an effort to learn about its structure, culture, language, customs, and beliefs.

I-2.6—To acknowledge families' childrearing values and their right to make decisions for their children.

I-2.7—To share information about each child's education and development with families and to help them understand and appreciate the current knowledge base of the early childhood profession.

I-2.8—To help family members enhance their understanding of their children and support the continuing development of their skills as parents.

I-2.9—To participate in building support networks for families by providing them with opportunities to interact with program staff, other families, community resources, and professional services.

Principles

P-2.1—We shall not deny family members access to their child's classroom or program setting unless access is denied by court order or other legal restriction.

P-2.2—We shall inform families of program philosophy, policies, curriculum, assessment system, and personnel qualifications, and explain why we teach as we do—which should be in accordance with our ethical responsibilities to children (see Section I).

P-2.3—We shall inform families of and, when appropriate, involve them in policy decisions.

P-2.4—We shall involve the family in significant decisions affecting their child.

P-2.5—We shall make every effort to communicate effectively with all families in a language that they understand. We shall use community resources for translation and interpretation when we do not have sufficient resources in our own programs.

P-2.6—As families share information with us about their children and families, we shall consider this information to plan and implement the program.

P-2.7—We shall inform families about the nature and purpose of the program's child assessments and how data about their child will be used.

P-2.8—We shall treat child assessment information confidentially and share this information only when there is a legitimate need for it.

P-2.9—We shall inform the family of injuries and incidents involving their child, of risks such as exposures to communicable diseases that might result in infection, and of occurrences that might result in emotional stress.

P-2.10—Families shall be fully informed of any proposed research projects involving their children and shall have the opportunity to give or withhold consent without penalty. We shall not permit or participate in research that could in any way hinder the education, development, or well-being of children.

P-2.11—We shall not engage in or support exploitation of families. We shall not use our relationship with a family for private advantage or personal gain, or enter into relationships with family members that might impair our effectiveness working with their children.

P-2.12—We shall develop written policies for the protection of confidentiality and the disclosure of children's records. These policy documents shall be made available to all program personnel and families. Disclosure of children's records beyond family members, program personnel, and consultants having an obligation of confidentiality shall require familial consent (except in cases of abuse or neglect).

P-2.13—We shall maintain confidentiality and shall respect the family's right to privacy, refraining from disclosure of confidential information and intrusion into family life. However, when we have reason to believe that a child's welfare is at risk, it is permissible to share confidential information with agencies, as well as with individuals who have legal responsibility for intervening in the child's interest.

P-2.14—In cases where family members are in conflict with one another, we shall work openly, sharing our observations of the child, to help all parties involved make informed decisions. We shall refrain from becoming an advocate for one party.

P-2.15—We shall be familiar with and appropriately refer families to community resources and professional support services. After a referral has been made, we shall follow up to ensure that services have been appropriately provided.

---

[3]The term *family* may include those adults, besides parents, with the responsibility of being involved in educating, nurturing, and advocating for the child.

Section III: Ethical Responsibilities to Colleagues

In a caring, cooperative workplace, human dignity is respected, professional satisfaction is promoted, and positive relationships are developed and sustained. Based upon our core values, our primary responsibility to colleagues is to establish and maintain settings and relationships that support productive work and meet professional needs. The same ideals that apply to children also apply as we interact with adults in the workplace.

A—Responsibilities to co-workers

Ideals

I-3A.1—To establish and maintain relationships of respect, trust, confidentiality, collaboration, and cooperation with co-workers.

I-3A.2—To share resources with co-workers, collaborating to ensure that the best possible early childhood care and education program is provided.

I-3A.3—To support co-workers in meeting their professional needs and in their professional development.

I-3A.4—To accord co-workers due recognition of professional achievement.

Principles

P-3A.1—We shall recognize the contributions of colleagues to our program and not participate in practices that diminish their reputations or impair their effectiveness in working with children and families.

P-3A.2—When we have concerns about the professional behavior of a co-worker, we shall first let that person know of our concern in a way that shows respect for personal dignity and for the diversity to be found among staff members, and then attempt to resolve the matter collegially and in a confidential manner.

P-3A.3—We shall exercise care in expressing views regarding the personal attributes or professional conduct of co-workers. Statements should be based on firsthand knowledge, not hearsay, and relevant to the interests of children and programs.

P-3A.4—We shall not participate in practices that discriminate against a co-worker because of sex, race, national origin, religious beliefs or other affiliations, age, marital status/family structure, disability, or sexual orientation.

B—Responsibilities to employers

Ideals

I-3B.1—To assist the program in providing the highest quality of service.

I-3B.2—To do nothing that diminishes the reputation of the program in which we work unless it is violating laws and regulations designed to protect children or is violating the provisions of this Code.

Principles

P-3B.1—We shall follow all program policies. When we do not agree with program policies, we shall attempt to effect change through constructive action within the organization.

P-3B.2—We shall speak or act on behalf of an organization only when authorized. We shall take care to acknowledge when we are speaking for the organization and when we are expressing a personal judgment.

P-3B.3—We shall not violate laws or regulations designed to protect children and shall take appropriate action consistent with this Code when aware of such violations.

P-3B.4—If we have concerns about a colleague's behavior, and children's well-being is not at risk, we may address the concern with that individual. If children are at risk or the situation does not improve after it has been brought to the colleague's attention, we shall report the colleague's unethical or incompetent behavior to an appropriate authority.

P-3B.5—When we have a concern about circumstances or conditions that impact the quality of care and education within the program, we shall inform the program's administration or, when necessary, other appropriate authorities.

C—Responsibilities to employees

Ideals

I-3C.1—To promote safe and healthy working conditions and policies that foster mutual respect, cooperation, collaboration, competence, well-being, confidentiality, and self-esteem in staff members.

I-3C.2—To create and maintain a climate of trust and candor that will enable staff to speak and act in the best interests of children, families, and the field of early childhood care and education.

I-3C.3—To strive to secure adequate and equitable compensation (salary and benefits) for those who work with or on behalf of young children.

I-3C.4—To encourage and support continual development of employees in becoming more skilled and knowledgeable practitioners.

Principles

P-3C.1—In decisions concerning children and programs, we shall draw upon the education, training, experience, and expertise of staff members.

P-3C.2—We shall provide staff members with safe and supportive working conditions that honor confidences and permit them to carry out their responsibilities through fair performance evaluation, written grievance procedures, constructive feedback, and opportunities for continuing professional development and advancement.

P-3C.3—We shall develop and maintain comprehensive written personnel policies that define program standards. These policies shall be given to new staff members and shall be available and easily accessible for review by all staff members.

P-3C.4—We shall inform employees whose performance does not meet program expectations of areas of concern and, when possible, assist in improving their performance.

P-3C.5—We shall conduct employee dismissals for just cause, in accordance with all applicable laws and regulations. We shall inform employees who are dismissed of the reasons for their termination. When a dismissal is for cause, justification must be based on evidence of inadequate or inappropriate behavior that is accurately documented, current, and available for the employee to review.

P-3C.6—In making evaluations and recommendations, we shall make judgments based on fact and relevant to the interests of children and programs.

P-3C.7—We shall make hiring, retention, termination, and promotion decisions based solely on a person's competence, record of accomplishment, ability to carry out the responsibilities of the position, and professional preparation specific to the developmental levels of children in his/her care.

P-3C.8—We shall not make hiring, retention, termination, and promotion decisions based on an individual's sex, race, national origin, religious beliefs or other affiliations, age, marital status/family structure, disability, or sexual orientation. We shall be familiar with and observe laws and regulations that pertain to employment discrimination. (Aspects of this principle do not apply to programs that have a lawful mandate to determine eligibility based on one or more of the criteria identified above.)

P-3C.9—We shall maintain confidentiality in dealing with issues related to an employee's job performance and shall respect an employee's right to privacy regarding personal issues.

Section IV: Ethical Responsibilities to Community and Society

Early childhood programs operate within the context of their immediate community made up of families and other institutions concerned with children's welfare. Our responsibilities to the community are to provide programs that meet the diverse needs of families, to cooperate with agencies and professions that share the responsibility for children, to assist families in gaining access to those agencies and allied professionals, and to assist in the development of community programs that are needed but not currently available.

As individuals, we acknowledge our responsibility to provide the best possible programs of care and education for children and to conduct ourselves with honesty and integrity. Because of our specialized expertise in early childhood development and education and because the larger society shares responsibility for the welfare and protection of young children,

we acknowledge a collective obligation to advocate for the best interests of children within early childhood programs and in the larger community and to serve as a voice for young children everywhere.

The ideals and principles in this section are presented to distinguish between those that pertain to the work of the individual early childhood educator and those that more typically are engaged in collectively on behalf of the best interests of children—with the understanding that individual early childhood educators have a shared responsibility for addressing the ideals and principles that are identified as "collective."

Ideal (Individual)

I-4.—To provide the community with high-quality early childhood care and education programs and services.

Ideals (Collective)

I-4.2—To promote cooperation among professionals and agencies and interdisciplinary collaboration among professions concerned with addressing issues in the health, education, and well-being of young children, their families, and their early childhood educators.

I-4.3—To work through education, research, and advocacy toward an environmentally safe world in which all children receive health care, food, and shelter; are nurtured; and live free from violence in their home and their communities.

I-4.4—To work through education, research, and advocacy toward a society in which all young children have access to high-quality early care and education programs.

I-4.5—To work to ensure that appropriate assessment systems, which include multiple sources of information, are used for purposes that benefit children.

I-4.6—To promote knowledge and understanding of young children and their needs. To work toward greater societal acknowledgment of children's rights and greater social acceptance of responsibility for the well-being of all children.

I-4.7—To support policies and laws that promote the well-being of children and families, and to work to change those that impair their well-being. To participate in developing policies and laws that are needed, and to cooperate with other individuals and groups in these efforts.

I-4.8—To further the professional development of the field of early childhood care and education and to strengthen its commitment to realizing its core values as reflected in this Code.

Principles (Individual)

P-4.1—We shall communicate openly and truthfully about the nature and extent of services that we provide.

P-4.2—We shall apply for, accept, and work in positions for which we are personally well-suited and professionally qualified. We shall not offer services that we do not have the competence, qualifications, or resources to provide.

P-4.3—We shall carefully check references and shall not hire or recommend for employment any person whose competence, qualifications, or character makes him or her unsuited for the position.

P-4.4—We shall be objective and accurate in reporting the knowledge upon which we base our program practices.

P-4.5—We shall be knowledgeable about the appropriate use of assessment strategies and instruments and interpret results accurately to families.

P-4.6—We shall be familiar with laws and regulations that serve to protect the children in our programs and be vigilant in ensuring that these laws and regulations are followed.

P-4.7—When we become aware of a practice or situation that endangers the health, safety, or well-being of children, we have an ethical responsibility to protect children or inform parents and/or others who can.

P-4.8—We shall not participate in practices that are in violation of laws and regulations that protect the children in our programs.

P-4.9—When we have evidence that an early childhood program is violating laws or regulations protecting children, we shall report the violation to appropriate authorities who can be expected to remedy the situation.

P-4.10—When a program violates or requires its employees to violate this Code, it is permissible, after fair assessment of the evidence, to disclose the identity of that program.

Principles (Collective)

P-4.11—When policies are enacted for purposes that do not benefit children, we have a collective responsibility to work to change these practices.

P-4.12—When we have evidence that an agency that provides services intended to ensure children's well-being is failing to meet its obligations, we acknowledge a collective ethical responsibility to report the problem to appropriate authorities or to the public. We shall be vigilant in our follow-up until the situation is resolved.

P-4.13—When a child protection agency fails to provide adequate protection for abused or neglected children, we acknowledge a collective ethical responsibility to work toward the improvement of these services.

STATEMENT OF COMMITMENT[4]

As an individual who works with young children, I commit myself to furthering the values of early childhood education as they are reflected in the ideals and principles of the NAEYC Code of Ethical Conduct. To the best of my ability I will

- Never harm children.
- Ensure that programs for young children are based on current knowledge and research of child development and early childhood education.
- Respect and support families in their task of nurturing children.
- Respect colleagues in early childhood care and education and support them in maintaining the NAEYC Code of Ethical Conduct.
- Serve as an advocate for children, their families, and their teachers in community and society.
- Stay informed of and maintain high standards of professional conduct.
- Engage in an ongoing process of self-reflection, realizing that personal characteristics, biases, and beliefs have an impact on children and families.
- Be open to new ideas and be willing to learn from the suggestions of others.
- Continue to learn, grow, and contribute as a professional.
- Honor the ideals and principles of the NAEYC Code of Ethical Conduct.

[4]This Statement of Commitment is not part of the Code but is a personal acknowledgment of the individual's willingness to embrace the distinctive values and moral obligations of the field of early childhood care and education. It is recognition of the moral obligations that lead to an individual becoming part of the profession.

Glossary of Terms Related to Ethics

Code of Ethics   Defines the core values of the field and provides guidance for what professionals should do when they encounter conflicting obligations or responsibilities in their work.

Values   Qualities or principles that individuals believe to be desirable or worthwhile and that they prize for themselves, for others, and for the world in which they live.

Core Values   Commitments held by a profession that are consciously and knowingly embraced by its practitioners because they make a contribution to society. There is a difference between personal values and the core values of a profession.

Morality   Peoples' views of what is good, right and proper; their beliefs about their obligations; and their ideas about how they should behave.

Ethics   The study of right and wrong, or duty and obligation, that involves critical reflection on morality and the ability to make choices between values and the examination of the moral dimensions of relationships.

Professional Ethics   The moral commitments of a profession that involve moral reflection that extends and enhances the personal morality practitioners bring to their work, that concern actions of right and wrong in the workplace, and that help individuals resolve moral dilemmas they encounter in their work.

Ethical Responsibilities   Behaviors that one must or must not engage in. Ethical responsibilities are clear-cut and are spelled out in the Code of Ethical Conduct (for example, early childhood educators should never share confidential information about a child or family with a person who has no legitimate need for knowing).

Ethical Dilemma   A moral conflict that involves determining appropriate conduct when an individual faces conflicting professional values and responsibilities.

Sources for Glossary Terms and Definitions

Feeney, S., & N. Freeman. 1999. *Ethics and the Early Childhood Educator: Using the NAEYC Code*. Washington, DC: NAEYC.

Kidder, R. M. 1995. *How Good People Make Tough Choices: Resolving the Dilemmas of Ethical Living*. New York: Fireside.

Kipnis, K. 1987. "How to Discuss Professional Ethics." *Young Children* 42 (4): 26–30.

Appendix B

NAEYC Guidelines for Developmentally Appropriate Practice in Early Childhood Programs Serving Children from Birth Through Age Eight

The purpose of this position statement is to promote excellence in early childhood education by providing a framework for best practice. Grounded both in the research on child development and learning and in the knowledge base regarding educational effectiveness, the framework outlines practice that promotes young children's optimal learning and development. Since its first adoption in 1986, this framework has been known as *developmentally appropriate practice.*[1]

The profession's responsibility to promote quality in the care and education of young children compels us to revisit regularly the validity and currency of our core knowledge and positions, such as this one on issues of practice. Does the position need modification in light of a changed context? Is there new knowledge to inform the statement? Are there aspects of the existing statement that have given rise to misunderstandings and misconceptions that need correcting?

Over the several years spent in developing this revision, NAEYC invited the comment of early childhood educators with experience and expertise from infancy to the primary grades, including a late 2006 convening of respected leaders in the field. The result of this broad gathering of views is this updated position statement, which addresses the current context and the relevant knowledge base for developmentally appropriate practice and seeks to convey the nature of such practice clearly and usefully.

This statement is intended to complement NAEYC's other position statements on practice, which include *Early Learning Standards* and *Early Childhood Curriculum, Assessment, and Program Evaluation,* as well as the *Code of Ethical Conduct* and *NAEYC Early Childhood Program Standards and Accreditation Criteria.*[2]

Note: Throughout this statement, the terms *teacher, practitioner,* and *educator* are variously used to refer to those working in the early childhood field. The word *teacher* is always intended to refer to any adult responsible for the direct care and education of a group of children in any early childhood setting. Included are not only classroom teachers but also infant/toddler caregivers, family child care providers, and specialists in other disciplines who fulfill the role of teacher. In more instances, the term *practitioner* is intended to also include a program's administrators. *Educators* is intended to also include college and university faculty and other teacher trainers.

Critical Issues in the Current Context

Since the 1996 version of this position statement, the landscape of early childhood education in the United States has changed significantly and a number of issues have grown in importance. Shortage of good care for children in the highly vulnerable infant and toddler years has become critical.[3] Issues of home language and culture, second language learning, and school culture have increased with the steady growth in the number of immigrant families and children in our population.[4] In addition, far more children with special needs (including those with disabilities, those at risk for disabilities, and those with challenging behaviors) participate in typical early childhood settings today than in the past.[5] As for teachers, the nation continues to struggle to develop and maintain a qualified teaching force.[6] This difficulty is especially acute in the underfunded early childhood arena, especially the child care sector, which is losing well-prepared teaching staff and administrators at an alarming rate.[7]

Looking forward, demographic trends predict a modest growth in the number of young children in the population, significant increases in the demand for early care and education, dramatic increases in children's cultural and linguistic diversity, and unless conditions change, a greater share of children living in poverty. Among these, the biggest single child-specific demographic change in the United States over the next twenty years is predicted to be an increase in children whose home language is not English.[8]

Also significant is that policy makers and the public are far more aware of the importance of the early childhood years in shaping children's futures. Based on this widespread recognition and the context of early childhood education today, it was decided this statement would highlight three challenges: reducing learning gaps and increasing the achievement of all children; creating improved, better-connected education for preschool and elementary children; and recognizing teacher knowledge and decision making as vital to educational effectiveness.

Reducing Learning Gaps and Increasing the Achievement of All Children

All families, educators, and the larger society hope that children will achieve in school and go on to lead satisfying and productive lives.

But that optimistic future is not equally likely for all of the nation's schoolchildren. Most disturbing, low-income and African American and Hispanic students lag significantly behind their peers on standardized comparisons of academic achievement throughout the school years, and they experience more difficulties while in the school setting.[9]

Behind these disparities in school-related performance lie dramatic differences in children's early experiences and access to good programs and schools. Often there is also a mismatch between the "school" culture and children's cultural backgrounds.[10] A prime difference in children's early experience is in their exposure to language, which is fundamental in literacy development and indeed in all areas of thinking and learning. On average, children growing up in low-income families have dramatically less rich experience with language in their homes than do middle-class children:[11] They hear far fewer words and are engaged in fewer extended conversations. By thirty-six months of age, substantial socioeconomic disparities already exist in vocabulary knowledge,[12] to name one area.

Children from families living in poverty or in households in which parent education is low typically enter school with lower levels of foundational skills, such as those in language, reading, and mathematics.[13] On starting kindergarten, children in the lowest socioeconomic group have average cognitive scores that are 60 percent below those of the most affluent group. Explained largely by socioeconomic differences among ethnic groups, average math achievement is 21 percent lower for African American children than for white children and 19 percent lower for Hispanic children than for non-Hispanic white children.[14] Moreover, due to deep-seated equity issues present in communities and schools, such early achievement gaps tend to *increase* rather than diminish over time.[15]

Concerns over the persistence of achievement gaps between subgroups are part of a larger concern about lagging student achievement in the United States and its impact on American economic competitiveness in an increasingly global economy. In comparisons with students of other industrialized countries, for example, America's students have not consistently fared well on tests of educational achievement.[16]

It is these worries that drive the powerful "standards/accountability" movement. Among the movement's most far-reaching actions has been the 2001 passing of No Child Left Behind (NCLB), which made it national policy to hold schools accountable for eliminating the persistent gaps in achievement between different groups of children. With the aim of ensuring educational equity, the law requires the reporting of scores disaggregated by student group; that is, reported separately for the economically disadvantaged, major racial and ethnic minorities, special education recipients, and English language learners.[17] By requiring the reporting of achievement by student group and requiring all groups to make achievement gains annually, NCLB seeks to make schools accountable for teaching *all* their students effectively.

Whether NCLB and similar "accountability" mandates can deliver that result is hotly debated, and many critics argue that the mandates have unintended negative consequences for children, teachers, and schools, including narrowing the curriculum and testing too much and in the wrong ways. Yet the majority of Americans support the movement's stated goals,[18] among them that *all* children should be achieving at high levels.[19] This public support—for the goals, if not the methods—can be viewed as a demand that educators do something to improve student achievement and close the gaps that all agree are damaging many children's future prospects and wasting their potential.

Learning standards and accountability policies have impinged directly on public education from grade K and up, and they are of growing relevance to preschool education, as well. As of 2007, more than three-quarters of the states had some sort of early learning standards—that is, standards for the years before kindergarten—and the remaining states had begun developing them.[20] Head Start has put in place a "child outcomes framework," which identifies learning expectations in eight domains.[21] National reports and public policy statements have supported the creation of standards-based curriculum as part of a broader effort to build children's school readiness by improving teaching and learning in the early years.[22] For its part, NAEYC has position statements defining the features of high-quality early learning standards, curriculum, and assessment.[23]

So we must close existing learning gaps and enable all children to succeed at higher levels—but *how*? While this question is not a new one, in the current context it is the focus of increased attention. As later outlined in "Applying New Knowledge to Critical Issues," accumulating evidence and innovations in practice now provide guidance as to the knowledge and abilities that teachers must work especially hard to foster in young children, as well as information on how teachers can do so.

Creating Improved, Better-Connected Education for Preschool and Elementary Children

For many years, preschool education and elementary education—each with its own funding sources, infrastructure, values, and traditions—have remained largely separate. In fact, the education establishment typically has not thought of preschool as a full-fledged part of American public education. Among the chief reasons for this view is that preschool is neither universally funded by the public nor mandatory.[24] Moreover, preschool programs exist within a patchwork quilt of sponsorship and delivery systems and widely varying teacher credentials. Many programs came into being primarily to offer child care for parents who worked. In recent years, however, preschool's educational purpose and potential have been increasingly recognized, and this recognition contributes to the blurring of the preschool-elementary boundary. The two spheres now have substantial reasons to strive for greater continuity and collaboration.

One impetus is that mandated accountability requirements, particularly third grade testing, exert pressures on schools and teachers at K–2,[25] who in turn look to teachers of younger children to help prepare students to demonstrate the required proficiencies later. A related factor is the growth of state-funded pre-kindergarten, located in schools or other community settings, which collectively serves more than a million three- and four-year-olds. Millions more children are in Head Start programs and child care programs that meet state pre-kindergarten require-ments and receive state pre-K dollars. Head Start, serving more than 900,000 children nationwide, is now required to coordinate with the public schools at the state level.[26] Title I dollars support preschool education and services for some 300,000 children. Nationally, about 35 percent of all four-year-olds are in publicly supported pre-kindergarten programs.[27]

For its part, the world of early care and education stands to gain in some respects from a closer relationship with the K–12 system. Given the shortage of affordable, high-quality programs for children under five and the low compensation for those staff, advocates see potential benefits to having more four-year-olds, and perhaps even three-year-olds, receive services in publicly funded schooling. Proponents also hope that a closer relation-ship between early-years education and the elementary grades would lead to enhanced alignment and each sphere's learning from the other,[28] thus resulting in greater continuity and coher-ence across the pre-K–3 span.

At the same time, however, preschool educators have some fears about the prospect of the K–12 system absorbing or radi-cally reshaping education for three-, four-, and five-year-olds, especially at a time when pressures in public schooling are intense and often run counter to the needs of young children. Many early childhood educators are already quite concerned about the current climate of increased high-stakes testing adversely affecting children in grades K–3, and they fear exten-sion of these effects to even younger children. Even learning standards, though generally supported in principle in the early childhood world,[29] are sometimes questioned in practice because they can have negative effects.

Early learning standards are still relatively new, having been mandated by Good Start, Grow Smart in 2002 for the domains of language, literacy, and mathematics. While some states have taken a fairly comprehensive approach across the domains of learning and development, others focus heavily on the man-dated areas, particularly literacy. When state standards are not comprehensive, the curriculum driven by those standards is less likely to be so, and any alignment will likely address only those few curriculum areas identified in the standards.

Such narrowing of curriculum scope is one shortcoming that can characterize a set of standards; there can be other defi-ciencies, too. To be most beneficial for children, standards need to be not only comprehensive but also address what is impor-tant for children to know and be able to do; be aligned across developmental stages and age/grade levels; and be consistent with how children develop and learn. Unfortunately, many state standards focus on superficial learning objectives, at times underestimating young children's competence and at other times requiring understandings and tasks that young children cannot really grasp until they are older.[30] There is also growing concern that most assessments of children's knowledge are exclusively in English, thereby missing important knowledge a child may have but cannot express in English.[31]

Alignment is desirable, indeed critical, for standards to be effective. Yet effective alignment consists of more than simplify-ing for a younger age group the standards appropriate for older children. Rather than relying on such downward mapping, developers of early learning standards should base them on what we know from research and practice about children from a variety of backgrounds at a given stage/age and about the processes, sequences, variations, and long-term consequences of early learning and development.[32]

As for state-to-state alignment, the current situation is chaotic. Although discussion about establishing some kind of national standards framework is gaining momentum, there is no common set of standards at present. Consequently, publishers competing in the marketplace try to develop curriculum and textbooks that address the standards of all the states. Then teachers feel compelled to cover this large array of topics, teach-ing each only briefly and often superficially. When such curricu-lum and materials are in use, children move through the grades encountering a given topic in grade after grade—but only shal-lowly each time—rather than getting depth and focus on a smaller number of key learning goals and being able to master these before moving on.[33]

Standards overload is overwhelming to teachers and chil-dren alike and can lead to potentially problematic teaching prac-tices. At the preschool and K–3 levels particularly, practices of concern include excessive lecturing to the whole group, frag-mented teaching of discrete objectives, and insistence that teach-ers follow rigid, tightly paced schedules. There is also concern that schools are curtailing valuable experiences such as problem solving, rich play, collaboration with peers, opportunities for emotional and social development, outdoor/physical activity, and the arts. In the high-pressure classroom, children are less likely to develop a love of learning and a sense of their own competence and ability to make choices, and they miss much of the joy and expansive learning of childhood.[34]

Educators across the whole preschool-primary spectrum have perspectives and strengths to bring to a closer collabora-tion and ongoing dialogue. The point of bringing the two worlds together is *not* for children to learn primary grade skills at an earlier age; it is for their teachers to take the first steps together to ensure that young children develop and learn, to be able to acquire such skills and understandings as they progress in school.

The growing knowledge base can shed light on what an exchanging of best practices might look like,[35] as noted later in "Applying New Knowledge to Critical Issues." Through increased communication and collaboration, both worlds can learn much that can contribute to improving the educational experiences of *all* young children and to making those experi-ences more coherent.

Recognizing Teacher Knowledge and Decision Making as Vital to Educational Effectiveness

The standards/accountability movement has led to states and other stakeholders spelling out what children should know and be able to do at various grade levels. Swift improvement in student achievement across all student subgroups has been demanded. Under that mandate, many policy makers and administrators understandably gravitate toward tools and strategies intended to expedite the education enterprise, including "teacher proofing" curriculum, lessons, and schedules. As a result, in some states and districts, teachers in publicly funded early childhood settings report that they are allowed far less scope in classroom decision making than they were in the past,[36] in some cases getting little to no say in the selection of curriculum and assessments or even in their use of classroom time.

How much directing and scaffolding of teachers' work is helpful, and how much teacher autonomy is necessary to provide the best teaching and learning for children? The answer undoubtedly varies with differences among administrators and teachers themselves and the contexts in which they work.

A great many school administrators (elementary principals, superintendents, district staff) lack a background in early childhood education, and their limited knowledge of young children's development and learning means they are not always aware of what is and is not good practice with children at that age. Teachers who have studied how young children learn and develop and effective ways of teaching them are more likely to have this specialized knowledge. Moreover, it is the teacher who is in the classroom every day with children. So it is the teacher (not administrators or curriculum specialists) who is in the best position to know the particular children in that classroom—their interests and experiences, what they excel in and what they struggle with, what they are eager and ready to learn. Without this particular knowledge, determining what is best for those children's learning, as a group and individually, is impossible.

But it must be said that many teachers themselves lack the current knowledge and skills needed to provide high-quality care and education to young children, at least in some components of the curriculum. Many factors contribute, including the lack of a standard entry-level credential, wide variation in program settings and auspices, low compensation, and high turnover.[37] With workforce parameters such as these, is it reasonable to expect that every teacher in a classroom today is capable of fully meeting the challenges of providing high-quality early care and education?

Expert decision making lies at the heart of effective teaching. The acts of teaching and learning are too complex and individual to prescribe a teacher's every move in advance. Children benefit most from teachers who have the skills, knowledge, and judgment to make good decisions and are given the opportunity to use them.

Recognizing that effective teachers are good decision makers, however, does not mean that they should be expected to make all decisions in isolation. Teachers are not well served when they are stranded without the resources, tools, and supports necessary to make sound instructional decisions, and of course children's learning suffers as well.

Ideally, well conceived standards or learning goals (as described previously) are in place to guide local schools and programs in choosing or developing comprehensive, appropriate curriculum. The curriculum framework is a starting place; then teachers can use their expertise to make adaptations as needed to optimize the fit with the children. Further, such curricular guidance gives teachers some direction in providing the materials, learning experiences, and teaching strategies that promote learning goals most effectively, allowing them to focus on instructional decision making without having to generate the entire curriculum themselves.

Even well-qualified teachers find it challenging to create from scratch a comprehensive curriculum that addresses all the required standards and important learning goals, as well as designing the assessment methods and learning experiences. This daunting task is even less realistic for those teachers with minimal preparation. Hence, there is value in providing teachers a validated curriculum framework and related professional development, as long as teachers have the opportunity to make individual adaptations for the diversity of children they teach.[38]

That good teaching requires expert decision making means that teachers need solid professional preparation, as well as ongoing professional development and regular opportunities to work collaboratively.[39] Since this level of preparation and training does not yet exist for many in the early childhood workforce, the question of how best to equip and support inadequately prepared teachers needs serious investigation. Research on critical factors in good teaching, as described in the next section of this statement, has powerful lessons to offer.

Applying New Knowledge to Critical Issues

Fortunately, a continually expanding early childhood knowledge base enables the field to refine, redirect, or confirm understandings of best practice. The whole of the present position statement reflects fresh evidence of recent years and the perspectives and priorities emerging from these findings. This section looks within that mass of new knowledge to a few lines of research specifically helpful in addressing the three critical issues for the field identified in this position statement.

First, new findings hold promise for reducing learning gaps and barriers and increasing the achievement of all children. More is now known about which early social and emotional, cognitive, physical, and academic competencies enable young children to develop and learn to their full potential. Such findings are useful in determining curriculum content and sequences for all children. But they are especially important in helping those children most likely to begin school with lower levels of the foundational skills needed to succeed and most likely to fall farther behind with time—among whom children of color, children growing up in poverty, and English language learners are overrepresented. Another key aspect is ensuring that children who have learning difficulties or disabilities receive the early intervention services they need to learn and function well in the classroom.

Research continues to confirm the greater efficacy of early action—and in some cases, intensive intervention—as compared with remediation and other "too little" or "too late" approaches. Changing young children's experiences can substantially affect their development and learning, especially when intervention starts early in life and is not an isolated action but a broad-gauged set of strategies.[40] For example, Early Head Start, a comprehensive two-generational program for children under age three and their families, has been shown to promote cognitive, language, and social and emotional development.[41] The success of Early Head Start illustrates that high-quality services for infants and toddlers—far too rare in the United States today—have a long-lasting and positive impact on children's development, learning abilities, and capacity to regulate their emotions.[42]

Although high-quality preschool programs benefit children (particularly low-income children) more than mediocre or poor programs do,[43] fewer children living in poverty get to attend high-quality preschool programs than do children from higher-income households.[44] Findings on the impact of teaching quality in the early grades show a similar pattern.[45] In addition to this relationship of overall program and school quality to later school success, research has identified a number of specific predictors of later achievement. Some of these predictors lie in language/literacy and mathematics; others are dimensions of social and emotional competence and cognitive functioning related to how children fare in school.

In the language and literacy domain, vocabulary knowledge and other aspects of oral language are particularly important predictors of children's reading comprehension.[46] Even when children with limited vocabulary manage to acquire basic decoding skills, they still often encounter difficulty around grade three or four when they begin needing to read more advanced text in various subjects.[47] Their vocabulary deficit impedes comprehension and thus their acquisition of knowledge necessary to succeed across the curriculum.[48] Clearly, children who hear little or no English in the home would have even more initial difficulty with comprehension in English.

To shrink the achievement gap, then, early childhood programs need to start early with proactive vocabulary development to bring young children whose vocabulary and oral language development is lagging—whatever the causes—closer to the developmental trajectory typical of children from educated, affluent families.[49] For these children to gain the vocabulary and the advanced linguistic structures they will need for elementary grade reading, their teachers need to engage them in language interactions throughout the day, including reading to them in small groups and talking with them about the stories. Especially rich in linguistic payoff is extended discourse; that is, conversation between child and adult on a given topic sustained over many exchanges.[50]

Compelling evidence has shown that young children's alphabet knowledge and phonological awareness are significant predictors of their later proficiency in reading and writing.[51] A decade ago, many preschool teachers did not perceive it as their role—or even see it as appropriate—to launch young children on early steps toward literacy, including familiarizing them with the world of print and the sounds of language. The early childhood profession now recognizes that gaining literacy foundations is an important facet of children's experience before kindergarten,[52] although the early literacy component still needs substantial improvement in many classrooms.

Like the teaching of early literacy, mathematics education in the early childhood years is key to increasing all children's school readiness and to closing the achievement gap.[53] Within the mathematics arena, preschoolers' knowledge of numbers and their sequence, for example, strongly predicts not only math learning but also literacy skills.[54] Yet mathematics typically gets very little attention before kindergarten.[55] One reason is that early childhood teachers themselves often lack the skills and confidence to substantially and effectively increase their attention to mathematics in the curriculum.[56]

Mathematics and literacy concepts and skills—and, indeed, robust content *across* the curriculum—can be taught to young children in ways that are engaging and developmentally appropriate.[57] It can be, but too often isn't; to achieve such improvements will require considerable strengthening of early-years curriculum and teaching. Failing to meet this challenge to improve all children's readiness and achievement will perpetuate the inequities of achievement gaps and the low performance of the U.S. student population as a whole.

Besides specific predictors in areas such as mathematics and literacy, another major thread in recent research is that children's social and emotional competencies, as well as some capabilities that cut across social and emotional and cognitive functioning, predict their classroom functioning. Of course, children's social, emotional, and behavioral adjustment is important in its own right, both in and out of the classroom. But it now appears that some variables in these domains also relate to and predict school success. For example, studies have linked emotional competence to both enhanced cognitive performance and academic achievement.[58] A number of factors in the emotional and social domain, such as independence, responsibility, self-regulation, and cooperation, predict how well children make the transition to school and how they fare in the early grades.[59]

A particularly powerful variable is self-regulation, which the early childhood field has long emphasized as a prime developmental goal for the early years.[60] Mounting research evidence confirms this importance, indicating that self-regulation in young children predicts their later functioning in areas such as problem solving, planning, focused attention, and metacognition, and thus contributes to their success as learners.[61] Moreover, helping children from difficult life circumstances to develop strong self-regulation has proven to be both feasible and influential in preparing them to succeed in school.[62]

The gains children make as a result of high-quality programs for children under six have been found to diminish in a few years if children do not continue to experience high-quality education in grades K–3.[63] This consistent finding makes clear the importance of improving quality and continuity all along the birth–eight continuum. As previously described, critical to developing a better-connected, more coherent preschool-elementary framework is aligning standards, curriculum, and assessment practices within that continuum.[64] (Ideally, such a framework would extend to infant and toddler care as well.)

Further, educators and researchers are beginning to consider how to unite the most important and effective elements of preschool education with those of K–3.[65] In this search for the "best of both worlds," policy makers and educators can look to the expanding body of knowledge on the aspects of early learning and development that enable children to do well in school and the practices that should be more prevalent across the entire pre-K–3 span.[66]

First, research evidence on the predictors of successful outcomes for children (highlighted earlier) suggests a number of learning goals and experiences that in some form ought to be incorporated across pre-K–3. These include, for example, robust curriculum content; careful attention to known learning sequences (in literacy, mathematics, science, physical education, and other domains); and emphasis on developing children's self-regulation, engagement, and focused attention. Also proven to yield positive results for children are practices familiar to early childhood educators, such as relationship-based teaching and learning; partnering with families; adapting teaching for children from different backgrounds and for individual children; active, meaningful, and connected learning;[67] and smaller class sizes.[68] Evidence of the benefits of these practices suggests that they should be extended more widely into the elementary grades.

A second source of knowledge about effectively connecting education across the preschool–grade three span comes from educational innovations now being piloted. Schools that encompass these grades and thoughtfully consider how to increase continuity, alignment, and coherence are emerging around the country, and some are being studied by researchers.[69]

Expansion of P–16 or P–20 commissions around the country, although not yet giving much attention to pre-kindergarten,[70] provides one vehicle for the conversations about continuity that need to take place. While there are entrenched practices and structures separating preschool and K–3 education, the current forces noted here provide considerable impetus and opportunity to achieve stronger, more coordinated pre-K–3 education.

The importance of teachers to high-quality early education, indeed to all of education, cannot be overemphasized. Although wise administrative and curricular decisions made upstream from the individual teacher significantly affect what goes on in the classroom, they are far from ensuring children's learning. Research indicates that the most powerful influences on whether and what children learn occur in the teacher's interactions with them, in the real-time decisions the teacher makes throughout the day.[71] Thus, no educational strategy that fails to recognize the centrality of the teacher's decisions and actions can be successful.

It is the teacher's classroom plans and organization, sensitivity and responsiveness to all the children, and moment-to-moment interactions with them that have the greatest impact on children's development and learning.[72] The way teachers design learning experiences, how they engage children and respond to them, how they adapt their teaching and interactions to children's background, the feedback they give—these matter greatly in children's learning. And none can be fully determined in advance and laid out in a curriculum product or set of lesson plans that every teacher is to follow without deviation. Teachers will always have moment-to-moment decisions to make.

To make these decisions with well-grounded intentionality, teachers need to have knowledge about child development and learning in general, about the individual children in their classrooms, and about the sequences in which a domain's specific concepts and skills are learned. Teachers also need to have at the ready a well-developed repertoire of teaching strategies to employ for different purposes.[73]

Directly following from this first lesson is a second: the imperative to make developing teacher quality and effectiveness a top priority. This investment must include excellent preservice preparation, ongoing professional development, and on-the-ground support and mentoring. For example, good curriculum resources are helpful when they specify the key skills and concepts for children and provide a degree of teaching guidance, but without overscripting. New or inadequately trained teachers and those encountering a new curriculum or set of standards may be particularly in need of such scaffolding.[74]

Another valuable form of scaffolding for teachers is interaction with mentors and peers. Meeting the needs of diverse learners and helping all children to develop and learn require significant time for teachers to collaborate with colleagues, discuss and observe best practices, and participate in meaningful professional development. Most teachers, including novice teachers, get too little time for such activities. While providing time and opportunity for teachers to do these things can be very challenging for administrators, it is critical.[75]

To act on this second "lesson"—the imperative to make teaching quality and effectiveness a top priority—means changing what happens in the classroom. But it also means establishing policies and committing public funds at the federal, state, and local levels, as described in "Policy Considerations," the concluding section of this position statement.

Core Considerations in Developmentally Appropriate Practice

Every day, early childhood practitioners make many great decisions, both long-term and short-term. As they do so, they need to keep in mind the identified goals for children's learning and development and be intentional in helping children achieve these goals. The core of developmentally appropriate practice lies in this intentionality, in the knowledge that practitioners consider when they are making decisions, and in their always aiming for goals that are both challenging and achievable for children.

Knowledge to Consider in Making Decisions

In all aspects of their work with children, early childhood practitioners must consider these three areas of knowledge:

1. What is known about child development and learning—referring to knowledge of age-related characteristics that permits general predictions about what experiences are likely to best promote children's learning and development. Teachers who are knowledgeable about child development and learning are able to make broad predictions about what children of a particular age group typically will be like, what they typically will and will not be capable of, and what strategies and approaches will most likely promote their optimal learning and development. With this knowledge, teachers can make preliminary decisions with some confidence about environment, materials, interactions, and activities. At the same time, their knowledge also tells them that specific groups of children and the individual children in any group always will be the same in some ways but different in others.

2. What is known about each child as an individual—referring to what practitioners learn about each child that has implications for how best to adapt and be responsive to that individual variation. To be effective, teachers must get to know each child in the group well. They do this using a variety of methods—such as observation, clinical interview (an extended dialogue in which the adult seeks to discern the child's concepts or strategies), examination of children's work, individual child assessments, and talking with families. From the information and insights gathered, teachers make plans and adjustments to promote each child's individual development and learning as fully as possible. Developmental variation among children is the norm, and any one child's progress also will vary across domains and disciplines, contexts, and time. Children differ in many other respects, too—including in their strengths, interests, and preferences; personalities and approaches to learning; and knowledge, skills, and abilities based on prior experiences. Children may also have special learning needs; sometimes these have been diagnosed and sometimes they have not. Among the factors that teachers need to consider as they seek to optimize a child's school adjustment and learning are circumstances such as living in poverty or homelessness, having to move frequently, and other challenging situations. Responding to each child as an individual is fundamental to developmentally appropriate practice.

3. What is known about the social and cultural contexts in which children live—referring to the values, expectations, and behavioral and linguistic conventions that shape children's lives at home and in their communities that practitioners must strive to understand in order to ensure that learning experiences in the program or school are meaningful, relevant, and respectful for each child and family. As we grow up in a family and in a broader social and cultural community, we all come to certain understandings about what our group considers appropriate, values, expects, admires. We learn this through direct teaching from our parents and other important people in our lives and through observing those around us. Among these understandings, we absorb "rules" about behaviors—such as how to show respect, how to interact with people we know well and those we have just met, how to regard time and personal space, how to dress, and countless other attitudes and actions. We typically absorb these rules very early and very deeply, so we live by them with little conscious thought. When young children are in a group setting outside the home, what makes sense to them, how they use language to interact, and how they experience this new world depend on the social and cultural contexts to which they are accustomed. A skilled teacher takes such contextual factors into account, along with the children's ages and their individual differences, in shaping all aspects of the learning environment.

To recap this decision-making process: An effective teacher begins by thinking about what children of the age and developmental status represented in the group are typically like. This knowledge provides a general idea of the activities, routines, interactions, and curriculum that will be effective with that group. The teacher also must consider each child, including looking at the child as an individual and within the context of family, community, culture, linguistic norms, social group, past experience (including learning and behavior), and current circumstances. Only then can the teacher see children *as they are* to make decisions that are developmentally appropriate for each of them.

Challenging *and* Achievable Goals

Meeting children where they are is essential, but no good teacher simply leaves them there. Keeping in mind desired goals and what is known about the children as a group and individually, the teacher plans experiences to promote children's learning and development.

Learning and development are most likely to occur when new experiences build on what a child already knows and is able to do and when those learning experiences also entail the child stretching a reasonable amount in acquiring new skills, abilities, or knowledge. After the child reaches that new level of mastery in skill or understanding, the teacher reflects on what goals should come next; and the cycle continues, advancing children's learning in a developmentally appropriate way.

Clearly, such effective teaching does not happen by chance. A hallmark of developmentally appropriate teaching is intentionality. Good teachers are intentional in everything they do—setting up the classroom, planning curriculum, making use of various teaching strategies, assessing children, interacting with them, and working with their families. Intentional teachers are purposeful and thoughtful about the actions they take, and they direct their teaching toward the goals the program is trying to help children reach.

Principles of Child Development and Learning That Inform Practice

Developmentally appropriate practice as defined in this position statement is not based on what we think might be true or what we want to believe about young children. Developmentally appropriate practice is informed by what we know from theory and literature about how children develop and learn. In particular, a review of that literature yields a number of well-supported generalizations, or principles.

No linear listing of principles—including the one below—can do justice to the complexity of the phenomenon that is child development and learning. While the list is comprehensive, it certainly is not all-inclusive. Each principle describes an individually contributing factor; but just as all domains of development and learning are interrelated, so too do the principles interconnect. For example, the influence of cultural differences and individual differences, each highlighted in a separate principle below, cuts across all the other principles. That is, the implication of any principle often differs as a function of cultural or individual givens.

A complete discussion of the knowledge base that informs developmentally appropriate practice is clearly beyond the scope of this document. Each of the principles rests on a very extensive research base that is only partially referenced here.[76]

All the limitations of such a list not withstanding, collectively the principles that follow form a solid basis for decision making—for decisions at all levels about how best to meet the needs of young children in general, and for decisions by teachers, programs, and families about the strengths and needs of individual children, with all their variations in prior experiences, abilities and talents, home language and English proficiency, personalities and temperaments, and community and cultural backgrounds.

1. All the domains of development and learning—physical, social and emotional, and cognitive—are important, and they are closely interrelated. Children's development and learning in one domain influence and are influenced by what takes place in other domains. Children are thinking, moving, feeling, and interacting human beings. To teach them well involves considering and fostering their development and learning in all domains.[77] Because this full spectrum of development and learning is fundamental to children's lives and to their future participation as members of society, early care and education must address all the domains.

Further, changes in one domain often facilitate or limit development in other areas.[78] For example, when children begin to crawl or walk, they gain new possibilities for exploring the world, and their mobility affects both their cognitive development and sense of autonomy. Likewise, children's language development influences their ability to participate in social interaction with adults and other children; such interactions, in turn, support their further language development.[79] A growing body of work demonstrates the relationship between emotional and social factors and children's academic competence[80] and thus the importance of all these areas in educating young children. In brief, the knowledge base documents the importance of a comprehensive curriculum and the interrelatedness of the developmental domains in children's well-being and success.

2. Many aspects of children's learning and development follow well-documented sequences, with later abilities, skills, and knowledge building on those already acquired. Human development research suggests that relatively stable, predictable sequences of growth and change occur in children during the first nine years of life.[81] Predictable changes occur in all domains of development, although the ways that these changes are manifested and the meaning attached to them may vary widely in different cultural and linguistic contexts.[82] Knowledge of how children within a given age span typically develop and learn provides a general framework to guide teachers in preparing the learning environment, considering curriculum, designing learning experiences, and teaching and interacting with children.

Also important for educators to know are the sequences in which children gain specific concepts, skills, and abilities, building on prior development and learning. In mathematics, for example, children's learning to count serves as an important foundation for their acquiring an understanding of numerals.[83] Familiarity with known learning sequences should inform curriculum development and teaching practice.

3. Development and learning proceed at varying rates from child to child, as well as at uneven rates across different areas of a child's individual functioning. Individual variation has at least two dimensions: the inevitable variability around the typical or normative course of development and the uniqueness of each child as an individual. Children's development follows individual patterns and timing; children also vary in temperament, personality, and aptitudes, as well as in what they learn in their family and within the social and cultural context or contexts that shape their experience.

All children have their own strengths, needs, and interests. Given the enormous variation among children of the same chronological age, a child's age is only a crude index of developmental abilities and interests. For children who have special learning needs or abilities, additional efforts and resources may be necessary to optimize their development and learning. The same is true when children's prior experiences do not give them the knowledge and skills they need to thrive in a specific learning environment.

Given this normal range of variation, decisions about curriculum, teaching, and interactions with children should be as individualized as possible. Rigid expectations of group norms do not reflect what is known about real differences in development and learning. At the same time, having high expectations for all children is essential, as is using the strategies and providing the resources necessary to help them meet these expectations.

4. Development and learning result from a dynamic and continuous interaction of biological maturation and experience. Development is the result of the interplay between the growing, changing child and the child's experiences in the social and physical worlds.[84] For example, a child's genetic makeup may predict healthy growth, but inadequate nutrition in the early years of life will keep this potential from being fulfilled. Conversely, the impact of an organic condition on a young child's learning and development can be minimized through systematic, individualized intervention. Likewise, a child's innate temperament—such as a predisposition to be either wary or outgoing—shapes and is shaped by how other children and adults interact with that child. In light of the power of biology and the effects of children's prior experiences, it is important for early childhood educators to maintain high expectations and employ all their knowledge, ingenuity, and persistence to find ways to help every child succeed.

5. Early experiences have profound effects, both cumulative and delayed, on a child's development and learning; and optimal periods exist for certain types of development and learning to occur. Children's early experiences, whether positive or negative, are cumulative. For example, a child's social experiences with other children in the preschool years may help him develop social skills and confidence that enable him or her to make friends in subsequent years, and these experiences further enhance the child's social competence and academic achievement. Conversely, children who fail to develop minimal social skills and thus suffer neglect or rejection from peers are at risk for later outcomes such as school dropout, delinquency, and mental health problems.[85] Similarly, early stimulation promotes brain development and the forming of neural connections, which in turn enable further development and learning. But if the very young child does not get this stimulation, he is less able to benefit from subsequent learning opportunities, and a cumulative disadvantage is set in motion.

Intervention and support are more successful the earlier a problem is addressed. Prevention of reading difficulties, for example, is far less difficult and expensive than remediation.[86] In addition, the literature shows that some aspects of development occur most efficiently at certain points in the life span. The first three years of life, for example, appear to be an optimal period for oral language development.[87] Ensuring that children get the needed environmental inputs and supports for a particular kind of learning and development at its "prime time" is always the most reliable route to desired results.

6. Development proceeds toward greater complexity, self-regulation, and symbolic or representational capacities. A pervasive characteristic of development is that children's functioning becomes increasingly complex—in language, social interaction, physical movement, problem solving, and virtually every other domain. Increased organization and memory capacity of the developing brain make it possible with age for children to combine simple routines into more complex strategies.[88] The younger the child, the more she or he tends to think concretely and in the here and now. Yet in some ways, young children's thinking can be quite abstract. For example, preschoolers know that adding always makes *more* and subtracting makes *less,* and they are able to grasp abstract ideas about counting objects such as the one-to-one principle.[89]

All young humans must negotiate the transition from total dependence on others at birth to competence and internal control, including learning to regulate their emotions, behaviors, and attention. For young infants, there are tasks such as learning to soothe themselves from arousal to a settled state. A few years later, self-regulation means developing the capacity to manage strong emotions and keep one's attention focused. Throughout the early years, adults play significant roles in helping children learn to self-regulate. Caregivers are important in helping very young children to modulate their emotional arousal; for example, soothing babies and then helping them learn to soothe themselves.[90] In the preschool years, teachers can help children develop self-regulation by scaffolding high-level dramatic play,[91] helping children learn to express their emotions, and engaging children in planning and decision making.[92]

During the early years of life, children move from sensory or behavioral responses to symbolic or representational knowledge.[93] For example, young children are able to navigate their homes and other familiar settings by recall and sensory cues, but later they come to understand and can use abstractions such as *left* and *right* or read a map of the house. It is around age two that children begin to represent and reconstruct their experiences and knowledge.[94] For example, children may use one object to stand for another in play, such as a block for a phone or a spatula for a guitar.[95] Their ability to use various modes and media to convey their meaning increases in range and scope. By the preschool years, these modes may include oral language, gestures and body movement, visual arts (drawing, painting, sculpting), construction, dramatic play, and writing. Their efforts to represent their ideas and concepts in any of these modes enhance the knowledge itself.[96]

7. Children develop best when they have secure, consistent relationships with responsive adults and opportunities for positive relationships with peers. From the earliest years of life, warm, nurturing relationships with responsive adults are necessary for many key areas of children's development, including empathy and cooperation, self-regulation and cultural socialization, language and communication, peer relationships, and identity formation.[97]

When children and caring adults have the opportunity to get to know each other well, they learn to predict each other's signals and behavior and establish attunement and trust.[98] The first and most important relationships are those a child forms with parents or other primary caregivers. Forming one or more such attachments sets the stage for other relationships, as children move into the wider world beyond their immediate family.[99] Young children benefit from opportunities to develop ongoing, trusting relationships with adults outside the family and with other children. Notably, positive teacher-child relationships promote children's learning and achievement, as well as social competence and emotional development.[100]

Nurturing relationships are vital in fostering high self-esteem and a strong sense of self-efficacy, capacity in resolving interpersonal conflicts cooperatively, and the sociability to connect with others and form friendships. Further, by providing positive models and the security and confidence to try new experiences and attempt new skills, such relationships support children's learning and the acquisition of numerous capabilities.[101]

8. Development and learning occur in and are influenced by multiple social and cultural contexts. Understanding children's development requires viewing each child within the sociocultural context of that child's family, educational setting, and community, as well as within the broader society.[102] These various contexts are interrelated, and all powerfully influence the developing child. For example, even a child in a loving, supportive family within a strong, healthy community is affected by the biases of the larger society, such as racism or sexism, and may show some effects of its negative stereotyping and discrimination.

Here *culture* is intended to refer to the customary beliefs and patterns of behavior, both explicit and implicit, that are inculcated by the society—or by a social, religious, or ethnic group within the society—in its members. Even though culture is discussed often in the context of diversity and immigrant or minority groups, all of us are members of cultures and are powerfully influenced by them. Every culture structures and interprets children's behavior and development in its own way.[103] Early childhood teachers need to understand the influence of sociocultural contexts and family circumstances on learning, recognize children's developing competencies, and be familiar with the variety of ways that children may demonstrate their developmental achievements.[104] Most importantly, educators need to be sensitive to how their own cultural experience shapes their perspective and to realize that multiple perspectives, not just their own, must be considered in decisions about children's development and learning.

As children grow up, they need to learn to function well in the society and in the increasingly global economy and to move comfortably among groups of people from backgrounds both similar and dissimilar to their own. Fortunately, children are capable of learning to function in more than one social or cultural context and to make behavioral or linguistic shifts as they move from one context to another, although this complex ability does not occur overnight and requires adult support. Acquiring a new language or the ability to operate in a new culture can and should be an additive process, rather than causing the displacement of the child's first language and culture.[105] For example, immigrant children are able to develop English proficiency without having to give up their home language, and it is important that they retain their fluency in the language of their family and community. Likewise, children who speak only English benefit from learning another language and can do so without sacrificing their English proficiency.[106]

9. Always mentally active in seeking to understand the world around them, children learn in a variety of ways; a wide range of teaching strategies and interactions are effective in supporting all these kinds of learning. Several prominent theories and bodies of research view cognitive development from the constructivist, interactive perspective.[107] That is, young children construct their knowledge and understanding of the world in the course of their own experiences, as well as from teachers, family members, peers and older children, and from books and other media. They learn from the concrete (e.g., manipulatives); they also apparently are capable of and interested in abstract ideas, to a far greater degree than was previously believed.[108] Children take all this input and work out their own understandings and hypotheses about the world. They try these out through interactions with adults and other children, physical manipulation, play, and their own thought processes—observing what happens, reflecting on their findings, imagining possibilities, asking questions, and formulating answers. When children make knowledge their own in these ways, their understanding is deeper and they can better transfer and apply their learning in new contexts.[109]

Using multiple teaching strategies is important in meeting children's different learning needs. The *Eager to Learn: Educating Our Preschoolers* report concluded:

> Good teachers acknowledge and encourage children's efforts, model and demonstrate, create challenges and support children in extending their capabilities, and provide specific directions or instruction. All of these teaching strategies can be used in the context of play and structured activities. Effective teachers also organize the classroom environment and plan ways to pursue educational goals for each child as opportunities arise in child-initiated activities and in activities planned and initiated by the teacher.[110]

Thus, children benefit when teachers have at their disposal a wide range of teaching strategies and from these teachers select the best strategy to use in a situation, depending on the learning goal, specific context, and needs of individual children at that moment, including children who may need much more support than others even in exploration and play.[111]

10. Play is an important vehicle for developing self-regulation as well as for promoting language, cognition, and social competence. Children of all ages love to play, and it gives them opportunities to develop physical competence and enjoyment of the outdoors, understand and make sense of their world, interact with others, express and control emotions, develop their symbolic and problem-solving abilities, and practice emerging skills. Research shows the links between play and foundational capacities such as memory, self-regulation, oral language abilities, social skills, and success in school.[112]

Children engage in various kinds of play, such as physical play, object play, pretend or dramatic play, constructive play, and games with rules. Observed in all young animals, play apparently serves important physical, mental, emotional, and social functions for humans and other species, and each kind of play has its own benefits and characteristics. From infancy, children act on the world around them for the pleasure of seeing what happens; for example, repeatedly dropping a spoon on the floor or pulling the cat's tail. At around age two, children begin to demonstrate symbolic use of objects—for instance, picking up a shell and pretending to drink as from a cup—at least when they have had opportunities to observe others engaging in such make-believe behavior.[113]

From such beginnings, children begin to engage in more mature forms of dramatic play, in which by the age of three to five they may act out specific roles, interact with one another in their roles, and plan how the play will go. Such play is influential in developing self-regulation, as children are highly motivated to stick to the roles and rules of the play, and thus grow in the ability to inhibit their impulses, act in coordination with others, and make plans.[114] High-level dramatic play produces documented cognitive, social, and emotional benefits.[115] However, with children spending more time in adult-directed activities and media use, forms of child play characterized by imagination and rich social interactions seem to be declining.[116] Active scaffolding of imaginative play is needed in early childhood settings if children are to develop the sustained, mature dramatic play that contributes significantly to their self-regulation and other cognitive, linguistic, social, and emotional benefits. Adults can use proven methods to promote children's extended engagement in make-believe play as well as in games with rules and other kinds of high-level play.[117] Rather than detracting from academic learning, play appears to support the abilities that underlie such learning and thus to promote school success.[118]

11. Development and learning advance when children are challenged to achieve at a level just beyond their current mastery, and also when they have many opportunities to practice newly acquired skills. Human beings, especially children, are motivated to understand or do what is just beyond their current understanding or mastery.[119] Effective teachers create a rich learning environment to activate that motivation, and they make use of strategies to promote children's undertaking and mastering of new and progressively more advanced challenges.[120]

In a task just beyond a child's independent reach, adults and more-competent peers contribute significantly to the child's development by providing the support or assistance that allows the child to succeed at that task. Once children make this stretch to a new level in a supportive context, they can go on to use the skill independently and in a variety of contexts, laying the foundation for the next challenge. Provision of such support, often called *scaffolding*,[121] is a key feature of effective teaching.[122]

At the same time, children need to be successful in new tasks a significant proportion of the time in order for their motivation and persistence to be maintained.[123] Confronted by repeated failure, most children will simply stop trying. Repeated opportunity to practice and consolidate new skills and concepts is also essential in order for children to reach the threshold of mastery at which they can go on to use this knowledge or skill and apply it in new situations. Young children engage in a great deal of practice during play and in other child-guided contexts.[124]

To set challenging, achievable goals for children and to provide the right amount and type of scaffolding require knowledge of child development and learning, including familiarity with the paths and sequences that children are known to follow in acquiring specific skills, concepts, and abilities. This general knowledge, along with what the teacher learns from close observation and probing of the individual child's thinking, is critical to matching curriculum and teaching experiences to that child's emerging competencies so as to be challenging but not frustrating.

12. Children's experiences shape their motivation and approaches to learning, such as persistence, initiative, and flexibility; in turn, these dispositions and behaviors affect their learning and development. The National Education Goals Panel and its Goal One Technical Planning Group identified "approaches to learning" as one of five aspects of school readiness.[125] Focused on the *how* rather than the *what* of learning, approaches to learning involve both children's feelings about learning (including their interest, pleasure, and motivation to learn) and children's behavior when learning (including attention, persistence, flexibility, and self-regulation).[126]

Even in the early years, children differ in their approaches to learning. These differences may influence children's school readiness and school success. For example, children who start school more eager to learn tend to do better in reading and mathematics than do less motivated children.[127] Children with more positive learning behaviors, such as initiative, attention, and persistence, later develop stronger language skills.[128] Moreover, children with greater self-regulation and other "learning-related skills" in kindergarten are more skilled in reading and mathematics in later grades.[129]

Although temperament and other inherent differences may affect children's approaches to learning, their experiences in families and early education programs have a major influence. Programs can implement evidence-based strategies that will promote positive approaches to learning. These strategies include strengthening relationships with children; working with families; and selecting effective curriculum, assessments, and teaching methods.[130]

Guidelines for Developmentally Appropriate Practice

Practice that promotes young children's optimal learning and development—what this statement terms *developmentally appropriate practice*—is grounded both in the research on child development and learning and in the knowledge base regarding educational effectiveness in early care and education.

But whether or not what actually happens in the classroom is, in practice, developmentally appropriate is the result of myriad decisions at all levels—by policy makers, administrators, teachers, and families—about the care and education of young children. Effective early childhood professionals draw on all the principles of child development and learning outlined, as well as the knowledge base on effective practices, and they apply the information in their practice.

The following guidelines address decisions that early childhood professionals make in the five key (and interrelated) areas of practice: (1) creating a caring community of learners, (2) teaching to enhance development and learning, (3) planning curriculum to achieve important goals, (4) assessing children's development and learning, and (5) establishing reciprocal relationships with families.

1. Creating a Caring Community of Learners

Because early childhood settings tend to be children's first communities outside the home, the character of these communities is very influential in development. How children expect to be treated and how they treat others is significantly shaped in the early childhood setting. In developmentally appropriate practice, practitioners create and foster a "community of learners" that supports *all* children to develop and learn. The role of the community is to provide a physical, emotional, and cognitive environment conducive to that development and learning. The foundation for the community is consistent, positive, caring relationships between the adults and children, among children, among teachers, and between teachers and families. It is the responsibility of all members of the learning community to consider and contribute to one another's well-being and learning.

To create a caring community of learners, practitioners ensure that the following occur for children from birth through the primary grades.

A. Each member of the community is valued by the others. By observing and participating in the community, children learn about themselves and their world and also how to develop positive, constructive relationships with other people. Each child has unique strengths, interests, and perspectives to contribute. Children learn to respect and acknowledge differences of all kinds and to value each person.

B. Relationships are an important context through which children develop and learn. Children construct their understandings about the world around them through interactions with other members of the community (both adults and peers). Opportunities to play together, collaborate on investigations and projects, and talk with peers and adults enhance children's development and learning. Interacting in small groups provides a context for children to extend their thinking, build on one another's ideas, and cooperate to solve problems. (Also see guideline 5, "Establishing Reciprocal Relationships with Families.")

C. Each member of the community respects and is accountable to the others to behave in a way that is conducive to the learning and well-being of all.

1. Teachers help children develop responsibility and self-regulation. Recognizing that such abilities and behaviors develop with experience and time, teachers consider how to foster such development in their interactions with each child and in their curriculum planning.

2. Teachers are responsible at all times for all children under their supervision, monitoring, anticipating, preventing, and redirecting behaviors not conducive to learning or disrespectful of the community, as well as teaching pro-social behaviors.

3. Teachers set clear and reasonable limits on children's behavior and apply those limits consistently. Teachers help children be accountable to themselves and to others for their behavior. In the case of preschool and older children, teachers engage children in developing their own community rules for behavior.

4. Teachers listen to and acknowledge children's feelings and frustrations, respond with respect in ways that children can understand, guide children to resolve conflicts, and model skills that help children to solve their own problems.

5. Teachers themselves demonstrate high levels of responsibility and self-regulation in their interactions with other adults (colleagues, family members) and with children.

D. Practitioners design and maintain the physical environment to protect the health and safety of the learning community members, specifically in support of young children's physiological needs for activity, sensory stimulation, fresh air, rest, and nourishment. The daily schedule provides a balance of rest and active movement. Outdoor experiences, including opportunities to interact with the natural world, are provided for children of all ages.

E. Practitioners ensure members of the community feel psychologically safe. The overall social and emotional climate is positive.

1. Interactions among community members (administrators, teachers, families, children), as well as the experiences provided by teachers, leave participants feeling secure, relaxed, and comfortable rather than disengaged, frightened, worried, or unduly stressed.

2. Teachers foster in children an enjoyment of and engagement in learning.

3. Teachers ensure that the environment is organized and the schedule follows an orderly routine that provides a stable structure within which development and learning

can take place. While the environment's elements are dynamic and changing, overall it still is predictable and comprehensible from a child's point of view.

4. Children hear and see their home language and culture reflected in the daily interactions and activities of the classroom.

2. Teaching to Enhance Development and Learning

From birth, a child's relationships and interactions with adults are critical determinants of development and learning. At the same time, children are active constructors of their own understanding of the world around them; as such, they benefit from initiating and regulating their own learning activities and from interacting with peers. Developmentally appropriate teaching practices provide an optimal balance of adult-guided and child-guided experiences. "*Adult-guided* experience proceeds primarily along the lines of the teacher's goals, but is also shaped by the children's active engagement; *child-guided* experience proceeds primarily along the lines of children's interests and actions, with strategic teacher support."[131] But whether a learning experience is adult- or child-guided, in developmentally appropriate practice it is the teacher who takes responsibility for stimulating, directing, and supporting children's development and learning by providing the experiences that each child needs.

The following describe teaching practices that are developmentally appropriate for young children from birth through the primary grades.

A. Teachers are responsible for fostering the caring learning community through their teaching.

B. Teachers make it a priority to know each child well, and also the people most significant in the child's life.

1. Teachers establish positive, personal relationships with each child and with each child's family to better understand that child's individual needs, interests, and abilities and that family's goals, values, expectations, and child-rearing practices. (Also see guideline 5, "Establishing Reciprocal Relationships with Families.") Teachers talk with each child and family (with a community translator, if necessary, for mutual understanding) and use what they learn to adapt their actions and planning.

2. Teachers continually gather information about children in a variety of ways and monitor each child's learning and development to make plans to help children progress. (Also see guideline 4, "Assessing Children's Development and Learning.")

3. Teachers are alert to signs of undue stress and traumatic events in each child's life and employ strategies to reduce stress and support the development of resilience.

C. Teachers take responsibility for knowing what the desired goals for the program are and how the program's curriculum is intended to achieve those goals. They carry out that curriculum through their teaching in ways that are geared to young children in general and these children in particular.

Doing this includes following the predictable sequences in which children acquire specific concepts, skills, and abilities and by building on prior experiences and understandings. (Also see guideline 3, "Planning Curriculum to Achieve Important Goals.")

D. Teachers plan for learning experiences that effectively implement a comprehensive curriculum so that children attain key goals across the domains (physical, social, emotional, cognitive) and across the disciplines (language literacy, including English acquisition, mathematics, social studies, science, art, music, physical education, and health).

E. Teachers plan the environment, schedule, and daily activities to promote each child's learning and development.

1. Teachers arrange firsthand, meaningful experiences that are intellectually and creatively stimulating, invite exploration and investigation, and engage children's active, sustained involvement. They do this by providing a rich variety of materials, challenges, and ideas that are worthy of children's attention.

2. Teachers present children with opportunities to make meaningful choices, especially in child-choice activity periods. They assist and guide children who are not yet able to enjoy and make good use of such periods.

3. Teachers organize the daily and weekly schedule to provide children with extended blocks of time in which to engage in sustained play, investigation, exploration, and interaction (with adults and peers).

4. Teachers provide experiences, materials, and interactions to enable children to engage in play that allows them to stretch their boundaries to the fullest in their imagination, language, interaction, and self-regulation as well as to practice their newly acquired skills.

F. Teachers possess an extensive repertoire of skills and strategies they are able to draw on, and they know how and when to choose among them, to effectively promote each child's learning and development at that moment. Those skills include the ability to adapt curriculum, activities, and materials to ensure full participation of *all* children. Those strategies include, but are not limited to, acknowledging, encouraging, giving specific feedback, modeling, demonstrating, adding challenge, giving cues or other assistance, providing information, and giving directions.

1. To help children develop initiative, teachers encourage them to choose and plan their own learning activities.

2. To stimulate children's thinking and extend their learning, teachers pose problems, ask questions, and make comments and suggestions.

3. To extend the range of children's interests and the scope of their thought, teachers present novel experiences and introduce stimulating ideas, problems, experiences, or hypotheses.

4. To adjust the complexity and challenge of activities to suit children's level of skill and knowledge, teachers increase the challenge as children gain competence and understanding.

5. To strengthen children's sense of competence and confidence as learners, motivation to persist, and willingness to take risks, teachers provide experiences for children to be genuinely successful and to be challenged.

6. To enhance children's conceptual understanding, teachers use various strategies, including intensive interview and conversation, that encourage children to reflect on and "revisit" their experiences.

7. To encourage and foster children's learning and development, teachers avoid generic praise ("Good job!") and instead give specific feedback ("You got the same number when you counted the beans again!").

G. Teachers know how and when to *scaffold* children's learning—that is, providing just enough assistance to enable each child to perform at a skill level just beyond what the child can do on his or her own, then gradually reducing the support as the child begins to master the skill, and setting the stage for the next challenge.

1. Teachers recognize and respond to the reality that in any group, children's skills will vary and they will need different levels of support. Teachers also know that any one child's level of skill and need for support will vary over time.

2. Scaffolding can take a variety of forms; for example, giving the child a hint, adding a cue, modeling the skill, or adapting the materials and activities. It can be provided in a variety of contexts, not only in planned learning experiences but also in play, daily routines, and outdoor activities.

3. Teachers can provide the scaffolding (e.g., the teacher models the skill) or peers can (e.g., the child's learning buddy models); in either case, it is the teacher who recognizes and plans for each child's need for support and assistance.

H. Teachers know how and when to use the various learning formats/contexts most strategically.

1. Teachers understand that each major learning format or context (e.g., large group, small group, learning center, routine) has its own characteristics, functions, and value.

2. Teachers think carefully about which learning format is best for helping children achieve a desired goal, given the children's ages, development, abilities, temperaments, etc.

I. When children have missed some of the learning opportunities necessary for school success (most often children from low-income households), programs and teachers provide them with even more extended, enriched, and intensive learning experiences than are provided to their peers.

1. Teachers take care not to place these children under added pressure. Such pressure on children already starting out at a disadvantage can make school a frustrating and discouraging experience, rather than an opportunity to enjoy and succeed at learning.

2. To enable these children to make optimal progress, teachers are highly intentional in use of time, and they

focus on key skills and abilities through highly engaging experiences.

3. Recognizing the self-regulatory, linguistic, cognitive, and social benefits that high-quality play affords, teachers do not reduce play opportunities that these children critically need. Instead, teachers scaffold and model aspects of rich, mature play.

J. Teachers make experiences in their classrooms accessible and responsive to *all* children and their needs—including children who are English language learners, have special needs or disabilities, live in poverty or other challenging circumstances, or are from different cultures.

1. Teachers incorporate a wide variety of experiences, materials and equipment, and teaching strategies to accommodate the range of children's individual differences in development, skills and abilities, prior experiences, needs, and interests.

2. Teachers bring each child's home culture and language into the shared culture of the learning community so that the unique contributions of that home culture and language can be recognized and valued by the other community members, and the child's connection with family and home is supported.

3. Teachers include all children in all of the classroom activities and encourage children to be inclusive in their behaviors and interactions with peers.

4. Teachers are prepared to meet special needs of individual children, including children with disabilities and those who exhibit unusual interests and skills. Teachers use all the strategies identified here, consult with appropriate specialists and the child's family, and see that the child gets the adaptations and specialized services he or she needs to succeed in the early childhood setting.

3. Planning Curriculum to Achieve Important Goals

The curriculum consists of the knowledge, skills, abilities, and understandings children are to acquire and the plans for the learning experiences through which those gains will occur. Implementing a curriculum always yields outcomes of some kind—but *which* outcomes those are and *how* a program achieves them are critical. In developmentally appropriate practice, the curriculum helps young children achieve goals that are developmentally and educationally significant. The curriculum does this through learning experiences (including play, small group, large group, interest centers, and routines) that reflect what is known about young children in general and about these children in particular, as well as about the sequences in which children acquire specific concepts, skills, and abilities, building on prior experiences.

Because children learn more in programs where there is a well planned and implemented curriculum, it is important for every school and early childhood program to have its curriculum in written form. Teachers use the curriculum and their knowledge of children's interests in planning relevant, engaging learning experiences; and they keep the curriculum in mind in their interactions with children throughout the day. In this way they ensure that children's learning experiences—in both adult-guided and child-guided contexts—are consistent with the program's goals for children and connected within an organized framework. At the same time, developmentally appropriate practice means teachers have flexibility—and the expertise to exercise that flexibility effectively—in how they design and carry out curricular experiences in their classrooms.[132]

The following describe curriculum planning that is developmentally appropriate for children from birth through the primary grades.

A. Desired goals that are important in young children's learning and development have been identified and clearly articulated.

1. Teachers consider what children should know, understand, and be able to do across the domains of physical, social, emotional, and cognitive development and across the disciplines, including language, literacy, mathematics, social studies, science, art, music, physical education, and health.

2. If state standards or other mandates are in place, teachers become thoroughly familiar with these; teachers add to these any goals to which the standards have given inadequate weight.

3. Whatever the source of the goals, teachers and administrators ensure that goals are clearly defined for, communicated to, and understood by all stakeholders, including families.

B. The program has a comprehensive, effective curriculum that targets the identified goals, including all those foundational for later learning and school success.

1. Whether or not teachers were participants in the decision about the curriculum, they familiarize themselves with it and consider its comprehensiveness in addressing all important goals.

2. If the program is using published curriculum products, teachers make adaptations to meet the learning needs of the children they teach.

3. If practitioners develop the curriculum themselves, they make certain it targets the identified goals and they use strong, up-to-date resources from experts to ensure that curriculum content is robust and comprehensive.

C. Teachers use the curriculum framework in their planning to ensure there is ample attention to important learning goals and to enhance the coherence of the classroom experience for children.

1. Teachers are familiar with the understandings and skills key for that age group in each domain (physical, social, emotional, cognitive), including how learning and development in one domain impact the other domains.

2. In their planning and follow-through, teachers use the curriculum framework along with what they know (from their observation and other assessment) about the children's

interests, progress, language proficiency, and learning needs. They carefully shape and adapt the experiences they provide children to enable each child to reach the goals outlined in the curriculum.

3. In determining the sequence and pace of learning experiences, teachers consider the developmental paths that children typically follow and the typical sequences in which skills and concepts develop. Teachers use these with an eye to moving all children forward in all areas, adapting when necessary for individual children. When children have missed some of the learning opportunities that promote school success, teachers must adapt the curriculum to help children advance more quickly.

D. Teachers make meaningful connections a priority in the learning experiences they provide children, to reflect that all learners, and certainly young children, learn best when the concepts, language, and skills they encounter are related to something they know and care about, and when the new learnings are themselves interconnected in meaningful, coherent ways.

1. Teachers plan curriculum experiences that integrate children's learning *within* and *across* the domains (physical, social, emotional, cognitive) and the disciplines (including language, literacy, mathematics, social studies, science, art, music, physical education, and health).

2. Teachers plan curriculum experiences to draw on children's own interests and introduce children to things likely to interest them, in recognition that developing and extending children's interests is particularly important during the preschool years, when children's ability to focus their attention is in its early stages.

3. Teachers plan curriculum experiences that follow logical sequences and that allow for depth and focus. That is, the experiences do not skim lightly over a great many content areas, but instead allow children to spend sustained time with a more select set.

E. Teachers collaborate with those teaching in the preceding and subsequent grade levels, sharing information about children and working to increase the continuity and coherence across ages/grades, while protecting the integrity and appropriateness of practices at each level.

F. In the care of infants and toddlers, practitioners plan curriculum (although they may not always call it that). They develop plans for the important routines and experiences that will promote children's learning and development and enable them to attain desired goals.

4. Assessing Children's Development and Learning

Assessment of children's development and learning is essential for teachers and programs in order to plan, implement, and evaluate the effectiveness of the classroom experiences they provide. Assessment also is a tool for monitoring children's progress toward a program's desired goals. In developmentally appropriate practice, the experiences and the assessments are linked (the experiences are developing what is being assessed, and vice versa); both are aligned with the program's desired outcomes or goals for children. Teachers cannot be intentional about helping children to progress unless they know where each child is with respect to learning goals.

Sound assessment of young children is challenging because they develop and learn in ways that are characteristically uneven and embedded within the specific cultural and linguistic contexts in which they live. For example, sound assessment takes into consideration such factors as a child's facility in English and stage of linguistic development in the home language. Assessment that is not reliable or valid, or that is used to label, track, or otherwise harm young children, is not developmentally appropriate practice.

The following describe sound assessment that is developmentally appropriate for children from birth through the primary grades.

A. Assessment of young children's progress and achievements is ongoing, strategic, and purposeful. The results of assessment are used to inform the planning and implementing of experiences, to communicate with the child's family, and to evaluate and improve teachers' and the program's effectiveness.

B. Assessment focuses on children's progress toward goals that are developmentally and educationally significant.

C. There is a system in place to collect, make sense of, and use the assessment information to guide what goes on in the classroom (formative assessment). Teachers use this information in planning curriculum and learning experiences and in moment-to-moment interactions with children—that is, teachers continually engage in assessment for the purpose of improving teaching and learning.

D. The methods of assessment are appropriate to the developmental status and experiences of young children, and they recognize individual variation in learners and allow children to demonstrate their competence in different ways. Methods appropriate to the classroom assessment of young children, therefore, include results of teachers' observations of children, clinical interviews, collections of children's work samples, and their performance on authentic activities.

E. Assessment looks not only at what children can do independently but also at what they can do with assistance from other children or adults. Therefore, teachers assess children as they participate in groups and other situations that are providing scaffolding.

F. In addition to this assessment by teachers, input from families as well as children's own evaluations of their work are part of the program's overall assessment strategy.

G. Assessments are tailored to a specific purpose and used only for the purpose for which they have been demonstrated to produce reliable, valid information.

H. Decisions that have a major impact on children, such as enrollment or placement, are never made on the basis of results from a single developmental assessment or screening instrument/device but are based on multiple sources of relevant information, including that obtained from observations of and interactions with children by teachers and parents (and specialists, as needed).

I. When a screening or other assessment identifies children who may have special learning or developmental needs, there is appropriate follow-up, evaluation, and, if indicated, referral. Diagnosis or labeling is never the result of a brief screening or one-time assessment. Families should be involved as important sources of information.

5. Establishing Reciprocal Relationships with Families

Developmentally appropriate practices derive from deep knowledge of child development principles and of the program's children in particular, as well as the context within which each of them is living. The younger the child, the more necessary it is for practitioners to acquire this particular knowledge through relationships with children's families.

Practice is not developmentally appropriate if the program limits "parent involvement" to scheduled events (valuable though these may be), or if the program/family relationship has a strong "parent education" orientation. Parents do not feel like partners in the relationship when staff members see themselves as having all the knowledge and insight about children and view parents as lacking such knowledge.

Such approaches do not adequately convey the complexity of the partnership between teachers and families that is a fundamental element of good practice. The following describe the kind of relationships that are developmentally appropriate for children (from birth through the primary grades), in which family members and practitioners work together as members of the learning community.

A. In reciprocal relationships between practitioners and families, there is mutual respect, cooperation, shared responsibility, and negotiation of conflicts toward achievement of shared goals. (Also see guideline 1, "Creating a Caring Community of Learners.")

B. Practitioners work in collaborative partnerships with families, establishing and maintaining regular, frequent two-way communication with them (with families who do not speak English, teachers should use the language of the home if they are able or try to enlist the help of bilingual volunteers).

C. Family members are welcome in the setting, and there are multiple opportunities for family participation. Families participate in program decisions about their children's care and education.

D. Teachers acknowledge a family's choices and goals for the child and respond with sensitivity and respect to those preferences and concerns, but without abdicating the responsibility that early childhood practitioners have to support children's learning and development through developmentally appropriate practices.

E. Teachers and the family share with each other their knowledge of the particular child and understanding of child development and learning as part of day-to-day communication and in planned conferences. Teachers support families in ways that maximally promote family decision-making capabilities and competence.

F. Practitioners involve families as a source of information about the child (before program entry and on an ongoing basis) and engage them in the planning for their child.

G. The program links families with a range of services, based on identified resources, priorities, and concerns.

Policy Considerations

Teachers and administrators in early childhood education play a critical role in shaping the future of our citizenry and our democracy. Minute to minute, day to day, month to month, they provide the consistent, compassionate, respectful relationships that our children need to establish strong foundations of early learning. By attending to the multiple domains of development and the individual needs of those in their care, early childhood professionals who employ developmentally appropriate practices engage young children in rich out-of-home early learning experiences that prepare them for future learning and success in life.

Regardless of the resources available, early childhood professionals have an ethical responsibility to practice according to the standards of their profession. It is unrealistic, however, to expect that they can fully implement those standards and practices without public policies and funding that support a system of early childhood education that is grounded in providing high-quality developmentally appropriate experiences for all children.

The goal must be advancement in both realms: more early childhood professionals engaging in developmentally appropriate practices, and more policy makers establishing policies and committing public funds to support such practices.

Many elements of developmentally appropriate practice should be reflected in our federal, state, and local policies. Policy areas that are particularly critical for developing a high-quality, well financed system of early childhood education, which includes the implementation of developmentally appropriate practice, must include at a minimum: early learning standards for children and related/aligned curricula and assessment; a comprehensive professional development and compensation system; a program quality rating and improvement system to improve program quality as well as to inform the families, the public, and policy makers about quality; comprehensive and coordinated services for children; attention to program evaluation; and commitment of additional public funds to support program affordability and quality in every setting.

NAEYC regularly provides information to inform advocates and policy makers in their efforts to establish sound policies in these areas.

In order for such information and recommendations to be up to date, NAEYC's policy-relevant summaries and information appear not in this position statement but in their own location on the Association's website at www.naeyc.org.

Notes

1. NAEYC. 1986. Position statement on developmentally appropriate practice in programs for 4- and 5-year-olds. *Young Children* 41 (6): 20–29; Bredekamp, S., ed. 1987. *Developmentally appropriate practice in early childhood programs serving children from birth through age 8*. Expanded edition. Washington, DC: NAEYC; NAEYC. 1996. Developmentally appropriate practice in early childhood programs serving children from birth through age 8. A position statement of the National Association for the Education of Young Children. In *Developmentally appropriate practice in early childhood programs,* Rev. ed., eds. S. Bredekamp & C. Copple, 3–30. Washington, DC: Author.

2. NAEYC & NAECS/SDE (National Association of Early Childhood Specialists in State Departments of Education). 2002. *Early learning standards: Creating the conditions for success*. Joint position statement. Online: www.naeyc.org/dap; NAEYC & NAECS/SDE (National Association of Early Childhood Specialists in State Departments of Education). 2003. *Early childhood curriculum, assessment, and program evaluation: Building an effective, accountable system in programs for children birth through age 8*. Joint position statement. Online: www.naeyc.org/dap; NAEYC. 2005. *Code of ethical conduct and statement of commitment*. Position statement. Online: www.naeyc.org/dap; NAEYC. 2005. *NAEYC early childhood program standards and accreditation criteria*. 11 vols. Washington, DC: Author.

Critical issues in the current context

3. Children's Defense Fund. 2005. *The state of America's children, 2005*. Washington, DC: Author.

4. Cochran, M. 2007. *Finding our way: The future of American early care and education*. Washington, DC: Zero to Three.

5. Sandall, S., M.L. Hemmeter, B.J. Smith, & M.E. McLean, eds. 2005. *DEC recommended practices: A comprehensive guide for practical application in early intervention/early childhood special education*. Longmont, CO: Sopris West, and Missoula, MT: Division for Early Childhood, Council for Exceptional Children; Hemmeter, M.L., L. Fox, & S. Doubet. 2006. Together we can: A program-wide approach to addressing challenging behavior. In *Social emotional development,* eds. E. Horn & H. Jones, Young Exceptional Children Monograph Series, vol. 8. Missoula, MT: Division for Early Childhood.

6. Gitomer, D.H. 2007. *Teacher quality in a changing policy landscape: Improvements in the teacher pool*. Princeton, NJ: Educational Testing Service. Online: www.ets.org/Media/Education_Topics/pdf/TQ_full_report.pdf.

7. Whitebook, M., C. Howes, & D. Phillips. 1990. *The national child care staffing study: Who cares? Child care teachers and the quality of care in America*. Final report. Oakland, CA: Child Care Employee Project.

8. Cochran, M. 2007. *Finding our way: The future of American early care and education*. Washington, DC: Zero to Three.

9. Klein, L.G., & J. Knitzer. 2006. Effective preschool curricula and teaching strategies. *Pathways to Early School Success,* Issue Brief No. 2. New York: Columbia University, National Center for Children in Poverty; Brooks-Gunn, J., C.E. Rouse, & S. McLanahan. 2007. Racial and ethnic gaps in school readiness. In *School readiness and the transition to kindergarten in the era of accountability,* eds. R.C. Pianta, M.J. Cox, & K.L. Snow, 283–306. Baltimore: Paul H. Brookes.

10. Heath, S.B. 1983. *Ways with words: Language, life, and work in communities and classrooms*. New York: Cambridge University Press; Vogt, L., C. Jordan, & R. Tharp. 1993. Explaining school failure, producing school success. In *Minority education: Anthropological perspectives,* eds. E. Jacob & C. Jordan, 53–65. Norwood, NJ: Ablex.

11. Hart, B., & T.R. Risley. 1995. *Meaningful differences in the everyday experience of young American children*. Baltimore: Paul H. Brookes; Hart, B., & T.R. Risley. 1999. *The social world of children learning to talk*. Baltimore: Paul H. Brookes.

12. Farkas, G., & K. Beron. 2004. The detailed age trajectory of oral vocabulary knowledge: Differences by class and race. *Social Science Research* 33: 464–97.

13. Barbarin, O., D. Bryant, T. McCandies, M. Burchinal, D. Early, R. Clifford, & R. Pianta. 2006. Children enrolled in public pre–K: The relation of family life, neighborhood quality, and socioeconomic resources to early competence. *American Journal of Orthopsychiatry* 76: 265–76; Zill, N., & J. West. 2001. *Entering kindergarten: Findings from the condition of education, 2000*. Washington, DC: U.S. Department of Education, National Center for Education Statistics.

14. Lee, V.E., & D.T. Burkam. 2002. *Inequality at the starting gate: Social background differences in achievement as children begin school*. New York: Economic Policy Institute.

15. Aber, L., K. Burnley, D.K. Cohen, D.L. Featherman, D. Phillips, S. Raudenbush, & B. Rowan. 2006. *Beyond school reform: Improving the educational outcomes of low-income children*. Report to the Spencer Foundation. Ann Arbor, MI: University of Michigan, Center for Advancing Research and Solutions for Society; Klein, L.G., & J. Knitzer. 2006. Effective preschool curricula and teaching strategies. *Pathways to Early School Success,* Issue Brief No. 2. New York: Columbia University, National Center for Children in Poverty.

16. See, e.g., Mullis, I.V.S., M.O. Martin, & P. Foy. 2009, in press. *TIMSS 2007 international report and technical report*. Chestnut Hill, MA: Lynch School of Education, Boston College, TIMSS & PIRLS International Study Center; NCES (National Center for Education Statistics). 2006. *Comparing mathematics content in the National Assessment of Educational Progress (NEAP), Trends in International Mathematics and Science Study (TIMSS), and Program for International Student Assessment (PISA) 2003 assessments: Technical report*. Washington, DC: U.S. Department of Education, National Center for Education Statistics, Institute of Education Sciences. Online: purl.access.gpo.gov/GPO/LPS70522.

17. U.S. Dept. of Education, Office of Elementary and Secondary Education. 2007. Title I—Improving the academic achievement of the disadvantaged; Individuals with Disabilities Education Act (IDEA): Final rule. *Federal Register* 72 (67): 17747–81. Online: www.ed.gov/legislation/FedRegister/finrule/2007-2/040907a.html.

18. Johnson, J., A.M. Arumi, & A. Ott. 2006. *Reality Check 2006—Education insights: A Public Agenda initiative to build momentum for improving American schools*. New York: Public Agenda.

19. The goals of NCLB—Goal 1: To strengthen the school's core academic program so that by 2013–2014 all students (in aggregate and for each subgroup) will demonstrate academic skills at the "proficient" level or above on the State's assessments and be engaged in high-quality teaching and learning. Goal 2: To increase the number of students making successful transitions between schools and school levels. Goal 3: To increase the level of parental involvement in support of the learning process via communication between school and home. Goal 4: To align staff capacities, school processes, and professional development

activities to implement effective methods and instructional practices that are supported by scientifically-based research. Goal 5: To recruit, staff, and retain highly qualified staff that will implement effective methods and instructional practices.

20. NIEER (National Institute for Early Education Research). 2007. *The state of preschool 2007: State preschool yearbook*. New Brunswick, NJ: Rutgers University, Graduate School of Education. Online: nieer.org/yearbook/pdf/yearbook.pdf.

21. U.S. Dept. of Health and Human Services, Administration on Children, Youth, and Families, & Head Start Bureau. 2003. *The Head Start path to positive child outcomes*. Washington, DC: Authors. Online: www.headstartinfo.org/pdf/hsoutcomespath28ppREV.pdf.

22. Bowman, B.T., S. Donovan, & M.S. Burns. 2000. *Eager to learn: Educating our preschoolers*. Washington, DC: National Academies Press; Shonkoff, J.P., & D.A. Phillips, eds. 2000. *From neurons to neighborhoods: The science of early child development*. A report of the National Research Council. Washington, DC: National Academies Press.

23. NAEYC & NAECS/SDE (National Association of Early Childhood Specialists in State Departments of Education). 2002. *Early learning standards: Creating the conditions for success*. Joint position statement. Online: www.naeyc.org/dap; NAEYC & NAECS/SDE (National Association of Early Childhood Specialists in State Departments of Education). 2003. *Early childhood curriculum, assessment, and program evaluation: Building an effective, accountable system in programs for children birth through age 8*. Joint position statement. Online: www.naeyc.org/dap.

24. Takanishi, R., & K. Kauerz. 2008. PK inclusion: Getting serious about a P–16 education system. *Phi Delta Kappan* 89 (7): 480–87.

25. Pedulla, J.J. 2003. State-mandated testing: What do teachers think? *Educational Leadership* 61 (3): 42–46; Goldstein, L.S. 2007. Embracing multiplicity: Learning from two practitioners' pedagogical responses to the changing demands of kinder-garten teaching in the United States. *Journal of Research in Childhood Education* 21 (4): 378–99; Goldstein, L.S. 2007b. Examining the unforgiving complexity of kindergarten teaching. *Early Childhood Research Quarterly* 22: 39–54.

26. U.S. House of Representatives and Senate. 2007. *Bill H.R.1429*. "The Improving Head Start for School Readiness Act." (P.L. 110–34). Online: www.washingtonwatch.com/bills/show/110_PL_110-134.html.

27. Takanishi, R., & K. Kauerz. 2008. PK inclusion: Getting serious about a P–16 education system. *Phi Delta Kappan* 89 (7): 480–87.

28. Graves, B. 2006. PK–3: What is it and how do we know it works? *Foundation for Child Development Policy Brief, Advancing PK–3* 4; Ritchie, S., K. Maxwell, & R.M. Clifford. 2007. FirstSchool: A new vision for education. In *School readiness and the transition to kindergarten in the era of accountability,* eds. R.C. Pianta, M.J. Cox, & K.L. Snow, 85–96. Baltimore: Paul H. Brookes; Takanishi, R., & K. Kauerz. 2008. PK inclusion: Getting serious about a P–16 education system. *Phi Delta Kappan* 89 (7): 480–87.

29. NAEYC & NAECS/SDE (National Association of Early Childhood Specialists in State Departments of Education). 2003. *Early childhood curriculum, assessment, and program evaluation: Building an effective, accountable system in programs for children birth through age 8*. Joint position statement. Online: www.naeyc.org/dap.

30. Neuman, S.B., K. Roskos, C. Vukelich, & D. Clements. 2003. *The state of state prekindergarten standards in 2003*. Report for the Center for the Improvement of Early Reading Achievement (CIERA). Ann Arbor, MI: University of Michigan.

31. NAEYC. 2005. *Screening and assessment of young English-language learners*. Supplement to the NAEYC and NAECS/SDE Joint Position Statement on Early Childhood Curriculum, Assessment, and Pro-gram Evaluation. Washington, DC: Author. Online: www.naeyc.org/dap.

32. NAEYC & NAECS/SDE (National Association of Early Childhood Specialists in State Departments of Education). 2002. *Early learning standards: Creating the conditions for success*. Joint position statement. Online: www.naeyc.org/dap.

33. NCTM (National Council of Teachers of Mathematics). 2006. *Curriculum focal points for prekindergarten through grade 8 mathematics: A quest for coherence*. Reston, VA: Author.

34. Wien, C.A. 2004. *Negotiating standards in the primary classroom: The teacher's dilemma*. New York: Teachers College Press.

35. See, e.g., Kagan, S.L., & K. Kauerz. 2007. Reaching for the whole: Integration and alignment in early education policy. In *School readiness and the transition to kindergarten in the era of accountability,* eds. R.C. Pianta, M.J. Cox, & K.L. Snow, 11–30. Baltimore: Paul H. Brookes; Ritchie, S., K. Maxwell, & R.M. Clifford. 2007. FirstSchool: A new vision for education. In *School readiness and the transition to kindergarten in the era of accountability,* eds. R.C. Pianta, M.J. Cox, & K.L. Snow, 85–96. Baltimore: Paul H. Brookes.

36. Goldstein, L.S. 2007a. Embracing multiplicity: Learning from two practitioners' pedagogical responses to the changing demands of kindergarten teaching in the United States. *Journal of Research in Childhood Education* 21 (4): 378–99; Goldstein, L.S. 2007b. Examining the unforgiving complexity of kindergarten teaching. *Early Childhood Research Quarterly* 22: 39–54.

37. Barnett, W.S. 2004. Better teachers, better preschools: Student achievement linked to teacher qualifications. *Preschool Policy Matters* 2: 2–7. Online: nieer.org/docs/?DocID=62.

38. NAEYC & NAECS/SDE (National Association of Early Childhood Specialists in State Departments of Education). 2003. *Early childhood curriculum, assessment, and program evaluation: Building an effective, accountable system in programs for children birth through age 8*. Joint position statement. Online: www.naeyc.org/dap.

39. Darling-Hammond, L., & J. Bransford. 2005. *Preparing teachers for a changing world: What teachers should learn and be able to do*. San Francisco: Jossey-Bass.

Applying new knowledge to critical issues

40. Klein, L.G., & J. Knitzer. 2006. Effective preschool curricula and teaching strategies. *Pathways to Early School Success,* Issue Brief No. 2. New York: Columbia University, National Center for Children in Poverty.

41. U.S. Dept. of Health and Human Services, Administration on Children, Youth, and Families, & Head Start Bureau. 2003. *The Head Start path to positive child outcomes*. Washington, DC: Authors. Online: www.headstartinfo.org/pdf/hsoutcomespath28ppREV.pdf.

42. NICHD (National Institute of Child Health and Human Development). 2003. The NICHD study of early child care: Contexts of development and developmental outcomes over the first seven years of life. In *Early child development in the 21st century,* eds. J. Brooks-Gunn, A.S. Fuligni, & L.J. Berlin, 181–201. New York: Teachers College Press.

43. NICHD (National Institute of Child Health and Human Development). 2001. *Quality of child care and child care outcomes*. Paper presented at the biennial meeting of the Society for Research in

Child Development. April 19–22, Minneapolis, MN; Klein, L.G., & J. Knitzer. 2006. Effective preschool curricula and teaching strategies. *Pathways to Early School Success,* Issue Brief No. 2. New York: Columbia University, National Center for Children in Poverty; Schweinhart, L.J., J. Montie, & Z. Xiang, W.S. Barnett, C.R. Belfield, & M. Mores. 2005. *Lifetime effects: The High/Scope Perry preschool study through age 40.* Monographs of the High/Scope Educational Research Foundation, vol. 14. Ypsilanti, MI: High/Scope Press.

44. Loeb, S., B. Fuller, S.L. Kagan, & B. Carrol. 2004. Child care in poor communities: Early learning effects of type, quality, and stability. *Child Development* 75 (1): 47–65.

45. Hamre, B.K., & R.C. Pianta. 2001. Early teacher-child relationships and the trajectory of children's school outcomes through eighth grade. *Child Development* 72 (2): 625–38; Hamre, B.K., & R.C. Pianta. 2005. Can instructional and emotional support in the first grade classroom make a difference for children at risk of school failure? *Child Development* 76 (5): 949–67.

46. Dickinson, D.K., & P.O. Tabors. 2001. *Beginning literacy with language: Young children learning at home and school.* Baltimore: Paul H. Brookes; NELP (National Early Literacy Panel). In press. *Developing early literacy: Report of the National Early Literacy Panel: A scientific synthesis of early literacy development and implications for intervention.* Washington, DC: National Institute for Literacy.

47. Snow, C.E. 2007. *Is literacy enough? Pathways to academic success for adolescents.* Baltimore: Paul H. Brookes.

48. Snow, C.E. 2005. From literacy to learning. *Harvard Education Letter* (July/August). Online: www.edletter.org/current/snow.shtml; Snow, C.E. 2007. *Is literacy enough? Pathways to academic success for adolescents.* Baltimore: Paul H. Brookes.

49. Snow, C.E. 2005. From literacy to learning. *Harvard Education Letter* (July/August). Online: www.edletter.org/current/snow.shtml.

50. Dickinson, D.K., & P.O. Tabors. 2001. *Beginning literacy with language: Young children learning at home and school.* Baltimore: Paul H. Brookes.

51. National Early Literacy Panel. In press. *Developing early literacy: Report of the National Early Literacy Panel: A scientific synthesis of early literacy development and implications for intervention.* Washington, DC: National Institute for Literacy.

52. See, e.g., IRA (International Reading Association) & NAEYC. 1998. *Learning to read and write: Developmentally appropriate practices for young children.* Joint position statement. Online: www.naeyc.org/dap; NAEYC & NAECS/SDE (National Association of Early Childhood Specialists in State Departments of Education). 2002. *Early learning standards: Creating the conditions for success.* Joint position statement. Online: www.naeyc.org/dap; Snow, C.E., M.S. Burns, & P. Griffin. 1998. *Preventing reading difficulties in young children.* Washington, DC: National Academies Press.

53. NAEYC & NCTM (National Council of Teachers of Mathematics. 2004. *Early childhood mathematics: Promoting good beginnings.* Joint position statement. Online: www.naeyc.org/dap; Ginsburg, H.P., J.S. Lee, & J.S. Boyd. 2008. Mathematics education for young children: What it is and how to promote it. *Social Policy Report* 22 (1): 3–11, 14–22.

54. Duncan, G.J., C.J. Dowsett, A. Claessens, K. Magnuson, A.C. Huston, P. Klebanov, L.S. Pagani, L. Feinstein, M. Engel, & J. Brooks-Gunn. 2007. School readiness and later achievement. *Developmental Psychology* 43 (6): 1428–46.

55. Early, D.M., O. Barbarin, D. Bryant, M. Burchinal, F. Chang, R. Clifford, G. Crawford, et al. 2005. Pre-kindergarten in eleven states: NCEDL's multi-state study of pre-kindergarten and study of statewide early education programs (SWEEP): Preliminary descriptive report. New York: The Foundation for Child Development. Online: www.fcd-us.org/usr_doc/Prekindergartenin 11States.pdf; Ginsburg, H.P., J.S. Lee, & J.S. Boyd. 2008. Mathematics education for young children: What it is and how to promote it. *Social Policy Report* 22 (1): 3–11, 14–22.

56. Clements, D.H. 2004. Major themes and recommendations. In *Engaging young children in mathematics: Standards for early childhood mathematics education,* eds. D.H. Clements, J. Sarama, & A.M. DiBiase, 7–72. Mahwah, NJ: Lawrence Erlbaum; Ginsburg, H.P., J.S. Lee, & J.S. Boyd. 2008. Mathematics education for young children: What it is and how to promote it. *Social Policy Report* 22 (1): 3–11, 14–22.

57. Roskos, K.A., J.F. Christie, & D.J. Richgels. 2003. The essentials of early literacy instruction. *Young Children* 58 (2): 52–60; Worth, K., & S. Grollman. 2003. *Worms, shadows and whirlpools: Science in the early childhood classroom.* Portsmouth, NH: Heinemann; Bennett-Armistead, V.S., N.K. Duke, & A.M. Moses. 2005. *Literacy and the youngest learner: Best practices for educators of children from birth to 5.* New York: Scholastic; Ginsburg, H.P., J.S. Lee, & J.S. Boyd. 2008. Mathematics education for young children: What it is and how to promote it. *Social Policy Report* 22 (1): 3–11, 14–22.

58. See, e.g., Linares, L.O., N. Rosbruch, M.B. Stern, M.E. Edwards, G. Walker, H.B. Abikoff, & J.M.J Alvir. 2005. Developing cognitive-social-emotional competencies to enhance academic learning. *Psychology in the Schools* 42 (4): 405–17; Raver, C.C., P.W. Garner, & R. Smith-Donald. 2007. The roles of emotion regulation and emotion knowledge for children's academic readiness: Are the links causal? In *School readiness and the transition to kindergarten in the era of accountability,* eds. R.C. Pianta, M.J. Cox, & K.L. Snow, 121–48. Baltimore: Paul H. Brookes.

59. McClelland, M.M., A.C. Acock, & F.J. Morrison. 2006. The impact of kindergarten learning-related skills on academic trajectories at the end of elementary school. *Early Childhood Research Quarterly* 21 (4): 471–90; McClelland, M., C. Cameron, C.M. Connor, C.L. Farris, A.M. Jewkes, & F.J. Morrison. 2007. Links between behavioral regulation and preschoolers' literacy, vocabulary, and math skills. *Developmental Psychology* 43 (4): 947–59; Snow, K.L. 2007. Integrative views of the domains of child function: Unifying school readiness. In *School readiness and the transition to kindergarten in the era of accountability,* eds. R.C. Pianta, M.J. Cox, & K.L. Snow, 197–214. Baltimore: Paul H. Brookes.

60. See, e.g., Montessori, M. 1949. *The absorbent mind.* Madras: Theosophical Publishing House; Hymes, J.L. 1955/1995. *A child development point of view: A teacher's guide to action.* Rev. ed. West Greenwich, RI: Consortium Publishing; Bredekamp, S., ed. 1987. *Developmentally appropriate practice in early childhood programs serving children from birth through age 8.* Expanded edition. Washington, DC: NAEYC.

61. DeLoache, J.S., & A.L. Brown. 1987. Differences in the memory-based searching of delayed and normally developing young children. *Intelligence* 11 (4): 277–89; Flavell, J.H. 1987. *Development of knowledge about the appearance-reality distinction.* Monographs of the Society for Research in Child Development, vol. 51, no. 1. Chicago: University of Chicago Press; Zimmerman, B.J., S. Bonner, & R. Kovach. 1996. *Developing self-regulated learners: Beyond achievement to self-efficacy.* Washington, DC: American Psychological Association; Ladd G.W., S.H. Birch, & E.S. Buhs. 1999. Children's social and scholastic lives in kindergarten: Related spheres of influence?

Child Development 70 (6): 1373–400; McClelland, M.M., A.C. Acock, & F.J. Morrison. 2006. The impact of kindergarten learning-related skills on academic trajectories at the end of elementary school. *Early Childhood Research Quarterly* 21 (4): 471–90; Blair, C., H. Knipe, E. Cummings, D.P. Baker, D. Gamson, P. Eslinger, & S.L. Thorne. 2007. A developmental neuroscience approach to the study of school readiness. In *School readiness and the transition to kindergarten in the era of accountability,* eds. R.C. Pianta, M.J. Cox, & K.L. Snow, 149–74. Baltimore: Paul H. Brookes.

62. Bodrova, E., & D.J. Leong. 2001. *The Tools of the Mind Project: A case study of implementing the Vygotskian approach in American early childhood and primary classrooms.* Geneva, Switzerland: International Bureau of Education, UNESCO; Bodrova, E., & D.J. Leong. 2003. Chopsticks and counting chips. *Young Children* 58 (3): 10–17; Diamond, A., W.S. Barnett, J. Thomas, & S. Munro. 2007. Preschool program improves cognitive control. *Science* 318 (5855): 1387–88.

63. Rathbun, A., J. West, & E.G. Hausken. 2004. *From kindergarten through third grade: Children's beginning school experiences.* Washington, DC: National Center for Education Statistics.

64. Bogard, K., & R. Takanishi. 2005. PK–3: An aligned and coordinated approach to education for children 3 to 8 years old. *Social Policy Report* 19 (3).

65. See, e.g., Graves, B. 2006. PK–3: What is it and how do we know it works? *Foundation for Child Development Policy Brief, Advancing PK–3* 4; Sadowski, M. 2006. Core knowledge for PK–3 teaching: Ten components of effective instruction. *Foundation for Child Development Policy Brief, Advancing PK–3* 5; Ritchie, S., K. Maxwell, & R.M. Clifford. 2007. FirstSchool: A new vision for education. In *School readiness and the transition to kindergarten in the era of accountability,* eds. R.C. Pianta, M.J. Cox, & K.L. Snow, 85–96. Baltimore: Paul H. Brookes.

66. Takanishi, R., & K.L. Bogard. 2007. Effective educational programs for young children: What we need to know. *Child Development Perspectives* 1: 40–45; Kauerz, K. Forthcoming. *P–3: What does it look like from a state policy perspective?* Denver, CO: Education Commission of the States.

67. Katz, L.G., & S.C. Chard. 2000. *Engaging children's minds: The project approach.* 2d ed. Norwood, NJ: Ablex.

68. AERA (American Education Research Association). 2003. Class size: Counting students can count. *Research Points: Essential Information for Education Policy* 1 (2). Online: www.aera .net/uploadedFiles/Journals_and_Publications/Research_Points/ RP_Fall03.pdf.

69. See, e.g., Maeroff, G.I. 2006. *Building blocks: Making children successful in the early years of school.* New York: Palgrave Macmillan; Ritchie, S., K. Maxwell, & R.M. Clifford. 2007. FirstSchool: A new vision for education. In *School readiness and the transition to kindergarten in the era of accountability,* eds. R.C. Pianta, M.J. Cox, & K.L. Snow, 85–96. Baltimore: Paul H. Brookes.

70. Takanishi, R., & K. Kauerz. 2008. PK inclusion: Getting serious about a P–16 education system. *Phi Delta Kappan* 89 (7): 480–87.

71. Bowman, B.T., S. Donovan, & M.S. Burns. 2000. *Eager to learn: Educating our preschoolers.* Washington, DC: National Academies Press; Hamre, B.K., & R.C Pianta. 2007. Learning opportunities in preschool and early elementary classrooms. In *School readiness and the transition to kindergarten in the era of accountability,*

eds. R.C. Pianta, M.J. Cox, & K.L. Snow, 49–83. Baltimore: Paul H. Brookes; Pianta, R.C. 2008. Neither art nor accident: A conversation with Robert Pianta. *Harvard Education Letter* (January/February). Online: www.edletter.org/insights/pianta .shtml.

72. Hamre, B.K., & R.C Pianta. 2007. Learning opportunities in preschool and early elementary classrooms. In *School readiness and the transition to kindergarten in the era of accountability,* eds. R.C. Pianta, M.J. Cox, & K.L. Snow, 49–83. Baltimore: Paul H. Brookes.

73. Horowitz, F.D., L. Darling-Hammond, J. Bransford., et al. 2005. Educating teachers for developmentally appropriate practice. In *Preparing teachers for a changing world: What teachers should learn and be able to do,* eds. L. Darling-Hammond & J. Bransford, 88–125. San Francisco: Jossey-Bass.

74. Layzer, J.I., C.J. Layzer, B.D. Goodson, & C. Price. 2007. *Evaluation of child care subsidy strategies: Findings from Project Upgrade in Miami-Dade County.* Washington, DC: U.S. Department of Health and Human Services, Administration for Children and Families, Office of Planning, Research and Evaluation.

75. Reeves, C., S. Emerick, & E. Hirsch. 2006. *Creating non-instructional time for elementary school teachers: Strategies from schools in North Carolina.* Hillsborough, NC: Center for Teaching Quality.

Principles of child development and learning that inform practice

76. For fuller reviews, see, e.g., Snow, C.E., M.S. Burns, & P. Griffin. 1998. *Preventing reading difficulties in young children.* Washington, DC: National Academies Press; Bowman, B.T., S. Donovan, & M.S. Burns. 2000. *Eager to learn: Educating our preschoolers.* Washington, DC: National Academies Press; Bransford, J., A.L. Brown, & R.R. Cocking. 1999. *How people learn: Brain, mind, experience, and school.* Washington, DC: National Academies Press; Shonkoff, J.P., & D.A. Phillips, eds. 2000. *From neurons to neighborhoods: The science of early child development.* A report of the National Research Council. Washington, DC: National Academies Press; Kilpatrick, J., J. Swafford, & B. Findell, eds. 2001. *Adding it up: Helping children learn mathematics.* Washington, DC: National Academies Press; Renninger, K.A., & I.E. Sigel, eds. 2006. *Handbook of child psychology, Vol. 4: Child psychology in practice.* 6th ed. New York: John Wiley & Sons.

77. Bransford, J., A.L. Brown, & R.R. Cocking. 1999. *How people learn: Brain, mind, experience, and school.* Washington, DC: National Academies Press; Shonkoff, J.P., & D.A. Phillips, eds. 2000. *From neurons to neighborhoods: The science of early child development.* A report of the National Research Council. Washington, DC: National Academy Press; ASCD (Association for Supervision and Curriculum Development). 2006. *The whole child in a fractured world.* Prepared by H. Hodgkinson. Alexandria, VA: Author. Online: www.ascd.org/ascd/pdf/fracturedworld.pdf.

78. Shonkoff, J.P., & D.A. Phillips, eds. 2000. *From neurons to neighborhoods: The science of early child development.* A report of the National Research Council. Washington, DC: National Academies Press.

79. Pellegrini, A.D., L. Galda, M. Bartini, & D. Charak. 1998. Oral language and literacy learning in context: The role of social relationships. *Merrill-Palmer Quarterly* 44 (1): 38–54; Dickinson, D.K., & P.O. Tabors. 2001. *Beginning literacy with language: Young children learning at home and school.* Baltimore: Paul H. Brookes.

80. La Paro, K.M., & R.C. Pianta. 2000. Predicting children's competence in the early school years: A meta-analytic review. *Review of Educational Research* 70 (4): 443–84; Howes, C., & K. Sanders. 2006. Child care for young children. In *Handbook of research on the education of young children,* 2d ed., eds. B. Spodek & O.N. Saracho, 375–92. Mahwah, NJ: Lawrence Erlbaum; Raver, C.C., P.W. Garner, & R. Smith-Donald. 2007. The roles of emotion regulation and emotion knowledge for children's academic readiness: Are the links causal? In *School readiness and the transition to kindergarten in the era of accountability,* eds. R.C. Pianta, M.J. Cox, & K.L. Snow, 121–48. Baltimore: Paul H. Brookes; Snow, K.L. 2007. Integrative views of the domains of child function: Unifying school readiness. In *School readiness and the transition to kindergarten in the era of accountability,* eds. R.C. Pianta, M.J. Cox, & K.L. Snow, 197–214. Baltimore: Paul H. Brookes; Pianta, R.C., K.M. La Paro, & B.K. Hamre. 2008. *Classroom assessment scoring system (CLASS).* Baltimore: Paul H. Brookes.

81. See, e.g., Erikson, E. 1963. *Childhood and society.* New York: Norton; Sameroff, A.J., & M.M. Haith. 1996. *The five to seven year shift: The age of reason and responsibility.* Chicago: University of Chicago Press; Bransford, J., A.L. Brown, & R.R. Cocking. 1999. *How people learn: Brain, mind, experience, and school.* Washington, DC: National Academies Press; Shonkoff, J.P., & D.A. Phillips, eds. 2000. *From neurons to neighborhoods: The science of early child development.* A report of the National Research Council. Washington, DC: National Academies Press.

82. Lynch, E., & M. Hanson. 2004. *Developing cross-cultural competence: A guide for working with children and their families.* 3d ed. Baltimore: Paul H. Brookes.

83. Wang, M.C., L.B. Resnick, & R.F. Boozer. 1970. *The sequence of development of some early mathematics behaviors.* Pittsburgh, PA: University of Pittsburgh, Learning Research and Development Center; Clements, D.H., J. Sarama, & A.M. DiBiase. 2004. *Engaging young children in mathematics: Standards for early childhood mathematics education.* Mahwah, NJ: Lawrence Erlbaum.

84. Scarr, S., & K. McCartney. 1983. How people make their own environments: A theory of genotype—environment effects. *Child Development* 54 (2). 425–35; Plomin, R. 1994. *Genetics and experience: The interplay between nature and nurture.* Thousand Oaks, CA: Sage Publications; Plomin, R. 1994b. Nature, nurture, and social development. *Social Development* 3: 37–53; Shonkoff, J.P., & D.A. Phillips, eds. 2000. *From neurons to neighborhoods: The science of early child development.* A report of the National Research Council. Washington, DC: National Academies Press.

85. Asher, S., S. Hymel, & P. Renshaw. 1984. Loneliness in children. *Child Development* 55 (4): 1456–64; Parker, J.G., & S.R. Asher. 1987. Peer relations and later personal adjustment: Are low-accepted children at risk? *Psychology Bulletin* 102 (3): 357–89.

86. Snow, C.E., M.S. Burns, & P. Griffin. 1998. *Preventing reading difficulties in young children.* Washington, DC: National Academies Press.

87. Kuhl, P. 1994. Learning and representation in speech and language. *Current Opinion in Neurobiology* 4: 812–22.

88. Nelson, C.A., & M. Luciana, eds. 2001. *Handbook of developmental cognitive neuroscience.* Cambridge, MA: MIT Press; Ornstein, P.A., C.A. Haden, & A.M. Hedrick. 2004. Learning to remember: Social-communicative exchanges and the development of children's memory skills. *Developmental Review* 24: 374–95.

89. Seo, K.H., & H.P. Ginsburg. 2004. What is developmentally appropriate in early childhood mathematics education? Lessons from new research. In *Engaging young children in mathematics: Standards for early childhood mathematics education,* eds. D.H. Clements, J. Sarama, & A.M. DiBiase, 91–104. Hillsdale, NJ: Lawrence Erlbaum; Gelman, R., & C.R. Gallistel. 1986. *The child's understanding of number.* Cambridge, MA: Harvard University Press.

90. Thompson, R.A. 1994. *Emotion regulation: A theme in search of a definition.* Monographs of the Society for Research in Child Development, vol. 59, nos. 2–3. Chicago: University of Chicago Press.

91. Bodrova, E., & D.J. Leong. 2005. Self-regulation: A foundation for early learning. *Principal* 85 (1): 30–35; Diamond, A., W.S. Barnett, J. Thomas, & S. Munro. 2007. Preschool program improves cognitive control. *Science* 318 (5855): 1387–88.

92. Kendall, S. 1992. *The development of autonomy in children: An examination of the Montessori educational model.* Doctoral dissertation. Minneapolis, MN: Walden University; Palfrey, J., M.B. Bronson, M. Erickson-Warfield, P. Hauser-Cram, & S.R. Sirin. 2002. *BEEPers come of age: The Brookline Early Education Project follow-up study.* Final Report to the Robert Wood Johnson Foundation. Chestnut Hill, MA: Boston College.

93. Bruner, J.S. 1983. *Child's talk: Learning to use language.* New York: Norton.

94. Piaget, J. 1952. *The origins of intelligence in children.* New York: International Universities Press; Piaget, J. 1962. *Play, dreams and imitation in childhood.* New York: Norton; Uzgiris, I.C., & J.M. Hunt. 1975. *Assessment in infancy: Ordinal scales of psychological development.* Urbana, IL: University of Illinois Press.

95. Fein, G. 1981. Pretend play in childhood: An integrative review. *Child Development* 52 (4): 1095–118; Fenson, L., P.S. Dale, J.S. Reznick, E. Bates, D.J. Thal, & S.J. Pethick. 1994. *Variability in early communicative development.* Monographs of the Society for Research in Child Development, vol. 59, no. 5. Chicago: University of Chicago Press.

96. Copple, C., I.E. Sigel, & R. Saunders. 1984. *Educating the young thinker: Classroom strategies for cognitive growth.* Hillsdale, NJ: Lawrence Erlbaum; Edwards, C.P., L. Gandini, & G. Forman, eds. 1998. *The hundred languages of children: The Reggio Emilia approach—Advanced reflections.* 2d ed. Greenwich, NJ: Ablex; Epstein, A.S. 2007. *The intentional teacher: Choosing the best strategies for young children's learning.* Washington, DC: NAEYC.

97. See, e.g., Dunn, J. 1993. *Young children's close relationships: Beyond attachment.* Newbury Park, CA: Sage Publications; Denham, S.A. 1998. *Emotional development in young children.* New York: Guilford; Shonkoff, J.P., & D.A. Phillips, eds. 2000. *From neurons to neighborhoods: The science of early child development.* A report of the National Research Council. Washington, DC: National Academies Press.

98. Fein, G., A. Gariboldi, & R. Boni. 1993. The adjustment of infants and toddlers to group care: The first 6 months. *Early Childhood Research Quarterly* 8: 1–14; Honig, A.S. 2002. *Secure relationships: Nurturing infant/toddler attachment in early care settings.* Washington, DC: NAEYC.

99. Bowlby, J. 1969. *Attachment and loss, Vol. 1: Attachment.* New York: Basic; Stern, D. 1985. *The psychological world of the human infant.* New York: Basic; Garbarino, J., N. Dubrow, K. Kostelny, & C. Pardo. 1992. *Children in danger: Coping with the consequences of community violence.* San Francisco: Jossey-Bass; Bretherton, I., & K.A. Munholland. 1999. Internal working models in attachment relationships: A construct revisited. In *Handbook of attachment theory, research, and clinical applications,* eds. J. Cassidy & P.R. Shaver, 89–114. New York: Guilford.

100. Pianta, R.C. 1999. *Enhancing relationships between children and teachers.* Washington, DC: American Psychological Association; Howes, C., & S. Ritchie. 2002. *A matter of trust: Connecting teachers and learners in the early childhood classroom.* New York: Teachers College Press.

101. Shonkoff, J.P., & D.A. Phillips, eds. 2000. *From neurons to neighborhoods: The science of early child development.* A report of the National Research Council. Washington, DC: National Academies Press.

102. Bronfenbrenner, U. 1979. *The ecology of human development: Experiments by nature and design.* Cambridge, MA: Harvard University Press; Bronfenbrenner, U. 1989. Ecological systems theory. In *Annals of child development, Vol. 6,* ed. R. Vasta, 187–251. Greenwich, CT: JAI Press; Bronfenbrenner, U. 1993. The ecology of cognitive development: Research models and fugitive findings. In *Development in context: Acting and thinking in specific environments,* eds. R.H. Wozniak & K.W. Fischer, 3–44. Hillsdale, NJ: Lawrence Erlbaum; Bronfenbrenner, U., & P.A. Morris. 2006. The bioecological model of human development. In *Handbook of child psychology, Vol. 1: Theoretical models of human development,* 6th ed., eds. R.M. Lerner & W. Damon, 793–828. Hoboken, NJ: John Wiley & Sons.

103. Tobin, J., D. Wu, & D. Davidson. 1989. *Preschool in three cultures: Japan, China, and United States.* New Haven, CT: Yale University Press; Rogoff, B. 2003. *The cultural nature of human development.* Oxford: Oxford University Press.

104. Bowman, B.T., & F. Stott. 1994. Understanding development in a cultural context: The challenge for teachers. In *Diversity and developmentally appropriate practices: Challenges for early childhood education,* eds. B. Mallary & R. New, 119–34. New York: Teachers College Press.

105. Gonzales-Mena, J. 2008. *Diversity in early care and education: Honoring differences.* 5th ed. Boston: McGraw-Hill; Tabors, P.O. 2008. *One child, two languages: A guide for early childhood educators of children learning English as a second language.* 2d ed. Baltimore: Paul H. Brookes.

106. Hakuta, K., & E.E. Garcia. 1989. Bilingualism and education. *American Psychologist* 44 (2): 374–79; Krashen, S.D. 1992. *Fundamentals of language education.* Torrance, CA: Laredo Publishing.

107. Dewey, J. 1916. *Democracy and education: An introduction to the philosophy of education.* New York: Macmillan; Piaget, J. 1952. *The origins of intelligence in children.* New York: International Universities Press; Vygotsky, L. 1978. *Mind in society: The development of higher psychological processes.* Cambridge, MA: Harvard University Press; Fosnot, C.T., ed. 1996. *Constructivism: Theory, perspectives, and practice.* New York: Teachers College Press; Malaguzzi, L. 1998. History, ideas, and basic philosophy. In *The hundred languages of children: The Reggio Emilia approach—Advanced reflections,* 2d ed., eds. C. Edwards, L. Gandini, & G. Forman, 49–97. Greenwich, NJ: Ablex.

108. Gelman, R., & C.R. Gallistel. 1986. *The child's understanding of number.* Cambridge, MA: Harvard University Press; Seo, K.H., & H.P. Ginsburg. 2004. What is developmentally appropriate in early childhood mathematics education? Lessons from new research. In *Engaging young children in mathematics: Standards for early childhood mathematics education,* eds. D.H. Clements, J. Sarama, & A.M. DiBiase, 91–104. Hillsdale, NJ: Lawrence Erlbaum.

109. Bransford, J., A.L. Brown, & R.R. Cocking. 1999. *How people learn: Brain, mind, experience, and school.* Washington, DC: National Academies Press.

110. Bowman, B.T., S. Donovan, & M.S. Burns. 2000. *Eager to learn: Educating our preschoolers.* Washington, DC: National Academies Press. 8.

111. Sandall, S., M.L. Hemmeter, B.J. Smith, & M.E. McLean, eds. 2005. *DEC recommended practices: A comprehensive guide for practical application in early intervention/early childhood special education.* Longmont, CO: Sopris West, and Missoula, MT: Division for Early Childhood, Council for Exceptional Children.

112. Davidson, J.I.F. 1998. Language and play: Natural partners. In *Play from birth to twelve and beyond: Contexts, perspectives, and meanings,* eds. D.P. Fromberg & D. Bergen, 175–83. New York: Garland; Bronson, M.B. 2000. *Self-regulation in early childhood: Nature and nurture.* New York: Guilford; Elias, C., & L.E. Berk. 2002. Self-regulation in young children: Is there a role for sociodramatic play? *Early Childhood Research Quarterly* 17 (1): 216–38; Clawson, M. 2002. Play of language: Minority children in an early childhood setting. In *Play and culture studies, Vol. 4: Conceptual, social-cognitive, and contextual issues in the fields of play,* ed. J.L. Roopnarine, 93–110. Westport, CT: Ablex. Fantuzzo, J., & C. McWayne. 2002. The relationship between peer-play interactions in the family context and dimensions of school readiness for low-income preschool children. *Journal of Educational Psychology* 94 (1): 79–87; Duncan, R.M., & D. Tarulli. 2003. Play as the leading activity of the preschool period: Insights from Vygotsky, Leont'ev, and Bakhtin. *Early Education and Development* 14: 271–92; Lindsey, E.W., & M.J. Colwell. 2003. Preschoolers' emotional competence: Links to pretend and physical play. *Child Study Journal* 33 (1): 39–52; Zigler, E.F., D.G. Singer, & S.J. Bishop-Josef, eds. 2004. *Children's play: The roots of reading.* Washington, DC: Zero to Three; Johnson, J.E., J.F. Christie, & F. Wardle. 2005. *Play, development, and early education.* Boston: Pearson; Diamond, A., W.S. Barnett, J. Thomas, & S. Munro. 2007. Preschool program improves cognitive control. *Science* 318 (5855): 1387–88; Hirsh-Pasek, K., R.M. Golinkoff, L.E. Berk, & D.G. Singer. 2009. *A mandate for playful learning in preschool: Presenting the evidence.* New York: Oxford University Press.

113. Fein, G. 1981. Pretend play in childhood: An integrative review. *Child Development* 52 (4): 1095–118.

114. Vygotsky, L. 1966/1977. Play and its role in the mental development of the child. In *Soviet developmental psychology,* ed. M. Cole, 76–99. Armonk, NY: M.E. Sharpe; Bronson, M.B. 2000. *Self-regulation in early childhood: Nature and nurture.* New York: Guilford; Elias, C., & L.E. Berk. 2002. Self-regulation in young children: Is there a role for sociodramatic play? *Early Childhood Research Quarterly* 17 (1): 216–38.

115. Isenberg, J.P., & N. Quisenberry. 2002. Play: Essential for all children. A position paper of the Association for Childhood Education International. *Childhood Education* 79 (1): 33–39; Fromberg, D.P., & D. Bergen, eds. 2006. *Play from birth to twelve: Contexts, perspectives, and meanings.* 2d ed. New York: Routledge; Diamond, A., W.S. Barnett, J. Thomas, & S. Munro. 2007. Preschool program improves cognitive control. *Science* 318 (5855): 1387–88.

116. Golinkoff, R.M., K. Hirsh-Pasek, & D.G. Singer. 2006. Why play = learning: A challenge for parents and educators. In *Play = learning: How play motivates and enhances children's cognitive and social-emotional growth,* eds. D. Singer, R.M. Golinkoff, & K. Hirsh-Pasek, 3–12. New York: Oxford University Press; Chudacoff, H.P. 2007. *Children at play: An American history.* New York: New York University Press.

117. Smilansky, S., & L. Shefatya. 1990. *Facilitating play: A medium for promoting cognitive, socioemotional, and academic development in young children*. Gaithersburg, MD: Psychosocial & Educational Publications; DeVries, R., B. Zan, & C. Hildebrandt. 2002. Group games. In *Developing constructivist early childhood curriculum: Practical principles and activities*, eds. R. DeVries, B. Zan, C. Hildebrandt, R. Edmiaston, & C. Sales, 181–91. New York: Teachers College Press; Bodrova, E., & D.J. Leong. 2007. *Tools of the mind: The Vygotskian approach to early childhood education*. 2d ed. Upper Saddle River, NJ: Pearson/Merrill Prentice Hall.

118. Bodrova, E., & D.J. Leong. 2001. *The Tools of the Mind Project: A case study of implementing the Vygotskian approach in American early childhood and primary classrooms*. Geneva, Switzerland: International Bureau of Education, UNESCO; Zigler, E.F., D.G. Singer, & S.J. Bishop-Josef, eds. 2004. *Children's play: The roots of reading*. Washington, DC: Zero to Three.

119. White, S.H. 1965. Evidence for a hierarchical arrangement of learning processes. In *Advances in child development and behavior*, eds. L.P. Lipsitt & C.C. Spiker, 187–220. New York: Academic Press; Vygotsky, L. 1978. *Mind in society: The development of higher psychological processes*. Cambridge, MA: Harvard University Press.

120. Bodrova E., & D.J. Leong. 2006. Vygotskian perspectives on teaching and learning early literacy. In *Handbook of early literacy research, Vol. 2*, eds. D.K. Dickinson & S.B. Neuman, 243–56. New York: Guilford; Berk, L.E., & A. Winsler. 2009, in press. *Scaffolding children's learning: Vygotsky and early childhood education*. Rev. ed. Washington, DC: NAEYC.

121. Wood, D., J. Bruner, & G. Ross. 1976. The role of tutoring in problem solving. *Journal of Child Psychology and Psychiatry and Allied Disciplines* 17: 89–100.

122. Vygotsky, L. 1978. *Mind in society: The development of higher psychological processes*. Cambridge, MA: Harvard University Press; Bodrova E., & D.J. Leong. 2006. Vygotskian perspectives on teaching and learning early literacy. In *Handbook of early literacy research, Vol. 2*, eds. D.K. Dickinson & S.B. Neuman, 243–56. New York: Guilford; Berk, L.E., & A. Winsler. 2009, in press. *Scaffolding children's learning: Vygotsky and early childhood education*. Rev. ed. Washington, DC: NAEYC.

123. Sanders, S.W. 2006. Physical education in kindergarten. In *K today: Teaching and learning in the kindergarten year*, ed. D.F. Gullo, 127–37. Washington, DC: NAEYC; Lary, R.T. 1990. Successful students. *Education Issues* 3 (2): 11–17; Brophy, J. 1992. Probing the subtleties of subject matter teaching. *Educational Leadership* 49 (7): 4–8.

124. Garner, B.P., & D. Bergen. 2006. Play development from birth to age four. In *Play from birth to twelve: Contexts, perspectives, and meaning*, 2d ed., eds. D.P. Fromberg & D. Bergen, 3–12. New York: Routledge; Johnson, J.E. 2006. Play development from ages four to eight. In *Play from birth to twelve: Contexts, perspectives,*

and meaning*, 2d ed., eds. D.P. Fromberg & D. Bergen, 13–20. New York: Routledge.

125. Kagan, S.L., E. Moore, & S. Bredekamp, eds. 1995. *Reconsidering children's early learning and development: Toward common views and vocabulary*. Report of the National Education Goals Panel, Goal 1 Technical Planning Group. ERIC, ED391576. Washington, DC: U.S. Government Printing Office; NEGP (National Education Goals Panel). 1997. *The National Education Goals report: Building a nation of learners*. Washington, DC: U.S. Government Printing Office.

126. Hyson, M. 2008. *Enthusiastic and engaged learners: Approaches to learning in the early childhood classroom*. New York: Teachers College Press.

127. NCES (National Center for Education Statistics). 2002. *Children's reading and mathematics achievement in kindergarten and first grade*. Washington, DC: Author. Online: nces.ed.gov/pubs2002/kindergarten/24.asp?nav=4.

128. Fantuzzo, J., M.A. Perry, & P. McDermott. 2004. Preschool approaches to learning and their relationship to other relevant classroom competencies for low-income children. *School Psychology Quarterly* 19 (3): 212–30.

129. McClelland, M.M., A.C. Acock, & F.J. Morrison. 2006. The impact of kindergarten learning-related skills on academic trajectories at the end of elementary school. *Early Childhood Research Quarterly* 21 (4): 471–90.

130. Frank Porter Graham Child Development Center. 2001. *The quality and engagement study. Final report*. R.A. McWilliam, principal investigator. Chapel Hill, NC: Author; Stipek, D. 2002. *Motivation to learn: Integrating theory and practice*. 4th ed. Boston: Allyn & Bacon; Rimm-Kaufman, S.E., K.M. La Paro, J.T. Downer, & R.C. Pianta. 2005. The contribution of classroom setting and quality of instruction to children's behavior in kindergarten classrooms. *Elementary School Journal* 105 (4): 377–94; Hyson, M. 2008. *Enthusiastic and engaged learners: Approaches to learning in the early childhood classroom*. New York: Teachers College Press.

Guidelines for developmentally appropriate practice

131. Epstein, A.S. 2007. *The intentional teacher: Choosing the best strategies for young children's learning*. Washington, DC: NAEYC. 3.

132. For a more complete discussion of principles and indicators of appropriate curriculum and assessment, see NAEYC & NAECS/SDE (National Association of Early Childhood Specialists in State Departments of Education). 2003. *Early childhood curriculum, assessment, and program evaluation: Building an effective, accountable system in programs for children birth through age 8*. Joint position statement. Online: www.naeyc.org/dap.

Appendix C

Time Line: The History of Early Childhood Education

1524   Martin Luther argued for public support of education for all children in his *Letter to the Mayors and Aldermen of All the Cities of Germany in Behalf of Christian Schools.*

1628   John Amos Comenius' *The Great Didactic* proclaimed the value of education for all children according to the laws of nature.

1762   Jean-Jacques Rousseau wrote *Émile,* explaining that education should take into account the child's natural growth and interests.

1780   Robert Raikes initiated the Sunday School movement in England to teach Bible study and religion to children.

1801   Johann Pestalozzi wrote *How Gertrude Teaches Her Children,* emphasizing home education and learning by discovery.

1816   Robert Owen set up a nursery school in Great Britain at the New Lanark Cotton Mills, believing that early education could counteract bad influences of the home.

1817   In Hartford, Connecticut, Thomas Gallaudet founded the first residential school for the deaf.

1824   The American Sunday School Union formed with the purpose of initiating Sunday Schools around the United States.

1836   William McGuffey published the *Eclectic Reader* for elementary school children. His writing had a strong impact on moral and literary attitudes in the nineteenth century.

1837   Friedrich Froebel established the first kindergarten in Blankenburgh, Germany. Frobel is known as the father of the kindergarten.

1837   Horace Mann began his job as secretary of the Massachusetts State Board of Education. Mann is often called the father of the common schools because of the role he played in helping set up the elementary school system in the United States.

1837   In France Edouard Seguin, influenced by Jean Itard, started the first school for the feebleminded.

1856   Mrs. Margaretha Schurz established the first kindergarten in the United States in Watertown, Wisconsin; the school was founded for children of German immigrants, and the program was conducted in German.

1860   Elizabeth Peabody opened a private kindergarten in Boston, Massachusetts, for English-speaking children.

1869   The first special education class for the deaf founded in Boston.

1871   The first public kindergarten opened in North America in Ontario, Canada.

1873   Susan Blow opened the first public school kindergarten in the United States in St. Louis, Missouri, as a cooperative effort with superintendent of schools William Harris.

1876   A model kindergarten was part of the Philadelphia Centennial Exposition.

1880   The first teacher-training program for teachers of kindergarten opened in Oshkosh Normal School, Philadelphia.

1884   The American Association of Elementary, Kindergarten, and Nursery School Educators founded to serve in a consulting capacity for other educators.

1892   The International Kindergarten Union (IKU) established.

1896   John Dewey started the Laboratory School at the University of Chicago, basing his program on child-centered learning with an emphasis on life experiences.

1905   Sigmund Freud wrote *Three Essays of the Theory of Sexuality,* emphasizing the value of a healthy emotional environment during childhood.

1907   In Rome, Maria Montessori started her first preschool, called Children's House; she based her now-famous teaching method on the theory that children learn best by themselves in a properly prepared environment.

1909   Theodore Roosevelt convened the first White House Conference on Children.

1911   Arnold Gesell, well known for his research on the importance of the preschool years, began his child development study at Yale University.

1911   Margaret and Rachel McMillan founded an open-air nursery school in Great Britain in which the class met outdoors; emphasis was on healthy living.

1912   Arnold and Beatrice Gesell wrote *The Normal Child and Primary Education.*

1915   In New York City Eva McLin started the first U.S. Montessori nursery school.

1915   The Child Education Foundation of New York City founded a nursery school using Montessori's principles.

1918   The first public nursery schools in Great Britain started.

1919   Harriet Johnson started the Nursery School of the Bureau of Educational Experiments, later to become the Bank Street College of Education.

1921   Patty Smith Hill started a progressive laboratory nursery school at Columbia Teachers College.

1921   A. S. Neill founded Summerhill, an experimental school based on the ideas of Rousseau and Dewey.

1922   With Edna Noble White as its first director, the Merrill-Palmer Institute Nursery School opened in Detroit, with the purpose of preparing women in proper child care. The Institute was known as the Merrill-Palmer School of Motherhood and Home Training.

1922   Abigail Eliot, influenced by the open-air school in Great Britain and basing her program on personal hygiene and proper behavior, started the Ruggles Street Nursery School in Boston.

1924   *Childhood Education,* the first professional journal in early childhood education, was published by the International Kindergarten Union (IKU).

1926   Patty Smith Hill at Columbia Teachers College founded the National Committee on Nursery Schools; now called the National Association for the Education of Young Children, it provides guidance and consultant services for educators.

1926   Founding of the National Association of Nursery Education (NANE).

1930   The International Kindergarten Union (IKU) changed its name to the Association for Childhood Education.

1933   The Works Projects Administration (WPA) provided money to start nursery schools so that unemployed teachers would have jobs.

1935   The first toy-lending library founded by Toy Loan in Los Angeles.

1940   The Lanham Act provided funds for child care during World War II, mainly for day care centers for children whose mothers worked in the war effort.

1943   Kaiser Child Care Centers opened in Portland, Oregon, to provide twenty-four-hour child care for children of mothers working in war-related industries.

1944   The National Association of Nursery Education published *Young Children.*

1946   Dr. Benjamin Spock wrote the *Common Sense Book of Baby and Child Care.*

1950   Erik Erickson published his writings on the eight ages or stages of personality growth and development and identified tasks for each stage of development; the information, known as Personality in the Making, formed the basis for the 1950 White House Conference on Children and Youth.

1952   Jean Piaget's *The Origins of Intelligence in Children* first published in English.

1955   Rudolf Flesch's *Why Johnny Can't Read* criticized the schools for their methodology in teaching reading and other basic skills.

1957   The Soviet Union launched *Sputnik,* sparking renewed interest in other educational systems and marking the beginning of the rediscovery of early childhood education.

1958   Congress passed The National Defense Education Act to provide federal funds for improving education in the sciences, mathematics, and foreign languages.

1960   Katharine Whiteside Taylor founded the American Council of Parent Cooperatives for those interested in exchanging ideas about preschool education; it later became the Parent Cooperative Preschools International.

1960   The Day Care and Child Development Council of America created to publicize the need for quality services for children.

1964   At its Miami Beach conference, the National Association of Nursery Education became the National Association for the Education of Young Children (NAEYC).

1964   Congress passed The Economic Opportunity Act of 1964, marking the beginning of the War on Poverty and the foundation for Head Start.

1965   Congress passed The Elementary and Secondary Education Act to provide federal money for programs for educationally deprived children.

1965   The Head Start program began with federal money allocated for preschool education; the early programs were known as child development centers.

1966   The Bureau of Education for the Handicapped established.

1967   The Follow Through program was initiated to extend Head Start into the primary grades.

1968   B. F. Skinner wrote *The Technology of Teaching,* which outlined a programmed approach to learning.

1968   The federal government established the Handicapped Children's Early Education Program to fund model preschool programs for children with disabilities.

1970   The White House Conference on Children and Youth.

1971   The Stride Rite Corporation in Boston was the first to start a corporate-supported child care program.

1972   The National Home Start Program began for the purpose of involving parents in their children's education.

1975   Congress passed Public Law–142, the Education for All Handicapped Children Act, mandating a free and appropriate education for all children with disabilities and extending many rights to the parents of such children.

1979   The International Year of the Child sponsored by The United Nations and designated by executive order.

1980   The first American *lekotek* (toy-lending library) opened its doors in Evanston, Illinois.

1980   The White House Conference on Families.

1981   Congress passed The Head Start Act of 1981 to extend Head Start and provide for effective delivery of comprehensive services to economically disadvantaged children and their families.

1981   Secretary of Education Terrell Bell announced the establishment of the National Commission on Excellence in Education.

1982   The Mississippi legislature established mandatory statewide public kindergartens.

1983   An Arkansas commission chaired by Hillary Clinton called for mandatory kindergarten and lower pupil–teacher ratios in the early grades.

1984   The HighScope Educational Foundation released a study that documented the value of high-quality preschool programs for poor children, a study cited repeatedly in later years by those favoring expansion of Head Start and other early-years programs.

1985   Head Start celebrated its twentieth anniversary with a joint resolution of the Senate and House "reaffirming congressional support."

1986   The U.S. Secretary of Education proclaimed this the Year of the Elementary School, saying, "Let's do all we can this year to remind this nation that the time our children spend in elementary school is crucial to everything they will do for the rest of their lives."

1986   Public Law 99–457 (the Education of the Handicapped Act Amendments) established a national policy on early intervention that recognizes its benefits, provides assistance to states to build systems of service delivery, and recognizes the unique roles of families in the development of their children with disabilities.

1987   Congress created the National Commission to Prevent Infant Mortality.

1988   Vermont announced plans to assess student performance on the basis of work portfolios as well as test scores.

1989   United Nations Convention adopted the Rights of the Child.

1990   The United Nations Convention on the Rights of the Child went into effect, following its signing by twenty nations.

1990   Head Start celebrated its twenty-fifth anniversary.

1991   Education Alternatives, Inc., a for-profit firm, opened South Pointe Elementary School in Miami, Florida, the first public school in the nation to be run by a private company.

1991   The Carnegie Foundation issued "Ready to Learn," a plan to ensure children's readiness for school.

1994   The United Nations declared 1994 the Year of the Indigenous Child.

1995   Head Start reauthorization established a new program, Early Head Start, for low-income pregnant women and families with infants and toddlers.

1999   As part of the effort to strengthen educational opportunities for America's six million students with disabilities, the Department of Education issued final regulations for implementing the Individuals with Disabilities Education Act (IDEA) of 1997.

1999   Florida became the first state in the nation to pass a statewide school voucher plan; the law gives children in academically failing public schools a chance to attend private, secular, or religious schools with public money.

2000   Head Start celebrated its thirty-fifth anniversary.

2002   President George W. Bush signed Public Law 107–110, the No Child Left Behind Act of 2001. NCLB contains four basic provisions: stronger accountability for results, increased flexibility and local control, expanded options for parents, and an emphasis on teaching methods that have been proven to work.

2003   The United Nations launched the Literacy Decade (2003–2012) in order to reduce world illiteracy rates. The theme is Literacy as Freedom.

2007   Congress passed the Improving Head Start for School Readiness Act of 2007, which reauthorized the Head Start program through 2012.

2009   President Barack Obama signed the American Reinvestment and Recovery Act of 2009, which provided more than $90 billion for education, nearly half of which went to local school districts to prevent layoffs and for school modernization and repair.

2010   Head Start Celebrated forty-five years of success.

Endnotes

Chapter 1

1. National Association for the Education of Young Children, *NAEYC Standards for Early Childhood Preparation Programs,* 2008, accessed December 16, 2009, from www.naeyc.org/.

2. Ibid.

3. Ibid.

4. Ibid.

5. Ibid.

6. Ibid.

7. L. J. Schweinhart, J. Montie, Z. Xiang, W. S. Barnett, C. R. Belfield, and M. Nores, *Lifetime Effects: The High/Scope Perry Preschool Study Through Age 40* (Ypsilanti, MI: High/Scope Press, 2005).

8. W. Barnett, D. J. Epstein, A. H. Friedman, K. Robin, and J. Hudstedt, *The State of Preschool: 2008 State Preschool Yearbook* (Rutgers, NJ: National Institute for Early Childhood Education Research, 2008); accessed January 13, 2010, at http://nieer.org/yearbook/pdf/yearbook.pdf.

9. U.S. Department of Education, National Center for Education Statistics, *Early Childhood Longitudinal Study, Birth Cohort (ECLS-B), Longitudinal 9-Month-Kindergarten*, October 2009. http://nces.ed.gov/pubs2010/2010005.pdf

10. W. Barnett, D. J. Epstein, A. H. Friedman, K. Robin, and J. Hudstedt, *The State of Preschool: 2008 State Preschool Yearbook* (Rutgers, NJ: National Institute for Early Childhood Education Research, 2008); accessed January 13, 2010, at http://nieer.org/yearbook/pdf/yearbook.pdf.

11. National Association for the Education of Young Children, *NAEYC Standards for Early Childhood Professional Preparation Programs* (Washington, DC: NAEYC, 2009), 11.

12. National Association for the Education of Young Children, *NAEYC Initial Licensure Standards*, "Initial Licensure Programs" (Washington, DC: NAEYC, 2009), 12.

13. Indiana Department of Education, "South Bend Educator Named 2009 Teacher of the Year," September 22, 2008, accessed December 21, 2009, at www.doe.in.gov/toy/pdf/Press_Release_2009_toy.pdf.

14. Indiana Department of Education, *Excellence in Education: 2009 Teacher of the Year*; accessed December 16, 2009, at www.doe.in.gov/toy/pdf/philosophies_2009.pdf.

15. L. Derman-Sparks and the A.B.C. Task Force, *Anti-Bias Curriculum: Tools for Empowering Young Children* (Washington, DC: NAEYC, 1998). Reprinted with permission from the National Association for the Education of Young Children (NAEYC). www.naeyc.org.

16. L. Derman-Sparks and J. Olsen Edwards, *Anti-Bias Education for Young Children and Ourselves* (Washington, DC: NAEYC, 2010).

17. Ibid.

18. A. Borys and L. Chiarello, *Promoting Disability Awareness and Acceptance in Childhood*; accessed December 16, 2009, at www.drexel.edu/cnhp/rehab_sciences/RHAB-Disability_Awareness_Manual.pdf.

19. Ibid.

20. National Association for the Education of Young Children, *NAEYC Initial Licensure Standards*, "Initial Licensure Programs" (Washington, DC: NAEYC, 2001), 19.

21. M. Henniger, "Cooking in the Classroom: Math . . . Science . . . FUN!" Accessed September 2, 2009, at www.primarily-kids.com/article_cooking.html.

22. The Associated Press, "Boy's 'Second Voice' Helps Him Communicate" (*Education Week*), January 4, 2010. Accessed January 5, 2010, at www.edweek.org/ew/articles/2010/01/02/321734kspnsecondvoice_ap.html?tkn=UUUFRokXNOZ5n55R8IUSpX3dnpkihVcAQiUM&print=1.

23. The Associated Press, "Program Pairs Autistic Students with Peer Tutors" (*Education Week*), December 3, 2009. Accessed December 17, 2009, at www.edweek.org/ew/articles/2009/12/03/316933idtutoringprogram_ap.html?r=1234616367.

24. T. Cheshier, "Improving Education Through Collaboration," (*The Jackson Sun*). December 21, 2009.

25. Ibid.

26. S. Sandall, M. L. Hemmeter, B. J. Smith, and M. E. McLean, *DEC Recommended Practices* (Longmont, CO: Sopris West, 2005), 113–118.

27. Vandalia-Butler City Schools—Demmitt Elementary School, "ABC's of Kindergarten," 2009. Accessed January 5, 2010, at http://vandaliabutlerschools.org/demmitt/pdf/2008-09/kindergarten/parentinfo/Microsoft%20Word%20-%20ABC'sofKindergarten.pdf.

28. Chapel Hill-Carrboro City School, "CHCCS Teachers of the Year 2009–2010"; accessed January 7, 2010, at www2.chccs.k12.nc.us/education/components/scrapbook/default.php?sectiondetailid=73341.

29. Ibid.

30. J. Fenton, "How to Get Started: Some Positive Steps to Starting the Year with Families." Teachers Network; accessed January 7, 2010, at http://teachersnetwork.org/NTNY/nychelp/mentorship/families.htm.

31. National Association for the Education of Young Children, *NAEYC Initial Licensure Standards*, "Initial Licensure Programs" (Washington, DC: NAEYC, 2001), 15.

32. AllThingsPLC, "Research, educational tools, and blog for building a professional learning community"; accessed November 23, 2009, at www.allthingsplc.info/evidence/pinewoodelementaryschool/index.php.

33. National Association for the Education of Young Children, *NAEYC Standards for Early Childhood Professional Preparation Programs* (Washington, DC: NAEYC, 2009), 16.

34. *Daily Herald*, "Teachers Awarded Grants for Innovative Teaching," October 3, 2008; accessed January 5, 2010, at www.dailyherald.com/story/?id=239576.

35. Indian Prairie School District, Robert E. Clow Elementary School, *Second Grade—Social Studies*; accessed January 6, 2010, at http://clow.ipsd.org/academics_2_soc.html.

36. National Council for Accreditation of Teacher Education, *NCATE Unit Standards* (Washington DC: NCATE, 2007).

37. Cumberland County Schools, "2009–2010 Teacher of the Year: Teaching Is Awesome Responsibility for Teacher of the Year Winner"; accessed January 8, 2010, at www.ccs.k12.nc.us/09-10-HP-Articles/9.10.09-2009TOY.htm.

38. M. Ackley, "Okemos Elementary School Teacher Named Michigan Teacher of the Year," May 14, 2009. Accessed January 8, 2010, at http://michigan.michigan.gov/mde/0,1607,7-140—214772—,00.html.

39. Ibid., 24.

40. Ibid., 24–25.

41. Contributed by Carole D. Moyer, National Board Certified Teacher, Early Childhood Coordinator, Shepard Center, Columbus, Ohio. Used with permission.

42. N. K. Freeman & S. Feeney, *Code of Ethical Conduct and Statement of Commitment* (Washington, DC: NAEYC, 2005). Used with permission.

43. S. Feeney and N. K. Freeman, *Ethics and the Early Childhood Educator: Using the NAEYC Code* (Washington, DC: NAEYC, 2005).

44. Ibid.

45. L. Killough, *Connecticut's 2010 Teacher of the Year Featured in the Advisor*, December 3, 2009; accessed January 8, 2010, at http://blogcea.org/2009/12/03/2010-teacher-of-the-year.

46. Georgia Justice Project, *GJP Hosts Back-2-School 2009 to Serve Community and Client Families*; accessed December 16, 2009, at www.gjp.org/news/back2school.

47. Used with the permission of Mary Nelle Brunson, Assistant Chair, Department of Elementary Education, Stephen F. Austin State University, Nacogdoches, Texas.

48. National Council for Accreditation of Teacher Education, *NCATE Unit Standards: Glossary* (Washington, DC: NCATE, 2006), 53.

49. Copple, C., & Bredekamp, S. (2009). *Developmentally Appropriate Practice in Early Childhood Programs*, 3e. Washington, D.C.: National Association for the Education of Young Children.

50. Universities.com, "Associate Degree in Early Childhood Education at Arkansas State University"; accessed November 23, 2009, at www.universities.com/edu/Associate_degree_in_Early_Childhood_Education_at_Arkansas_State_University_Heber_Springs_AR.html.

51. Northern Illinois University, *Illinois Teacher of the Year Linda Smerge Provides Wisdom on Teaching at Alma Mater,"* September 14, 2009; accessed December 16, 2009, at www.niu.edu/northerntoday/2009/sept14/smerge.shtml

52. Carrie Downie Elementary School, "2009–2010 Teacher of the Year"; accessed December 22, 2009, at www.e2t2c2.net/carriedownie/sitepages/cdTeachOY.htm.

53. New Mexico Public Education Department, "Rio Rancho Teacher Named New Mexico Teacher of the Year," November 4, 2008; accessed January 11, 2010, at www.rrps.net/PDF/TeacheroftheYear2008-2009.pdf.

54. Second Grade Teachers, "An online community for second grade level teachers and support staff," http://second-grade-teachers.ning.com/.

55. The Partnership for 21st Century Skills, "Press Release 1/28/2010: The Partnership's Statement on the State of the Union," January 28, 2010; accessed February 16, 2010, at www.21stcenturyskills.org/index.php?option=com_content&task=view&id=883&Itemid=64.

56. DEC/NAEYC. (2009). *Early childhood inclusion: A joint position statement of the Division for Early Childhood (DEC) and the National Association for the Education of Young Children (NAEYC)*. Chapel Hill: The University of North Carolina, FPG Child Development Institute.

57. Ibid.

Chapter 2

1. National Association for the Education of Young Children, *NAEYC Standards for Early Childhood Professional Preparation Programs*, July 2009, 11–19.

2. Ibid.

3. The White House, *Education*; accessed October 28, 2009, at www.whitehouse.gov/issues/Education/.

4. Children's Defense Fund, CDF Mission Statement; accessed October 27, 2009, at http://cdf.pub30.convio.net/.

5. CYFERnet, *Findings from the National School Readiness Indicators Initiative A 17 State Partnership*; accessed August 31, 2009, at http://cyfernet.ces.ncsu.edu/cyfdb_abstracts/abstracts/8016.php.

6. P. Eisler and B. Morrison, *USA Today*, "26,500 School Cafeterias Lack Required Inspections" (December 16, 2009), 1A, 6A.

7. Ed.gov, "The Early Learning Challenge: Raising the Bar"; accessed November 11, 2009, at www.ed.gov/news/speeches/2009/11/11182009.html.

8. National Institute for Early Education Research, *State-Funded Preschool Enrollment Passes One Million Mark, Yet Most 3- and 4-Year-Olds are Denied Access to Public Preschool Programs*, Mar 19, 2008; accessed September 1, 2009, at http://nieer.org/mediacenter/index.php?PressID=80.

9. U. Bronfenbrenner, *The Ecology of Human Development: Experiments by Nature and Design* (Cambridge, MA: Harvard University Press, 1979).

10. W. Jeynes, Center for Disease and Prevention, *Parent, School Success and Health*, August 3, 2009; accessed January 5, 2010, at www2c.cdc.gov/podcasts/player.asp?f=13471.

11. *Ocala News and Announcements*, "Students to Receive Free Books for Family Literacy Night at Pinewood," October 8, 2009; accessed January 5, 2010, at www.americantowns.com/fl/ocala/news/students-to-receive-free-books-for-family-literacy-night-at-pinewood-elementary-219804.

12. *Child Health USA*, "Population Characteristics" (2006), 17.

13. M. Brick, TinyEYE Therapy Services, "Overview," January 28, 2009; accessed January 6, 2010, at www.scribd.com/doc/11476769/TinyEYE-Collaborating-With-Families-for-Preschool-.

14. C. Rivera, "Teachers' Stress Linked to Preschool Expulsions," *Los Angeles Times*, January 11, 2008; accessed January 8, 2010, at http://articles.latimes.com/2008/jan/11/local/me-expulsions11?pg=2.

15. National Center for Family Literacy, "Toyota: Committed to Moving Families Forward"; accessed October 20, 2009, from www.famlit.org/toyota.

16. *Science Daily*, "Number of Stay-at-Home Dads Increasing," July 17, 2007; accessed August 27, 2009, at www.sciencedaily.com/upi/index.php?feed=TopNews&article=UPI-1-20070617-12130500-bc-us-fathers.xml.

17. Department of Health and Human Services: Centers for Disease Control and Prevention, "NCHS Data on Teenage Pregnancy" (October 2008); accessed September 2009 at www.cdc.gov/nchs//data/infosheets/infosheet_teen_preg.htm.

18. Centers for Disease Control and Prevention, "Marriage and Divorce," March 6, 2009; accessed October 18, 2010, at http://www.cdc.gov/nchs/nvss/marriage_divorce_tables.htm.

19. "School Family Community Partnership Ideas" (n.d.); accessed January 8, 2010, at www.naperville203.org/parents-students/ProgramIdeasPS.asp.

20. Center for the Improvement of Child Caring, "Parenting Skill-Building Programs" (n.d.); accessed January 8, 2010, at www.ciccparenting.org/cicc_sbp_11.asp.

21. Centers for Disease Control and Prevention, "Preventing Teen Pregnancy: An Update in 2009," August 10, 2009; accessed August 27, 2009, at www.cdc.gov/reproductivehealth/AdolescentReproHealth/AboutTP.htm.

22. United States Global Health Policy, *Adolescent Fertility Rate*, 2009, accessed October 28, 2009, at www.globalhealthfacts.org/topic.jsp?i=90.

23. *US News*, "Teen Birth Rate Up in 26 States in 2006," January 7, 2009; accessed October 28, 2009, at http://health.usnews.com/health-news/family-health/womens-health/articles/2009/01/07/teen-birth-rate-up-in-26-states-in-2006.html.

24. F. Pompa and S. Jayson, *USA Today*, "Teen Birth Rates Up in 26 States," January 7, 2009; accessed January 6, 2010, at www.usatoday.com/news/health/2009-01-07-teenbirths_N.htm.

25. *Education News*, "Poor Schools and Poor Kids?" January 5, 2010; accessed January 6, 2010, at www.educationnews.org/commentaries/20787.html.

26. United States of Department of Health and Human Services, *The 2009 HHS Poverty Guidelines*; accessed September 2, 2009, at http://aspe.hhs.gov/POVERTY/09poverty.shtml.

27. G. Kenney and S. Dorn, "Health Care Reform for Children with Public Coverage: How Can Policymakers Maximize Gains and Prevent Harm?" June 2009; accessed October 6, 2009, at www.urban.org/UploadedPDF/411899_children_healthcare_reform.pdf

28. Peter Eisler and Elizabeth Weise, USA Today, 5A, June 11, 2009.

29. S. Fass and N. K. Cauthen, *Who Are America's Poor Children?* National Center for Children in Poverty, November 2007; accessed August 31, 2009, at www.nccp.org/publications/pub_787.html.

30. Robert Wood Johnson Foundation, "America's Health Starts with Healthy Children: How Do States Compare?" October 2008, accessed January 6, 2010, at www.commissiononhealth.org/Documents/ChildrensHealth_Chartbook.pdf.

31. Ibid.

32. A. Wigton and A. Weil, *Snapshots of America's Families II: A View of the Nation and 13 States from the National Survey of America's Families*; accessed August 31, 2009, at http://www.urban.org/publications/900841.html.

33. University of Michigan, "Inner City Schooling" (2004); accessed February 9, 2010, at http://sitemaker.umich.edu/mitchellyellin.356/parent_involvement.

34. Earth Times, National Teacher Survey Indicates High Number of U.S. Children Too Hungry to Learn, November 23, 2009; accessed November 24, 2009, at www.earthtimes.org/articles/show/national-teacher-survey-indicates-high,1059357.shtml.

35. U.S. Census Bureau, "Region, Division and Type of Residence—Poverty Status for People in Families with Related Children Under 18 by Family Structure: 2007," *Current Population Survey*, August 2008; http://pubdb3.census.gov/macro/032008/pov/new43_100_01.htm.

36. "Census: Fewer Americans Lack Health Insurance," CNNhealth.com, August 26, 2008; www.cnn.com/2008/HEALTH/08/26/census.uninsured/index.html.

37. "How the Physiological Effects of Poverty on Young Children Takes Its Toll on Health," *Medical News Today*, November 8, 2007; www.medicalnewstoday.com/articles/88146.php.

38. University of Washington, "Researcher Links Rising Tide of Obesity to Food Prices," *Science Daily*, January 5, 2004; accessed August 31, 2009, at www.sciencedaily.com/releases/2004/01/040105071229.htm.

39. National Governors Association, "State Strategies to Reduce Child and Family Poverty," June 5, 2008; www.nga.org/Files/pdf/0806POVERTYBRIEF.PDF.

40. Ibid.

41. Centers for Disease Control and Prevention, *Secondhand Smoke*; accessed September 8, 2009, at www.cdc.gov/tobacco/data_statistics/fact_sheets/secondhand_smoke/general_facts/index.htm.

42. U.S. Department of Housing and Urban Development Office of Policy Development and Research, "Affordable Housing Needs 2005: Report to Congress," May 2007; accessed August 31, 2009, at www.huduser.org/Publications/pdf/AffHsgNeeds.pdf.

43. National Center for Healthy Housing, *Healthier Homes, Stronger Families: Public Policy Approaches to Healthy Housing*; accessed August 31, 2009, at www.centerforhealthyhousing.org/html/healthier_homes_stronger_famil.htm.

44. V. Wright, M. Chau, and Y. Aratani, "Who Are America's Poor Children?" National Center for Children in Poverty, January 2010; accessed February 8, 2010, at www.nccp.org/publications/pdf/text_912.pdf.

45. U.S. Department of Housing and Urban Development Office of Policy Development and Research, "Affordable Housing Needs 2005: Report to Congress," May 2007; accessed August 31, 2009, at www.huduser.org/Publications/pdf/AffHsgNeeds.pdf.

46. ChildStats.gov, "America's Children: Key National Indicators of Well-Being," 2009; accessed August 31, 2009, at www.childstats.gov/americaschildren/phenviro4.asp.

47. K. Kopko, "The Effects of the Physical Environment on Children's Development," March 30, 2009, Cornell University; accessed October 2009 at www.parenting.cit.cornell.edu/documents/Physical-Environment-Evans.pdf.

48. B. Bloom and R. A. Cohen, Summary Health Statistics for U.S. Children: National Health Interview Survey, 2007. "The State of Childhood Asthma—United States, 1980–2005," *Advance Data from Vital and Health Statistics*, 381 (2009), U.S. Department of Health and Human Services; accessed August 31, 2009, at www.cdc.gov/nchs/data/series/sr_10/sr10_239.pdf.

49. Centers for Disease Control and Prevention, "Lead," June 1, 2009; accessed August 31, 2009, at www.cdc.gov/nceh/lead.

50. Ibid.

51. N. L. Wolfe, "Mattel Knowingly Imported Poison," October 25, 2009; accessed January 6, 2010, at http://newsblaze.com/story/20091025095134tsop.nb/topstory.html.

52. M. Fetterman, G. Farrell, and L. Petrecca, "Recall of China-Made Toys Unnerves Parents," *USA Today*, August 3, 2007; accessed August 31, 2009, at www.usatoday.com/money/industries/retail/2007-08-02-toy-fright_N.htm.

53. J. Pritchard, "Tests Reveal Toxic Cadmium in Kids' Jewelry from China; U.S. to Investigate," *Star Tribune*, January 11, 2010; accessed January 11, 2010, at www.startribune.com/lifestyle/health/81095207.html?elr=KArks7PYDiaK7DUvDE7aL_V_BD77:DiiUiacyKUnciaec8O7EyUr.

54. "Senator Obama and Rep. Slaughter Introduce Legislation to Protect Children from Lead Poisoning," Barack Obama Official Website, July 18, 2007; accessed August 31, 2009, at http://obama.senate.gov/press/070718-senator_obama_a/.

55. Centers for Disease and Control and Prevention, "Childhood Overweight and Obesity," August 19, 2009, accessed October 6, 2009, at www.cdc.gov/obesity/childhood/.

56. Obesity America, "Understanding Obesity," The Endocrine Society; accessed October 6, 2009, at www.obesityinamerica.org/understandingObesity/index.cfm.

57. "Obesity and Overweight," University of Michigan Health System, February 2007; accessed August 31, 2009, at www.med.umich.edu/1libr/yourchild/obesity.htm.

58. This is the formula for body mass index: BMI = [Weight in pounds/(Height in inches) × (Height in inches)] × 703. However, because children's body fat changes over the years and because maturing girls and boys differ in body fat, the BMI for children and teens is plotted on gender-specific growth charts.

59. A. Natenshon, *The "Skinny" on Childhood Obesity*, 2007; accessed September 9, 2009, at www.empoweredparents.com/1prevention/prevention_07.htm.

60. J. Foster, "Many Reasons for Childhood Obesity," Netwellness, April 12, 2009; accessed October 6, 2009, at www.netwellness.org/healthtopics/obesity/childhoodobesity.cfm.

61. New York State Department of Health, *Preventing Childhood Obesity: Tips for Child Care Professionals*, April 2006; accessed August 31, 2009, at www.health.state.ny.us/prevention/nutrition/resources/obchcare.htm.

62. Ibid.

63. Ibid.

64. Nutritional and Physical Fitness, "Active Start—Physical Activity Guidelines for Birth to Five Years," May 2006. www.journal.naeyc.org/btj/200605/NASPEGuidelinesBTJ.pdf.

65. V. Iannelli, *Preventing Childhood Obesity, Too Little Too Late for Too Many Overweight Kids?* January 26, 2008; accessed September 8, 2009, at http://pediatrics.about.com/cs/nutrition/a/childhd_obesity.htm.

66. Animal Trackers—A Preschool Motor Skills and Physical Activity Curriculum. Contributed by Christine L. Williams, MD, MPH, director, Children's Cardiovascular Health Center, Columbia University, Children's Hospital.

67. C. Bafile, "Teacher Feature," *Education World*, 2008; accessed January 8, 2010, at www.educationworld.com/a_curr/teacher_feature/teacher_feature178.shtml.

68. Contributed by Rae Pica, children's physical activity specialist and author of *Experiences in Movement* (3rd ed.) and *Your Active Child*.

69. Elizabeth Englander, *Cyberbullying and Bullying in Massachusetts; Frequency & Motivations*, 2008; accessed October 28, 2009, at https://webhost.bridgew.edu/marc/MARC%20findings%20summary%202008.pdf.

70. Mike Donlin, "How to Prevent Cyberbullying: From the Home to the Homeroom," Quest Communications, 2008; accessed March 1, 2010, at www.incredibleinternet.com/user_files/cyberbullying_full.pdf.

71. National Center for Mental Health Promotion and Youth Violence Prevention, Preventing Cyber Bullying in the School and the Community," August 2009; accessed November 30, 2009, at www.promoteprevent.org/Publications/center-briefs/Cyberbullying%20Prevention%20Brief.pdf.

72. B. Hayes, "Increasing the Representation of Underrepresented Minority Groups in U.S. Colleges and Schools of Pharmacy," *American Journal of Pharmaceutical Education*, 72(1), February 15, 2008, 14.

73. Charlotte-Mecklenburg Schools, *ESL Program*, January 2008; retrieved October 20, 2009, from www.cms.k12.nc.us/mediaroom/aboutus/documents/english%20as%20a%20second%20Language%20(ESL).pdf.

74. S. Dewan, "Southern Schools Mark Two Majorities," *New York Times*, January 6, 2010; accessed January 8, 2010, at www.nytimes.com/2010/01/07/us/07south.html.

75. K. A. Magnuson, H. R. Sexton, P. E. Davis-Kean, and A. C. Huston, "Increases in Maternal Education and Young Children Language Skills,"

Merrill-Palmer Quarterly, Jul 2009; accessed February 22, 2010, at http://findarticles.com/p/articles/mi_qa3749/is_200907/ai_n32127514/.

76. www.scaoda.state.wi.us/docs/main/CulturalCompetencyDefinition.pdf

77. Council for Exceptional Children; Cultural and Linguistic Diversity; accessed October 20, 2009, at www.cec.sped.org/AM/Template.cfm?Section=Cultural_and_Linguistic_Diversity&Template=/TaggedPage/TaggedPageDisplay.cfm&TPLID=36&ContentID=5541.

78. Individuals with Disabilities Education Act Improvement Amendments of 2004 (PL 108–144).

79. H. L. Hodgkinson, *Leaving Too Many Children Behind, A Demographer's View on the Neglect of America's Youngest Children*, Institute for Educational Leadership, April 2003; accessed September 8, 2009, at www.factsinaction.org/pageone/p1nov03.htm.

80. P. Johnson, Educational Leadership, *Teaching for 21st Century Skills*, September 2009, vol. 67 no. 1, 11.

81. N. Walser, *Harvard Education Letter*, Teaching 21st Century Skills, (3) September/October 2008; accessed October 28, 2009, at www.siprep.org/prodev/documents/21stCenturySkills.pdf.

82. Green Building Council, "Green Building Research" (2008); accessed September 14, 2009, from www.usgbc.org/DisplayPage.aspx?CMSPageID=1718.

83. *The Baltimore Sun*, "Schools Going Green Big-Time" (September 7, 2009); accessed September 14, 2009, from www.baltimoresun.com/features/green/bal-md.gr.greenschool07sep07,0,5804340.story.

84. Green Schools Recognition Program, "Congratulations Green Schools!" (May 21, 2009); accessed September 14, 2009, from www.ourgreenschools.com/congratulations-green-schools/.

85. *St. Louis Post-Dispatch*, "Growing Minds Love Growing Gardens" (September 9, 2009); accessed September 14, 2009, from STLToday.com.

86. G. Morrison, How the Rise of China Will Change Everything, Fall 2008, Issue 81, Jola Montessori; accessed November 2, 2009, at www.jola-montessori.com/psm/81/articles/morrison.html.

87. Science, Technology, Engineering & Math, State Educational Technology Directors Association, September 2008, "Why Is Stem Education Important?" Accessed October 28, 2009, at www.setda.org/web/guest/2020/stem-education.

88. United States Department of Education, "Early Childhood Education"; accessed November 2, 2009, at www.ed.gov/parents/earlychild/ready/resources.html.

Chapter 3

1. National Association for the Education of Young Children, *NAEYC Standards for Early Childhood Professional Preparation Programs*, July 2009, 11–19.

2. Teacher Lingo, Lingo Message Boards, *Assessment*; accessed November 5, 2009, from http://teacherlingo.com/forums/post/210359.aspx.

3. M. Sommerville, *Kindergarten's 3 R's: Respect, Resources and Rants*, April 12, 2008; accessed November 6, 2009, from http://kidney-garden.blogspot.com/.

4. M. Sommerville, *Kindergarten's 3 R's: Respect, Resources and Rants*, April 12, 2008; accessed November 6, 2009, from http://kidney-garden.blogspot.com/2008/04/that-time-of-yearkindergarten-roundup.html.

5. University of Oregon Reading Department, "How to Access the Big Ideas of Early Literacy," 2009; accessed April 6, 2009, from http://reading.uoregon.edu/assessment/assess_types.php.

6. National Association for the Education of Young Children, *Overview of the NAEYC Early Childhood Program Standards*: 2008, 1.

7. National Association for the Education of Young Children (2009). *Developmentally Appropriate Practice in Early Childhood Programs: Serving Children from Birth Through Age 8*, 3rd ed. C. Copple and S. Bredekamp, eds. Washington, DC: 22.

8. Ibid.

9. Ibid.

10. From Kentucky Early Childhood Data System, "Selecting the Most Appropriate Assessment Tool," and Kentucky Department of Education (2004), *Building a Strong Foundation for School Success: Kentucky's Early Childhood Continuous Assessment Guide.* Used with permission.

11. NMSA, C. Garrison and M. Ehringhaus, *Formative and Summative Assessments in the Classroom*; accessed January 25, 2010, from www.nmsa.org/Publications/WEbexclusive/Assessment/tabid/1120/Default.aspx.

12. Ibid.

13. *Education Week*, On Special Education, "In Virginia 'Portfolio' Testing on the Rise," June 8, 2009; accessed July 24, 2009, from http://blogs.edweek.org/edweek/speced/2009/06/in_virginia_portfolio_testing_1.html?qs=e+portfolios.

14. Texas Education Agency, Texas Essential Knowledge and Skills for English Language Arts and Reading: Subchapter A: Elementary, 2008; accessed August 4, 2009, from http://ritter.tea.state.tx.us/rules/tac/chapter110/ch110a.pdf.

15. M. Rose, "Make Room for Rubrics," accessed July 23, 2009, at http://teacher.scholastic.com/professional/assessment/roomforubrics.htm.

16. J. M. Hintze and W. J. Matthews (2004). "The Generalizability of Systematic Direct Observations across Time and Setting: A Preliminary Investigation of the Psychometrics of Behavioral Observation." *School Psychology Review, 33*(2).

17. NMSA, C. Garrison and M. Ehringhaus, *Formative and Summative Assessments in the Classroom*; accessed January 25, 2010, from www.nmsa.org/Publications/WEbexclusive/Assessment/tabid/1120/Default.aspx

18. Ibid.

19. Ibid.

20. CO ST §22-1-116 http://mb2.ecs.org/reports/Report.aspx?id=31.

21. CO ST §22-7-504 http://mb2.ecs.org/reports/Report.aspx?id=31.

22. J. O'Brian, "How Screening Assessment Practices Support Quality Disabilities Services in Head Start," *Head Start Bulletin*, 70 (April 2001): 20–24.

23. *Education Week, Teacher Magazine*, Living in Dialogue, "Performance Pay—What Do Teachers Say?" July 8, 2008; accessed July 24, 2009, from http://blogs.edweek.org/teachers/living-in-dialogue/2008/07/performance_pay_what_do_teache.html?qs=assessments+are+often+used+inappropriately.

24. *USA Today*, "Teachers' Pay Would Be Tied to Test Scores Under Obama Plan," 7/23/2009; accessed November 5, 2009, from www.usatoday.com/news/education/2009-07-23-racetop_N.htm.

25. *Journal Sentinel*, "Teacher Merit Pay Essential, Obama Says," March 11, 2009, accessed November 5, 2009, from www.jsonline.com/news/usandworld/41068832.html.

26. Ibid.

27. Ibid.

28. Ibid.

29. U.S. Department of Education, *Structure of the U.S. Education System: Curriculum and Content Standards*, February 2008; accessed August 7, 2009, from www.ed.gov/about/offices/list/ous/international/usnei/us/edlite-structure-us.html.

30. P. Hartigan, "Pressure-Cooker Kindergarten," *The Boston Globe*, August 30, 2009; accessed November, 5, 2009, from www.boston.com/community/moms/articles/2009/08/30/pressure_cooker_kindergarten/?page=1.

31. Bagnato, S. J., Neisworth, J. T., Pretti-Frontczak, K. (2009). *LINKing Authentic Assessment and Early Childhood Intervention: Best Measures for Best Practices*. (4th edition). Baltimore, MD: Paul Brookes.

32. W. J. Yeung, M. R. Linver, and J. Brooks-Gunn, "How Money Matters for Young Children's Development: Parental Investment and Family Processes," *Child Development* 73, no. 6 (November/December 2002): 1861–1879.

33. Testimony of Ben Allen, Ph.D., Research and Evaluation Director, National Head Start Association Before the National Research Council Committee on Developmental Outcomes and Assessments for Young Children. July 6, 2007; accessed November 5, 2009, from http://policy.gmu.edu/currents/volume8/issue01/NHSABenAllen Testimony.pdf.

34. National Education Association, *NEA Policy Brief: English Language Learners Face Unique Challenges*, 2008; accessed August 10, 2009, from www.nea.org/assets/docs/mf_PB05_ELL.pdf.

35. Ibid.

36. Ibid.

37. Ibid.

38. Ibid.

39. WIDA Consortium, *WIDA Focus on Language and Culture: Variables Affecting Individual Academic Achievement*; accessed August 10, 2009, from www.wida.us/resources/focus/Bulletin1.pdf.

40. Ibid.

41. Ibid.

42. *The Seattle Times*, "Seattle Special-Ed Teachers Suspended for Refusal to Give Test," March 6, 2009; accessed July 24, 2009, from http://seattletimes.nwsource.com/html/education/2008819875_suspension06m.html.

Chapter 4

1. National Association for the Education of Young Children, *NAEYC Standards for Early Childhood Professional Preparation Programs*, July 2009, 11–19.

2. Ibid.

3. B. Beatty, "Past, Present and Future," *The American Prospect, Online Edition*; November 2004; accessed September 4, 2007, at www.prospect.org/cs/articles?article=past_present_and_future.

4. S. Broughman, N. Swaim, and P. Keaton, "Characteristics of Private Schools in the United States: Results from the 2007–2008 Private School Universe Survey," National Center for Education Statistics, March 2009; accessed August 13, 2009, from http://nces.ed.gov/pubs2009/2009313.pdf.

5. J. A. Comenius, *The Great Didactic of John Amos Comenius,* ed. and trans. M. W. Keating (New York: Russell & Russell, 1967), 58.

6. J. Rousseau, *Émile; Or, Education,* trans. B. Foxley (New York: Dutton, Everyman's Library, 1933), 5.

7. *Newsweek*, "Should Children Redshirt Kindergarten?" September 3, 2009, accessed November 6, 2009, from http://blog.newsweek.com/

blogs/nurtureshock/archive/2009/09/03/should-children-redshirt-kindergarten.aspx.

8. Roger DeGuimps, *Pestalozzi: His Life and Work* (New York: Appleton, 1890), 196.

9. *Chapter 1: Shipyard Day Care Centers of World War II: The Kaiser Experiment*; accessed January 29, 2010, from http://wwiishipyard daycare.tripod.com/intro.htm.

10. K. Wellhousen and J. Kieff, (2002). *A Constructivist Approach to Block Play in Early Childhood*. NY: Delmar.

11. Froebel gifts and blocks; accessed September 4, 2007, at www.froebelgifts.com.

12. R. D. Archambault, ed., *John Dewey on Education—Selected Writings* (New York: Random House, 1964), 430.

13. M. Montessori, *The Discovery of the Child,* trans. M. J. Costelloe (Notre Dame, IN: Fides, 1967), 22.

14. M. Montessori, *The Montessori Method,* trans. A. E. George (Cambridge, MA: Bentley, 1967), 38.

15. Montessori, *The Discovery of the Child,* 28.

16. Forest Schools; accessed February 8, 2010, from www.forestschools.com/history-of-forest-schools.php.

17. M. G. Yudof, *Exploring A New Role For Federal Government In Higher Education*; accessed February 8, 2010, from www.aplu.org/NetCommunity/Document.Doc?id=1932.

18. P. Johnson, Educational Leadership, *Teaching for 21st Century Skills*, September 2009, pg. 11, volume 67, no. 1.

19. eSchool News, *Support grows for common standards,* May 5th, 2009; accessed February 9, 2010, from www.eschoolnews.com/2009/05/05/support-grows-for-common-standards/.

20. *Time*, "How to Raise the Standard in America's Schools," April 15, 2009; accessed February 9, 2010, from www.time.com/time/nation/article/0,8599,1891468,00.html#ixzz0f3dMXA0b

21. US Department of Education, *Improving Basic Programs Operated by Local Educational Agencies (Title I, Part A);* accessed February 10, 2010, from www2.ed.gov/programs/titleiparta/index.html.

22. *The Washington Post*, "Educators Await Obama's Mark on No Child Left Behind," January 9, 2010; accessed February 24, 2010, from www.washingtonpost.com/wp-dyn/content/article/2010/01/08/AR2010010802165.html.

23. US Department of Education Archives, *A Nation At Risk: The Imperative for Educational Reform*, April 1983, www2.ed.gov/pubs/NatAtRisk/index.html.

24. National Association for the Education of Young Children. (2009). *Developmentally Appropriate Practice In Early Childhood Programs: Serving Children from Birth Through Age 8*, 3rd ed. C. Copple and S. Bredekamp, eds. Washington, DC: xii.

25. S. Mintz, *Huck's Raft: A History of American Childhood* (Cambridge, MA: Belknap Press, 2004), 7–13.

26. Fox News, *Suri Cruise Isn't Only Toddler Wearing High Heels, Doctors Warn of Dangers*, January 14, 2010, accessed February 3, 2010, from www.foxnews.com/story/0,2933,583021,00.html.

27. D. Elkind, *The Hurried Child: Growing Up Too Fast Too Soon* (Reading, MA: Addison-Wesley, 1981).

28. Fox News, *Suri Cruise Isn't Only Toddler Wearing High Heels, Doctors Warn of Dangers*, January 14, 2010, accessed February 3, 2010, from www.foxnews.com/story/0,2933,583021,00.html.

29. Mintz, *Huck's Raft,* 7–13.

30. J. Locke, *An Essay Concerning Human Understanding* (New York: Dover, 1999), 92–93.

31. Troxel v. Granville (99-138) 530 U.S. 57 (2000) 137 Wash. 2d 1, 969 P.2d 21, affirmed. From www.law.cornell.edu/supct/html/99-138.ZS.html.

32. New York Life, Adult Children Moving Back Home: Don't Let "Boomerang Kids" Derail Your Goals, 2010, from www.newyorklife.com/nyl/v/index.jsp?contentId=13762&vgnextoid=d0bd47bb939d2210a2b3019d221024301cacRCRD.

33. California Department of Education, American Indian Early Childhood Education Program; accessed December 10, 2007, at www.cde.ca.gov/sp/ai/ec/.

34. FindLaw, U.S. Supreme Court, *Plessy v. Ferguson (1896), 163 U.S. 537 (1896) 163 U.S. 537*; accessed August 11, 2009, from http://caselaw.lp.findlaw.com/cgi-bin/getcase.pl?court=us&vol=163&invol=537.

35. FindLaw, U.S. Supreme Court, *Brown v. Board of Education (1954) 347 U.S. 483 (1954) 347 U.S. 483*; accessed August 11, 2009, from http://caselaw.lp.findlaw.com/scripts/getcase.pl?court=US&vol=347&invol=483.

36. Associated Press—Education Week, *Achievement Gap Still Separates White, Black Students*, July 14, 2009; accessed August 12, 2009, from www.edweek.org/ew/articles/2009/07/14/287503usblackwhitechievement_ap.html?qs=minority+education.

37. G. Orfield, "Reviving the Goal of an Integrated Society: A 21st Century Challenge." The Civil Rights Project, UCLA, January 2009; accessed October 8, 2009, from www.projectcensored.org/top-stories/articles/2-us-schools-are-more-segregated-today-than-in-the-1950s-source/.

38. Ibid.

39. McKinsey and Co. (2009). *The Economic Impact of the Achievement Gap in America's Schools: Summary of Findings*; accessed August 20, 2009, from www.mckinsey.com/App_Media/Images/Page_Images/Offices/SocialSector/PDF/achievement_gap_report.pdf

40. FindLaw, *Title IX and Education*; accessed August 11, 2009, from http://library.findlaw.com/1996/Jan/11/126069.html.

41. Ibid.

42. Education Week, *Stereotype of Mathematical Inferiority Still Plagues Girls*, August 22, 2008; accessed August 12, 2009, from www.edweek.org/ew/articles/2008/08/27/01girls_ep.h28.html?qs=gender+differences+in+education.

43. J. Rehmeyer, "Gender Equality Closes Math Gap," *ScienceNews*, June 5th, 2008; accessed October 12, 2009, from www.sciencenews.org/view/generic/id/32949/title/Math_Trek__Gender_equality_closes_math_gap.

44. Ibid.

45. National Center for Learning Disabilities, *What is FAPE and What Can it Mean to my Child?* February 25 2009; accessed August 14, 2009, from www.ncld.org/at-school/your-childs-rights/laws-protecting-students/what-is-fape-and-what-can-it-mean-to-my-child.

46. Ibid.

47. Ibid.

48. Ibid.

49. Oxford OH Press, *Unemployed Pushing Out Disabled Residents for Jobs*, August 30, 2009, from www.oxfordpress.com/news/oxford-business-news/unemployed-pushing-out-disabled-residents-for-jobs-272553.html.

50. Ibid.

51. L. J. Schweinhart, J. Montie, Z. Xiang, W. S. Barnett, C. R. Belfield, and M. Nores, *Lifetime Effects: The High/Scope Perry Preschool Study Through Age 40* (monographs of the High/Scope Educational Research Foundation, 14) (Ypsilanti, MI: High/Scope Press, 2004), 3.

52. ASCD, The Whole Child Initiative; accessed April 1, 2010 from www.ascd.org/Programs/The_Whole_Child/The_Whole_Child.aspx.

Chapter 5

1. National Association for the Education of Young Children, *NAEYC Standards for Early Childhood Professional Preparation Programs*, July 2009, 11–19.

2. Ibid.

3. Siegler, DeLoache, and Esienberg. (2010). *How Children Develop*, 3rd ed. New York: Worth.

4. D. M. Brodzinsky, I. E. Sigel, and R. M. Golinkoff, "New Dimensions in Piagetian Theory and Research: An Integrative Perspective," in I. E. Sigel, D. M. Brodzinsky, and R. M. Golinkoff, eds., *New Directions in Piagetian Theory and Practice* (Hillsdale, NJ: Erlbaum, 1981), 5.

5. M. A. Spencer Pulaski, *Understanding Piaget* (New York: Harper & Row, 1980), 9.

6. P. G. Richmond, *An Introduction to Piaget* (New York: Basic Books, 1970), 68.

7. Ibid.

8. National Association for the Education of Young Children. (2009). *Developmentally Appropriate Practice in Early Childhood Programs: Serving Children from Birth Through Age 8*, 3rd ed. C. Copple and S. Bredekamp, eds. Washington, DC: 11.

9. Ibid., 12.

10. L. S. Vygotsky, *Mind in Society* (Cambridge, MA: Harvard University Press, 1978), 244.

11. J. R. H. Tudge, "Processes and Consequences of Peer Collaboration: A Vygotskian Analysis," *Child Development*, 63, (1992): 1365.

12. Ibid.

13. Vygotsky, *Mind in Society,* 90.

14. Tudge, "Processes and Consequences," 1365.

15. "Nutrition—Feeding Your Child's Brain!" *More 4 Kids*, February 28, 2007; accessed December 10, 2007, at www.more4kids.info/362/brain-nutrition-for-your-child/.

16. U.S. Department of Agriculture, Nutrition and Brain Function; accessed April 5, 2010, from www.ars.usda.gov/is/AR/archive/aug07/aging0807.htm.

17. Geopolitical and Economic News and Analysis, DEVELOPMENT: Hunger Feeds More Hunger, January 22, 2010; accessed April 5, 2010, from http://globalgeopolitics.net/wordpress/2010/01/22/development-hunger-feeds-more-hunger/.

18. Ibid.

19. M. Hegarty, "Supporting School Success: Fueled to Succeed"; accessed December 10, 2007, at http://content.scholastic.com/browse/article.jsp?id=1297.

20. USDA, Kids, Fast Food, and Obesity; accessed April 5, 2010, from www.ars.usda.gov/is/AR/archive/oct09/kids1009.htm.

21. USDA, Food Insecurity in Households with Children: Prevalence, Severity, and Household Characteristics, 2009; accessed April 5, 2010, from www.ers.usda.gov/Publications/EIB56/.

22. NAEYC, *Principles of Child Development and Learning That Inform Developmentally Appropriate Practice*; accessed December 10, 2007, at www.naeyc.org/about/positions/dap3.asp.

23. B. K. Hamre and R. C. Pianta, "Early Teacher-Child Relationships and the Trajectory of Children's School Outcomes Through Eighth Grade," *Child Development* 72 (2001): 625–638.

24. G. W. Ladd and K. B. Burgess, "Do Relational Risks and Protective Factors Moderate the Linkages Between Childhood Aggression and Early Psychological and School Adjustment?" *Child Development* 72 (2001): 1579–1601.

25. Ibid.

26. Based on Taylor, John F. (1979). "Encouragement vs. Praise," unpublished manuscript. Praise v. Encouragement, Gratitude; accessed April 5, 2010, from www.noogenesis.com/malama/encouragement.html.

27. P. Tarr, "Consider the Walls," *Young Children, Beyond the Journal* (May 2004); accessed December 10, 2010, from http://prim.ncwiseowl.org/curriculum___instruction/k-2_best_practices/consider_the_walls_of_your_classroom/.

28. G. Boeree, "Erik Erikson"; accessed February 22, 2010, from http://webspace.ship.edu/cgboer/erikson.html.

29. *Child Development*, November/December 2008, Volume 79, Number 6, Pages 1802–1817.

30. *Education Week*, Preschoolers Expelled From School at Rates Exceeding That of K–12; accessed April 5, 2010, from www.edweek.org/login.html?source=http://www.edweek.org/ew/articles/2005/05/18/37prek.h24.html&destination=http://www.edweek.org/ew/articles/2005/05/18/37prek.h24.html&levelId=2100.

31. R. R. Lange, R *The Truth about Grade Level Retention*, accessed February 22, 2010, from www.fcarweb.org/grade_level_retention.htm.

Chapter 6

1. National Association for the Education of Young Children, *NAEYC Standards for Professional Preparation Programs,* 2009; accessed April 6, 2010, from www.naeyc.org/.

2. Ibid.

3. National Association for the Education of Young Children, *Accreditation Matters*, www.naeyc.org/academy/AccreditationMattersWhyEarn.asp.

4. National Association for the Education of Young Children, *Summary of NAEYC-Accredited Programs for Young Children*; accessed April 6, 2010, at http://oldweb.naeyc.org/academy/summary/center_summary.asp.

5. W. Sentell, "Pre-K Classes Popularity Explodes," *Advocate News,* August 2, 2005.

6. A. Chaudhuri and M. Potepan, *Key to Economic Success in the 21st Century: Investment in Early Childhood Programs* (San Francisco, CA: 2009); accessed April 6, 2010, at www.bayareacouncil.org/docs/Early_Childhood_Report.pdf.

7. Ibid.

8. Ibid.

9. B. Obama, "Organizing for America: Education"; accessed February 17, 2010, at www.barackobama.com/issues/education/.

10. A. Chaudhuri and M. Potepan, *Key to Economic Success in the 21st Century: Investment in Early Childhood Programs* (San Francisco, CA: 2009); accessed February 17, 2010, at www.bayareacouncil.org/docs/Early_Childhood_Report.pdf

11. Ibid.

12. Ibid.

13. Ibid.

14. M. Montessori, *Dr. Montessori's Own Handbook* (New York: Schocken, 1965), 133.

15. M. Montessori, *The Secret of Childhood,* trans. M. J. Costello (Notre Dame, IN: Fides, 1966), 20.

16. Ibid., 46.

17. M. Montessori, *The Absorbent Mind,* trans. Claude A. Claremont (New York: Holt, Rinehart and Winston, 1967), 25.

18. Montessori, *Dr. Montessori's Own Handbook,* 131.

19. North American Montessori Teachers' Association, Montessori and Special Education: Converging Disciplines (Conference), Minneapolis, MN, November 12–15, 2009; accessed March 24, 2010, at www.montessori-namta.org/NAMTA/conferences/Minneapolis2009.pdf.

20. L. J. Schweinhart, J. Montie, Z. Xiang, W. S. Barnett, C. R. Belfield, and M. Nores, *Lifetime Effects: The HighScope Perry Preschool Study Through Age 40* (Ypsilanti, MI: HighScope Press, 2005).

21. Reprinted by permission of High/Scope Educational Research Foundation, 600 N. River St., Ypsilanti, MI 48198-2898.

22. Ibid.

23. Ibid.

24. "Educational Programs: Early Childhood"; accessed April 5, 2010, at www.highscope.org/Content.asp?ContentId=63.

25. Regional Early Childhood Center; accessed April 5, 2010, at www.howard.k12.md.us/res/recc.html.

26. This section is adapted from L. Gandini, "Foundations of the Reggio Emilia Approach," in J. Hendrick, ed., *First Steps Toward Teaching the Reggio Way* (Upper Saddle River, NJ: Merrill/Prentice Hall, 1997), 14–25.

27. Reprinted by permission from L. Malaguzzi, "No Way. The Hundred Is There," trans. L. Gandini, in *The Hundred Languages of Children: The Reggio Emilia Approach*, eds. C. Edwards, L. Gandini, and S. Forman (Greenwich, CT: Ablex), 3.

28. The College School: Early Childhood Atelier, "The Atelier"; accessed March 24, 2010, at www.thecollegeschool.org/page.cfm?p=66.

29. R. K. Edmiaston and L. M. Fitzgerald, "How Reggio Emilia Encourages Inclusion," *Educational Leadership,* 58(1), 2000, 66. Update contributed by Valerie Dolezal, principal of Grant Early Childhood Center, in Cedar Rapids, IA on January 14, 2010. http://grant.cr.k12.ia.us/grant_facts.htm.

30. H. Helm and L. Katz, *Young Investigators: The Project Approach in the Early Years* (New York: Teachers College Press, 2001).

31. McKinsey and Co. (2009). *The Economic Impact of the Achievement Gap in America's Schools: Summary of Findings*; accessed August 20, 2009, from www.mckinsey.com/clientservice/socialsector/achievement_gap_report.pdf.

32. Ibid.

33. Ibid.

Chapter 7

1. National Association for the Education of Young Children, *NAEYC Standards for Early Childhood Professional Preparation Programs,* July 2009, 11–19.

2. Ibid.

3. National Association of Child Care Resource & Referral Agencies, *Swine Flu (H1N1) and Child Care: Resources to Help You Prepare for, Plan and Respond to a Possible Outbreak,* September 10, 2009; accessed November 16, 2009, at www.naccrra.org/news/swine-flu.

4. V. Wright, M. Chau, and Y. Artani, "Who Are America's Poor Children?" National Center for Children in Poverty, January 2010; accessed January 21, 2010, at www.nccp.org/publications/pdf/text_912.pdf.

5. Ibid.

6. Bureau of Labor Statistics, U.S. Department of Labor, "Employment Characteristics of Families Summary," May 27, 2009; accessed November 8, 2009, at www.bls.gov/news.release/famee.nr0.

7. Baby Center, "How Much You'll Spend" (2007); accessed May 10, 2010, at www.babycenter.com/0_how-much-youll-spend-on-childcare_1199776.bc and National Association of Child Care Resource & Referral Agencies, "Price of Child Care" (2008); accessed May 20, 2010, at www.naccrra.org/randd/docs/2008_Price_of_Child_Care.pdf.

8. Bureau of Labor Statistics, U.S. Department of Labor, "Employment Status of Mothers with Own Children Under 3 Years Old by Single Year of Age of Youngest Child and Marital Status, 2007–2008 Annual Averages" (2007–08); www.bls.gov/news.release/famee.t06.htm.

9. National Association of Child Care Resource and Referral Agencies, "The Child Care Workforce"; accessed November 24, 2009, at www.naccrra.org/policy/background_issues/cc_workforce.php.

10. P. J. Sainz, "Latino Children Are Behind in Preschool Enrollment," June 20, 2008; accessed November 25, 2009, at www.preschool california.org/media-center/latino-children-are-behind-in-preschool-enrollment.html.

11. National Association of Child Care Resource & Referral Agencies, "Unequal Opportunities for Preschoolers," February 2009, http://issuu.com/naccrra/docs/unequalopportunities?mode=embed&layout=white.

12. National Association of Child Care Resource & Referral Agencies, "Child Care in America Fact Sheet," Introduction, 2008; accessed November 24, 2009, at www.kaccrra.org/PDFs/FAMpdfs/childcareinamericafactsheet.pdf.

13. L. Lippman, S. Vandivere, J. Keith, and A. Atienza, Child Trends Research Brief, Child Care Used by Low-Income Families; Variations Across States, June 2008; accessed November 24, 2009, at www.childtrends.org/Files/Child_Trends2008_07_02_RB_Child CareLowIncome.pdf.

14. National Association of Child Care Resource & Referral Agencies, Child Care in America Fact Sheet, April 14, 2009; accessed November 16, 2009, at www.naccrra.org/docs/childcareinamericafactsheet.pdf.

15. S. Shellenbarger, "When Granny Is Your Nanny," *Wall Street Journal,* June 24, 2009; accessed January 12, 2010, at http://online.wsj.com/article/SB10001424052970204621904574245973124738260.html.

16. E. Brandon, "When Your Nanny Is Granny," April 17, 2009; accessed November 25, 2009, at http://images.usnews.com/money/personal-finance/retirement/articles/2009/08/17/when-your-nanny-is-granny.html.

17. "State Fact Sheets for Grandparents and Other Relatives Raising Children, October 2008; accessed January 12, 2010, at www.grand factsheets.org/doc/Texas%20New%20Template%2008.pdf.

18. State Fact Sheets for Grandparents and Other Relatives Raising Children, October 2007; accessed January 12, 2010, at www.grandfactsheets.org/doc/California%2007.pdf.

19. C. Thompson, "Grandparents Raising Grandchildren," Baby Zone, June 1, 2009; accessed January 12, 2010, at www.babyzone.com/mom_dad/love_friendship/grandparents-and-extended/article/raising-grandchildren.

20. National Association of Child Care Resource & Referral Agencies, Child Care in America Fact Sheet; accessed November 16, 2009, at www.naccrra.org/policy/docs/childcareinamericafactsheet.doc.

21. Florida Family Child Care Home Association, "What Is Family Child Care?" (n.d) accessed November 21, 2009, at www.familychildcare.org/index.php?page=parents. FFCCHA is a non-profit state association. Used with permission.

22. Contributed by Martha Magnia, owner/director of Magnia Family Child Care and adjunct faculty member at Fresno City College, where she teaches a child development and family child care course.

23. Family Education, "Family Day Care" (n.d) accessed April 1, 2010, at http://life.familyeducation.com/working-parents/child-care/40377.html.

24. Sarah Hutcheon Child Development, "Helping Youth Avoid Risky Behavior: Family-Based Program," May 19, 2009; accessed January 15, 2010, at www.medicalnewstoday.com/articles/150150.php; Florida Family Child Care Association, "What Is Family Child Care?" (n.d) accessed November 21, 2009, at www.familychildcare.org/index.php?page=parents.

25. T. Scott, "No New Abuse Cases Reported Against Missoula Daycare Provider: Accused Rapist Remains in Jail," *Missoulian*, April 9, 2010; accessed April 13, 2010, at www.missoulian.com/news/local/article_99f2dc36-4391-11df-8e9e-001cc4c002e0.html.

26. S. Brink, Good for Each Other, *Los Angeles Times*, Section F, December 5, 2005; accessed November 16, 2009, at www.onegeneration.org/onegen1pdf.pdf.

27. National Child Care Information and Technical Assistance Center, Statistical Information on Child Care in the United States, March 2008; nccic.acf.hhs.gov/poptopics/statistics.pdf.

28. Kidco Annual Report, "Kidco Fact Sheet" p. 7, June 2008; accessed February 3, 2010, at www.kidco-childcare.org/Annual%20Reports/Annual%20Report%2007-08%20Final.pdf.

29. S. GreenHouse, "Recession Drives Women Back to the Work Force," *New York Times*, September 19, 2009; accessed February 3, 2010, at www.nytimes.com/2009/09/19/business/19women.html.

30. Virginia Kids Count, "Business on Board with Childcare," October 30, 2009; accessed January 12, 2010, at www.wvkidscountfund.org/documents/ApplicationPacket-Final.pdf.

31. Lee McIntyre, "Childcare on Board," Federal Reserve Bank of Boston (2000); accessed January 12, 2010, at www.bos.frb.org/economic/nerr/rr2000/q3/daycare.htm.

32. Virginia Kids Count, "Business on Board with Childcare," October 30, 2009; accessed January 12, 2010, at www.wvkidscountfund.org/documents/ApplicationPacket-Final.pdf.

33. Ibid.

34. Bristol-Myers Squibb, "Bristol-Myers Squibb Named a 2009 Working Mother 100 Best Company," September 22, 2009; accessed January 11, 2010, at www.bms.com/news/features/2009/Pages/2009_working_mother.aspx=83.

35. Quadrennial Quality of Life Review, *Child Care Incentives*, January 2009; accessed November 8, 2009, at www.militaryonesource.com/Portals/0/Content/Service_Provider_Tools/QQLR%20Documents/4c.DoD_Initiatives_ChildCare.pdf.

36. Department of Defense Education Activities, "Pentagon Ceremony Honors Top Teachers," November 18, 2009; accessed January 22, 2010, at www.dodea.edu/teachers/2010/index.cfm.

37. Military Homefront, *Welcome to the Child Care Home Page* (n.d); accessed November 8, 2009, at www.militaryhomefront.dod.mil/portal/page/mhf/MHF/MHF_HOME_1?id=20.60.500.100.0.0.0.

38. "Before & After School Care," *Broward County Public Schools*, May 24, 2008; accessed November 11, 2009, at www.broward.k12.fl.us/k12programs/bascc.

39. "Kindergarten Wraparound Program" (n.d); accessed January 11, 2010, at www.town.raynham.ma.us/Public_Documents/RaynhamMA_Recreation/Childcare%20Program%20Description.

40. Maricopa School District, "Copa Kids Care" (2009–1010); accessed January 12, 2010, at www.maricopausd.org/filestore/CopaKidsParentHandbook0910.pdf.

41. "The Exchange Top 40 North America's Largest For-Profit Child Care Organizations," Child Care Exchange, January/February 2009, p. 23, www.childcareexchange.com/library/5018521.pdf.

42. "Knowledge Learning Corporation Fact Sheet," Knowledge Learning Corporation; accessed November 8, 2009, at www.knowledgelearning.com/pdf/corporate-fact-sheet.pdf.

43. The Exchange Top 40 North America's Largest For-Profit Child Care Organizations," Child Care Exchange, January/February 2009, p. 23, www.childcareexchange.com/library/5018521.pdf.

44. J. P. Bianchi, Colorado's Children Campaign, Quality Child Care: An Investment in Families, an Investment in Colorado's Economy, March 2009; accessed November 16, 2009, at www.coloradokids.org/includes/downloads/qualitychildcarereport.pdf.

45. "The Critical Importance of Cultural and Linguistic Continuity for Infants and Toddlers"; accessed March 31, 2010, at http://condor.admin.ccny.cuny.edu/~mmcenter/tk/gwilgus/linguisticdevelopment.htm.

46. I. Koo, "Infectious Diseases," October 29, 2008; accessed April 14, 2010, at http://infectiousdiseases.about.com/od/kidsinfections/a/Daycare_prev.htm.

47. M. Story, K. Kaphingst, R. Robinson-O'Brien, and K. Glanz, Creating Healthy Food and Eating Environments: Policy and Environmental Approaches, Annual Review Public Health, November 21, 2007; accessed April 1, 2009, at http://publhealth.annualreviews.org.

48. All for Natural Health, "Organic Food Benefits Children Too" (2007–2010); accessed February 4, 2010, at www.all4naturalhealth.com/organic-food-benefits.html.

49. Little Dreamers, Big Believers, "Organic Food Day Care," June 2, 2008; accessed February 4, 2010, at www.littledreamersdaycare.org/tag/organic-food-day-care/.

50. Centers for Disease Control and Prevention, "Potential Exposure to Lead in Artificial Turf: Public Health Issues, Actions, and Recommendations," June 18, 2008; accessed January 21, 2010, at www2a.cdc.gov/HAN/ArchiveSys/ViewMsgV.asp?AlertNum=00275.

51. Ibid.

52. J. Pritchard, "Cadmium Found in Kid's Jewelry," January 11, 2010; accessed January 11, 2010, at www.thonline.com/article.cfm?id=269455.

53. Centers for Disease Control and Prevention, "Reducing Pesticide Exposure at Schools," 2007; accessed January 21, 2010, at www.cdc.gov/niosh/docs/2007-150/.

54. "Healthy Classroom Fact Sheet," May 2007; accessed January 21, 2010, at www.in.gov/idem/healthy_classroom_fact_sheet.pdf.

55. National Resource Center for Health and Safety in Child Care, University of Colorado Health Sciences Center at Fitzsimons, "A Parent's Guide to Choosing a Safe and Healthy Child Care"; accessed March 31, 2010, at http://nrckids.org/RESOURCES/ParentsGuide.pdf.

56. Ibid.

57. Kiddie Academy, About Us, 2008; accessed March 31, 2010, at www.kiddieacademy.com/aboutus/choose_child-care-services-resources.aspx.

58. School of Graduate Studies & Continuing Education, "Creating a Safe and Engaging Classroom Climate," 2006; accessed January 15, 2010, at www.uww.edu/learn/diversity/safeclassroom.php.

59. National Council of La Raza, "Early Care and Education Policy," accessed November 24, 2009, at www.nclr.org/content/policy/detail/55516/.

60. Ibid.

61. Contributed by Amy Turcotte, developmental specialist.

62. Read, Play and Learn, "Supportive Environment" (n.d); accessed January 15, 2010, at www.readplaylearn.com/philosophy/environment.htm.

63. Texas Association for the Education of Young Children, "Comments/Recommendations Texas Day Care Minimum Standards Revisions" October 2009; accessed January 20, 2010, at www.texasaeyc.org/docs/Texas%20Minimum%20Standards%20Revisions%20Comments%20TAEYC%20October%202009.doc.

64. NICHD Early Child Care Research Network, "Child Outcomes When Child Care Center Classes Meet Recommended Standards for Quality," *American Journal of Public Health*, 88(7), 1998, 1072–77.

65. K. McCartney, E. Dearing, B. A. Taylor and K. L. Bub, "Quality Child Care Supports the Achievement of Low-Income Children: Direct and Indirect Pathways Through Caregiving and the Home Environment" July 24, 2007; accessed November 17, 2009, at www.sciencedirect.com/science?_ob=MImg&_imagekey=B6W52-4P89846-1-1&_cdi=6558&_user=452995&_orig=search&_coverDate=12%2F31%2F2007&_sk=999719994&view=c&wchp=dGLzVtb-zSkWA&md5=e2c01726876bdf4a065443b9b250bdca&ie=/sdarticle.pdf.

66. American Red Cross, "California Child Care" 2007; accessed April 1, 2010, at www.sdarc.org/TakeAClass/IndividualTraining/CaliforniaChildCarePediatricFirstAidCPR/tabid/140/Default.aspx.

67. NAEYC, Accreditation by the National Academy of Early Childhood Programs (Washington: Author, 2008).

68. NAEYC, "Why NAEYC Accreditation?" accessed May 10, 2010, at www.naeyc.org/academy/interested/whyaccreditation.

69. Contributed by Stephanie Fanjul, Smart Start Communications & Development Director, The North Carolina Partnership for Children, Inc., February 24, 2010.

70. Ibid.

71. *Community Development: Journal of the Community Development Society,* Vol. 37, No. 2, Summer 2006; accessed February 9, 2010, at http://government.cce.cornell.edu/doc/pdf/53-70%20meyers%20jordan.pdf.

72. Ibid.

73. Ibid.

74. Ibid.

75. *Journal of Family Issues*, Vol. 29, No. 9, 1161–1184 (2008); accessed February 9, 2010, at http://jfi.sagepub.com/cgi/content/refs/29/9/1161.

76. Ibid.

77. E. K. Shriver, National Institute of Child Health and Human Development, "Study of Early Child Care and Youth Development," May 24, 2007; accessed November 21, 2009, at www.nichd.nih.gov/health/topics/seccyd.cfm.

78. Marilou Hyson, *Enthusiastic and Engaged Learners,* Teachers College Press, May 2008, p. 86.

79. The Early Childhood Initiative Foundation (ELC) in Florida. Accessed July 28, 2010, at www.teachmorelovemore.org/index.asp.

80. Sensory Integration Cindy Hatch-Rasmussen, 2005. Accessed July 28, 2010, at www.pathfindersforautism.org/upload/Sensory-Integration. pdf.

Chapter 8

1. National Association for the Education of Young Children, *NAEYC Standards for Professional Preparation Programs,* 2009; accessed April 30, 2009, from www.naeyc.org/.

2. Ibid.

3. Ibid.

4. Ibid.

5. "Fiscal Year 2010 Budget Summary and Background Information," Department of Education; accessed June 17, 2010, at www2.ed.gov/about/overview/budget/budget10/summary/10summary.pdf.

6. The White House, "Education"; accessed December 3, 2009, at www.whitehouse.gov/issues/education.

7. Committee of Ways and Means: Headstart; accessed June 17, 2010, at http://waysandmeans.house.gov/media/pdf/110/head.pdf.

8. U.S. Department of Health and Human Services, Administration for Children and Families, "About the Office of Head Start"; accessed April 19, 2010, at www.acf.hhs.gov/programs/ohs/about/index.html.

9. Ibid.

10. United States Department of Education, "FY 2010 ED Budget: Elementary and Secondary Education," https://ed.gov/about/overview/budget/budget10/summary/edlite-section3a.html#title1lea.

11. Pre-K Now, "ARRA Overview." www.preknow.org/documents/arra_overview.pdf.

12. Ibid.

13. U.S. Department of Health and Human Services, "Head Start: Promoting Early Childhood Development," 2002; accessed July 8, 2007, at www.hhs.gov/news/press/2002pres/headstart.html.

14. Pre-K Now, "Head Start and Pre-K Collaboration," 2007; accessed April 30, 2010, at www.preknow.org/policy/headstart.cfm.

15. U.S. Department of Health and Human Services, Administration for Children and Families; accessed June 15, 2010, from www.acf.hhs.gov/programs/ohs/legislation/HS_act.html.

16. National Institute for Early Education Research (NIEER), Cost of providing quality preschool education to America's 3- and 4-year olds, 2010; accessed April 30, 2010, at http://nieer.org/resources/facts/index.php?FastFactID=5.

17. Head Start Program Fact Sheet. HHS/ACF/OHS. 2010; accessed March 29, 2010, at http://eclkc.ohs.acf.hhs.gov/hslc/About%20Head%20Start/fHeadStartProgr.htm.

18. Center for the Child Care Workforce, A Project of the AFT Educational Foundation (CCW/AFTEF), "President Obama's 2011 Budget Requests," January & February 2010; accessed February 19, 2010, at www.ccw.org/index.php?option=content&task=view&id=170&Itemid=70.

19. N. Pelosi, "American Recovery and Reinvestment Act of 2009," 2009; accessed February 19, 2010, at www.speaker.gov/newsroom/legislation?id=0273.

20. D. Arrieta, *Head Start Center to Open on EPCC Campus*, April 6, 2010; accessed April 19, 2010, at www.elpasotimes.com/education/ci_14831883.

21. U.S. Department of Health and Human Services, "Head Start Program Performance Standards and Other Regulations," Administration for Children and Families; accessed December 3, 2009, at http://eclkc.ohs.acf.hhs.gov/hslc/Program%20Design%20and%20Management/Head%20Start%20Requirements/Head%20Start%20Requirements/1306/45%20CFR%201306_ENG.pdf.

22. U.S. Department of Health and Human Services, Early Head Start National Resource Center, "What Is Early Head Start?"; accessed March 12, 2010, at www.ehsnrc.org/aboutus/ehs.htm.

23. U.S. Department of Health and Human Services, "45 CFR Part 1306-Head Start Staffing Requirements and Program Options," Administration for Children and Families; accessed March 10, 2010, at http://eclkc.ohs.acf.hhs.gov/hslc/Program%20Design%20and%20Management/Management%20and%20Administration/Eligibility%20%26%20Enrollment/Program%20Options/45%20CFR%201306_ENG.pdf.

24. Ibid.

25. Illinois Head Start Association, "Program Options," *Head Start Program Framework*; accessed April 20, 2010, at www.ilheadstart.org/options.html.

26. Early Childhood Learning and Knowledge Center, "Proposed Regulation on Family Child Care Homes as a Head Start Program Option," 2009; accessed March 10, 2010, at http://eclkc.ohs.acf.hhs.gov/hslc/Family%20and%20Community%20Partnerships/Community%20Partnership/Program%20Options/famcom_ime_00052a1_062005.html.

27. Early Childhood Learning and Knowledge Center, "Quality Early Head Start Services: A Summary of Research-Based Practice that Support Children's Families and Expectant Parents," 2009; accessed March 10, 2010, at http://eclkc.ohs.acf.hhs.gov/hslc/Early%20Head%20Start/Approach%20%26%20Program%20Design/ehs%20quality%20final%203-02%20(2).pdf.

28. Ibid.

29. Ibid.

30. Ibid.

31. Madera County Community Action Agency, "Fresno Migrant Head Start Program," 2010; accessed April 30, 2010, at www.maderacap.org/headstart_fresno.html.

32. Aleutian Pribilof Islands Association, "Human Services: Head Start Program"; accessed May 12, 2010, at www.apiai.org/headstart.asp.

33. Ibid.

34. M. Galley, Academy for Educational Development, "New AED Examines Barriers Some Head Start Teachers Face in Securing College Degrees—and Makes Recommendations for Overcoming Them," February 23, 2010; accessed March 16, 2010, at www.aed.org/News/Releases/headstart-whitepaper.cfm.

35. Ibid.

36. Ibid.

37. U.S. Department of Health and Human Services (2010, January). Head Start Impact Study Final Report, xxiii–xxvi from www.acf.hhs.gov/programs/opre/hs/impact_study/reports/impact_study/hs_impact_study_tech_rpt.pdf

38. Ibid.

39. Ibid.

40. Ibid.

41. Ibid.

42. Ibid.

43. Child Trends, "Early Childhood Highlights." Volume 1, Issue 2; May 10, 2010, at www.childtrends.org/Files//Child_Trends-2010_05_10_HL_EarlyHeadStart.pdf

44. United States Department of Agriculture Food and Nutrition Service. Quick Facts: National School Lunch Program; accessed April 14, 2010, at www.fns.usda.gov/cga/factsheets/NSLP_Quick_Facts.htm.

45. V. Watson, "AISD Sends Sweets Packing," *Reporter News*; April 22, 2010, at www.reporternews.com/news/2010/apr/22/aisd-sends-sweets-packing/?print=1.

46. United States Department of Agriculture Food and Nutrition Service, "SY 2009-2010 Income Eligibility Requirements for National School Lunch Program"; accessed May 3, 2010, at www.fns.usda.gov/cnd/governance/notices/iegs/IEGs09-10.pdf.

47. U.S. Department of Education, Title I, Part A Program; accessed April 20, 2010, at www2.ed.gov/programs/titleiparta/index.html.

48. Columbia Public Schools, "CPS Title I Preschool Program: Welcome to Title I Preschool"; accessed April 14, 2010, at www.columbia.k12.mo.us/titleone/Index.htm.

49. Contributed by Karen Owens, Title I Specialist, dated May 3, 2010. Cactus View Elementary, Phoenix, AZ.

50. J. Rosenberg and W. B. Wilcox, *The Importance of Fathers in the Healthy Development of Children*, Office on Child Abuse and Neglect, U.S. Children's Bureau, 2006; accessed May 12, 2010, at www.childwelfare.gov/pubs/usermanuals/fatherhood/chaptertwo.cfm.

51. U.S. Department of Defense, "Military Homefront-Overview"; accessed May 4, 2010, at www.militaryhomefront.dod.mil/portal/page/mhf/MHF/MHF_HOME_1?section_id=20.40.500.94.0.0.0.0.0.

52. National Association of Child Care Resource and Referral Agencies, "What Program Is Right for Your Family?" accessed May 4, 2010, at www.naccrra.org/MilitaryPrograms/army/fee-assistance-programs/.

53. Stripes—Military Moms, "Sure Start"; accessed May 4, 2010, at http://militarymoms.stripes.com/resources/education/dod-education-resources-101.

54. Department of Defense Education Activity, "Early Childhood Education: Welcome to Sure Start"; accessed May 4, 2010, at www.dodea.edu/curriculum/eChildhood.cfm?cId=ss.

Chapter 9

1. National Association for the Education of Young Children, *NAEYC Standards for Professional Preparation Programs*, 2009; accessed December 16, 2009, from www.naeyc.org/.

2. Ibid.

3. J. Klinkner, *Cultural Sensitivity When Caring for Infants and Toddlers*. Wisconsin Child Care Improvement Project, Inc.; accessed December 28, 2006, at www.wccip.org/tips/Infant_Toddler/Cultural_Sensitive_Info.html.

4. American Association of Pediatrics, Breastfeeding; accessed June 4, 2010, from www.aap.org/healthtopics/breastfeeding.cfm.

5. World Health Organization, Breastfeeding, accessed August 4, 2010, from www.who.int/topics/breastfeeding/en/.

6. www.aap.org/publiced/BR_ToiletTrain.htm.

7. *CNN*, Spanking Detrimental to Children, Study Says, September 16, 2009; accessed April 6, 2010, from www.cnn.com/2009/HEALTH/09/16/spanking.children.parenting/index.html?iref=allsearch

8. Ibid.

9. Ibid.

10. Ibid.

11. Ibid.

12. J. Huttenlocher, "Language Input and Language Growth," *Preventive Medicine: An International Journal Devoted to Practice and Theory*, 27(2), 1998, 195–99.

13. P. Kuhl, *How Babies Acquire Building Blocks of Speech Affects Later Reading, Language Ability,* July 2001; accessed July 18, 2007, at www.sciencedaily.com/releases/2001/07/010730080042.htm.

14. Professionals and Researchers: Quick Reference and Fact Sheets. March of Dimes Birth Defects Foundation; accessed June 16, 2007, at www.marchofdimes.com/professionals/14332_1206.asp.

15. *Time*, TV for Babies: Does It Help or Hurt? March 3, 2009; accessed March 30, 2010, at www.time.com/time/health/article/0,8599,1882560,00.html?iid=sphere-inline-sidebar.

16. Ibid.

17. Eric H. Lenneberg, "The Biological Foundations of Language," in Mark Lester, ed., *Readings in Applied Transformational Grammar* (New York: Holt, Rinehart and Winston, 1970), 8.

18. Linda Acredolo and Susan Goodwyn, *Baby Signs: How to Talk with Your Baby Before Your Baby Can Talk.* (Chicago: Contemporary Books, 1996).

19. T. R. Hart and B. Risley, *Meaningful Differences in the Everyday Experience of Young American Children* (Maryland MD: Paul H. Brooks Co., 1995).

20. E. L. Newport, "Mother, I'd Rather Do It Myself: Some Effects and Non-Effects on Maternal Speech Style," in C. E. Snow and C. A. Ferguson, eds., *Talking to Children* (Cambridge: Cambridge University Press, 1977), 112–129.

21. T.R. Hart and B. Risley, *Meaningful Differences in the Everyday Experience of Young American Children* (Maryland MD: Paul H. Brooks Co., 1995).

22. R. Brown, *A First Language* (Cambridge, MA: Harvard University Press, 1973), 281.

23. L. Bloom, *Language Development: Form and Function in Emerging Grammars* (Cambridge, MA: MIT Press, 1970).

24. J. Portner, "Two Studies Link High-Quality Day Care and Child Development," *Education Week* (April 19, 1995), 6.

25. S. Bredekamp and C. Copple, eds., *Developmentally Appropriate Practice in Early Childhood Programs,* rev. ed. (Washington, DC: NAEYC, 1997), 9.

26. Erik Erikson, *Childhood and Society,* 2nd ed. (New York: Norton, 1963; first pub., 1950), 249.

27. MyChildWithoutLimits.org, Early Intervention, 2010; accessed April 16, 2010, from www.mychildwithoutlimits.org/?page=early-intervention&gclid=CJWQzu23iaECFc9Y2godPXB-NA.

28. Ibid.

29. Ibid.

30. Ibid.

31. Ibid.

32. ACHIEVA, Early Intervention Services, www.achieva.info/achievaei.php.

33. MyChildWithoutLimits.org, Early Intervention, 2010; accessed April 16, 2010, from www.mychildwithoutlimits.org/?page=early-intervention&gclid=CJWQzu23iaECFc9Y2godPXB-NA.

34. Ibid.

35. TheFreeLibrary.com, Parenting Predictors of Father-Child Attachment Security: Interactive Effects of Father Involvement and Fathering Quality; accessed April 16, 2010, from www.thefreelibrary.com/Parenting+predictors+of+father-child+attachment+security%3a+interactive...-a0172831835.

36. A. Thomas, S. Chess, and H. Birch, "The Origin of Personality," *Scientific American* (1970): 102–109.

37. Charles J. Zeanah, Jr., "Towards a Definition of Infant Mental Health," *Zero to Three,* 22(1), 2001, 13–20.

38. *AndhraNews*, Babies recognise emotions by 7 months, March 2010; accessed April 13, 2010, at www.andhranews.net/Technology/2010/March/27-Babies-recognise-emotions-8237.asp.

39. Ibid.

40. A. Mehrabian, "Communication Without Words," *Psychol. Today*, vol. 2, no. 4, pp. 53–56, 1968.

41. Bredekamp and Copple, *Developmentally Appropriate Practice,* 9.

42. Ibid.

43. N. Engineer, C. Percaccio, and M. Kilgard, "Environment Shapes Auditory Processing," *New Horizons for Learning*, June 2004; accessed June 20, 2007, at www.newhorizons.org/neuro/engineer%20percaccio%20kilgard.htm.

44. U.S. Department of Health and Human Services Administration for Children and Families, *FY 2007 PRISM Protocol: Safe Environments*, 2007.

45. NAEYC, Supportive Care for Infants and Toddlers; accessed April 6, 2010, at http://journal.naeyc.org/btj/200607/Huffman706BTJ.pdf.

46. *Parents Magazine*, Encouraging Toddler Friendships, 2009; accessed April 6, 2010, at www.parents.com/toddlers-preschoolers/development/social/encouraging-toddler-friendships/?page=6.

47. *Beyond the Journal*, Young Children on the Web; July 2006 from http://journal.naeyc.org/btj/200607/Gillespie709BTJ.pdf.

48. Ibid.

49. Ibid.

50. Ibid.

51. Ibid.

52. Ibid.

53. Ibid.

54. Ibid.

55. Parents as Teachers, Helping Your Child Learn Self Regulation Through Play; accessed March 30, 2010, from www.parentsasteachers.org/site/pp.asp?c=ekIRLcMZJxE&b=307151.

56. Ibid.

Chapter 10

1. National Association for the Education of Young Children, *NAEYC Standards for Professional Preparation Programs*, 2009; accessed May 14, 2010, at www.naeyc.org/.

2. Ibid.

3. Ibid.

4. National Institute for Early Education Research. *2009 State of Preschool Yearbook* (2009). http://nieer.org/yearbook/pdf/yearbook.pdf.

5. American Federation of Teachers–A Union of Professionals, *Welcome Early Childhood Educators and Child Care Providers,* 2009; accessed June 22, 2009, at http://aft.org/earlychildhood/index.htm.

6. W. T. Dickens, I. Sawhill, and J. Tebbs, *Policy Brief #153: The Effects of Investing in Early Childhood Education on Economic Growth* (Washington, DC: The Brookings Institution, April 2006), www.brookings.edu/comm/policybriefs/pb153.pdf.

7. Ibid.

8. California Department of Education, *Preschool for All: A First-Class Learning Initiative*, 2006, www.cde.ca.gov/eo/in/se/yr05preschoolwp.asp?print=yes.

9. L. J. Calman and L. Tarr-Whelan, *Early Childhood Education for All: A Wise Investment* (New York: Legal Momentum, April 2005), http://web.mit.edu/workplacecenter/docs/Full%20Report.pdf.

10. Ibid.

11. K. Uhlig, "Wausau-Report: Early Spending Pays Off in Education," *Wausau Daily Herald,* October 19, 2005.

12. National Center for Children in Poverty, *Child Poverty* (2009); www.nccp.org/topics/childpoverty.html

13. Pew Center on the States, "Economy Threatens Impressive Expansion of State Pre-K Programs," April 8, 2009; accessed May 18, 2010, at www.pewcenteronthestates.org/news_room_detail.aspx?id=50884.

14. B. Bowman, M. S. Donovan, and M. S. Burns, *Eager to Learn: Educating Our Preschoolers* (Washington, DC: National Academy Press, 2001), 25–28.

15. Montgomery County Public Schools, *PEP Program Description* (2009); accessed May 14, 2010, at www.montgomeryschoolsmd.org/curriculum/pep/description.shtm.

16. Ibid.

17. Healy Communications, Inc., *First-Ever National Preschool Teacher of the Year Award Winners Announced by Story Reader*, September 18, 2006; accessed June 22, 2009, from www.pubint.com/about/dsp_pr_PTOTYWinnersReleaseFINAL.cfm.

18. Ibid.

19. National Institute for Early Education Research, "Executive function: A critical skill for preschoolers." *Preschool Matters,* 4(5) 2006; accessed May 2, 2010, at http://nieer.org/psm/index.php?article=171.

20. Culver City Unified School District, *News and Announcements*, April 20, 2009; accessed June 22, 2009, at http://ccusd.org/apps/news/show_news.jsp?REC_ID=93423&id=0.

21. U.S. Department of Health and Human Services, Administration for Children and Families, *Head Start Child Outcomes Framework Domain 6: Social and Emotional Development*, March 4, 2005; accessed October 24, 2007, at www.headstartinfo.org/leaders_guideeng/domain6.htm.

22. Child Trends, "Early Childhood Highlights: A Review of School Readiness Practices in the States," Volume 1, Issue 3, June 17, 2010; accessed June 21, 2010, at www.childtrends.org/_docdisp_page.cfm?LID=70467B6D-CD19-491A-A0AFC6E4F9611771.

23. Florida Department of Education, Office of Early Learning, "Florida Voluntary Prekindergarten Education Standards," August 19, 2008; accessed June 21, 2010, at www.fldoe.org/earlylearning/perform.asp.

24. Basque Research (2010, March 17). Behind a child with aggressive behavior there is a negative family environment. *ScienceDaily*. Retrieved August 5, 2010, from www.sciencedaily.com/releases/2010/03/100317101346.htm.

25. National Center for Family and Community Connections with Schools. *Readiness: School, Community, and Family Connections* (2004). www.sedl.org/connections/resources/readiness-synthesis.pdf.

26. Micheal Conn-Powers *The Early Childhood Briefing Paper Series: All Children Ready for School: Approaches to Learning,* Indiana University Bloomington 2006. Retrieved August 5, 2010, from www.iidc.indiana.edu/styles/iidc/defiles/ECC/SRUD-ApproachestoLearning.pdf.

27. Ibid.

28. Based on information constructed by Lesley Mandel Morrow, professor and coordinator of early childhood programs, Rutgers University.

29. M. Parten, "Social Participation Among Pre-School Children," *Journal of Abnormal and Social Psychology,* 27, 1933, 243–269.

30. The Grove School, 2010. http://blog.groveschool.com/.

31. L. L. Flynn and J. Kieff, "Including *Everyone* in Outdoor Play," *Young Children* 57(3), 2002: 20–26. Reprinted with permission from the National Association for the Education of Young Children (NAEYC). www.naeyc.

32. S. Urahn and S. Watson, "A Movement Transformed," November 19, 2007; www.prospect.org/cs/articles?article=a_movement_transformed.

33. Children's Alliance, *The achievement gap starts before kindergarten*, July 17, 2009; accessed May 10, 2010, at www.childrensalliance.org/blog/achievement-gap-starts-kindergarten.

34. S. Urahn and S. Watson, "A Movement Transformed," November 19, 2007; www.prospect.org/cs/articles?article=a_movement_transformed.

35. California Department of Education, "Preschool for All"; accessed October 24, 2007, at www.cde.ca.gov/eo/in/se/yr05preschoolwp.asp.

36. M. Martin, *Passion for childcare leads to chain of 'palaces'*, May 6, 2010; www.courierlifenews.com/articles/2010/05/06/features/00gorka.txt.

37. Love A Lot Preschool, 2010; www.lovealotpreschool.com/program_pages/specialty.html.

38. Nobel Learning Communities, *NLCI PE Program Keeps Preschoolers Active and Healthy,* March 30, 2009; www.nobellearning.com/Default.aspx?DN=1699716d-d2db-42a8-8e87-6d147202631e.

39. C. J. McVicker, "Young Readers Respond: The Importance of Child Participation in Emerging Literacy," *Young Children 62*(3), 2007, 18.

40. National Early Literacy Panel, *Developing Early Literacy: Report of the National Early Literacy Panel* (Washington, DC: National Institute for Literacy, 2008).

41. Ibid.

42. Ibid.

43. Ibid.

44. Ibid.

45. Based on the online reading program *Alphabet Strategy Bank* (2004).

46. W. Ellis, *Phonological Resources* (Phonological Awareness Resources, 1993).

47. Madison Metropolitan School District, *Concepts of Print* (2005).

48. L. Indiana, *Vocabulary Activities* (Teachers Net Gazette, 2003).

49. K. Lowry, *Discourse Planning Skills* (Thames Valley Children's Center, 1994).

50. Crawmer's Critterz Preschool, 2010. http://bendpreschool.com/index.html.

51. Albany Children's Center, 2010. http://acc-ausd.ca.schoolloop.com/cms/page_view?d=x&piid=&vpid=1225554129399.

52. L. Braunt and California Preschool Instructional Network, *Transitions: Preschool to Kindergarten and Beyond*, 2006; accessed May 14, 2010, at www.cpin.us/docs/mod_transitionsfinal2.10.06.pdf.

53. Gertie Belle Rogers Elementary, *Mrs. Christensen's Page* (2010); accessed May 14, 2010, at http://ac069.k12.sd.us/.

54. Kokomo Center Schools, *Kindergarten Round-up 2010–2011;* www.kokomo.k12.in.us/.

55. HighScope, *Lifetime Effects: The HighScope Perry Preschool Study Through Age 40* (2005); www.highscope.org/content.asp?contentid=219.

56. The Chicago Child–Parent Center Program; www.waisman.wisc.edu/cls/Program.htm.

57. National Institute for Early Education Research. *The APPLES Blossom: Abbott Preschool Program Longitudinal Effects Study (APPLES) Preliminary Results through 2nd grade* (June 2009); http://nieer.org/pdf/apples_second_grade_results.pdf.

58. C. Rivera, "L.A. Study Affirms Benefits of Preschool," April 19, 2010. *Los Angeles Times*; www.latimes.com/news/local/la-me-0420-preschool-20100419,0,2289045.story.

Chapter 11

1. National Association for the Education of Young Children, *NAEYC Standards for Early Childhood Professional Preparation Programs*, July 2009, 11–19.

2. Ibid.

3. Ibid.

4. Ibid.

5. Wake County Public School System, "Fuller Elementary Teacher is 2010 Wake County Teacher of the Year," May 13, 2010; accessed May 18, 2010, at www.wcpss.net/news/2010_may13_toy/.

6. Norms Notes, "2010–2011 Teacher of the Year Finalist: Abby Lowe," April 16, 2010; accessed May 19, 2010, at http://normsnotessps.blogspot.com/2010/04/2010-2011-teacher-of-year-finalist-abby.html.

7. NEA Education and Policy Practice Department, "Full Day Kindergarten Helps Close Achievement Gaps," 2008; accessed November 20, 2009, at www.nea.org/assets/docs/mf_PB12_FullDayK.pdf.

8. Rhode Island Kids Count Factbook "Full Day Kindergarten," 2010; accessed April 25, 2010, at www.rikidscount.org/matriarch/documents/10_Factbook_Indicator_49.pdf.

9. G. Yara, "Kyrene, Tempe School Districts to Maintain All-Day Kindergarten," AzCentral, February 5, 2010; accessed February 16, 2010, at www.azcentral.com/community/tempe/articles/2010/02/05/20100205tr-all-day-kindergarten-06-ON.html.

10. NAE Education and Policy Practice Department, "Full Day Kindergarten Helps Close Achievement Gaps," 2008; accessed November 20, 2009, at www.nea.org/assets/docs/mf_PB12_FullDayK.pdf.

11. Newcastle School, "Kindergarten Pressure," 2009; accessed February 17, 2010, at http://newcastleschool.com/parent-resources/early-childhood-ed/kindergarten-pressure-reason-for-concern/.

12. E. Miller and J. Almon, "Crisis in Kindergarten: Why Children Need to Play in School," 2009; accessed February 16, 2010, at www.allianceforchildhood.org/sites/allianceforchildhood.org/files/file/kindergarten_report.pdf.

13. International Reading Association & National Association for the Education of Young Children, "Learning to Read and Write," 9.

14. Anne Arundel County Public Schools, "Kindergarten FAQs," 2009; accessed January 28, 2010, at www.aacps.org/earlychildhood/mdlaw.asp.

15. Getting Ready for Kindergarten or Academically Redshirted," 2009; accessed December 15, 2009, at http://teacher.haywood.k12.nc.us/nolte/files/2009/06/071406-kindergarten-readiness.pdf.

16. R. Haas, "Redshirting: Examining the New Trend of Holding School Aged Children Back A Year," February 23, 2007; accessed February 16, 2010, at www.associatedcontent.com/article/152514/redshirting_examining_the_new_trend.html?cat=4.

17. Illinois Early Learning Project, "What Are the Effects of Academic Redshirting?" April 2009; accessed December 21, 2009, at http://illinoisearlylearning.org/faqs/redshirting.htm.

18. L. Leonard, "Starting Kindergarten Later Gives Students Only a Fleeting Edge," (p. 3) *Handprints*, Winter 2009, Vol. 4, Issue 3, accessed February 2, 2009, at www.partnershipforchildren.org/handprints/Newsletter%20-%2009%20winter.pdf.

19. Health and Human Services, "Massachusetts Chapter 766," 2010; accessed May 19, 2010, at www.mass.gov/?pageID=eohhs2terminal&L=4&L0=Home&L1=Government&L2=Laws%2C+Regulations+and+Policies&L3=Massachusetts+Commission+for+the+Blind+-+Related+Laws+and+Regulations&sid=Eeohhs2&b=terminalcontent&f=mcb_g_chapter_766&csid=Eeohhs2.

20. Scholastic Testing Service Inc, "Readiness Assessment," 2010; accessed January 16, 2010, at http://ststesting.wordpress.com/category/school-readiness-testing/.

21. Troy School District, "Developmental Kindergarten Program," 2010–2011, accessed February 16, 2010, at www.troy.k12.mi.us/tsdnews/dkbrochure.pdf.

22. The Honor Roll School, "Transition Kindergarten," n.d.; accessed February 16, 2010, at www.thehonorrollschool.com/page.cfm?p=19548.

23. C. Peck, "Multiage Classrooms Aid Both Students, Teachers," *Arizona Republic*, January 17, 2010; accessed February 18, 2010, at www.azcentral.com/arizonarepublic/local/articles/2010/01/17/20100117edpeck0117.html.

24. Contributed by Lauren Gonzales, Denton Independent School District Teacher

25. *Psychology Today*, May 20, 2008; accessed February 2, 2010, at www.psychologytoday.com/blog/digital-children/200805/kindergarten-retention

26. Ibid.

27. N. Xia and S. Kirby, RAND Education, "Retaining Students in Grade: A Literature Review of the Effects of Retention on Students' Academic and Nonacademic Outcome," 2009; accessed April 29, 2010, at www.rand.org/pubs/technical_reports/2009/RAND_TR678.sum.pdf.

28. Council of Chief State School Officers, "Addressing the Challenges: A Safe, Supportive, and Healthy School Environment," January 27, 2009; accessed January 27, 2009, at www.ccsso.org/Projects/school_health_project/addressing_the_challenges/6498.cfm.

29. G. Hopkins, "School Wide Handwashing Campaign Cut Germs, Absenteeism," *Education World*, April 30, 2009; accessed January 13, 2010, at www.educationworld.com/a_admin/admin/admin431.shtml.

30. M. Story, K. Kaphingst, R. Robinson-O'Brien, and K. Glanz, "Creating Healthy Food and Eating Environments: Policy and Environmental Approaches," Annual Review Public Health,

November 21, 2007; accessed November 1, 2009, at http://publhealth.annualreviews.org.

31. D. Lau Whela, "With America's Kids in Danger of Becoming Obese, a Growing Number of Schools Are Thinking Outside the Lunchbox," June 1, 2008; accessed January 21, 2010, at www.schoollibraryjournal.com/article/CA6565675.html.

32. Ibid.

33. D. Weaver, *Atlantic Press*, "Long Beach Island Schools Ban Treats with Birthday Celebrations," December 28, 2009; accessed May 19, 2010, at www.pressofatlanticcity.com/news/press/ocean/article_a67b3bbd-868d-5ae3-9f62-4f2f648bd3bd.html.

34. D. Lau Whela, "With America's Kids in Danger of Becoming Obese, a Growing Number of Schools Are Thinking Outside the Lunchbox," June 1, 2008; accessed January 21, 2010, at www.schoollibraryjournal.com/article/CA6565675.html.

35. S. White, *Organic*, "Lesson Plan on Organic Food" July 24, 2007; accessed January 21, 2010, at http://organic.lovetoknow.com/Lesson_Plan_on_Organic_Food.

36. Dawson, Elizabeth, www.SantaMariaPreschool.com, Santa Maria, CA. Casa dei Bambini Montessori, 2010.

37. Council of Chief State School Officers, "Addressing the Challenges: A Safe, Supportive, and Healthy School Environment," January 27, 2009; accessed February 18, 2010, at www.ccsso.org/projects/School_Health_Project/Addressing_the_Challenges/6498.cfm.

38. M. Bredngen, B. Wanner, and F. Vitaro, "Verbal Abuse by the Teacher and Child Adjustment from Kindergarten Through Grade 6," *Pediatrics*, 117(5), 2006, 1585–98.

39. Council of Chief State School Officers, "Addressing the Challenges: A Safe, Supportive, and Healthy School Environment," January 27, 2009; accessed February 18, 2010, at www.ccsso.org/projects/School_Health_Project/Addressing_the_Challenges/6498.cfm

40. B. Caldwell, "What is a Good Kindergarten?" 2010; accessed May 2, 2010, at www.fisher-price.com/fp.aspx?st=4081&e=expertadvice&content=57470.

41. Ibid.

42. S. Greenspan, "Meeting Learning Challenges: Creating an All Inclusive Classroom," 2005; accessed May 3, 2010, at www2.scholastic.com/browse/article.jsp?id=3746102.

43. G. Thorton, J. Kempster, and E. Sternfield, "It's Child's Play," November 5, 2009; accessed May 4, 2010, at http://nyteachers.wordpress.com/2009/11/05/it%E2%80%99s-child%E2%80%99s-play/.

44. M. Ferrer and A. Fugate, "Working with School-Aged Children: Promoting Friendship," 2009; accessed May 4, 2010, at www.education.com/reference/article/Ref_Working_School_Age/.

45. P. Jennings and M. Greenburg, "The Prosocial Classroom: Teacher Social and Emotional Competence in Relation to Student and Classroom Outcomes," December 29, 2008; accessed May 4, 2010, at http://rer.sagepub.com/cgi/content/full/79/1/491.

46. Glenwood Elementary School, "Positive Behavior Support," 2008; accessed May 4, 2010, at www2.chccs.k12.nc.us/education/components/scrapbook/default.php?sectiondetailid=77033&&PHPSESSID=33b10693c22fd87c63d5b8699b9a0c4a.

47. Arizona Educational Foundation, 2010 Ambassador of Excellence, accessed February 2, 2010, at www.azedfoundation.org/10tingle.php.

48. CASRC, "How Can I Help My Child Get Ready for Kindergarten?" 2008; accessed December 22, 2009, at www.howkidsdevelop.com/developKindergarten.html.

49. Education Portal, "Illiteracy: The Downfall of American Society," July 24, 2007; accessed February 2, 2010, at http://education-portal.com/articles/Illiteracy:_The_Downfall_of_American_Society.html.

50. Reading Rockets, "NELP Report: Developing Early Literacy," National Early Literacy Panel, 2009; accessed February 18, 2010, at www.readingrockets.org/articles/31095.

51. K. Swick, "Promoting School and Life Success Through Early Childhood Family Literacy," February 25, 2009; accessed February 18, 2010, at www.springerlink.com/content/010n88151554vg40/fulltext.pdf.

52. Ibid.

53. S. Mead, Early Ed First, "Early Education Is the First Pillar in President's Education Plan," March 10, 2009; accessed February 18, 2010, at www.newamerica.net/blog/early-ed-watch/2009/early-education-first-pillar-presidents-education-plan-10551.

54. *Journal of Research in Childhood Education*, "Increasing the Literacy Behaviors of Preschool Children Through Environmental Modification and Teacher Mediation," September 22, 2007; accessed April 29, 2010, at http://goliath.ecnext.com/coms2/gi_0199-7222031/Increasing-the-literacy-behaviors-of.html.

55. L. Espinosa, "Challenging Common Myths About Young English Language Learners," *Foundation for Child Development*, January 2008; accessed February 18, 2010, at www.fcd-us.org/usr_doc/MythsOfTeachingELLsEspinosa.pdf.

56. Ibid.

57. J. Harmon, K. Wood, W. Hedrick, J. Vintinner, and T. Williford, "Interactive Word Walls: More Than Just Reading the Writing on the Walls," *Journal of Adolescent & Adult Literacy*, February 2009; accessed February 16, 2010, at www.scribd.com/doc/16127639/Interactive-Word-Walls.

58. National Institute for Literacy, "Developing Early Literacy: Report of the National Early Literacy Panel," 2008; accessed January 26, 2009, at www.nifl.gov/publications/pdf/NELPReport09.pdf.

59. Dolch Sight Words, accessed April 27, 2010, at http://dolchsightwords.org.

60. W. A. Hoover, "The Importance of Phonemic Awareness in Learning to Read," *SEDL Letter* 14 (3); accessed November 1, 2009, at www.sedl.org/pubs/sedl-letter/v14n03/3.html.

61. Ibid., 8.

62. J. E. Brown, "A Balanced Approach to Reading and Writing Across the Curriculum," August 21, 2007; accessed January 28, 2010, at www.paisd.org/Curriculum/Webpage%20for%20C%20&%20I/A_Balanced_Approach_to_Reading_and_Writing_Final.ppt.

63. Entire section on shared reading adapted from J.David Cooper, *Literacy,* 5th ed., 157–167. Copyright © 2003 Houghton Mifflin Company. Used with permission.

64. Contributed by Lauren Gonzales, Denton Independent School District.

65. V. Spandel, *Creating Writers Through 6-Trait Writing Assessment and Instruction,* 4th ed. Allyn and Bacon, 2004.

66. Timmons Times, "Readers Workshop," October 16, 2007; accessed May 4, 2010, at http://timmonstimes.blogspot.com/2007/10/video-streaming-readers-workshop.html.

67. National Council of Teachers of Mathematics, *Curriculum Focal Points for Prekindergarten Through Grade 8 Mathematics*, 2006;

accessed February 1, 2009, at www.nctmmedia.org/cfp/front_matter.pdf.

68. San Mateo-Foster City School District, "Mathematics Framework for California Public Schools, Kindergarten–Mathematics Content Standards," accessed June 22, 2010, at www.smfc.k12.ca.us/standards/kmathstand.pdf.

69. L. M. Melber, "Young Learners at Natural History Museums," *Dimensions of Early Childhood*, Winter 2008, Vol. 36, No.1.

70. Contributed By Lori Cadwaller, Kindergarten Teacher, Garrett Park Elementary, Garrett Park, Maryland.

71. National Council for Social Studies, "About NCSS," accessed November 1, 2009, at www.socialstudies.org/about/.

Chapter 12

1. National Association for the Education of Young Children, *NAEYC Standards for Professional Preparation Programs*, 2009; accessed December 16, 2009, from www.naeyc.org/.

2. Ibid.

3. T. W. Briggs, "All-USA teachers strive to give confidence, changes." November 6, 2007; accessed May 25, 2010, from www.usatoday.com/news/education/2007-10-17-teacher-team_N.htm?csp=34.

4. Arkansas Department of Education, "Milken Family Foundation, National Educator Awards," October 10, 2008; accessed June 28, 2009, at http://arkansased.org/about/pdf/releases/milken_release_111009.pdf.

5. Milken Family Foundation "Milken Educator–Elizabeth Parker"; accessed May 25, 2010, at www.mff.org/mea/mea.taf?page=recipient&meaID=22570.

6. T. W. Briggs, "All-USA teachers strive to give confidence, changes." November 6, 2007; accessed May 25, 2010, at www.usatoday.com/news/education/2007-10-17-teacher-team_N.htm?csp=34.

7. The Council of Chief State School Officers News, 2010 National Teacher of the Year Finalists Chosen, January 12, 2010; accessed May 25, 2010, from www.ccsso.org.

8. U. Neisser, ed., *The Rising Curve: Long-Term Gains in IQ and Related Measures* (American Psychological Association, 1998); accessed May 6 2010, at http://home.comcast.net/~neoeugenics/TRC.htm.

9. U.S. Census Bureau, "Historical Poverty Tables," accessed May 25, 2010, from www.census.gov/hhes/www/poverty/histpov/perindex.html.

10. Child Development Institute, Stages of Social-Emotional Development in Children and Teenagers; accessed May 24, 2010, from www.childdevelopmentinfo.com/development/erickson.shtml.

11. T. Strine, C. Okoro, L. McGuire, and L. Balluz, "The Associations Among Childhood Headaches, Emotional and Behavior Difficulties, and Health Care Use," *Pediatrics*, 117(5), 2006, 1728–1735.

12. M. Lu, *Children's Literature in a Time of National Tragedy* (ERIC Clearinghouse on Reading, English, and Communication Digest); accessed June 28, 2010, at http://permanent.access.gpo.gov/websites/eric.ed.gov/ERIC_Digests/ed457525.htm.

13. "Childhood Depression: Tips for Parents," *Mental Health America*, May 6, 2010, at www.nmha.org/index.cfm?objectid=C7DF9240–1372–4D20-C81D80B5B7C5957B.

14. "Depression in Children," *Mental Health America*, May 6, 2010, at www.mentalhealthamerica.net/index.cfm?objectid=CA866E0D-1372–4D20-C8872863D2EE2E90.

15. S. K. Bhatia and S. C. Bhatia, "Childhood and Adolescent Depression," *American Family Physician*, 75(1), 2007, 74.

16. L. Kohlberg, "The Claim to Moral Adequacy of a Highest Stage of Moral Judgment," *Journal of Philosophy*, 70(18), 1973, 630–46.

17. Georgia Character Education Law, Official Code of Georgia 20-2-145; accessed May 24, 2010, from https://public.doe.k12.ga.us/DMGetDocument.aspx/characterpercent20educationpercent20law.pdf?p=6CC6799F8C1371F66F2E68DB4B620C7235394D3860ACC9198382B2AD1F16C70A&Type=D.

18. Contributed by Carol Cates, first grade teacher, Hillcrest Elementary School, North Carolina, and 1999 North Carolina Educator of the Year.

19. Contributed by Gary W. Baird, principal, Lead Mine Elementary School, Raleigh, North Carolina.

20. Kxan.com news, E-textbooks May Soon Be Reality: Traditional Hardbacks Lost in Wave of Future, May 18, 2010; accessed May 24, 2010, from www.kxan.com/dpp/news/education/the-web-could-soon-replace-textbooks.

21. National Center of Response to Intervention; accessed May 24, 2010, from www.rti4success.org/.

22. Ibid.

23. Ibid.

24. Ibid.

25. Ibid.

26. Edweek, RTI Said to Pay Off in Gains for English Learners, Vol. 29, Issue 19, pp. 1,10; accessed April 27, 2010, from www.edweek.org/ew/articles/2010/01/22/19rtiells_ep.h29.html?tkn=Wpercent5bYCLqVUfF0pqicVwkwTVkZdlSyTBmx7rRRb.

27. Ibid.

28. C. Gewertz, National Database Rounds Up Schools with Extended Time, *Education Week*, December 9, 2009.

29. The Annie E Casey Foundation, EARLY WARNING! Why Reading by the End of Third Grade Matters; accessed May 24 from aecf.org.

30. Contributed by Candice M. Bookman, first grade teacher, Lawrence Elementary School, Mesquite Independent School District, Mesquite, Texas, 2010.

31. Ibid.

32. Ibid.

33. Ibid.

34. Ibid.

35. Ibid.

36. Ibid.

37. US Department of Education, Assisting Students Struggling with Reading: Response to Intervention (RtI) and Multi-Tier Intervention in the Primary Grades, 2009; accessed May 24, 2010, from http://ies.ed.gov/ncee/wwc/pdf/practiceguides/rti_reading_pg_021809.pdf.

38. Ibid.

39. Ibid.

40. Mathematics Learning in Early Childhood: Paths Toward Excellence and Equity; accessed May 6, 2010, at www.nap.edu/openbook.php?record_id=19&page=1 a.

41. S. Feeney and K. Kipnis, *Code of Ethical Conduct and Statement of Commitment* (Washington, DC: National Association for the Education of Young Children, 1998). Used with permission.

42. Mathematics Learning in Early Childhood: Paths Toward Excellence and Equity; accessed May 6, 2010, at www.nap.edu/openbook.php?record_id=19&page=1.

43. Ibid.

44. US Department of Education, Nation's Report Card; accessed May 24, 2010, from http://nces.ed.gov/nationsreportcard/.

45. *Education Week*, "Hong Kong's Math Found More Difficult Than Massachusetts'," May 20, 2009; accessed May 4, 2010.

46. Ibid.

47. Ibid.

48. *Education Week*, "Market for S. Korean Math Texts Remains Elusive for US Educator," May 13, 2009; accessed May 4, 2010.

49. Singapore Math, accessed May 4, 2010, from www.singaporemath.com/.

50. *The Daily Riff*, "Singapore Math Demystified! Can Solving Problems Unravel Our Fear Of Math?" March 27, 2010; accessed May 4, 2010, from www.thedailyriff.com/2010/03/singapore-math-demystified-part-2-philosophy.php.

51. Singapore Math, accessed May 4, 2010, from www.singaporemath.com/.

52. *The Daily Riff*, "Singapore Math Demystified! Can Solving Problems Unravel Our Fear Of Math?" March 27, 2010; accessed May 4, 2010, from www.thedailyriff.com/2010/03/singapore-math-demystified-part-2-philosophy.php.

53. "Inquiry in the National Science Education Standards"; accessed May 6, 2010, at http://books.nap.edu/html/inquiry_addendum/ch2.html.

54. 2010-11 PUSD Teachers of the Year Press Release, March 23 2010; accessed May 24, 2010, from www.pwayusd.com/news/TOY/TOY_2010-11.shtml.

55. The White House Blog, Educate to Innovate; accessed May 4, 2010, from www.whitehouse.gov/issues/education/educate-innovate.

56. *Education Week*, "Obama Unveils Projects to Bolster STEM Teaching," January 11, 2010; accessed May 4, 2010, from www.edweek.org/ew/articles/2010/01/07/18stem_ep.h29.html?tkn=PRXFatrETzl8ApLuOI HyoVcOWhBvzwDgx533.

57. Ibid.

58. S. Feeney and N. K. Freeman, *Ethics and the Early Childhood Educator: Using the NAEYC Code* (Washington, DC: National Association for the Education of Young Children, 2005).

59. Accessed May 6, 2010, at www.dpi.state.nc.us/curriculum/.

60. Used with the permission of Mary Nelle Brunson, Assistant Chair, Department of Elementary Education, Stephen F. Austin State University, Nacogdoches, Texas.

61. US Department of Education, Treasury, Education Departments Announce Initiatives to Raise Awareness About Financial Education; accessed May 6, 2010, from www2.ed.gov/news/pressreleases/2002/10/10032002.html.

62. MyCentralJersey, Green Brook Second-Graders Learn the Ups and Downs of Personal Banking, May 3, 2010; accessed May 6, 2010, from www.mycentraljersey.com/article/20100503/NEWS/5030325/-1/newsfront/Green-Brook-second-graders-learn-the-ups-and-downs-of-personal-banking.

63. Science Daily, School Bullying Affects Majority of Elementary Students; accessed May 10, 2010, from www.sciencedaily.com/releases/2007/04/070412072345.htm.

64. Ibid.

65. *The Baltimore Sun*, Bullying, Suicide Attempt Reported at Elementary School, April 27, 2010; accessed May 6, 2010, from http://articles.baltimoresun.com/2010-04-27/news/bs-ci-school-bullying-20100427_1_bullying-suicide-attempt-gilmor-elementary.

66. CBS News, Boy, 9, Found Hanged in Texas School, Jan. 22, 2010; accessed May 6, 2010, from www.cbsnews.com/stories/2010/01/22/national/main6130070.shtml.

67. Kamaron Institute, Bullying Prevention Program Results; accessed May 11, 2010, from http://kamaron.org/KC3-Program-Results.

68. SmartBean, What Are 21st Century Skills? Accessed May 11, 2010, from www.thesmartbean.com/magazine/21st-century-skills-magazine/what-are-21st-century-skills/.

69. Massachusetts Department of Elementary and Secondary Education, Task Force Recommends Integration of 21st Century Skills Throughout K12 System; accessed May 11, 2010, from www.doe.mass.edu/news/news.aspx?id=4429.

70. SmartBean, What Are 21st Century Skills? Accessed May 11, 2010, from www.thesmartbean.com/magazine/21st-century-skills-magazine/what-are-21st-century-skills/.

71. Ibid.

72. *Time*, "Postcard: Minneapolis," November 23, 2009; accessed May 11, 2010.

73. *The Salt Lake Tribune*, "Murray Elementary Kids Going Bilingual," September 9, 2009; accessed May 25, 2010, from www.sltrib.com/midvalley/ci_13301286.

74. *Journal Sentinel*, "Building Bridges to Families," accessed May 11, 2010, from www.jsonline.com/news/education/78108377.html.

75. American Hospice Foundation, *Talking to Children About Grief*, accessed January 28, 2010, from www.americanhospice.org/media/upload/Talkingpercent20topercent20Childrenpercent20Aboutpercent20Grief.pdf.

76. Ibid.

Chapter 13

1. National Association for the Education of Young Children, *NAEYC Standards for Professional Preparation Programs,* 2009; accessed February 24, 2010, from www.naeyc.org/.

2. Ibid.

3. K. Chaffin, "Visitors See Technology in Classroom," November 21, 2009; accessed March 4, 2010, at www.salisburypost.com/News/112109-Technology-in-classroom-visitors.

4. D. Mattiola, *Wall Street Journal*, "Recommended Reading: Using Technology in the Classroom," October 22, 2007; accessed April 20, 2010, at http://online.wsj.com/article/SB119247579234659595.html.

5. A. Kamenetz, *Fast Company*, "A is for App: How Smartphones, Handheld Computers, Sparked an Educational Reform," April 1, 2010; accessed April 18, 2010, at http://fastcompany.com/magazine/144/a-is-for-app.htlm.

6. Ibid.

7. S. Jayson, "iGeneration Has No Off Switch," *USA Today*, Section D, February 10, 2010.

8. Ibid.

9. Ibid.

10. Ibid.

11. C. An, "Walnut School Adds iPod Touch to Three R's," *SGVTribune*, January 10, 2010; accessed May 18, 2010, at www.sgvtribune.com/news/ci_14161816.

12. A. Kamenetz, *Fast Company*, "A is for App: How Smartphones, Handheld Computers, Sparked an Educational Reform," April 1, 2010; accessed April 18, 2010, at http://fastcompany.com/magazine/144/a-is-for-app.htlm.

13. B. R. Jones-Kavalier and S. L. Flannigan, "Connecting the Digital Dots: Literacy of the Twenty-first Century," *Educause*, Volume 29, Number 2 (2006); accessed May 5, 2010, at www.educause.edu/EDUCAUSE+Quarterly/EDUCAUSEQuarterlyMagazineVolum/ConnectingtheDigitalDotsLitera/157395.

14. J. Blanchard and T. Moore, "The Digital World of Young Children: Impact on Emergent Literacy," Person Foundation, Arizona State University (March 2010); accessed May 5, 2010, at www.pearsonfoundation.org/downloads/EmergentLiteracy-ExecutiveSummary.pdf.

15. Ibid.

16. R. Thurlow, "Improving Emergent Literacy Skills: Web Destinations for Young Children," November 20, 2009; accessed June 28, 2010, at http://pdfserve.informaworld.com/528224_731199542_917054959.pdf.

17. J. Blanchard and T. Moore, "The Digital World of Young Children: Impact on Emergent Literacy" Person Foundation, Arizona State University (March 2010); accessed May 5, 2010, at www.pearsonfoundation.org/downloads/EmergentLiteracy-ExecutiveSummary.pdf.

18. C. McHenry, "E-Textbooks May Soon be Reality," May 18, 2010; accessed May 24, 2010, at http://kxan.com/dpp/news/education/the-web-could-soon-replace-textbooks.

19. A. Collins, M.A., and J. Bronte-Tinkew, Ph.D., Child Trends, March 2010; accessed May 6, 2010, at www.childtrends.org/Files//Child_Trends-2010_03_01_RB_TechnologyOST.pdf.

20. Apple, "Accessibility Features," 2010; accessed May 6, 2010, at www.apple.com/ipad/features/accessibility.html.

21. Peters Township School District, 2008; accessed May 19, 2010, at www.ptsd.k12.pa.us/PT_technology.htm

22. C. An, "Walnut School Adds iPod Touch to Three R's," *SGVTribune*, January 10, 2010; accessed April 18, 2010, at http://sgvtribune.com/news/ci_14161816.

23. H. Pitler, E. R Hubbell, M. Kuhn, and K. Malenoski, "Using Technology with Classroom Instruction that Works," 2007; accessed March 16, 2010, at http://books.google.com/books?id=tUk1L-cYEDMC&printsec=frontcover&dq=elizabeth+hubbell+and+technology&source=bl&ots=k-Xs_GV74d&sig=so9bt_GOxFC5vePi4L8jkxL8H-xc&hl=en&ei=xcmfS-WCGIXGlQex-YSQBA&sa=X&oi=book_result&ct=result&resnum=3&ved=0CA0Q6AEwAg#v=onepage&q=&f=false.

24. The US Technology-Related Assistance for Individuals with Disabilities Act of 1988, Section 3.1. Public Law 100-407, August 9, 1988 (renewed in 1998 in the Clinton Assistive Technology Act) http://section508.gov/docs/AT1998.html#3.

25. K. Ash, "Assistive Tech Connections," *Education Week*, October 14, 2009; www.edweek.org/dd/articles/2009/10/21/01autistictech.h03.html.

26. "Assistive Technology Device," U.S. Department of Education, Building the Legacy: IDEA 2004, Title I/A/602/1, 2004; accessed May 5, 2010, from http://idea.ed.gov/explore/view/p/%2Croot%2Cstatute%2CI%2CA%2C602%2C1%2C.

27. J. Lam, "Technology in the Classroom," 2007; accessed March 11, 2010, at www.teach-nology.com/tutorials/techinclass/print.htm.

28. State Educational Technology Directors Association, "Science, Technology, Engineering and Mathematics," 2008; accessed March 11, 2010, at www.setda.org/c/document_library/get_file?folderId=270&name=DLFE-257.pdf.

29. Ibid.

30. Prince William County School (6/22/09); accessed May 5, 2010, at www.pwcs.edu/admin/infoguide/instructional_opener.html#http://www.pwcs.edu/admin/infoguide/instructional_opener.html.

31. State Educational Technology Directors Association, "Science, Technology, Engineering and Mathematics," 2008; accessed March 11, 2010, at www.setda.org/c/document_library/get_file?folderId=270&name=DLFE-257.pdf.

32. Ibid.

33. L. Champion, "School's 'Engineering is Elementary' Inspires Third Graders," December 5, 2008; accessed May 6, 2010, at www.leominsterchamp.com/news/2008-12-05/schools/013.html.

34. eInstruction. CPS Pulse. www.einstruction.com/products/assessment/pulse/index.html. Accessed September 1, 2010.

35. Entire section contributed by Karla Burkholder and Cathy Faris, director of technology and technology coach at Northwest I.S.D, Fort Worth, Texas.

36. Entire section contributed by Pamela Beard, ESL specialist, Forest Ridge Elementary.

37. Ibid.

38. Contributed by Andrea J. Spillett-Maurer, kindergarten teacher, Arovista Elementary, Brea, California.

39. Ibid.

40. Ibid.

41. Ibid.

42. T. Wasil, "Mr. Wasil's Class," 2009; accessed May 4, 2010, at http://staff.bbhcsd.org/wasilt/

43. K. Cassidy, Mrs. Cassidy's Classroom Blog, August 16, 2009; accessed May 9, 2010, from http://classblogmeister.com/blog.php?blogger_id=1337.

44. A. Hix, First Grade Newsletter, May 10, 2009; accessed May 5, 2010, from http://moberly.k12.mo.us/blogs/ahix/2009/05/10/first-grade-newsletter-6.

45. A. Rebora, Reinventing Teacher Development in Tough Times, *EdWeek*, March 16, 2009; accessed February 4, 2010, at www.edweek.org/tsb/articles/2009/03/16/02pd_budget.h02.html.

46. Northwest ISD, "Long-Range Plan for Technology" 2009, p. 7; accessed May 6, 2010, at www.nisdtx.org/120710425142221763/lib/120710425142221763/2008-2011_NISD_LRTP_.doc.

47. Inspiration Software, Inc. "Case Study: Fairfield Elementary School," accessed March 11, 2010, at www.inspiration.com/sites/default/files/images/case_studies/CaseStudy_Kids_Fairview.pdf.

48. M. Ryan, "Ipods Touch Salem-Keizer Schools," *Statesman Journal*, March 21, 2010; accessed April 19, 2010, at http://statesmanjournal.com/fdcp/?1270481703736.

49. Madison Metropolitan School District, "Stephens Elementary," August 17, 2009; accessed May 6, 2010, at www.madison.k12.wi.us/032.htm and http://boeweb.madison.k12.wi.us/policies/3721.

50. Angel Oak Elementary, "Internet—Terms and Conditions" (n.d.); accessed May 6, 2010, at http://angeloak.ccsdschools.com/userpolicy.

51. Polk City Schools Technology Plan, 2007; accessed April 15, 2010, at www.polk-schools.com/Polk%20County%20Schools%20Technology%20Plan.doc.

52. *Education World*, "Teacher-Created Web Sites Link Home and School—Virtually!" (n.d.) accessed May 23, 2010, at www.educationworld.com/a_tech/tech008.shtml.

53. PECS was developed by Lori Frost and Andrew Bondy. A. S. Bondy and L. A. Frost, "The Picture Exchange Communication System." *Focus on Autistic Behavior, 9*(3), 1994, 1–19.

Chapter 14

1. National Association for the Education of Young Children, *NAEYC Standards for Professional Preparation Programs,* 2009; www.naeyc.org/.

2. Ibid.

3. National Institute for Early Education Research, "Executive Function: A Critical Skill for Preschoolers." *Preschool Matters, 4*(5), 2006; accessed May 2, 2010, at http://nieer.org/psm/index.php?article=171.

4. P. Tough, "Can the Right Kinds of Play Teach Self-Control?" *New York Times*, September 25, 2009; accessed May 27, 2010, at www.nytimes.com/2009/09/27/magazine/27tools-t.html?pagewanted=1&_r=1.

5. A. Duckworth and M. E. P. Seligman, "Self-Discipline Outdoes IQ Predicting Academic Performance of Adolescents." *Journal of Psychological Science, 16*(12), 2005, 939–944.

6. S. E. Rimm-Kaufman, R. C. Pianta, and M. J. Cox, "Teachers' Judgments of Problems in the Transition to Kindergarten." *Early Childhood Research Quarterly, 15*(2), 2000, 147–166.

7. P. Tough, "Can the Right Kinds of Play Teach Self-Control?" *New York Times,* September 25, 2009; accessed May 27, 2010, at www.nytimes.com/2009/09/27/magazine/27tools-t.html?pagewanted=1&_r=1.

8. W. Reinke, J. Splett, E. Robeson, and C. Offutt, "Combining school and family interventions for the prevention and early intervention of disruptive behavior problems in children: A public health perspective," *Psychology in the Schools, 46*(1), 33–43, 2008; retrieved May 18, 2009, from www.preventionaction.org/what-works/helping-schools-be-better-parents/1006.

9. M. Tilley, "Civility in America; Can't We All Just Get Along," Children's Theater Company, September 5, 2007; accessed May 26, 2010, at www.associatedcontent.com/article/362551/civility_in_america_cant_we_all_just.html?cat=9.

10. S. Wolk, "Hearts and Minds," *Educational Leadership*, September 2003, Vol. 61, No. 1, pp. 14–18; accessed May 25, 2010, at www.ascd.org/publications/educational_leadership/sept03/vol61/num01/Hearts_and_Minds.aspx.

11. J. Green, *Future Looks Bright for Bridgeton's Broad Street School Students Honored for Exceptional Kindness,* May 25, 2010; www.nj.com/cumberland/index.ssf/2010/05/future_looks_bright_for_bridge.html.

12. L. R. Roehler and D. J. Cantlon, *Scaffolding: A Powerful Tool in Social Constructivist Classrooms* (1996); http://ed-web3.educ.msu.edu/literacy/papers/paperlr2.html.

13. L. E. Berk and A. Winsler, *Scaffolding Children's Learning: Vygotsky and Early Childhood Education* (Washington, DC: NAEYC, 1995), 45–46.

14. Temple of Kriya Yoga-Chicago, "Y Is for Yoga: First- and Third-Grade Yogis at Jefferson Elementary School, Berwyn," March–April 2007, www.yogachicago.com/mar07/jefferson.shtml.

15. National Sleep Foundation, *How Much Sleep Do We Really Need?* (2009). www.sleepfoundation.org/article/how-sleep-works/how-much-sleep-do-we-really-need.

16. B. K. Hamre and R. C. Pianta, "Early Teacher–Child Relationships and the Trajectory of Children's School Outcome Through Eighth Grade," *Child Development 72,* 2001, 625–638.

17. G. W. Ladd and K. B. Burgess, "Do Relational Risks and Protective Factors Moderate the Linkages Between Childhood Aggression and Early Psychological and School Adjustment?" *Child Development 72,* 2001, 1579–1601.

18. Ibid.

19. Global Initiative to End All Corporal Punishment of Children, *Progress Towards Prohibiting All Corporal Punishment in North America,* November 2009. www.endcorporalpunishment.org/pages/pdfs/charts/Chart-NorthAmerica.pdf.

20. American Academics of Pediatrics, *Where We Stand: Spanking,* 2010. www.healthychildren.org/English/family-life/family-dynamics/communication-discipline/pages/Where-We-Stand-Spanking.aspx?nfstatus=401&nftoken=00000000-0000-0000-0000-000000000000&nfstatusdescription=ERROR%3a+No+local+token.

21. C. Taylor et al., "Mothers' Spanking of 3-Year-Old Children and Subsequent Risk of Children's Aggressive Behavior," *Pediatrics 125*(5), 2010, e1057–e1065.

Chapter 15

1. National Association for the Education of Young Children, *NAEYC Standards for Professional Preparation Programs,* 2009; accessed May 11, 2010, from www.naeyc.org/.

2. Ibid.

3. U.S. Census Bureau, "U.S. Interim Projections by Age, Sex, Race, and Hispanic Origin" (2008); accessed May 18, 2010, at www.census.gov/.

4. M. Marcus, "Marriages Mix Races or Ethnicities More than Ever," June 4, 2010; accessed June 7, 2010, at http://content.usatoday.net/dist/custom/gci/InsidePage.aspx?cId=floridatoday&sParam=38765158.story.

5. A. Dodson, "English Language Learners Fastest-Growing Segment of U.S. Population," *Diverse Education*, January 18, 2008; accessed May 17, 2010, at http://diverseeducation.com/artman/publish/article_10516.shtml.

6. D. Aleman, J. Johnson Jr, and L. Perez, "Winning Schools for ELLs," *Educational Leadership*, April 2009, pp. 66–69.

7. Contributed by Jeanette O'Neal.

8. Ibid.

9. MSNBC, "Minority Babies Set to Become Majority in 2010," March 10, 2010; accessed June 1, 2010, at www.msnbc.msn.com/id/35793316/.

10. H. El Nasser, "Minority Kids Grow to Majority in Some Countries," *USA Today*, June 17, 2009; accessed June 1, 2010, at www.usatoday.com/news/nation/2009-06-16-youngminorities_N.htm.

11. G. Scharrer and J. Lacoste-Caputo, "School Enrollments Foreshadow Texas Future," May 16, 2010; accessed June 1, 2010, at www.mysanantonio.com/news/education/School_enrollments_foreshadow_Texas_future_93903929.html.

12. Minneapolis Foundation, "Africa–Focus on Somalis" (n.d); accessed June 1, 2010, at www.minneapolisfoundation.org/immigration/Africa.htm.

13. A. Terrazas, "Haitian Immigrants in the United States," Migration Policy Institute, January 2010; accessed June 1, 2010, at www.migrationinformation.org/USfocus/display.cfm?id=770.

14. T. Melendez, National Association for Bilingual Education Press Conference Release, February 3, 2010; accessed June 3, 2010, at www2.ed.gov/news/speeches/2010/02032010.html.

15. National Center for Cultural Competence, "Conceptual Frameworks/Models, Guiding Values and Principals" (n.d.); accessed June 1, 2010, at http://nccc.georgetown.edu/foundations/frameworks.html.

16. C. Chew, "Incoming IRA President Aims to Prepare Literacy Teachers to Instruct Diverse Classrooms," *Diverse Education*, April 22, 2010; accessed June 1, 2010, at http://diverseeducation.com/article/13728/incoming-ira-president-aims-to-prepare-literacy-teachers-to-instruct-diverse-classrooms.html.

17. National Association for Multi-Cultural Education, "Definitions of Multi-Cultural," 2010; accessed June 2, 2010, at http://nameorg.org/names-missio/definition-of-multicultural-education/.

18. "Teaching Kids Cultural Awareness," February 21, 2010; accessed May 17, 2010, at www.news4jax.com/news/22624613/detail.html.

19. Bright Hub, "Preschool Lesson Plans," March 24, 2010; accessed June 10, 2010, at www.brighthub.com/education/early-childhood/articles/66983.aspx.

20. J. Gonzales and D. Tobiassen, "Teaching Diversity: A Place to Begin," *Scholastic World*, (n.d); accessed June 2, 2010, at http://content.scholastic.com/browse/article.jsp?id=3499.

21. W. Tulinsky, "Baleros in the Classroom," (n.d.); accessed June 3, 2010, at www.lessonplanspage.com/LASSPEMDBaleros InTheClassroomK12.htm.

22. C. Read, "F Is for Flexibility" March 2, 2010; accessed June 7, 2010, at http://carolread.wordpress.com/2010/03/02/f-is-for-flexibility/.

23. J. Miller, "Schools Matter," April 9, 2010; accessed June 3, 2010, at www.schoolsmatter.info/2010/04/teacher-in-florida.html.

24. *Education World*, "Student Led Conferences Successful in Elementary and Middle School Grades," October 1, 2009; accessed May 18, 2010, at www.educationworld.com/a_admin/admin/admin326.shtml.

25. C. Metzler, "Teaching Children about Diversity," PBS, March 11, 2010; accessed May 26, 2010, at www.pbs.org/parents/experts/archive/2009/02/teaching-children-about-divers.html.

26. Alain Locke Elementary, "Students Celebrate Culture Day," 2010; accessed May 26, 2010, at http://alainllocke.org/2010/03/students-celebrate-cultural-day/.

27. T. R. Benson, "Integrated Teaching Units," September 2004; accessed July 12, 2010, at www.pbs.org/teachers/earlychildhood/articles/integratedunits.html.

28. J. Lardeni, "Getting to Know You with Toilet Paper," 2010; accessed June 8, 2010, at www.lessonplanspage.com/OBeginSchoolGetting ToKnowYouToiletPaperIdeaK12.htm.

29. H. Barrett, "Special Characteristics," 2010; accessed June 8, 2010, at www.lessonplanspage.com/OGettingToKnowStudentSpecial CharacteristicsBeginSchoolIdeaP12.htm.

30. A. Bayer, "Kids Are Asked to Make Largest Mural Ever," November 24, 2009; accessed June 8, 2010, at www.examiner.com/examiner/x-28900-Minneapolis-Homeschooling-Examiner~y2009m11d24-Kids-are-asked-to-help-make-the-worlds-longest-mural.

31. R. Houston, "All About Me Scrapbooks," 2010; accessed June 8, 2010, at www.lessonplanspage.com/OBeginningOfSchoolAll AboutMePhotoSymbolJournalExpectationsScrapbook512.htm.

32. K. Radel, "Ideas for Teaching about Different Countries and Cultures," 2010; accessed June 8, 2010, at www.lessonplanspage.com/SSLAOCICountriesandCulturesIdeas18.htm.

33. P. Ammonds Newcomb, "ASFL Students have ePals Around the World," *Huntsville Times*, May 24, 2010; accessed June 9, 2010, at http://blog.al.com/breaking/2010/05/asfl_students_have_epals_aroun.html.

34. California State Board of Education, "English Language Arts Content Standards for California Public Schools," June 2009; accessed June 7, 2010, at www.cde.ca.gov/be/st/ss/.

35. Florida Department of Education, "Benchmark Standards," revised December 2008; accessed June 7, 2010, at www.floridastandards.org/Standards/PublicPreviewBenchmark2936.aspx?kw=culture.

36. *Federal Register* (August 11, 1975), 33803.

37. *Federal Register* (June 4, 1975), 24128.

38. Mason Elementary School, "School Activities," 2010; accessed June 9, 2010, at www.gwinnett.k12.ga.us/schooldom/MasonES/gcps-schooltemplate.nsf/Pages/Students.

39. D. Baker, "Teaching for Gender Difference," 2010; accessed June 3, 2010, at www.narst.org/publications/research/gender.cfm

40. Based on *Before Push Comes to Shove; Building Conflict Resolution Skills with Children,* by N. Carlsson-Paige and D. Levin, 1998, St. Paul, MN: Red Leaf Press.

41. A. Clutter and A. Zubieta, "Understanding the Latino Culture," 2009; accessed May 27, 2010, at http://ohioline.osu.edu/hyg-fact/5000/pdf/5237.pdf.

42. E. Olivos, "Intervention in School and Clinic: Collaboration with Latino Families," Sage Publications 45:109 (2009).

43. M. Thao, "Parent Involvement in School," December 2009; accessed May 27, 2010, at www.wilder.org/download.0.html?report=2262.

44. "No Child Left Behind Act," *National Association for Bilingual Education*, 2010; accessed May 26, 2010, at www.nabe.org/advocacy.html.

45. National Clearinghouse for English Language Acquisition, "Educating English Language Learners: Building Teachers' Capacity," 2008; accessed June 9, 2010, at www.ncela.gwu.edu/files/uploads/3/EducatingELLsBuildingTeacherCapacityVol1.pdf.

46. National Clearinghouse for English Language Acquisition and Language Instruction Educational Programs, M. Bowles and C. Stanfield, "A Practical Guide to Standards-Based Assessment

in the Native Language," 2008; accessed June 9, 2010, at www.ncela.gwu.edu/files/uploads/11/bowles_stansfield.pdf.

47. National Clearinghouse for English Language Acquisition and Language Instruction Educational Programs (NCELA), Department of Education, "Types of Language Instructional Programs" (n.d.); accessed May 26, 2010, at www.ncela.gwu.edu/files/uploads/5/Language_Instruction_Educational_Programs.pdf.

48. *The ELL Outlook*, "When an ELL Has Difficulty Learning, Is the Problem a Disability or the Second-Language Acquisition Process?" accessed May 20, 2010, from www.coursecrafters.com/ELL-Outlook/2004/mar_apr/ELLOutlookITIArticle4.htm.

49. TEA Student Assessment Division, "ELL Update," accessed June 7, 2010, at http://ritter.tea.state.tx.us/student.assessment/resources/conferences/tac/2008/ell_assessment_update.pdf.

Chapter 16

1. National Association for the Education of Young Children, *NAEYC Standards for Professional Preparation Programs,* 2009; accessed May 17, 2010, from www.naeyc.org/.

2. Ibid.

3. Ibid.

4. Public Law 105–17 (1997).

5. Individuals with Disabilities Education Act Amendments of 2004, P.L. 108–44, 20 U.S.C. §§ SEC. 602, 1401 et seq.; accessed May 21, 2010.

6. U.S. Department of Education, Office of Special Education Programs, Data Analysis System (DANS), OMB #1820043: "Children with Disabilities Receiving Special Education Under Part B of the Individuals with Disabilities Education Act," 1998–2007. Data updated as of July 15, 2008; accessed May 21, 2010.

7. National Dissemination Center for Children with Disabilities, Part B of IDEA; accessed June 10, 2010, from www.nichcy.org/Laws/IDEA/Pages/PartB.aspx.

8. Ibid.

9. Ed.gov accessed June 10, 2010.

10. U.S. Department of Education, Office of Special Education and Rehabilitative Services, Office of Special Education Programs, *28th Annual Report to Congress on the Implementation of the Individuals with Disabilities Education Act, 2006,* vol. 1, Washington, DC, 2009.

11. *The ELL Outlook*, When an ELL Has Difficulty Learning, Is the Problem a Disability or the Second-Language Acquisition Process? Accessed June 10, 2010, from www.coursecrafters.com/ELL-Outlook/2004/mar_apr/ELLOutlookITIArticle4.htm.

12. Ibid.

13. Ibid.

14. Council for Exceptional Children, *National Special Education Teacher of the Year to Be Honored at Convention*, March 11, 2009; accessed May 21, 2010, from www.cec.sped.org/Content/NavigationMenu/ProfessionalDevelopment/ConventionExpo/Press/National_Special_Edu.htm.

15. Council for Exceptional Children, 1996; accessed June 2, 2010, at www.cec.sped.org.

16. Material in this section on itinerant special educators contributed by Faith Haertig Sadler, M.Ed., itinerant special education teacher in Seattle, Washington.

17. The National Human Genome Research Institute, Learning about Autism; accessed June 10, 2010, from www.genome.gov/25522099.

18. Autism Society of America, *What Is Autism?* Accessed June 10, 2010, at www.autism-society.org/site/PageServer?pagename=about_whatis.

19. American Psychiatric Association, *Diagnostic and Statistical Manual of Mental Disorders: DSM-IV-TR* (Washington, DC: Author, 2000).

20. Autism Society of America, *What Is Autism?* Accessed June 10, 2010, at www.autism-society.org/site/PageServer?pagename=about_whatis.

21. Autism Speaks, *Building a Community of Hope, About Autism,* 2007; accessed June 10, 2010, at www.autismspeaks.org/docs/Autism_Speaks_Annual_Report_2007.pdf.

22. Ibid.

23. J. J. Woods and A. M. Wetherby, "Early Identification of and Intervention for Infants and Toddlers Who Are At Risk for Autism Spectrum Disorder," *Language, Speech, and Hearing Services in Schools, 34*, 2003, 180–293.

24. S. Mastrangelo, "Play and the Child with Autism Spectrum Disorder: From Possibilities to Practice, " *International Journal of Play Therapy, 18*(1), 2009, 13–30.

25. K. Painter, "Science Getting to the Roots of Autism," *USA Today*, January 12, 2004; accessed June 10, 2010, at www.usatoday.com/news/health/2004-01-12-autism-main x.htm.

26. Autism Society of America, *What Is Autism?* Accessed June 10, 2010, at www.autism-society.org/site/PageServer?pagename=about_whatis.

27. The National Human Genome Research Institute, Learning about Autism; accessed June 10, 2010, from www.genome.gov/25522099.

28. The Associated Press, "Gene Clues from Mideast Suggest Autism Occurs When Brain Cannot Learn Properly from Early Life," *The International Herald Tribune*, July 11, 2008; accessed June 10, 2010, from www.iht.com/bin/printfriendly.php?id=14407868.

29. K. L. Spittler, "New Evidence Supports Theory of an Environmental Trigger for Autism." *NeuroPsychiatry Reviews*, 2009, 6.

30. The National Human Genome Research Institute, Learning about Autism; accessed June 10, 2010, from www.genome.gov/25522099.

31. J. J. Woods and A. M. Wetherby, "Early Identification of and Intervention for Infants and Toddlers Who Are At Risk for Autism Spectrum Disorder," *Language, Speech, and Hearing Services in Schools, 34*, 2003, 180–293.

32. S. Mastrangelo, "Play and the Child with Autism Spectrum Disorder: From Possibilities to Practice, " *International Journal of Play Therapy, 18*(1), 2009, 13–30.

33. T. Wigram and C. Gold, "Music Therapy in the Assessment and Treatment of Autistic Spectrum Disorder: Clinical Application and Research Evidence," *Child Care, Health and Development, 32*(5), 2005, 535–542.

34. Centers for Disease Control, *Attention Deficit/Hyperactivity Disorder: Facts about ADHD*, May 25, 2010; accessed June 10, 2010, from www.cdc.gov/ncbddd/adhd/facts.html.

35. Mental Health America, *Fact Sheet: Adult AD/HD in the Work Place*; accessed June 10, 2010, from www.mentalhealthamerica.net/go/information/get-info/ad/hd/adult-ad/hd-in-the-workplace/adult-ad/hd-in-the-workplace.

36. Centers for Disease Control, *Attention Deficit/Hyperactivity Disorder: Facts about ADHD*, May 25, 2010; accessed June 10, 2010, from www.cdc.gov/ncbddd/adhd/facts.html.

37. Reprinted with permission from the *Diagnostic and Statistical Manual of Mental Disorders, Fourth Edition, Text Revision* (Copyright 2000), American Psychiatric Association.

38. Ibid.

39. Ibid.

40. Ibid.

41. Ibid.

42. Ibid.

43. B. Bloom, R. A. Cohen, and G. Freeman, *Summary Health Statistics for U.S. Children: National Health Interview Survey, 2008*. National Center for Health Statistics. Vital Health Stat 10(244), 2009.

44. C. Adams, Girls and ADHD, *Instructor, 116* (6), 2007, 31–35.

45. Ibid.

46. Ibid.

47. Mental Health America, *Fact Sheet: Adult AD/HD in the Work Place*; accessed June 10, 2010, from www.mentalhealthamerica.net/go/information/get-info/ad/hd/adult-ad/hd-in-the-workplace/adult-ad/hd-in-the-workplace.

48. Centers for Disease Control, *Attention Deficit/Hyperactivity Disorder: Facts about ADHD*, May 25, 2010; accessed June 10, 2010, from www.cdc.gov/ncbddd/adhd/facts.html.

49. U.S. Office of Special Education Programs, *Teaching Children with Attention Deficit Hyperactivity Disorder: Instructional Strategies and Practices*, 2008; accessed June 10, 2010, at www2.ed.gov/rschstat/research/pubs/adhd/adhd-teaching.html.

50. Ibid.

51. Information in this section from the U.S. Department of Education, *Teaching Children with Attention Deficit Hyperactivity Disorder: Instructional Strategies and Practices*, 2008; accessed June 10, 2010, at www2.ed.gov/rschstat/research/pubs/adhd/adhd-teaching.html.

52. Indiana's Academic Standards—Mathematics, *Core Standards, Standard Indicators: 1.1.1, 1.1.4,* March 12, 2009; accessed June 24, 2009, from www.Edroundtable.State.In.Us/Meetings/2009docs/March%2025%202009%20Meeting/Math_Standards_3-12-09.Pdf.

53. Ibid.

54. *Pittsburg Post-Gazette*, "Modified PSSA Test in Math Offered for 1st Time," April 18, 2010; accessed June 10, 2010, from www.post-gazette.com/pg/10108/1051042-454.stm#ixzz0oUfbWXWV.

55. Jacob K. Javits Gifted and Talented Students Education Act of 1988; accessed June 10, 2010, at www2.ed.gov/programs/javits/index.html.

56. *Los Angeles Times*, "L.A. Schools On Sharper Lookout for Gifted Students—And They Find Them," May 9, 2010; accessed June 10, 2010, from http://articles.latimes.com/2010/may/09/local/la-me-0509-gifted-20100509,full.story.

57. Ibid.

58. U. S. Department of Health & Human Services Administration for Children and Families Administration on Children, Youth and Families Children's Bureau, accessed October 19, 2010, from http://www.acf.hhs.gov/programs/cb/pubs/cm08/cm08.pdf.

59. *Pediatrics*, "Child Abuse Statistics," accessed June 10, 2010, from http://pediatrics.about.com/od/childabuse/a/05_abuse_stats.htm.

60. U.S. Statutes at Large, vol. 88, pt. 1 (Washington, DC: U.S. Government Printing Office, 1976), 5.

61. *Pediatrics*, "Child Abuse Statistics," accessed June 10, 2010, from http://pediatrics.about.com/od/childabuse/a/05_abuse_stats.htm.

62. eMedicine, Child Abuse & Neglect, Physical Abuse; accessed June 10, 2010, from http://emedicine.medscape.com/article/915664-overview.

63. *Pediatrics*, "Child Abuse Statistics," accessed June 10, 2010, from http://pediatrics.about.com/od/childabuse/a/05_abuse_stats.htm.

64. Ibid.

65. *Darkness to Light*, "Statistics Surrounding Child Sexual Abuse"; accessed May 18, 2010, from www.darkness2light.org/KnowAbout/statistics_2.asp.

66. Ibid.

67. Ibid.

68. Ibid.

69. Ibid.

70. "How Many People Experience Homelessness?" NCH Fact Sheet #2, National Coalition for the Homeless; accessed June 10, 2010, at www.nationalhomeless.org/publications/facts/How_Many.pdf.

71. The National Center on Family Homelessness, *America's Youngest Outcasts: State Report Card on Child Homelessness,* March 2009; accessed June 10, 2010, from www.homelesschildrenamerica.org/pdf/rc_full_report.pdf.

72. K. Kingsbury, "Keeping Homeless Kids in School," *Time*, March 23, 2009, 42–43.

73. The National Center on Family Homelessness, *America's Youngest Outcasts: State Report Card on Child Homelessness,* March 2009; accessed June 10, 2010, from www.homelesschildrenamerica.org/pdf/rc_full_report.pdf.

74. Ibid.

75. Public Law 100-77, McKinney–Vento Homeless Education Act, Title VII-Subtitle B-Education for Homeless Children and Youths, 2001.

76. K. Kingsbury, "Keeping Homeless Kids in School," *Time*, March 23, 2009, 42–43.

77. The National Center on Family Homelessness, *America's Youngest Outcasts: State Report Card on Child Homelessness,* March 2009; accessed June 10, 2010, from www.homelesschildrenamerica.org/pdf/rc_full_report.pdf.

78. K. Kingsbury, "Keeping Homeless Kids in School," *Time*, March 23, 2009, 42–43.

79. E. Burmaster, State of Wisconsin Department of Public Instruction, *Homeless Bulletin Series 01*, August 18, 2003; accessed April 29, 2009, from www.caction.org/indicators/reports/hmls_identification.pdf.

Chapter 17

1. National Association for the Education of Young Children, *NAEYC Standards for Professional Preparation Programs,* 2009; www.naeyc.org/.

2. Ibid.

3. Community Foundation for Greater New Haven, *Recipients of the NewAlliance Bank Teacher Excellence Award,* 2010; accessed June 1, 2010, at www.cfgnh.org/News/ReadArticle/tabid/312/smid/895/ArticleID/77/reftab/207/t/2010-Recipients-of-the-NewAlliance-Bank-Teacher-Excellence-Award/Default.asp

4. E. Nermeen, E. Nokali, H. J. Bachman, and E. Votruba-Drzal, "Parent Involvement Continues to be Important in Elementary Years," *ScienceDaily,* May 20, 2010; retrieved June 24, 2010, from www.sciencedaily.com/releases/2010/05/100514074915.htm.

5. W. J. Bushaw and J. A. McNee, The 41st Annual Phi Delta Kappa/Gallup Poll of the Public's Attitudes Toward the Public Schools, August 26, 2009; www.docstoc.com/docs/10425651/Phi-Delta-KappaGallup-Poll-of-the-Public%E2%80%99s-Attitudes-Toward-the-Public-Schools.

6. E. Nermeen, E. Nokali, H. J. Bachman, and E. Votruba-Drzal, "Parent Involvement Continues to be Important in Elementary Years," *ScienceDaily,* May 20, 2010; retrieved June 24, 2010, from www.sciencedaily.com/releases/2010/05/100514074915.htm.

7. CovNews.com, "Porterdale Elementary's Parent University Has Several Programs Planned." January 27, 2010; accessed June 10, 2010, at http://covnews.com/news/archive/10804/

8. ChildStats.gov, *America's Children: Key Indicators of Well Being,* 2009; accessed June 17, 2010, at www.childstats.gov/americaschildren/famsoc2.asp.

9. U.S. Census Bureau, Custodial Mothers and Fathers and Their Child Support, November 2009; accessed June 9, 2010, from http://singleparents.about.com/gi/o.htm?zi=1/XJ&zTi=1&sdn=singleparents&cdn=parenting&tm=62&gps=420_139_1657_867&f=20&su=p284.9.336.ip_p504.3.336.ip_&tt=11&bt=0&bts=0&zu=http%3A//www.census.gov/prod/2009pubs/p60-237.pdf.

10. Ibid.

11. *The McDowell News,* "Volunteers Honored With Awards," May 24, 2010; accessed June 16, 2010, at www2.mcdowellnews.com/news/2010/may/24/volunteers-honored-awards-ar-168070/.

12. C. Millner, *Parent Volunteers Help Lift San Jose Schools,* June 6, 2010; accessed June 16, 2010, at http://articles.sfgate.com/2010-06-06/opinion/21779254_1_parents-low-performing-schools-neighborhood-school.

13. J. S. Coleman, *Parental Involvement in Education* (Washington, DC: U.S. Department of Education, 1991), 7.

14. U.S. Census Bureau, Custodial Mothers and Fathers and Their Child Support, November 2009; accessed June 9, 2010, from http://singleparents.about.com/gi/o.htm?zi=1/XJ&zTi=1&sdn=singleparents&cdn=parenting&tm=62&gps=420_139_1657_867&f=20&su=p284.9.336.ip_p504.3.336.ip_&tt=11&bt=0&bts=0&zu=http%3A//www.census.gov/prod/2009pubs/p60-237.pdf.

15. S. Jayson, "Non-resident, but Present," *USA Today,* June 16, 2010.

16. National Fatherhood Initiative, *Overview: School-based Programming,* 2010; www.fatherhood.org/Page.aspx?pid=654.

17. B. Thatcher, "Colorado Program Helps Dads Become Better Men," June 16, 2010, at www.9news.com/seenon9news/article.aspx?storyid=141157&catid=509.

18. N. Roshan, "Dads Enjoy 'DOG' Days at Bellows Spring," June 10, 2010, at www.explorehoward.com/education/72430/dads-enjoy-dog-days-bellows-spring/.

19. Barnes and Noble, Books. *My Fathers Knows the Names of Things, by Jane Holden,* 2010; accessed June 21, 2010, at http://search.barnesandnoble.com/My-Father-Knows-the-Names-of-Things/Jane-Yolen/e/9781416948957/.

20. Penguin Group USA, *My Father is Taller than a Tree,* 2008; accessed June 21, 2010, at http://us.penguingroup.com/nf/Book/BookDisplay/0,,9780803731738,00.html?strSrchSql=my+father+is+taller+than+a+tree/My_Father_Is_Taller_than_a_Tree_Joseph_Bruchac.

21. Generations United, "Fact Sheet: Multigenerational Households," June 2010; www.gu.org/documents/A0/Multigenerational Households_2009.pdf.

22. Pew Research Center, "Millenials: Portraits of the Generation Next," February 2010; accessed June 10, 2010, at http://pewsocialtrends.org/assets/pdf/millennials-confident-connected-open-to-change.pdf.

23. Pew Research Center, "The Return of the Multi-generational Family Household," March 8, 2010; accessed June 10, 2010, at http://pewsocialtrends.org/assets/pdf/752-multi-generational-families.pdf.

24. Generations United, "GrandFacts: Data, Interpretations, and Implications for Caregivers," April 2010; accessed June 10, 2010, at www.gu.org/documents/A0/GrandFacts_Fact_Sheet.pdf.

25. S. Plummer, "Future Cowboys," *Tulsa World,* June 11, 2010; www.tulsaworld.com/news/article.aspx?subjectid=11&articleid=20100611_11_A11_Veteri115080.

26. J. Klockenga, "Life's a Picnic When You Have a Grandma to Talk To," June 4, 2010, accessed June 16, 2010, at www.desmoinesregister.com/article/20100604/NEWS/6040312/1001/NEWS/Life-s-a-picnic-when-you-have-a-grandma-to-talk-to.

27. Reprinted by permission from J. González-Mena, "Taking a Culturally Sensitive Approach in Infant-Toddler Programs," *Young Children,* 1 (1992): 8–9.

28. C. Bowers, *Teen Pregnancies End Decade-Long Decline,* January 26, 2010; accessed June 14, 2010, at www.cbsnews.com/stories/2010/01/26/eveningnews/main6144496.shtml.

29. A. Dizon, "Seven Local Moms Overcome Stats to Graduate from High School," May 25, 2010; accessed June 14, 2010, at http://lubbockonline.com/education/2010-05-25/seven-local-moms-overcome-stats-graduate-high-school.

30. C. Kieffer, "Dropout Reduction Aim of New Programs," *Tupelo News;* June 7, 2010, at http://nems360.com/view/full_story/7821316/article-Dropout-reduction-aim-of-new-programs?instance=news_special_coverage_right_column.

31. *Pittsburg Post-Gazette,* "What Happens to Kids Raised by Gay Parents? Research Suggests that They Turn Out About the Same, No Better, No Worse and No More Likely to be Gay than Other Kids," June 10, 2007; accessed June 8, 2010, from www.post-gazette.com/pg/07161/793042-51.stm#ixzz0qHEotsZP.

32. *CNN,* "Kids of Lesbians Have Fewer Behavioral Problems, Study Suggests," June 7, 2010; accessed June 8, 2010, from http://edition.cnn.com/2010/HEALTH/06/07/lesbian.children.adjustment/index.html.

33. The Gay, Lesbian and Straight Education Network, "LGBT Parents Involved In, Excluded From K–12 Schools; Children Often Harassed," 2008; accessed June 9, 2010, from www.glsen.org/cgi-bin/iowa/all/library/record/2271.html?state=research&type=research.

34. Ibid.

35. *Pittsburg Post-Gazette*, "What Happens to Kids Raised by Gay Parents? Research Suggests that They Turn Out About the Same, No Better, No Worse and No More Likely to be Gay than Other Kids," June 10, 2007; accessed June 8, 2010, from www.post-gazette.com/pg/07161/793042-51.stm#ixzz0qHEotsZP.

36. About.com, "Gay Adoption Statistics Based on U.S. Census 2000, the National Survey of Family Growth (2002), and the Adoption and Foster Care Analysis and Reporting System (2004)"; accessed June 8, 2010, from http://adoption.about.com/od/gaylesbian/f/gayparents.htm.

37. Ibid.

38. The Gay, Lesbian and Straight Education Network, "LGBT Parents Involved In, Excluded From K–12 Schools; Children Often Harassed," 2008; accessed June 9, 2010, from www.glsen.org/cgi-bin/iowa/all/library/record/2271.html?state=research&type=research.

39. Ibid.

40. National Military Family Association, "Supporting Children," accessed June 21, 2010, from www.militaryfamily.org/get-info/support-children/.

41. D. Fassler, "My Turn: Children in Active Military Families: Tips for Parents and Teachers," June 18, 2010; accessed June 18, 2010, at www.burlingtonfreepress.com/article/20100618/OPINION02/6180318/My-Turn-Children-in-active-military-families-Tips-for-parents-and-teachers.

42. Department of Defense, "Family Support During Deployment," accessed June 22, 2010, from http://fhp.osd.mil/deployment Tips.jsp.

43. *Times Observer*, "Youngsville Woman Starts Pennies for Postage to Help Get Packages to Service Personnel," accessed June 22, 2010, from www.timesobserver.com/page/content.detail/id/531862.html

44. DODEA, "Sure Start: It Takes a Community," accessed June 22 2010, from www.dodea.edu/instruction/curriculum/ece/pubs/community/community-portrait.pdf.

45. Enidnews.com, "Program Helps Children of Military Through Moving," accessed June 22, 2010, from http://enidnews.com/state/x1174310405/Program-helps-children-of-military-through-moving.

46. KMBC, "Help Kids in Military Families Cope: Psychiatrist Offers Tips to Support Children," accessed June 22, 2010, from www.kmbc.com/military-service/2107168/detail.html.

47. *Military Money*, "Children in Military Families," accessed June 22, 2010, from www.militarymoney.com/home/1101923157.

48. Bureau of Justice Statistics, "Total Correctional Population," accessed September 2, 2010, from http://bjs.ojp.usdoj.gov/index.cfm?ty=tp&tid=11

49. Minnesota Fathers and Families Network, "Families with Incarcerated Families Fact Sheet," 2010; accessed June 21, 2010, at www.mnfathers.org/FamiliesOfIncarceratedFACTSHEET final.pdf.

50. R. Jervis, "Prison Dads Learn Meaning of 'Father'," June 18, 2010, *USA Today*; accessed June 21, 2010, at www.usatoday.com/news/nation/2010-06-17-prison-dads_N.htm.

51. Ibid.

52. Personal communication and telephone interview with Maria Costanzo Palmer, June 22, 2010; maria@getonthebus.us.

53. Ibid.

54. D. Samfield, "When It Comes to Reading, LAW Students Go Above and Beyond," June 18, 2010; accessed June 18, 2010, at www.nashobapublishing.com/shirley_news/ci_15325076

55. California Healthy Families Program, "About Healthy Families," 2010; accessed June 18, 2010, at www.healthyfamilies.ca.gov/HFProgram/default.aspx.

56. *Cape May County Herald*, "Families to Graduate from Parenting Program," June 4, 2010, at www.capemaycountyherald.com/article/court+house/62996-families+graduate+parenting+program.

57. AVANCE, "The AVANCE Model," 2010; www.avance.org/why-avance/model/.

58. K. Horner, "Dallas-area Services Aim to Help Families Prevent Child Abuse," *Dallas Morning News,* May 16, 2010; accessed June 10, 2010, at www.dallasnews.com/sharedcontent/dws/news/localnews/stories/DN-parenthelp_16met.ART.State.Bulldog.a211d69.html.

59. E. Richards, "Teachers Make House Calls to Forge Stronger Partnerships," *Milwaukee Wisconsin Journal Sentinel Online,* December 1, 2009; accessed June 15, 2010, at www.jsonline.com/news/education/78193777.html.

60. R. J. Stiggins, *Student-Centered Classroom Assessment,* 2nd ed. (Upper Saddle River, NJ: Merrill/Prentice Hall, 1997), 499.

61. M. McGowan, "Mrs. Marci McGowan's First Grade Website," 2010; accessed June 17, 2010, at www.mrsmcgowan.com/index.html.

62. The Teachers' Podcast, "Twitter Used to Develop Second Graders' Writing Skills"; accessed April 23, 2009, from http://teachers podcast.org/2009/03/31/ep-36-digital-catchup-and-21st-century-learning-debate.

63. INFOlathe, Unified School District 233, "Students Partner with Parents, Teachers in High-Tech Conferences," April 6, 2009; accessed May 21, 2009, from www.olatheschools.com/index.php?option=com_content&task=view&id=1370&Itemid=47.

64. M. Sacchetti, "Teachers Take Bulletin Boards Online: Blogs Reaching Out to Students, Parents," *Boston Globe,* September 7, 2006; accessed May 21, 2009, from www.mackenty.org/images/uploads/boston_globe_blogging.pdf.

65. C. Johnson, "Oakland Literacy Program Needs Your Help," May 18, 2010; http://articles.sfgate.com/2010-05-18/bay-area/20902770_1_reading-nights-free-book-reading-events.

66. Ibid.

67. Durham Public Schools, "Business Leaders Get Involved in Durham," accessed June 4, 2009, from www.dpsnc.net/news/community-news/business-leaders-get-involved-in-durham.

68. Oregon School District 24J, Salem-Keizer Public Schools, "Business Partnerships," January 8, 2008; accessed May 21, 2009, from www.salkeiz.k12.or.us/content/business-partnerships?page=1.

69. *The Wall Street Journal*, "Businesses Emerge to Help School Fund-Raisers Go Green," July 15, 2008; accessed June 5, 2009, from http://online.wsj.com/article/SB121607802464352547.html?mod=us_business_biz_focus_hs.

70. Education Commission of the States, "The Progress of Education Reform," February 2010; www.ecs.org/clearinghouse/84/20/8420.pdf.

71. NCCP, "A National Portrait of Chronic Absenteeism in the Early Grades," accessed June 22, 2010, from www.nccp.org/publications/pub_771.html.

Glossary

Absorbent mind The idea that the minds of young children are receptive to and capable of learning. The child learns unconsciously by taking in information from the environment.

Accommodation Changing or altering existing schemes or creating new ones in response to new information.

Active learning Involvement of the child with materials, activities, and projects in order to learn concepts, knowledge, and skills.

Active learning theory The view that children develop knowledge and learn by being physically and mentally engaged in learning activities.

Adaptation The cognitive process of building schemes through interaction with the environment. Consists of two complementary processes—assimilation and accommodation.

Adaptive education Modifications in any classroom, program, environment, or curriculum that help students achieve desired educational goals.

Adult–child discourse The talk between an adult and a child, which includes adult suggestions about behavior and problem solving.

Advocacy The act of engaging in strategies designed to improve the circumstances of children and families. Advocates move beyond their day-to-day professional responsibilities and work collaboratively to help others.

Alignment The arrangement of standards, curriculum, and tests so they are in agreement.

Alphabetic knowledge (AK) Knowledge of the names and sounds associated with printed letters.

American Recovery and Reinvestment Act of 2009 (ARRA) Seeks to reform education by investing quickly in America's youngest children. Provides funding for several programs proposed during President Obama's administration that benefit young children.

Anecdotal record A brief written recording of student behavior that includes only what a teacher sees or hears, not what he or she thinks or infers.

Antibias education (ABE) An approach that seeks to provide children with an understanding of social and behavioral problems related to prejudice and seeks to provide them with the knowledge, attitude, and skills needed to combat prejudice.

Applied behavior analysis (ABA) ABA is based on the learning theory of Behaviorism, which states that all behavior is motivated by a purpose and is learned through systematic reinforcement.

Approaches to learning How children react to and engage in learning and activities associated with school.

Assessment The cognitive process of collecting information about children's development, learning, behavior, academic progress, need for special services, and achievement in order to make decisions.

Assimilation The process of fitting new information into existing schemes.

Assistive technology Any device used to promote the learning of children with disabilities.

Atelier A special area or studio for creating projects.

Atelierista A teacher trained in the visual arts, who works with teachers and children.

Attachment An emotional tie between a parent/caregiver and an infant that endures over time.

Attention Deficit Hyperactivity Disorder (ADHD) Difficulty with attention and self-control, which leads to problems with learning, social functioning, and behavior that occur in more than one situation and have been present for a significant length of time.

Autism A developmental disability that typically appears during the first three years of life and is the result of a neurological disorder that affects the normal functioning of the brain, impacting development in the areas of social interaction and communication skills.

Autism spectrum disorder A neurological developmental disorder characterized by a deficit in communication and social interactions, as well as by the presence of restricted and repetitive behaviors.

Auto-education The idea that children teach themselves through appropriate materials and activities.

Autonomy An Erikson concept that says as toddlers mature physically and mentally, they want to do things by themselves.

Baby signing Teaching babies to use signs or gestures to communicate a need or emotion.

Behavior guidance The processes by which children are helped to identify appropriate behaviors and use them.

Bias-free An environment, classroom setting, or program that is free of prejudicial behaviors.

Blank tablet The belief that at birth the mind is blank and that experience creates the mind.

Bloom's Taxonomy Refers to a classification of different objectives that educators set for students in three domains: affective, psychomotor, and cognitive.

Bonding A parent's initial emotional tie to an infant.

Book and print concepts Activities that show how books look and how they work.

Brown v. Board of Education Court ruling that stated, "Segregation of children in public schools solely on the basis of race deprives children of the minority group of equal educational opportunities, even though the physical facilities and other 'tangible' factors may be equal.

Center-based child care Child care and education provided in a facility other than a home.

Cephalocaudal development The principle that development proceeds from the head to the toes.

Challenging environments Environments that provide achievable and "stretching" experiences for all children.

Checklists Lists of behaviors identifying children's skills and knowledge.

Child as sinful View that children are basically sinful, need supervision and control, and should be taught to be obedient.

Child care Comprehensive care and education of young children outside their homes.

Child development associate (CDA) An individual who has successfully completed the CDA assessment process and has been awarded the CDA credential. CDAs are able to meet the specific needs of children and work with parents and other adults to nurture children's physical, social, emotional, and intellectual growth in a child development framework.

Child-centered Term meaning that every child is a unique and special individual; that all children have a right to an education that helps them grow and develop to their fullest; that children are active participants in their own education and development; and teachers should consider children's ideas, preferences, learning styles, and interests in planning for and implementing instructional practices.

Childhood depression A disorder affecting as many as one in thirty-three children that can negatively impact feelings, thoughts, and behavior and can manifest itself with physical symptoms of illness.

Children as blank tablets View that presupposes no innate genetic code or inborn traits exist and the sum of what a child becomes depends on the nature and quality of experience.

Children as growing plants View of children popularized by Froebel, which equates children to plants and teachers and parents to gardeners.

Children as investments View that investing in the care and education of children reaps future benefits for parents and society.

Children as miniature adults Belief that children are similar to adults and should be treated as such.

Children as property Belief that children are literally the property of their parents.

Children with disabilities IDEA defines children with disabilities as those children with mental retardation, hearing impairments (including deafness), speech or language impairments, visual impairments (including blindness), serious emotional disturbance, orthopedic impairments, autism, developmental delays, traumatic brain injury, other health impairments, or specific learning disabilities, and who, by reason thereof, need special education and related services.

Children's house Montessori's first school especially designed to implement her ideas.

Chronosystem The environmental contexts and events that influence children over their lifetimes, such as living in a technological age.

Civil behavior Polite, courteous, and respectful behavior.

Civil Rights Act of 1964 Included a provision that protects the constitutional rights of individuals in public facilities, including public education.

Collaboration Working jointly and cooperatively with other professionals, parents, and administrators.

Collaborative planning Planning used by groups of teachers at the grade levels or across grade levels to plan curriculum daily, weekly, and monthly. Also called *team planning*.

Concrete operations stage The stage of cognitive development during which children's thought is logical and can organize concrete experiences.

Constructivism Theory that emphasizes the active role of children in developing their understanding and learning.

Consultation Seeking advice and information from colleagues.

Content knowledge The content and subjects teachers plan to teach.

Continuity of care The ongoing nurturing relationship between a child and his or her caregiver.

Conventional literacy skills Skills such as decoding (turning written words into spoken words), oral reading fluency, reading comprehension, writing, and spelling.

Cultural awareness The appreciation for and understanding of people's cultures, socioeconomic status, and gender.

Cultural competence The ability and confidence to interact effectively with children, families, and colleagues of different cultures.

Cultural competency The process of developing proficiency in effectively responding in a crosscultural text. It is the process by which individuals respond respectfully and effectively to diverse cultures.

Cultural infusion Culturally aware and culturally sensitive education permeates the curriculum to alter or affect the way young children and teachers think about diversity issues.

Culturally appropriate practice An approach to education based on the premise that all peoples in the United States should receive proportional attention in the curriculum.

Culture A group's way of life, including basic values, beliefs, religion, language, clothing, food, and practices.

Curriculum alignment The process of making sure that what is taught matches the standards.

Data-driven instruction The analysis of assessment data to make decisions about how best to meet the instructional needs of each child.

Developmental kindergarten (DK) A kindergarten designed to provide children with additional time for maturation and physical, social, emotional, and intellectual development.

Developmentally and culturally responsive practice (DCRP) Teaching based on the ability to respond appropriately to children's and families' developmental, cultural, and ethnic backgrounds and needs.

Developmentally appropriate practice (DAP) Practice based on how children grow and develop and on individual and cultural differences.

Differentiated instruction (DI) An approach that enables teachers to plan strategically to meet the needs of every student in order to teach to the needs of each child and allow for diversity in the classroom.

Discourse skills Activities that encourage telling stories and explaining how the world works.

Documentation Records of children's work, including recordings, photographs, art, work samples, projects, and drawings.

Early childhood professional An educator who successfully teaches all children, promotes high personal standards, and continually expands his or her skills and knowledge.

Early Head Start A federal program serving pregnant women, infants, toddlers, and their families.

Early intervention A system of educational and social services that support families and children's growth and development; for example early Head Start.

Economic Opportunity Act of 1964 (EOA) Implemented several social programs to promote the health, education, and general welfare of people of low socioeconomic backgrounds.

Education of All Handicapped Children Act (EAHC) Mandated that in order to receive federal funds, states must develop and implement policies that assure a Free Appropriate Public Education (FAPE) for all children with disabilities.

Elementary and Secondary Education Act of 1965 (ESEA) Federal legislation that funds primarily elementary and secondary education.

Embedded instruction Instruction that is included as an integral part of normal classroom routines.

Emergent literacy Children's communication skills are in an emerging state—in the process of developing.

Émile Jean-Jacques Rousseau's famous book that outlines his ideas about how children should be reared.

Encouraging classroom A classroom environment that rewards student accomplishment and independence.

Entitlement programs Programs and services children and families are entitled to because they meet the eligibility criteria for the services.

Environmentalism The theory that the environment, rather than heredity, exerts the primary influence on intellectual growth and cultural development.

Equilibrium A balance between existing and new schemes, developed through assimilation and accommodation of new information.

Ethical conduct Responsible behavior toward students and parents that allows you to be considered a professional.

Event sampling A form of assessment that systematically observes a specific behavior during a particular period of time that is based on the ABC model.

Executive function See **self-regulation.**

Exosystems Environments or settings in which children do not play an active role but which nonetheless influence their development.

Expanding horizons approach Also called the *expanding environments approach*, an approach to teaching social studies where the student is at the center of the expanding horizons and initial units, and at each grade level is exposed to an ever-widening environment.

Family child care Home-based care and education provided by a nonrelative outside the child's home; also known as *family care.*

Family involvement The participation of parents and other family members in all areas of their children's education and development, based on the premise that parents are the primary influence in children's lives.

Family-centered teaching Instruction that focuses on meeting the needs of students through the family unit.

Fantasy play Play involving unrealistic notions and superheroes.

Fatherhood initiatives Various efforts by federal, state, and local agencies to increase and sustain fathers' involvement with their children and families.

Forest schools Programs with the belief that by participating in engaging, motivating, and achievable tasks and activities in a woodland environment, each child has an opportunity to develop intrinsic motivation and sound emotional and social skills.

Formative assessment The ongoing process of gathering information about students during learning and teaching. Also called informal assessment, performance assessment, and authentic assessment.

Free and appropriate public education (FAPE) Education suited to children's age, maturity, condition of disability, past achievements, and parental expectations.

Full inclusion An approach whereby students with disabilities receive all instruction and support services in a general classroom.

Gift of time The practice of giving children more time in a program or at home to develop physically, emotionally, socially, and cognitively as preparation for kindergarten.

Gifts Ten sets of learning materials designed to help children learn through play and manipulation.

Goodness of fit How well a teacher recognizes and responds or adapts to a child's temperament—also affects the learning of self-regulation.

Grandfamilies Children living with their grandparents.

Guidelines (standards) Preschool statements of what children should know and be able to do.

Head Start A federally funded program for children from low socioeconomic backgrounds.

Head Start Program Performance Standards Federal guidelines for Head Start and Early Head Start, designed to ensure that all children and families receive high-quality services.

Healthy environments Environments that provide for children's physical and psychological health, safety, and sense of security.

Heteronomy The stage of moral thinking in which children are governed by others regarding matters of right and wrong.

Hierarchy of needs Maslow's theory that basic needs must be satisfied before higher-level needs can be satisfied.

HighScope educational model A program for young children based on Piaget's and Vygotsky's ideas.

High-stakes testing An assessment test used to either admit children into programs or promote them from one grade to the next.

Holophrases The single words children use to refer to what they see, hear, and feel (e.g., *up, doll*).

Implementation Committing to a certain action based on interpretations of observational data.

Impulse control See **self-regulation**.

Inclusion Generally defined as educating students with disabilities in the regular classroom.

Individualization of instruction Providing for students' specific needs, disabilities, and preferences.

Individualized education program (IEP) A plan for meeting an exceptional learner's educational needs, specifying goals, objectives, services, and procedures for evaluating progress.

Individualized family service plan (IFSP) A plan designed to help families reach their goals for themselves and their children, with varied support services.

Individuals with Disabilities Education Act (IDEA) A federal act providing a free and appropriate public education to youth between ages three and twenty-one with disabilities.

Infancy The first year of life.

Infant/toddler mental health The overall health and well-being of young children in the context of family, school, and community relationships.

Informal (free) play Play in which children play in activities of interest to them.

Inquiry learning Involvement of children in activities and processes that lead to learning.

Instrumental-relativist orientation The second stage of preconventional moral development, when children's actions are motivated by satisfaction of their needs.

Intentional teaching Developing plans, selecting instructional strategies, and teaching to promote learning.

Interactive word wall A collection of frequently used words in the classroom that children use to make sentences or use in other classroom literacy activities.

Interpretation Forming a conclusion based on observational and assessment data with the intent of planning and improving teaching and learning.

Intersubjectivity A Vygotskian theory based on the idea that individuals come to a task, problem, or conversation with their own subjective experiences and ways of thinking. Through discussing their different viewpoints, children can build a shared understanding.

Interview A common way that observers and researchers engage children in discussion through questions to obtain information.

Itinerant teachers Professionals who travel from school to school, providing assistance and teaching students.

Key developmental indicators (KDIs) In the HighScope approach, activities that foster developmentally important skills and abilities.

Kindergarten The name Friedrich Froebel gave to his system of education for children ages three through six; means "garden of children."

Learned helplessness A condition that can develop when children perceive that they are not doing as well as they can or as well as their peers and lose confidence in their abilities and achievement, and then attribute their failures to a lack of ability. These children are passive and have learned to feel they are helpless.

Learning Cognitive and behavioral changes that result from experiences.

Learning centers Areas of the classroom set up to promote student-centered, hands-on, active learning, organized around student interests, themes, and academic subjects.

Least restrictive environment (LRE) The education of students with disabilities with students who do not have disabilities.

Linguistically diverse parents Individuals whose English proficiency is minimal and who lack a comprehensive knowledge of the norms and social systems in the United States.

Literacy circles Discussion groups in which children meet regularly to talk about books.

Literacy education Teaching that focuses on reading, writing, speaking, and listening.

Locus of control The source of control over personal behavior, either internal or external.

Looping A single-graded class of children staying with the same teacher for two or more years.

Macrosystem In Bronfenbrenner's ecological theory, the broader culture in which children live (e.g., democracy, individual freedom, and religious freedom).

Mastery-oriented attributions Attributions that include effort (industriousness), paying attention, determination, and perseverance.

Mesosystem Links or interactions between microsystems.

Microsystem In Bronfenbrenner's ecological theory, the environmental settings in which children spend a lot of their time (e.g., children in child care spend about thirty-three hours a week there).

Middle childhood Describes children in Erikson's industry versus inferiority stage of social-emotional development, ages six to nine years, during which time they gain confidence and ego satisfaction from completing demanding tasks.

Migrant and Seasonal Head Start A federal program designed to provide educational and other services to children and families who earn income in agricultural work.

Migrant family A family with school-age children that moves from one geographic location to another to engage in agricultural work.

Mixed-age grouping Students in two or three grade levels combined in one classroom with one teacher.

Model early childhood program An exemplary approach to early childhood education that serves as a guide to best practices.

Modes of response The various ways children respond to books and conversations.

Montessori method A system of early childhood education founded on the ideas and practices of Maria Montessori.

Motherese (parentese) The way parents and others speak to young children in a slow, exaggerated way that includes short sentences and repetition of words and phrases.

Multicultural awareness Developing in all children an appreciation and understanding of other people's cultures, socioeconomic status, and gender, including their own.

Multicultural infusion Making multiculturalism an explicit part of curriculum and programs.

Multigenerational families Living arrangements in which three or more generations share a common housing unit.

National Defense Education Act (NDEA) Provided federal funding for science, technology, engineering, math (S.T.E.M.), and foreign language education and is considered by many to be the beginning of federal standards in education.

Naturalism Education that follows the natural development of children and does not force the educational process on them.

Naturalistic teaching strategies Incorporating instruction into opportunities that occur naturally or routinely in the classroom.

Negative reinforcement Taking away something to promote or diminish a behavior, such as removing your attention from someone (ignoring them).

Neural shearing (pruning) The selective elimination of synapses.

No Child Left Behind Act (NCLB) Federal law passed in 2001 that has significantly influenced early childhood education.

Object permanence The concept that people and objects have an independent existence beyond the child's perception of them.

Observation Observation is the intentional, systematic act of looking at the behavior of a child in a particular setting, program, or situation.

Occupations Froebelian learning materials designed to engage children in learning activities.

Open-air nursery school School established by the McMillan sisters, who believed in education where young children could explore their imaginations, develop their sensory and perceptual faculties, and care for gardens and pets.

Operation In Piaget's cognitive theory, a reversible mental action.

Orbis Pictus (***The World in Pictures***) Considered the first picture book for children.

Parent–teacher conferences or **family–teacher conferences** Meetings between parents and early childhood professionals to inform the parents of the child's progress and allow them to actively participate in the educational process.

Partial inclusion An approach whereby students with disabilities receive some instruction in a general classroom and some in a specialized setting.

Pedagogical content knowledge The teaching skills teachers need to help all children learn.

Pedagogical knowledge The ability to apply pedagogical and content knowledge to develop meaningful learning experiences for children.

Philosophy of education A set of beliefs about how children develop and learn and what and how they should be taught.

Phonological awareness (PA) The ability to detect, manipulate, or analyze the auditory aspects of spoken language (including the ability to distinguish or segment words, syllables, or phonemes), independent of meaning.

Phonological memory (PM) The ability to remember spoken information for a short period of time.

Plan-do-review In the HighScope approach, a sequence in which children, with the help of the teacher, initiate plans for projects or activities; work in learning centers to implement their plans; and then review what they have done with the teacher and their fellow classmates.

Play therapy A developmentally appropriate practice and model to incorporate social experiences and enjoyable interactions to enhance a child's pretend skills, joint attention, communication skills, and appropriate behavior.

Portfolio A compilation of children's work samples, products, and teacher observations collected over time.

Positive classroom A classroom environment that promotes appropriate behavior and success.

Positive reinforcement Adding something to promote or diminish a behavior, such as giving a high-five for a job well done.

Poverty The condition of having insufficient income to support a minimum standard of living.

Practical life Montessori activities that teach skills related to everyday living.

Preconventional level The first level in Kohlberg's theory of moral development, when morality is based on punishment and rewards.

Pre-kindergarten A class or program preceding kindergarten for children usually from three to four years old.

Preoperational stage In Piaget's theory, the stage of cognitive development in which young children are capable of mental representations.

Prepared environment A classroom or other space that is arranged and organized to support learning in general and/or special knowledge and skills.

Preschool years The period from three to five years of age, before children enter kindergarten and when many children attend preschool programs.

Primary circular reactions Repetitive actions that are centered on the infant's own body.

Private speech Self-directed speech that children use to plan and guide their behavior.

Professional development A process of studying, learning, changing, and becoming more professional.

Professional dispositions The values, commitments, and professional ethics that influence behaviors toward students, families, colleagues, and communities and affect student learning, motivation, and development as well as the educator's own professional growth.

Professional learning community (PLC) A team of early childhood professionals working collaboratively to improve teaching and learning.

Progressivism Dewey's theory of education that emphasizes the importance of focusing on the needs and interests of children rather than teachers.

Project Approach An in-depth investigation of a topic worth learning more about.

Proximodistal development The principle that development proceeds from the center of the body outward.

Public policy All the plans that local, state, and national governmental and nongovernmental organizations have for implementing their goals.

Punishment and obedience orientation The first stage of preconventional moral development, when children make moral decisions based on physical consequences.

Rapid automatic naming (RAN) of letters or digits The ability to rapidly name a sequence of random letters or digits.

Rapid automatic naming (RAN) of objects or colors The ability to rapidly name a sequence of repeating random sets of pictures or objects (e.g., "car," "tree," "house," "man") or colors.

Rating scales Usually numeric scales that contain a list of descriptors for a set of behaviors or goals.

Receptive language Ability to understand and use spoken, written, and visual communication.

Redshirting The practice of postponing the entrance into kindergarten of age-eligible children to allow extra time for social-emotional, intellectual, or physical growth.

Reflective practice The active process of thinking before teaching, during teaching, and after teaching in order to make decisions about how to plan, assess, and teach.

Reggio Emilia An approach to education based on the philosophy and practice that children are active constructors of their own knowledge.

Relations of constraint Children's reliance on others to determine right and wrong.

Relations of cooperation Children's engagement with others in making decisions about good, bad, right, or wrong.

Resource teachers Professionals who provide assistance with materials and planning for teachers of exceptional students.

Respectful environments Environments that show respect for each individual child and for their culture, home language, individual abilities or disabilities, family context, and community.

Respect-reflect-relate model A responsive curriculum for infants and toddlers in which teachers show respect for children, reflect on what children need, and relate to them by providing appropriate care and education.

Response to intervention/Response to instruction (RTI) A multi-tiered approach to the early identification and support of students with learning and behavior needs.

Responsive relationships The relationship that exists between yourself, children, and their families where you are responsive to their needs and interests.

Rubric Scoring guide that differentiates among levels of performance.

Running record A detailed narrative of a child's behavior that focuses on a sequence of events that occur over a period of time. Includes both factual observations and teacher's inferences.

Scaffolding The process of providing various types of support, guidance, or direction during the course of an activity.

Schemes Organized units of knowledge.

Screening A type of summative assessment that gives a broad picture of what children know and are able to do, as well as their physical health and emotional status.

Seasonal family A family with children who are engaged primarily in seasonal agricultural labor and who have not changed their residence to another geographic location in the preceding two-year period.

Secondary circular reactions Repetitive actions focused on the qualities of objects, such as their shapes, sizes, colors, and noises.

Self-actualization An inherent tendency to reach one's true potential.

Self-regulation A child's ability to gain control of bodily functions, manage emotions, maintain focus and attention, and integrate cognitive, physical, and social-emotional abilities.

Self-regulation (executive function) The ability of preschool children to control their emotions and behaviors, to delay gratification, and to build positive social relations with each other.

Self-talk Speech directed to oneself that helps guide one's behavior.

Sensitive period In the Montessori method, a relatively brief time during which learning is most likely to occur. Also called a critical period.

Sensorimotor stage The stage during which children learn through the senses and motor activities.

Sensory education Learning experiences involving the five senses: seeing, touching, hearing, tasting, and smelling.

Sensory materials Montessori learning materials designed to promote learning through the senses and to train the senses for learning.

Sexism Prejudice or discrimination based on sex.

Sexual harassment Unwelcome sexual behavior and talk.

Shared reading A teaching method in which the teacher and children read together from text that is visible to all.

Skill deficit When a child has not learned how to perform a particular skill or behavior.

Social constructivist approach Approaches to teaching that emphasize the social context of learning and behavior.

Social play Play of children with others and in groups.

Social story A personalized, detailed, and simple script that breaks down behavior and provides rules and directions.

Sociodramatic play Play involving realistic activities and events.

Sputnik The world's first satellite.

Summative assessments Assessments given periodically to determine at a particular point in time what students know and are able to do. Examples of summative assessments include: state, end of year, and end of grading period assessments.

Supportive environments Environments in which professionals believe each child can learn, and that help children understand and make meaning of their experiences.

Sure Start A Department of Defense Education Activity (DoDEA) program based on the Head Start program model for children at overseas installations.

Symbolic play The ability of a young child to have an object stand for something else.

Symbolic representation The ability to use mental images to stand for something else.

Synaptogenesis The rapid development of neural connections.

Technological literacy The ability to understand and apply technological devices to reading and writing.

Technology The application of tools and information used to support learning.

Telegraphic speech Two-word sentences that express actions and relationships (e.g., "Milk gone").

Temperament A child's general style of behavior.

Tertiary circular reactions In Piaget's theory, the repetition of actions resulting in the modifications of behavior.

Theory A set of explanations of how children develop and learn.

Time sampling Authentic means to assess children that involves focusing on a particular behavior over a continuous period of time.

Title I Provided monies to help educate children from low-income families under the Elementary Secondary Education Act.

Title IX Also known as Title IX of the Education Amendment Act of 1972 that states, "No person in the United States shall, on the basis of sex, be excluded from participation in, be denied the benefits of, or be subjected to discrimination under any program or activity receiving federal financial assistance."

Toddlerhood Children twelve to twenty-four months.

Transdisciplinary team model Professionals from various disciplines working together to integrate instructional strategies and therapy and to evaluate the effectiveness of their individual roles.

Transition A passage from one learning setting, grade, or program to another.

Transition kindergarten A kindergarten designed to serve children who may be old enough to go to first grade but are not quite ready to handle all of its expectations.

Twice exceptional Students with dual exceptionalities.

Typically developing When children achieve the majority of developmental milestones at the time when most young children achieve them without deficits in social or communication areas.

Unfolding Process by which the nature of children—what they are to be—develops as a result of maturation according to their innate developmental schedules.

Universal design (UD) A broadspectrum solution that produces buildings, products and environments that are usable and effective for everyone, not just people with disabilities.

Universal kindergarten The availability of publicly funded kindergarten to all children.

Utopian The belief that by controlling circumstances and consequent outcomes of child rearing and other social processes, it is possible to build a new and more perfect society.

Vocabulary knowledge Activities that emphasize words and their meanings.

Warmth Displaying or exhibiting kindness and genuine affection.

Whole-language approach Philosophy of literacy development that advocates the use of all dimensions of language—reading, writing, listening, and speaking—to help children become motivated to read and write.

Word wall A collection of words displayed on a wall or another display place in the classroom designed to promote literacy learning.

Work sample or **student artifact** An example of children's work that demonstrates what they know and are able to do. Such examples are used as evidence to assess student abilities. Work samples can be physical or electronic and come in many different forms.

Zone of proximal development The range of tasks that are too difficult to master alone but that can be learned with guidance and assistance.

Index

Photo Credits

Jasmine Montgomery, p. iv; iStockphoto, pp. 2, 64 (bottom), 89, 102, 104, 183, 189; Pearson Scott Foresman, pp. 12 (bottom), 301, 303, 341, 395, 398, 399, 402, 416; Thinkstock, pp. 8, 334 (center); Michael Newman/PhotoEdit, pp. 12 (top), 94, 470; Karen Mancinelli/Pearson Learning Photo Studio, pp. 13, 480; SMART Technologies, p. 29; Shutterstock, pp. 34, 57, 100, 126, 143 (top, 2nd from top), 150, 158, 174, 196, 201, 224, 236 (3rd from right), 262, 298, 330, 366, 382, 388, 410, 420, 428, 462; Krista Greco/Merrill, pp. 37 (left), 83, 107, 145, 242; George Dodson/PH College, pp. 37 (right), 43, 153 (bottom); Cynthia Cassidy/Merrill, p. 38 (bottom); Mary Kate Denny/PhotoEdit, p. 45; Fotolia, LLC–Royalty Free, pp. 62, 226 (both), 227 (right), 236 (left, 2nd from left, 3rd from left, 2nd from right, right), 238, 258, 334 (left, right), 335 (left), 343 (2nd from top), 358, 376 (top); EyeWire Collection/Getty Images–Photodisc, pp. 64 (top), 143 (2nd from bottom); Bob Daemmrich/Bob Daemmrich Photography, Inc., p. 64 (2nd from top); David Mager/Pearson Learning Photo Studio, pp. 64 (center), 162; Anthony Magnacca/Merrill, p. 64 (2nd from bottom); Patrick White/Merrill, pp. 66, 143 (bottom), 314, 393 (both); Courtesy of the Centenary of the Montessori Movement, pp. 105, 111; Library of Congress, p. 110; Mark Richards/PhotoEdit, pp. 113, 220; © Ellen B. Senisi, pp. 120, 188, 217; Elizabeth Crews/Elizabeth Crews Photography, pp. 155, 375 (top); Michele Sanderson/A. Sophie Rogers Laboratory School, The Ohio State University, p. 166 (all); © BananaStock Ltd., pp. 154, 192; Annie Pickert/Pearson, pp. 153 (top), 274, 343 (bottom left, 2nd from top, top right); Vanessa Davies © Dorling Kindersley, p. 153 (center); Andrew D. Brosig/The Daily Sentinel/AP Wide World Photos, p. 215; Courtesy of Monica Beyer, p. 241; Dreamstime LLC–Royalty Free, p. 227 (left); © Picture Contact/Alamy, p. 268; David Young-Wolff/PhotoEdit, p. 276; Laura Bolesta/Merrill, p. 284; Barb Tingle, Sahuarita Primary School, Tucson, Arizona, Kindergarten Teacher, pp. 296 (both), 297 (both), 308 (both), 309 (both); Katelyn Metzger/Merrill, pp. 313, 339; Scott Cunningham/Merrill, p. 346; © 2010 The LEGO Group. Used with permission, p. 357; Rayna Freedman, p. 335 (center, right); Graphic, JumpStart® Baby, used with permission of Knowledge Adventure, Inc., p. 368; ELMO Document Camera TT-02RX. Courtesy of ELMO USA CORP., p. 375 (bottom); Courtesy of einstruction® student response system, pp. 376 (bottom), 377 (bottom); Stief & Schnare/Superstock Royalty Free, p. 377 (top); © Myrleen Pearson/Alamy, p. 414; Lori Whitley/Merrill, p. 440; Silver Burdett Ginn Needham, p. 444; Bob Daemmrich/The Image Works, p. 489; © Steven May/Alamy, p. 464; PhotoDisc/Getty Images, p. 467; Superstock Royalty Free, p. 481.